NEW ENGLAND INSTITUTE
OF TECHNOLOGY
LEARNING RESOURCES CENTER

# *STRESS*

# THE SERIES IN CLINICAL AND COMMUNITY PSYCHOLOGY

*CONSULTING EDITORS*

## Charles D. Spielberger and Irwin G. Sarason

## IN PREPARATION

# STRESS
## *Psychological and Physiological Interactions*

*Edited by*

## Susan R. Burchfield
University of Washington

● HEMISPHERE PUBLISHING CORPORATION
*Washington    New York    London*

DISTRIBUTION OUTSIDE THE UNITED STATES
McGRAW-HILL INTERNATIONAL BOOK COMPANY
*Auckland    Bogotá    Guatemala    Hamburg    Johannesburg*
*Lisbon    London    Madrid    Mexico    Montreal*
*New Delhi    Panama    Paris    San Juan    São Paulo*
*Singapore    Sydney    Tokyo    Toronto*

STRESS: Psychological and Physiological Interactions

2 3 4 5 6 7 8 9 0    E B E B    8 9 8 7 6

This book was set in Press Roman by Hemisphere Publishing Corporation. The
editors were Christine Flint, Bettie Loux Donley, and Janet Mais; the
production supervisor was Miriam Gonzalez; and the typesetter was Sandra Watts.
Edwards Brothers, Inc. was printer and binder.


*Library of Congress Cataloging in Publication Data*

Main entry under title:

Stress: psychological and physiological interactions.

(The series in clinical and community psychology)
Includes bibliographies and index.
1. Stress (Psychology) 2. Stress (Physiology)
I. Burchfield, Susan R., date. II. Series.
[DNLM: 1. Stress—Physiopathology. 2. Stress,
Psychological—Physiopathology. QT 162.S8 S915]
BF575.S75S7735    1984        616.9'8        83-12971
ISBN 0-89116-267-4
ISSN 0146-0846

*This book is dedicated to*

**Irwin G. Sarason**

*for encouraging me to edit a book on stress*

**Janet Crump** *and* **Tammy Rayburn**

*for typing endless letters and manuscripts*

*and to*

*my husband,* **William C. Holliday,**

*for his patience and support throughout this undertaking*

# Contents

### III
### *MODERATION OF THE STRESS RESPONSE*

## CONCLUSIONS

# Contributors

*ALFRED A. AMKRAUT*, Alza Pharmaceuticals, Palo Alto, California, USA

*FRANK ANDRASIK*, Department of Psychology, State University of New York, Albany, Albany, New York, USA

*HYMIE ANISMAN*, Department of Psychology, Carleton University, Ottawa, Ontario, Canada K1S 5B6

*JAMES C. ASCOUGH*, Wabash Valley Hospital Mental Health Center *and* Department of Psychology, Purdue University, West Lafayette, Indiana, USA

*EDWARD B. BLANCHARD*, Department of Psychology, State University of New York, Albany, Albany, New York, USA

*JAMES A. BLUMENTHAL*, Department of Psychiatry, Duke University Medical Center, Durham, North Carolina, USA

*SUSAN R. BURCHFIELD*, Department of Psychology, University of Washington, Seattle, Washington, USA

*KARL C. CORLEY, JR.*, Department of Physiology, Medical College of Virginia, Richmond, Virginia, USA

*S. REBECCA EDLUND*, Department of Psychology, State University of New York, Albany, Albany, New York, USA

*JOHN J. FUREDY*, Department of Psychology, University of Toronto, Toronto, Ontario, Canada M5S 1A1

*THOMAS F. GARRITY*, Department of Behavioral Science, College of Medicine, University of Kentucky, Lexington, Kentucky, USA

*KATHY L. HAMILTON*, Department of Psychology, University of Kentucky, Lexington, Kentucky, USA

*THOMAS L. HANEY*, Department of Psychiatry, Duke University Medical Center, Durham, North Carolina, USA

*JAMES H. JOHNSON*, Department of Clinical Psychology, University of Florida, Gainesville, Florida, USA

*LARRY KOKKINIDIS*, Department of Psychology, University of Saskatchewan, Saskatoon, Saskatchewan, Canada

*ROBERT S. LAVEY*, Department of Psychiatry, Duke University Medical Center, Durham, North Carolina, USA

MARTIN B. MARX, Department of Family Practice, College of Medicine, University of Kentucky, Lexington, Kentucky, USA

DIANE M. RILEY, Department of Psychology, University of Toronto, Toronto, Ontario, Canada M5S 1A1

ROBERT T. RUBIN, Department of Psychiatry, University of California, Los Angeles, and Harbor General Hospital, Torrance, California, USA

CURT A. SANDMAN, Department of Psychiatry and Psychobiology, University of California, Irvine, and Fairview Hospital, Costa Mesa, California, USA

BARBARA R. SARASON, Department of Psychology, University of Washington, Seattle, Washington, USA

IRWIN G. SARASON, Department of Psychology, University of Washington, Seattle, Washington, USA

DEANE H. SHAPIRO, JR., Department of Psychiatry and Human Behavior, University of California, Irvine, Orange, California, USA

LAWRENCE S. SKLAR, Department of Psychology, Carleton University, Ottawa, Ontario, Canada K1S 5B6

RONALD E. SMITH, Department of Psychology, University of Washington, Seattle, Washington, USA

GEORGE F. SOLOMON, Department of Psychiatry, University of California, San Francisco, and Fresno County Department of Health, Fresno, California, USA

LESLIE J. STEIN, Department of Psychology, University of Washington, Seattle, Washington, USA

C. BARR TAYLOR, Department of Psychiatry and Stanford Heart Disease Prevention Program, Stanford University School of Medicine, Stanford, California, USA

JANE VEITH-FLANIGAN, Department of Psychology, Washington State University, Pullman, Washington, USA

JOHN F. WILSON, Department of Behavioral Science, College of Medicine, University of Kentucky, Lexington, Kentucky, USA

MARLENE M. WILSON, Department of Physical and Life Sciences, University of Portland and University of Oregon Health Sciences Center, Portland, Oregon, USA

# *Preface*

When preparing to teach a graduate seminar on stress, I realized that there were no multidisciplinary books available that discussed both the psychological and physiological aspects of the stress response. There were several books about stress on the market, but each one espoused its author's theory and tended to ignore contradictory evidence or data collected by researchers in different fields. The more I searched for an appropriate book integrating research on stress, the more it became evident to me that such a volume did not exist. When I expressed by frustration to Irwin Sarason, he suggested I write my own book. That was several years ago. Time passed, and still no such book appeared on the market. In the meantime, I had been considering Irwin's suggestion and finally decided to act on it. After many discussions and false beginnings, I came up with an outline I believed would meet the needs of researchers and advanced students in the field. I wanted to include chapters representative of stress research in different fields, the major premise being that life events and stress increase susceptibility to illness.

The book expands on this theme by examining the physiological mechanisms underlying this relationship and the psychological factors involved in modulating it. The book concludes with research on treatment of the stress response. This section is based on the hypothesis that if stress increases illness susceptibility and if certain psychological and physiological factors can prevent or diminish stress-induced illness, then application of these principles to treatment should result in decreased morbidity. Four treatment modalities and the parameters within which they are effective are examined to evaluate this hypothesis.

The goal of this book is to approach the concept of stress within a biopsychosocial framework. This framework is representative of Meyer's (cf. Meyer & Brady, 1979) psychobiology, which is based on the principle that the living man can only be studied as a whole person in action. In psychobiology, all systems must be examined and incorporated into the final product. Meyer, reacting to mechanistic medicine, believed that every person is unique and that categorizations are more often detrimental than helpful. The philosophy underlying this current book is that individuals must be studied in toto, that they are unique, but that much can be learned by examining similarities between people and other organisms. Although each of us is unique, we are all members of the species *Homo sapiens* and thus share many characteristics.

This book is divided into four parts and a final summary chapter. The parts are arranged to follow one another naturally, with the final chapter integrating the material presented earlier. The first part is a general one on mind–body interactions. The two chapters in this part focus on whether monism or dualism is better supported by the research literature. The first chapter, by Riley and Furedy, discusses this issue within a general context, whereas Burchfield, Stein, and Hamilton in the second chapter use a specific emotional state (test anxiety) as a basis for determining whether the psychological, physiological, or inter-actionistic approach has more explanatory power.

Part II deals with the psychobiology of stress. It contains primarily physio-logical research, although, given the nature of stress per se, psychological concomitants are also included. The part is arranged to begin with a discussion of neurotransmission, followed by chapters on immunity, hormones, and the autonomic nervous system's cardiovascular effects. Anisman, Kokkinidis, and Sklar (Chap. 3) focus on changes in the catecholamines after stress. Solomon, Amkraut, and Rubin (Chap. 4) discuss neural effects on immunity; their chapter delineates several mechanisms for stress-induced illness susceptibility. M. Wilson (Chap. 6) and Veith-Flanigan and Sandman (Chap. 5) both discuss hormones and stress. M. Wilson deals with regulation of a specific hormonal system, whereas Veith-Flanigan and Sandman give a broad overview of how and why hormones are involved in the stress response. They also integrate information from neuropharmacology to discuss the role of endorphins and peptides in neuro-transmission and reaction to stress. Corley's chapter (Chap. 7) concludes this part by showing the effects of stress on the cardiovascular system. He reviews the executive monkey research and describes the cardiac pathology of both the worker and executive monkeys. Corley found that different kinds of stress affect the cardiac tissue in different ways, a finding echoed in the other chapters in regard to other physiological systems.

Chapter 8, by Haney and Blumenthal, on the cardiovascular system, differs from the previous discussion of cardiac pathology in that now the psychological and behavioral characteristics of cardiac-prone (Type A) people are discussed. From there, Garrity and Marx (Chap. 9) discuss the life stress–illness relationship and factors that moderate it. Moderating variables they have investigated include psychophysiological strain, Type A behavior, and social supports. Sarason, Sarason, and Johnson (Chap. 10) also outline research on moderator variables in the life stress–illness relationship. They differ from Garrity and Marx, however, in their choice of measurement instruments and methodological techniques.

Part III concludes with Chapter 11 by J. Wilson, who also identifies moderating variables, yet, with a unique approach. Instead of using relatively healthy undergraduates and correlating measures of stress with those of psycho-logical or physiological malaise, he has gone into a health care setting and worked with patients awaiting surgery. His outcome measures include length of hospitalization, hormonal secretion, and number of medications given for pain. In addition to simply assessing psychosocial characteristics of surgery patients, he has, in other studies, used different intervention strategies to prepare them for surgery. In this way, Wilson applies theoretical knowledge to an ill population and assesses its impact. All chapters in this part depict different aspects and methodologies of assessing life stress and understanding psychosocial factors that moderate its influence.

Part IV deals with treatment of the stress response. Four different treatment approaches are described. Each one is based on the premise that, to reduce the stress response, arousal and anxiety must first be decreased. Chapter 12 delineates a physiological technique for lowering arousal. Andrasik, Blanchard, and Edlund describe biofeedback and the parameters within which it is effective. Shapiro (Chap. 13) describes a cognitive technique, meditation, that, by relaxing the mind, relaxes the body. The remaining two chapters employ techniques with both psychological and physiological components. Lavey and Taylor (Chap. 14) review their work on a method of relaxation that consists of both muscle relaxation and inner focusing, or mental relaxation. Smith and Ascough (Chap. 15) conclude Part IV by describing their stress-management treatment program, which includes cognitive restructuring, coping-skills training, and induced affect (e.g., induced physiological arousal). Step-by-step presentation of this treatment package is useful for understanding its structure and for easy replication by interested practitioners. At this point, the book has come full circle: from general chapters on the nature of cognitive–physiological interactions to specific chapters examining its component parts and integrating the information in terms of treatment strategies.

This book is aimed at scientists in all areas of stress research. Because expertise in one area does not confer expertise in others, some chapters will be difficult reading for those not well-versed in their topics. Yet each author has tried to include general information that is not too technical and summary paragraphs to help the novice reader understand the gist of the chapter. The variety of technical chapters was included because of the perceived need for a book that integrated all aspects of the problem.

The book was thus designed as a source book so that people would have, under one cover, access to research articles on a variety of subjects. Not only does this book attempt to integrate many different areas but, by providing diversity, it should encourage diversity of thinking among scientists. It is time to integrate the research on stress and provide a framework for the study of the total organism. In turn, new areas of research may be suggested, and the mechanisms whereby psychological processes increase or decrease disease susceptibility may be better understood.

*Susan R. Burchfield*

# REFERENCE

Meyer, E., III, & Brady, J. V. (Eds.). *Research in the psychobiology of human behavior.* Baltimore: Johns Hopkins Press, 1979.

# I

# COGNITIVE–
# PHYSIOLOGICAL
# INTERACTIONS

Because this volume attempts to integrate psychological and physiological research on stress, Part I was designed to examine psychological and physiological interactions in general. The chapters explore the interdependency of these systems and determine what theoretical framework best explains the literature. This part is the only one in which the theme of all chapters is the integration of psyche and soma.

Riley and Furedy (Chap. 1) discuss monism and dualism and elaborate on their theory of learning in the cognitive and physiological modalities. By postulating that the learning processes involved in the various psychological and physiological systems may differ, they are able to explain many disparate results in the literature.

Burchfield, Stein, and Hamilton (Chap. 2) explore the issue of cognitive-physiological interactions in another way. Their chosen topic, test anxiety, has been well researched but still evokes controversy over the relative contributions of cognitive and physiological processes. By examining the literature, Burchfield et al. conclude that test anxiety has both cognitive and physiological components. Their chapter brings up an important question about the role of psychological and physiological systems in emotions: If emotions stem from an interaction between these systems, why are treatments that focus on only one system effective? By what mechanism do they work? Riley and Furedy offer an answer to this question based on their research on learning differences between systems.

These two chapters serve as an introduction to this book in that they integrate a variety of research to show that psychological and physiological systems are inseparable. In Parts II and III, these systems are dissected, and variables affecting each one are examined. Finally, all these data are reintegrated in the form of treatment protocols (Part IV) and a model for understanding stress (Part V).

# 1

# Psychological and Physiological Systems

## Modes of Operation and Interaction

*Diane M. Riley and John J. Furedy*
*University of Toronto, Toronto, Canada*

## INTRODUCTION

### Philosophic Background

No issue is as readily shelved by psychologists as that of the nature of the relationship between mind (psychology) and body (physiology). While such a move postpones having to grapple with a difficult problem, it does not solve it. Indeed, by failing to address the issue explicitly, one necessarily adopts an implicit stance, which may lead all too often to theoretical inconsistency and empirical problems. Such inconsistency is not only the basis of poor scientific theory but a source of serious errors in any pragmatic approach to human responding (Marx, 1963). Consideration of the relationship between the mind and the body is vital to both the scientific understanding and the practical treatment of psychological and physiological processes.

The range of positions available regarding mind–body relationships is wide and diverse (e.g., Borst, 1970; Burchfield—this volume, chap. 2), but they can generally be characterized as variants of three major ones. First, one may regard psychological and physiological processes as different sorts of events occurring quite independently of one another. This is known as *parallelism*. If one considers that the psychological and the physiological are not totally independent of each other, one may adopt some variant of a second position, *epiphenomenalism*. According to such a position, one set of events is a by-product or epiphenomenon of the other, being totally dependent upon, but not affecting, the other set of events. Third, if one thinks that the psychological and the physiological affect each other, then one logically has to take a position in which the mind and the body are indeed capable of interacting, which is the position of *interactionism*. One form of interactionism is *dualistic*, according to which the mind and the body are in two fundamentally different worlds, as in Cartesian dualism. The main problem with this variant of interactionism is that one must cogently address the issue of how it is that two fundamentally different worlds,

Preparation of this chapter was facilitated by a grant from the Natural Sciences and Engineering Council of Canada to JJF. We owe a special intellectual debt of gratitude to Shelley Parlow for a critical reading of earlier drafts of the manuscript.

Diane M. Riley is now at Addiction Research Foundation, Toronto, Canada.

the mind and the body, do interact. Specification of the form of the interaction of the different worlds, a specification of both logical and practical import, has remained an insurmountable problem for dualist interactionists (e.g., Borst, 1970; Shaffer, 1967).

Finally, one may avoid the theoretical problems associated with the interaction of two fundamentally different realms and remain logically consistent by adopting a *monist* stance. According to this position, the mind and the body are not different worlds but simply different systems within the same world. The monist-interactionist position is one that regards the physiological and the psychological as different organizations of fundamentally identical events. By way of example, consider an ant and an elephant. While these organisms represent very different organizations of constituents, they are still of the same world and capable of interacting. An important characteristic of interactionism of a monistic form is that the systems involved are indeed different systems in the same world, but one system is not simply reducible to the other. If it were the case that the psychological could be completely reduced to the physiological or vice versa, then there could be no interaction of the two, but only a unitary, main effect.

Parallelist or epiphenomenalist accounts of psychophysiological relationships would propose that the psychological and the physiological cannot interact. For a parallelist account to be viable, it would need to be demonstrated that the psychological and the physiological do indeed operate totally independently of one another. That is, the psychological systems would have to be ineffective in changing physiological activity and vice versa. An epiphenomenalist account, on the other hand, would not require total independence, inasmuch as changing the underlying set of systems could affect the epiphenomenal set. Epiphenomenalism does require, however, that the epiphenomenal systems be ineffective in changing the activity of the underlying system. Consequently, if it is demonstrated that the psychological affects the physiological and that the physiological affects the psychological, parallelism and both possible forms of epiphenomenalism cannot be regarded as viable positions on the mind–body relationship. The position we advocate here is one of interactionism, and in the following sections evidence for such a psycnophysiological relationship is presented. We discuss the specific implications of an interactionist position for the analysis and modification of the response to stress, with particular reference to the modes of operation of the different systems involved.

## Definitional Issues

Accepting that the psychological and the physiological do interact may seem intuitively satisfying, but in order to increase scientific understanding of a phenomenon, it is not sufficient merely to feel more familiar with it. Rather, it is necessary to be able to state the nature of the conditions that are held to be necessary and sufficient for the occurrence of the phenomenon and thereby to afford more adequate explanations of observed effects. For this sort of understanding to be a valid one, it is first necessary systematically to manipulate factors so that effects can be reliably and unequivocally assessed. Systematic manipulation in turn requires that the factor to be examined can be identified, and to identify any factor it is necessary first to provide some minimal conceptual definition and operational specification.

Advocates of the operational-definition approach sometimes imply that operational specification per se is enough, so that one can scientifically define a concept in terms of the experimental manipulations used in an attempt to produce it. Specification in terms of operations alone, however, is not sufficient for analyzing complex concepts. For example, one cannot adequately define or understand "cognitive dissonance" by stating it simply to be a process that is associated with certain experimental situations because such a definition does not include any minimal conception of what cognitive dissonance is like. For adequate definition of a term, it is necessary to provide some idea of the differences between the term and other processes that may be occurring. If it is not specified that a factor is of some form and not of some other, effects may be attributed to it that are, in fact, the result of some completely different process. The importance of adequate conceptual definition is illustrated by Harré and Secord (1973) in their lucid critique of logical positivism. In discussing the definition of cognitive dissonance, Harré and Secord write that

> *The experimenter treats the experimental paradigm as if its operations represent the concepts themselves.* Dissonance *remains unanalysed. And in the absence of a clear account of what dissonance is, there can be no set of precise rules that a scientist can use for generating a series of dissonance inducing experiments. Without such rules he cannot tell whether his experiment has succeeded or failed. (p. 36)*

The need for conceptual analysis is thus apparent, for without it one cannot specify what it is that one's operations are intended to measure, leaving one to interpret experimental results in a subjective manner.

This said, we attempt here to provide conceptual definitions of key terms used in the course of this chapter. The first of these is the word *cognitive*, a term that enjoys frequent use yet has been poorly defined in recent approaches to psychology. While it is usually stated that events such as those of imaging, problem solving, and reasoning are cognitive events, there is little attempt made to specify in what sense these are examples of the cognitive and not some other psychological process. Some specification is provided through equating the cognitive with the higher mental processes, but this in itself is not an adequate definition because we do not know what is required for a mental process to be characterizable as "higher." Furthermore, it is not often made clear what psychological processes are *not* characterizable as cognitive, and hence it is difficult to determine the unique features of such events (see Searle, 1980, for an extensive analysis of these issues). "Cognition" has frequently been used as though it were synonymous with "information processing" (e.g., Haugeland, 1978; Simon, 1969), a substitution which only serves to remove the problem one step. *Information processing* is itself a term that is so generally used and variously defined that it can be taken to refer to any function of the organism that involves input and output, and such generality does not allow for adequate specification. Similarly, characterization of the cognitive as involving "symbol manipulation" fails to do more than delay a solution to the problem of what sort of symbol manipulation is being considered. It would seem that unless one can differentiate the "cognitive" from other processes occurring in the organism, one can only furnish very general descriptions of behavior, with no basis for a delineation of the possible different mechanism involved in different processes. Such generality does not allow for a realistic account of the complexity of behavior (see, e.g., Harré & Secord, 1973); and even from a postpositivistic view, it is suggested that a more precise analysis can be attempted (e.g., Koch, 1980; Meehl, 1978). For adequate explanation, clear definition is first needed (see, e.g., Harré & Secord, 1973; Marx, 1963). If a term such as *cognitive* is to be used meaningfully, one should indicate what the term can in fact contribute to our understanding of psychological processes.

The use of the term *cognitive* in this chapter is in keeping with traditional epistemological usage (e.g., Armstrong, 1973; Lacey, 1976). That is, *cognitive* is limited to those mental processes that involve propositional relationships between events. *Propositional relationships* involve statements about the manner in which events occur. They thus involve assertions about the way the world is and can therefore be meaningfully called true or false. Propositional relationships are standardly represented by the form "$X$ is $Y$." The predicate ($Y$) states something about the subject ($X$), and to such relationships it is meaningful to apply expressions of truth, belief, and evidence (Scheffler, 1965). Thus, for an organism to be genuinely spoken of as "knowing" (cognizing), its behavior must be meaningfully describable as involving processing of propositional relationships. So cognition involves a special kind of information processing, and *propositional information* is a term that refers to this form of information. Tolman's (1948) expectancies and cognitive maps are, therefore, cognitive in this sense, as are O'Keefe and Nadel's (1979) more recently proposed "locale" systems involving processing of propositional relationships by the organism rather than simple responding to stimuli. Cognition is thus activity involving sign-significate relationships: in other words, there is something about the system that represents something in the world rather than the system simply reacting to the world. Noncognitive processes, on the other hand, involve processing of information that is nonpropositional in nature (Lacey, 1976). These processes, such as affection, involve the organism simply reacting or expressing, and these are behaviors that cannot be meaningfully described as involving processing of propositional relationships and to which the true–false category does not apply. Consequently, in cases of cognition one can say that the organism *knows* that $X$ is $Y$. Where there is no such knowledge and the organism is simply responding, one can only say that the organism is able to do $R$ in response to $X$.[1] This is not a purely

---

[1] This distinction between knowledge and ability does not ignore the "knowing how" class of events. According to the characterization presented here, "knowing how" (Ryle, 1949), or procedural (Dreyfus, 1972; Goodman, 1978) or "tacit" knowledge, (Polanyi, 1962) is classifiable as knowledge only to the extent that it involves behavior that can be meaningfully described in terms of propositional relationships. The part of the skill or performance that cannot be so described is, according to the definition used here, ability. Thus, from the point of view of the describer of the behavior, "knowing how" is an instance of "knowing that" because, on strict epistemological grounds, it is only the latter process that can properly be characterized as "knowledge." We suggest that the common confusion between knowing "that" and "how" would be clarified if the describer's knowledge of the subject's behavior were clearly distinguished from the subject's knowledge. It is often the case that a subject's behavior exhibits "marks of cognition," or, in our terms, is characterizable (by the describer) propositionally; and yet the subject *cannot* characterize his own behavior propositionally. In such a situation the subject may report that "I know *how* to do it, but I don't know the principles/rules/propositions (i.e., knowing "that") that I have been using." It may also be that some cognition is nonpropositional, involving analogue symbolic representation rather than discrete data structures (see Kolers & Smythe, 1979). For the purposes of this discussion, however, specific consideration of such nonpropositional "cognitive" processes is not necessary. It is necessary only to recognize that only some processes involve propositional information, whereas others do not. The specific names of those nonpropositional processes are, for our present purposes, unimportant.

metaphysical issue but an empirical one, as indicated by the maze-learning experiments of Tolman and his students in the forties and the more recent work of Olton (Olton, Becker, Handelmann, & Mitchell, 1979) and of O'Keefe and Nadel (1979).

Of course processes may be based not on propositional relationships but on *contiguity relationships*, including temporal association. The Hullian S-R system was based on such associations, "cognition" being eliminated. It is not meaningful to apply true–false assertions to contiguity-based processes. Rather, one may only speak of pairing a response with an event. Many psychological and physiological events involve nonpropositional relationships and are thus noncognitive according to the present definition. For example, the affective, motivational, and autonomic systems cannot be meaningfully characterized as processing propositional information but only as reacting. When noncognitive processes are referred to in this chapter, the term *response* is often used. When cognitive approaches are referred to, the term *propositional* is often used, the approaches discussed being concerned exclusively with propositional relationships between events.

A number of important theoretical and practical issues relate to the adequate definition of terms. For example, the foregoing definition of *cognitive* makes it clear that several systems associated with processing of information can be differentiated. Information processing does not always involve propositional relationships (knowledge), sometimes only response. All psychological effects need not be regarded as being due to cognitive factors. Furthermore, problems with such a unitary approach become evident when effects are predicted in a system, following certain psychological manipulations, and they do not occur. Such a failure is often ascribed to some methodological flaw, but it could equally well reflect the falsity of the (often implicit) assumption that all psychological systems operate according to cognitive principles. One of the basic premises of the following argument is that an analysis of different principles of operation of different systems may prove of some value in explaining the ineffectiveness of traditional cognitive approaches in producing behavioral change.

Historically, it is quite understandable that the psychological processes generally have come to be regarded as "cognitive" and that processing of propositional information by the organism is therefore of primary concern. The impact of information theory and cybernetics on psychology has led to a focusing on the "higher" mental processes. This emphasis on the cognitive, however, has resulted in the failure of modern psychology to acknowledge that the "lower" mental functions of affection and motivation are also important determinants of behavior (see, e.g., Berlyne, 1960; Leventhal, 1979; Zajonc, 1980). Further, learning has become equated with the processing of propositional information—the acquisition of knowledge (e.g., Rescorla, 1969; Schwartz, 1978)—to the exclusion of ability. Although such approaches have greatly improved our understanding of processes such as memory and reasoning, they have done little to further our understanding either of how the organism as a whole responds to environmental demands or of the processes that underlie the actions of the organism (see Kolers & Smythe, 1979; Martin and Levy, 1968).

Recently, however, researchers such as Leventhal (1979) and Zajonc (1980) have returned to an examination of the distinctive features of the affective and motivational processes, arguing that these processes not only are "pre-cognitive" but operate according to quite different principles from the cognitive system. The notion that there are different psychological systems that operate differently and that can be independent of the cognitive system has very important implications for the analysis and treatment of the response to stress. One may benefit similarly by making a distinction between the types of physiological systems involved in a response, for it is probable that they too differ in nature and in principles of responding. One such difference relates to whether or not the physiological system in question is capable of being under cognitive control, the somatic system generally being under extensive control, the autonomic system is not (e.g., Guyton, 1976). A further difference lies in the biochemical characteristics of a system, the sympathetic (adrenergic) nervous system being quite distinctive in terms of its neurotransmission. Such differences lead to behavioral effects, as indicated below, and need to be taken into account when analyzing and changing behavior (see Dismukes, 1979; Pribram, 1971; Riley, 1980).

In sort, ignoring noncognitive systems leads only to an unrealistic emphasis on thinking and memory—the organism has much to cogitate with, but we cannot teach it *how* to *do* anything. As has been argued elsewhere (Furedy, 1979, pp. 212-213), Guthrie's jibe at the insufficiency of Tolman's propositional theory of learning is applicable to more recent cognitive approaches to behavior, including the area of biofeedback. These approaches would seem to leave not only the rat but also the human subject "buried in thought," unable to act. In the following sections we attempt to redress this imbalance by focusing on the behavior of the total organism (cognitive, affective, and motivational and the various forms of physiological processes) in the response to stress.

## THE RESPONSE TO STRESS

When an organism is exposed to a psychological or physiological stressor, a number of bodily changes are observed; they are psychological, physiological, and overt behavioral in nature. With respect to psychological events, there are three main aspects. Cognitively, one may observe anxiety; affectively, feelings of distress and arousal; and motivationally, evidence of a strong tendency to avoid the situation. With respect to the physiological events, one sees significant changes in cortical measures, such as electroencephalographic activity, and in peripheral measures such as heart rate (HR), blood pressure (BP), electrodermal activity, catecholamine levels, and so forth. There is usually little correlation between these various physiological measures (Lacey, 1967). With respect to the overt behavioral responses, one sees trembling, stuttering, and physical avoidance of the stressor (for a detailed account of these various changes, see, e.g., in addition to this book, Lang, 1977a; Levi, 1975; Marks, 1969; Selye, 1956). There is often little concordance between these various measures of anxiety and fear. It is, for example, quite possible for a subject to show many signs of physiological arousal associated with anxiety and yet report low-anxiety cognitions and feelings, or vice versa (e.g., Gatchel, 1979; Hodgson & Rachman, 1974; Marks, 1969).

As a consequence of this diverse activity, the response to stress cannot be considered a simple response in a single system. Rather, the response to stress comprises a number of different variables and appears as a complex pattern of responding in different systems. A number of views of this multidimensional nature of emotional behavior such as that in the response to stress have been put forward, and generally these point to a complex interaction of psychological, physiological, and behavioral systems (e.g., Lang, 1977a; Lang, Rice, & Sternbach, 1972; Marks, 1969; Rachman, 1968). The lack of synchrony between these various systems is also well-documented, there being little relationship between subjective, overt behavioral and internal physiological systems in the response to a wide variety of stressors (e.g., Gatchel, 1979; Hodgson & Rachman, 1974; Lang et al., 1972; Öhman, 1979a; Riley & Cupchik, 1980). The lack of concordance between the different systems is particularly well-documented in the fear response of phobics, where at the cognitive level the subject may express no fear and acknowledge the irrationality of his or her behavior, yet autonomic responding indicates a state of extreme fear (e.g., Hodgson & Rachman, 1974; Marks, 1969; Öhman & Hugdahl, 1979).

The data generally indicate that the response to stress is multidimensional, involving very different forms of responding in different systems, different individuals, and different situations. Such complexity raises a number of empirical and pragmatic issues with respect to the stress response. For example, questions arise as to the nature of interactions between systems, the extent of generalization across systems, the modes of operation of different systems, and the importance of individual differences. All of these issues need to be taken into account when investigating the behavior of the total organism. Further, because the response to stress comprises a complex pattern of responding in a number of interacting but nonsynchronous systems, a single measure of responding cannot be considered a valid measure of the effects of a stressor. Not only is the activity in different systems often poorly correlated, but there is the fact that different psychological and physiological systems may obey quite different principles of operation (see, e.g., Dismukes, 1979; Furedy & Riley, 1982; Kolers & Smythe, 1979; Leventhal, 1979; Pribram, 1971; Riley, 1980). It is consequently important to consider the modes of operation of, and interactions between, *all* systems involved in the response to stress or any other event involving the total organism. In order to examine the possibility of different modes of operation, we turn next to a consideration of some situations in which different response systems behave quite differently.

## Modes of Systems Operation

We have suggested that the modes of operation of the different psychological and physiological systems involved in the response to stress are often radically different. The nature of these differences can be shown here by considering data on the nature of responding of different systems in a variety of experimental situations: human Pavlovian autonomic conditioning, signaling of noxious unmodifiable events, and phobic research.

*Human Pavlovian autonomic conditioning.* As detailed elsewhere (Furedy, 1973), the recent shift from S–R behaviorism to cognitivism in psychology has led many researchers to espouse cognitivistic epiphenomenalism to replace what was behavioristic epiphenomenalism. That is, from considering cognitive learning of the contingency between the conditional stimulus (CS) and unconditional stimulus (US) as merely an unimportant by-product or epiphenomenon of a conditional autonomic response such as the electrodermal response (EDR), there is now a tendency to consider EDR conditioning a mere reflection of cognitive (propositional) or "relational" learning (Dawson, 1973). On this view of an unlimited "cognitive control" (Furedy, 1973, p. 108), the functioning of the cognitive and autonomic systems is identical, inasmuch as the former completely controls the latter, which is just an index of the controlling cognitive process.[2]

One set of facts that has been taken to confirm the strong cognitive-control position is that only those subjects show conditioning of an autonomic response such as the EDR who are aware of the CS–US relationship or contingency; unaware subjects show no evidence of EDR conditioning (e.g., Fuhrer & Baer, 1965). These data are taken to confirm the cognitive-control position because this position can be formulated in causal terms, wherein contingency learning ($A$) is stated to cause EDR conditioning ($B$). Evidence for $A$ being necessary for $B$ of the sort provided by Fuhrer and Baer does indeed confirm an $A$-causes-$B$ position.

The cognitive-control position, however, has other consequences that are refuted by sets of well-documented facts. The first of these consequences is that the extent of awareness of the CS–US contingency of "relational learning" should be highly and positively correlated with the extent of EDR conditioning. Thus, although $A$ being correlated with $B$ does not imply that $A$ causes $B$, the causal claim requires (as a minimal condition) that $A$ and $B$ be correlated. This correlational requirement between knowledge of contingency and EDR conditioning has been examined in a number of instances over a variety of conditioning paradigms and has been uniformly found not to hold (Furedy & Schiffmann, 1971, 1973, 1974; Schiffmann & Furedy, 1972, 1977). Nor have there been any published criticisms of these denials of any correlation between these cognitive and autonomic processes. In this respect, then, the cognitive and autonomic systems do not function in the same manner.

Another consequence of the cognitive-control position stems directly from one of its most influential and systematically formulated variants, the contingency account of Pavlovian conditioning (Rescorla, 1967, 1969; see also Prokasy, 1965, for an earlier and less well-known version). This account favors a contingency over a pairings view of all Pavlovian conditioning, and it sees the organism as a "contingency analyzer" (see Furedy, 1973, p. 109), reacting only in terms of the propositional information inherent in the contingency between the CS and the US. A methodological corollary of the contingency account is that the proper control for the CS associated with the US (i.e., the $CS^+$) is not the conventional

---

[2] The sort of cognitivism that sees propositional processing as the only relevant determinant in the behavior of the organism is "imperialistic" in the same way as the Hullians of the 1940s and 1950s were imperialistic with respect to the purportedly universal role of S–R processes in determining behavior. The S–R imperialism of those days attempted to employ the response concept so widely that a construct like the Hullian fractional-anticipatory-goal response ($r_G$) appeared to be able to do all that Tomanian expectancy could do in accounting for such apparently cognitive phenomena as latent learning. The breadth enjoyed by the $r_G$ construct was thought by most Hullians to be a positive feature (see, e.g., Kendler, 1952). As Ritchie (1953) in his satirical response to the Hullians pointed out, however, the price for this sort of "circumnavigation" of genuinely cognitive phenomena was great. It amounted to giving up a genuine scientific understanding of behavior, because the $r_G$ concept was so broad as to be compatible with *any* behavioral outcome and was thus unfalsifiable. We suggest, mutatis mutandis, that the price for "circumnavigating" genuine noncognitive phenomena, a fashion popular in our times, is the same.

explicitly unpaired CS⁻ (which is negatively correlated with the US and is therefore a signal of US absence). In a propositional, or contingency, account of learning, the proper control is the truly random CS⁻ that has a zero correlation with the US and is therefore a signal neither of US presence nor absence (Rescorla, 1967).

The propositional, or contingency, account thus implies certain performance differences between responses elicited by the two kinds of control CSs. These performance differences have been examined in autonomic variables such as the EDR and the peripheral vasomotor response (VMR) over a wide range of conditions. This consequence of the cognitive-control position has, like the correlational consequence, been uniformly disconfirmed, there being no differences between responses to explicitly unpaired and truly random CS⁻s (Furedy, 1971; Furedy & Schiffmann, 1971, 1973, 1974; Schiffmann & Furedy, 1972, 1977). In addition, recent studies with decelerative heart-rate Pavlovian conditioning (Furedy & Klajner, 1978) have also failed to produce performance differences when responding to the truly random and explicitly unpaired CS⁻ conditions is compared (Szalai & Furedy, 1978; Westergren & Furedy, 1978).

It bears emphasis that, in all of these Pavlovian autonomic-conditioning studies, the human subjects were aware of the contingency difference between the two control CS⁻s. They were consequently sensitive to the negative-contingency difference between the truly random CS⁻ (zero contingency) and the explicitly unpaired CS⁻ (negative contingency). It is only the autonomic nervous system that appears to be insensitive to negative-contingency variation.[3] That is, while the subjects *knew* that there was a difference in the relationship between stimuli, this knowledge of propositional relationships was not reflected by the noncognitive autonomic system. This again supports the notion that, contrary to an extreme cognitive-control position, in which the entire organism is viewed as a contingency analyzer, the cognitive and autonomic systems do not operate in the same way.

*Signaling of noxious unmodifiable events.* Another instance in which the cognitive system and the autonomic nervous system (ANS) appear, on examination, to be quite disparate is during "informational control," which has been defined as occurring when a preceding signal of a noxious event reduces the

---

[3] Although explanations in terms of adaptiveness are postdictive rather than predictive, it may be worth noting that it makes little sense for the autonomic nervous system (ANS) to be sensitive to negative-contingency variation just because the cognitive component of the CNS is so sensitive. In terms of the acquisition of knowledge about the world, an organism that cannot distinguish between a stimulus that is a signal for the absence of another stimulus and one that is neutral with respect to occurrence of the other stimulus is an organism that is not likely to be well-adapted to the complex cognitive demands of a rapidly changing environment. On the other hand, in terms of ANS effectiveness, it may well be that discriminating between events that are (positive) signals for significant other events (i.e., a CS⁺ in conditioning terms) need only be discriminated by the ANS from the remaining class of events. A reflex like the flight-or-fight reaction, at least in its autonomic components, could function quite efficiently this way without having also to be sensitive to the negative-contingency differences to which the cognitive system reacts. That is, in terms of the energy requirements of the organism in times of danger, it would be safer for the ANS to prepare for mobilization when it was not, in fact, necessary than to have the functional capacity *not* to respond appropriately. The failure of the ANS to process propositional information reduces the probability of an error of inappropriate nonresponding at the expense of inappropriate responding.

perceived impact of that event. The notion that signals have this sort of beneficial effect is in line with the current "cognitivism" zeitgeist, which emphasizes the importance of propositional, declarative information (see Kolers & Smythe, 1979). It can be shown, however, that signaling a shock or loud noise does not reduce the rated intensity, nor are signaled shocks or noises preferred over unsignaled ones (Furedy, 1975). In fact, only autonomic evidence appears to support the notion of informational control. Lykken (1962), for example, interpreted the fact that rats gave smaller EDRs to signaled than to unsignaled shocks as evidence for reduction in perceived impact owing to signaling. Also, both the EDR and the peripheral VMRs show this reduction owing to signaling in human subjects (e.g., Furedy, 1970; Furedy & Doob, 1971; Riley & Champion, 1978) when shock-elicited ANS responding is the measure. Thus there is, once again, a discrepancy between autonomic and cognitive measures.

*Phobia.* Finally, the discrepancies between cognitive and noncognitive systems are perhaps most clearly evident in the phobic fear reaction and, in particular, in the "irrational" aspects of the phobic response (e.g., Marks, 1969; Öhman, 1979a). That is, the subject reports that she or he knows that the phobic stimulus will not be, in fact, damaging, but total bodily reaction does not reflect this rational response, the autonomic components in particular indicating instead great fear of the phobic stimulus.

These differences between response systems in reacting to propositional information in this case are properly regarded as problematic for cognitive accounts of phobia (see Eysenck, 1979; Marks, 1969). Further, such accounts fail to explain why EDRs to potentially phobic stimuli used in Pavlovian conditioning analogues of phobia do not extinguish more rapidly with addition of instructions about the removal of the aversive unconditioned stimulus (e.g., Öhman & Hugdahl, 1979).[4] The insensitivity of autonomic indexes to propositional information would, however, be predicted if one assumes that there are different principles of operation in the different systems. While the human organism may be regarded as "rational" at the level of reason and other higher mental processes (i.e., that which is referred to here as "cognitive"), there is much more involved in the response to stress than just cognition. The behavior of the total organism involves many systems, not all of which have the structural and functional capacity to process the kind of information associated with rationality.

Although the behavior of phobics might appear irrational when considering the contingencies between stimuli, it is quite understandable when considering

---

[4] It should be noted that failures of the ANS to respond to instructional manipulations need not simply be due to the inability of the ANS to process the verbal aspect of the information. Such failures may be due to a failure to process the propositional aspect. That the failure of the ANS to behave in the same manner as the cognitively controlled systems during extinction is not simply due to failure to process verbal information is demonstrated by the fact that autonomic components behave differently even when the information is not verbal. Presentation of the CS alone is nonverbal, propositional information about the absence of the US, but such presentation is itself not sufficient for extinction of autonomic responses. Thus true extinction instructions (i.e., the CS is no longer paired with the US) may fail to produce extinction in the ANS either because the nonverbal propositional information of the US no longer following the CS is not processed or because the verbal extinction instructions are not processed. Verbal and propositional information, therefore, should not be conceptually equated.

the temporal associations between stimuli and responses. For the non-propositional systems, the relationship between the fear-relevant stimulus and the fear response is firmly established, either through direct pairing on a number of occasions or, because of the salience of the stimulus, on a single occasion. Indeed, because of the marked salience of phobic stimuli, direct exposure to the phobic stimulus itself is not necessary, pictures or other representations being sufficient to evoke the fear response in some form (e.g., Öhman, 1979a). Although one can point to phobic reactions to a wide variety of stimuli, not necessarily those classifiable as "potentially phobic" (such as spiders and snakes), the most common phobic reactions are to a class of stimuli traditionally associated with fear. Fear, like anxiety, is a difficult response to diminish, precisely because it is an example of a multidimensional response to a stressor, involving a great deal of autonomic activity, especially in the sympathetic branch. Thus, not only does the fear response involve a number of psychological and physiological systems; it also involves systems that operate quite differently. Some of these systems are not sensitive to contingency manipulations (stimulus-stimulus relationships), but are only sensitive to temporal associations (stimulus response relationships). Because of these different sensitivities to information, differences between systems in terms of responding are predictable. These different principles apply not only to different systems but to different aspects of the learning process. In the following section, the nature of these principles and possible neurochemical bases for them are considered.

## Principles of Operation

Any discussion of the principles of conditioning and learning requires adequate definition of terms. Grings (1977) has recently noted with respect to the current disputes over what is learned in autonomic conditioning that "the major reasons for ambiguity are lack of explicit definition of terms and a tendency to overgeneralise from limited empirical demonstrations" (p. 343). We attempt, therefore, to clarify terms we use here and to indicate why overgeneralization from limited paradigms has posed serious problems for stress research and treatment. *Conditioning* refers here to a change in behavior owing to a consistent pairing of stimuli (see Champion, 1969). *Learning* here refers to a relatively permanent change in behavior acquired through practice, which may include exposure to the repeated pairings of two stimuli (Champion, 1969).

Recent cognitive-contingency accounts of classical conditioning (e.g., Mackintosh, 1974; Rescorla, 1967) have viewed the arrangements of the CS and the US as relations of contingency rather than just temporal pairings. These cognitive accounts suggest that Pavlovian (classical) conditioning should be viewed as a process of contingency, stimulus-stimulus (S-S) learning. A contingency account, however, is not necessarily applicable to the behavior of all of the response systems in the organism. Even if the CS–US arrangements are described procedurally as contingency arrangements, it does not follow that for conditioning, learning, or both to occur in a response system, the organism must have learned the contingency. That is, it is not necessary for the organism to learn the proposition that "Stimulus $X$ (the CS) is a sign of Stimulus $Y$ (the US)" in order to respond to Stimulus $X$. Even if one believes that the contingency between stimuli is responsible for observed conditioning, it does not follow that what the system has learned is *knowledge* about that contingency. Knowledge, as we define it, involves the processing of propositional relationships. In such processing, the organism demonstrates that it perceives one stimulus as a sign (representation) of another stimulus. This complex form of processing can only be carried out by the cognitive systems. The noncognitive systems cannot themselves learn such relationships, for they appear to be unable to process such propositional information (see, e.g., Furedy, 1973; Furedy & Schiffmann, 1971, 1973, 1974). The noncognitive systems can, however, be used to demonstrate or provide evidence for the existence of such knowledge in the organism, at least to the extent that the noncognitive systems react to the cognitive systems. For example, EDRs have been used as an index of the organism's recognition of a stimulus as having signal value or significance (Bernstein, 1979), which suggests that the electrodermal system is sensitive to cognitive events.

We suggest, however, that noncognitive processes, including autonomic activity, can demonstrate conditioning and learning of a form quite independent of that of cognitive processes. In stressing the distinction between conditioning of responses to stimuli and the acquisition of information about the contingencies between these stimuli, S–R approaches to conditioning and learning differ markedly from many current cognitive approaches. These latter approaches focus more or less exclusively on the cognitive or "intellectual" aspects of the conditioning process (see Öhman, 1979b). That is, they concentrate on the learning of S-S (propositional) relationships at the expense of S–R relationship.

The differences in emphasis between the cognitive and a more behavioristic approach has obvious implications for the study and manipulation of behavior. The study of learning as a purely cognitive process—the acquisition of knowledge alone (S-S learning) rather than of ability (S–R learning) as well—leads to a concern with those parameters that are optimal for cognitive processes and may disregard the needs of the particular response system being studied (see Grings, 1977; Martin & Levey, 1968; Öhman, 1979b). With respect to this emphasis on cognitive factors, Prokasy (1977) notes that

> One may be interested in what information is being abstracted from the pairing of stimuli and how it is recalled and employed in subsequent trials or settings. Under these circumstances, the response selected for measurement is not particularly critical, provided that the index of change employed in measurement is one which is demonstrably a unique result of the conditioning paradigm. (p. 361)

If one is interested in examining the behavior of the total organism, however, exclusive concern with either the cognitive or the noncognitive alone is not adequate. That is, a real-world understanding of the organism as a complex hierarchy of interacting systems cannot afford to disregard any source of information.

Before continuing, it is necessary to consider in some detail the interaction of noncognitive systems with cognitive ones. We have stated that the autonomic system can be used to demonstrate relationships between stimuli. This does not mean that the autonomic system itself learns those relationships. We have split the organism conceptually into different systems, and the behavior of each system can thus be considered separately. We stress the fact that the autonomic system learns to react to stimuli themselves; and in addition, perhaps through different pathways, this system can react to the cognitive system's knowledge of what a stimulus represents. The activity of the ANS can thus be viewed as a composite of the many forms of stimulation to which it responds. For example, the ANS does indeed react to the CS as a sign of the US, reflecting the prior cognitive processing.[5] The ANS, however, also reacts directly to the CS as a stimulus at a pre-cognitive stage. Thus measures of autonomic activity reflect the complex interplay of cognitive and noncognitive information processing. If one accepts the composite nature of such indexes, then a purely cognitive account of learning and conditioning is seen to give only an incomplete account of autonomic activity.

In the language of conditioning, it appears that, whereas the cognitive system learns the contingency relationships between the stimuli in conditioning (S-S), the noncognitive systems simply learn to give a response to the conditional stimulus (S-R). Noncognitive systems do not respond to the CS because it is a sign of the US, but because it is paired with a response to the US. Thus, in addition to reacting to processing by the cognitive system, noncognitive systems react to the CS as a substitute for the US, learning thereby to produce a response (the CR) that is independent of propositional knowledge.

The early S-R school of behaviorism, which included such theorists as Hull and Spence, tended to focus solely on the noncognitive aspects of the acquisition process, emphasizing contiguity rather than contingency as the central factor in conditioning. For this reason, S-R accounts of learning were not more adequate than S-S ones. Of late, there has been an almost total reversal of the early position, focusing on the cognitive aspects of conditioning and learning to the exclusion of all others (e.g., Öhman, 1979b; Rescorla, 1967; Stern & Walrath, 1977). Neither kind of account considers the total bodily response. Of course, a purely cognitive account will be reasonably accurate when the organism is in a situation that is almost totally cognitive in nature, such as during mild test anxiety (e.g., Wine, 1971), or phobic conditioning with fear-irrelevant conditional stimuli and weak shock (Öhman, 1979a). In fact, most conventional human autonomic conditioning preparations can probably be described as cognitive in nature and not extensively involving noncognitive processes in the way that fear- or anxiety-provoking situations do (e.g., Dawson, 1973). Nevertheless, even in Pavlovian autonomic conditioning preparations, a strictly cognitive account can be shown to be inadequate. We refer to the previously considered evidence that refutes the notion that the ANS can be considered to be under the complete "cognitive control" of the CNS. To repeat, it has been shown that, in the conditional EDR, relational awareness and EDR conditioning are not highly

---

[5] These differences in the form of information processing between systems would relate to the very different capacities of the neuronal processes involved. For example, the very dense, multiply-interconnected neuronal networks of CNS mechanisms important in autonomic functioning, such as the hypothalamus and amygdala, would allow for considerable interaction between different components. Processing taking place in such networks might be of the analogue, complex symbolic form, which is labeled "context-dependent" by Pribram (1971). Such processing would be prominently involved in highly evocative events such as feelings and other "ineffable" processes. Alternatively, the relatively well-separated neuronal networks of the higher CNS, such as the association cortex, would be more suitable for discrete, denotative processing of the kind labeled "context-independent" by Pribram (1971). Such processing would frequently involve signs and would be associated with the discursive, declarative processes of linguistic and other propositional systems (Pribram, 1971).

correlated and that the ANS, unlike the higher CNS, is not sensitive to negative contingency differences. This means that a purely cognitive account is not adequate for an explanation of EDR conditioning that apparently involves processes that are different from those involved in the learning of propositional relationships.

Another ANS-CNS discrepancy that emerges in the acquisition of conditioning is the role of the interstimulus interval (ISI). Traditional S-R accounts focus on parameters that are important for the attachment of responses to stimuli. Hence the ISI, which is the interval between CS onset and US onset, is considered critical (see, e.g., Kimble, 1961).[6] Cognitive approaches, on the other hand, emphasize parameters of importance for the learning of propositions about the relationship between stimuli, that is, between CS and US. These approaches consequently stress factors such as CS-US associability. Hence, rather than focusing on the ISI, a cognitive approach like that of Öhman (1979a, 1979b) focuses on such associability-related aspects as whether the conditioning paradigm is trace or delay, with separated stimuli (trace) being harder to associate than stimuli present in short-term memory at the same time (delay).

It is a fact, however, that some response systems do not conform to the cognitive view that the ISI is unimportant. In differential EDR and vasomotor conditioning, for example, a 7.5-sec ISI group was significantly inferior to a 0.75-sec group (Furedy, 1970, esp. Fig. 1). In HR decelerative conditioning with negative body tilt as the US, a 5-sec ISI produced no conditioning over eight repeated sessions, whereas a 0.5-sec ISI produced reliable conditioning over one session (Furedy & Poulos, 1976). Finally, it is found in human eyelid conditioning that if the ISI is 2 sec or more, no conditioning is obtained.

Because in most response systems there is at least some level of responding produced during acquisition with long ISIs, differences between response systems have not been marked enough to cause serious problems for cognitive accounts of the acquisition part of conditioning procedures. That is, during acquisition, noncognitive and cognitive systems respond similarly. For the extinction procedure, however, serious problems have arisen (see Eysenck, 1979; Öhman, 1979b) because, in contrast to the acquisition case, it appears that the noncognitively controlled systems behave in a manner totally unlike that of cognitive systems during extinction. Studies of phobic fear and neurotic anxiety have disclosed an unexpected failure of the autonomic system to respond to instructional manipulation (e.g., Eysenck, 1979; Marks, 1969; Öhman, 1979a). During the extinction of responses to fear-inducing stimuli, the autonomic system responds in a manner "quite independent of cognitive manipulations" (Öhman, 1979b, p. 465). After having been informed that the US will not be presented, subjects still produce autonomic responses to the CS for a number of trials; these

---

[6] In fact, the most radical S-R approach, the contiguity-reinforcement account (Jones, 1962; also cf. Champion, 1969), stresses temporal relationships between stimuli (e.g., CS) and response (e.g., UR) so that it is not the CS-US but the CS-UR interval that is deemed critical. This yields differential predictions from conventional pairings approaches in that a US-CS arrangement with a long-latency UR is viewed as a forward CS-UR arrangement and therefore capable of producing conditioning (e.g., Champion & Jones, 1962). For present purposes, however, these relatively minor variations between the pairings approaches are unimportant, as all approaches differ from the contingency approaches in that the former stress temporal rather than contingency (propositional) relations.

responses gradually diminish in the same manner as those of unistructed subjects (e.g., Öhman & Hugdahl, 1979). Thus, in the terms used here, although the subject *knows* that the primary stressor will not be presented, he or she is not able to control the response, that is, to behave in a totally nonfearful manner. With respect to the behaviorist account, this gradual extinction would be predicted rather than the on-instruction extinction predicted by a cognitive account, inasmuch as the phenomenon is based on a noncognitive system. Over the extinction trials, this system learns to associate the CS with a new, nonexcitatory response rather than with the excitatory response previously elicited by the US during acquisition. This would account for the gradual shift, as new learning supersedes old, and because, according to a behavioral account, the system is regarded as not capable of processing propositional information such as that in the instructions, there can be no extinction through instructional manipulation. This would explain the outcome of various experiments involving procedures similar to those of Öhman and Hugdahl (1979). Researchers interested in the extinction rather than the acquisition of behavior have had to turn to behaviorist S-R theories (e.g., Kimble, 1961; Miller, 1948; Mowrer, 1940; Razran, 1956), to explain this phenomenon, postulating the gradual learning of competing responses to the CS through contiguity rather than contingency.

There is a second anomaly of the extinction process in autonomic conditioning, however, that poses difficulties not only for cognitive accounts but for traditional behaviorist accounts (see, e.g., Eysenck, 1979; Marks, 1969). When autonomic responses to strong stressors are examined in subjects with phobic or neurotic disorders or during conditioning with high shock levels, one may fail to observe response diminution over trials. Indeed sometimes extinction produces an intensification of the response to the CS (for a review, see, e.g., Eysenck, 1979; Wood, 1974). This latter intensification of responding, found only when very strong stressors are used as the US, is known as "incubation," and a number of accounts have been proposed in an attempt to explain it (e.g., Eysenck, 1979; Marks, 1969). For example, attempts have been made to explain the phenomenon in terms of the fear-inducing properties of the CS (Eysenck, 1979), but no adequate mechanism of such an effect has been proposed (see, e.g., Wolpe, 1979).

Acknowledging the different modes of operation of systems allows for postulation of a mechanism of incubation and can explain a total absence of extinction. Such an account would begin with the idea of an S-R competing response in stating that extinction depends on a system learning to produce a response to the CS during extinction. But whereas most traditional accounts would maintain that this response would automatically be a new, competing response owing to the absence of the US, we suggest a systemic-competing-response account that postulates that a new response in a system will only be learned if the properties of the system do in fact allow for a new state to be produced in that particular system (see, e.g., Razran, 1956). Thus some central change in the cognitive system is not sufficient to produce new competing responses automatically in all of the systems of the organism. Each system changes according to its different principles of operation. That is, for systems that are slow to change in response to a change in stimulation, there is less probability of learning a new response than with rapidly changing systems. If the state of a noncognitive response system does not change at all during the extinction period, then no new response can be learned by that system and extinction will not be observed. This is because noncognitive systems learn by being shown how to respond, and such demonstration cannot occur unless the desired response is actually produced by changing the state of that response system. Similarly, if the manipulations during extinction are such as to produce a state of increased activation in the system, the response learned will be one of increasing magnitude (incubation) rather than decreasing magnitude (extinction).

Consequently, a systemic account that takes note of the different modes of operation of different systems proposes that a noncognitive system has to be shown how to respond in a manner that is tailored to the constraints of that particular response system. This demonstration in the extinction case requires that the system learn nonexcitation in the presence of the CS rather than the excitation learned during acquisition. Because the noncognitive systems cannot learn sign-significance relationships of a propostional nature, they cannot learn this nonexcitation simply through learning "that" the CS now represents a stimulus not associated with excitation. The noncognitive systems must learn *how* to respond in a nonexcitatory manner through actually being in a state of decreased excitation owing to the absence of the excitatory US. Simple absence of the US, however, is not sufficient to ensure decreased excitation. The fact that the cognitive system can be shown to change states rapidly on instruction (e.g., Öhman & Hugdahl, 1979) does not mean that the noncognitive systems also do so. In fact, assumption of a central change in "drive" state that would affect all systems equally was the main weakness of traditional S–R accounts of extinction.

We have noted that, in addition to the removal of the US, there must be a decreased level of excitation, and the data presented here on different modes of operation of systems show that such a decrease does not necessarily follow. The system can remain in a state of activation through stimulation other than that associated with presence of the US. The system, for example, may remain excited by the presence of the CS alone, as is normally the case for the beginning of extinction. In systems where excitation diminishes quickly, either through diminution or active inhibition, a new response to the CS can develop rapidly because a new state is introduced into the system during the latter part of the intertrial interval. In systems that have slow diminution of excitation, there will be a long period of excitation to the CS. If this activation is not allowed to subside before presentation of the next CS, then further activation rather than reduction of activation will result in the presence of the next CS. Thus, in modifying systems with long periods of activation, such as the sympathetic nervous system, practical considerations such as longer periods between presentations of the CS should be allowed to ensure extinction of the excitatory response to the CS.

For response systems that are primarily sympathetic in innervation, account must be taken of the long period of activation elicited by strong stimulation that is characteristic of this system. A more detailed analysis of the properties of the sympathetic branch of the autonomic nervous system will allow for a clearer understanding of the mechanism involved in the systemic-competing-response approach to extinction. The long period of sympathetic activation such as that evidenced in response to a strong stressor is due to the nature of one of the neurotransmitters involved in the operation of this system. The majority of the postganglionic neurons of the sympathetic system release norepinephrine, and the effects of this and of epinephrine in their blood-borne form can last up to several minutes (Guyton, 1976). The sympathetic system may thus require a long period of time for the reduction of excitation in response to a CS made highly noxious through previous pairing with a highly noxious US. Note should be taken of the duration of sympathetic activation when measuring from response systems that are primarily sympathetic, such as the vasomotor and the electrodermal ones.[7] These response systems will follow the same principles as the nervous system that regulates them, and modification of their activity will require recognition of the constraints of the sympathetic nervous system (SNS).

If the CS is presented when a system is still active, as in the instance of an intense stressor or a highly reactive individual, then overlaying of additional activation could produce a net effect of an increased level of activation relative to that shown on the previous trial. The effect of this sympathetic activation would be represented, for example, electrodermally as an increase in magnitude of the response, an increase in number of spontaneous fluctuations in skin conductance, or both. More generally, the overt behavioral effects would be those of increased fear and anxiety—the incubation phenomenon.

Traditionally, neither cognitive nor S-R experimental approaches have taken into account the importance of the intertrial interval during extinction, although clinicians have noted its pragmatic importance during treatment of phobia with systematic desensitization (Rimm & Masters, 1979). In experimental investigations of learning phenomena, the time between presentations of the (brief) CSs is generally on the order of 40–50 sec. This period is long enough for the extinction of cognitively controlled responses such as those of the somatic system, inasmuch as these can be changed immediately by propositional information (e.g., Öhman & Hugdahl, 1979). For example, Brady (1975) and his associates have observed that the motor system shows rapid extinction during extinction of the conditioned suppression of bar pressing in monkeys. This short period between CSs is also adequate for extinction of the primarily parasympathetically (cholinergic) innervated response systems, inasmuch as the period of activation of these is relatively short owing to the rapid destruction of the neurotransmitter acetylcholine (Guyton, 1976). In the parasympathetic case, however, although the period between presentations of the CS may be adequate for reduction of activation, this is not sufficient for extinction. Because this system cannot learn propositions about the absence of the US, it will need a number of trials to learn how to respond.

The behavior of sympathetically innervated systems during extinction will depend on the level of activation produced by the stressor during acquisition. Where the sympathetic response to a stimulus is weak, as in the case of a weak US, then a 40- to 50-sec interval between CS presentations will also be adequate for extinction, the activation to the CS having diminished before the next CS presentation. As in the parasympathetic instance, however, the noncognitive sympathetic system will require a number of trials before extinction will be

---

[7] Although the electrodermal system is peripherally cholinergic, it is a sympathetic system and hence responds with the rest of the sympathetic nervous system (SNS). The anatomic organization of the SNS is such that in most instances large parts of the system are activated at the same time (Guyton, 1976). The present argument therefore holds for all sympathetically innervated responses irrespective of the peripheral neurotransmitter involved.

completed. Such gradual extinction is demonstrated in the electrodermal and vasomotor systems during phobic conditioning with fear-relevant stimuli and weak shock (e.g., Fredrikson & Öhman, 1979). Very slow extinction of sympathetic responses is particularly notable with intense stressors, such as the strong-shock USs used in animal studies. For example, Brady (1975) and his associates, examining the conditioned emotional response in monkeys, noted that, whereas the suppressing of the motor response (lever-press) underwent rapid extinction in 10 trials, the sympathetically mediated BP and HR changes did not show any evidence of extinction for some 40 additional trials.

In some instances, however, even the repeated brief presentations of the CS alone at short intervals may not be sufficient for sympathetically innervated systems to undergo extinction. The period between the CS presentations must also be adequate, and the standard 40- to 50-sec interval can be far too short in cases where the stressor is extremely intense or the individual highly reactive. This inadequacy of the interval between CS presentation is evident in the incubation phenomenon and in systematic desensitization with short periods between exposure to a brief CS (e.g., Wood, 1974). In cases of very intense sympathetic activity, a minimum period of several minutes is necessary for the adrenergic response to the stressor to begin to dissipate. In such cases, extremely long intervals between CS presentations or long exposure to the CS itself will allow for a deactivation response to be learned and for extinction to occur (e.g., Marks, 1977; Wood, 1974).

Further examination of the implications of the systemic-competing-response account of extinction are presented in the next section, which deals with treatment of the response to stress. Briefly, such an account accommodates the finding that "flooding" (prolonged exposure to the CS during which the subject experiences high levels of anxiety) is a highly efficient means of treating phobics, although the technique seems cognitively counterintuitive (e.g., Marks, 1977). In terms of the systemic account, flooding works because the subject learns a total bodily reaction, not just a cognition. Cognitively she or he learns that the CS is not actually followed by a US, other than fear itself; and this fear is allowed to dissipate before the CS is removed. Noncognitively the subject learns how to produce nonfearful (nonactivation) responses in the presence of the fear-inducing CS. The learning of these responses is important for phobics in that "fear of fear itself" is an important component of this disorder (e.g., Marks, 1969). The learning of these nonactivation responses can only result if the system is (1) exposed to the stressor and activation of relevant systems is produced and (2) exposure is long enough to allow dissipation of the anxiety in the presence of the stimulus, for removing the subject too soon can cause failure of extinction or incubation. Meeting of both of these conditions has in fact been found to be necessary for the effective use of flooding (e.g., Eysenck, 1979; Marks, 1977).

Consideration of the above data results in refutation of the notion that systems like the higher central, somatic, and autonomic nervous systems have the same modes of operation.[8] An ANS index such as electrodermal activity cannot

---

[8] The differences in modes of operation of different systems are quite predictable given their very different structures and functions. The slow inhibition of the sympathetic branch of the ANS is well-suited to the ensuring of continued preparedness for dealing with danger and is hence adaptive. The functioning of the ANS generally is adapted to the long-term

be regarded as under complete cognitive control, as a mere index of the higher-CNS cognitive processes. The fact that the ANS can operate in a manner different from the cognitive system has, however, often been overlooked. One of the reasons for this has been the finding that relational learning of the CS–US contingency (a higher-CNS function) is necessary for electrodermal conditioning (e.g., Fuhrer & Baer, 1965; see also Dawson & Furedy, 1976). It has therefore been concluded from this fact that electrodermal conditioning is a simple consequence of cognitive conditioning. Such a conclusion, however, assumes an identity of higher-CNS and ANS principles of operation, and this is not the case. By way of illustration, consider an electrodermal conditioning experiment in which the discriminanda ($CS^+$ and $CS^-$) are red and green lights with equal brightness and saturation. In such an arrangement, having a non-red-green-color-blind visual system would be necessary for electrodermal conditioning. It would not be concluded from this, however, that ANS functioning followed the same principles as, or was merely an index of, visual-system functioning. Electrodermal effects "do not seem to be *all* stimulus change determined, *all* mechanistically determined by stimulus pairing, or *all* the result of verbal-cognitive reaction, thinking or problem solving" (Grings, 1977, p. 349). The ANS is not an epiphenomenon of the CNS; they and other systems in the organism operate in different ways and interact with each other in a complex manner.[9]

## Interaction of Systems

There are complex interactions occurring between the various systems involved in the response to stress, and these are of both empirical and pragmatic import. At this point, we return to the question posed initially as to the relationship between psychological and physiological systems, and in order to support the argument for psychophysiological interaction rather than parallelism or epiphenomenalism, we present a number of brief examples. For more extensive reviews of response-system interactions, the reader is referred to the other chapters in this volume and, for example, to Lang, Rice and Sternbach (1972), Levi (1975), Marks (1969), Selye (1956), and Zimbardo (1969).

Modification of psychological components can affect physiological aspects of the response as well as other psychological systems, and there are numerous

---

well-being of the organism, and failure to respond to propositional information ensures that error through superstitious learning of potentially harmful behaviors (such as failure to avoid or be activated) cannot occur. On the other hand, the cognitive system and systems under its control are adapted to rapid change in a rapidly changing environment, and propositional information must therefore be processed by these. Inasmuch as these systems are not vital to the survival of the organism in terms of mobilization of energy, possible error owing to superstitious learning would not be maladaptive in the sense that it would be in the ANS. The different forms of neuromodulators and neuronal networks involved are likewise suited to the different roles served by different systems (see Dismukes, 1979; Pribram, 1971). Thus there is a need to consider the function of a system as well as its structure in order to have an idea of its principles of operation, and we suggest that this would lead to better understanding of both cognitive and noncognitive systems.

[9] This is not to imply that the CNS is not involved in autonomic conditioning and learning. The point being emphasized is that, when the autonomic system is also involved in the responding of a system, differences in the modes of operation of systems begin to emerge.

examples of this. Lazarus (1967), for example, using scenes of operation or injury as the stressful stimulus, found that instructions to "deny" or "intellectualize" the scene reduced the level, not only of self-reported anxiety, but of various measures of autonomic responding. Again, with respect to the effects of psychological manipulations on autonomic responses, it has been found that incentive affects HR. For example, Bouchard and Corson (1976) reported that "success" feedback signals (delivered on achieving the target HR) were associated with HR increases in humans during operant conditioning, regardless of whether the subjects were actually instructed to increase or decrease HR. Signals of "failure" had the opposite effect, leading to HR decrease regardless of the nature of the instruction—results with obvious implications for the biofeedback methodology. Also with respect to incentive effects on physiology, Malmo and Bélanger (1967) have reported that HR increases with an increase in the number of hours of water deprivation in rats, and this difference is not merely due to changes in physical effort.

Electrodermal activity (see review by Fowles, 1980) and catecholamine levels (see review by Frankenhäuser, 1975) are also found to change in response to a variety of psychological manipulations. In addition, there are instances where two or more psychological systems interact. For example, Meichenbaum (1977) and his colleagues have manipulated the affective components of the cold-pressor test and have found that an increase in the "coping level" of cognitions results in a decrease in negative affect and self-reported anxiety. Silverman and Cohen (1960), investigating responses to a high-gravity stressor, report that manipulation of affect in low-tolerance, high-anxiety subjects results in an increased tolerance of gravity stress and decreased anxiety.

Similarly, the manipulation of physiological factors leads to changes in both physiological and psychological systems. An instance of physiological-psychological interaction is given in the work of Landis and Hunt (1932), who demonstrated that the manipulation of catecholamine levels affected cognitions and feelings. These researchers found that epinephrine in small-to-moderate doses produced subjective responses similar in a number of respects to emotional changes associated with real-life stressors. Also with respect to physiological manipulations, operant conditioning of HR has been found to affect physiological systems. For example, Cacioppo and his associates (Cacioppo, Sandman, & Walker, 1978) found that conditioned HR change was associated with cognitive change. They reported more counterarguments and resistance to persuasion in an "attitude change" situation during HR acceleration training than during deceleration training, indicating the importance of physiological activity for cognitive elaboration.

The nature of these interactions between systems is not only diverse but exceedingly complex. This complexity is demonstrated by the work of Sirota, Schwartz, and Shapiro (1974, 1976) in the modification of anxiety through the reduction of HR acceleration. Lower ratings of shock intensity were reported by subjects who decreased HR than by those who increased HR, but these ratings were lower only in those subjects classified as "cardiac aware," suggesting a complex interaction between cognition and physiological responding. The work of Schacter and Singer (1962) on emotion also indicates this complexity of interrelationships. These researchers found that subjects given low doses of epinephrine reported a rise in nonspecific arousal, and the label given to this arousal depended on the nature of the environmental cues present. For example, if the subject was in an experimentally manipulated anger-provoking situation, he or she reported "anger," but if in an anxiety-provoking situation, she or he reported "anxiety." The fact that such cognitive labeling may only be important for low levels of arousal and not for intense ones (see, e.g., Lang et al., 1972) adds a further degree of complexity to the situation.

Catecholamine-manipulation studies also indicate the importance of considering both peripheral and central physiological changes when investigating psychophysiological interactions. For example, Frankenhäuser (1975) gave epinephrine infusions over a 35-min period and found no clearly consistent relationship for individuals between changes in subjective stress, HR, BP, and other measures. Frankenhäuser concluded that "this discrepancy indicates that the magnitude of the subjective response was only partly determined by that of the physiological reaction" (p. 223). The apparent absence of physiological effects owing to the manipulation of either physiological or psychological events, however, may be the result of measuring only peripheral physiological activity and not central changes, such as those involving cortical activity (see Lader & Tyrer, 1975). Central mechanisms such as those of the thalamus and limbic system are extremely important for affection and motivation and thus should also be considered, even though it may be methodologically difficult at the present to do so. Assessment of physiological states should consequently not be based solely on peripheral measures but should include observation of the full complexity of responding throughout the organism and the interactions between *all* relevant systems (see Lang et al., 1972).

There are innumerable other instances of psychological and physiological variables affecting each other as well as interactions between systems within each category. In our opening argument on the nature of relationships between the psychological and the physiological, we noted that, to reject the parallelist and epiphenomenalist positions, falsification of those positions is required. For that falsification, only a single instance, if convincing, of the psychological affecting the physiological and the physiological affecting the psychological would be necessary. We contend that the foregoing examples provide multiple evidence of the fallibility of the parallelist and epiphenomenalist positions, and we propose that interactionism is a viable, and indeed the only reasonable, alternative.

## TREATMENT: MODIFYING THE RESPONSE TO STRESS

### Cognitive Approaches

Cognitive approaches to the treatment of the response to stress concentrate, naturally enough, on the modification of the cognitive systems, with consideration of the noncognitive processes only insofar as these are modifiable by cognitive manipulation. That is, such approaches view the cognitive system to be of primary concern in stress-related behavior, the rationale being that a change in this system will result in a change in other systems as well. These cognitive approaches have been found effective for modifying certain forms of behavior. It thus appears that treatment of one response system alone *can* lead to reduced anxiety, but this has been reliably found only for mild levels of stress (see, e.g., Lang et al., 1972). An example of this is test anxiety, which responds well to cognitive manipulations provided that the level of autonomic arousal is not excessive (Wine, 1971). Also it is clear that in this case the response system that is most involved in the stress reaction is the cognitive one, the test situation involving attention, problem solving, and other cognitive processes. When the cognitive system is not central to the problem, however, as with many phobias and neuroses, cognitive approaches alone have not proven successful (see, e.g., Eysenck, 1979; Marks, 1977; Öhman, 1979b). In discussing the limitations of a purely cognitive account of phobia, Öhman clearly indicates the problems of overemphasizing the learning of propositional relationships without considering the noncognitive reactions. Of the "intellectual" approach to learning, Öhman writes:

> There is a body of experimental data, however, which poses problems for the present approach. Öhman and his associates (see review by Öhman, 1979a) have demonstrated that fear-relevant CSs such as pictures of snakes and spiders have some very special properties during aversive SCR [skin conductance response] conditioning. In particular, responses in this context appear quite independent of cognitive manipulations. (1979b, p. 465)

Failure to acknowledge the role of noncognitive systems and the very different principles involved in their operation can lead to ineffective and inefficient methodologies for stress treatment. This may explain some of the difficulties associated with biofeedback, which is applied to responses that cannot necessarily be changed using only information of the propostional form that is traditionally provided. While biofeedback has produced placebo effects, there is little evidence of its specific efficacy (see Katkin & Goldband, 1979). According to a narrow definition, the biofeedback phenomenon is said to occur if and only if the increase in control of the target response is the result of the provision of a response-contingent signal (i.e., the feedback). As we have argued in detail elsewhere, such specific effects require for their demonstration that a non-contingent control condition be used, in order that the observed effects can unequivocally be said to be the result of the response-reinforcement contingency (Furedy & Riley, 1980). When such a control is run, however, specific effects fail to emerge in the majority of response systems, with instructional effects accounting for the observed changes (London & Schwartz, 1980; Riley & Furedy, 1981; Shapiro & Surwit, 1976).

In addition to demonstrating the importance of adequately specifying what the necessary and sufficient conditions for an effect are, the narrow definition of biofeedback and the subsequent investigation of the role of reinforcement in conditioning also point to the need to acknowledge different learning principles. Central to the biofeedback methodology is the notion that provision of response-contingent signals will lead to an increase in control or regulation of that response. Biofeedback methods generally employ feedback in the form of propositional information. For example, a light or tone is the signal that the system is in some specified state (i.e., that $X$ is $Y$). Provision of such propositional, declarative information requires that the subject can actually use this form of information to change the target response (TR) in the desired manner. Such an assumption will hold for systems that can operate on such information—for cognitively controlled systems such as the somatic system. This assumption would also hold in a system where all forms of information were logically equatable and operated in the same manner. In the human system, however, there does not seem to be a common language of discrete data structures that is operated on by all systems (Dreyfus, 1972; Kolers & Smythe, 1979). There would not appear to be a "mentalese" into which all forms of information can be translated (Harman, 1975). Provision of propositional information about the TR may fail to have its intended effect on the TR, even though the subject may be aware of the intended meaning of the message. This failure, in information-theoretical terms, is a translation problem–a failure of information to be conveyed through the nervous system and the resulting inaccurate transmission of the intended meaning to the destination (see Furedy & Riley, 1980).

In evaluating approaches such as that of biofeedback, it is consequently necessary to assess whether the information provided to the subject can be expected to have the intended effect. In the case of cognitively controlled systems, such as the somatic, the problem of the nontranslatability of propositional information does not arise.[10] In the case of noncognitive systems, the propositional information may not be sufficient for production of the TR. To the extent that a system such as the autonomic one is under cognitive control, the propositional information may allow the subject to formulate strategies for production of the TR by the mediation of a cognitively controlled system. For example, to produce an increase in HR, the subject can simply tense muscles or increase respiration rate. The declarative information of the feedback display tells the subject that some already learned strategy $(X)$ is effective in producing the target response $(Y)$. The information thus tells the subject *that* some response is required. Such information, however, is not sufficient for teaching the subject *how* to respond in order to produce the TR. This latter process involves ability, not knowledge, and we have already shown that knowledge of propositional relationships is not sufficient for noncognitive learning. For example, while the subject may know *that* a long interbeat interval means slower HR, this does not mean the subject can, therefore, produce slower HR. The subject may not be able to bring the desired response under cognitive control and will thus need to be taught how to produce it through the use of noncognitive techniques. Failure to provide information of a suitable form for processing by noncognitive systems can thus result in failure to modify the response (see Tursky, 1982).

## Noncognitive Approaches

Noncognitively controlled systems such as the affective and the autonomic operate through reaction rather than cognition. That is, rather than processing

---

[10] There is an additional problem regarding the biofeedback methodology that pertains to the use of the information provided. The subject is not passively responding to signals but actively processing information, formulating cognitive and affective strategies in an attempt to gain reinforcement. In such cases, although the TR may be effectively regulated, the message has not had its intended feedback effect on the system. The message is here being used not as feedback but as *feedforward*, that is, as information for control of the TR by higher processes, such as cognitive strategies (Anliker, 1977). Such feedforward-control situations have practical significance because, in such situations, the elaborate and precise information of the kind provided in the biofeedback methodology (e.g., exact change in HR on a beat-by-beat basis) is unnecessary and therefore wasteful (see Riley & Furedy, 1982; Tursky, 1982).

information about the relationship between events (propositions), they simply respond to events. Modification of the responding of these systems requires, as we have noted, concentration on the manner in which the response is attached to the stimuli (S-R) rather than on the manner in which stimuli are related (S-S). Noncognitive approaches are concerned with temporal, contiguity relationships between the stimulus and the response rather than with propositional, or contingency, relationships between stimuli. The emphasis of the two forms of treatment approach thus clearly differs.

There is a rather obvious procedural or methodological difference between the contiguity approaches to response learning and the propositional approaches. Whereas contiguity approaches stress temporal relationships between stimuli, the contingency approaches stress contingency (propositional) relationships. Thus what Rescorla (1967) called the older "pairings" position stressed the importance of having short ISIs between CS and US onsets for response acquisition. On the other hand, a contingency approach like the Rescorla-Wagner (1972) model does not even have the ISI as one of its critical parameters and focuses rather on the propositional, or contingency, relationship between CS and US for both acquisition and extinction (e.g., Öhman, 1979b). The two sorts of approaches do generate different predictions, and as already noted, whereas contingency approaches account well for the behavior of cognitive systems, noncognitive systems are better explained by contiguity approaches.

The critical difference between the contiguity and contingency approaches, and one that is not always explicitly brought out, lies in what each approach considers to be learned as a result of conditioning. To take Pavlovian conditioning as an example, a contiguity approach assumes that what is learned is the attachment of responses (i.e., the CR) to stimuli (i.e., CS), and this learning is taken to occur through the temporal association of *pairing* the elements to be learned. The propositional, or contingency, approach, on the other hand, sees the stimulus-stimulus learning as the learning of a sign-significate relationship, a contingency relationship, or in Tolman's terms, a "cognitive map" (the "locale" system of O'Keefe & Nadel, 1979). This type of S-S learning is propositional, although this label is seldom explicitly applied.

A further important difference between contiguity and contingency approaches is that in the former the target response is often elicited from the subject. This elicitation is used because provision of propositional information is not sufficient for production of the response. According to a noncognitive account, what is necessary for teaching some responses in noncognitive systems is showing the subject how to produce the response through procedural means. An instance where cognitive approaches have proved ineffective has been the production of large-magnitude HR decelerations in humans. Neither instructions nor conventional biofeedback have been successful (see, e.g., Lang, 1977b). On the other hand, a noncognitive approach like that of "response learning" (Furedy, 1979) has been more successful. In this approach, the target behavior (phasic HR deceleration) is first elicited unconditionally and massively by such USs as negative tilting (Furedy & Poulos, Experiment I, 1976). Then, various forms of Pavlovian conditioning, of which the most powerful is the "imaginational" one (Furedy & Klajner, 1978), are used to teach the subject to produce the decelerative response as a CR by pairing a CS with the tilt US. Only after this Pavlovian operation is the cognitive approach introduced by providing (verbal) feedback (propositional information) to the subject about how much his HR has decelerated each CS trial (e.g., Furedy, 1977).

Noncognitive approaches to the treatment of stress also lead to the efficient usage of techniques that appear, in a strictly "intellectual" propositional account, to be counterintuitive and not usable. For example, it has been demonstrated that one of the most effective techniques for the treatment of phobias is flooding (Eysenck, 1979; Marks, 1977). Flooding involves long durations of exposure to the feared object, with an initial period of intense anxiety. According to a propositional view, such an approach should be no more effective than instructing the subject that the feared stimulus will not have an aversive effect. Flooding is, however, far more effective than instructional manipulations, which, as we have illustrated, do not work at all with high levels of fear (Öhman, 1979a). According to a contiguity view, which takes into account the different principles of operation of different systems, the effectiveness of flooding is quite predictable. The noncognitive sympathetic nervous system requires a long period in which to produce a response of deactivation in the presence of a stressor, and simply instructing the subject as to the absence of an aversive outcome is not sufficient to produce this response. That is, just as with more traditional approaches to the treatment of phobic responding, such as systematic desensitization, the subject is taught *how* to respond in the presence of the stressor. The subject learns a response of nonfear to the fear-provoking stimulus. For the subject to learn this response, actual responding is required in the relevant situations.

In other words, the correct S–R association has to be learned, rather than a propositional S–S contingency of the form "This feared event is not really harmful." According to this contiguity, or S–R, view, a number of facts about the necessary conditions for successful treatments of fear and anxiety become more understandable. For example, it is the case that the subject must be exposed to the phobia-arousing situation for a considerable time (Eysenck, 1979; Marks, 1977). In other words, the CS must be presented for a long enough time to allow the increased sympathetic activity elicited by the CS to dissipate and therefore to allow the attachment of the new nonfear R to the CS. Extinction, in this view, is the learned substitution of a new CR (deactivation) for the old CR (activation). It is also the case that the treatment is ineffective if the CS initially does not elicit considerable fear, no matter how convincing the intellectual, propositional information might be that, in fact, the CS should not be feared at all. In a contiguity, or S–R, account, this again is more understandable. The deactivation to-be-learned CR must be attached to the original CS, which has, as its essential property, that of being feared, or *arousing*. It is to an arousing S that the patient must learn to attach the deactivating R, rather than learning propositional S–S information about the "real" harmlessness of the feared stimulus.

Noncognitive approaches also emphasize the importance of the provision of nonpropositional information in biofeedback. One means of avoiding the translation problem—failure of the intended meaning of a message to be accurately conveyed throughout the various systems—is to provide information that can be processed by the target system. In the noncognitive cases, this will require nonpropositional information. One such method is to provide information directly to the target system through the afferent pathways, thereby obviating the problem of translating propositional information. Research on BP changes and sphincter control (e.g., Tursky, 1982) and HR deceleration (Furedy, 1979, pp. 215-216) using direct feedback to the system to be modified does attest to the efficacy of approaches that use nonpropositional information.

Just as the cognitive approaches have limited application to noncognitive systems, the contiguity approaches are restricted in their application, being effective only for reactive, not cognitive, systems. Because noncognitive systems do operate in a manner that is different from cognitive ones, however, it is necessary to include noncognitive techniques where the nature of the response to stress is such as to implicate the importance of other than cognitively controlled systems.

The response to stress is a total bodily reaction and hence based on a multiplicity of complexity interacting systems that operate according to different principles. Neither cognitive nor noncognitive approaches alone are therefore adequate either for the investigation or for the modification of the stress response. A recent remark that "a therapeutic intervention which alters only one measure ... should be regarded with little enthusiasm" (Hodgson & Rachman, 1974, p. 320) is consistent with this multidimensional, complex, interactive view of the stress response. No single measure can be regarded as reflecting the organism as whole, because the organism is composed of different systems that work differently. Thus a purely intellectual, propositional measure of the efficacy of phobic treatment wherein the subject shows himself or herself to be totally intellectually convinced that his or her fears have no rational basis is not, in itself, a guarantee that other noncognitive systems have also been successfully treated for the phobia. A response-system–specific approach takes into account the different modes of operation of differently innervated systems, as well as other differences such as that between acquisition and extinction processes. In some cases, the focus may be on the systems most relevant for the overall stress response, with the treatment mode being dictated by the specific mode of operation of each system. Furthermore, because there are wide individual differences in the relative sensitivities of various systems (e.g., some subjects respond electrodermally, whereas others respond more in terms of peripheral vasomotor measures), the appropriate forms of response modification for any given person would need to be tailored to her or his specific systems of reactivity as well as degree of cognitive control over the various systems and the extent of the interaction of various systems.

In terms of pragmatics, a multidimensional, interactive approach to the response to stress allows for the development of efficient, cost-effective treatment methods. In terms of the monetary and time considerations for both patients and health care staff, it is becoming increasingly important to develop interventions that are inexpensive as well as efficacious. This involves establishing that procedures work not just for one response system but for all sysems that require treatment. Further, this requires that effects are being produced in the most efficient possible way, once again indicating the need for correct control procedures in testing out the techniques (see Furedy & Riley, 1980; Katkin & Goldband, 1979). If it is not demonstrated unequivocally that a method is producing effects because of some identifiable factor, then it may well be the case that we are employing methods that are unnecessarily expensive in both senses of the term. Thus, as in the biofeedback case, if we do not precisely determine what it is that the effects are attributable to, we will be using techniques that involve expensive equipment and elaborate methodology for the purposes of nothing more specific than placebo effects in many response systems. As we have argued elsewhere (Furedy & Riley, 1980), an efficient technology is one that is founded on sound scientific method.

It is particularly important in the case of modification of the stress response to investigate thoroughly the modes of operation and interaction of systems because it is one of the primary areas in which intuitive notions as to what is important are so prevalent and yet so often mistaken. As in the flooding example, many therapists are reluctant to accept, for ethicointuitive reasons, that the provocation of anxiety can lead to its effective elimination. Also, being bequeathed the Platonic-Cartesian tradition of the "rational," cogitating human, we tend to often forget that we also feel and act. The learning of human behavior involves ability as well as knowledge and therefore involves noncognitive as well as cognitive systems. To study behavior, the activity of the total organism must be realistically appraised with the goal of determining the principles of operation and interaction of all pertinent systems. Only through such realistic methods can we furnish adequate explanations and control of the response to stress in all psychological and physiological systems of the organisms.

# REFERENCES

Anliker, J. Biofeedback from the perspectives of cybernetics and systems science. In J. Beatty & H. Legewie (Eds.), *Biofeedback and behavior.* New York: Plenum, 1977.

Armstrong, D. M. *Belief, truth and knowledge.* Cambridge: Cambridge University Press, 1973.

Berlyne, D. E. *Conflict, arousal and curiosity.* New York: McGraw-Hill, 1960.

Bernstein, A. S. The orienting reflex as novelty *and* significance detector: Reply to O'Gorman. *Psychophysiology,* 1979, *16,* 263–273.

Borst, C. V. (Ed.). *The mind/brain identity theory.* London: Macmillan, 1970.

Bouchard, C., & Corson, J. Heart rate regulation with success and failure signals. *Psychophysiology,* 1976, *13,* 69–74.

Brady, J. V. Toward a behavioral biology of emotion. In L. Levi (Ed.), *Emotions: Their parameters and measurement.* New York: Raven, 1975.

Cacioppo, J. T., Sandman, C. A., & Walker, B. B. The effects of operant heart rate conditioning on cognitive elaboration and attitude change. *Psychophysiology,* 1978, *15,* 330–338.

Champion, R. A. *Learning and activation.* Sydney: Wiley, 1969.

Champion, R. A., & Jones, J. E. Drive level (D) and extinction in classical aversive conditioning. *Journal of General Psychology,* 1962, *67,* 61–67.

Dawson, M. E. Can classical conditioning occur without contingency learning? A review and evaluation of the evidence. *Psychophysiology,* 1973, *10,* 82–86.

Dawson, M. E., & Furedy, J. J. The role of awareness in human differential autonomic classical conditioning: The necessary-gate hypothesis. *Psychophysiology,* 1976, *13,* 50–53.

Dismukes, R. Key. New concepts of molecular communcation among neurons. *Behavioral and Brain Sciences,* 1979, *2,* 409–448.

Dreyfuss, H. L. *What computers can't do: The limits of artificial intelligence.* New York: Harper, 1972.

Eysenck, H. J. The conditioning model of neurosis. *Behavioral and Brain Sciences,* 1979, *2,* 155–199.

Fowles, D. C. The three arousal model: Implications of Gray's two-factor learning theory for heart rate, electrodermal activity, and psychopathy. *Psychophysiology,* 1980, *17,* 87–104.

Frankenhäuser, M. Experimental approaches to the study of catecholamines and emotion. In L. Levi (Ed.), *Emotions: Their parameters and measurement.* New York: Raven, 1975.

Fredrikson, M., & Öhman, A. Cardiovascular and electrodermal responses conditioned to fear-relevant stimuli. *Psychophysiology,* 1979, *16,* 1–7.

Fuhrer, M. J., & Baer, P. E. Differential classical conditioning: Verbalization of stimulus contingencies. *Science,* 1965, *150,* 1479–1481.

Furedy, J. J. CS and UCS intervals and orders in human autonomic classical differential trace conditioning. *Canadian Journal of Psychology,* 1970, *24,* 417–426.

Furedy, J. J. Explicitly unpaired and truly random CS⁻ controls in human classical differential autonomic conditioning. *Psychophysiology,* 1971, *8,* 497–503.

Furedy, J. J. Some limits of the cognitive control of conditioned autonomic behavior. *Psychophysiology,* 1973, *10,* 108–111.

Furedy, J. J. An integrative progress report on informational control in humans: Some laboratory findings and methodological claims. *Australian Journal of Psychology,* 1975, *27,* 61–83.

Furedy, J. J. Pavlovian and operant-biofeedback procedures combined produce large-magnitude conditional heart rate decelerations. In J. Beatty & H. Legewie (Eds.), *Biofeedback and behavior.* New York: Plenum, 1977.

Furedy, J. J. Teaching self-regulation of cardiac function through imaginational Pavlovian and biofeedback conditioning: Remember the response. In N. Birnbaumer & H. D. Kimmel (Eds.), *Biofeedback and self-regulation.* Hillsdale, N.J.: Erlbaum, 1979.

Furedy, J. J., & Doob, A. N. Autonomic responses and verbal reports in further tests of the preparatory-adaptive-response interpretation of reinforcement. *Journal of Experimental Psychology,* 1971, *89,* 258–264.

Furedy, J. J., & Klajner, F. Imaginational Pavlovian conditioning of large-magnitude cardiac decelerations with tilt as US. *Psychophysiology,* 1978, *15,* 538–543.

Furedy, J. J., & Poulos, C. X. Heart rate decelerative Pavlovian conditioning with tilt as US: Towards behavioral control of cardiac dysfunction. *Biological Psychology,* 1976, *4,* 93–106.

Furedy, J. J., & Riley, D. M. Classical and operant conditioning in the enhancement of biofeedback: Specifics and speculations. In L. White & B. Tursky (Eds.), *Clinical biofeedback: Efficacy and mechanisms.* New York: Guilford, 1982.

Furedy, J. J., & Schiffmann, K. Test of the propriety of the traditional discriminative control procedure in Pavlovian electrodermal and plethysmographic conditioning. *Journal of Experimental Psychology,* 1971, *91,* 161–164.

Furedy, J. J., & Schiffmann, K. Concurrent measurement of autonomic and cognitive processes in a test of the traditional discriminative control procedure for Pavlovian electrodermal conditioning. *Journal of Experimental Psychology,* 1973, *100,* 210–217.

Furedy, J. J., & Schiffmann, K. Interrelationships between human classical differential electrodermal conditioning, orienting reaction, responsivity, and awareness of stimulus contingencies. *Psychophysiology,* 1974, *11,* 58–67.

Gatchel, R. J. Biofeedback and the treatment of fear and anxiety. In R. J. Gatchel & K. P. Price (Eds.), *Clinical applications of biofeedback: Appraisal and status.* Elmsford, N.Y.: Pergamon, 1979.

Goodman, N. *Ways of worldmaking.* Indianapolis: Hackett, 1978.

Grings, W. W. Orientation, conditioning and learning. *Psychophysiology,* 1977, *14,* 343–349.

Guyton, A. C. *Textbook of medical physiology.* Philadelphia: Saunders, 1976.

Harman, G. Language, thought, and communication. In K. Gunderson (Ed.), *Language, mind and knowledge.* Minneapolis: University of Minnesota Press, 1975.

Harré, R., & Secord, P. F. *The explanation of social behavior.* Oxford: Blackwell, 1973.

Haugeland, J. The nature and plausability of cognitivism. *Behavioral and Brain Sciences,* 1978, *1,* 215–260.

Hodgson, R. J., & Rachman, S. Desynchrony in measures of fear. *Behaviour Research and Therapy,* 1974, *12,* 319–326.

Jones, J. E. Contiguity and reinforcement in relation to CS–UCS intervals in classical aversive conditioning. *Psychological Review,* 1962, *69,* 176–186.

Katkin, E. S., & Goldband, S. The placebo effect and biofeedback, In R. J. Gatchel & K. P. Price (Eds.), *Clinical applications of biofeedback: Appraisal and status.* Elmsford, N.Y.: Pergamon, 1979.

Kendler, H. H. "What is learned?" A theoretical blind alley. *Psychological Review,* 1952, *59,* 269–277.

Kimble, G. A. *Hilgard and Marquis' conditioning and learning* (2nd ed. New York: Appleton, 1961.

Koch, S. *A possible psychology for a possible postpositivist world.* Paper presented at the 88th meeting of the American Psychological Association, Montreal, September 1980.

Kolers, P. A., & Smythe, W. E. Images, symbols and skills. *Canadian Journal of Psychology,* 1979, *33,* 158–184.

Lacey, A. *A dictionary of philosophy.* London: Routledge & Kegan Paul, 1976.

Lacey, J. I. Somatic response patterning and stress: Some revisions of activation theory. In M. H. Appley & R. Trumbull (Eds.), *Psychological stress: Issues in research.* New York: Appleton, 1967.

Lader, M., & Tyrer, P. Vegetative system and emotion. In L. Levi (Ed.), *Emotions: Their parameters and measurement.* New York: Raven, 1975.

Landis, C., & Hunt, W. A. Adrenalin and emotion. *Psychological Review,* 1932, *39,* 467–485.

Lang, P. J. The psychophysiology of anxiety. In H. Akiskal (Ed.), *Psychiatric diagnosis: Exploration of biological criteria.* Holliswood, N.Y.: Spectrum, 1977. (a)

Lang, P. J. Research on the specificity of feedback training: Implications for the use of biofeedback-treatment of anxiety and fear. In J. Beatty & H. Legewie (Eds.), *Biofeedback and behavior.* New York: Plenum, 1977. (b)

Lang, P. J., Rice, D. G., & Sternbach, R. A. The psychophysiology of emotion. In N. S. Greenfield & R. A. Sternbach (Eds.), *Handbook of psychophysiology.* New York: Holt, 1972.

Lazarus, R. S. Cognitive and personality characteristics underlying threat and coping. In M. H. Appley & R. Trumbull (Eds.), *Psychological stress: Issues in research.* New York: Appleton, 1967.

Leventhal, H. A perceptual-motor processing model of emotion. In P. Pliner, K. Blankstein, & I. M. Spigel (Eds.), *Perception of emotion in self and others* (vol. 5). New York: Plenum, 1979.

Levi, L. (Ed.). *Emotions: Their parameters and measurement.* New York: Raven, 1975.

London, M. D., & Schwartz, G. E. The interaction of instruction components with cybernetic effects in the voluntary control of human heart rate. *Psychophysiology,* 1980, *17,* 437–443.

Lykken, D. T. Perception in the rat: Autonomic responses to shock as a function of the length of warning interval. *Science,* 1962, *137,* 665–666.

Mackintosh, N. J. *The psychology of animal learning.* New York: Academic, 1974.

Malmo, R. B., & Bélanger, D. Related physiological and behavioral changes: What are their determinants? *Research Publications of the Association for Research in Nervous and Mental Disease,* 1967, *45,* 288–318.

Marks, I. M. *Fears and phobias.* London: Heinemann, 1969.

Marks, I. M. Phobias and obsessions: Clinical phenomena in search of a laboratory model. In J. D. Maser & M. E. P. Seligman (Eds.), *Psychopathology: Experimental models.* San Francisco: W. H. Freeman, 1977.

Martin, I., & Levey, A. *The genesis of the classical conditioned response.* Oxford: Pergamon, 1968.

Marx, M. H. *Theories in contemporary psychology,* New York: Macmillan, 1963.

Meehl, P. E. Theoretical risks and tabular asterisks: Sir Karl, Sir Ronald and the slow progress of soft psychology. *Journal of Consulting and Clinical Psychology,* 1978, *46,* 806–834.

Meichenbaum, D. *Cognitive behavior modification.* New York: Plenum, 1977.

Miller, N. E. Studies of fear as a learnable drive: I. Fear as motivation and fear reduction as reinforcement in the learning of new responses. *Journal of Experimental Psychology,* 1948, *38,* 89–101.

Mowrer, O. H. Anxiety-reduction and learning. *Journal of Experimental Psychology,* 1940, *27,* 497–516.

Öhman, A. Fear relevance, autonomic conditioning, and phobias: A laboratory model. In P. O. Sjoden, S. Bates, & W. S. Dockens III (Eds.), *Trends in behavior therapy.* New York: Academic, 1979. (a)

Öhman, A. The orienting response, attention and learning: An information-processing perspective. In H. D. Kimmel, E. H. van Olst, & J. F. Orlebeke (Eds.), *The orienting reflex in humans.* Hillsdale, N.J.: Erlbaum, 1979. (b)

Öhman, A., & Hugdahl, K. Instructional control of autonomic respondents: Fear relevance as a critical factor. In N. Birnbaumer & H. D. Kimmel (Eds.), *Biofeedback and self-regulation.* Hillsdale, N.J.: Erlbaum, 1979.

O'Keefe, J., & Nadel, L. Precis of O'Keefe and Nadel's *The hippocampus as a cognitive map. Behavioral and Brain Sciences,* 1979, *2,* 487–533.

Olton, D. S., Becker, J. T., Handelmann, G. E., & Mitchell, S. J. Hippocampus, space and memory. *Behavioral and Brain Sciences,* 1979, *2,* 313–365.

Polanyi, M. *Personal knowledge.* New York: Harper, 1962.

Pribram, K. *Languages of the brain: Experimental paradoxes and principles in neuro-psychology.* Englewood Cliffs, N.J.: Prentice-Hall, 1971.

Prokasy, W. F. Classical eyelid conditioning: Experimenter operations, task demands, and response shaping. In W. F. Prokasy (Ed.), *Classical conditioning.* New York: Appleton, 1965.

Prokasy, W. F. First interval skin conductance responses: Conditioned or orienting responses? *Psychophysiology,* 1977, *14,* 360–367.

Rachman, S. *Phobias: Their nature and control.* Springfield, Ill.: Thomas, 1968.

Razran, G. Extinction re-examined and re-analysed: A new theory. *Psychological Review,* 1956, *63,* 39–52.

Rescorla, R. A. Pavlovian conditioning and its proper control procedures. *Psychological Review,* 1967, *74,* 71–80.

Rescorla, R. A. Pavlovian conditioned inhibition. *Psychological Bulletin,* 1969, *72,* 77–94.

Rescorla, R. A., & Wagner, A. R. A theory of Pavlovian conditioning: Variations in the effectiveness of reinforcement and non-reinforcement. In A. H. Black & W. F. Prokasy (Eds.), *Classical conditioning* (Vol. 2). New York: Appleton, 1972.

Riley, D. M. *On the role of cognitive, affective, and motivational processes in determining behaviour: Some important distinctions for psychophysiology.* In W. Grings (Chair), Cognitive Psychophysiology, a symposium presented at the meeting of the Society for Psychophysiological Research, Vancouver, October 1980.

Riley, D. M., & Champion, R. A. *Emergence of electrodermal preparatory response in humans.* In Signalling Noxious Events: Status of Evidence and Status of Paradigms, a symposium presented at the American Psychological Association Meetings, Toronto, September 1978.

Riley, D. M., & Cupchik, G. *Cognitive, motor and autonomic interrelationships and sex differences in emotion.* Paper presented at the meeting of the Society for Psychophysiological Research, Vancouver, October 1980.

Riley, D. M., & Furedy, J. J. Effects of instructions and contingency of reinforcement on the operant conditioning of human phasic heart-rate change. *Psychophysiology,* 1981, *18,* 75–81.

Riley, D. M., & Furedy, J. J. Reply to Mulholland. In L. White & B. Tursky (Eds.), *Clinical biofeedback: Efficacy and mechanisms.* New York: Guilford, 1982.

Rimm, D. C., & Masters, J. C. *Behavior therapy.* New York: Academic, 1979.

Ritchie, B. The circumnavigation of cognition. *Psychological Review,* 1953, *60,* 216–221.

Ryle, G. *The concept of mind.* Harmondsworth: Penguin, 1949.

Schacter, S., & Singer, J. E. Cognitive, social, and physiological determinants of emotional state. *Psychological Review,* 1962, *69,* 379–399.

Scheffler, I. *Conditions of knowledge.* Chicago: University of Chicago Press, 1965.

Schiffmann, K., & Furedy, J. J. Failures of contingency and cognitive factors to affect long-interval differential Pavlovian autonomic conditioning. *Journal of Experimental Psychology,* 1972, *96,* 215–218.

Schiffmann, K., & Furedy, J. J. The effect of CS-US contingency variation on GSR and on subjective CS-US relational awareness. *Memory and Cognition,* 1977, *5,* 273–277.

Schwartz, B. *Psychology of learning and behavior.* Toronto: McCLeod, 1978.

Searle, J. R. Minds, brains, and programs. *Behavioral and Brain Sciences,* 1980, *3,* 417–458.

Selye, H. *The stress of life.* New York: McGraw-Hill, 1956.

Shaffer, J. Mind–body problem. In P. Edwards (Ed.), *The encyclopaedia of philosophy* (Vol. 5). New York: Macmillan and Free Press, 1967.

Shapiro, D., & Surwit, R. S. Learned control of physiological function and disease. In H. Leitenberg (Ed.), *Handbook of behavior modification and behavior therapy.* Englewood Cliffs, N.J.: Prentice-Hall, 1976.

Silverman, A. J., & Cohen, S. L. Affect and vascular correlates to catecholamines. In L. J. West & M. Greenblat (Eds.), *Explorations in the physiology of emotions* (Psychiatric Research Reports of the American Psychological Association, No. 12). Washington: APA, 1960.

Simon, H. A. *The sciences of the artificial.* Cambridge, Mass.: MIT Press, 1969.

Sirota, A. D., Schwartz, G. E., & Shapiro, D. Voluntary control of human heart rate: Effect on reaction to aversive stimulation. *Journal of Abnormal Psychology*, 1974, *83*, 261–267.

Sirota, A. D., Schwartz, G. E., & Shapiro, D. Voluntary control of human heart rate: Effect on reaction to aversive stimulation: A replication and extension. *Journal of Abnormal Psychology*, 1976, *85*, 473–477.

Stern, J. A., & Walrath, L. C. Orienting responses and conditioning of electrodermal responses. *Psychophysiology*, 1977, *14*, 334–342.

Szalai, J. P., & Furedy, J. J. Is the effective tilt US onset merely coy and elusive or should we welcome back backward conditioning—Pavlov's prodigal son? *Psychophysiology*, 1978, *15*, 272. (Abstract)

Tolman, E. C. Cognitive maps in rats and men. *Psychological Review*, 1948, *55*, 189–208.

Tursky, B. An engineering approach to biofeedback. In L. White & B. Tursky (Eds.), *Clinical biofeedback: Efficacy and mechanisms.* New York: Guilford, 1982.

Westergren, B., & Furedy, J. J. Importance of the instructed eye-movement component of the complex imaginational CS in Pavlovian conditioning of cardiac function with negative tilt as US. *Psychophysiology*, 1978, *15*, 266. (Abstract)

Wine, J. Text anxiety and direction of attention. *Psychological Bulletin*, 1971, *76*, 97–104.

Wolpe, J. Commentary on H. J. Eysenck: The conditioning model of neurosis. *Behavioral and Brain Sciences*, 1979, *2*, 155–199.

Wood, D. J. Paradoxical enhancement of learned anxiety responses. *Psychological Reports*, 1974, *35*, 295–304.

Zajonc, R. B. Feeling and thinking: Preferences need no inferences. *American Psychologist*, 1980, *35*, 151–175.

Zimbardo, P. G. *The cognitive control of motivation.* Glenview, Ill.: Scott, Foresman, 1969.

# 2

# Test Anxiety

## A Model for Studying Psychological and Physiological Interrelationships

**Susan R. Burchfield and Leslie J. Stein**
*University of Washington, Seattle, United States*

**Kathy L. Hamilton**
*University of Kentucky, Lexington, United States*

The purpose of studying psychological and physiological interrelationships is to understand their contributions to behavior, emotions, emotional illnesses, and psychophysiological diseases. Many investigators (Fehr & Stern, 1970; Funkenstein, King, & Drolette, 1957; Greene, Conron, Schalch, & Schreiner, 1970; Knight, Atkins, Eagle, Evans, Finkelstein, Fukushima, Katz, & Weiner, 1979) have attempted to clarify this interrelationship, and although much data is available, many discrepancies exist. The most frequently used paradigm involves the experimenter manipulating an external psychological stressor and measuring concomitant physiological changes. Unfortunately, most of these studies have used physiological measures too indirectly related to the central change or unresponsive to the presumed cognitive change (Johansson, 1976; Petry & Desiderato, 1978; Rahe, Ryman, & Biersner, 1976). Additionally, because investigators measure different physiological and psychological variables, interpretations of trends and patterns across studies are difficult. Between-studies differences are often attributed to situation-specific physiological responding, whereas similarities are interpreted as response-specific processing. Little can be learned about the processing of physiological and psychological systems by examining diverse studies that measure only one psychological or physiological variable. Differences between studies examining similar variables may be owing to anything, ranging from the type of measurement technique used to differences in reactivity of the variable of interest. Thus, for this chapter, we decided that a more useful way to examine psychological and physiological interrelationships was to choose one emotional event or situation about which a large quantity of research has been generated and to examine that portion of the research that bears on the psychological and physiological components of the situation. Presumably, studying a specific situation should provide insight into psychological and physiological systems in general and into methodological flaws common to all studies of psychological and physiological interrelationships.

We chose test anxiety as a model from which to examine these interrelationships because it has been extensively investigated and because there is an ongoing controversy among test anxiety theorists concerning the nature of the psychological and physiological components of test anxiety. This controversy exemplifies the more general controversy of whether physiological and psychological systems act in parallel or interact. Test anxiety, employed as a model to study psychological and physiological processing, can be conceptualized as primarily a cognitive event, a physiological event, or an interaction between the two. The first two positions are consistent with a parallel-processing theory of psychological and physiological systems; the third position corresponds to the interactionist model. This chapter deals with the test anxiety research that bears on this issue.[1]

## THEORIES OF PSYCHOLOGICAL AND PHYSIOLOGICAL PROCESSES

### General Models

There are two general models that can explain the relationship between psychological and physiological processing: parallel processing and interactionism, both discussed in detail in Chap. 1 and hence only briefly here. The parallel-processing model (Borst, 1970; Robinson, 1976) proposes that physiological and psychological systems act in parallel, that is, they react concurrently to input but at different levels that never intersect. The two systems can be conceptualized as being independent; events in one do not influence events in the other. The interactive model (Borst, 1970; Robinson, 1976) asserts that these systems are interdependent. In actuality the interactive model is transactional in that one system may directly or indirectly (through behavior) affect the other. Changes in the other system then feed back and produce changes in the originally activated one.

Differences between these two perspectives and support for one of them can be demonstrated using the test anxiety literature. Treatments of test anxiety can be distinguished as primarily acting on either a psychological or a physiological level. A psychological treatment is defined here as one geared toward changing a person's psychological reaction to an event; a physiological treatment is one that focuses on changing the physiological response to an event. Examples of psychological treatments include cognitive behavior modification, modeling, counseling, and psychodrama. Physiological treatments are relaxation, systematic desensitization, implosive therapy, meditation, tranquilizing agents, and physical exertion.

Two predictions concerning the outcome of treatment-intervention studies are derived from the parallel-processing model. If it is presumed that the two systems are independent and do not interact, then interventions that treat one system only should not effect the other one. The epiphenomenalist position within this model is that both systems react simultaneously to stimuli in a parallel fashion because one system accompanies the other and is caused by it (i.e., is an epiphenomenon). This position predicts that if one modality, physiological, for

---

[1] We presume readers are familiar with the construct of test anxiety and the psychological-behavioral research that has been done. For more information about test anxiety, see Sarason (1972, 1980) and Wine (1971).

example, is the epiphenomenon of the other, then a psychological treatment will produce concurrent changes in both psychological and physiological processes; but a physiological treatment will only produce changes within the physiological system.

The interactive model, on the other hand, predicts that a change in one system is followed by a change in the other, and thus, either psychologically or physiologically oriented treatments should be equally effective. If the results of treatment-outcome studies are those predicted by one perspective and not by the other, then it can be concluded that that perspective has more explanatory power and is probably more valid than the other.

## Test Anxiety Models

As stated earlier, classification of theories of text anxiety as a psychological or physiological phenomenon fall into separate categories. One category, neither physiological nor psychological, is a null set and thus is not discussed further. A second category, test anxiety as a physiological event only, implies that parallel processing occurs. According to this perspective, high- and low-test-anxious people do not differ systematically in their cognitive reactions to testing, but they do exhibit significant differences in physiological arousal. There is no evidence in the test anxiety literature to support this view of test anxiety. This lack of support is, in part, definitional. Test anxiety is based on the presence of psychological differences between people (e.g., high vs. low anxiety). It is definitionally impossible for a high-test-anxious person to have the same psychological reaction as a low-test-anxious one. Similar cognitions and different physiological reactions do occur, however, in other situations. Repressors (Weinberger, Schwartz, & Davidson, 1979) do not differ from true low-anxious people on self-report instruments. Under stress, however, they are physiologically more aroused than the true low-anxious. Low-test-anxious people may similarly consist of two groups: true low-anxious and repressors. This hypothesis, that some people who report low test anxiety are highly aroused and others (the true low-anxious) are not, has never been investigated. It deserves some attention, for it may help explain discrepant results reported in several studies (Hollandsworth, Glazeski, Kirkland, Jones, & Van Norman, 1979; Holroyd, Westbrook, Wolf, & Badhorn, 1978; Montgomery, 1977). Given that, at present, no one has proposed that test anxiety is primarily a physiological event, we do not discuss it further here.

The third proposition, that test anxiety is primarily a cognitive event (also supportive of a parallel-processing model), has received the most support in the literature. This model presupposes that high- and low-test-anxious people do not differ in physiological arousal but do differ significantly in their cognitions about and during the event. The proponents of this hypothesis (Sarason, 1980; Wine, 1971) suggest that high-test-anxious subjects have more task-irrelevant thoughts that prevent them from focusing on the task. These ruminative, self-deprecatory thoughts are the major distinguishing variable between high- and low-test-anxious students. If the cognitive position is correct, then one would predict that cognitively focused (e.g., psychological) treatments would be more effective in reducing test anxiety than physiological treatments.

The interactive model of test anxiety—that highly test-anxious people are more highly psychologically and physiologically aroused than low-test-anxious people—is derived from the interactionist perspective of psychological and physiological processing. Interactive theories of test anxiety, although abundant in the earlier literature (Epstein, 1972; Sarason, 1972; Spielberger, 1972) have only been tested in three studies (Hollandsworth et al., 1979; Holroyd et al., 1978; Montgomery, 1977). Interactive theorists, although accepting that test anxiety is primarily a cognitive event, hypothesize that physiological changes are also present. Test anxiety presumably arises from inner-directed, maladaptive thinking, and these thoughts cause a change in physiological arousal, which then excites and affects the nature of the cognitions. Although many studies (Hollandsworth et al., 1979; Holroyd et al., 1978; Sarason, 1973, 1975) have reported that high-test-anxious people have more maladaptive thoughts than low-test-anxious ones, no differences have been found in physiological arousal. Because of methodological flaws in these studies (discussed later), however, the possibility of an interaction cannot be ruled out. If the interactionist model is correct, then psychological and physiological treatments of text anxiety should be equally effective.

## TEST ANXIETY AS A MULTIDIMENSIONAL CONSTRUCT

Several authors (Lent & Russell, 1978; Mitchell & Ng, 1972) have suggested that test anxiety is a multidimensional construct. Like other emotional states, it can be conceived of as encompassing cognitive, affective, physiological, and behavioral components. Generally, it is assumed that the cognitive component is worry, the affective component is anxiety—presumably formed by pairing worry and arousal (cf. Liebert & Morris, 1967; Schachter & Singer, 1962), and the behavioral component is study skills and test-taking behaviors. The physiological component does not contribute to differences between high- and low-test-anxious people according to the cognitive perspective; but according to the interactive position, it does. The different dimensions that test anxiety is presumed to involve include worry and emotionality (Liebert & Morris, 1967), facilitative and debilitative anxiety (Alpert & Haber, 1960), reactive and conditioned anxiety (Nietzel, 1981), and study-skills deficits (Hollandsworth et al., 1979). The differences between these terms and their implications are discussed in this section.

The term *test anxiety* actually refers to debilitative anxiety: that which interferes with test taking. Anxiety, or arousal, may also be facilitative and may increase motivation and drive to perform well. Thus, anxiety may be channeled in either a task-oriented direction or an inner-oriented, ruminative one. Alpert and Haber (1960) designed a test anxiety questionnaire (The Achievement-Anxiety Test) to measure both debilitative and facilitative anxiety. They found that two scales on this questionnaire correlated −.48 with each other and that the debilitative scale correlated .64 with the Test Anxiety Questionnaire (Mandler & S. Sarason, 1952). The Test Anxiety Scale (Sarason, 1958, 1978) and the Test Anxiety Questionnaire measure debilitative anxiety only, and scores on these scales do not reflect the amount of facilitative anxiety that a person is experiencing. It is possible for a person to be low in test anxiety and high in facilitative anxiety. If this is the case, then one might not expect to find any gross differences in physiological arousal between high- and low-test-anxious

subjects, as has been reported (Holroyd et al., 1978). The pattern of physiological activation may be different between these two types of anxiety, however,
and this difference may contribute to the attention-focusing differences between
high- and low-test-anxious subjects. It is also expected that successful treatment
of test anxiety results in a decrease of debilitative and an increase of facilitative
anxiety. Many investigators (Allen, 1971; Deffenbacher & Michaels, 1980; Harris
& Johnson, 1980) have reported these changes in high-test-anxious subjects who
had undergone a treatment program. The exact nature of facilitative and
debilitative anxiety remains, however, to be elucidated.

Another potentially confusing aspect of the multidimensionality concept of
test anxiety is that test anxiety may actually represent conditioned or reactive
anxiety or both. Most investigators probably conceptualize test anxiety as
conditioned anxiety, that is, as a learned response to testing situations (see
Sarason, 1972). Yet it may also represent the intense anxiety of people who are
not prepared for a test. In these cases, it is expected that study-skills training
would reduce anxiety and improve performance. In students with conditioned
anxiety, however, study-skills training may have no effect. For these students,
structuring the testing situation so as to reduce its evaluative component should
result in improved performance and less anxiety. If some students reporting high
test anxiety are experiencing reactive anxiety instead of the more common
conditioned anxiety, then this difference might explain why some investigators
(Kirkland & Hollandsworth, 1980) find study-skills training alone sufficient to
reduce test anxiety, whereas other investigators (Cornish & Dilley, 1973; Horne
& Matson, 1977) find that it has no effect. The final aspect of the dimensions
encompassed by test anxiety involves the independence of the cognitive and
physiological components. Liebert and Morris (1967) factor-analyzed the Test
Anxiety Questionnaire and identified two factors. These components, worry and
emotionality, were conceptualized as cognitive concern about one's performance
and autonomic reactivity, respectively. Liebert and Morris found that worry was
inversely related to performance expectancy, whereas emotionality was not.
Clarification of the relationship of these factors to reactive and facilitative anxiety
may be useful for understanding the nature of test anxiety.

## TREATMENT–OUTCOME STUDIES

Treatment studies have theoretical implications because, if parallel processing
exists, then treatments dealing with one modality should have no effect on
reactions in the other modality. If the cognitive perspective is correct, then
treatments reducing maladaptive thinking should be more effective than those
decreasing physiological arousal. Based on the presumptions that arousal is
equivalent in high- and low-test-anxious people and that arousal is necessary for
good performance (see Yerkes & Dodson, 1908), some investigators (see, Sarason,
1980) have suggested that decreasing arousal in high-test-anxious students results
in poor performance, and they therefore do not recommend physiological
treatments. There is, however, much evidence that shows that high-test-anxious
subjects improve their grades after receiving a physiological treatment (Barrios &
Shigetomi, 1979; Deffenbacher, Mathis, & Michaels, 1979). The interaction
theories of test anxiety predict that physiological and psychological treatments
are equally effective because, when reactions of one system are modified, those

of the other system are also changed. This perspective predicts that treatments result in change not only of the targeted system but of the nontargeted system, whereas the cognitive theory predicts that either no such concomitant changes of the nontargeted system occur or, if they do, they are irrelevant. Before discussing the results of treatment-outcome studies, it is important to note the methodological flaws inherent in these experiments.

## Methodological Issues

Most studies of the treatment of high test anxiety have compared one type of treatment to a no-treatment control group. Such studies have generally reported that the treatment successfully decreased test anxiety. Successful treatments include music (Stanton, 1973), relaxation (Deffenbacher, 1976), cognitive restructuring (Sarason & Johnson, 1976), modeling (Sarason, 1973), meditation (Linden, 1973), and hypnotism (Nemenef & Rothman, 1974). Because no attention control group was included in these studies or in others not cited, it is not possible to conclude that these treatments are any more effective than a placebo treatment. The only way to clarify this issue is to examine studies that have compared treatments and determined which is most effective: a cognitive, a physiological, or a combination treatment. Very few studies of this nature have been performed, and the results from these are inconclusive.

One of the most obvious problems with treatment-outcome studies that examine the effectiveness of physiological treatments (relaxation, systematic desensitization, etc.) is that no pre- and posttreatment measurement of physiological arousal is ever obtained. Thus, although a treatment may have successfully reduced test anxiety, it may not have reduced physiological arousal. As a result, the possibility exists that its effectiveness may have been due to cognitive changes induced by the treatment. Future studies examining the effectiveness of relaxation-type treatments should include several physiological-outcome measures to insure that the conclusion—that the treatment reduced arousal—is valid. Until this data is available, it is possible to conclude that relaxation changes a person's cognitions or interpretations of a situation, in which case, the effectiveness of relaxation therapy supports the cognitive perspective. For the purposes of this chapter, the effectiveness of physiological treatments is ascribed to their relaxation effects.

## Results

To determine the general trends of results of treatment-outcome studies, we grouped them according to type (psychological or physiological) of treatments evaluated within the study. The text summarizes the findings; tables provide additional information concerning the exact treatment used, the design (group vs. case history), the number of subjects, the assessment channel, and the post-treatment and follow-up results. Self-report assessments included the following materials: the Test Anxiety Scale (Sarason, 1958, 1978), the Achievement-Anxiety Test (Alpert & Haber, 1960), the State-Trait Anxiety Inventory (Spielberger, 1972), the Suinn Test Anxiety Behavior Scale (Suinn, 1969); and the S–R Inventory of Anxiousness (Endler, Hunt, & Rosenstein, 1962). Behavioral assessments involved examining between-group and pre- and posttreatment differences in grade-point average, performance on college tests, performance on a test (digit symbol, anagrams) in an experimental situation, or combinations of these. Occasionally physiological variables (HR, skin resistance) were also measured. If many measures within one assessment channel were taken and the results differed across instruments, then conclusions of treatment effectiveness were determined by the direction of change of the instruments specifically measuring test anxiety. When computing overall effectiveness of treatments within a category, only results on the self-report measures were included unless the study used only behavioral measures; in which case, these were also included. To clarify the validity of self-reports compared with behavioral assessments, the results are also discussed in terms of percentage of studies using behavioral or self-report measures or both and reporting positive results.

*Physiological treatment versus no treatment.* It is apparent that most of the studies comparing a treatment to a no-treatment (NT) control used a physiological treatment. Because so few psychological-treatment versus NT studies exist, we discuss those that are under the heading "Psychological versus Psychological, NT." Of the 13 studies that simply used one treatment and examined pre- and posttreatment differences or else included an NT control group, 11 (85%) reported that the treatment significantly reduced test anxiety. Whereas 6 of these studies used both self-report and behavioral measures, 5 used only self-report, and 2 used only behavioral dependent measures. Of the 11 studies that used a self-report measure, 9 (82%) reported that the treatment was effective, whereas 6 of 8 (75%) that used behavioral measures reported significant differences. These data are summarized in Table 2.1. Self-report and behavioral measures appear equally effective in determining posttreatment changes in studies comparing a physiological treatment to a control group.

*Physiological versus physiological, NT.* Of the 18 studies that used paradigms in which one type of physiological treatment was compared with another, 15 included a control group. Of the 18, 17 (94%) reported that one physiological treatment equaled or surpassed the other in effectiveness and that both, or one, was significantly different from controls. All 18 studies used self-report inventories; 14 also used behavioral-assessment channels, and 8 of these (57%) reported that one or more physiological treatments differed from the NT group. Comparison of the percentage of positive results obtained using self-report versus behavioral techniques reveals a significant difference ($p < .01$) between the two measures. Because of this difference, it is difficult to determine the validity of either assessment channel in these studies. These data are summarized in Table 2.2.

*Psychological versus psychological, NT.* Of the five studies that compared one psychological treatment with another psychological treatment, an NT control, or both, three (60%) reported that one psychological treatment surpassed or equaled the other and that both were significantly different from the NT group. One out of three (33%) of the studies using self-report measures reported that the psychological treatment group differed significantly from the NT group. All four studies that included behavioral assessments reported that one or more psychological treatments were effective. One of these studies did not use a control group, however, pre- and posttreatment comparisons were used instead. These data are reported in Table 2.3. Apparently, studies comparing the effectiveness of two psychological treatments are more likely to report positive results if they use

*Table 2.1* Physiological versus NT studies

| Authors | Design | Conditions compared | Assessment channel | Posttreatment outcome | Follow-up |
|---|---|---|---|---|---|
| Deffenbacher (1976) | Case<br>$n = 4$ | AR | Self-report<br>Behavioral | AR<br>AR | NA<br>NA |
| Deffenbacher & Rivera (1976) | Case<br>$n = 2$ | AR | Self-report<br>Behavioral | AR<br>AR | AR<br>AR |
| Deffenbacher & Snyder (1976) | Case<br>$n = 11$ | AR | Self-report<br>Behavioral | AR<br>AR | NA<br>NA |
| James & James (1973) | Group<br>$n = 144$ | CDZ<br>HPL<br>P<br>NT | Self-report<br>Physiological<br>Behavioral | CDZ = HPL = P = NT<br>CDZ = HPL = P = NT<br>HPL = P > CDZ > NT | NA<br>NA<br>NA |
| Linden (1973) | Group<br>$n = 26$ | MT<br>NT | Self-report<br>Behavioral | MT > NT<br>MT = NT | NA<br>NA |
| Marchetti, McGlynn, & Patterson (1977) | Group<br>$n = 33$ | CC<br>AT<br>NT | Self-report<br>Physiological | CC = AT = NT<br>CC = AT = NT | NA<br>NA |

| Study | n | Groups | Measure | | |
|---|---|---|---|---|---|
| McGlynn, Kinjo, & Doherty (1978) | Group $n = 28$ | CC AT NT | Self-report | CC = AT > NT | CC = AT > NT |
| Nemenef & Rothman (1974) | Case $n = 3$ | H | Self-report | H | NA |
| Russell, Miller & June (1974) | Case $n = 9$ | CC | Self-report | CC | NA |
| Russell & Sipich (1973) | Case $n = 1$ | CC | Self-report | CC | CC |
| Russell & Sipich (1974) | Case $n = 1$ | CC | Self-report / Behavioral | CC / CC | NA / NA |
| Stanton (1973) | Group $n = ?$ | MU | Behavioral | MU | NA |
| Stanton (1975) | Group $n = 162$ | MU NT | Behavioral | MU > NT | NA |

*Note.* Abbreviations for Tables 2.1–2.6: AMT, anxiety management training; AR, applied relaxation; AT, attention control; Att-relax, attribution therapy-relaxed attribution; Att-stim, attribution therapy-stimulant attribution; B, electromyographic biofeedback; C, counseling; CBM, cognitive behavior modification; CC, cue-controlled relaxation; CDZ, Chlordiazepoxide; F, flooding; H, hypnosis; HPL, haloperidol; IT, implosion therapy; M, modeling; M-d, modeling and problem description; M-p, modeling and problem solving with underlying principles; MCC, minimal contact control; MT, meditation; MU, music; NT, no treatment; P, placebo; PE, prolonged exposure; PE–PI, physical exertion and positive imagery; R, relaxation; SCD, self-controlled desensitization; SD, systematic desensitization; SP, structured psychodrama; SS, study skills; TB, taped EMG biofeedback; WC, wait-list controls.

43

Table 2.2  Physiological versus physiological, NT studies

| Authors | Design | Conditions compared | Assessment channel | Posttreatment outcome | Follow-up |
|---|---|---|---|---|---|
| Barrios, Ginter, & McKnight (1979) | Group $n = 18$ | AR<br>CC (cognitive)<br>CC (conditional) | Self-report<br>Behavioral | AR = CC (cognitive) = CC (conditional)<br>AR = CC (cognitive) = CC (conditional) | NA<br>NA |
| Bedell (1976) | Group $n = 50$ | SD-high expectancy<br>SD-low expectancy<br>R-high expectancy<br>R-low expectancy<br>NT | Self-report<br>Behavioral | SD-high = SD-low = R-high = R-low > NT<br>SD-high = SD-low = R-high = R-low = NT | NA<br>NA |
| Bedell, Archer, & Rosmann (1979) | Group $n = 10$ | SD<br>R | Self-report | SD = R | NA |
| Chang-Liang & Denney (1976) | Group $n = 81$ | AR<br>SD<br>R<br>NT | Self-report<br>Behavioral | AR = SD = R > NT<br>AR > SD = R = NT | NA<br>NA |
| Counts, Hollandsworth & Alcorn (1978) | Group $n = 40$ | CC<br>CC and B<br>AT<br>NT | Self-report<br>Behavioral | CC = CC and B > AT = NT<br>CC = CC and B > AT = NT | NA<br>NA |
| Deffenbacher, Mathis, & Michaels | Group $n = 69$ | SD<br>R<br>WC | Self-report<br>Behavioral | R = SD > WC = NT<br>R = SD = WC = NT | NA<br>NA |
| Deffenbacher & Michaels (1980) | Group $n = 69$ | R<br>SD<br>NT | Self-report<br>Behavioral | NA<br>NA | SD = R > NT<br>SD = R = NT |
| Deffenbacher, Michaels, Michaels, & Daley (1980) | Group $n = 62$ | SCD<br>AMT<br>NT<br>WC | Self-report<br>Behavioral | AMT = SCD > NT = WC<br>AMT = SCD > NT = WC | NA<br>NA |

| Study | Group n | AMT conditions | Measure | AMT = SD | AMT > SD |
|---|---|---|---|---|---|
| Deffenbacher & Shelton (1978) | Group n = 40 | AMT, SD | Self-report | | |
| Denney & Rupert (1977) | Group n = 86 | SCD, SD, AT, NT | Self-report | SCD > SD > AT = NT | NA |
| | | | Behavioral | SCD > SD > AT = NT | SCD > SD > AT = NT |
| Reed & Saslow (1980) | Group n = 27 | R, R and B, NT | Self-report | R = R and B > NT | NA |
| | | | Physiological | R = R and B > NT | NA |
| Romano & Cabianca (1978) | Group n = 40 | SD and B, R and B, SD, NT | Self-report | SD and B = R and B > SD > NT | NA |
| | | | Behavioral | SD and B = R and B = SD > NT | NA |
| Russell, Miller, & June (1975) | Group n = 31 | CC, SD, NT | Self-report | CC = SD > NT | NA |
| | | | Behavioral | CC = SD = NT | NA |
| Russell, Wise, & Stratoudakis (1976) | Group n = 19 | CC, SD, NT | Self-report | CC = SD = NT | NA |
| | | | Behavioral | CC = SD = NT | NA |
| Ryan, Krall, & Hodges (1976) | Group n = 72 | SD, R, NT | Self-report | SD = R > NT | NA |
| Snyder & Deffenbacher (1977) | Group n = 43 | AR, SCD, NT | Self-report | AR = SCD > NT | NA |
| | | | Behavioral | AR = SCD = NT | NA |
| Spiegler, Cooley, Marshall, Prince, Puckett, & Skenazy (1976) | Group n = 47 | SCD, SD, NT | Self-report | SCD > SD = NT | NA |
| Zemore (1975) | Group n = 40 | SCD, SD, NT | Self-report | SCD = SD > NT | NA |
| | | | Behavioral | SCD = SD > NT | NA |

*Note.* For abbreviations, see note to Table 2.1.

45

*Table 2.3* Psychological versus psychological, NT studies

| Authors | Design | Conditions compared | Assessment channel | Posttreatment outcome | Follow-up |
|---|---|---|---|---|---|
| Holroyd (1978) | Group $n = 250$ | Att.-relax Att.-stim. | Self-report Behavioral | Att.-relax = Att.-stim. Att.-relax = Att.-stim. | |
| Hussian & Lawrence (1978) | Group $n = 48$ | CBM (test) CBM (general) AT NT | Self-report Behavioral | CBM (test) = CBM (general) = AT = NT CBM (test) = CBM (general) > AT = NT | CBM (test) = CBM (general) = AT > NT NA |
| Malec, Park, & Watkins (1976) | Group $n = 21$ | M NT | Self-report | M > NT | NA |
| Sarason (1973) | Group $n=120$ | M M-d M-p AT | Behavioral | M-p > M-d = M = AT | NA |
| Sarason (1975) | Group $n = 40$ | M (coping anxiety) M (noncoping anxiety) M (low test anxiety) M (neutral) NT | Behavioral | M (coping anxiety) > M (non-coping anxiety) = M (low test anxiety) = M (neutral) = NT | NA |

*Note.* For abbreviations, see note to Table 2.1.

a behavioral-assessment channel than a self-report channel, whereas studies comparing two physiological treatments are more likely to report positive results when using self-report instruments.

*Physiological versus psychological, NT.* All six studies in this category compared effectiveness of a physiological treatment, a cognitive treatment, and a control group (either NT or wait-list). All studies used self-report measures, and four included a behavioral assessment. On the self-report channel, two out of six studies (33%) found that the physiological treatment surpassed the psychological one (Anton, 1976; Doctor, Aponte, Burry, & Welch, 1970), whereas one study (17%) reported that the psychological treatment was most effective (Meichenbaum, 1972). Three studies (50%) reported that there was no difference between the two treatments but that both were significantly more effective than controls (Goldfried, Lineham & Smith, 1978; Kipper & Giladi, 1978; Kostka & Galassi, 1974). Using the behavioral measures, 50% reported no difference between any of the three techniques (Anton, 1976; Kostka & Galassi, 1974), and the remaining 50% reported that, although the experimental treatments did not differ, they were significantly different from the controls (Doctor et al., 1970; Meichenbaum, 1972). Table 2.4 describes the studies in this category. In general, it can be tentatively concluded that there is no difference in effectiveness of psychological and physiological treatments. More research is needed using this paradigm before any conclusion can be definitive.

*Combined versus psychological, physiological, NT.* Nine studies compared the effectiveness of a combined treatment, containing both cognitive and physiological techniques, to a physiological, a psychological, a control group, or some combination. In general, these studies used better controls than studies in the other categories. As in the category physiological versus psychological, no definitive conclusions can be drawn because the results of these studies are so disparate. All studies used self-report techniques, and seven also used a behavioral assessment. On the self-report channel, two studies (22%) compared a combined treatment with an NT group (Sarason & Johnson, 1976; Thompson, Griebstein, & Kuhlenschmidt, 1980), both reporting significant results. One study (11%) reported that a combined treatment was more effective than a physiological treatment (Driscoll, 1976), whereas three studies (33%) reported that the combined treatment equaled the physiological treatment and equaled (Finger & Galassi, 1977; Wine, 1970) or surpassed (Mitchell & Ng, 1972) the psychological treatment. All treatments in these studies differed from the controls. Lastly, three studies (33%) reported that the psychological treatment surpassed the combined treatment (Holroyd, 1976; Kaplan, McCordick, & Twitchell, 1979; Pesta & Zwettler, 1977). Examination of the behavioral-assessment channel revealed that two studies (Finger & Galassi, 1977; Kaplan et al., 1979) (29%) reported no difference between any treatment group and controls; three studies (Mitchell & Ng, 1972; Sarason & Johnson, 1976; Thompson et al., 1980) (43%) reported that combined treatments differed significantly from controls; and two studies (Holroyd, 1976; Wine, 1970) reported that a psychological treatment was more effective than a combined or a physiological treatment. These studies are described further in Table 2.5.

The most appropriate conclusion from these results is that combined treatments are effective although psychological treatments may be more effective. Exactly how effective combined treatments are is difficult to determine. Some

Table 2.4  Physiological versus psychological, NT studies

| Authors | Design | Conditions compared | Assessment channel | Posttreatment outcome | Follow-up |
|---|---|---|---|---|---|
| Anton (1976) | Group $n = 54$ | SD<br>C<br>NT | Self-report<br>Behavioral | SD > C = NT<br>SD = C = NT | NA<br>NA |
| Doctor, Aponte, Burry, & Welch (1970) | Group $n = 25$ | C<br>SD<br>NT | Self-report<br>Behavioral | SD > C<br>SD = C > NT | NA |
| Goldfried, Lineham, & Smith (1978) | Group $n = 36$ | CBM<br>PE<br>NT | Self-report | CBM = PE > NT | CBM = PE |
| Kipper & Giladi (1978) | Group $n = 36$ | SD<br>SP<br>WC | Self-report | SD = SP > WC | NA |
| Kostka & Galassi (1974) | Group $n = 23$ | SD<br>CBM<br>NT | Self-report<br>Behavioral | SD = CBM > NT<br>NT = CBM > SD | NA<br>NA |
| Meichenbaum (1972) | Group $n = 21$ | SD<br>CBM<br>NT | Self-report<br>Behavioral | CBM > SD > NT<br>CBM = SD > NT | CBM > SD > NT<br>NA |

*Note.* For abbreviations, see note to Table 2.1.

Table 2.5 Combined versus others, NT studies

| Authors | Design | Conditions compared | Assessment channel | Posttreatment outcome | Follow-up |
|---|---|---|---|---|---|
| Driscoll (1976) | Group n = 16 | SD PE–PI PE PI NT | Self-report | PE–PI > SD | NA |
| Finger & Galassi (1977) | Group n = 50 | CBM CBM and R R NT | Self-report | R = CBM and R = CBM > NT | NA |
|  |  |  | Behavioral | CBM = CBM and R = R = NT | NA |
| Holroyd (1976) | Group n = 53 | CBM SD CBM and SD AT NT | Self-report | CBM > CBM and SD = SD = AT > NT | CBM > CBM and SD = SD = AT > NT |
|  |  |  | Behavioral | CBM > CBM and SD > SD = AT > NT | CBM > CBM and SD > SD = AT > NT |
| Kaplan, McCordick, & Twitchell (1979) | Group n = 24 | CBM and SS SD and SS CBM and SD and SS NT | Self-report | CBM and SS > CBM and SD and SS > SD and SS > NT | NA |
|  |  |  | Behavioral | CBM and SS = CBM and SD and SS = SD and SS = NT | NA |
| Mitchell & Ng (1972) | Group n = 30 | SD C SD–serial and C SD–combined and C NT | Self-report | SD = SD–combined and C = SD–serial and C > C = NT | NA |
|  |  |  | Behavioral | SD–serial and C = SD–combined and C > SD = C = NT | NA |

(See note on p. 50.)

49

Table 2.5  Combined versus others, NT studies (Continued)

| Authors | Design | Conditions compared | Assessment channel | Posttreatment outcome | Follow-up |
|---|---|---|---|---|---|
| Pesta & Zwettler (1977) | Group n = 48 | R<br>CBM<br>CBM and R<br>NT | Self-report | CBM > R = CBM and R > NT | NA |
| Sarason & Johnson (1976) | Group n = 19 | CBM and R<br>NT | Self-report<br>Behavioral | CBM and R > NT<br>CBM and R = NT | NA<br>NA |
| Thompson, Griebstein, & Kuhlenschmidt (1980) | Group n = 19 | AMT and B<br>AMT and TB<br>CBM and B<br>CBM and TB<br>NT | Self-report<br><br>Behavioral | AMT and B = AMT and TB =<br>  CBM and B = CBM and TB > NT<br><br>AMT and B = AMT and TB =<br>  CBM and B | NA<br><br>NA |
| Wine (1970) | Group n = ? | CBM<br>CBM and R<br>AT | Self-report<br>Behavioral | CBM = CBM and R > AT<br>CBM = CBM and R > AT | NA<br>NA |

Note. For abbreviations, see note to Table 2.1.

authors (Holroyd, 1976; Wine, 1971) have suggested that the effectiveness of a combined treatment is simply due to the cognitive component of the treatment; the physiological component does not add anything (Finger & Galassi, 1977; Mitchell & Ng, 1972; Pesta & Zwettler, 1977) and may, in some cases, reduce overall treatment effectiveness (Holroyd, 1976; Kaplan et al., 1979; Wine, 1970). Although the results from these studies do not support the interactionist position, they do not support the cognitive model either. If the physiological component was actually irrelevant, then one would expect to find several studies in which the cognitive treatment equaled or surpassed the combined, which, in turn, was more effective than the physiological one. This result was, however, only reported in one study (Kaplan et al., 1979). On the behavioral-outcome measure of this study, no groups differed from controls. Additional confounding in this study accrued from the use of study-skills training as an adjunct to all groups. Until more studies are carried out using a combined treatment group, results from studies in this category cannot be viewed as supportive of either perspective.

*Study-skills training versus Others.* The last group of studies reviewed were studies that used a group receiving study-skills training. These studies addressed test anxiety as consisting, at least partially, of reactive anxiety. One problem with this approach is that when study-skills training is shown to improve performance in high-test-anxious subjects—so their performance becomes equal to that of low-test-anxious subjects—the most appropriate control is not included. Low-anxious students should also receive study-skills training. If their performance is also improved, then a study-skills deficit cannot be postulated as a basis for test anxiety. Instead, it must be viewed as a possible covariate that may or may not be present in all highly test anxious subjects. Despite this fact, studies investigating study-skills training included psychological or physiological treatments or a combination as comparison groups and, thus, they are useful to examine here.

Nine studies attempted to test the hypothesis that test anxiety merely reflects poor study habits. All nine studies used behavioral measures; all but one (Bruch, 1978) also included self-report instruments. No differences of treatment effectiveness between study-skills and other treatments (physiological, psychological) were revealed in 50% of the self-reports and 55% of the behavioral assessments. These treatments all differed significantly from controls. One (12.5%) of the studies using self-report measures reported that study-skills training was more effective than a physiological treatment (Kirkland & Hollandsworth, 1980); one (12.5%) reported that a psychological treatment was more effective than study skills (Horne & Matson, 1977); and two (25%) reported that a physiological treatment was more effective (Cornish & Dilley, 1973; Osterhouse, 1972). Examining the behavioral channel, it is apparent that two (22%) studies (Horne & Matson, 1977; Kirkland & Hollandsworth, 1980) found that study-skills training was more effective than a physiological treatment, whereas one (11%) (Harris & Johnson, 1980) reported that a cognitive treatment, which included a study-skills program, was more effective than study skills alone. Osterhouse (1972) reported that subjects who underwent study-skills training did more poorly on a test than NT controls. These data are detailed in Table 2.6.

From these results it appears that study-skills training probably does not harm a highly test anxious person, but it may not help, either. The possibility that

Table 2.6  Study skills versus others, NT studies

| Authors | Design | Conditions compared | Assessment channel | Posttreatment outcome | Follow-up |
|---|---|---|---|---|---|
| Allen (1971) | Group n = 67 | AT SD SS SD and SS NT MCC | Self-report | SD = SS = SD and SS = AF > NT = MCC | NA |
| | | | Behavioral | SD and SS = AT = SD = SS > MC = NT | NA |
| Allen (1973) | Group n = 84 | SS and R (group) SS (group) AT (group) SS and R (individual) SS (individual) NT MCC | Self-report | SS and R (group) = SS (group) = SS and R (individual) = SS (individual) > AT (group) = NT = MCC | NA |
| | | | Behavioral | SS and R (group) = SS (individual) = SS (group) = SS and R (individual) > AT (group) = NT = MCC | NA |
| Bruch (1978) | Group n = 60 | SS CBM M NT | Behavioral | SS = CBM > M | NA |
| Cornish & Dilley (1973) | Group n = 39 | SS SD IT NT | Self-report Behavioral | SD > SS = IT > NT SD = SS = IT > NT | NA NA |

| Study | Group / n | Conditions | Measure | Result | |
|---|---|---|---|---|---|
| Harris & Johnson (1980) | Group n = 48 | SS SCD and SS CBM and SS NT | Self-report | CBM and SS = SCD and SS = SS > NT | NA |
| | | | Behavioral | CBM and SS > SCD and SS = NT = SS | NA |
| Horne & Matson (1977) | Group n = 100 | M SD F SS NT | Self-report | M > SD > F > SS > NT | NA |
| | | | Behavioral | SS < F > NT | NA |
| Kirkland & Hollandsworth (1980) | Group n = 50 | CC MT SS AT | Self-report | SS > MT = CC = AT | NA |
| | | | Behavioral | SS > MT = CC = AT | NA |
| Lent & Russell (1978) | Group n = 57 | SS SD and SS CC and SS NT | Self-report | SD and SS = CC and SS > SS = NT | SD and SS = CC and SS > SS = NT |
| | | | Behavioral | SD and SS = CC and SS > NT | NA |
| Osterhouse (1972) | Group n = 60 | SD SS NT | Self-report | SD > NT | NA |
| | | | Behavioral | NT > SS = SD | NA |

*Note.* For abbreviations, see note to Table 2.1.

some high-test-anxious people suffer from study deficits is suggested by the multidimensional conceptualization of test anxiety. Study-skills training probably helps these people and does not affect the others. Until researchers begin to pre-test high-test-anxious people for study-skills deficits and include low-anxious study-skill–deficit people as controls, the utility of study-skills training as a treatment for test anxiety will remain unknown.

*Conclusion.* An examination of the self-report channels of all studies that compared physiological, psychological, or combined treatments with study-skills training, NT controls, or both reveals: 24% of these studies (5 of 21) reported that a psychological treatment was most effective in decreasing test anxiety; 19% (4 of 21) reported that a physiological treatment was most effective; only one (5%) reported a combined treatment superior; and 48% reported no difference in effectiveness between the experimentel treatments. Similar results were found using the behavioral-assessment channel. These data stand alone as proof that test anxiety is improved equally by psychological and physiological treatments and thus is probably due to an interaction between the two systems. As mentioned earlier, however, because no one measured arousal pre- and posttreatment, it is possible that the physiological treatments did not modify physiological arousal but instead only affected cognitive processing. Probably the type of study that would best determine the validity of the cognitive and interactive positions is that which concurrently measures psychological and physiological reactions of high- and low-test-anxious subjects during evaluative stress. No such studies exist, but three have approached this ideal.

## MEASUREMENT OF PHYSIOLOGICAL RESPONSE TO A TESTING SITUATION

To assess physiological changes accurately during evaluative stress, several principles must be followed. Lacey and Lacey (1958) have shown that people react to stressful stimuli using one system or organ more than another. Some people may tend to react with dramatic increases in HR, whereas others may react with increased muscle tension. This organ-specificity hypothesis accounts for the between-subject variability seen in studies that use only one physiological dependent variable. To control for these individual differences, researchers have been urged to measure variables in two or more systems. When this procedure is not followed, conclusions that certain subjects are not physiologically aroused are not valid.

Because the internal environment is constantly changing, an accurate physiological picture can be obtained only by taking frequent measures of the variables of interest. Using techniques that require that large amounts of data be averaged together over a long time span decreases the power of the data and increases the likelihood of obtaining spurious results. For example, plasma catecholamines increase within 3 sec of stressor onset and may return to base line within 2 min if the stressor is acute. If an investigator obtained a blood sample 5 min after the stressor, plasma catecholamines would not differ from their basal values, and the conclusion that catechols do not increase after stress would be invalid. It is best to measure frequently as many physiological variables as possible. Finally, because a certain physiological behavior may arise as a result of different mechanisms, one should include measurement of variables that may be relevant to the behavior of interest. For example, HR may be increased directly by increased sympathetic input to the heart or indirectly by changes in composition and volume of the blood. The meaning of the HR change depends on what mechanisms are involved. Further, to conclude that two people are equally aroused based on a measure of HR is to ignore potential differences in variables controlling HR and in other systems.

To perform a good psychophysiological study, all of the above potential confounds must be controlled. Additionally, subjects in a psychophysiological study often experience arousal in response to the novelty of the laboratory setting. To gather valid base-line measures, the subject should be given time to habituate to the instrumentation. Differences owing to failure to control for the aforementioned variables in the three studies reviewed below are probably tantamount in explaining differences of results.

Holroyd et al. (1978) measured ANS arousal in testing situations in an attempt to clarify the components of test anxiety and to examine the various test anxiety theories. Base-line electrodermal response, HR, and HR variability were measured before the task and four times during the task. The task consisted of the Stroop Color Word Test followed by an anagrams test. Presentation order was never varied. Mean response for every 15-min period served as the index of physiological reactivity. Dependent variables included self-report of anxiety, performance, and amount of time spent worrying. The results indicated that high-test-anxious women reported more anxiety, showed poorer performance, and spent more time worrying than did low-test-anxious women. There was no difference between high- and low-test-anxious women in HR and EDR, but HR variability was higher in low-test-anxious women. The results were interpreted as supporting Wine's (1971) theory of test anxiety in which test anxiety is viewed as an attentional deficit and not related to maladaptive arousal patterns. Yet the design was inadequate to test this hypothesis because within-subjects' physiological changes were not reported (or correlated with the subject's anxiety level), nor were any cognitive measures taken during the task. In addition, Holroyd et al. mentioned that one reason for lack of physiological differences between groups may have been the subjects' unfamiliarity with the physiological procedures.

Hollandsworth et al. (1979) chose six women from an introductory psychology class on the basis of extreme scores on the Test Anxiety Scale and near-mean scores on the General Anxiety Scale (Sarason, 1972). Subjects were individually exposed to a testing situation composed of a 5-min adaptation period, a 2-min anticipatory period after the test directions were read, another 2-min anticipatory period after stress-inducing instructions were given, and then a 40-min period to complete the test (the Otis-Lennon Mental Ability Test [Otis & Lennon, 1968]). Heart rate, EDR, and respiration were monitored continuously. Subjects were videotaped; after test completion, they viewed the videotape with the experimenter and described their thoughts and feelings during the test. The results indicate that both high- and low-test-anxious subjects were aroused during the testing period. All three physiological variables were reported in terms of average response every 2–5 min. Because there were only three subjects per group, no statistical analyses were performed, although "average trends" were discussed. Unfortunately, the large intersubject physiological variability precluded meaningful between-group comparisons. Although the physiological data appeared similar between groups, the psychological data did not. High-test-anxious students made more debilitative self-statements than did low-anxious students, who reported more facilitative, task-oriented cognitions. Hollandsworth et al. (1979) also concluded that their results supported Wine's (1971) attentional-deficit hypothesis, although like Holroyd et al. (1978), they measured average HR differences from base line—a technique that loses valuable physiological data. Additionally, they used only three subjects per group, which reduced generalizability and validity. Their tour de force, however, was videotaping—making it to examine cognitive and physiological concomitants—which, sadly, they did not do. Clarification of physiological changes made during or after debilitating and facilitating self-statements would have been very enlightening. Although this research favors the cognitive viewpoint, its shortcomings preclude definitiveness.

A study by Montgomery (1977) controlled for many of the previously mentioned confounding variables. He examined high- and low-test-anxious subjects under evaluative and nonstress conditions. There was no difference in performance on a slide-presented anagrams task between groups or across conditions. There were, however, significant between-group differences of anticipatory cardiac response within the evaluative stress condition. Montgomery measured the second-by-second HR before a 1-sec warning tone, through an 8-sec anticipatory interval, and after exposure to the anagram, which the subject had 30 sec to solve. Results indicated that the biphasic cardiac wave form of high-test-anxious subjects peaked later and higher and decelerated less than did that of low-anxious subjects. These results were interpreted by Montgomery as supporting the attentional-deficit model of test anxiety. The high-test-anxious subjects were presumably more preoccupied with inner ruminations and displayed poorer attentional control. These differences were reflected in their cardiac response. Montgomery noted that the experimental design could not isolate the effects of evaluative stress from unfamiliarity with the laboratory, so that interpretation of results should be cautious. Despite Montgomery's assertion that his results favored the cognitive hypothesis, it is clear that he did find significant between-group differences. These differences cannot be accounted for by Wine's theory; they reflect, instead, the interactive role of physiological and psychological systems. There are several other studies that tend to corroborate this interpretation.

Lacey and Lacey (1979) reported their studies of second-to-second HR changes in which they found that deceleration of HR occurs during cognitive processing and attention focusing. Their hypothesis, that baroreceptor discharge is inhibitory to sensorimotor activity and facilitative of internalized cognitive activities, was supported by their research, which found that HR and BP decreased when detection of, and response to, external stimuli was required and increased when there was "motivated inattention" to these stimuli. Lacey and Lacey, thus, provide an explanation for the differences in the pattern of HR variability reported by Montgomery (1977) and alluded to by Holroyd et al. (1978).

Fenz (1975) described the series of experiments performed with sport parachutists in which he identified differences of HR between novice and experienced parachutists. During the morning of the jump, novice parachutists' HRs increased significantly above base line, did not peak until the time of the jump, and then slowly decelerated. On the other hand, HRs of experienced parachutists peaked and decelerated before the jump, so that, at the time of the jump, they were near basal levels. This pattern also differentiated between good and poor jumpers. Additionally, the novice jumpers reported more anxiety and performed more poorly on word-association and reaction-time tasks before the jump than did experienced parachutists.

Given that Montgomery's (1977) results were similar to Fenz's (1975), it seems probable that people who experience high state anxiety, which prevents them from focusing on a task, display anticipatory cardiac changes that differ from those of people who experience task-oriented, facilitative anxiety. These data suggest that test anxiety is primarily a cognitive event in which physiological changes occur concomitantly and feed back to affect perceptions and cognitions. This transaction can be accounted for by the interactive model but not by the parallel-processing one.

Future research on the physiological response to evaluative stress should include continuous measurement of variables within several systems beginning before stressor exposure and including basal measurements taken at a separate time. More direct measures of autonomic arousal may provide valuable data concerning differences of central processing of cognitive events.

In conclusion, only three studies have examined the physiological response to evaluative stress in high- and low-test-anxious people. Two of these studies (Hollandsworth et al., 1979; Holroyd et al., 1978) reported no difference of arousal between groups, although the authors concede that methodological problems may be responsible for these results. The third study (Montgomery, 1977), which examined more specific physiological changes, reported between-group differences in cardiac wave forms. The pattern of results of other investigations of cardiac response to stress (Fenz, 1975; Lacey & Lacey, 1979) is similar to Montgomery's findings, increasing the probability that his results are valid. From the review of the treatment-outcome studies and of these latter studies, we conclude that the cognitive model does not adequately explain the available data. The data supports the position that test anxiety is primarily a cognitive event and that high-test-anxious subjects focus less attention on the task than do low-test-anxious subjects. Yet it also supports the contention that physiological arousal contributes to test anxiety and interacts with the cognitive modality.

For the cognitive model to be proved correct, it would be necessary to show that cognitive treatments are more effective than physiological ones. It was found, however, that 48% of the treatment-outcome studies comparing psychological, physiological, or combined treatments with study-skills training, NT controls, or both reported no differences in effectiveness between treatments. This result alone casts serious doubt on the validity of the cognitive model. The most parsimonious explanation of this result is that both systems transact and, through excitatory and inhibitory mechanisms, affect each other. Until disconfirmatory evidence is presented, the interactive model of test anxiety must be accepted.

Future studies of physiological treatments of test anxiety should include measurement of physiological variables to determine whether these treatments act on a physiological or on a cognitive level. If it is found that they act primarily on a physiological level, then the interactive model will be validated. Additionally, the wide variability in results of treatment-outcome studies may be due to the multidimensionality of test anxiety. Until investigators determine differences in reactive and conditioned anxiety in highly test anxious people, outcome differences in performance and emotionality, especially in studies using study-skills training, will vary greatly. Controlling for all of the above differences is an important step in clarifying the interactionist model of test anxiety. The shortcomings of the test anxiety research are similar to those of other studies investigating psychological and physiological interactions. Much research is still needed before the mechanisms of psychological and physiological interactions can be understood.

## CONCLUSIONS

The methodological problems seen in test anxiety research exemplify those of any study of psychological and physiological interrelationships. The following suggestions, aimed at improving studies of psychological and physiological variables, are inferred from the difficulties inherent in the studies of test anxiety.

1. Variables should be measured as directly as possible. For example, instead of just examining HR and EDR, plasma catecholamines should also be measured at meaningful intervals. A corollary of this suggestion is to measure the primary variable thought to be involved or reactive. More information is gained by measuring plasma epinephrine and norepinephrine than by measuring finger pulse volume. Similarly, measurements of end products, such as urinary epinephrine, provide less information about physiological arousal than does measurement of a compound closer to the system of interest. This is not to say that measurements of end products and of hormonal actions are irrelevant; they provide information about the feedback between degradation and synthesis of a compound. Unless the original compounds are also measured, however, it becomes more difficult to determine if increases of the end product indicate that the primary compound is increased or if a step somewhere in between has been altered (possibly increased enzymatic action or alterations in another chain that also results in the same end product).

2. To accomplish the first objective, plasma samples should be obtained. Because taking blood is often involved and stressful in and of itself and may thus confound results, the methodology must control for this procedure. The use of portable blood-withdrawal pumps seems, at present, a most effective way to control for the negative psychological effects resulting from blood withdrawal. Because the pump withdraws blood automatically, the subject is not aware of when the blood is being withdrawn; and because it is portable and can be programmed to withdraw several samples over a set amount of time, it can be worn by the subject during a period of stressor presentation. Other methods using indwelling intravenous catheters are also acceptable, although caution must be exercised to avoid hormonal conditioning to the technician's approach immediately before a blood sample is to be withdrawn.

3. Precise psychological measures should be taken concurrently (or a few minutes before) physiological measures are obtained. Correlations between these variables are then more valid.

4. If possible, several physiological and psychological measures should be taken concurrently. When a blood sample is taken, it is relatively easy to include measurement of several blood constituents. With the advent of assay kits, the

cost of assaying hormones and neurotransmitters has decreased considerably. Because evidence of arousal may be exhibited in only one or two systems, it is important to take as wide a variety of measures as possible so that the results are more meaningful. Similarly, psychological measures should be varied. It may be that a subject's physiological arousal correlates well with one psychological variable but not with another.

5. A within-subjects design should be used (e.g., Lazarus & Golden, in press). Repeated measures taken from the same subject are the best way to achieve understanding of psychological and physiological interactions. Only after sufficient within-subjects data have been collected, can between-subjects comparisons begin to provide useful information. Although subjects often differ in arousability, there is usually a measurable between-subjects trend in reactivity.

6. If a between-subjects design is to be used, then investigators should try to reduce variability by maximizing differences between groups and by collecting all relevant background information. For example, an investigator using endocrinologic dependent measures should determine if any subjects have endocrinologic disorders or habits that may affect their hormonal reactivity. In addition, by examining special populations (e.g., those exhibiting high or low test anxiety or Type A or Type B behavior patterns), selective contributions to the pattern of the stress response may be illuminated.

Using test anxiety as a model and classifying treatment-outcome studies by the modality they presumably primarily effect is a method that provides insight into the theoretical formulations of test anxiety and into the nature of cognitive and physiological interactions in general. Given that each modality can affect the other, the parallel-processing model of psychological and physiological systems is not supported. Within the test anxiety literature, this model is represented by the attentional-deficit theory. Although test anxiety is primarily a cognitive event, it is not independent of physiological processing. High arousal may be either facilitative or debilitative, but as Montgomery (1977) showed, the pattern of physiological reactivity differs between the two. Although these results were investigated in the context of test anxiety, there is no reason to assume they would not generalize to other states that have both cognitive and physiological components. Hence, one would assume that the interactive model is more appropriate than the parallel-processing one in all cases.

The use of test anxiety as a model has supported the interactive-processing perspective. Riley and Furedy (this volume, chap. 1) also concluded that an interactive model receives the most support from the research literature. There are still questions to be answered about the nature of psychological and physiological interactions in general and about test anxiety specifically. Yet, given the improved availability of physiological measurement instruments, many of these questions may be answered in the near future.

## REFERENCES

Allen, G. J. Effectiveness of study counseling and desensitization in alleviating test anxiety in college students. *Journal of Abnormal Psychology,* 1971, *77,* 282–289.

Allen, G. J. Treatment of test anxiety by group-administered and self-administered relaxation and study counseling. *Behavior Therapy,* 1973, *4,* 349–360.

Alpert, R., & Haber, R. N. Anxiety in academic achievement situations. *Journal of Abnormal and Social Psychology,* 1960, *61,* 207–215.

Anton, W. D. An evaluation of outcome variables in the systematic desensitization of test anxiety. *Behaviour Research and Therapy*, 1976, *14*, 217–224.

Barrios, B. A., Ginter, E. J., & McKnight, R. R. *Effectiveness of coping skills training in the management of test anxiety.* Unpublished manuscript, University of Utah, 1979.

Barrios, B. A., & Shigetomi, C. C. Coping-skills training for the management of anxiety: A critical review. *Behavior Therapy*, 1979, *10*, 491–522.

Bedell, J. R. Systematic desensitization, relaxation-training, and suggestion in the treatment of test anxiety. *Behaviour Research and Therapy*, 1976, *14*, 309–311.

Bedell, J. R., Archer, R. P., & Rosmann, M. Relaxation therapy, desensitization and the treatment of anxiety-based disorders. *Journal of Clinical Psychology*, 1979, *35*, 840–843.

Borst, C. V. (Ed.). *The mind/brain identity theory.* London: Macmillan, 1970.

Bruch, M. A. Type of cognitive modeling, imitation of modeled tactics, and modification of test anxiety. *Cognitive Therapy and Research*, 1978, *2*, 147–164.

Chang-Liang, R., & Denney, D. R. Applied relaxation as training in self-control. *Journal of Counseling Psychology*, 1976, *23*, 183–189.

Cornish, R. D., & Dilley, J. S. Comparison of three methods of reducing test anxiety: Systematic desensitization, implosive therapy, and study counseling. *Journal of Counseling Psychology*, 1973, *20*, 499–503.

Counts, D., Hollandsworth, J. G., Jr., & Alcorn, J. D. Use of electromyographic feedback and cue-controlled relaxation in the treatment of test anxiety. *Journal of Consulting and Clinical Psychology*, 1978, *46*, 990–996.

Deffenbacher, J. L. Relaxation in vivo in the treatment of test anxiety. *Journal of Behavior Therapy and Experimental Psychiatry*, 1976, *7*, 289–292.

Deffenbacher, J. L., Mathis, H., & Michaels, A. C. Two self-control procedures in the reduction of targeted and non-targeted anxieties. *Journal of Counseling Psychology*, 1979, *26*, 120–127.

Deffenbacher, J. L., & Michaels, A. C. Two self-control procedures in the reduction of targeted and non-targeted anxieties: A year later. *Journal of Counseling Psychology*, 1980, *27*, 9–15.

Deffenbacher, J. L., Michaels, A. C., Michaels, T., & Daley, P. C. Comparison of anxiety management training and self-control desensitization. *Journal of Counseling Psychology*, 1980, *27*, 232–239.

Deffenbacher, J. L., & Rivera, N. A behavioral self-control treatment of test anxiety in minor populations: Some cases and issues. *Psychological Reports*, 1976, *39*, 1188–1190.

Deffenbacher, J. L., & Shelton, J. L. Comparison of anxiety management training and desensitization in reducing test and other anxieties. *Journal of Counseling Psychology*, 1978, *25*, 277–282.

Deffenbacher, J. L., & Snyder, A. L. Relaxation as self-control in the treatment of test and other anxieties. *Psychological Reports*, 1976, *39*, 379–385.

Denney, D. R., & Rupert, P. A. Desensitization and self-control in the treatment of test anxiety. *Journal of Counseling Psychology*, 1977, *24*, 272–280.

Doctor, R. M., Aponte, J., Burry, A., & Welch, R. Group counseling versus behavior therapy in treatment of college underachievement. *Behavior Research and Therapy*, 1970, *8*, 87–90.

Driscoll, R. Anxiety reduction using physical exertion and positive images. *Psychological Record*, 1976, *26*, 87–94.

Endler, W. S., Hunt, J. McV., & Rosenstein, A. J. An S-R inventory of anxiousness. *Psychological Monographs*, 1962, *76*(17, Whole No. 536).

Epstein, S. The nature of anxiety with emphasis upon its relationship to expectancy. In C. D. Spielberger (Ed.), *Anxiety: Current trends in theory and research* (Vol. 2). New York: Academic, 1972.

Fehr, F. S., & Stern, J. A. Peripheral physiological variables and emotion: The James-Lange theory revisited. *Psychological Bulletin*, 1970, *74*, 411–424.

Fenz, W. D. Strategies for coping with stress. In I. G. Sarason & C. D. Spielberger (Eds.), *Stress and anxiety* (Vol. 2). Washington: Hemisphere, 1975.

Finger, R., & Galassi, J. P. Effects of modifying cognitive versus emotionality responses in the treatment of test anxiety. *Journal of Consulting and Clinical Psychology*, 1977, *45*, 280–287.

Funkenstein, D., King, S., & Drolette, M. (Eds.). *Mastery of stress.* Cambridge, Mass.: Harvard University Press, 1957.

Goldfried, M. R., Lineham, M. M., & Smith, J. L. Reduction of test anxiety through cognitive restructuring. *Journal of Consulting and Clinical Psychology,* 1978, *46,* 32–39.

Greene, W. A., Conron, G., Schalch, D. S., & Schreiner, B. F. Psychologic correlates of growth hormone and adrenal secretory responses of patients undergoing cardiac catheterization. *Psychosomatic Medicine,* 1970, *32,* 599–614.

Harris, G., & Johnson, S. B. Comparison of individualized covert modeling, self-control desensitization, and study skills training for alleviation of test anxiety. *Journal of Consulting and Clinical Psychology,* 1980, *48,* 186–194.

Hollandsworth, J. G., Jr., Glazeski, R. C., Kirkland, K., Jones, G. E., & Van Norman, L. R. An analysis of the nature and effects of test anxiety: Cognitive, behavioral, and physiological components. *Cognitive Therapy and Research,* 1979, *3,* 165–180.

Holroyd, K. A. Cognition and desensitization in the group treatment of test anxiety. *Journal of Consulting and Clinical Psychology,* 1976, *44,* 991–1001.

Holroyd, K. A. Effectiveness of an "attribution therapy" manipulation with test anxiety. *Behavior Therapy,* 1978, *9,* 526–534.

Holroyd, K. A., Westbrook, T., Wolf, M., & Badhorn, E. Performance, cognition, and physiological responding in test anxiety. *Journal of Abnormal Psychology,* 1978, *87,* 442–451.

Horne, A. M., & Matson, J. L. A comparison of modeling, desensitization, flooding, study skills, and control groups for reducing test anxiety. *Behavior Therapy,* 1977, *8,* 1–8.

Hussian, R. A., & Lawrence, P. S. The reduction of test, state, and trait anxiety by test-specific and generalized stress inoculation training. *Cognitive Therapy and Research,* 1978, *2,* 25–37.

James, B., & James, N. N. Tranquilizers and exam stress. *Journal of the American College Health Association,* 1973, *21,* 241–243.

Johansson, G. Subjective wellbeing and temporal patterns of sympathetic-adrenal medullary activity. *Biological Psychology,* 1976, *4,* 157–172.

Kaplan, R. M., McCordick, S. M., & Twitchell, M. Is it the cognitive or the behavioral component which makes cognitive-behavior modification effective in test anxiety? *Journal of Counseling Psychology,* 1979, *26,* 371–377.

Kipper, D. A., & Giladi, D. Effectiveness of structured psychodrama and systematic desensitization in reducing test anxiety. *Journal of Counseling Psychology,* 1978, *25,* 499–505.

Kirkland, K., & Hollandsworth, J. G., Jr. Effective test-taking: Skills acquisition versus anxiety-reduction techniques. *Journal of Consulting and Clinical Psychology,* 1980, *48,* 431–439.

Knight, R. B., Atkins, A., Eagle, C. J., Evans, N., Finkelstein, J. W., Fukushima, D. K., Katz, J. L., & Weiner, H. Psychological stress, ego defenses, and cortisol production in children hospitalized for elective surgery. *Psychosomatic Medicine,* 1979, *41,* 40–49.

Kostka, M. P., & Galassi, J. P. Group systematic desensitization versus covert positive reinforcement in the reduction of test anxiety. *Journal of Counseling Psychology,* 1974, *21,* 464–468.

Lacey, J. I., & Lacey, B. C. Verification and extension of the principle of autonomic response stereotypy. *American Journal of Psychology,* 1958, *71,* 50–73.

Lacey, J. I., & Lacey, B. C. Somatopsychic effects of interoception. In E. Meyer III and J. V. Brady (Eds.), *Research in the psychobiology of human behavior.* Baltimore: Johns Hopkins Press, 1979.

Lazarus, R. S., & Golden, G. The function of denial in stress, coping, and aging. In S. Breznitz (Ed.), *Denial of stress.* New York: International Universities Press, in press.

Lent, R. W., & Russell, R. K. Treatment of test anxiety by cue-controlled desensitization and study-skills training. *Journal of Counseling Psychology,* 1978, *25,* 217–224.

Liebert, R. M., & Morris, L. W. Cognitive and emotional components of test anxiety: A distinction and some initial data. *Psychological Reports,* 1967, *20,* 975–978.

Linden, W. Practicing of meditation by school children and their levels of field dependence–independence, test anxiety, and reading achievement. *Journal of Consulting and Clincical Psychology,* 1973, *41,* 139–143.

Malec, J., Park, T., & Watkins, J. T. Modeling with role playing as a treatment for test anxiety. *Journal of Consulting and Clinical Psychology,* 1976, *44,* 679.

Mandler, G., & Sarason, S. B. A study of anxiety and learning. *Journal of Abnormal and Social Psychology,* 1952, *47,* 166–173.

Marchetti, A., McGlynn, F. D., & Patterson, A. S. Effects of cue-controlled relaxation, a placebo treatment, and no treatment on changes in self-reported and psychophysiological indices of test anxiety among college students. *Behavior Modification*, 1977, *1*, 47–72.

McGlynn, F. D., Kinjo, K., & Doherty, G. Effects of cue-controlled relaxation, a placebo treatment, and no treatment on changes in self-reported test anxiety among college students. *Journal of Clinical Psychology*, 1978, *34*, 707–714.

Meichenbaum, D. H. Cognitive modification of test anxious college students. *Journal of Consulting and Clinical Psychology*, 1972, *39*, 370–380.

Mitchell, K. R., & Ng, K. T. Effects of group counseling and behavior therapy on the academic achievement of test-anxious students. *Journal of Counseling Psychology*, 1972, *19*, 491–497.

Montgomery, G. K. Effects of performance evaluation and anxiety on cardiac response in anticipation of difficult problem solving. *Psychophysiology*, 1977, *14*, 251–257.

Nemenef, H., & Rothman, I. Acupuncture and hypnotism: Preliminary experiments and a warning. *American Journal of Clinical Hypnosis*, 1974, *16*, 156–159.

Nietzel, M. T. Personal communication, 1981.

Osterhouse, R. A. Desensitization and study-skills training as treatment for two types of test anxious students. *Journal of Counseling Psychology*, 1972, *19*, 301–307.

Otis, A. S., & Lennon, R. T. *Otis-Lennon Mental Ability Test: Manual for Administration.* New York: Harcourt Brace Jovanovich, 1968.

Pesta, T., & Zwettler, S. Influence of cognitive desensitization on test anxiety in school children: A therapeutic comparison. *Zeitschrift für klinische Psychologie*, 1977, *6*, 130–143.

Petry, H. M., & Desiderato, O. Changes in heart rate, muscle activity, and anxiety level following shock threat. *Psychophysiology*, 1978, *15*, 398–402.

Rahe, R. H., Ryman, D. H., & Biersner, R. J. Serum uric acid, cholesterol, and psychological moods throughout stressful naval training. *Aviation, Space, and Environmental Medicine*, 1976, *47*, 883–888.

Reed, M., & Saslow, C. The effects of relaxation instructions and EMG biofeedback on test anxiety, general anxiety, and locus of control. *Journal of Clinical Psychology*, 1980, *36*, 683–690.

Robinson, D. N. (Ed.). *An intellectual history of psychology.* New York: Macmillan, 1976.

Romano, J. L., & Cabianca, W. A. EMG biofeedback training versus systematic desensitization for test anxiety reduction. *Journal of Counseling Psychology*, 1978, *25*, 8–13.

Russell, R. K., Miller, D. E., & June, L. N. Group cue-controlled relaxation in the treatment of test anxiety. *Behavior Therapy*, 1974, *5*, 572–573.

Russell, R. K., Miller, D. E., & June, L. N. A comparison between group systematic desensitization and cue-controlled relaxation in the treatment of test anxiety. *Behavior Therapy*, 1975, *6*, 172–177.

Russell, R. K., & Sipich, J. F. Cue-controlled relaxation in the treatment of test anxiety. *Journal of Behavior Therapy and Experimental Psychiatry*, 1973, *4*, 47–49.

Russell, R. K., & Sipich, J. F. Treatment of test anxiety by cue-controlled relaxation. *Behavior Therapy*, 1974, *5*, 673–676.

Russell, R. K., Wise, F., & Stratoudakis, J. P. Treatment of test anxiety by cue-controlled relaxation and systematic desensitization. *Journal of Counseling Psychology*, 1976, *23*, 563–566.

Ryan, V. L., Krall, C. A., & Hodges, W. F. Self-concept change in behavior modification. *Journal of Consulting and Clinical Psychology*, 1976, *44*, 638–645.

Sarason, I. G. Interrelationships among individual different variables, behavior in psychotherapy and verbal conditioning. *Journal of Abnormal and Social Psychology*, 1958, *56*, 339–344.

Sarason, I. G. Experimental approaches to test anxiety: Attention and the uses of information. In C. D. Spielberger (Ed.), *Anxiety: Current trends in theory and research* (Vol. 2). New York: Academic, 1972.

Sarason, I. G. Test anxiety and cognitive modeling. *Journal of Personality and Social Psychology*, 1973, *28*, 58–61.

Sarason, I. G. Test anxiety and the self disclosing coping model. *Journal of Consulting and Clinical Psychology*, 1975, *43*, 148–153.

Sarason, I. G. The Test Anxiety Scale: Concept and research. In C. D. Spielberger & I. G. Sarason (Eds.), *Stress and anxiety* (Vol. 5). Washington: Hemisphere, 1978.

Sarason, I. G. (Ed.). *Test anxiety: Theory, research, and applications.* Hillsdale, N.J.: Erlbaum, 1980.

Sarason, I. G., & Johnson, J. H. *Coping with academic stressors: A pilot study* (Tech. Rep. SCS-CS-001). Seattle: University of Washington, Psychology Department, December 1976.

Schachter, S., & Singer, J. E. Cognitive, social, and physiological determinants of emotional state. *Psychological Review*, 1962, *69*, 379–399.

Snyder, A. L., & Deffenbacher, J. L. Comparison of relaxation as self-control and systematic desensitization in the treatment of test anxiety. *Journal of Consulting and Clinical Psychology*, 1977, *45*, 1202–1203.

Spiegler, M. D., Cooley, E. J., Marshall, G. J., Prince, H. T., Puckett, S. P., & Skenazy, J. A. A self-control versus a counterconditioning paradigm for systematic desensitization: An experimental comparison. *Journal of Counseling Psychology*, 1976, *23*, 83–86.

Spielberger, C. D. Current trends in theory and research on anxiety. In C. D. Spielberger (Ed.), *Anxiety: Current trends in theory and research* (Vol. 1). New York: Academic, 1972.

Stanton, H. E. The effect of music on test anxiety. *Australian Psychologist*, 1973, *8*, 220–228.

Stanton, H. E. Music and test anxiety: Further evidence for an interaction. *British Journal of Educational Psychology*, 1975, *45*, 80–82.

Suinn, R. M. The STABS, a measure of test anxiety for behavior therapy: Normative data. *Behaviour Research and Therapy*, 1969, *7*, 335–339.

Thompson, J. G., Griebstein, M. G., & Kuhlenschmidt, S. L. *Journal of Counseling Psychology*, 1980, *27*, 97–106.

Weinberger, D. A., Schwartz, G. E., & Davidson, R. J. Low-anxious, high-anxious, and repressive coping styles: Psychometric patterns and behavioral and physiological responses to stress. *Journal of Abnormal Psychology*, 1979, *88*, 369–380.

Wine, J. *Investigations of an attentional interpretation of test anxiety.* Unpublished doctoral dissertation, University of Waterloo, 1970.

Wine, J. Test anxiety and direction of attention. *Psychological Bulletin*, 1971, *76*, 92–104.

Yerkes, R. M., & Dodson, J. D. The relation of strength of stimulus to rapidity of habit formation. *Journal of Comparative Neurology and Psychology*, 1908, *18*, 459–482.

Zemore, R. Systematic desensitization as a method of teaching a general anxiety-reducing skill. *Journal of Consulting and Clinical Psychology*, 1975, *43*, 157–161.

# II

# PSYCHOBIOLOGY OF STRESS

Having opened this book with evidence showing that cognitive and physio logical systems interact and are inseparable in the discussion of emotions, we now turn to the specific nature of these interactions as they relate to stress. The five chapters in this part discuss four different biologic systems (neural, hormonal, immune, and cardiovascular) and their involvement in the stress response. Given that no system acts in a vacuum, it is clear that the chapters and their themes must overlap in an interdependent way. For example, although Anisman, Kokkinidis, and Sklar (Chap. 3) focus on neurotransmitter changes after stress, the remaining chapters also bridge this topic to clarify stress-induced alterations in other systems. Readers with a background in physiology will find the detail useful and will be able to integrate information given in each chapter into a broad perspective. Readers with little background in physiology should also be able to assimilate the important information with the aid of the summaries and general statements about the system of interest.

Anisman et al. (Chap. 3) discuss the differential release of norepinephrine based on length of stressor exposure. Because of the pervasiveness and importance of the catecholaminergic system, their research has many implications for understanding behavioral and hormonal stress reactions. Solomon, Amkraut, and Rubin (Chap. 4) continue the discussion of neural involvement in the stress response, although they are primarily interested in the effects on immunity. They show how stress can suppress the immune response both directly and indirectly. In so doing, they tie together research on hormonal and neural interrelationships. Veith-Flanigan and Sandman (Chap. 5) describe the hormonal system in general, citing several interesting hypotheses concerning mechanisms of response to stress. They present the hormonal-response and stimulus-specificity hypotheses in great detail so as to encourage researchers to explore this field. They also discuss the role of the endorphins and other peptides (ACTH and melanocyte-stimulating hormone) in terms of their psychological effects and contribution to the physiological stress response. M. Wilson (Chap. 6) integrates the theme of neural regulation of the endocrine system by describing in detail the role of the hippocampus in regulating the pituitary-adrenocortical system. The glucocorticoids (e.g., cortisol) are extremely important hormones involved in the reaction to stress. By specifically describing this system, Wilson enables us to integrate knowledge obtained in the previous chapters and understand the stress response in terms of a specific subsystem. The final chapter also describes the mechanisms involved in a specific system.

The part closes with Corley's (Chap. 7) discussion of the cardiovascular response to stress; Part III begins by describing the cardiovascular system. Corley describes the physiological mechanisms involved in the stress response, whereas Chap. 8 is concerned with the psychological factors that characterize those at risk for cardiac pathology.

# 3

# Neurochemical Consequences of Stress

## Contributions of Adaptive Processes

*Hymie Anisman*
*Carleton University, Ottawa, Canada*

*Larry Kokkinidis*
*University of Saskatchewan, Saskatoon, Canada*

*Lawrence S. Sklar*
*Carleton University, Ottawa, Canada*

The response of an organism to aversive stimulation appears to reflect adaptive changes to meet environmental demands. In addition to behavioral attempts to cope with stress, several physiological changes occur that might prevent pathologies that would otherwise be induced by a stressor. When behavioral attempts to cope with stress are ineffective, the contribution of physiological mechanisms to coping processes is further increased. The effectiveness of these physiological changes appears, however, to be limited inasmuch as stress-induced pathologies do frequently occur. The precise physiological alterations that occur not only vary between species, and strains within a species, but depend on several psychological, environmental, and organismic variables. Accordingly, it is not accurate to think of the stress response as a unitary one. Rather, the stress reaction should be considered in the context of a broad range of modifier variables.

Following our discussion of the conditions that lead to neurochemical and hormonal changes, we consider the way in which these physiological alterations may prevent or provoke pathologies. It will become apparent that, although the stress response tends to protect the organism from the immediate health threat of the stressor, this directed mobilization of resources may also dispose the organism to other adverse consequences.

## STRESS AND NEUROCHEMICAL CHANGES

Aversive stimuli result in a multiplicity of neurochemical changes, the duration of which depend on the particular neurotransmitter in question. Of course, a wide variety of factors has been shown to modify stress-induced alterations of neurochemical functioning, including stress severity, the organism's ability to

Preparation of this chapter was supported by Grants A9845 and A7042 from the Natural Sciences and Engineering Research Council and MT-6486 from the Medical Research Council.

cope with stress, stress chronicity, as well as its previous stress history. Furthermore, the influences of these variables on neurochemical change are also determined by the social conditions that prevail as well as by genetic factors.

*Norepinephrine.* When animals are exposed to stressors of moderate severity, it has been observed that levels of brain norepinephrine (NE) initially increase and return to basal levels shortly thereafter. With more severe stress, a transient increase in amine levels will also be evident but will fall below control values (see Welch & Welch, 1970). We suggested that the initial increase of amine levels reflects adaptive changes to meet environmental demands. More explicitly, to ensure adequate stores of NE, monoamine oxidase (MAO), the enzyme that degrades monoamines intraneuronally, is thought to be transiently inhibited (Welch & Welch, 1970). Indeed, Welch and Welch (1970) indicated that soon after stress the proportion of NE metabolites catabolized extraneuronally by catechol-*O*-methyl transferase are increased relative to the NE products degraded through MAO. Thus, although the actual turnover of NE is not altered by a mild stress, the NE that is present may be used more efficiently.

With somewhat more severe stress, however, both the synthesis and the use (i.e., turnover) of NE are increased. As seen in Table 3.1, NE changes occur following any number of stressors including footshock, tailshock, heat, cold, restraint, noxious smells, limb ischemia, rotation, and shaking (see review in Stone, 1975a). The conclusion that increased amine synthesis occurs is based on the fact that various stressors will increase the formation of 3-H-NE formed from the exogenously administered precursor [3]H-tyrosine (Gordon, Spector, Sjoerdsma, & Undenfriend, 1966; Huszti & Kenessey, 1976; Thierry, 1973; Thierry, Fekete, & Glowinski, 1968). Moreover, it has frequently been reported that stress will increase the activity of the synthetic enzymes tyrosine hydroxylase and dopamine β-hydroxylase involved in the NE production (Kobayashi, Palkovits, Kizer, Jacobowitz, & Kopin, 1976; Van Loon, 1976). Evidence showing increased NE utilization induced by stress was derived from several different techniques. For example, following inhibition of tyrosine hydroxylase, the rate of NE disappearance is enhanced by stress, suggesting augmented amine utilization (R. M. Brown, Snider, & Carlsson, 1974; Clarke & Sampath, 1973; Corrodi, Fuxe, & Hokfelt, 1968; Gordon et al., 1966; Korf, Aghajanian & Roth, 1973; Otto & Paalzow, 1975; Stolk, Conner, Levine, & Barchas, 1974). Further to the same point, metabolites of NE, namely normetanephrine and 3-methoxy-4-hydroxyphenylethyleneglycol (MHPG), are increased after stress exposure (Stone, 1971, 1973, 1975a, 1975b). Finally, stress increases the disappearance of exogenously administered [3]H-NE (Thierry, 1973).

As indicated earlier, if the stressor is sufficiently severe, then depletion of NE will occur. Such an effect is produced by any of a number of stressors (see Anisman, 1978; Stone, 1975a) and has been noted in a variety of brain regions (Bliss & Zwanziger, 1966; Thierry, Javoy, Glowinski, & Kety, 1968; Weiss, Glazer, & Pohorecky, 1976) and across different species (Anisman & Sklar, 1979; Bliss, Thatcher, & Alion, 1972; Saarela et al., 1977; Weiss, Glazer, & Pohorecky, 1976). It appears that if the stress is sufficiently severe, then amine synthesis may not keep pace with utilization, consequently resulting in the NE depletion

*Table 3.1*  Norepinephrine changes with acute stress

| | Level | Synthesis[a] | Utilization[b] |
|---|---|---|---|
| Footshock | | | |
| Anisman, Pizzino, & Sklar, 1980 | ↓ | ↑ | |
| Anisman & Sklar, 1979 | ↓ | | |
| Barchas & Freedman, 1963 | 0 | | |
| Bliss, Ailion, & Zwanzieger, 1968 | ↓ | | ↑ |
| Bliss & Zwanziger, 1966 | ↓ | | |
| R. M. Brown et al., 1974 | ↓ | ↑ | ↑ |
| Fulginiti & Orsingher, 1971 | ↓ | | |
| Gold & Van Buskirk, 1978 | ↓ | | |
| Javoy, Thierry, Kety, & Glowinski, 1968 | 0 | ↑ | |
| Korf, 1976 | ↓ | | ↑ |
| Korf et al., 1973 | | | ↑ |
| Maynert & Levi, 1964 | ↓ | | |
| Moore & Lariviere, 1964 | ↓ | | |
| Ordy, Samorajski, & Schroeder, 1966 | ↓ | | |
| Paré & Livingston, 1970 | ↓ | | |
| Paulsen & Hess, 1963 | ↓ | | |
| Ray & Barrett, 1975 | ↓ | | |
| Ritter & Pelzer, 1978 | ↓ | | |
| Ritter & Ritter, 1977 | ↓ | | |
| Sauter, Baba, Stone, & Goldstein, 1978 | ↓ | ↑ | |
| Schutz, Barros-Schutz, Orsingher, & Izquierdo, 1979 | ↓ | | |
| Stolk et al., 1974 | ↓ | ↑ | ↑ |
| Stone, 1975a | | | ↑ |
| Taylor & Laverty, 1969a | ↓ | | ↑ |
| Taylor & Laverty, 1969b | ↓ | | ↑ |
| Thierry, 1973 | ↓ | ↑ | ↑ |
| Thierry, Blanc, & Glowinski, 1970 | ↓ | ↑ | ↑ |
| Thierry, Javoy, Glowinski, & Kety, 1968 | 0 | ↑ | ↑ |
| Weiss, Glazer, & Pohorecky, 1976 | ↓ | ↑ | ↑ |
| Weiss, Glazer, Pohorecky, Brick, & Miller, 1975 | ↓ | | ↑ |
| Weiss, Stone, & Harrell, 1970 | ↓ | ↑ | ↑ |
| Zigmond & Harvey, 1970 | ↓ | | |
| Avoidance-escape | | | |
| Anisman, Pizzino, & Sklar, 1980 | 0 | | |
| Fulginiti & Orsingher, 1971 | 0 | ↑ | |
| Fuxe & Hanson, 1967 | 0 | | ↑ |
| Hurwitz, Robinson, & Barofsky, 1971 | 0 | | ↑ |
| Saito, Morita, Miyazaki, & Takegi, 1976 | 0 | | |
| Weiss, Glazer, Pohorecky, Brick, & Miller, 1976 | 0 | ↑ | ↑ |
| Weiss, Stone, & Harrell, 1970 | 0 | | |
| Restraint | | | |
| Bliss & Zwanziger, 1966 | ↓ | | |
| Carr & Moore, 1968 | 0 | | ↑ |
| Corrodi et al., 1968 | ↓ | | ↑ |
| Hrubes & Benes, 1969 | ↓ | | |
| Huszti & Kenessey, 1976 | | ↑ | ↑ |
| Keim & Sigg, 1976 | ↓ | | |
| Keim & Sigg, 1977 | ↓ | | |
| Kobayashi et al., 1976 | ↓[c] | | |
| Kvetnansky, Mitro, Palkovits, Vigaš, Albreacht, Torda, & Mikulaj, 1975 | ↓[c] | | |

(*See footnotes on p. 70.*)

*Table 3.1*   Norepinephrine changes with acute stress (*Continued*)

| | Level | Synthesis[a] | Utilization[b] |
|---|---|---|---|
| **Restraint (*Continued*)** | | | |
| Kvetnansky, Palkovits, Mitro, Torda, & Mikulaj, 1977 | ↓[c] | | |
| Lidbrink, Corrodi, Fuxe, & Olson, 1972 | ↓ | | ↑ |
| Moore & Lariviere, 1964 | 0 | | |
| Saavedra, Kvetnansky, & Kopin, 1979 | ↓[c] | | |
| Saito et al., 1976 | ↓ | | |
| Welch & Welch, 1968 | 0 | | ↑ |
| **Cold** | | | |
| Beley, Beley, Rochette, & Bralet, 1977 | ↓ | ↑ | ↑ |
| Corrodi, Fuxe, & Hokfelt, 1967 | 0 | | 0 |
| Corrodi et al., 1967 | ↓ | | ↑ |
| Goldstein & Nakajima, 1966 | 0 | | ↑ |
| Ingenito & Bonnycastle, 1967 | ↓ | | ↑ |
| Reid, Volicer, Smookler, Beaven, & Brodie, 1966 | 0 | | ↓ |
| Saarela, Hissa, Hohtola, & Jeronen, 1977 | | | ↑ |
| Simmonds, 1969 | 0 | | |
| **Swimming** | | | |
| Barchas & Freedman, 1963 | ↓ | | |
| Bliss & Zwanziger, 1966 | 0 | | |
| Moore & Lariviere, 1964 | ↓ | | |
| Stone, 1970 | ↓ | | ↑ |
| **Forced running** | | | |
| Barchas & Friedman, 1963 | 0 | | |
| Gordon et al., 1966 | ↓ | | ↑ |
| Stone, 1971 | ↓ | ↑ | ↑ |
| Stone, 1973 | | ↑ | ↑ |
| **Shaking** | | | |
| Lee, Morita, Saito, & Takagi, 1973 | ↓ | | ↑ |
| Rosecrans, 1969 | ↓ | | ↑ |
| Saito et al., 1976 | ↓ | | |
| **Noise** | | | |
| Moore & Lariviere, 1964 | 0 | | |
| Spyraki, Papadopailou-Daifoti, & Petounis, 1978 | ↓ | | |
| **Formalin** | | | |
| Carr & Moore, 1968 | ↓ | | ↑ |
| Kobayashi et al., 1976 | ↓[c] | 0 | |
| **Limb ischemia** | | | |
| Stoner & Elsen, 1971 | ↓ | | ↑ |
| Stoner & Hunt, 1976a | ↓ | ↑ | ↑ |
| Stoner & Hunt, 1976b | ↓ | ↑ | ↑ |
| **Burns** | | | |
| Stoner & Elsen, 1971 | ↓ | | ↑ |
| **Sleep deprivation** | | | |
| Stone, 1971 | 0 | | 0 |
| **Handling** | | | |
| Van Loon, 1976 | | ↑ | |

*Note.* Obviously, if NE levels are maintained and utilization is increased, then synthesis rate must be increased as well.

[a]Synthesis was determined in the various studies either by activity of tyrosine hydroxylase or dopamine β-hydroxylase, or by formation of 3-H-NE from ³H-tyrosine and ³H-dopa.

[b]Utilization in various studies was determined either by disappearance of NE following tyrosine hydroxylase or dopamine β-hydroxylase inhibition, formation of the NE metabolite MHPG, or rate of disappearance of exogenously administered 3-H-NE.

[c]NE levels were determined in discrete brain nuclei.

(Thierry, 1973; Thierry, Javoy, Glowinski, & Kety, 1968). It might be noted that the amine pool from which NE is released is dependent on stress severity. Moderate stress will increase release of 3-H-NE exogenously administered or formed from $^3$H-tyrosine administered 20 min earlier. 3-H-NE synthesized 180 min earlier from $^3$H-tyrosine is not, however, affected by moderate stress. In contrast, severe stress increased utilization of both newly synthesized and previously stored NE. Accordingly, it was hypothesized that moderate stress increases release of NE only from the functional storage pools containing the newly formed amine, whereas severe stress will result in the mobilization of NE from main storage pools containing previously stored amine as well as from the functional pools (Thierry, 1973; Thierry, Javoy, Glowinski, & Kety, 1968).

It appears likely that the NE cell bodies in the locus coeruleus, among others, are activated by stress. It was shown that the NE reductions ordinarily produced by tyrosine hydroxylase inhibition among stressed animals were abolished on the side of the brain ipsilateral to a locus coeruleus lesion (Korf, 1976; Korf et al., 1973). Because the locus coeruleus is composed of NE cell bodies with terminals in the ipsilateral cerebral cortex and hippocampus (Andén, Dhalstrom, Fuxe, Larsson, Olson, & Ungerstedt, 1966; Korf et al., 1973; Ungerstedt, 1971), the NE changes induced in these regions following stress exposure involve stimulation of the locus coeruleus (Korf, 1976). Furthermore, the changes in NE activity provoked by stress may be related to stress-induced cholinergic alterations inasmuch as acetylcholine neurons have been shown to innervate the locus coeruleus (Kuhar, Atweh, & Bird, 1978).

*Epinephrine.* Although epinephrine is found in much lower concentrations in the brain than is NE, the contribution of this neurotransmitter to activity of neuroendocrine processes must be considered. As in the case of brain NE, exposure to stress in the form of restraint was found to have profound effects on epinephrine in the hypothalamus, and these effects were nucleus-dependent (Kvetnansky, Kopin, & Saavedra, 1978). In particular, neither 20 nor 240 min of immobilization influenced epinephrine in the supraoptic, the paraventricular, or the dorsomedial nuclei. In the median eminence, 20 min of restraint caused a small but significant rise of epinephrine. The increase may have been due to peripheral epinephrine circulation owing to an inefficient blood-brain barrier for this region; it is noteworthy, however, that small, nonsignificant increases occur in other nuclei as well. With 240 min of immobilization, very pronounced depletions of epinephrine were seen in the periventricular, arcuate, ventromedial, and anterior nuclei. These effects are reminiscent of those seen in the case of NE, but it is significant that NE depletion is seen in the ventromedial nucleus and in the supraoptic nucleus within 20 min of immobilization (Kvetnansky, Mitro, Palkovits, Brownstein, Torda, Vigaš, & Mikulaj, 1976). Accordingly, it appears that the amounts of stress necessary to provoke NE and epinephrine depletions are not comparable and moreover that the NE alterations are induced in different nuclei than those in which the epinephrine depletions are observed. As such, it is highly unlikely that the epinephrine changes are a direct consequence of the NE alterations.

As in the hypothalamus, immobilization stress has been shown to influence both NE and epinephrine content of brainstem neurons. Whereas 240 min of immobilization decreased epinephrine in A1 and A2 areas, nucleus commissuralis, and the anterior part of the nucleus tractus solitarii, NE depletion was only seen in the latter nuclei. Moreover, 20 min of immobilization stress did not influence either epinephrine or NE in any of these regions (Saavedra et al., 1979). These data indicate that brainstem nuclei are less susceptible to depletion by stress and point to the independent action of stress on NE and epinephrine neurons. Parenthetically, 20 min of stress in this study was found to be sufficient to increase plasma epinephrine, NE, and corticosterone, but the catecholamines do not penetrate into the brain.

Although the NE and epinephrine depletions in the brainstem appear to be independent of one another, this does not imply that epinephrine-containing neurons have no influence on the stress reaction in NE-containing neurons. It has been shown (Sauter et al., 1978) that stress will decrease epinephrine in the locus coeruleus and hypothalamus as well as the C1 and C2 cell groups of reticular cell bodies in the medulla oblongata. The extent of the depletion was further enhanced by inhibition of phenylethanolamine N-methyltransferase. Interestingly enough, although the enzyme inhibition alone did not alter NE levels in these various regions, it substantially exacerbated the NE depletion provoked by stress. These data were taken to indicate that epinephrine terminals in the locus coeruleus are inhibitory so that alterations in the activity of these neurons will increase NE turnover in the dorsal NE pathway.

*Dopamine.* The changes of dopamine (DA) activity provoked by stress are considerably less pronounced than those of NE. Moreover, inconsistent results have been reported with respect to DA alterations following stress (see Table 3.2). Whereas some investigators have found that stress enhances the depletion of DA produced by tyrosine hydroxylase inhibition (R. M. Brown et al., 1974), other investigators have reported stress to be without effect (Otto & Paalzow, 1975). Thierry, Blanc, and Glowsinski (1971) reported that stress increased conversion of $^3$H-tyrosine to $^3$H-DA in the brainstem; these changes may, however, have reflected increased activity in NE rather than DA neurons.

More recent evaluations of stress-induced changes have indicated rather subtle changes of DA activity. In particular, Kobayashi et al. (1976) and Kvetnansky et al., 1977) reported that stress may provoke depletion of DA, but this occurs exclusively in the arcuate nucleus of the hypothalamus. Given the limited representation of the arcuate in analysis of the hypothalamus, it is not surprising that determination of DA did not reveal depletion in the relatively large brain region. It should be noted that the tuberoinfundibular DA system, which originates in the arcuate nucleus, sends its projections to the median eminence and is responsible for the regulation of several pituitary hormones or their releasing factors (Terry & Martin, 1978). Thus, DA changes in the arcuate may play an essential role in determining stress-related pathology.

As reported by Kobayashi et al. (1976), other investigators (Thierry, Tassin, Blanc, & Glowinski, 1976) found that footshock stress may result in pronounced region-specific DA changes. Although stress did not influence turnover of nigrostriatal DA, or DA in the tuberculum olfactorium, a 25 percent decline was noted in the nucleus accumbens and a 60 percent depletion in the frontal cerebral cortex among rats pretreated with a tyrosine hydroxylase inhibitor. This effect was noted even after 6-OHDA lesion that depleted forebrain NE, suggesting that the DA depletion was unrelated to NE changes. In accordance with these results, it has been reported that stress will increase accumulation of 3,4-dihydroxyphenylacetic acid, the primary metabolite of DA, in the nucleus

*Table 3.2* Dopamine changes with acute stress

| | Level | Synthesis[a] | Utilization[b] |
|---|---|---|---|
| Footshock | | | |
| Anisman, Pizzino, & Sklar, 1980 | 0 | | |
| Blanc et al., 1980 | | | ↑[c] |
| Bliss & Ailion, 1971 | 0 | | ↑ |
| Bliss, Ailion, & Zwanziger, 1968 | 0 | | 0 |
| Bliss & Zwanziger, 1966 | 0 | | |
| R. M. Brown et al., 1974 | 0 | | ↑ |
| Fadda, Argiolas, Melis, Tissari, Onali, & Gessa, 1978 | 0 | | ↑ |
| Fekete et al., 1981 | | | ↑[c] |
| Herman et al., 1982 | | | ↑[c] |
| Lavielle et al., 1978 | | | ↑[c] |
| Moore & Lariviere, 1964 | ↓ | | |
| Saavedra, 1982 | | | ↑[e] |
| Schutz et al., 1978 | ↓ | | |
| Taylor & Laverty, 1969a | ↓ | | |
| Taylor & Laverty, 1969b | | | ↑ |
| Thierry, Blanc, & Glowinski, 1970 | | | ↑ |
| Thierry, Blanc, & Glowinski, 1971 | | | ↑ |
| Thierry, Javoy, Glowinski, & Kety, 1968 | 0 | | 0 |
| Thierry, Tassin, Blanc, & Glowinski, 1976 | 0[c] | | ↑[d] |
| Tissari, Argiolas, Fadda, Serra, & Gessa, 1979 | 0[c] | | ↑[c] |
| Avoidance-escape | | | |
| Fuxe & Hanson, 1967 | 0 | | 0 |
| Hurwitz et al., 1971 | 0 | | |
| Saito et al., 1976 | 0 | | |
| Restraint | | | |
| Carr & Moore, 1968 | 0 | | 0 |
| Corrodi et al., 1968 | 0 | | |
| Hrubes & Benes, 1969 | 0 | | |
| Keim & Sigg, 1976 | | | |
| Kobayashi et al., 1976 | ↓[d] | | |
| Kvetnansky, Mitro, Palkovits, Vigaš, Albrecht, Torda, & Mikulaj, 1975 | ↓[d] | | |
| Kvetnansky, Mitro, Palkovits, Brownstein, Torda, Vigaš, & Mikulaj, 1976 | ↓[d] | | |
| Kvetnansky, Palkovits, Mitro, Torda, Torda, & Mikulaj, 1977 | ↓[d] | | |
| Lidbrink et al., 1972 | ↑ | | ↓ |
| Moore & Lariviere, 1964 | 0 | | |
| Saito et al., 1976 | ↑ | | |
| Saavedra et al., 1979 | 0 | | |
| Welch & Welch, 1970 | ↑ | | 0 |
| Cold | | | |
| Corrodi et al., 1967 | ↓ | | |
| Goldstein & Nakajima, 1966 | 0 | | |
| Ingenito, 1967 | 0 | | 0 |
| Ishii, Homma, & Yhoshigawa, 1975 | 0 | | |
| Juorio, 1979 | | | |
| Kobayashi et al., 1976 | ↓[d] | | |
| Reid et al., 1966 | | | 0 |
| Saarela et al., 1977 | | | ↑ |
| Saito et al., 1976 | 0 | | |

*(See footnotes on p. 74.)*

Table 3.2  Dopamine changes with acute stress (Continued)

|  | Level | Synthesis[a] | Utilization[b] |
|---|---|---|---|
| Heat |  |  |  |
| Corrodi et al., 1967 | 0 |  | 0 |
| Ingenito & Bonnycastle, 1967 | ↑ |  |  |
| Saarela et al., 1977 |  |  | ↓ |
| Swimming |  |  |  |
| Moore & Lariviere, 1964 | 0 |  |  |
| Shaking |  |  |  |
| Lee et al., 1973 | 0 |  | 0 |
| Saito et al., 1976 | 0 |  |  |
| Noise |  |  |  |
| Moore & Lariviere, 1964 | 0 |  |  |
| Formalin |  |  |  |
| Carr & Moore, 1968 | 0 |  | 0 |
| Kobayashi et al., 1976 | ↓$^d$ |  |  |

[a]Synthesis was determined in the various studies either by activity of tyrosine hydroxylase or by formation of $^3$H-DA from $^3$H-tyrosine.
[b]Utilization was determined either by disappearance of DA following tyrosine hydroxylase inhibition, formation of DA metabolites, or rate of disappearance of exogenously administered $^3$H-DA.
[c]Effects were restricted to the nucleus accumbens or mesolimbic frontal cortex.
[d]Effects were restricted to the arcuate nucleus.
[e]Effects were restricted to the lateral septal nucleus.

accumbens and mesolimbic frontal cortex indicating increased DA utilization (Blanc, Herve, Simon, Lisoprawski, Glowinski, & Taasin, 1980; Fadda, Argiolas, Melis, Tissari, Onali, & Gessa, 1978; Fekete, Szentendrei, Kanyicska, & Palkovits, 1981; Herman, Guillonneau, Dantzer, Scatton, Semerdjian-Rouquier, & Le Moal, 1982; Lavielle, Tassin, Thierry, Blanc, Herve, Barthelemy, & Glowinski, 1978). Finally, it has been reported that exposure to a stressor may also result in a decline of DA concentrations in the lateral septal nucleus, without altering concentrations of the amine in other septal regions (Saavedra, 1982).

*Serotonin.* As in the case of NE, utilization and synthesis of 5-hydroxytryptamine (5-HT), or serotonin, is increased by stress (see Table 3.3). More specifically, after stress exposure, levels of the 5-HT metabolite 5-hydroxyindoleacetic acid (5-HIAA) are increased (Bliss, Thatcher, & Ailion, 1972; Ladisch, 1974); and predictably, the decline of 5-HT induced by the tryptophan hydroxylase inhibitor parachlorophenylalanine (PCPA) is enhanced (Telegdy & Vermes, 1976; Thierry, 1973). Thierry and her associates (Thierry, 1973; Thierry, Fekete, & Glowinski, 1968; Thierry, Javoy, Glowinski, & Kety, 1968) also demonstrated that stress increased $^3$H-5-HT formed from $^3$H-5-HTP while it decreased levels of exogenously administered $^3$H-5-HT. The data reported by Thierry et al. indicated that, although in many ways changes in 5-HT parallel those of NE, 5-HT neurons appear less sensitive than NE neurons in response to stress.

Consistent with the hypothesis that mild stress inhibits MAO activity, increased levels of 5-HT are evident shortly after inception of a weak stressor (Welch & Welch, 1970). With sufficiently severe stress, a slight depletion of 5-HT is evident in the whole brain (Saito et al., 1976), and a more extensive

Table 3.3 Serotonin changes with acute stress

| | Level | Synthesis[a] | Utilization[b] |
|---|---|---|---|
| Footshock | | | |
| Bliss, Thatcher, & Ailion, 1972 | 0 | | ↑ |
| R. M. Brown et al., 1974 | ↓ | ↑ | ↑ |
| Ladisch, 1974 | ↑ | | ↑ |
| Maynert & Levi, 1963 | ↑ | | |
| Petty & Sherman, 1982 | ↓ | | |
| Ray & Barrett, 1975 | ↓ | ↑ | ↑ |
| Telegdy & Vermes, 1976 | 0 | | |
| Thierry, 1973 | 0 | ↑ | ↑ |
| Thierry, Fekete, & Glowinski, 1968 | 0 | ↑ | ↑ |
| Thierry, Javoy, Glowinski, & Kety, 1968 | 0 | ↑ | ↑ |
| Avoidance-escape | | | |
| Aprison, Kariya, Hingtgen, & Toru, 1968 | ↓ | | |
| Saito et al., 1976 | 0 | | |
| Restraint | | | |
| Bliss, Thatcher, & Ailion, 1972 | | | ↑ |
| Morgan, Rudeen, & Pfeil, 1975 | 0 | | ↑ |
| Palkovits, Brownstein, Kizer, Saavedra, & Kopin, 1976 | ↓[c] | | |
| Saito et al., 1976 | ↓↑[d] | | |
| Telegdy & Vermes, 1976 | ↑↓[d] | | |
| Welch & Welch, 1970 | ↑↓[d] | | ↑ |
| Cold | | | |
| Ingenito, 1967 | 0 | | |
| Saarela et al., 1977 | ↓ | | |
| Saito et al., 1976 | ↑ | | |
| Telegdy & Vermes, 1976 | ↑↓[d] | | |
| Heat | | | |
| Saarela et al., 1977 | 0 | | |
| Swimming | | | |
| Barchas & Freedman, 1963 | ↑ | | ↑ |
| Bliss, Thatcher, & Ailion, 1972 | | | |
| Forced running | | | |
| Barchas & Freedman, 1963 | 0 | | |
| Shaking | | | |
| Rosecrans, 1969 | ↓ | | ↑ |
| Formalin | | | |
| Palkovits et al., 1976 | ↑[c] | | |
| Sleep deprivation | | | |
| Bliss, Thatcher, & Ailion, 1972 | | | ↑ |
| Food deprivation | | | |
| Kantak, Wagner, Tilson, & Sved, 1977 | ↓ | | ↑ |
| Ether | | | |
| Telegdy & Vermes, 1976 | ↓↑[d] | | |
| Surgery | | | |
| Telegdy & Vermes, 1976 | ↓ | | |

[a]Synthesis was determined by formation of $^3$H-5-HT from $^3$H-5-HTP.

[b]Utilization was determined either by rate of disappearance of 5-HT following tryptophan hydroxylase inhibition, formation of 5-HT metabolites, or rate of disappearance of $^3$H-5-HT.

[c]Determined in restricted brain nuclei.

[d]Variations were either dependent on temporal factors or stress severity.

depletion in the hypothalamus was noted (Telegdy & Vermes, 1976). Likewise, it has been shown that stress will result in 5-HT depletion in the median eminence, lateral amygdaloid nucleus, hippocampus, cingulate cortex, and dorsal-raphe nucleus (Palkovits et al., 1976; see also Thierry, 1973). In light of the effects of stress on serotonin synthesis and utilization, it is likely that the depletion occurs because the organism is using the transmitter at a faster rate than it can produce it.

*Histamine.* Contradictory results have been reported with respect to the effects of stress on brain histamine levels. Whereas some investigators reported decreased histamine concentrations in the hypothalamus following cold exposure or restraint (Snyder & Taylor, 1972), others have found no effect either in the whole brain after restraint (Eroglu, 1979) or in hypothalamus after either cold exposure or restraint (Kobayashi & Kopin, 1974). Curiously, increased histamine concentrations were observed after electric shock (Campos & Jurupe, 1970). Although several explanations are possible for the paradoxical results, Mazurkiewicz-Kwilecki and Taub (1978) found that stress effects on histamine varied not only as a function of brain region but with the duration of the stress session and the number of stress sessions applied. Mild stress for 5 min decreased histamine levels in the midbrain, whereas an increase of hypothalamic histamine was seen after 15 min of stress. If rats received 15 min of stress twice daily over 4 days, the increase in hypothalamic histamine was not longer evident.

*Acetylcholine.* Relative to the monoamines, considerably less information is available concerning the effects of stress on acetylcholine (ACh). It has been demonstrated that exposure to cold stress will alter the turnover of ACh in the frontal cortex and hypothalamus (Costa, Tagliomonte, Brunello, & Cheney, 1980). Moreover, footshock has been shown to increase high affinity choline uptake and ACh turnover, but such an effect varied between different lines of rats (Schmidt, Cooper, & Barrett, 1980). Several investigators (Karczmar, Scudder, & Richardson, 1973; Saito et al., 1976, Zajaczkowska, 1975) have found that stress increases levels of this transmitter. This increase in ACh levels occurs after various forms of stress but does not occur until some time after stress termination (Saito et al., 1976; Zajaczkowska, 1975).

*Gamma-aminobuytric Acid.* It has been reported that stress increases the level of γ-aminobutyric acid (GABA) (Bliss & Zwanziger, 1966). Chattopadhyay and Uniyal (1975) likewise reported an increase after stress; the increase of GABA was apparent, however, after three, five, or seven stress sessions but not after a single session.

*Opiate Peptides.* Stressors have been shown to increase the secretion of endorphins from the anterior pituitary, consequently decreasing the concentration present in this region (Baizman, Cox, Osman, & Goldstein, 1979; Millan, Tsang, Przewlocki, Hollt, & Herz, 1981), while increasing concentrations of endorphins in blood (Przewlocki, Millan, Gramsch, Millan, & Herz, 1982). It has been reported that stress leads to reductions of hypothalamic concentrations of immunoreactive endorphin or leu-enkephalin (Rossier, Guillemin, & Bloom, 1878; Rossier, French, Rivier, Ling, Guillemin, & Bloom, 1977); however, other investigators have observed an increase in the concentration of dynorphin or β-endorphin in the hypothalamus (Millan et al., 1981; Przewlocki et al., 1982). Morever, it has been shown that binding of exogenously administered 3H-leu-enkephalin was decreased by stressors, possibly as a result of increased availability of the endogenous peptide (Chance, White, Krynock, & Rosecrans, 1978; Christie, Chesher, & Bird, 1981). It appears that the alterations of endogenous opioids in both the pituitary and the brain are sensitive to the severity and chronicity of the stressor. In particular, Barta and Yashpal (1981) have demonstrated that the application of moderate stress results in increased endorphin concentrations in the brain coupled with reductions in the pituitary. With severe stress the increase endorphin concentrations in the brain were magnified, but the reductions seen in the pituitary were minimized. Among mice that received the moderate stress treatment repeatedly (21 days), adaptation was evident in the brain and the pituitary; however, the adaptation in the brain was not evident after repeated exposure to the more severe stress. In fact, under such conditions the enhancement of endorphin concentrations was further increased. Clearly, the effectiveness of stressors in altering endorphin concentrations varies with the animal's previous stress history, as well as the severity of the stressor.

## Coping Factors as a Determinant

In considering the neurochemical consequences of stress it is important to distinguish between escapable and inescapable stressors. Although many stressors elicit comparable types of changes (see Anisman, 1978; Stone, 1975b), the animal's ability to cope with the stress largely influences the nature of the neurochemical changes. For example, it has been found that, although exposure of rats to inescapable shock reduced NE levels in several brain regions, an identical amount of escapable shock either had no effect or in fact increased levels of NE (Weiss, Glazer, & Pohorecky, 1976; Weiss, Goodman, Losito, Corrigan, Charry, & Bailey, 1981). Likewise, as seen in Fig. 3.1, work conducted in our laboratory has revealed similar effects in mice.

In this particular experiment, one group of mice received 60 trials in which escape from shock was possible 5 sec after shock onset, and the shock was terminated when the animal traversed a hurdle. Shock onset and offset in a second, yoked group occurred concomitantly with that of mice in the first group irrespective of their responses. Thus the mice in both groups received an identical amount of shock, but only mice in the first group had control over the stress. Because NE depletion was only evident among the mice that received yoked inescapable shock, it appears that shock per se was not the critical variable responsible for the amine depletion. Rather, the animal's inability to control shock offset was the major factor responsible for the variations of NE levels.

In a second experiment (see Fig. 3.2), it was found that the NE depletion in the hippocampus and cortex induced by inescapable stress could be prevented if animals were initially trained in a task where escape was possible. This again indicates the importance of coping factors in the NE depletion elicited by stress. Apparently, experience with stress of a controllable nature will abrogate the NE depletion produced by a similar stress of an uncontrollable nature. It has yet to be determined whether such transfer effects are evident when the stressors employed during the two sessions differ from one another.

In evaluating the biochemical basis for the differential NE effects produced by escapable and inescapable shock, Weiss et al. (1976) found that the rate of disappearance of exogenously administered 3-H-NE was greater among inescapably shocked rats than rats exposed to escapable shock, indicating faster

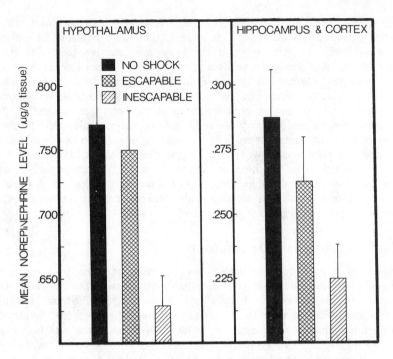

*Figure 3.1*   Mean NE levels in the hypothalamus and in the hippocampus
and cortex of Swiss Webster mice exposed to either 60 escapable
shocks (150 μA); 60 yoked, inescapable shocks; or no shock.
Mice were decapitated, and tissue was dissected immediately
after stress; NE was determined radioenzymatically. (From
"Coping with Stress, Norepinephrine Depletion and Escape
Performance" by H. Anisman, A. Pizzino, and L. S. Sklar, *Brain
Research*, 1980, *191*, 583–588. Copyright 1980 by Elsevier
Science Publishing Co., Inc. Reprinted by permission.)

utilization among the animals that could not cope behaviorally with the stress. In
addition, it was found that reuptake of NE was greater among mice in the
inescapable shock condition, indicating that the effect of stress on the disappearance of NE was not restricted to the rate of amine release.

In accordance with the proposition that coping factors are important in
determining the amine depletion, it has been reported that abrogation of the
shock effect will occur among rats given the opportunity to fight (Stolk et al.,
1974). Furthermore, NE levels were inversely related to the number of fights in
which rats had been engaged. These investigators provisionally suggested that
fighting acts as a coping mechanism much in the same way as escape does,
thereby preventing the amine depletion. It is significant in this respect that
fighting has also been found to reduce the extent of gastric ulceration induced
by shock (Weiss, Pohorecky, Salman, & Gruenthal, 1976), lending support to the
proposition that fighting acts as a coping mechanism.

As in the case of NE, coping factors may influence cholinergic changes
induced by stress. Karczmar et al. (1973) found that levels of ACh were
increased after inescapable shock; but in an independent group of rats that

received avoidance-escape training, no such effect was evident. Likewise, Aprison and Hingtgen (1970) reported increased levels of ACh during the early trials of Sidman avoidance training (i.e., before the avoidance response was acquired), whereas this effect was not evident among well-trained animals. Although the contribution of coping factors in determining ACh changes have not as yet been conducted within a single experimental paradigm (e.g., the yoked design), it appears likely that changes in ACh level, like those of NE, depend on whether the stress is escapable or inescapable.

Limited data are available concerning the contribution of coping factors in determining the alterations of DA and 5-HT provoked by stressors. Petty and Sherman (1982), however, have demonstrated that reductions of 5-HT in septum and in the anterior cortex are not readily induced by escapable footshock, whereas pronounced reductions were evident in these regions following an equivalent amount of inescapable shock. Moreover, these investigators found the reductions of 5-HT to persist as long as 5 days following application of the stressor. In the case of DA, comparison between animals exposed to escapable and inescapable shock have not been reported where the amine was determined in the arcuate nucleus, nucleus accumbens, or mesolimbic frontal cortex—regions in which inescapable shock influences DA activity. It was reported, however, that receptor binding in the mesolimbic frontal cortex was influenced by 4 days of

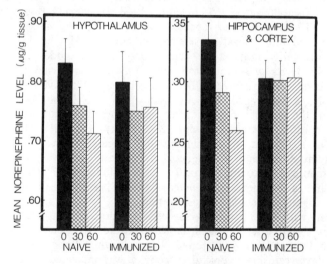

Figure 3.2   Mean NE levels among mice as a function of prior stress. Mice received either 0, 30, or 60 inescapable shocks (150 μA, 6-sec duration) 24 h after 30 escape trials (immunized) or NT (naive). Note that the initial escape training largely prevented the depletion otherwise produced by inescapable shock. (From "Coping with Stress, Norepinephrine Depletion and Escape Performance" by H. Anisman, A. Pizzino, and L. S. Sklar, *Brain Research*, 1980, *191*, 583–588. Copyright 1980 by Elsevier North-Holland Biomedical Press. Reprinted by permission.)

inescapable shock (8 h/day), whereas an equivalent amount of escapable shock was without effect (Cherek, Lane, Freedman, & Smith, 1980).

Summarizing, it it our contention that neurochemical changes that occur upon stress exposure reflect one of a series of coping mechanisms used to meet environmental demands. That is to say, when faced with a stressor, the organism makes accommodation through both behavioral responses and increased synthesis and utilization of catecholamines. Under conditions where behavioral responses are ineffective in reducing the impact of the stress, the neurochemical effects persist and may even increase. As a result, utilization of the amines will come to exceed synthesis and hence result in depletion. In contrast, if environmental demands can be met through behavioral means, amine-utilization rates will remain stable or decline, resulting in either minimal change or increase in amine levels.

## Neurochemical Adaptation after Stress

Following chronic exposure to stress, utilization and synthesis of cate-cholamines is increased as in the case of acute stress. Following the chronic stress regimen, however, reductions in levels of DA and NE are not apparent. It has been shown that following chronic cold exposure, for example, the rate of NE utilization remains substantially increased. The rate of NE synthesis was also increased, however, surpassing that of utilization and leading to increased levels of brain NE (see Bhagat, 1969; Ingenito, 1968; Ingenito & Bonnycastle, 1967; Reid et al., 1966). Likewise, repeated immobilizations of short duration or a single protracted immobilization session did not result in the depletions of NE that were ordinarily induced by acute stress. Indeed under these conditions increased NE levels were found in several hypothalamic nuclei (Kvetnansky, Mitro, Palkovits, Vigaš, Albrecht, Torda, & Mikulaj, 1975; Kvetnansky, Palkovits, Mitro, Torda, & Mikulaj, 1977). As in the case of NE, the DA depletion that occurred in the arcuate nucleus after acute immobilization was not evident following repeated restraint sessions (Kvetnansky, Palkovits, Mitro, Torda, & Mikulaj, 1977). In light of the finding that repeated stress results in increased tyrosine hydroxylase and dopamine β-hydroxylase activity (Kobayashi et al., 1976; Kvetnansky, Palkovits, Mitro, Torda, & Mikulaj, 1977; Thoenen, 1970), it is likely that a compensatory increase in the synthesis of the amines was responsible for the catecholamine adaptation.

Consistent with other stressors, the NE depletion evident after a single shock session was absent after repeated shock exposure. As seen in Fig. 3.3, Weiss, Glazer, and Pohoracky (1976) found that, following shock administered on 15 successive days, tyrosine hydroxylase activity was increased, a finding reported by other investigators as well (see Huttenen, 1971; Kvetnansky, Mitro, Palkovits, Brownstein, Torda, Vigaš, & Mukulaj, 1976; Kvetnansky, Mitro, Palkovits, Vigaš, Albrecht, Torda, & Mikulaj, 1975; Nielson & Fleming, 1968; Thoenen, 1970). In addition, it was found that the rate of NE reuptake was appreciably reduced with chronic stress (see Fig. 3.3). Within-session adaptation in terms of NE reuptake has also been reported to occur (Hendley, Burrows, Robinson, Heiden-reich, & Bulman, 1977).

A series of experiments revealed that the neurochemical variations provoked by chronic stress varied over time following the last stress session (Irwin, Bowers,

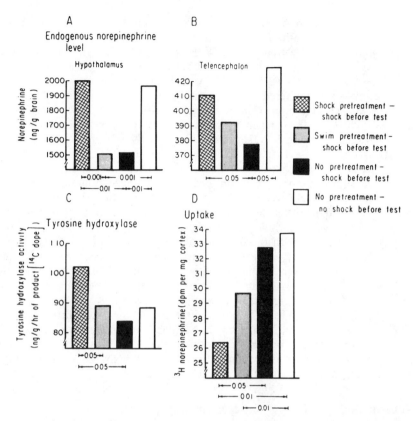

*Figure 3.3* Mean NE levels, tyrosine hydroxylase activity, and ³H-NE uptake
among rats exposed to either a single session of inescapable shock,
shock applied on 14 occasions before the inescapable shock session,
swim stress on 14 occastions before the inescapable shock session, or
NT. Note that the NE changes elicited by acute stress were absent
among rats chronically exposed to shock. (From "Effects of Chronic
Exposure to Stressors on Avoidance-Escape Behavior and on Brain
Norepinephrine" by J. M. Weiss, H. I. Glazer, L. A. Pohorecky,
J. Brick, & N. E. Miller, *Psychosomatic Medicine,* 1975, *37,* 522–534.
Copyright 1975 by Elsevier Science Publishing Co., Inc. Reprinted by
permission.)

Zacharko, & Anisman, 1982). In particular, among mice decapitated immediately
after the last session, NE concentrations were comparable to those of nonstressed
mice and higher than those of mice that received a single stress session. Within
24 h of the last stress session the concentrations of NE appreciably exceeded
those of naive animals. Evaluation of NE turnover indicated that soon after
application of the last stress the rate of amine utilization was appreciably
increased, and was apparently met with increased synthesis. The rates of NE
utilization 24 h later, however, were reduced relative to that of nonstressed
animals, while synthesis evidently continued at a relatively high rate. It appears
as if two compensatory processes are operative following application of a
repeated stress regimen. Upon inception of the stressor the utilization of NE

increases, presumably in order to meet the immediate environmental demands, and rate of amine synthesis keeps pace with utilization in order to assure adequate supplies of the transmitter. With the termination of the stressor the utilization of NE decreases, thereby resulting in increased amine concentrations that may be necessary to deal effectively with impending insults.

In addition to the altered rates of turnover, further adaptive changes will occur with the repeated appliation of stressors. In particular, it was reported that following a chronic stress regimen the sensitivity of β-NE receptors declines (Nomura, Watanabe, Ukei, & Nakazawa, 1981; Stone, 1978, 1979; Stone & Platt, 1982). It is conceivable that the excessive turnover of NE following repeated stress application results in excessive neuronal stimulation. Consequently, the NE receptor subsensitivity may occur in order to minimize potential maladaptive consequences attributable to the enhanced NE activity. In fact, Stone and Platt (1982) reported that the ulcerogenic and anorexic effects evident after acute stress were absent after chronic application of the stressor, and the reduction of pathology corresponded with the development of receptor subsensitivity.

Taken together, there appear to exist adaptive mechanisms that assure adequate supplies of catecholamines following protracted, uncontrollable stress. The mechanism responsible for maintaining catecholamine levels appears to be an increase in the activity of synthetic enzymes. In addition, reuptake of NE is reduced, resulting in more efficient utilization of the transmitter substance. Finally, once the increased synthesis of NE has compensated for the increased release of this amine, further adaptation occurs in the form of receptor subsensitivity in order to assure that the continued high NE release results in only normal responsiveness at the postsynaptic sites.

## Neurochemical Changes on Reexposure to Stress

Although the NE depletion that occurs following stress is relatively transient (Barchas & Freedman, 1963; Maynert & Levi, 1964; Paulsen & Hess, 1963), the magnitude of the neurochemical changes becomes progressively more pronounced with repeated stress sessions administered over successive days (Keim & Sigg, 1976). Moreover, although amine concentrations on each day return to basal levels, the rapidity with which the depletion occurs is accentuated with repeated stress. Data collected in our laboratory (Anisman & Sklar, 1979) revealed that reexposure to a limited stress resulted in a rapid and pronounced depletion of hypothalamic NE. Figure 3.4 depicts NE concentrations in the hypothalamus of mice that had been exposed to either: a single session of 60 shocks (6 sec, 150 $\mu$A) 24 h earlier, 10 shocks (6 sec each) immediately before decapitation; 60 shocks followed 24 h later by 10 shocks, or no shock on either day. It should be noted that when NE levels are determined immediately after the 60-shock treatment, a depletion of NE in the magnitude of 25% had been observed. As seen in Fig. 3.4, NE levels among mice that received 60 shocks 24 h earlier did not differ from that of nonshocked animals. Among naive animals, application of 10 shocks likewise did not alter NE levels; 10 shocks, however, substantially reduced hypothalamic NE among previously stressed mice, Evidently, NE levels are readily reduced on reexposure to a stressor even when the second stress session itself is insufficient to produce any appreciable change in amine levels. Recent data reported by Cassens, Kuruc, Orsulak, and Schildraut (1979) are

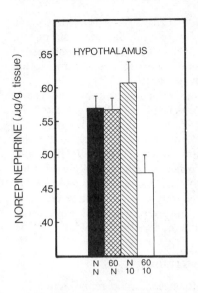

*Figure 3.4*  Mean NE levels in the hypothalamus among mice that received either: no treatment (Group N-N), 60 shocks of 150 µA, 6-sec duration followed by NT 24 h later (Group 60-N), NT and 10 shock trials 24 h later (Group N-10), or 60 shocks followed 24 h later by 10 shocks (Group 60-10). A depletion in the magnitude of 20–25 percent is ordinarily evident in mice decapitated immediately after 60 shocks. This depletion could be reinstated by 10 shocks, which ordinarily has no effect, among mice previously exposed to the 60-shock treatment. (From "Catecholamine Depletion upon Reexposure to Stress: Mediation of the Escape Deficits Produced by Inescapable Shock" by H. Anisman and L. S. Sklar, *Journal of Comparative and Physiological Psychology*, 1979, *93*, 610–625. Copyright 1979 by the American Psychological Association. Reprinted by permission.)

consistent with our earlier findings. These investigators reported that a cue (CS) paired with shock increased the accumulation of MHPG sulfate in the brain. Similarly, it has been found that a CS that had been paired with shock in a conditioned emotional response (CER) paradigm may come to elicit increases of ACh levels (Hingtgen, Smith, Shea, Aprison, & Gaff, 1976). Finally, Chance et al. (1978) found that cues reliably associated with shock decreased binding of [3]H-N-leu-enkephalin in the rat brain, while Herman et al. (1982) reported that cues associated with footshock increased the utilization of DA in frontal mesolimbic regions.

Taken together, the aforementioned findings indicate that NE, ACh, and opiate peptide activity are subject to either sensitization or conditioning. Regardless of which of these processes is responsible for the stress-reexposure effects, it is abundantly clear that the response to a stressor depends on the organism's prior stress history. Thus, depending on the organism's previous experience, a seemingly innocuous stimulus can come to have profound effects on neurochemical activity.

## Social Conditions as a Determinant

Social housing conditions may influence neurochemical activity and might act as a modifier of the effects of other stressors (Welch & Welch, 1970). Isolation was found to produce a decrease in utilization of NE (Modigh, 1974; Welch & Welch, 1970) as well as a corresponding decline in the synthesis of this amine among mice (Modigh, 1973). With respect to 5-HT, conflicting reports are available as to the effects of isolation among mice (Modigh, 1976; Welch & Welch, 1970).

The effects of isolation among rats do not entirely coincide with those seen in mice. Isolation increased synthesis and utilization of NE and 5-HT in the brainstem and telencephalon (Stolk et al., 1974) and increased concentrations of NE in the whole brain (Geller, Yuwiler, & Zolman, 1965; Nishikawa, Kajiwara,

Kono, Sano, Nagasaki, Tanaka, & Norda, 1974). Effects similar to those seen among mice are observed among rats, however, when more discrete brain regions are examined. Indeed, under these conditions, both increases and decreases of DA and NE concentrations have been found, and decreased amine turnover has been noted among rats (Thoa, Tizabi, & Jacobowitz, 1977).

In view of the effects of housing conditions on amine turnover, it is not particularly surprising that stress effects on neurochemical activity interact with housing condition (Modigh, 1973, 1974, 1976; Thoa et al., 1977; Weiss, Glazer, & Pohorecky, 1976; Welch & Welch, 1970). For example, Welch and Welch (1968) reported that restraint increased the utilization of DA and NE among mice raised in isolation but had an opposite effect among group-housed mice. Likewise, Weiss, Glazer, and Pohorecky (1976) found shock stress reduced NE levels in group-housed rats but not in isolated rats. The protective effect of isolation in this latter study was mitigated, however, when different shock parameters were employed (see Weiss, Glazer, Pohorecky, Brick, & Miller, 1975).

## Genetic and Ontogenetic Factors as Determinants

In view of the numerous variables that influence catecholamine activity, it should come as no surprise that the magnitude of stress effects depends on the age of the organism and will also vary as a function of strain. It is known, for example, that catecholamine turnover decreases with age (Finch, 1973), and furthermore, stress in the form of cold-water immersion provoked a greater NE depletion in 7-month-old animals than in 3-month-old animals. Predictably, recovery of NE levels was slower in the older animals as well (Ritter & Pelzer, 1978).

Turning briefly to genetic differences, numerous studies have revealed strain differences in biogenic-amine levels and their associated enzymes (see review in Anisman, 1978). Strain differences have also been observed with respect to the neurochemical consequences of stress. For example, Wimer, Norman, and Eleftherious (1974) found that an amount of stress that decreased 5-HT and did not affect NE levels in DBA/2J mice resulted in increases of these amines among C57BL/6J mice. In a similar fashion, Ray and Barrett (1975) found that stress differentially influenced turnover of biogenic amines in two rat strains while Blanc et al. (1980) reported differences in DA turnover between strains of mice following exposure stress. In general, however, it seems that comparable changes occur between strains within a species following exposure to stressors. The differences that do occur appear to be in degree rather than in nature. Of course, the possibility should be considered that the strain effect may also vary with the form of the stressor employed. After all, the effects of stressors such as cold, for example, might be expected to vary with the natural habitat of the strain or species. In light of the importance of such factors, an analysis of the potential consequences of stress for behavioral and physiological pathology clearly must consider the contribution of organismic variables.

## STRESS AND HORMONAL CHANGES

It is well-documented that stress will influence hormonal activity and that hormonal activity varies with neurochemical change. Because much of this work is presented in detail in Chap. 5 in this volume, we present only a limited review here. Acute exposure to a variety of stressors results in enhanced secrection of ACTH and adrenal corticosteroids (Bassett & Cairncross, 1975; Brush & Levine, 1966; Conner, 1972; Coover, Ursin, & Levine, 1973; Knigge, 1960; Kvetnansky, Mitro, Palkovits, Brownstein, Torda, Vigaš, 1976; Kvetnansky, Mitro, Palkovits, Vigaš, Albrecht, Torda, & Mikulaj, 1975; Levine, 1972; Németh, 1973; Van Loon, 1976), β-endorphin (Rossier, French, Rivier, Line, Guillemin, & Bloom, 1977), prolactin (PRL) (Ajika, Kalra, Fawcett, Krulich, & McCann, 1972; Van Vugt, Bruni, & Meites, 1978), thyrotropin (TSH) (Del Conte, Ravello, & Stux, 1955; Ducommun, Vale, Sakiz, & Guillemin, 1967; J. W. Mason, Maher, Hartley, Mougey, Perlow, & Jones, 1976; McCann, Ajika, Fawcett, Hefco, Illner, Negro-Villar, Orias, Watson, & Krulich, 1973; Taché, Ruisseau, Ducharme, & Collu, 1978), growth hormone (GH) (G. M. Brown & Reichlin, 1972; J. W. Mason et al., 1976; McCann, Ajika, Fawcett, Hefco, Illner, Negro-Villar, Orias, Watson, & Krulich, 1973), leuteinizing hormone (LH) (McCann, Ajika, Fawcett, Hefco, Illner, Negro-Villar, Orias, Watson, & Krulich, 1973), and renin (Sigg, Keim, & Sigg, 1978).

As in the case of the neurochemical alterations produced by stress, the stress-induced hormonal changes appear to depend on stress chronicity. Following repeated exposure to cold, restraint, or shock stress, the ACTH and adrenal corticosteroid release seen after acute stress was greatly reduced (Feldman & Brown, 1975, 1976; Keim & Sigg, 1976; Kvetnansky, Mitro, Palkovits, Brownstein, Torda, Vegaš, & Mikulaj, 1976; Kvetnansky, Mitro, Palkovits, Vigaš, Albrecht, Torda, & Mikulaj, 1976; Levine, Madden, Conner, Moskal, & Anderson, 1973; J. W. Mason et al., 1976; Mikulaj, Kvetnansky, Murgas, Parizkova, & Vencel, 1976; Taché et al., 1978; Weiss, Glazer, Pohorecky, Brick, & Miller, 1975), as was the GH release evident after restraint stress (J. W. Mason et al., 1976) and the cold-induced TSH release (Martin, 1974). It should be noted that, unlike central transmitters, the adaptation is a reflection of reduced secretion of these hormones rather than increased synthesis (Bassett & Cairncross, 1976a, 1976b; Keim & Sigg, 1976; Leduc, 1961; Mikulaj et al., 1976).

The parallel between hormonal and neurochemical changes induced by stress is evident when considering the contribution of coping factors. Inescapable shock increased levels of plasma corticosterone to a much larger degree than did shock stress that could be controlled behaviorally (Weiss, 1971a, 1971b). In these studies, a yoked paradigm was employed, such that the animals received identical amounts of shock but differed with respect to their ability to control shock offset. It appears that the ability to cope with stress behaviorally reduced adrenal activity. The role of stress controllability in secretion of other hormones has as yet not been established.

## Neurochemical and Hormonal Interactions

Although we have discussed the neurochemical and hormonal effects of stress independently, it appears that their activity is interdependent. Considerable data are available indicating neurochemical involvement in hormonal regulation. Tuberoinfundibular neurons of the hypothalamus contain the peptide-releasing factors that act on the anterior pituitary via median-eminence capillaries to produce synthesis and secretion of ACTH, β-endorphin, TSH, PRL, LH, and GH

(Guillenmin, 1978; Terry & Martin, 1978). Moreover, it seems that secretion of these releasing factors is under neural control of DA, NE, 5-HT, histamine, ACh, and GABA (Terry & Martin, 1978). The congruency between the conditions under which stress provokes neurochemical and hormonal changes leads to the suggestion that changes in one system are secondary to changes in the other system.

Release of corticotropin-releasing factor (CRF), and thus ACTH and adrenal corticosteroids, was stimulated by both ACh and 5-HT in vitro (Bennett & Edwardson, 1975; Jones, Hillhouse, & Burden, 1976) and in vivo (Ganong, 1976; Meyer, Buckholtz, & Boggan, 1978). Morever, CRF and ACTH release were inhibited by NE and DA in vitro (Bennett & Edwardson, 1975; Edwardson & Bennett, 1974) and tonically inhibited by NE in vivo (Ganong, 1976; Scapagnini, Annunziato, & Preziosi, 1973; Van Loon, 1976). In effect, when concentrations of NE, DA, or both in the hypothalamus are reduced, CRF release is increased, and ACTH secretion is promoted. Conversely, when brain concentrations of ACh, 5-HT, or both are increased, ACTH secretion is promoted. Accordingly, the possibility exists that the stress-induced alteration of ACTH and corticosteroids is, at least to some extent, due to reductions of hypothalamic DA, NE, or both (e.g., Kobayashi et al., 1976; Kvetnansky, Mitro, Palkovits, Vigaš, Albrecht, Torda, & Mikulaj, 1975; Kvetnansky, Palkovits, Mitro, Torda, & Mikulaj, 1977) and increased ACh availability (Aprison & Hingtgen, 1966, 1969, 1970; Aprison, Hingtgen, & McGride, 1968; Aprison, Kariya, Hingtgen, & Toru, 1975; Karczmar et al., 1973; Zajaczkowska, 1975).

In addition, because stress has been found to result in β-endorphin secretion from the anterior pituitary (e.g., Rossier, French, Rivier, Ling, Guillemin, & Bloom, 1977), and because β-endorphins are located in the same secretory cells as ACTH (Weber, Voigt, & Martin, 1978), it seems likely that β-endorphin release is regulated by the same neural systems involved in ACTH secretion.

Prolactin release appears to be tonically inhibited by DA and stimulated by 5-HT and histamine (see review in Terry & Martin, 1978). Because pharmacological manipulations that influence brain DA alter PRL release (Martin, Lal, Tolis, & Friesen, 1974; Vijayan, & McCann, 1978), the possibility should be considered that the stress-induced increase of PRL release is secondary to DA alterations. When DA is reduced in the arcuate nucleus by stress (Kobayashiet al., 1976; Kvetnansky, Mitro, Palkovits, Vigaš, Albrecht, Torda, & Mikulaj, 1975; Kvetnansky, Palkovits, Mitro, Torda, & Mikulaj, 1977), the secretion of prolactin from the pituitary may be disinhibited. Moreover, the fact that the PRL secretion induced by restraint was attenuated by histamine-receptor blockage as well (McCann, Krulich, Ojeda, & Vijayan, 1978) suggests that stress-induced alterations in histamine activity (Mazurkiewicz-Kwilecki, & Taub, 1978) might also be responsible for the increased PRL secretion.

Neurochemical manipulations suggest that GH-releasing factor, and thus GH, are stimulated by DA, NE, 5-HT, and ACh (W. A. Brown, Krieger, Van Woert, & Ambani, 1974; Chambers, & G. M. Brown, 1976; Jacoby, Greenstein, Sassin, & Weitzman, 1974). The finding that hypothalamic DA and NE appear to stimulate GH release might account for the transient enhancement of GH secretion induced by stress (G. M. Brown, Schalch, & Reichlin, 1971; J. W. Mason et al., 1976). That is, at stress inception, the initial DA and NE release promotes GH secretion, whereas the catecholamine depletion that occurs following more-protracted stress results in inhibition of the hormone release.

Summarizing briefly, it appears that stress has predictable effects on neuro-chemical and hormonal activity. The alterations in these systems induced by stress seem to be subject to similar manipulations. In both instances, coping factors and stress chronicity are critical elements in determining the nature and magnitude of the physiological changes. This is not to say that the functions of these substances are redundant, nor that they must necessarily occur in conjunction with one another. Rather, it is our contention that analysis of stress-induced pathology should consider neurochemical and hormonal functioning (as well as immunologic; see Sklar & Anisman, 1981) in the context of coping processes.

## SUMMARY AND IMPLICATIONS

It would appear that when an animal is faced with a stressor, a variety of neurochemical and hormonal changes occur. As indicated in the introductory remarks, we view some of these neurochemical and hormonal changes as adaptive consequences whose purpose is either to meet environmental demands, to reduce the aversiveness of the stimulation, or to alleviate maladaptive physiological or behavioral consequences of the stress. Reiterating briefly, the most notable physiological consequences of stress from this perspective are as follows:

1. Shortly after stress inception, catecholamine levels increase, possibly owing to MAO inhibition, ensuring adequate supplies of the amines. Concurrently, amine release is increased. The initial increase in amine utilization probably has the function of aiding the animal in coping behaviorally with the stress. For example, the neurochemical release could aid the adoption of evasive maneuvers (depending on species, these could take the form of flight, freezing or camouflage, or aggressive postures). In addition, it is thought that a second pain system in addition to an opioid-mediated one exists and that this system may be subserved by a biogenic amine (e.g., Lewis, Cannon, & Liebeskind, 1980). Thus, while one neurotransmitter might have the effect of aiding the animal to evade the aversive stimulation, the role of a second neurotransmitter might be one of reducing the actual sensory impact of the stimulus.

2. Concurrent with the initial catecholamine rise, the utilization and synthesis of amines are increased. Needless to say, the function of the increased utilization is to meet environmental demands. The effectiveness of these neurochemical changes appears, however, to be limited. That is to say, when the stress is uncontrollable but relatively brief, neurochemical factors may be sufficient to protect the organism. By the same token, if the stress is controllable, then the necessity of neurochemical adaptive changes is diminished. When the stress is sufficiently protracted and behavioral coping is not possible, amine utilization may come to exceed synthesis, resulting in net amine depletion. Under these conditions, maladaptive changes in terms of physiology and behavior can be expected. It is known, for example, that deficits in escape tasks are common under such conditions (Anisman & Sklar, 1979; Maier & Seligman, 1976; Weiss, Glazer, & Pohorecky, 1976), gastric ulceration is readily induced (Weiss, 1971a, 1971b, 1971c), immunosuppression occurs (Monjan & Collector, 1977), and growth of transplanted tumors is exacerbated (Sklar & Anisman, 1979).

Despite the apparent adaptive failure, other changes with seemingly positive attributes also occur. For instance, enkephalin and endorphin release is increased centrally and peripherally, resulting in an analgesic reaction. Sympathetic and parasympathetic reactions to stress occur (mediated by epinephrine and acetylcholine) whose function is sustaining cardiovascular activity as well as activity of other peripheral organs. Finally, a variety of hormonal and steroid changes occur, some of which may have adaptive significance by increasing oxygen metabolism and energy production (e.g., mobilization of fatty acids, carbohydrate metabolism, protein metabolism) (see Guyton, 1971).

3. With repeated stress exposure, tyrosine hydroxylase and dopamine $\beta$-hydroxylase activity is increased, and reuptake of NE is reduced. As a result, levels of NE and DA are increased (i.e., the depletion is abrogated), and the effectiveness of the released neurotransmitter is augmented. Under these conditions, some of the adverse consequences derived from the amine depletion will be negated. For example, the deficits of escape behavior that have been observed after an acute session of uncontrollable shock are not evident after repeated shock (Weiss, Glazer, & Pohorecky, 1976), supporting the contention that reduced catecholamine levels are responsible for the behavioral deficits (Anisman, Remington, & Sklar, 1979; Weiss, Glazer, & Pohorecky, 1976). Furthermore, following chronic stress, immunofacilitation occurs (Monjan & Collector, 1977), and the enhancement of tumor growth produced by acute stress is prevented (Sklar & Anisman, 1978, 1979). Whether the latter changes are a result of neurotransmitter and neuroendocrine variations has yet to be determined, although this possibility has been entertained (see Sklar & Anisman, 1981). Interestingly enough, following chronic stress, there is a reduction in the accumulation of NE-sensitive cyclic AMP, suggesting decreased sensitivity of NE receptors. In effect, the increased NE activity that may eventually prove maladaptive is compensated for by a decrease of receptor sensitivity.

In assessing the various adaptive changes that occur in response to aversive stimulation, it is important to differentiate variations that occur to meet environmental demands from those that come about as a result of physiological needs. Thus, the initial increase of NE activity during acute stress helps the organism evade the aversive insult; if amine utilization is too great (i.e., exceeding synthesis), however, or if receptor stimulation is sustained for too long a period, then the physiological well-being of the organism may become threatened, necessitating further physiological accommodation. For instance, if the depletion of catecholamines is sufficiently great, as would occur in the absence of increased tyrosine hydroxylase activation, any number of behavioral or psychological disturbances might ensue (e.g., deficits of feeding, sexual behavior, attention, responsiveness to further stress, as well as affective disturbances; see Anisman & Lapierre, 1980; S. T. Mason & Iversen, 1979; Stricker & Zigmond, 1974; Zigmond & Stricker, 1975). Conversely, if catecholamine-receptor stimulation were too intense over a protracted period, then irregularities of hormone secretion, energy metabolism, and possibly immune functions might occur (Sklar & Anisman, 1981). In addition, psychotic behaviors might result, like those observed following chronic drug-induced receptor stimulation (see Kokkinidis & Anisman, 1981; Segal & Janowsky, 1978). According to this view, the tyrosine hydroxylase activation is induced to compensate for the initial amine depletion and to prevent the development of pathologies resulting from the depletion. Such adaptation is not intended for protracted periods, however, and receptor subsensitivity eventually occurs to reduce potential hazards associated with excessive stimulation.

Three additional points warrant further note. Most of the maladaptive consequences of stress occur under conditions where the organism is unable to cope behaviorally with aversive insults. Clearly, then, coping factors represent one key feature in determining neurochemical change and consequent physiological variations. Accordingly, therapy aimed at alleviating or preventing stress-induced pathology might consider behavioral programs in which people acquire coping styles and strategies.

The second issue deals with the theoretical views that can be taken in assessing the role of stress controllability in determining behavioral and physiological pathology. It has been suggested that uncontrollable stress will result in the organism learning that it is "helpless" in determining outcomes (Maier & Seligman, 1976). It has further been argued that these feelings of "helplessness" provoke illness such as clinical depression. It is true that some depressed patients report feelings of "helplessness" and "hopelessness," but it is likely that these feelings simply represent symptoms of the depression rather than antecedent conditions (Anisman & Lapierre, 1980). It is our view that an analysis of stress-induced pathology is better served by consideration of quantifiable neurochemical and hormonal changes than by loosely defined cognitive models.

Finally, the fact that our summary is concerned primarily with catecholamines, with scant attention devoted to the other neurotransmitter changes, should not be taken to indicate that the contribution of other transmitters to adaptive processes is less essential. It is simply the case that catecholamines have been evaluated most extensively, and hence conclusions pertaining to these transmitters can be drawn with a greater degree of confidence. The fact that several transmitters in addition to the catecholamines are influenced by stress, and further, that these transmitters influence hormonal activity, implicates complex serial interactive effects in the precipitation of stress-related pathologies.

# REFERENCES

Ajika, K., Kalra, S. P., Fawcett, C. P., Krulich, L., & McCann, S. M. The effect of stress and Nembutal on plasma levels of gonadotropins and prolactin in ovariectomized rats. *Endocrinology,* 1972, *90,* 707–715.

Andén, N. E., Dahlstrom, A., Fuxe, K., Larsson, K., Olson, L., & Ungerstedt, U. Ascending monoamine neurons to the telencephalon and diencephalon. *Acta Physiologica Scandinavica,* 1966, *67,* 313–326.

Anisman, H. Neurochemical changes elicited by stress. In H. Anisman & G. Bignami (Eds.), *Psychopharmacology of aversively motivated behavior.* New York: Plenum, 1978.

Anisman, H., & Lapierre, Y. Stress and depression: Formulations and caveats. In W. J. M. Neufeld (Ed.), *Stress and psychopathology.* New York: McGraw-Hill, 1981.

Anisman, H., Pizzino, A., & Sklar, L. S. Coping with stress, norepinephrine depletion and escape performance. *Brain Research,* 1980, *191,* 583–588.

Anisman, H., Remington, G., & Sklar, L. S. Effects of inescapable shock on subsequent escape performance: Catecholaminergic and cholinergic mediation of response initiation and maintenance. *Psychopharmacology,* 1979, *61,* 107–124.

Anisman, H., & Sklar, L. S. Catecholamine depletion upon reexposure to stress: Mediation of the escape deficits produced by inescapable shock. *Journal of Comparative and Physiological Psychology,* 1979, *93,* 610–625.

Aprison, M. H., & Hingtgen, J. N. Neurochemical correlates of behavior: V. Differential effects of drugs on approach and avoidance behavior in rats with related changes in brain serotonin and norepinephrine. *Recent Advances in Biological Psychiatry,* 1966, *8,* 87–100.

Aprison, M. H., & Hingtgen, J. N. Brain acetylcholine and excitation in avoidance behavior. *Biological Psychiatry,* 1969, *1,* 87–89.

Aprison, M. H., & Hingtgen, J. N. Evidence of a central cholinergic mechanism functioning during drug-induced excitation in avoidance behavior. In E. Heilbronn & A. Winter (Eds.), *Drugs and cholinergic mechanisms in the CNS.* Forsavarets Stockholm-Sansalt: Forskning, 1970.

Aprison, M. H., Hingtgen, J. N., & McBride, W. J. Serotonergic and cholinergic mechanisms during disruption of approach and avoidance behavior. *Federation Proceedings,* 1975, *34,* 1813-1822.

Aprison, M. H., Kariya, T., Hingtgen, J. N., & Toru, M. Changes in acetylcholine, norepinephrine and 5-hydroxytryptamine concentration in several discrete brain areas of the rat during behavioral excitation. *Neurochemistry,* 1968, *15,* 1131-1139.

Baizman, E. R., Cox, B. M., Osman, O. H., & Goldstein, A. Experimental alterations of endorphin levels in rat's pituitary. *Neuroendocrinology,* 1979, *28,* 403-424.

Barchas, J. D., & Freedman, D. X. Brain amines: Response to physiological stress. *Biochemical Pharmacology,* 1963, *12,* 1232-1235.

Barta, A., & Yashpal, K. Regional redistribution of β-endorphin in the rat brain. The effect of stress. *Progress in Neuro-Psychopharmacology,* 1981, *5,* 595-598.

Bassett, J. R., & Cairncross, K. D. Time course for plasma 11-hydroxycorticosteroid evaluations in rats during stress. *Pharmacology Biochemistry and Behavior,* 1975, *3,* 139-142.

Bassett, J. R., & Cairncross, K. D. Endogenous levels of catecholamines in the rat myocardium following exposure to stress. *Pharmacology, Biochemistry and Behavior,* 1976, *4,* 35-38. (a)

Bassett, J. R., & Cairncross, K. D. Myocardial sensitivity to catecholamines following exposure of rats to irregular, signalled footshock. *Pharmacology, Biochemistry and Behavior,* 1976, *4,* 27-33. (b)

Beley, A., Beley, P., Rochette, L., & Bralet, J. Time-dependent changes in the rate of noradrenaline synthesis in various rat brain areas during cold exposure. *Pflugers Archives,* 1977, *368,* 225-229.

Bennett, G. W., & Edwardson, J. A. Release of corticotropin-releasing factor and other hypophysiotropic substances from isolated nerve endings (synaptosomes). *Journal of Endocrinology,* 1975, *65,* 33-44.

Bhagat, B. Effect of chronic cold stress on catecholamine levels in rat brain. *Psychopharmacology,* 1969, *16,* 1-4.

Blanc, G., Herve, D., Simon, H., Lisoprawski, A., Glowinski, J., & Tassin, J. P. Response to stress of mesocortical-frontal dopaminergic neurons after long-term isolation. *Nature,* 1980, *284,* 265-276.

Bliss, E. L., & Ailion, J. Relationship of stress and activity to brain dopamine and homovanillic acid. *Life Sciences,* 1971, *10,* 1161-1169.

Bliss, E. L., Ailion, J., & Zwanziger, J. Metabolism of norepinephrine, serotonin, and dopamine in rat brain with stress. *Journal of Pharmacology and Experimental Therapeutics,* 1968, *164,* 122-134.

Bliss, E. L., Thatcher, W., Ailion, J. Relationship of stress to brain serotonin and 5-hydroxyindoleacetic acid. *Journal of Psychiatric Research,* 1972, *9,* 71-80.

Bliss, E. L., & Zwanziger, J. Brain amines and emotional stress. *Journal of Psychiatric Research,* 1966, *4,* 189-198.

Brown, G. M., & Reichlin, S. Psychologic and neural regulation of growth hormone secretion. *Psychosomatic Medicine,* 1972, *34,* 45-61.

Brown, G. M., Schalch, D. S., & Reichlin, S. Hypothalamic mediation of growth hormone and adrenal stress response in the squirrel monkey. *Endocrinology,* 1971, *89,* 694-703.

Brown, R. M., Snider, S. R., & Carlsson, A. Changes in biogenic amine synthesis and turnover induced by hypoxia and/or footshock stress: II. The central nervous system. *Journal of Neural Transmission,* 1974, *35,* 293-305.

Brown, W. A., Krieger, D. T., Van Woert, M. E., & Ambani, L. M. Dissociation of growth hormone and cortisol release following apomorphine. *Journal of Clinical Endocrinology and Metabolism,* 1974, *38,* 1127-1130.

Brush, F. R., & Levine, S. Adrenocortical activity and avoidance learning as a function of time after fear conditioning. *Physiology and Behavior,* 1966, *1,* 309-311.

Campos, H. A., & Jurupe, J. Evidence for a cholinergic mechanism inducing histamine increase in the rat brain in vivo. *Experientia,* 1970, *26,* 746-747.

Carr, L. A., & Moore, K. E. Effects of reserpine and α-methyltyrosine on brain cate-cholamines and the pituitary-adrenal response to stress. *Neuroendocrinology,* 1968, *3,* 285–302.

Cassens, G., Kuruc, A., Orsulak, P. J., & Schildkraut, J. J. Conditioning of stress-induced alterations of norepinephrine metabolism in rat brain: Studies in progress. *Society for Neuroscience Abstracts,* 1979, *5,* 331.

Chambers, J. W., & Brown, G. M. Neurotransmitter regulation of growth hormone and ACTH in the rhesus monkey: Effects of biogenic amines. *Endocrinology,* 1976, *98,* 420–428.

Chance, W. T., White, A. C., Krynock, G. M., & Rosecrans, J. A. Conditional fear-induced and antinociception and decreased binding of [³H] N-leu-enkephalin to rat brain. *Brain Research,* 1978, *141,* 371–374.

Chattopadhyay, S., & Uniyal, M. The interaction of stress and corticosteroid on the hypothalamus as reflected by gamma aminobutyric acid content. *Proceedings of the Fifth Asia and Oceania Congress of Endocrinology,* 1975.

Cherek, D. R., Lane, J. D., Freedman, M. E., & Smith, J. E. Receptor changes following shock avoidance. *Society for Neuroscience Abstracts,* 1980, *6,* 543.

Christie, M. J., Chesher, G. B., & Bird, K. D. The correlation between swim-stress induced antinociception and [³H] leu-enkephalin binding to brain homogenates in mice. *Pharmacology, Biochemistry and Behavior,* 1981, *15,* 853–857.

Clarke, D. E., & Sampath, S. S. Studies on the functional role of intraneuronal monoamine oxidase. *Journal of Pharmacology and Experimental Therapeutics,* 1973, *187,* 539–549.

Conner, R. L. Hormones, biogenic amines and aggression. In S. Levine (Ed.), *Hormones and behavior.* New York: Academic, 1972.

Coover, G. D., Ursin, H., & Levine, S. Plasma corticosterone levels during active avoidance learning in rats. *Journal of Comparative and Physiological Psychology,* 1973, *82,* 170–174.

Corrodi, H., Fuxe, K., & Hokfelt, T. A possible role played by central monoamine neurones in thermo-regulation. *Acta Physiologica Scandinavica,* 1967, *71,* 224–232.

Corrodi, H., Fuxe, K., & Hokfelt, T. The effect of immobilization stress on the activity of central monoamine neurons. *Life Sciences,* 1968, *7,* 107–112.

Costa, E., Tagliomonte, A., Brunello, N., & Cheney, D. L. Effect of stress on the metabolism of acetylcholine in the cholinergic pathways of extrapyramidal and limbic systems. In E. Usdin, R. Kvetnansky, & I. J. Kopin (Eds.), *Catecholamines and Stress: Recent Advances,* New York: Elsevier, 1980.

Del Conte, E., Ravello, J. J., & Stux, M. The increase of circulating thyrotrophin and the activation of the thyroid by means of electroshock in guinea pigs. *Acta Endocrinologica,* 1955, *18,* 8–14.

Ducommun, P., Vale, W., Sakiz, W., & Guillemin, R. Reversal of the inhibition of TSH secretion due to acute stress. *Endocrinology,* 1967, *80,* 953–956.

Edwardson, J. A., & Bennett, G. W. Modulation of corticotropin releasing factor (CRF) release from hypothalamic synaptosomes. *Nature,* 1974, *251,* 425–427.

Eroglu, L. Effect of morphine on the brain histamine levels in stress-exposed rats. *Psychopharmacology,* 1979, *63,* 13–15.

Fadda, F., Argiolas, A., Melis, M. R., Tissari, A. H., Onali, P. L., & Gessa, G. L. Stress-induced increase in 3,4-dihydroxyphenylacetic acid (DOPAC) levels in the cerebral cortex and in n. accumbens: Reversal by diazepam. *Life Sciences,* 1978, *23,* 2219–2224.

Fekete, M. I. K., Szentendrei, T., Kanyicska, B., & Palkovits, M. Effects of anxiolytic drugs on the catecholamine and DOPAC (3,4-dihydroxyphenylacetic acid) levels in brain cortical areas and on corticosterone and prolactin secretion in rats subjected to stress. *Psychoneuroendocrinology,* 1981, *6,* 113–120.

Feldman, J., & Brown, G. M. Cortisol and growth hormone responses to electric shock and avoidance conditioning in the rhesus monkey. *First Pacific Congress of Psychiatry, the Australian and New Zealand College of Psychiatrists with the American Psychiatric Association,* 1975, *118.* (Abstract)

Feldman, J., & Brown, G. M. Endocrine responses to electric shock and avoidance conditioning in the rhesus monkey: Cortisol and growth hormone. *Psychoneuroendocrinology,* 1976, *1,* 231–242.

Finch, C. E. Catecholamine metabolism in the brains of aging male mice. *Brain Research,* 1973, *52,* 261–276.

Fulginiti, S., & Orsingher, O. A. Effects of learning, amphetamine and nicotine on the level and synthesis of brain noradrenaline in rats. *Archives International Pharmacodynamics,* 1971, *190,* 291.

Fuxe, K., & Hanson, L. C. F. Central catecholamine neurons and conditioned avoidance behavior. *Psychopharmacologia,* 1967, *11,* 439.

Ganong, W. F. The role of catecholamines and acetylcholine in the regulation of endocrine function. *Life Sciences,* 1976, *15,* 1401–1414.

Geller, E., Yuwiler, A., & Zolman, Z. F. Effects of environmental complexity on constituents of brain and liver. *Journal of Neurochemistry,* 1965, *12,* 949–955.

Gold, P. E., & Van Buskirk, R. Posttraining brain norepinephrine concentrations: Correlation with retention performance of avoidance training and with peripheral epinephrine modulation of memory processing. *Behavioral Biology,* 1978, *23,* 509–520.

Goldstein, M., & Nakajima, K. The effect of disulfiram on the biosynthesis of catecholamines during exposure of rats to cold. *Life Sciences,* 1966, *5,* 175–179.

Gordon, R., Spector, S., Sjoerdsma, A., & Undenfriend, S. Increased synthesis of norepinephrine and epinephrine in the intact rat during exercise and exposure to cold. *Journal of Pharmacology and Experimental Therapeutics,* 1966, *153,* 440–447.

Guillemin, R. Peptides in the brain: The new endocrinology of the neuron. *Science,* 1978, *202,* 390–402.

Guyton, A. C. *Textbook of medical physiology.* Toronto: Saunders, 1971.

Hendley, E. D., Burrows, G. H., Robinson, E. S., Heidenreich, K. A., & Bulman, C. A. Acute stress and the brain norepinephrine uptake mechanism in the rat. *Pharmacology, Biochemistry and Behavior,* 1977, *6,* 197–202.

Herman, J. P., Guillonneau, D., Dantzer, R., Scatton, B., Semerdjian-Rouquier, L., & LeMoal, M. Differential effects of inescapable footshocks and stimuli previously paired with inescapable footshocks on dopamine turnover in cortical and limbic areas of the rat. *Life Sciences,* 1982, *30,* 2207–2214.

Hingtgen, J. N., Smith, J. E., Shea, P. A., Aprison, M. H., & Gaff, T. M. Cholinergic changes during conditioned suppression in rats. *Sciences,* 1976, *193,* 332–334.

Hrubes, V., & Benes, V. The time course of metabolic changes during prolonged stress in rats. *Journal of Psychosomatic Research,* 1969, *13,* 327.

Hurwitz, D. A., Robinson, S. M., & Barofsky, I. The influence of training and avoidance performance on disulfiram induced changes in brain catecholamines. *Neuropharmacology,* 1971, *10,* 447.

Huszti, Z., & Kenessey, A. 3-H-tyrosine incorporation into proteins and catecholamines in immobilized rats. In E. Usdin, R. Kvetnansky, & I. J. Kopin (Eds.), *Catecholamines and stress.* Oxford: Pergamon, 1976.

Huttenen, M. O. Persistent alteration of turnover of brain noradrenaline in the offspring of rats subjected to stress during pregnancy. *Nature,* 1971, *230,* 53–55.

Ingenito, A. J. The effect of acute and prolonged cold exposure on the brain amine depleting action of reserpine. *Archives Internationale Pharmacodynamie et de Therapie,* 1967, *166,* 324–332.

Ingenito, A. J. Norepinephrine levels in various areas of rat brain during cold acclimatization. *Proceedings of the Society for Experimental Biology and Medicine,* 1968, *127,* 74–76.

Ingenito, A. J., & Bonnycastle, D. D. The effects of exposure to heat and cold upon rat brain catecholamine and 5-hydroxytryptamine levels. *Canadian Journal of Physiology and Pharmacy,* 1967, *45,* 733–743.

Irwin, J., Bowers, W., Zacharko, R. M., & Anisman, H. Stress-induced alterations of norepinephrine: Cross-stressor sensitization. *Society for Neuroscience Abstracts,* 1982, *8,* 359.

Ishii, Y., Homma, M., & Yhoshigawa, A. Effect of a dopamine-beta-hydroxylase inhibitor on tissue catecholamine levels in spontaneously hypertensive rats subject to immobilization-cold stress. *Neuropharmacology,* 1975, *14,* 155–157.

Jacoby, J. H., Greenstein, M., Sassin, J. F., & Weitzman, E. D. The effect of monoamine precursors on the release of growth hormone in the rhesus monkey. *Neuroendocrinology,* 1974, *14,* 95–102.

Javoy, F., Thierry, A. M., Kety, S. S., & Glowinski, J. The effect of amphetamine on the turnover of brain norepinephrine in normal and stressed rats. *Communications in Behavioral Biology,* 1968, *1A,* 43–48.

Jones, M. T., Hillhouse, E. W., & Burden, J. Effect of various putative neurotransmitters on the secretion of corticotropin releasing hormone from the rat hypothalamus in vitro: A model of the neurotransmitters involved. *Journal of Endocrinology,* 1976, *69,* 1–10.

Juorio, A. V. Effect of stress and L-dopa administration on mouse striatal tyramine and HVA levels. *Brain Research,* 1979, *179,* 186–189.

Kantak, K. M., Wagner, M. J., Tilson, H. A., & Sved, A. Turnover of [3]H-5-hydroxytryptamine and [3]H-5-hydroxyindoleacetic acid and [3]H-5-methoxyindoles in nondeprived and 24 h food deprived rats. *Pharmacology, Biochemistry and Behavior,* 1977, *6,* 221–225.

Karczmar, A. G., Scudder, C. L., & Richardson, D. L. Interdisciplinary approach to the study of behavior in related mice types. In S. Ehrenpreis & I. J. Kopin (Eds.), *Chemical approaches to brain function.* New York: Academic, 1973.

Keim, K. L., & Sigg, E. B. Physiological and biochemical concomitants of restraint stress in rats. *Pharmacology, Biochemistry and Behavior,* 1976, *4,* 289–297.

Keim, K. L., & Sigg, E. B. Plasma corticosterone and brain catecholamines in stress: Effect of psychotropic drugs. *Pharmacology, Biochemistry and Behavior,* 1977, *6,* 79–85.

Knigge, K. M. Neuroendocrine mechanisms influencing ACTH and TSH secretion and their role in cold acclimation. *Federation Proceedings,* 1960, *5,* 45–49.

Kobayashi, R. M., & Kopin, I. J. The effects of stress and environmental lighting on histamine in the rat brain. *Brain Research,* 1974, *74,* 356–359.

Kobayashi, R. M., Palkovits, M., Kizer, J. S., Jacobowitz, D. M., & Kopin, I. J. Selective alterations of catecholamines and tyrosine hydroxylase activity in the hypothalamus following acute and chronic stress. In E. Usdin, R. Kvetnansky, & I. J. Kopin (Eds.), *Catecholamines and stress.* Oxford: Pergamon, 1976.

Kokkinidis, L., & Anisman, H. Amphetamine models of paranoid schizophrenia: An overview and elaboration of animal experimentation. *Psychological Bulletin,* 1981, *88,* 551–579.

Korf, J. Locus coeruleus, noradrenaline metabolism and stress. In E. Usdin, R. Kvetnansky, & I. J. Kopin (Eds.), *Catecholamines and stress.* Oxford: Pergamon, 1976.

Korf, J., Aghajanian, G. K., & Roth, R. H. Increased turnover of norepinephrine in the rat cerebral cortex during stress: Role of locus coeruleus. *Neuropharmacology,* 1973, *12,* 933–938.

Kuhar, M. J., Atweh, S. F., & Bird, S. J. Studies of cholinergic-monoaminergic interactions in rat brain. In L. L. Butcher (Ed.), *Cholinergic-Monoaminergic Interactions in the Brain.* New York: Academic, 1978.

Kvetnansky, R., Kopin, I. J., & Saavedra, J. M. Changes in epinephrine in individual hypothalamic nuclei after immobilization stress. *Brain Research,* 1978, *155,* 387–390.

Kvetnansky, R., Mitro, A., Palkovits, M., Brownstein, M., Torda, T., Vigaš, M., & Mikulaj, L. Catecholamines in individual hypothalamic nuclei in stressed rats. In E. Usdin, R. Kvetnansky, & I. J. Kopin (Eds.), *Catecholamines and stress.* Oxford: Pergamon, 1976.

Kvetnansky, R., Mitro, A., Palkovits, M., Vigaš, M., Albrecht, I., Torda, T., & Mikulaj, L. Effects of stress on catecholamines in individual hypothalamic nuclei and ACTH in rats. *Symposium of the International Society of Psychoendocrinology,* Visegrad, 1975.

Kvetnansky, R., Palkovits, M., Mitro, A., Torda, T., & Mikulaj, L. Catecholamines in individual hypothalamic nuclei of acutely and repeatedly stressed rats. *Neuroendocrinology,* 1977, *23,* 257–267.

Ladisch, W. Effect of stress upon serotonin metabolism in various regions of the rat brain. *Arzneimittel-Forschung,* 1974, *24,* 1025–1027.

Lavielle, S., Tassin, J. P., Thierry, A. M., Blanc, G., Herve, D., Barthelemy, C., & Glowinski, J., Blockade by benzodiazepines of the selective high increase in dopamine turnover induced by stress in mesocortical dopaminergic neurons of the rat. *Brain Research,* 1978, *168,* 585–594.

Leduc, J. Catecholamine production and release in exposure and acclimation to cold. *Acta Physiologica Scandinavica,* 1961, *53*(Suppl. 183), 1–101.

Lee, C. H., Morita, A., Saito, H., & Takagi, K. Changes in catecholamine levels of mouse brain during oscillation-stress. *Chemistry and Pharmacy Bulletin,* 1973, *21,* 2768–2770.

Levine, S. (Ed.). *Hormones and behavior.* New York: Academic, 1972.

Levine, S., Madden, J., IV, Conner, R. L., Moskal, J. R., & Anderson, D. C. Physiological and behavioral effects of prior aversive stimulation (preshock) in the rat. *Physiology and Behavior,* 1973, *10,* 467–471.

Lewis, J. W., Cannon, J. T., & Liebeskind, J. C. Opioid and nonopioid mechanisms of stress analgesia. *Science*, 1980, *208*, 623–625.

Lidbrink, P., Corrodi, H., Fuxe, K., & Olson, L. Barbituates and meprobamate: Decreases in catecholamine turnover of central dopamine and noradrenaline neuronal systems and the influence of immobilization stress. *Brain Research*, 1972, *45*, 507–524.

Madden, J., IV, Akil, H., Patrick, R. L., & Barchas, J. D. Stress-induced parallel changes in central opioid levels and pain responsiveness in the rat. *Nature*, 1977, *265*, 358–360.

Maier, S. F., & Seligman, M. E. P. Learned helplessness: Theory and evidence. *Journal of Experimental Psychology: General*, 1976, *105*, 3–46.

Martin, J. B. Regulation of the pituitary-thyroid axis. In S. M. McCann (Ed.), *Endocrine physiology*. London: Butterworth, 1974.

Martin, J. B., Lal, S., Tolis, G., & Friesen, H. G. Inhibition by apomorphine of prolactin secretion in patients with elevated serum prolactin. *Journal of Clinical Endocrinology and Metabolism*, 1974, *39*, 180–182.

Mason, J. W., Maher, J. T., Hartley, L. H., Mougey, E. H., Perlow, M. J., & Jones, L. G. Selectivity of corticosteroid and catecholamine responses to various natural stimuli. In G. Serban (Ed.), *Psychopathology of human adaptation*. New York: Plenum, 1976.

Mason, S. T., & Iversen, S. D. Theories of the dorsal bundle extinction effect. *Brain Research Review*, 1979, *1*, 107–137.

Maynert, E. W., & Levi, R. Stress-induced release of brain norepinephrine and its inhibition by drugs. *Journal of Pharmacology and Experimental Therapeutics*, 1964, *143*, 90–95.

Mazurkiewicz-Kwilecki, I. M., & Taub, H. Effect of stress on brain histamine. *Pharmacology, Biochemistry and Behavior*, 1978, *9*, 465–468.

McCann, S. M., Ajika, K., Fawcett, C. P., Hefco, E., Illner, P., Negro-Villar, A., Orias, R., Watson, J. T., & Krulich, L. Hypothalamic control of the adenohypophyseal response to stress by releasing and inhibitory neurohormones. In S. Németh (Ed.), *Hormones, metabolism and stress*. Bratislava: Slovak Academy of Sciences, 1973.

McCann, S. M., Krulich, L., Ojeda, S. R., & Vijayan, E. Control of prolactin release by putative synaptic transmitters. In C. Robyn & M. Harter (Eds.), *Progress in prolactin physiology and pathology*. New York: Elsevier-North Holland, 1978.

Meyer, J. S., Buckholtz, N. S., & Boggan, W. O. Serotonergic stimulation of pituitary-adrenal activity in the mouse. *Neuroendocrinology*, 1978, *26*, 312–324.

Mikulaj, L., Kvetnansky, R., Murgas, K., Parizkova, J., & Vencel, P. Catecholamines and corticosteroids in acute and repeated stress. In E. Usdin, R. Kvetnansky, & I. J. Kopin (Eds.), *Catecholamines and stress*. Oxford: Pergamon, 1976.

Millan, M. J., Tsang, Y. F., Przewlocki, V., Hollt, V., & Herz, A. The influence of foot-shock stress upon brain, pituitary and spinal cord pools of immunoreactive dynorphin in rats. *Neuroscience Letters*, 1981, *24*, 75–79.

Modigh, K. Effects of isolation and fighting in mice on the rate of synthesis of noradrenaline, dopamine, and 5-hydroxytryptamine in the brain. *Psychopharmacologia*, 1973, *33*, 1–17.

Modigh, K. Effects of social stress on the turnover of brain catecholamines and 5-hydroxy-tryptamine in mice. *Acta Pharmacologica Toxicologica*, 1974, *34*, 97–105.

Modigh, K. Influence of social stress on brain catecholamine mechanisms. In E. Usdin, R. Kvetnansky, & I. J. Kopin (Eds.), *Catecholamines and stress*. Oxford: Pergamon, 1976.

Monjan, A. A., & Collector, M. I. Stress-induced modulation of the immune response. *Science*, 1977, *196*, 307–308.

Moore, K. E., & Lariviere, E. W. Effects of stress and d-amphetamine on rat brain catecholamines. *Biochemical Pharmacology*, 1964, *13*, 1098–1100.

Morgan, W. W., Rudeen, P. K., & Pfeil, K. A. Effect of immobilization stress on serotonin content and turnover in regions of the rat brain. *Life Sciences*, 1975, *17*, 143–150.

Neilson, H. C., & Fleming, R. M. Effect of electroconvulsive shock and prior stress on brain amine levels. *Experimental Neurology*, 1968, *20*, 21–30.

Németh, S. *Hormones, metabolism and stress: Recent progress and perspectives*. Bratislava: Slovak Academy of Sciences, 1973.

Nishikawa, I., Kajiwara, Y., Kono, Y., Sano, T., Nagasaki, N., Tanaka, M., & Norda, Y. Isolation-induced general behavioral changes and brain monoamine levels in rat. *Kurume Medical Journal*, 1974, *21*, 117–121.

Nomura, S., Watanabe, M., Ukei, N., & Nakazawa, T. Stress and $\beta$-adrenergic receptor binding in the rat's brain. *Brain Research,* 1981, *224,* 199–203.

Ordy, J. M., Samorajski, T., & Schroeder, D. Concurrent changes in hypothalamic and cardiac catecholamine levels after anesthetics, tranquilizers and stress in subhuman primates. *Journal of Pharmacology and Experimental Therapeutics,* 1966, *152,* 445–457.

Otto, U., & Paalzow, L. Effect of stress on the pharmacokinetics of sodium salicylate and quinidine sulphate in rats. *Acta Pharmacologica Toxicologica,* 1975, *36,* 415–426.

Palkovits, M., Brownstein, M., Kizer, J. S., Saavedra, J. M., & Kopin, I. J. Effect of stress on serotonin and tryptophan hydroxylase activity of brain nuclei. In E. Usdin, R. Kvetnansky, & I. J. Kopin (Eds.), *Catecholamines and stress.* Oxford: Pergamon, 1976.

Páré, W. P., & Livingston, A. Brain norepinephrine and stomach ulcers in rats exposed to chronic conflict. *Physiology and Behavior,* 1970, *5,* 215–220.

Paulsen, E. C., & Hess, S. M. The rate of synthesis of catecholamines following depletion in guinea pig brain and heart. *Journal of Neurochemistry,* 1963, *10,* 453–459.

Petty, F., & Sherman, A. A neurochemical differentiation between exposure to stress and the development of learned helplessness. *Drug Development Research,* 1982, *2,* 43–45.

Przewiocki, R., Millan, M. J., Gramsch, Ch., Millan, M. H., & Herz, A. The influence of selective adeno- and neurointermedio-hypophysectomy upon plasma and brain levels of $\beta$-endorphin and their response to stress in rats. *Brain Research,* 1982, *242,* 107–117.

Ray, O. S., & Barrett, R. J. Behavioral, pharmacological, and biochemical analysis of genetic differences in rats. *Behavioral Biology,* 1975, *15,* 391–418.

Reid, W. D., Volicer, L., Smookler, H., Beaven, M. A., & Brodie, B. B. Brain amines and temperature regulation. *Pharmacology,* 1966, *1,* 329–344.

Ritter, S., & Pelzer, N. L. Magnitude of stress-induced norepinephrine depletion varies with age. *Brain Research,* 1978, *152,* 170–175.

Ritter, S., & Ritter, R. C. Protection against stress-induced brain norepinephrine depletion after repeated 2-deoxy-D-glucose administration. *Brain Research,* 1977, *127,* 179–184.

Rosecrans, J. A. Brain amine changes in stressed and normal rats pretreated with various drugs. *Archives of International Pharmacodynamics,* 1969, *180,* 460–470.

Rossier, J., French, E. D., Rivier, C., Ling, N., Guillemin, R., & Bloom, F. E. Foot-shock induced stress increases $\beta$-endorphin levels in blood but not brain. *Nature,* 1977, *270,* 618–620.

Rossier, J., Guillemin, R., & Bloom, F. E. Footshock induced stress decreases leu[5]-enkephalin immunoreactivity in rat hypothalamus. *European Journal of Pharmacology,* 1978, *48,* 465–466.

Saarela, S., Hissa, R., Hohtola, E., & Jeronen, E. Effect of $\alpha$-methylparatyrosine and temperature stress on monoamine and metabolite levels in the pigeon. *Journal of Thermal Biology,* 1977, *2,* 121–129.

Saavedra, F. M., Kvetnansky, R., & Kopin, I. J. Adrenaline, noradrenaline and dopamine levels in specific brain stem areas of acutely immobilized rats. *Brain Research,* 1979, *160,* 271–280.

Saavedra, J. M. Changes in dopamine, noradrenaline and adrenaline in specific septal and preoptic nuclei after acute immobilization stress. *Neuroendocrinology,* 1982, *35,* 396–401.

Saito, H., Morita, A., Miyazaki, I., & Takagi, K. Comparison of the effects of various stresses on biogenic amines in the central nervous system and animal symptoms. In E. Usdin, R. Kvetnansky, & I. J. Kopin (Eds.), *Catecholamines and stress.* Oxford: Pergamon, 1976.

Sauter, A. M., Baba, Y., Stone, E. A., & Goldstein, M. Effect of stress and of phenylethanol-amine-N-methyltransferase inhibition on central norepinephrine and epinephrine levels. *Brain Research,* 1978, *144,* 415–419.

Scapagnini, U., Annunziato, L., & Preziosi, P. Role of brain norepinephrine in stress regulation. In S. Németh (Ed.), *Hormones, metabolism and stress.* Bratislava: Slovak Academy of Sciences, 1973.

Schmidt, D. E., Cooper, D. O., & Barrett, R. J. Strain specific alterations in hippocampal cholinergic function following acute footshock. *Pharmacology, Biochemistry and Behavior,* 1980, *12,* 277–280.

Schutz, R. A., Barros-Schutz, M. T., Orsingher, O. A., & Izquierdo, I. Brain dopamine and noradrenalin levels in rats submitted to four different aversive behavioral tests. *Psychopharmacology,* 1978, *63,* 289–292.

Segal, D. S., & Janowsky, D. S. Psychostimulant-induced behavioral effects: Possible models of schizophrenia. In Morris A. Lipton, A. Dimascio, & K. F. Killam (Eds.), *Psychopharmacology: A generation of progress*. New York: Raven, 1978.

Sigg, E. B., Keim, K. L., & Sigg, T. D. On the mechanism of renin release by restraint stress in rats. *Pharmacology, Biochemistry and Behavior*, 1978, *8*, 47–50.

Simmonds, M. A. Effect of environmental temperature on the turnover of noradrenaline in hypothalamus and other areas of the rat brain. *Journal of Physiology* (London), 1969, *203*, 199–210.

Sklar, L. S., & Anisman, H. Transplanted carcinoma development and growth: Effects of isolation, inescapable shock, and coping style. *Society for Neuroscience Abstracts*, 1978, *4*, 400.

Sklar, L. S., & Anisman, H. Stress and coping factors influence tumor growth. *Science*, 1979, *205*, 513–515.

Sklar, L. S., & Anisman, H. Contributions of stress and coping to cancer development and growth. In K. Bammer & B. H. Newberry (Eds.), *Stress and cancer*. Toronto: Hogrefe, 1981.

Snyder, S. H., & Taylor, K. M. *Perspective in neuropharmacology*. New York: Oxford University Press, 1972.

Spyraki, Ch., Papadopoulou-Daifoti, Z., & Petounis, A. Norepinephrine levels in rat brain after infrasound exposure. *Physiology and Behavior*, 1980, *21*, 447–448.

Stolk, J. M., Conner, R. L., Levine, S., & Barchas, J. D. Brain norepinephrine metabolism and shock induced fighting behavior in rats: Differential effects of shock and fighting on the neurochemical response to a common footshock stimulus. *Journal of Pharmacology and Experimental Therapeutics*, 1974, *190*, 193–209.

Stone, E. A. Behavioral and neurochemical effects of acute swim stress are due to hypothermia. *Life Sciences*, 1970, *9*, 877–888.

Stone, E. A. Hypothalamic norepinephrine after acute stress. *Brain Research*, 1971, *35*, 260–263.

Stone, E. A. Adrenergic activity in rat hypothalamus following extreme muscular exertion. *American Journal of Physiology*, 1973, *224*, 165–169.

Stone, E. A. Effect of stress on sulfated glycol metabolites of brain norepinephrine. *Life Sciences*, 1975, *16*, 1725–1730. (a)

Stone, E. A. Stress and catecholamines. In A. J. Friedhoff (Ed.), *Catecholamines and behavior* (Vol. 2). New York: Plenum, 1975. (b)

Stone, E. A. Effect of stress on norepinephrine-stimulated accumulation of cyclic AMP in rat brain slices. *Pharmacology, Biochemistry and Behavior*, 1978, *8*, 583–591.

Stone, E. A. Reduction by stress of norepinephrine-stimulated accumulation of cyclic AMP in rat cerebral cortex. *Journal of Neurochemistry*, 1979, *32*, 1335–1337. (a)

Stone, E. A. Subsensitivity to norepinephrine as a link between adaptation to stress and antidepressant therapy: An hypothesis. *Research Communications in Psychology, Psychiatry and Behavior*, 1979, *4*, 241–255. (b)

Stone, E. A., & Platt, J. E. Brain adrenergic receptors and resistance to stress. *Brain Research*, 1982, *237*, 405–414.

Stoner, H. B., & Elson, P. M. The effect of injury on monoamine concentrations in the rat hypothalamus. *Journal of Neurochemistry*, 1971, *18*, 1837.

Stoner, H. B., & Hunt, A. The effect of hind-limb ischemia on the concentration of 4-hydroxy-3-methoxyphenylethylene glycol, sulphate (MOPEG-SO4) in the hypothalamus and hind-brain of the rat. In E. Usdin, R. Kvetnansky, & I. J. Kopin (Eds.), *Catecholamines and stress*. Oxford: Pergamon, 1976.

Stoner, H. B., & Hunt, A. The effect of trauma on the activity of central noradrenergic neurons. *Brain Research*, 1976, *112*, 337–346. (b)

Stricker, E. M., & Zigmond, M. J. Effects on homeostasis of intraventricular injection of 6-hydroxydopamine in rats. *Journal of Comparative and Physiological Psychology*, 1974, *86*, 973–994.

Taché, Y., Ruisseau, P. D., Ducharme, J. R., & Collu, R. Pattern of adenohypophyseal hormone changes in male rats following chronic stress. *Neuroendocrinology*, 1978, *26*, 208–219.

Taylor, K. M., & Laverty, R. The effect of chlordiazepoxide, diazepam and nitrazepam on catecholamine metabolism in regions of the rat brain. *European Journal of Pharmacology*, 1969, *8*, 296. (a)

Taylor, K. M., & Laverty, R. The metabolism of tritiated dopamine in regions of the rat brain in vivo: II. The significance of the neutral metabolites of catecholamines. *Journal of Neurochemistry*, 1969, *16*, 1367. (b)

Telegdy, G., & Vermes, I. Changes induced by stress in the activity of the serotonergic system in limbic brain structures. In E. Usdin, R. Kvetnansky, & I. J. Kopin (Eds.), *Catecholamines and stress*. Oxford: Pergamon, 1976.

Terry, L. C., & Martin, J. B. Hypothalamic hormones: Subcellular distribution and mechanisms of release. *Annual Review of Pharmacology and Toxicology*, 1978, *18*, 111–123.

Thierry, A. M. Effects of stress on the metabolism of serotonin and norepinephrine in the central nervous system of the rat. In S. Németh (Ed.), *Hormones, metabolism and stress*. Bratislava: Slovak Academy of Sciences, 1973.

Thierry, A. M., Blanc, G., & Glowinski, J. Preferential utilization of newly synthesized norepinephrine in the brain stem of stressed rats. *European Journal of Pharmacology*, 1970, *10*, 139.

Thierry, A. M., Blanc, G., & Glowinski, J. Effect of stress on the disposition of catecholamines localized in various intraneuronal storage forms in the brain stem of the rat. *Journal of Neurochemistry*, 1971, *18*, 449–461.

Thierry, A. M., Fekete, M., & Glowinski, J. Effects of stress on the metabolism of noradrenaline, dopamine and serotonin (5-HT) in the central nervous system of the rat: II. Modifications of serotonin metabolism. *European Journal of Pharmacology*, 1968, *4*, 384–389.

Thierry, A. M., Javoy, J., Glowinski, J., & Kety, S. S. Effects of stress on the metabolism of norepinephrine, dopamine and serotonin in the central nervous system of the rat: I. Modifications of norepinephrine turnover. *Journal of Pharmacology and Experimental Therapeutics*, 1968, *163*, 163–171.

Thierry, A. M., Tassin, J. P., Blanc, G., & Glowinski, J. Selective activation of the mesocortical DA system by stress. *Nature*, 1976, *263*, 242–244.

Thoa, N. B., Tizabi, Y., & Jacobowitz, D. M. The effect of isolation on catecholamine concentration and turnover in discrete areas of the rat brain. *Brain Research*, 1977, *131*, 259–269.

Thoenen, H. Induction of tyrosine hydroxylase in peripheral and central adrenergic neurons by cold exposure. *Nature*, 1970, *228*, 861–862.

Tissari, A. H., Argiolas, A., Fadda, F., Serra, G., & Gessa, G. L. Footshock stress accelerates nonstriatal dopamine synthesis without activating tyrosine hydroxylase. *Archives of Pharmacology*, 1979, *308*, 155–158.

Ungerstedt, U. Postsynaptic supersensitivity after 6-hydroxydopamine induced degeneration of the nigrostriatal dopamine system. *Acta Physiologica Scandanavica*, 1971, *357*(Suppl), 69–93.

Van Loon, G. R. Brain dopamine beta hydroxylase activity: Response to stress, tyrosine hydroxylase inhibition, hypophysectomy and ACTH administration. In E. Usdin, R. Kvetnansky, & I. J. Kopin (Eds.), *Catecholamines and stress*. Oxford: Pergamon, 1976.

Van Vugt, D. A., Bruni, J. F., & Meites, J. Naloxone inhibition of stress-induced increase in prolactin secretion. *Life Sciences*, 1978, *22*, 85–90.

Vijayan, E., & McCann, S. M. The effect of systemic administration of dopamine and apomorphine on plasma LH and prolactin concentrations in conscious rats. *Neuroendocrinology*, 1978, *25*, 221–235.

Weber, E., Voigt, K. H., & Martin, R. Concomitant storage of ACTH and endorphin-like immunoreactivity in secretory granules of anterior pituitary corticotrophs. *Brain Research*, 1978, *157*, 385–390.

Weiss, J. M. Effects of coping behavior in different warning signal conditions on stress pathology in rats. *Journal of Comparative and Physiological Psychology*, 1971, 77, 1–13. (a)

Weiss, J. M. Effects of coping behavior with and without a feedback signal on stress pathology in rats. *Journal of Comparative and Physiological Psychology*, 1971, 77, 23–30. (b)

Weiss, J. M. Effects of punishing the coping response (conflict) on stress pathology in rats. *Journal of Comparative and Physiological Psychology*, 1971, 77, 14–21. (c)

Weiss, J. M., Glazer, H. I., & Pohorecky, L. A. Coping behavior and neurochemical changes:

An alternative for the original "learned helplessness" experiments. In G. Serban & A. Kling (Eds.), *Animal models in human psychobiology*. New York: Plenum, 1976.

Weiss, J. M., Glazer, H. I., Pohorecky, L. A., Brick, J., & Miller, N. E. Effects of chronic exposure to stressors on avoidance-escape behavior and on brain norepinephrine. *Psychosomatic Medicine*, 1975, *37*, 522–534.

Weiss, J. M., Goodman, P. A., Losito, B. G., Corrigan, S., Charry, J. M., & Bailey, W. H. Behavioral depression produced by an uncontrollable stressor. Relationship to norepinephrine, dopamine and serotonin levels in various regions of rat brain. *Brain Research Reviews*, 1981, *3*, 161–191.

Weiss, J. M., Pohorecky, L. A., Salman, S., & Gruenthal, M. Attenuation of gastric lesions by psychological aspects of aggression in rats. *Journal of Comparative and Physiological Psychology*, 1976, *90*, 252–259.

Weiss, J. M., Stone, E. A., & Harrell, N. Coping behavior and brain norepinephrine level in rats. *Journal of Comparative and Physiological Psychology*, 1970, *72*, 153–160.

Welch, B. L., & Welch, A. S. Differential activation by restraint stress of a mechanism to conserve brain catecholamines and serotonin in mice differing in excitability. *Nature*, 1968, *218*, 575–577.

Welch, B. L., & Welch, A. S. Control of brain catecholamines and serotonin during acute stress and after d-amphetamine by natural inhibition of monoamine oxidase: An hypothesis. In E. Costa & S. Garattini (Eds.), *Amphetamines and related compounds*. New York: Raven, 1970.

Wimer, R. E., Norman, R., & Eleftheriou, B. E. Serotonin levels in hippocampus: Striking variations associated with mouse strain and treatment. *Brain Research*, 1974, *63*, 397–401.

Zajaczkowska, M. N. Acetylcholine content in the central and peripheral nervous system and its synthesis in the rat brain during stress and post-stress exhaustion. *Acta Physiologica Polska*, 1975, *26*, 493–497.

Zigmond, M. J., & Harvey, J. A. Resistance to central norepinephrine depletion and decreased mortality in rats chronically exposed to electric footshock. *Journal of Neuro-visceral Relations*, 1970, *31*, 373–381.

# 4

# Stress, Hormones, Neuroregulation, and Immunity

George F. Solomon
*University of California, San Francisco*

Alfred A. Amkraut
*Alza Pharmaceuticals, Palo Alto, California*

Robert T. Rubin
*University of California, Los Angeles*

## HISTORICAL BACKGROUND ON OUR WORK ON STRESS, THE CNS, AND IMMUNITY

The notion of "resistance" to disease, particularly infectious, is ancient and ubiquitous, and the idea that such resistance can be modified by life experience and by emotional states is likewise old and common. For example, Ayurveda, ancient Indian medicine, the basic writings of which data back two milllenia, avoids Cartesian dichotomization of mind and body; contains the concepts of natural and acquired immunity, the latter influenced by experience; and approaches the treatment of disease through the restoration of a healthy balance of life forces and an integrated relationship to the environment (Shukla, Solomon, & Doshi, 1979). Relatively modern psychosomatic observation began with emotional factors as related to the onset and course of pulmonary tuberculosis, "unhappiness" being cited, for example, as a cause of lower resistance (Day, 1951).

Our own work in "psychoimmunology" began with a series of studies (Moos & Solomon, 1964a, 1964b, 1965a, 1965b, 1965c, 1966) in collaboration with Moos on personality and emotional factors in the pathogenesis of a disease associated with an immunologic dysfunction, rheumatoid arthritis. We found that personality factors seem predisposing, that onset of disease could be correlated with life events, and that a more malignant course was related to failure of psychological defenses. We found (Solomon & Moos, 1965) that healthy relatives of rheumatoid patients with rheumatoid factor (an IgM anti-IgG autoantibody) in their serums were particularly emotionally healthy, implying that a combination of emotional decompensation and immunologic predisposition led to overt

An edited version of this chapter was published as "Stress and Psychoimmunological Response" by G. F. Solomon, A. A. Amkraut, and R. T. Rubin in *Mind and Cancer Prognosis*, edited by B. A. Stoll. Chichester: John Wiley and Sons, Ltd., 1979.

disease. Other investigators (Engel, 1953; McClary, Meyer, & Weitzman, 1955) found similar patterns in other diseases with autoimmune features. Auto-immunity was discovered to be associated with relative immunologic incom-petence (Dixon, Feldman, & Vasquez, 1959, 1961). [(Such "incompetence" is now felt to be related largely to dysfunction of suppressor T cells (Allison & Denman, 1976).] At any rate, the creative leap in our thinking (if that is what it was) occurred with the mental juxtaposition of this knowledge about relative immunologic deficiency in autoimmune disease with evidence that stress, emo-tional decompensation, and depression are associated with elevation of adrenal corticosteroid hormones (Hamburg, 1962) and, of course, the awareness that cortisol can be immunosuppressive (Hirschhorn, Bach, Kolodny, Firschein, & Hashem, 1963). Finally, we noted that psychological factors similar to those we and others documented in rheumatoid arthritis had been observed in patients with cancer (Leshan & Worthington, 1956) and that there was ever-growing evidence that there is immunologic resistance to cancer (Fudenberg, 1968; Habel, 1963). Many patients with cancer seem to have decreased immunity, and immunity-boosting procedures may have some therapeutic effect (Hellstrom, Hellstrom, Sjogren, & Werner, 1971; Smith, 1971). The cancer cell, a mutant whether occurring spontaneously or by the influence of virus, radiation, or chemical carcinogen, might be expected to be rejected as "foreign" by a surveillance mechanism based on recognition by T cells of a new surface antigen in the mutant cell. Minimal weakness of this mechanism might permit "sneaking through" of tumor cells (Old, Boyse, Clarke, & Carswell, 1962).

The other side of the coin in our psychoimmunologic interests has been the relationship of immunologic abnormalities, including alteration in immuno-globulin levels; morphological abnormalities in lymphocytes; and presence of autoantibodies, including antibrain antibodies, in mental illness, particularly schizophrenia (Amkraut, Solomon, Allansmith, McClellan, & Rappaport, 1973; Fessel, 1963; Fessel & Grunbaum, 1961; Fessel & Hirata-Hibi, 1963; Fessel, Hirata-Hibi, & Shapiro, 1965; Heath & Krupp, 1967; Solomon, Allansmith, McClellan, & Amkraut, 1969). Schizophrenia appears to protect from rheumatoid arthritis (Pilkington, 1956; Rothermich & Philips, 1963; Trevethan & Tatum, 1954), and the incidence of cancer may be lower in schizophrenia (Katz, Kunofsky, Patton, & Alloway, 1967; Roppel, 1978). Discussion of these findings, the significance of which remains quite unclear, would lead us astray. Suffice it to say, clinical evidence suggests that emotional distress might alter immunity and that psychiatric conditions of profound emotional disturbance have immuno-logic concomitants. A role of the CNS in immune function is, thus, indirectly suggested.

## Stress and Disease

The cause of disease is multifactorial, even of those diseases with clearly established "etiologic agents." *Mycobacterium tuberculosis* fulfills Koch's postu-lates as the etiologic agent of tuberculosis, yet we know of a variety of factors other than the organism itself that relate to the onset and course of disease following exposure to the organism. Genetic factors play a role. Jews, more susceptible individuals among them probably having died out in centuries of ghetto living, appear relatively resistant; whereas, Native Americans are susceptible, having only been relatively recently exposed. Living conditions such as overcrowding, climate, diet, life stress, and as already mentioned, emotional factors, particularly depression, play a role.

There has long been an interest in the role of stress in production of disease, dating in modern times especially to Selye. We are concerned with the effects of psychological, rather than physiological stress in immune resistance to disease, although the differentiation between the two can be difficult. Stress-induced behavior can lead to changes in nutrition, for example. In the human, distress is a more relevant concept than stress, because what is stressful to one person may not be to another (e.g., a parachute jump to an experienced skydiver).

In clinical studies, emotions, especially depression (Schmale, 1958), and social factors (Mutter & Schleifer, 1966) have been linked to susceptibility to, and recovery from, infectious diseases. Families of ill children were found to have been more disorganized during the prior 6-month period and to have exposed their children to a greater number of psychological and social changes, which were threatening and had a disruptive impact, than was the case with a comparison group of healthy children. Delayed recovery from infectious mononucleosis has been correlated with deficient ego-strength (Greenfield, Roessler, & Crosley, 1966), and prolonged convalescence from brucellosis (Imboden, Carter, Leighton, & Trevor, 1959) and influenza (Imboden, Carter, & Leighton, 1961) has been correlated with depression. Normal bacterial flora may be modified by emotional state. An increase in total oral streptococcus and in $\beta$-hemolytic streptococcus counts were associated with masochistic mechanisms of meeting dependency strivings in one longitudinal study (Kaplan, Gottschalk, & Fleming, 1957). Dentists are quite familiar with the occurrence of acute necrotizing gingivitis at times of stress. With this disease normal flora become invasive under conditions of immunosuppression (Cohen-Cole, Cogen, Stevens, Kirk, Gaitan, Hain, & Freeman, 1981).

Currently, there is a great interest in documenting the relationship of recent life events to illnesses of any sort, at least some of which may be caused by alteration in immune states (Holmes & Rahe, 1967). The area remains controversial (Minter & Kimball, 1978), but the occurrence within a relatively short period of time of a number of major life changes requiring adaptation seems particularly to dispose to illness, and ability to cope successfully may be protective. Current life-event methodology opens the way to predictive clinical studies, which are essential to tie experimental data convincingly to diverse occurrence in humans (Gunderson & Rahe, 1974).

There are numerous reports (Rasmussen, Spencer, & Marsh, 1957; Yamada, Jensen, & Rasmussen, 1964) on the effects of experimental stress on infectious disease, without specific reference to immunologic factors, a topic insightfully reviewed by S. B. Friedman and Glasgow (1966), who pointed out the difficulty of defining stress-induced mechanisms responsible for modifications, either positive or negative, of infectious disease. In the case of viral disease, the relationship of stress to interferon production, as well as its relationship to immune defenses, must be considered.

We have previously discussed the many defenses that must be considered in microbial or parasitic diseases, from the adaptive immune response to consistency of mucous barriers, blood flow, clotting, and so forth. This multiple nature of the physiological defenses makes it very difficult to use these complex disease processes as paradigms for identifying the mechanisms of stress-mediated effects on the immune system.

Cancer presents a similar, albeit perhaps somewhat less diffuse, problem. The difficulty with this decrease is the as-yet-not-clearly-understood role of the immune system in the defense of the organism against neoplasm. The effect of stress on tumors has been reviewed by LaBarba (1970), and since that review appeared, many other reports on stress effects on cancer have been published (e.g., Newberry, Frankie, Beatty, Maloney, & Gilchrist, 1972). Particularly interesting is a series of studies by Riley (1975) and associates. Altering environmental conditions markedly changed incidence of spontaneous mammary tumors in mice, and adequate protection from stress reduced mammary-tumor occurrence (Riley & Spackman, 1974). These investigators postulate stress effects on immune surveillance (Riley, Spackman, & Santisteban, 1975). Biologic stress (administration of a relatively benign nononcogenic virus that temporarily increases plasma corticosterone) also enhances growth of melanoma (Riley & Spackman, 1976). Similar observations were made by Henry, Stephens, & Watson (1975), who demonstrated a very rapid appearance of mammary cancer in mice of a low-incidence strain placed in a highly stressful social situation. We (Amkraut & Solomon, 1972) have shown a modification of Moloney virus–induced sarcoma by a variety of stresses, including shock stress and differential housing conditions. The course of this tumor is clearly determined by immune factors. The immune response of Balb/C mice is very rapid and leads almost invariably to the rejection of the tumor. The variables measured, however, are tumor size and appearance, and these could be very significantly influenced nonimmunologically by the stresses applied. Ader and Friedman (1965) found that preweaning handling significantly decreased the rate of development of Walker 256 carcinosarcoma in the rat. We (Solomon, Levine, & Kraft, 1968) had found early handling enhanced primary and secondary antibody response in the rat.

With this short background of how we have been led to hypothesize a role of the CNS and neuroendocrines in the regulation of immunity, including a brief review of clinical and experimental observations on the role of stress and emotions in the onset and course of autoimmune, infectious, and neoplastic diseases, we proceed to call attention to brain–environment interaction in CNS development; to discuss some issues about the concept of stress and its neurochemical and endocrine concomitants; to mention rhythmicity of endocrine function, which may have implications for immunology; to describe results of animal experiments on stress effects on immunity; to point out what little evidence there is for stress-related alteration of immunity in humans; to outline our as-yet-fragmentary knowledge of neuroendocrine influences on specific components of the immune response; and to discuss, somewhat speculatively, mechanisms of stress-induced effects on the immune response.

## CNS DEVELOPMENT AND ENVIRONMENT

A developing area of research that can broaden our perspective on psycho-neuroendocrine-immune relationships is early brain development. It is known that brain–environment interactions in the human occur at least as early as the first minutes after birth (Condon & Sander, 1974; Lipsitt, Mustaine, & Zeigler, 1977;

Meltzoff & Moore, 1977; Wolff, 1976). The actual morphological development of the brain has been shown to depend on environmental stimulation (Weiner, 1972). This is true not only for gross sensory deficits, such as the disturbed brain maturation following the blinding of experimental animals, but for more subtle influences, such as the richness of dendritic branching in the developing brain of experimental animals which depends on the intensity of psychosocial stimulation after birth (Schapiro & Vukovich, 1970). It also appears that discrete, time-limited changes in the chemical milieu of the brain can result in long-lasting alterations of brain function. The exposure of the developing brain to androgens—most probably from the fetal gonad in the normal human male—is the most likely determinant of "male" (tonic) hypothalamic function, at least with respect to the hypothalamopituitary-gonadal axis (Gorski, 1971). The neonatal exposure of experimental animals to exogenous glucocorticoids can delay considerably the maturation of the hypothalamopituitary–adrenal cortical axis (A. N. Taylor, Lorenz, & Turner, 1976). Because glucocorticoids are an important hormonal influence on immune mechanisms, it is possible to hypothesize that intrauterine changes in the glucocorticoid milieu of the human fetus, perhaps brought about by psychologically induced adrenocortical stress responses in the mother, could result in altered maturation of the hypothalamopituitary–adrenal cortical axis in the offspring, leading to altered immune mechanisms, especially in view of evidence for hypothalamic regulation of immunity (Korneva & Khai, 1963). This sequence is, of course, pure speculation at present.

We (Solomon, Levine, & Kraft, 1968) have referred to our own work on early infantile stimulation altering adult humoral immunity in the rat, which most likely is based on experiential effects on maturation of hypothalamic function in view of the fact that other physiological parameters modified by early experience are thought to have hypothalamic mediation (Levine, 1966).

## PSYCHOLOGICAL STRESS: SPECIFIC OR NONSPECIFIC?

Selye (1973) has stated, "Everybody knows what stress is, and nobody knows what it is." In these words, Selye summed up decades of debate about the nature of stress. Following on Cannon's classic formulation of the activation of the sympathoadrenal medullary axis as part of the fight-or-flight reaction to environmental threat, Selye discovered activation of the pituitary–adrenocortical axis in many instances of physical and psychological stress. So frequent and nonspecific was this hormonal response that he termed it the *general adaptation syndrome*. Further, Selye (1973) defined stress as "the non-specific response of the body to any demand made on it," and he defined as *stressors* the demands themselves. Selye's semantics, however, have not gained widespread acceptance; the term *stress* is used, in the main, to denote pressing external demands on the organism, not its response (Mason, 1975b). Attempts at physiological reductionism of the stress concept, such as considering stress as any circumstance that causes adrenocortical activation (Ganong, 1963), lack heuristic value because they are tautologous. A host of experimental stress situations, both naturally occurring and contrived in the laboratory, have been used to provoke measurable physiological responses (Levi, 1972). Social as well as physical parameters differ considerably among these situations, so that descriptors must be sought that characterize each situation individually. Perhaps the best operational approach to the concept of stress in humans is the decomposition of external environmental demands into several dimensions of social interaction, for example, relationships (involvement, peer cohesion, support), personal development (autonomy, responsibility, practical orientation), and system maintenance (organization, clarity, control, work pressure, innovation or change) (Kiritz & Moos, 1974). Such an operational social definition of stress permits the correlation of dimensions such as activity and coping behavior with physiological changes such as adrenocortical activation (Gal & Lazarus, 1975).

Of considerable practical importance is the consideration of the relative specificity versus nonspecificity of stress responses; in other words, do all stress situations provoke the same physiological responses? Historically, as mentioned, the early work of Cannon and Selye suggested that major components of all stress reactions were the sympathoadrenal medullary fight-or-flight response and the pituitary–adrenocortical general adaptation response. The latter, particularly, was said to respond to a host of diverse, noxious stimuli, some of which even were opposite, such as hot and cold environments. A series of carefully controlled experiments by Mason (Mason, 1971, 1975a; Mason, Maher, Hartley, 1976, Mougey, Perlow, & Jones, 1976) over a 15-year period, using chair-restrained monkeys, has shown, however, that the adrenocortical response to different stresses is specific, being enhanced during cold exposure; suppressed during heat exposure; unchanged during fasting when nonnutritive food pellets were provided; and of crucial importance, increased in all those situations with a psychological stress component, such as capture, chair restraint, and footshock avoidance. In humans, studies (Gal & Lazarus, 1975; Miller, Rubin, Clark, Crawford, & Arthur, 1970; Rahe, Rubin, & Arthur, 1974; Rubin, Rahe, Arthur, & Clark, 1969) of naturally occurring stresses indicated that adrenocortical activation precedes an unfamiliar experience, undergoes rapid adaptation as mastery over the situation is gained, and is higher when some kind of task performance (coping) is required. Here, the operational definition of stress along the aforementioned social-interactional dimensions (duration, intensity, ambient noise and temperature, etc.) permits the delineation of specific factors that result in activation of this hormonal axis. The multiplicity of other hormone responses to stress we consider in a later section.

## NEUROTRANSMITTERS AND STRESS

Since the 1960s considerable research has focused on the effect of environmental stress on neurotransmitter function in the brain and the importance of neurotransmitters in brain–body mechanisms. The putative CNS neurotransmitters that have been most extensively investigated are the catecholamines DA and NE the indoleamine 5-HT, and ACh. These are but four of a host of postulated CNS neurotransmitters, including these and other biogenic amines; amino acids such as $\gamma$-aminobutyric acid, glycine, and histamine; and polypeptides such as the pituitary-hormone releasing and inhibiting factors, endorphins, and enkephalins (Barchas, Akil, Elliott, Holman, & Watson, 1978). With reference to just one neurotransmitter believed important in CNS arousal and alerting, NE, studies (Bliss & Ailion, 1969; Bliss & Zwanziger, 1966; Bliss, Ailion, & Zwanziger, 1968; Smookler & Buckley, 1969; K. M. Taylor & Laverty, 1969; Thierry, Javoy,

Glowinski, & Kety, 1968) in animals have demonstrated directly that there is an increased turnover of brain NE under various experimental stress conditions. Analogous studies are very difficult in humans because CNS neurotransmission must be measured indirectly. Because the same neurotransmitters exist in much greater amounts throughout the rest of the body, assay of these substances and their metabolites in most body fluids does not suffice for elucidating neurotransmitter changes in the CNS. Two possibilities are the measurement of neurotransmitters and their metabolites in the CSF and the measurement of those metabolites relatively specific for CNS neurotransmission. With reference to the former, the levels of CSF metabolites determined from lumbar puncture do not reflect regional CNS neurotransmitter activity but, rather, are more or less integrated measures of such activity throughout the entire CNS, including the spinal cord. With reference to the latter possibility, much attention has focused on urine and CSF MHPG as the NE metabolite best reflecting CNS, as opposed to peripheral, NE metabolism (Ebert & Kopin, 1975). Increased urine MHPG excretion has been found in normal, young, adult men (naval aviators) during a high-stress situation (aircraft carrier landings) (Rubin, Miller, Clark, Poland, & Arthur, 1970), suggesting that a stress-related increase in CNS NE turnover can occur in humans as well as in laboratory animals. The concentration of NE, as well as of other biogenic amine neurotransmitters, is particularly high, as already mentioned, in the hypothalamus, an area in which lesions have been shown to alter immune responsivity via neural and hormonal pathways (Stein, Schiavi, & Camerino, 1976). Therefore, CNS neurotransmitter alterations in humans under stress conditions might result in important neural and hormonal changes that could alter susceptibility to the development of cancer.

## STRESS–ENDOCRINE INTERRELATIONS

Some historical aspects of stress-endocrine relationships already have been presented, in particular Cannon's (1932) and Selye's (1973) concepts of increased adrenal medullary and adrenolcortical hormone secretion, respectively. Research on these two endocrine axes has continued to the present time. Some older constructs have been discarded, for example, the idea that "anger in" as an emotional response is associated with a greater urine epinephrine: NE excretion ratio than "anger out." Other constructs have been refined by newer data, for example, that adrenocortical activation occurs in those situations with a psychological stress component (Mason, 1971, 1975; Mason, Maher, Hartley, Mougey, Perlow, & Jones, 1976), particularly as an anticipatory response; that it can be chronic, but with fairly rapid adaptation to superimposed discrete stresses (Rubin, Rahe, Arthur, & Clark, 1969); and that it tends to be greater when task performance is part of the stress situation (Gal & Lazarus, 1975; Miller et al., 1970). More recently, development of radioimmunoassays for the measurement of many steroid and polypeptide hormones (Yalow, 1978) has permitted the investigation of stress effects on a number of individual hormone axes.

## ACTH

As already mentioned, the common denominator for the provocation of ACTH and cortisol secretion by environmental demands is the presence of psychological stress, frequently as an anticipatory reaction to an impending, novel situation. This acute stress can be superimposed on a chronic adrenocortical stress reaction, as exemplified by the study of Navy underwater demolition-team trainees (Rubin, Rahe, Arthur, & Clark, 1969). Other stresses, such as surgery, regulaly evoke an adrenocortical response (Ichikawa, Kawagoe, Nichikai, Yoshida, & Homma, 1971; Newsome & Rose, 1971; Yalow, Versano-Aharon, Echemendia, & Berson, 1969), but the pharmacological effects of premedication and anesthesia complicate the psychological stress component of the surgical experience. Physical exercise per se can produce a moderate release of cortisol (Brandenberger & Follenius, 1975). Although ACTH and β-lipotropin-β-melanacyte-stimulating hormone (MSH) are secreted together in most instances (Hirata, Sakamoto, Matsukura, & Imura, 1975), there may be circumstances in which their secretion is dissociated (Kastin, Beach, Hawley, Kendall, Edwards, & Schally, 1973).

## GH

GH secretion is provoked by a variety of stimuli, related both to stress and to caloric homeostasis (G. M. Brown & Reichlin, 1972). By and large, the ACTH and GH responses to stress are dissimilar (G. M. Brown & Reichlin, 1972; Charters, Odell, & Thompson, 1969; Greene, Conron, Schalch, & Schreimer, 1970; Ichikawa et al., 1971; Newsome & Rose, 1971; Yalow et al., 1969). GH stress responsivity may be related to such personality characteristics as "neuroticism" (Miyabo, Asato, & Mizushima, 1977; Miyabo, Hisada, Asato, Mizushima, & Ueno, 1976), field independence (W. A. Brown & Heninger, 1976), and "coronary-proneness" (M. Friedman, Byers, Rosenman, & Neuman, 1971), but these dimensions of individual personality are rather evanescent, being, in part, constructs derived from experimental methodology. In the main, the determinants of GH stress responsivity have proven to be rather elusive. One interesting correlation is the low GH secretion and small stature associated with emotional deprivation in young children ("psychosocial dwarfs") (Powell, Hopwood, & Barratt, 1973). Although these children do respond to environmental (including nutritional) enrichment with catch-up growth, the long-term ramifications of the deprivation on the maturation of other endocrine systems and immune mechanisms is yet unknown.

## PRL

PRL also is a stress-responsive anterior pituitary hormone in humans (Noel, Dimond, Earll, & Frantz, 1976; Noel, Suh, Stone, & Frantz, 1972; Sowers, Raj, Hershman, Carlson, & McCallum, 1977), with a secretion pattern different from that of GH (Miyabo, Asato, & Mizushima, 1977). The metabolic importance of stress-related PRL secretion is mostly unknown, although one endocrine consequence is stress-induced galactorrhea (Corenblum & Whitaker, 1977). Possible relationships between hormone-sensitive mammary neoplasias and stress-induced alterations of PRL remain speculative.

## TSH and Thyroid Hormones

Early studies of thyroid function during stress situtations in humans yielded conflicting data, but the general impression was that stress induced an acute increase in thyroid activity (Dwehurst, Kabir, Harris, & Mandelbrote, 1968). That hyperthyroidism (Graves's disease) sometimes acutely follows an emotional stress, particularly an object loss, is a relatively old observation (Mandelbrote & Wittkower, 1955). Direct measurement of TSH by radioimmunoassay has indicated, however, that very small increases in TSH, if any, follow psychological stress situations, such as anticipation of severe exercise (Charters et al., 1969; Mason, Hartley, Kotchen, Wherry, Pennington, & Jones, 1973). Whereas cold stress produces a prompt increase in TSH secretion in infants and children, this response appears to be lost in the human adult (Fisher & Odell, 1971). A history of postpartum illness in the mother is sometimes obtained in hyperthyroid patients, perhaps implying early maternal neglect and raising the question whether loss or threat of loss may be associated with a physiological response to cold in some people.

Volpe (1978) strongly supports the notion of a relationship of stress to Graves's disease and, most relevantly, suggests than an immunosuppressive mechanism may be involved. Immunosuppressive therapy can initiate hyperthyroidism (McDougall, Greie, Gray, & Smith, 1971). Volpe speculates that stress might suppress the surveillance capacity of specific suppressor T cells in genetically predisposed people, rendering it impossible for a particular clone of thyroid-directed "helper" T cells to be suppressed. Once initiated, hyperthyroidism itself may be a "stress" that could be immunosuppressive, and there is some evidence that thyroxine may effect T-cell function (Sorkin & Besedovsky, 1976).

## Gonadotropins, LH, FSH, and Gonadal Steroids

Although a number of stress studies have found variable changes in gonadotropin levels in blood (Carstensen, Amer, Wide, & Amer, 1973; Charters et al., 1969; Guevara, Luria, & Wieland, 1969; Matsumoto, Takeyasu, Mizutani, Hamanaka, & Uozumi, 1970; Monden, Koshiyama, Tanaka, Mizutani, Aono, Hamahaka, Uozumi, & Matsumoto, 1972; Nakashima, Koshiyama, Uozumi, Monden, Hamanaka, Kurachi, Aono, Mizutani, & Matsumoto, 1975; Oyama, Maeda, & Kudo, 1976), most such studies have shown a clear decrease in testosterone levels during stress, with a poststress recovery to normal levels (Kreuz, Rose, & Jennings, 1972; Matsumoto et al., 1970; Monden et al., 1972; Nakashima et al., 1975; Rose, Bourne, Poe, Mougey, Collins, & Mason, 1969). As with the other hormones, the metabolic significance of this stress-induced testosterone decrease is not known, although hypotheses about it have been put forward (*vide infra*).

Other hormones as well have been shown to be stress-responsive. Both pain and induced motion sickness cause secretion of the posterior pituitary hormone basopressin (Felsl, Gottsmann, Eversmann, Jehle, & Uhlich, 1978; Kendler, Weitzman, & Fisher, 1978), and a general stress-antidiuresis has been recognized for a long while. In nonhuman primates glucagon secretion also has been shown to be stress-responsive, but each appears to have its own stress-related secretion pattern.

Imporant questions, addressed comprehensively by Mason (1968), are how these multiple hormone responses may be interrelated and what their ultimate metabolic effects at the target tissue level may be. Many of these hormones have competing metabolic effects, for example, the protein-catabolic–gluconeogenic effect of adrenal glucocorticoids and the protein-anabolic effect of gonadal steroids and insulin. The ultimate metabolic consequences of a given hormone most probably are influenced strongly by the existing overall hormonal milieu. For example, it has been suggested (Rubin, 1975) that the large slow-wave sleep-related secretory peak of GH in the first few hours of the night, occurring at a time when glucocorticoid secretion is at its 24-hr nadir, plays a role in brain-protein synthesis and consolidation of memory for the prior day's events.

Mason (1975a), again on the basis of considerable experimental evidence, has suggested that the multiple endocrine responses to an acute stress are organized in a catabolic–anabolic sequence. Using the stress paradigms of 72-hr footshock exposure in chair-restrained monkeys and naturally occurring stress situations in humans, Mason found immediate increases in the output of protein-catabolic energy-promoting hormones, including cortisol, GH, epinephrine, and NE. Concomitantly, protein-anabolic hormones, including the gonadal steroids and insulin, were suppressed. Following the stress, the former group of hormones returned to base line, while the output of the latter group increased. Mason considers this pattern of responses to be organized around on overall hormone balance resulting in enhanced availability of energy substrate (glucose) during the stress, as a preparation for fight-or-flight, and then poststress restoration of protein and other tissue stores (e.g., glycogen) via the anabolic hormones. From these data Mason (1968) suggested that there is a CNS "organizer" of these multiple hormone responses, via the ANS and the hypothalamopituitary endocrine axes.

## CHRONOBIOLOGY OF ENDOCRINE RESPONSES

It now is well known that most hormones are secreted in a pulsatile, episodic fashion. Many hormones have unique 24-h secretion rhythms, some of which are entrained to the sleep–wake cycle. For example, in the normal adult, PRL secretion increases during nocturnal sleep and daytime naps; GH is secreted in conjunction with slow-wave (Stage 3–4) sleep; TSH and parathyroid hormone secretion increase during sleep; and ACTH and cortisol secretion increase markedly during the last few hours of nocturnal sleep (Rubin, 1975; Rubin & Poland, 1976). Some biologic rhythms, such as ACTH-cortisol and body temperature, are considered truly *circadian* in that they remain close to a 24-h rhythm when subjects are studied in special environments without light–dark or time cues. Other 24-h rhythms, which are entrained by the light–dark (and wake–sleep) cycle, break up when they become free-running under these experimental circumstances (Halberg, 1975). In mammals these rhythms are neurally controlled, both by an "internal oscillator" in the brain, which maintains circadian rhythms when entraining cues are absent, and by the light–dark cycle, which appears to influence rhythms directly via a retinohypothalamic pathway (R. Y. Moore, 1978).

The rhythmic nature of hormone-secretion patterns adds another dimension to stress-endocrine interrelations. In the preceding section considered the organization of psychoendocrine responses with particular emphasis on the catabolic-anabolic sequence of hormone responses, first in preparation for fight-or-flight activity and then for restoration of body stores and function. Implicit in this catabolic–anabolic sequence is the concept of homeostasis; that is, the organism's balanced physiology is perturbed by stress and restored poststress. It also may be, however, that stress-induced alterations of normal phase relations among endocrine rhythms have an adverse impact on overall hormone balance, leading to prolonged disturbances in physiological function (Curtis, 1972). These chronobiologic alterations could come about as a result of disrupted living schedules, such as stress-induced sleep–wake alterations, with interindividual differences in the ability to synchronize hormone and other rhythms to the environmental cycles. In one study (Lund, 1974), 7 of 34 subjects living under constant conditions without time cues showed internal desynchronization of activity and temperature rhythms; during this time, these 7 subjects scored significantly higher on neuroticism and physical-ailment questionnaires than did the other 27 subjects.

Mechanisms of immunity also show a 24-h periodicity, most likely in response to neural, hormonal, and other influences. It is well-known that the lymphocyte count in peripheral blood varies inversely with the circadian rhythm of cortisol. It also has been shown, however, that the transformability of lymphocytes by phytohemagglutinin (PHA) (and by tuberculin–purified protein derivative (PPD), etc.) varies directly with the cortisol rhythm (Tavadia, Fleming, Hume, & Simpson, 1975). In 180 normal human volunteers, the area of skin induration in response to tuberculin–PPD was positively related to the circadian corticosteroid rhythm in blood, with the greatest immune responses occurring when the tests were done at 0700–0800 h (Cove-Smith, Kabler, Pownall, & Knapp, 1978). Thus, in spite of reduced numbers, lymphocytes stimulated by high circulating glucocorticoids appear to contribute to an enhanced, overall, cell-mediated immune response. The implications of these findings for the chronobiology of immune mechanisms undoubtedly are important but remain to be elucidated.

## STRESS AND IMMUNITY

Isolation of stress-dependent elements of the immune system is likely to require simple models that reflect relatively limited areas of the immune system. Minimally, one can divide the immune response into two spheres or branches: that concerned with the induction of immunity (the afferent branch) and that which refers to the effects of the immune system, once activated, on invaders and on the immunized organism itself (the efferent branch). The elements of the immune response proper are T cells, B cells, and macrophages. The end products are antibodies and effector lymphocytes that act in a variety of ways to remove noxious stimuli. Suppression or enhancement of this first branch would thus lead to an increase or a decrease in the production of antibodies and of immune-effector cells.

The second, or effector, branch of the immune response involves antibodies attaching to noxious stimuli, thereby either activating complement components that act directly on toxic agents or causing activation of phagocytes that serve to remove such agents. Antibodies of a particular type, IgE, are those chiefly responsible for direct toxic (i.e., allergic) effects within the organism. These effects are mediated by *mast cells*, which are induced to release a number of toxic factors, among them 5-HT, when an antigen interacts with cell-bound IgE. The second mediating element of this effector branch is the *lymphokines*, which are materials produced by T cells and which can activate macrophages, enhance B-cell antibody-producing capacity, and kill cells directly. Killing of cells can also occur through their direct contact with T cells or with a different kind of lymphocytes known as K cells; the latter require antibody for effector action. ["Natural" killer (NK) cells, thought to be the first line of defense against cancer-cells, do not require antibodies.] Interference with the effector branch of the response thus could result in enhancement or decrease of complement factors, protection of the targets of the products of complement, modification of the effects of complement on chemotaxis or on phagocyte activation, and ensuing release of hydrolytic enzymes. The effects of lymphokines could be interfered with by reducing their production at the level of the T cell or by inhibiting their effects on other cells, lymphocytes, or macrophages. Finally, toxic consequences of T-cell action, such as direct killing of target cells or release of hydrolytic enzymes from macrophages, could be inhibited by steroids. These possibilities have been studied to some extent; others, such as the effect on K cells, are currently being investigated (Strom & Carpenter, 1977).

It is clear that experiments that specifically study either the induction phase or the effector phase of the immune response, rather than disease entities, are more likely to lead to the identification of stress-responsive mechanisms. A further level of definition is obtained by in vitro experiments, which in the last 15 years have opened up the field of cellular immunology. This approach has lead to the identification of a number of different T- and B-cell populations and of the various cell-to-cell interactions that regulate the immune system. It has also led to the definition of a number of mutually regulatory factors produced by these cells.

Following is a very brief outline of the elements of the immune system and their development. Both lymphocytic cell lines—T cells and B cells—are produced in the bone marrow. The T cell is differentiated in the thymus in several steps driven by thymic hormones (Luckey, 1973). During differentiation the cell becomes progressively more susceptible to damage by corticosteroids (Claman, 1975). It is released into the bloodstream and undergoes further changes, in particular in lymphoid tissues. The end result of this differentiation in the periphery are cell populations prepared to respond to antigens. These T-cell populations can be clearly classified into three subclasses: one concerned with the "helper" function, a function that consists in recognizing foreign materials and in assisting B cells in the task of making antibodies; a second concerned with a cytotoxic or suppressor function; and a third that serves as a precursor of the other two and acts in graft rejection (Canter & Boyse, 1977). The cytotoxic action results in the elimination of unwanted target cells, such as tumor cells, virus-infected cells, and allogeneic cells. The suppressor action is a feedback mechanism that suppresses the proliferation of other T cells as well as that of B cells; that is, it leads to suppression of immune response. The B cell has the primary function of producing antibody. It is reported, however, to be steroid responsive; and both enhancement of activity (Fauci, Pratt, & Whalen, 1977) and damage (Dumont & Barrois, 1977) by steroids have been reported.

The macrophage plays a central role in the immune response, serving to present antigens to both T and B cells for recogntiion and subsequent induction of immune responses. It also is the prime effector cell of the immune response, carrying out the mandates of the immune system by ingesting and digesting noxious stimuli or by releasing lysosomal hydrolytic enzymes in focuses of infection and tumor growth. It can also release factors that serve to repress or stimulate the immune response (Unaure, 1972). The macrophage has been shown to be steroid responsive (Hunninghake & Fauci, 1977), being both activated and deactivated depending on the level of steroids.

## Animal Experiments

Gisler and co-workers (Gisler, Bussard, Mazie, & Hess, 1971; Gisler, Schenkel, & Hullinger, 1971) have carried out a series of very interesting in vitro experiments on the immunologic effects of stress. The model is an acutely stressed mouse, from which the spleen is removed at various periods following stress. The spleen was used as a source of immunocompetent cells for induction of cells producing antibody against spleen erythrocytes. It was shown that the stress severely represses the capacity of donor spleens to mount the in vitro response for 24–72 h. The stress affects the settling out of injected B cells in the spleen. B cells supplemented to the in vitro system can, to some extent, reverse the effects of stress, but macrophages appear to be essential to obtain this effect. Thus, it is quite possible that an important direct effect of stress is on the macrophages of the stressed animal. Experiments (Gisler, Schenkel, & Hullinger, 1971) indicated that this effect could be approximately mimicked by ACTH administration and that it may be counteracted by somatotropin. Neither Gisler nor we have been able to repress in vivo responses significantly by such hormone administration in mice. Possibly feedback actions, which may limit the response in normal animals, are also affected by the stress, making the end result the same in both groups. Alternatively, the response in stressed animals could occur mainly in the lymph nodes and not in the spleen.

Monjan and Collector (1977) have shown that the response of lymphocytes to a lymphoproliferative agent (PHA) in vitro is severely affected by sound stress administered to the cell donor. A significant decrease in response, which with continuous stress is reversed, is followed by an increase in stimulation and finally by a further and perhaps permanent decrease. The authors postulate that direct effects on T cells account for the phenomena observed. As this stimulation is known to be macrophage-dependent (H. Friedman, 1978), it would have been of interest to supplement macrophages of normal animals to the assay system. Direct effects on T cells were demonstrated, however, by the decrease of the cytotoxic effects of immune lymphocytes on target cells. This type of experiment offers an important model for further studies of hormonal influences on immune responses. In our hands, crowding of rats, which can affect steroid levels (Amkraut, Solomon, & Kraemer, 1971), has not given rise to changes in this response (unpublished data); but others (Joasoo & McKenzie, 1976) have shown suppressive effects in that system. It is clear from Monjan's experiments that the time factor must be given serious consideration. Folch and Waksman (1974), also postulated that suppression of PHA-induced proliferation following stress was due to an effect of T cells. Supplementing the assay system with macrophages counteracted this effect, however, and the possibility that these were indeed the population chiefly affected by stress must be contemplated.

The effect of stress on antibody production in the whole animal has been studied by a number of investigators. We (Solomon, 1969) have shown that antibodies to flagellin can be significantly suppressed by stress, but it is of importance to note that, of four stresses applied, only one was effective in causing a significant reduction. These experiments showed that both primary and secondary antibody responses were inhibited, indicating that the effects were probably on both T and B cells. We (Solomon, Levine, & Kraft, 1968) furthermore have shown that early experience—daily handling of rats from birth to 21 days—increases response to primary and secondary challenge, the former more pronouncedly. We have also shown that stress-induced antibody suppression occurs only if stress is administered immediately before and immediately after the inoculation with antigen. Stress applied several days following inoculation is ineffective. This result replicates findings with many immunosuppressive agents.

Aside from these in vitro experiments, little direct experimentation has been carried out to determine the effect of stress on cell-mediated immunity as reflected in the generation of helper and cytotoxic lymphocytes. It should be noted that the above-mentioned suppression of in vitro cytotoxicity may very well reflect the killer ability of the cells rather than the number of effector lymphocytes present in the assay system.

We (Amkraut & Solomon, 1973) have studied the effects of alterations of feeding schedules, which present a significant and steroidogenic stress for the animal, on the immune response. For this purpose we sued the graft-versus-host (GVH) reaction, a response measured by increase in popliteal lymph node weight following footpad injection of parenteral lymphocytes in $F_1$ hybrids. Because the recipient possesses all the histocompatibility antigens of the donor, but not vice versa, the response is initiated by the donor lymphocytes introduced into the "foreign" system. Elements of the recipient—macrophages and lymphocytes—will, however, compound the response once the introduced lymphocytes start producing effector substances that attract other cells. Stress applied for 7 days before and during the response significantly reduces the lymph node size. Discontinuing stress on the day of injection abolishes stress effect; on the other hand, stress applied for 3 days after injection significantly depresses the response. We have shown by $^{125}$I-desoxyuridine uptake and by second-transfer experiments that donor lymphocytes are capable of proliferation. We therefore concluded that the major effects of this stress were on the ability of the donor cells to recruit elements of the host for the response. Although this would indicate that the bulk of the effects of stress lie in this instance in the effector branch, such effects, in the case of this reaction, cannot however, be readily divorced from those impinging on induction of the response. The anatomic structure of a site, which controls cell-cell interactions, is of fundamental importance in the induction phase. Lymphokines and macrophage effector substances also contribute significantly to the nature and magnitude of this phase. That stress can affect effector reactions was shown by us in several experiments. The stress of overcrowding or group housing causes significant increase in the inflammation of adjuvant-induced arthritis (Amkraut, Solomon, & Kraemer, 1971). We have already mentioned our experiments on Moloney virus–induced sarcoma. Stress effects on maximal tumor size are most probably indicative of a disturbance of effector functions. We have also shown (Rosenberg, Amkraut, & Solomon, 1970) that housing stress can increase complement levels in animals (group-housed male Balb/C mice), which may lead to increased inflammation in the presence of antigen-antibody reactions.

## Human Studies

Bartrop (Bartrop, Luckhurst, Lazarus, Kiloh, & Penny, 1977) investigated the effects on immune function of the loss of a spouse in 26 bereaved subjects compared with normal controls. [Bereavement has been shown to be associated with increased mortality and morbidity (Parkes & Brown, 1972; Rees & Lutkins, 1967).] He found lymphocyte response to PHA in spouses significantly suppressed at 8 weeks; to concanavalin A, at 6 weeks. There were no significant differences, however, between bereaved and control groups in terms of T- and B-cell numbers, serum immunoglobulin and $\alpha_2$ macroglobulin concentrations, immunoglobulins, the presence of four autoantibodies, and delayed skin hypersensitivity. Moreover, differences were not observed in mean serum concentration of thyroxine, triiodothyronine, cortisol, PRL, and GH between bereaved and control groups. The surprising endocrine findings, contrary to the general consensus that adrenal cortical and thyroid hormones are elevated for weeks or months following great stress, may be due to a single blood sample being used for hormone assays (Hamburg, Hamburg, & Barchas, 1975). At the follow-up 6 months later, only one mitogen-induced lymphocyte response reached significance, and by 12 months dose-response curves between subjects and controls could not be separated. A subsequent study (Bartrop, 1979) in 43 bereaved spouses and 39 controls of antibody response to tetanus immunization showed significantly lower base-line antibody levels and a decreased antibody response to tetanus toxoid among bereaved. Thus, psychological stress has been demonstrated to affect both T and B-cell function in humans, as it has in animals.

Palmblad and co-workers of the Karolinska Institute have studied a variety of immunologic and endocrine parameters during experimental stress in humans. They (Palmblad, Levi, Burger, Malander, Westgren, Schenk, & Skude, 1977) found that 10 days of "total energy withdrawal" (i.e., fasting) in healthy, normal-weight-men resulted in early, marked reduction in $T_3$ and elevation of reverse $T_3$, small reductions of blood TSH, pronounced increase in levels of GH but a return toward preexposure levels even before discontinuation of starvation, a minor and gradual enhancement of blood cortisol levels, and an increase in nocturnal urinary-epinephrine excretion. The same starvation stress resulted in significant depression of DNA synthesis by subjects' lymphocytes stimulated in vitro by low doses of pokeweed mitogen and PPD; whereas, there was no effect on the response to concanavalin A. No change was noted in the percentages and total numbers of circulating B and T lymphocytes and monocytes (Holm & Palmblad, 1976). Delayed skin reactivity following intradermal PPD and mumps antigen did not differ from that of nonstarving controls. Implications of those results are somewhat unclear. Pokeweed mitogen stimulates mainly B lymphocytes; concanavalin A, mainly T cells. These results differ from studies (Law, Dudrick, & Abdou, 1973) of people suffering from long-term food deficiencies, in whom depressed response to mitogen has been consistently found and interpreted as T-lymphocyte deficiency. It will be recalled that we (Amkraut, Solomon, Allensmith, McClellan, & Rappaport, 1973) found that the stress of a limited feeding schedule in recipient animals significantly reduced the GVH response; and we contended that the stress was not completely the result of nutritional deprivation, was not mediated exclusively through corticosteroids, chiefly affected either host-cell population composition or the GVH-enhancing release of mediators or both, and might reduce a donor-"suppressor" T-cell population. Palmblad (1976) also found that fasting depressed the bactericidal capacity of polymorphonuclear granuloyctes and, in other work (Palmblad, Cantell, Strander, Fröberg, Karlsson, Levi, Granstrom, & Unger, 1976), that phagocytosis by peripheral blood phagocytes showed a decrease during a 77-h vigil with postexposure "rebound" above preexposure levels. Previously, decreased phagocytosis by granulocytes and macrophages had been shown in surgical patients and in malnourished and obese subjects (Jarstrand, Lahnborg, & Palmblad, 1978).

Palmblad and others (Palmblad, Cantell, Holm, Norberg, Strander, & Sunblad, 1977) also studied the effects of a 77-h vigil on interferon-producing capacity in eight healthy women. Previously, we (Solomon, Merigan, & Levine, 1967) found that the stress of repeated, random electrical shocks preceded by a warning buzzer administered for 5 h before virus inoculation significantly enhanced interferon production in mice. ACTH or corticosterone administered to produce circulatory levels just greater than maximal physiological levels did not alter interferon production; in contrast, adrenalectomized mice had relatively high interferon titers that were not altered by particular corticosterone replacement therapy. We wondered whether antecedent stress "exhausted" the adrenal cortex, producing less adrenal response to the virus insult. Our results are compatible both with Jensen and Rasmussen's (1963) observation of increased resistance to virus infection after two daily periods of sound stress and with Marsh and others' (Marsh, Lavender, Chang, & Rasmussen, 1963) finding of decreased susceptibility to poliomyelitis after 24 h of stress. Palmblad's group's work in human stress conforms to ours in an animal system. The ability of lymphocytes to produce interferon in response to the addition of Sendai virus to blood samples rose during the 77-h vigil and was highest just afterward, when serum cortisol values had reached their lowest level. It seems quite unclear telologically why stress should suppress both humoral and cellular immunity as well as phagocytosis while enhancing production of interferon, which of course is a primary defense against viral infections. That interferon may play a feedback role in regulative control of immune response has been suggested (Baron & Johnson, 1978; Ranney, 1975). Interferon can be stimulated by nonviral antigens. Thus, stress-induced elevation of interferon might be associated with immunosuppression even in the absence of viral disease.

## CNS, HORMONES, AND NEUROREGULATORS AFFECTING IMMUNE RESPONSES

Hormonal mechanisms mediating stress effects on the immune system are still far from being fully understood. Furthermore, different stresses lead to very different effects, and tracing the mechanisms is extremely difficult. One might bridge this gap between the psychological input and the immunologic output by looking at direct effects of CNS manipulations and at effects of neuroendocrines and neuroregulators on the immune response.

Korneva and her group (Korneva & Khai, 1963) have studied the effect on the immune response of hypothalamic stimulation and ablation. They have shown that a destructive lesion in a specific portion of the dorsal hypothalamus leads to complete suppression of primary antibody response and prolonged retention of antigen in the blood, prolonged graft retention, and inability to induce streptococcal-antigen myocarditis in rabbits. The effects can be reversed by growth hormones. Electrical stimulation of the same hypothalamic region enhances antibody response (Korneva, 1967). This group (Konovalov, Korneva, & Khai, 1971) also found that ablation of a hypothalamic region augmented experimental allergic polyneuritis, which is related to the absence of complement-fixing antibodies, which are protective. Macris, Schiavi, Camerino, and Stein (1970) found protection against lethal analphylaxis, low antibody titers, and decreased cutaneous delayed hypersensitivity in guinea pigs with symmetrical lesions in the anterior basal hypothalamus. Earlier, Fessel and Forsyth (1963) had demonstrated changes in $\gamma$-globulin levels by electrical stimulation of the lateral hypothalamus. In our laboratories, Kaspar (Kaspar, Solomon, & Amkraut, 1970) has shown that simultaneous electrolytic lesions of the ventral-medial and posterior nuclei of the hypothalamus significantly impaired the GVH response in the recipient. On the other hand, lesions of the preoptic or anterior nuclei did not change the response. The effective lesions tended to increase thymus and spleen weights rather than decrease them, whereas stress in general significantly decreased thymus weights. Jankovic and Isakovic (1973) also found important depression of immune responses following hypothalamic lesioning. The field has recently been reviewed by Stein et al. (1976).

An important and interesting hypothesis has recently been put forth by Besedovsky and Sorkin (1977) and by Pierpaoli and Maestroni (1977). These authors postulate an effect of the immune response on the endocrine system that would serve as an additional feedback-control system. To prove this point, Besedovsky and Sorkin showed that corticosteroid levels were elevated and thyroxine levels decreased briefly on Days 5–8 following the injection of antigen (Besedovsky & Sorkin, 1977) or skin grafting (Besedovsky, Sorkin, & Keller, 1978)— that is, at a critical point in the immune response. It may be of interest that this point appears to be that at which the effects of $\beta$-adrenergic agents in the graft-rejection response are maximal (Henney & Witzke, 1977) but much beyond the interval during which those agents affect the antibody response (Melmon, Weinstein, Bourne, Shearer, Poon, Kraany, & Segal, 1976). This observation may reflect an effect of these hormones, or of others not measured in these experiments, at points of differentiation of lymphocytes that differ from each other. These authors (Besedovsky, Sorkin, Felix, & Haas, 1977) have reinforced their hypothesis by the demonstration of neuronal responses in the hypothalamus at the same time interval. Similar neuronal responses have been reported by Korneva and Klimenko (1973). In both cases, these responses were detected by implantation of electrodes and the measurement of neuron firings. Besedovsky and Sorkin have shown that this hypothalamic activity was not due to circulating corticosteroids, but possible effects of ACTH were not excluded.

Pierpaoli and Maestroni (1977) showed a rapid rise (2 h) of LH following injection of allogeneic (but not of syngeneic) cells. Earlier, Pierpaoli and Sorkin (1967) had shown that in ontogeny the thymus influences the development of the endocrine system. They suggest that the thymus controls the establishment of self-tolerance via the endocrine system during embryonic development and that it retains some control over endocrine functions in response to antigen administration into adult life. The thymus is a highly stress-responsive organ, and rapid atrophy under acute stress has been frequently found by others and by us.

Although the observation of endocrine effects of induction of immunity is new, the release of neuroregulators, including histamine, 5-HT, and other amines, in the efferent branch of the response is well known. Possible profound effects of such mediators on the CNS should be given serious consideration. In allergic attacks, massive amounts of histamine and 5-HT can be released from mast cells.

These may cause significant effects on the CNS, and psychiatric symptoms accompanying such allergy attacks have been described. Whether such CNS effects can be generated beyond the blood-brain barrier and whether these regulators can affect the immune system through some feedback loop are questions that remain to be answered. The possible role of other stress-responsive factors, for example, endorphins and enkephalins, also requires investigation.

A fruitful area of investigation of the relationship of the CNS to immune response was opened up by the work of Ader and Cohen (1975). They conditioned rats through taste aversion accompanied by cyclophosphamide to respond to the CS as a suppressive agent, as though *it* were accompanied by cyclophosphamide. This observation was confirmed by others (Rogers, Reich, Strom, & Carpenter, 1976). Wayner, Flannery, & Singer (1978) have found that conditioned immunosuppression affects T cell-dependent antigens and, most interestingly, is dependent on the presence of a behavioral response. A number of Soviet authors have claimed in the past to be able to induce specific antibodies by conditioned reflex (Luk'Yanenko, 1961). This observation was puzzling in that it would require from the CNS a complexity in recognition ability similar to that of the immune system. Conditioning of immunosuppression, especially if no specificity is claimed, is quite acceptable, but the interpretation is difficult. Possibly an explanation may be found in the neuroendocrine–immune system feedback loop discussed above, in that a particular constellation of immuno-regulatory hormones is released when conditioner and cyclophosphamide are administered simultaneously and that it is this endocrine constellation that is recalled when the CS is administered alone.

## MECHANISMS OF STRESS–INDUCED EFFECTS ON THE IMMUNE SYSTEM

Knowledge of stress effects on endocrines is greater than that of immunologic effects of the variety of stress-responsive hormones on specific components of the immune response. Because of their many known effects on the immuno-competent cells and their relative reliability as stress indicators, adrenocortico-steroids are most frequently adduced as the prime endocrine intermediate in stress-induced changes in the immune system. There has been excessive emphasis on the effects of corticosteroids; other stress-responsive hormones are probably equally important. Following are some of our reasons for this belief:

Corticosteroids are known not only to suppress but to enhance immunologic functions. Likely, there is an optimal range of corticosteroid level for effective immunologic function, both excessively high or low levels being suppressive, as may well be the case for other stress-responsive hormones. The effects of corticosteroids on the many different aspects of the immune system are not well-understood. Furthermore, there appears to be built into the immune system the ability to resist the action of these hormones (M. R. Moore, Goodrum, Couch, & Berry, 1978).
We (Amkraut & Solomon, 1973) have shown that the effects of food-deprivation stress on the GVH reaction cannot be accurately mimicked by injection of ACTH.
The highly variable response to corticosteroids of different sublines of lympho-

cytes in different species (Clamen, 1972) makes it necessary to look very critically at their effect.

Direct influence of many hormones on immune responses have been demonstrated. Some of these may be modulated by corticosteroids, but their intrinsic importance should be investigated and understood. The importance of receptors for many neuroendocrines and for neuroregulators on immunocompetent cells must be further explored, a most promising area of current research.

Corticosteroid levels in stressed subjects have served, and served well, as the main indicator for the effective induction of stress responses, but we would urge caution in making such elevation a sine qua non requirement in experimentation or interpretation. These hormones may even be somewhat deceptive if used as the sole indicators of stress, as we have shown (Amkraut & Solomon, 1972). Nonetheless, the effects of steroids on the immune system are extensive and probably constitute a large part of the stress-responsive mechanism even though other stress-responsive hormones may be equally important.

Receptors on lymphocytes for catecholamines, prostaglandins, somatostatic hormone, histamine, and insulin have been described (Melmon et al., 1976). β-adrenergic agonists can suppress cytotoxic action of and lymphokine release from lymphocytes. These effects are generally believed to be mediated by elevation of cyclic AMP, which is known to exert this effect. Effects of prostaglandins and catecholamines on macrophages (Ignarro, 1977), which are also steroid-dependent (H. Friedman, 1978) have been reported. Mast cells' release of histamine, 5-HT and slow reactive substance-A (SRS-A) can be inhibited readily by raising intracellular AMP levels (Bourne, Lichtenstein, Melmon, Henney, Weinstein, & Shearer, 1974).

The importance of β-adrenergic and other hormone receptors on lymphocytes is beginning to be understood. Agents that raise intracellular cyclic nucleotide levels have been shown to enhance antibody production (Mozes, Weinstein, Bourne, Melmon, & Shearer, 1974) and graft rejection (Henney & Witzke, 1977), but these materials must be administered in a "window" of 6- to 48-h duration in which the immune response can be significantly altered by the administration of such agents. This window does not occur at the same time in all responses; it can be very close to the administration of the antigen several days later. Obviously, the effect of stresses, particularly intermittent ones, on adrenergic agents must be better understood before the importance of this factor in stress responses can be properly evaluated. It is possible that the existence of a number of such windows explains the general difficulty in obtaining reliable stress effects. It seemed to us often in the course of our experiments that a number of different stresses would have different effects and that the high variability, not so much from animal to animal, but from experiment to experiment, indicates that some factors, perhaps environmental, mediate the direction and magnitude of effects.

Immunosuppressive effects of stress might result from neuroendocrine *enhancement* of any of the variety of biologic inhibitors of lymphoid cell division that function to regulate the immune response. Ranney (1975) outlined a basic concept of continuous, negative regulation of proliferation during the resting state and of cortisol withdrawal following stimulation, with the concomitant appearance of antiactivators (which prevent spurious responses by the division-vulnerable, residual lymphoid clones). Specific and nonspecific inhibitors include low-molecular-weight factors released by lymphoid tissues, macrophage factors, suppression due to cell-to-cell interaction by both stimulated and unstimulated cells, and immunoregulatory γ-globulin, γ-fetoprotein, interferon, and others.

The effects of hormones on the effector branch of the immune response are doubtless significantly mediated by adrenergic receptors on lymphocytes and, in particular, on those mast cells. Elevation of AMP levels leads to inhibition of secretion in both cell systems. Although in some of the assays applied to it, it appears that the macrophage is rather resistant to many outside influences, it nonetheless seems reasonable to investigate its possible role as the main target of stress effects in view of a number of the observations we have mentioned. Many immunologists now ascribe to the macrophage a central role in the immune response. It has also been shown that effects on its various functions may be dissociated and that measuring one will not necessarily yield information on the state of the others (Hadden & England, 1977). The macrophage is known to produce a number of factors that control the immune response, among them a thymus-differentiating factor (Beller, Farr, & Unaure, 1978), a glucocorticoid-resistance factor (M. R. Moore et al., 1978) and immunosuppressive and immuno-enhancing factors (Unaure, 1972). The macrophage is also known to play a key role in immune recognition (Feldmann, Erb, & Dunkley, 1976), and new information indicates that it does indeed play a central role in defenses from tumors (Hibbs, 1974). It has been shown that tumors produce materials that repress macrophages (Normann & Sorkin, 1976). Thus, if a stress of short duration is applied at the point in time at which a tumor cell appears, it may reduce macrophage action. This reduction may allow tumors that would normally have been eliminated to reach the stage where they can effectively suppress first-line defenses by macrophages.

We have already mentioned that the redistribution of lymphocytes is affected by corticosteroids (Spry, 1972). Experiments on this parameter with other hormones are still lacking. The cellular arrangements within the lymphoid system are of such fundamental importance in the immune response that investigation of this aspect of stress effects is sorely needed.

A possible mode of action of noncorticosteroid hormones is on the development of the T-cell. It has been shown that differentiation in the T-cell series mediated by at least one of the thymus factors, thymopoietin, can also be induced by β-adrenergic agonists or by cAMP (G. Goldstein, Scheid, Boyse, Brand, & Gilmour, 1976). Thymopoietin effects in vivo can be demonstrated only in systems that are immunodepressed, and a combination of corticosteroid-induced peripheral suppression and adrenergic effects might lead to notable increases in depression. Inasmuch as adrenergic actions are frequently biphasic depending on dose, one may also expect to see neutralization of otherwise immunosuppressive interventions. Stress effects in thymectomized animals and in those supplemented with thymic factors should be studied. The possibility exists that thymopoietin or other polypeptide thymic hormones comprising "thymosin" might be true neuroendocrines under direct CNS regulation. These hormones act at several points in the maturation of T cells to assure their development and function. Lack of thymic factors may cause immune imbalance and contribute to the etiology of a number of diseases, including possibly cancer (A. L. Goldstein, Thurman, Low, Rossio, & Trivers, 1978). As sensitive assays of circulatory levels of these substances become available, studies should be made of their correlation with levels of stress-responsive hormones in a variety of emotional states in humans and under conditions of experimental stress in animals.

In the 15 years that the pattern of neuroendocrine and immune-system interactions has been emerging, the introduction of new ideas and experimental methods has expanded the vistas of the two underlying sciences tremendously. The current state in this interdisciplinary era is reminiscent of the early days of cellular immunology. New concepts frequently in conflict with long-established ideas are emerging based on experiments that require difficult techniques and are difficult to reproduce. But observations that reinforce each other are being made in different laboratories and are coalescing into a sensible, useful, and exciting pattern.

An unraveling of the nature and mechanisms of stress effects on the immune response may provide a key for understanding psychosomatic aspects of infectious, autoimmune, and neoplastic diseases, and we hope it will have implications for prevention and even amelioration of disease by appropriate psychological intervention in conditions of stress and emotional distress. The emerging field of psychoneuroimmunology can serve to enhance a holistic understanding of the human being's intrinsically interwoven psyche and soma.

# REFERENCES

Ader, R., & Cohen, N. Behaviorally conditioned immunosuppression. *Psychosomatic Medicine*, 1975, *37*, 333–340.

Ader, R., & Friedman, S. B. Differential early experiences and susceptibility to transplanted tumor in the rat. *Journal of Comparative Physiological Psychology*, 1965, *59*, 361–364.

Allison, A. C., & Denman, A. M. Self-tolerance and autoimmunity. *British Medical Bulletin*, 1976, *32*, 124.

Amkraut, A. A., & Solomon, G. F. Stress and murine sarcoma virus (Moloney)–induced tumors. *Cancer Research*, 1972, *32*, 1428–1433.

Amkraut, A. A., & Solomon, G. F. Effects of stress and of hormonal intervention on the graft-versus-host response. In B. D. Jankovic & K. Isakovic (Eds.), *Microenvironmental aspects of immunity*. New York: Plenum, 1973.

Amkraut, A. A., Solomon, G. F., Allansmith, M., McClellan, B., & Rappaport, M. Immunoglobulins and improvement in acute schizophrenic reactions. *Archives of General Psychiatry*, 1973, *28*, 673–677.

Amkraut, A. A., Solomon, G. F., & Kraemer, H. C. Stress, early experience and adjuvant-induced arthritis in the rat. *Psychsomatic Medicine*, 1971, *3*, 203–214.

Barchas, J. D., Akil, H., Elliott, G. R., Holman, R. B., & Watson, S. J. Behavioral neurochemistry: Neuroregulators and behavioral states. *Science*, 1978, *200*, 964.

Baron, S., & Johnson, H. M. 1978. Does interferon help regulate immunity? *Sciences*, 1978, *18*, 18–20, 29.

Bartrop, R. W., Luckhurst, E., Lazarus, L., Kiloh, L. G., & Penny, R. Depressed lymphocyte function after bereavement. *Lancet*, 1977, 834–836.

Bartrop, R. W. An integrated model of bereavement. Personal communication, 1979.

Beller, D. I., Farr, A. G., & Unaure, E. R. Regulation of lymphocyte differentiation proliferation and differentiation by macrophages. *Federal Proceedings*, 1978, *37*, 91.

Besedovsky, H., & Sorkin, E. Network of immune-neuroendocrine interactions. *Clinical and Experimental Immunology*, 1977, *27*, 1–12.

Besedovsky, H., Sorkin, E., Felix, D., & Haas, H. Hypothalamic changes during the immune response. *European Journal of Immunology*, 1977, *7*, 323–325.

Besedovsky, H., Sorkin, E., & Keller, M. Changes in the concentration of corticosterone in the blood during skin-graft rejection in the rat. *Journal of Endocrinology*, 1978, *76*, 175–176.

Bliss, E. L., & Ailion, J. Response of neurogenic amines to aggregation and strangers. *Journal of Pharmacology and Experimental Therapeutics*, 1969, *168*, 258.

Bliss, E. L., Ailion, J., & Zwanziger, J. Metabolism of norepinephrine, serotonin, and dopamine in rat brain with stress. *Journal of Pharmacology and Experimental Therapeutics*, 1968, *164*, 122.

Bliss, E. L., & Zwanziger, J. Brain amines and emotional stress. *Journal of Psychiatric Research*, 1966, *4*, 189.

Bourne, H. R., Lichtenstein, L. M., Melmon, K. L., Henney, C. S., Weinstein, Y., & Shearer, G. M. Modulation of inflammation and immunity by cyclic AMP. *Science*, 1974, *184*, 19–28.

Brandenberger, G., & Follenius, M. Influence of timing and intensity of muscular exercise on temporal patterns of plasma cortisol levels. *Journal of Clinical Endocrinology and Metabolism*, 1975, *40*, 845.

Brown, G. M., & Reichlin, S. Psychologic and neural regulation of growth hormone secretion. *Psychosomatic Medicine*, 1972, *34*, 45–61.

Brown, W. A., & Heninger, G. Stress-induced growth hormone release: Psychologic and physiologic correlates. *Psychosomatic Medicine*, 1976, *38*, 145.

Cannon, W. B. *The wisdom of the body.* New York: Norton, 1932.

Canter, H., & Boyse, E. A. Regulation of immune response by T-cell subclasses. *Immunobiology*, 1977, *1*, 47.

Carstensen, H., Amer, I., Wide, L., & Amer, B. Plasma testosterone, LH and FSH during the first 24-hours after surgical operations. *Journal of Steroid Biochemistry*, 1973, *4*, 605.

Charters, A. C., Odell, W. D., & Thompson, J. C. Anterior pituitary function during surgical stress and convalescence: Radioimmunoassay measurement of blood TSH, LH, FSH and growth hormone. *Journal of Clinical Endocrinology and Metabolism*, 1969, *29*, 63.

Claman, H. N. Corticosteroids and lymphoid cells. *New England Journal of Medicine*, 1972, *287*, 388–397.

Claman, H. N. How corticosteroids work. *Journal of Allergy and Clinical Immunology*, 1975, *55*, 145.

Cohen-Cole, S., Cogeh, R., Stevens, A., Kirk, K., Gaitan, F., Hain, J., & Freeman, A. Psychosocial, endocrine, and immune factors in acute necrotizing ulcerative gingivitis ("trenchmouth"). *Psychosomatic Medicine*, 1981, *43*, 91.

Condon, W. S., & Sander, L. W. Neonate movement is synchronized with adult speech: Interactional participation and language acquisition. *Science*, 1974, *181*, 99.

Corenblum, B., & Whitaker, M. Inhibition of stress-induced hyperprolactinemia. *British Medical Journal*, 1977, *2*, 1328.

Cove-Smith, J. R., Kabler, P., Pownall, R., & Knapp, M. S. Circadian variation in an immune response in man. *British Medical Journal*, 1978, *2*, 253.

Curtis, G. C. Psychosomatics and chronobiology: Possible implications of neuroendocrine rhythms. *Psychosomatic Medicine*, 1972, *34*, 235.

Day, G. The psychosomatic approach to pulmonary tuberculosis. *Lancet*, 1951, 6663.

Dewhurst, K. E., el Kabir, D. J., Harris, G. W., & Mandelbrote, B. M. A review of the effect of stress on the activity of the central nervous-pituitary-thyroid axis in animals and man. *Confina Neurologica*, 1968, *30*, 161.

Dixon, F. J., Feldman, J., & Vasquez, J. Immunology and pathogenesis of experimental serum sickness. In *Cellular and humoral aspects of hypersensitive states.* New York: 1959.

Dixon, F. J., Feldman, J., & Vasquez, J. Experimental glomerulonephritis. *Journal of Experimental Medicine*, 1961, *113*, 899.

Dumont, F., & Barrois, R. Electrokinetic properties and mitogen responsiveness of mouse splenic B and T lymphocytes following hydrocortisone treatment. *International Archives of Allergy and Applied Immunology*, 1977, *53*(4), 283.

Ebert, M. H., & Kopin, I. J. Differential labelling of origins of urinary catecholamine metabolites by dopamine-$C^{14}$. *Transactions of the Association of American Physicians*, 1975, *88*, 256.

Engel, G. Studies of ulcerative colitis: III. Nature of psychologic process. *American Journal of Medicine*, 1953, *19*, 231–256.

Fauci, A. S., Pratt, K. R., & Whalen, G. Activation of human B lymphocytes: IV, Regulatory effects of corticosteroids on the triggering signal in the plaque-forming cell response of human peripheral blood B lymphocytes to polyclonal activation. *Journal of Immunology,* 1977, *119*(2), 598.

Feldmann, M., Erb, P., & Dunkley, M. Lymphocyte and macrophage receptor interaction. In Roland F. Beers, Jr. & Edward G. Basse (Eds.), *For viruses, antigens and antibodies, polypeptide hormones, and small molecules.* New York: Raven, 1976.

Felsl, I., Gottsmann, M., Eversmann, T., Jehle, W., & Uhlich, E. Influence of various stress situations on vasopressin secretion in man. *Acta Endocrinologica,* 1978, *87,* 122.

Fessel, W. J. "Antibrain" factors in psychiatric patients' sera: I. Further studies with hemagglutination techniques. *Archives of General Psychiatry,* 1963, *8,* 614–621.

Fessel, W. J., & Forsyth, R. P. Hypothalamic role in control of gamma globulin levels. *Arthritis and Rheumatism,* 1963, *6,* 770 (abstract).

Fessel, W. J., & Grunbaum, B. W. Electrophoretic and analytical ultracentrifuge studies in sera of psychotic patients: Elevation of $\gamma$-globulins and macroglubulins and splitting of $\alpha_2$-globulins. *Annals of Internal Medicine,* 1961, *54,* 1134.

Fessel, W. J., & Hirata-Hibi, M. Abnormal leukocytes in schizophrenia. *Archives of General Psychiatry,* 1963, *9,* 91–103.

Fessel, W. J., Hirata-Hibi, M., & Shapiro, I. M. Genetic and stress factors affecting the abnormal lymphocyte in schizophrenia. *Journal of Psychiatric Research,* 1965, *3,* 275–283.

Fisher, D. A., & Odell, W. D. Effect of cold on TSH secretion in man. *Journal of Clinical Endocrinology and Metabolism,* 1971, *33,* 859.

Folch, H., & Waksman, H. The splenic suppressor cell: I. Activity of thymus-dependent adherent cells: Changes with age and stress. *Journal of Immunology,* 1974, *113,* 127.

Friedman, H. Macrophages in immunity. *Federal Proceedings,* 1978, *37,* 102.

Friedman, M., Byers, S. O., Rosenman, R. H., & Neuman, R. Coronary-prone individuals (Type A behavior pattern): Growth hormone responses. *Journal of the American Medical Association,* 1971, *217,* 929.

Friedman, S. B., & Glasgow, L. A. Psychologic factors and resistance to infectious disease. *Pediatric Clinics of North America,* 1966, *13,* 315–335.

Fudenberg, H. H. Are autoimmune diseases immunologic deficiency states? *Hospital Practice,* 1968, *3,* 43.

Gal, R., & Lazarus, R. S. The role of activity in anticipating and confronting stressful situations. *Journal of Human Stress,* 1975, *1*(4), 4.

Ganong, W. F. The central nervous system and the synthesis and release of adrenocorticotropic hormone. In A. Nalbandov (Ed.), *Advances in neuroendocrinology.* Urbana: University of Illinois Press, 1963.

Gisler, R. H., Bussard, A. E., Mazie, J. C., & Hess, R. Hormonal regulation of the immune response: Induction of an immune response in vitro with lymphoid cells from mice exposed to acute system stress. *Cellular Immunology,* 1971, *2,* 634–645.

Gisler, R. H., Schenkel, B., & Hullinger, L. Hormonal regulation of immune response: II. Influence of pituitary and activity on immune responsiveness in vivo. *Cellular Immunology,* 1971, *2,* 646.

Goldstein, A. L., Thurman, G. B., Low, T. L., Rossio, J. L., & Trivers, G. E. Hormonal influences on the reticuloendothelial system: Current status of the role of thymosin in the regulation and modulation of immunity. *Journal of the Reticuloendothelial Society,* 1978, *23,* 253–265.

Goldstein, G., Scheid, M., Boyse, A. A., Brand, A., & Gilmour, D. G. Thymopoietin and bursopoietin: Induction signals regulating early lymphocyte differentiation. *Cold Spring Harbor Symposia on Quantitative Biology,* 1976, *41.*

Gorski, R. Gonadal hormones and the perinatal development of neuroendocrine function. In L. Martini & W. Ganong (Eds.), *Frontiers in neuroendocrinology.* New York: Oxford University Press, 1971.

Greene, W. A., Conron, G., Schalch, D. S., & Schreimer, B. F. Psychologic correlates of growth hormone and adrenal secretory responses of patients undergoing cardiac catheterization. *Psychosomatic Medicine,* 1970, *32,* 599–614.

Greenfield, N. S., Roessler, R., & Crosley, A. P., Jr. Ego strength and length of recovery from infectious mononucleosis. *Journal of Nervous and Mental Disease,* 1966, *128,* 125–131.

Guevara, A., Luria, M. H., & Wieland, R. G. Serum gonadotropin levels during medical stress (myocardial infarction). *Metabolism,* 1969, *19,* 79.

Gunderson, E. K., & Rahe, R. H. *Life stress and illness.* Springfield, Ill.: Thomas, 1974.
Habel, K. Immunologic aspects of oncogenesis by polyoma virus. In *Conceptual advances in immunology and oncology.* New York: Harper, 1963.
Hadden, J. W., & England, A. Molecular aspects of macrophage activation and proliferation. In *Immunopharmacology.* 1977.
Halberg, F. Biological rhythms. *Advances in Experimental Medicine and Biology,* 1975, *54,* 1.
Hamburg, D. A. Plasma and urinary corticosteroid levels in naturally occurring psychologic stresses. *Research Publications of the Association Research in Nervous and Mental Disease,* 1962, *40,* 406–413.
Hamburg, D. A., Hamburg, B. A., & Barchas, J. D. In L. Levi (Ed.), *Emotions: Their parameters and measurement.* New York: Raven, 1975.
Heath, R. G., & Krupp, I. M. Schizophrenia as an immunologic disorder. *Archives of General Psychiatry,* 1967, *16,* 1–9.
Hellstrom, K. E., Hellstrom, I., Sjogren, H. O., & Werner, G. A. Cell-mediated immunity to human tumor antigens. In B. Amos (Ed.), *Progress in immunology.* New York: Academic, 1971.
Henney, C. S., & Witzke, F. M. Cholera-enterotoxin induced suppression of effector T-cell function *in vivo* and *in vitro.* In D. Schlessinger (Ed.), *Microbiology.* Bethesda, Md.: American Society for Microbiology, 1977.
Henry, J. P., Stephens, P. M., & Watson, F. M. C. Force breeding, social disorder, and mammary tumor formation in cBA/USC. Mouse colonies: A pilot study. *Psychosomatic Medicine,* 1975, *37,* 277–283.
Hibbs, J. B. Discrimination between neoplastic and non-neoplastic cells in vitro by activated macrophages. *Journal of the National Cancer Institute,* 1974, *53,* 1487.
Hirata, Y., Sakamoto, N., Matsukura, S., & Imura, H. Plasma levels of $\beta$-MSH and ACTH during acute stresses and metyrapone administration in man. *Journal of Clinical Endocrinology and Metabolism,* 1975, *41,* 1092.
Hirschhorn, K., Bach, F., Kolodny, R., Firschein, I., & Hashem, N. Immune response and mitosis of human peripheral blood lymphocytes in vitro. *Science,* 1963, *142,* 1185–1187.
Holm, G., & Palmblad, J. Acute energy deprivation in man: Effect on cell-mediated immunological reactions. *Clinical and Experimental Immunology,* 1976, *25,* 207–211.
Holmes, T. H., & Rahe, R. H. The Social Readjustment Rating Scale. *Journal of Psychosomatic Research,* 1967, *11,* 213.
Hunninghake, G. W., & Fauci, A. S. Immunologic reactivity of the lung: Effects of corticosteroids on alveolar macrophage cytotoxic effector cell function. *Journal of Immunology,* 1977, *118*(1), 136.
Ichikawa, Y., Kawagoe, M., Nishikai, M., Yoshida, K., & Homma, M. Plasma corticotropin (ACTH), growth hormone (GH), and 11-OHCS (hydroxycorticosteroid) response during surgery. *Journal of Laboratory and Clinical Medicine,* 1971, *78,* 882.
Ignarro, J. L. Regulation of polymorphonuclear leukocytes, macrophages and platelets. In *Immunopharmacology.* 1977.
Imboden, J. B., Carter, A., & Leighton, E. C. Convalescence from influenza: A study of the psychological and clinical determinants. *Archives of Internal Medicine,* 1961, *108,* 115–121.
Imboden, J. B., Carter, A., Leighton, E. C., & Trevor, R. W. Brucellosis: III. Psychologic aspects of delayed convalescence. *Archives of Internal Medicine,* 1959, *103,* 406–414.
Jankovic, B. D., & Isakovic, K. Neuro-endocrine correlates of immune response: I. Effects of brain lesions on antibody production: Arthus reactivity and delayed hypersensitivity in the rat. *International Archives of Allergy,* 1973, *45,* 360–372.
Jarstrand, C., Lahnborg, G., & Palmblad, J. Phagocyte function in various situations in surgery. *Acta Chirurgica Scandinavica,* 1978, *482* (Suppl.), 79–82.
Jensen, M. M., & Rasmussen, A. F., Jr. Stress and susceptibility to viral infections. *Journal of Immunology,* 1963, *90,* 21.
Joasoo, A., & McKenzie, J. M. Stress and the immune response in rats. *International Archives of Allergy and Applied Immunology,* 1976, *50,* 659.
Kaplan, S. M., Gottschalk, L. A., & Fleming, D. E. Modifications of oropharyngeal bacteria with changes in the psychodynamic state. *AMA Archives of Neurology and Psychiatry,* 1957, *78,* 656–664.

Kaspar, P., Solomon, G. F., & Amkraut, A. A. Effects of hypothalamic lesions on cellular immunity. Unpublished data, 1970.

Kastin, A. J., Beach, G. D., Hawley, W. D., Kendall, J. W., Edwards, M. S., & Schally, A. V. Dissociation of MSH and ACTH release in man. *Journal of Clinical Endocrinology and Metabolism*, 1973, *36*, 770.

Katz, J., Kunofsky, S., Patton, R., & Alloway, N. Cancer mortality among patients in New York mental hospitals. *Cancer*, 1967, *20*, 2194–2199.

Kendler, K. S., Weitzman, R. E., & Fisher, D. A. The effect of pain on plasma arginine vasopressin concentrations in man. *Clinical Endocrinology*, 1978, *8*, 89.

Kiritz, S., & Moos, R. H. Physiological effects of social environments. *Psychosomatic Medicine*, 1974, *36*, 96–114.

Konovalov, G. V., Korneva, E. A., & Khai, L. M. Effect of destruction of the posterior hypothalamic area on experimental allergic polyneuritis. *Brain Research*, 1971, *29*, 383–386.

Korneva, E. A. The effect of stimulating different mesancephalic structures on protective immune response patterns. *Fiziologicheskii Zhurnal SSSR Simen: I. M. Sechnova*, 1967, *53*, 42–47.

Korneva, E. A., & Khai, L. M. Effect of destruction of hypothalamic areas on immunogenesis. *Fiziologicheskii Zhurmal SSSR imeni I. M. Sechnova*, 1963, *49*, 42–46.

Korneva, E. A., & Klimenko, V. M. Neuronale Hypothalamusaktivitat und homoostatische Reaktionen. *Ergebnisse experimentallen Medizen*, 1973, *23*, 373–382.

Kreuz, L. E., Rose, R. M., & Jennings, J. R. Suppression of plasma testosterone levels and psychological stress: A longitudinal study of young men in officer candidate school. *Archives of General Psychiatry*, 1972, *26*, 479–482.

LaBarba, R. C. Experiential and environmental factors in cancer: A review of research with animals. *Psychosomatic Medicine*, 1970, *32*, 259.

Law, D. K., Dudrick, S. J., & Abdou, N. I. Immunocompetence of patients with protein-calorie malnutrition. *Annals of Internal Medicine*, 1973, *79*, 545.

Leshan, L. L., & Worthington, R. E. Personality as a factor in pathogenesis of cancer: Review of literature. *British Journal of Medical Psychology*, 1956, *29*, 49.

Levi, L. (Ed.). Stress and distress in response to psychosocial stimuli: Laboratory and real life studies on sympathoadrenomedullary and related reactions. *Acta Medica Scandinavica*, 1972, Suppl. 528.

Levine, S. Infantile stimulation and adaptation to stress. In Association for Research in Nervous and Mental Disease (Ed.), *Endocrines and the central nervous system.* Baltimore: Williams & Wilkins, 1966.

Lipsitt, L. P., Mustaine, M. G., & Zeigler, B. Effects of experience on the behavior of the young infant. *Neuropädiatrie*, 1977, *8*, 107.

Luckey, T. D. *Thymic hormones.* Baltimore: University Park Press, 1973.

Luk'Yanenko, V. The problem of conditioned reflex regulation of immunobiological reactions. *Uspekhi Sovremenno: Biologii*, 1961, *51*, 170.

Lund, R. Personality factors and desynchronization of circadian rhythms. *Psychosomatic Medicine*, 1974, *36*, 224.

Macris, N. T., Schiavi, R. C., Camerino, M. S., & Stein, M. Effect of hypothalamic lesions on immune processes in the guinea pig. *American Journal of Physiology*, 1970, *219*, 1205.

Mandelbrote, B. M., & Wittkower, E. Emotional factors in Graves' disease. *Psychosomatic Medicine*, 1955, *17*, 109–117.

Marsh, J. T., Lavender, J. F., Chang, S. S., & Rasmussen, A. F. Poliomyelitis in monkeys: Decreased susceptibility after avoidance stress. *Science*, 1963, *140*, 1414.

Mason, J. W. Over-all hormonal balance as a key to endocrine organization. *Psychosomatic Medicine*, 1968, *30*, 791.

Mason, J. W. A re-evaluation of the concept of "non-specificity" in stress theory. *Journal of Psychiatric Research*, 1971, *8*, 323.

Mason, J. W. Emotion as reflected in patterns of endocrine integration. In L. Levi (Ed.), *Emotions: Their parameters and measurement.* New York: Raven, 1975. (a)

Mason, J. W. A historical view of the stress field. I and II. *Journal of Human Stress*, 1975, *1*(1), 6; *1*(2), 22. (b)

Mason, J. W., Hartley, L. H., Kotchen, T. A., Wherry, F. E., Pennington, L. L., & Jones, L. G. Plasma thyroid-stimulating hormone response in anticipation of muscular exercise in the human. *Journal of Clinical Endocrinology and Metabolism*, 1973, *37*, 103.

Mason, J. W., Maher, J. T., Hartley, L. H., Mougey, E. H., Perlow, M. J., & Jones, L. G. Selectivity of corticosteroid and catecholamine responses to various natural stimuli. In G. Serban (Ed.), *Psychopathology of human adaptation.* New York: Plenum, 1976.

Matsumoto, K., Takeyasu, K., Mizutani, S., Hamanaka, Y., & Uozumi, T. Plasma testosterone levels following surgical stress in male patients. *Acta Endocrinologica,* 1970, *65,* 11.

McClary, A. R., Meyer, E., & Weitzman, D. J. Observations on role of mechanism of depression in some patients with disseminated lupus erythematosus. *Psychosomatic Medicine,* 1955, *17,* 311-321.

McDougall, I. R., Greig, W. R., Gray, H. W., & Smith, J. F. Thyrotoxicosis developing during cyclophosphamide theory. *British Medical Journal,* 1971, *4,* 275.

Melmon, K. L., Weinstein, Y., Bourne, H. R., Shearer, G. M., Poon, T., Kraany, L., & Segal, S. Isolation of cells with specific receptors for amines. In R. F. Beers & E. G. Basset (Eds.), *Opportunities and problems in cell membrane receptors for viruses, antigens and antibodies, polypeptide hormones and small molecules.* New York: Academic, 1976.

Meltzoff, A. N., & Moore, M. K. Imitation of facial and manual gestures by human neonates. *Science,* 1977, *198,* 75.

Miller, R. G., Rubin, R. T., Clark, B. R., Crawford, W. R., & Arthur, R. J. The stress of aircraft carrier landings: I. Corticosteroid responses in naval aviators. *Psychosomatic Medicine,* 1970, *32,* 581.

Minter, R. E., & Kimball, C. P. Life events and illness onset: A review. *Psychosomatic Medicine,* 1978, *19,* 334-339.

Miyabo, S., Asato, T., & Mizushima, N. Prolactin and growth hormone responses to psychological stress in normal and neurotic subjects. *Journal of Clinical Endocrinology and Metabolism,* 1977, *44,* 947.

Miyabo, S., Hisada, T., Asato, T., Mizushima, N., & Ueno, K. Growth hormone and cortisol responses to psychological stress: Comparison of normal and neurotic subjects. *Journal of Clinical Endocrinology and Metabolism,* 1976, *42,* 1158.

Monden, Y., Koshiyama, K., Tanaka, H., Mizutani, S., Aono, T., Hamanaka, Y., Uozumi, T., & Matsumoto, K. Influence of major surgical stress on plasma testosterone, plasma LH and urinary steroids. *Acta Endocrinologica,* 1972, *69,* 542.

Monjan, A. A., & Collector, M. I. Stress-induced modulation of the immune response. *Science,* 1977, *196,* 307.

Moore, M. R., Goodrum, K. J., Couch, R., & Berry, L. J. Factors affecting macrophage function: Glucocorticoid antagonizing factor. *Journal of Ref. Endocrin Society*, 1978, *23,* 321.

Moore, R. Y. Central neural control of circadian rhythms. In W. Ganong & L. Martini (Eds.), *Frontiers in neuroendocrinology* (Vol. 5). New York: Raven, 1978.

Moos, R. H., & Solomon, G. F. Minnesota Multiphasic Personality Inventory response patterns in patients with rheumatoid arthritis. *Journal of Psychosomatic Research,* 1964, *8,* 17-18. (a)

Moos, R. H., & Solomon, G. F. Personality correlates of the rapidity of progression of rheumatoid arthritis. *Annals of Rheumatic Diseases,* 1964, *23,* 145-151.

Moos, R. H., & Solomon, G. F. Personality correlates of the degree of functional incapacity of patients with physical disease. *Journal of Chronic Diseases,* 1965, *18,* 1019-1038. (b)

Moos, R. H., & Solomon, G. F. Psychologic comparisons between women with rheumatoid arthritis and their non-arthritic sisters: I. Personality test and interview rating data. *Psychosomatic Medicine,* 1965, *27,* 135-149. (b)

Moos, R. H., & Solomon, G. F. Psychologic comparisons between women with rheumatoid arthritis and their non-arthritic sisters: II. Content analysis of interviews. *Psychosomatic Medicine,* 1965, *27,* 150-164. (c)

Moos, R. H., & Solomon, G. F. Social and personal factors in rheumatoid arthritis: Pathogenic considerations. *Clinical Medicine,* 1966, *73,* 19-23.

Mozes, E., Weinstein, Y., Bourne, H. R., Melmon, K. L., & Shearer, G. M. *In vitro* correction of antigen induced immune suppression: Effects of histamine, dibutyryl cAMP and cholera toxin. *Cellular Immunology,* 1974, *11,* 57.

Mutter, A. Z., & Schleifer, M. J. The role of psychological and social factors in the onset of somatic illness in children. *Psychosomatic Medicine,* 1966, *28,* 333-343.

Nakashima, A., Koshiyama, K., Uozumi, T., Monden, Y., Hamanaka, Y., Kurachi, K., Aono, T., Mizutani, S., & Matsumoto, K. Effects of general anesthesia and severity of surgical stress on serum LH and testosterone in males. *Acta Endocrinologica,* 1975, *78,* 258.

Newberry, B. H., Frankie, G., Beatty, P. A., Maloney, B. D., & Gilchrist, J. C. Shock stress and DMBA-induced mammary tumor. *Psychosomatic Medicine*, 1972, *34*, 295–303.

Newsome, H. H., & Rose, J. C. The response of human adrenocorticotropic hormone and growth hormone to surgical stress. *Journal of Clinical Endocrinology and Metabolism*, 1971, *33*, 481.

Noel, G. L., Dimond, R. C., Earll, J. M., & Frantz, A. G. Prolactin, thyrotropin, and growth hormone release during stress associated with parachute jumping. *Aviation Space and Environmental Medicine*, 1976, *47*, 543.

Noel, G. L., Suh, H. K., Stone, G., & Frantz, A. G. Human prolactin and growth hormone release during surgery and other conditions of stress. *Journal of Clinical Endocrinology and Metabolism*, 1972, *35*, 840.

Normann, S., & Sorkin, E. Cell-specific defect in monocyte function during tumor growth. *Journal of the National Cancer Institute*, 1976, *57*, 135–140.

Old, L. J., Boyse, E. A., Clarke, D. A., & Carswell, E. A. Antigenic properties of chemically induced tumors. *Annals of the New York Academy of Science*, 1962, *101*, 80.

Oyama, T., Maeda, A., & Kudo, T. Effect of premedication halothane anesthesia and surgery on plasma luteinizing hormone levels in man. *Agressologie*, 1976, *17*, 119.

Palmblad, J. Fasting (acute energy deprivation) in man: Effect on polymorphonuclear granulocyte functions, plasma iron and serum transferrin. *Scandinavian Journal of Hämatology*, 1976, *17*, 217–226.

Palmblad, J., Cantell, K., Holm, G., Norberg, R., Strander, H., & Sunbald, L. Acute energy deprivation in man: Effect on serum immunoglobulins, antibody response, complement Factors 3 and 4, acute phase reactants and interferon-producing capacity of blood lymphocytes. *Clinical and Experimental Immunology*, 1977, *30*, 50–55.

Palmblad, J., Cantell, K., Strander, H., Fröberg, J., Karlsson, C., Levi, L., Granstrom, M., & Unger, P. Stressor exposure and immunological response in man: Interferon-producing capacity and phagocytosis. *Journal of Psychosomatic Research*, 1976, *20*, 193–199.

Palmblad, J., Levi, L., Burger, A., Melander, A., Westgren, U., Schenck, H. von, & Skude, G. Effects of total energy withdrawal (fasting) on the levels of growth hormone, thyrotropin, cortisol, adrenaline, noradrenaline, $T_4$, $T_3$ and $rT_3$ in healthy males. *Acta Medica Scandinavica*, 1977, *201*, 15–22.

Parkes, C. M., & Brown, R. J. Health after bereavement. *Psychosomatic Medicine*, 1972, *34*, 449.

Pierpaoli, W., & Maestroni, G. J. Pharmacological control of the immune response by blockade of the early hormonal changes following antigen injection. *Cellular Immunology*, 1977, *31*, 355–363.

Pierpaoli, W., & Sorkin, E. Relationship between thymus and hypophysis. *Nature*, 1967, *215*, 834.

Pilkington, T. L. Coincidence of rheumatoid arthritis and schizophrenia. *Journal of Nervous and Mental Disease*, 1956, *124*, 604.

Powell, G. F., Hopwood, N. J., & Barratt, E. S. Growth hormone studies before and during catch-up growth in a child with emotional deprivation and short stature. *Journal of Clinical Endocrinology and Metabolism*, 1973, *37*, 674.

Rahe, R. H., Rubin, R. T., & Arthur, R. J. The three investigators study: Serum uric acid, cholesterol, and cortisol variability during stresses of everyday life. *Psychosomatic Medicine*, 1974, *36*, 258.

Ranney, D. F. Biological inhibitors of lymphoid cell division. *Advances in Pharmacology and Chemotherapy*, 1975, *13*, 359.

Rasmussen, A. F., Jr., Spencer, E. S., & Marsh, J. T. Increased susceptibility to herpes simplex in mice subjected to avoidance-learning stress or restraint. *Proceedings of the Society for Experimental Biology and Medicine*, 1957, *96*, 183.

Rees, W. D., & Lutkins, S. G. Mortality of bereavement. *British Medicol. Journal*, 1967, *4*, 13–16.

Riley, V. Mouse mammary tumors: Alterations of incidence as apparent function of stress. *Science*, 1975, *189*, 465–467.

Riley, V., & Spackman, D. Modifying effects of a benign virus on the malignant process and the role of physiological stress on tumor incidence. In *Fogarty International Center Proceedings* No. 28 (DHEW Publication No. 77-893). Washington: U.S. Government Printing Office, 1974.

Riley, V., & Spackman, D. Melanoma enhancement by viral-induced stress. *Pigment Cell,* 1976, *2*, 163–173.

Riley, V., Spackman, D., & Santisteban, G. The role of physiological stress on breast tumor incidence in mice. *Proceedings of the American Association of Cancer Research,* 1975, *16*, 152.

Rogers, M., Reich, P., Strom, T., & Carpenter, C. Behaviorally conditioned immunosuppression. *Psychosomatic Medicine,* 1976, *38*, 447–451.

Roppel, R. M. Cancer and mental illness. *Science,* 1978, *201*, 398.

Rose, R. M., Bourne, P. G., Poe, R. O., Mougey, E. H., Collins, D. R., & Mason, J. W. Androgen responses to stress: II. *Psychosomatic Medicine,* 1969, *31*, 418.

Rosenberg, L. T., Amkraut, A. A., & Solomon, G. F. Stress effects on complement levels. 1970. Unpublished data.

Rothermich, N. O., & Philips, V. K. Rheumatoid arthritis in criminal and mentally ill populations. *Arthritis and Rheumatism,* 1963, *6*, 639–640.

Rubin, R. T. Sleep-endocrinology studies in man. In W. H. Gispen, T. B. van Wimersma Greidanus, B. Bohus, & D. de Wied (Eds.), *Hormones, homeostasis and the brain* (Progress in Brain Research, Vol. 42). Amsterdam: Elsevier, 1975.

Rubin, R. T., Miller, R. G., Clark, B. R., Poland, R. E., & Arthur, R. J. The stress of aircraft carrier landings: II. 3-methoxy-4-hydroxyphenylglycol excretion in naval aviators. *Psychosomatic Medicine,* 1970, *32*, 589–597.

Rubin, R. T., & Poland, R. E. Synchronies between sleep and endocrine rhythms in man and their statistical evaluation. *Psychoneuroendocrinology,* 1976, *1*, 281–290.

Rubin, R. T., Rahe, R. H., Arthur, R. J., & Clark, B. R. Adrenal cortical activity changes during underwater demolition team training. *Psychosomatic Medicine,* 1969, *31*, 553–564.

Schapiro, S., & Vukovich, K. R. Early experience effects upon cortical dendrites: A proposed model for development. *Science,* 1970, *167*, 292.

Schmale, A. H., Jr. The relation of separation and depression to disease. *Psychosomatic Medicine,* 1958, *20*, 259.

Selye, H. The evolution of the stress concept. *American Scientist,* 1973, *61*, 692.

Shukla, H. C., Solomon, G. F., & Doshi, R. P. The relevance of some Ayurvedic (traditional Indian medical) concepts to modern holistic health. *Journal of Holistic Health,* 1979, *4*, 125–131.

Smith, R. T. Potentials for immunologic intervention. In B. Amos (Ed.), *Progress in immunology.* New York: Academic, 1971.

Smookler, H. H., & Buckley, J. P. Relationships between brain catecholamine synthesis, pituitary adrenal function and the production of hypertension during prolonged exposure to environmental stress. *International Journal of Neuropharmacology,* 1969, *8*, 33.

Solomon, G. F. Stress and antibody response in rats. *International Archives of Allergy and Applied Immunology,* 1969, *35*, 97–104.

Solomon, G. F., Allansmith, M., McClellan, B., & Amkraut, A. Immunoglobulins in psychiatric patients. *Archives of General Psychiatry,* 1969, *20*, 272–278.

Solomon, G. F., Levine, S., & Kraft, J. K. Early experience and immunity. Nature, 1968, *220*, 821–822.

Solomon, G. F., Merigan, T. C., & Levine, S. Variations in adrenal cortical hormones within physiologic ranges, stress and interferon production in mice. *Proceedings of the Society for Experimental Biology and Medicine,* 1967, *126*, 74–79.

Solomon, G. F., & Moos, R. H. The relationship of personality to the presence of rhematoid factor in asymptomatic relatives of patients with rheumatoid arthritis. *Psychosomatic Medicine,* 1965, *27*, 350–360.

Sorkin, E., & Besedovsky, H. Hormonal control of immune processes. *Proceedings of the 5th International Congress of Endocrinology,* Hamburg: Excerpts Medica, 1976.

Sowers, J. R., Raj, R. P., Hershman, J. M., Carlson, H. E., & McCallum, R. W. The effect of stressful diagnostic studies and surgery on anterior pituitary hormone release in man. *Acta Endocrinologica,* 1977, *86,* 25.

Spry, C. J. F. Inhibition of lymphocyte recirculation by stress and corticotropin. *Cellular Immunology,* 1972, *4,* 86.

Stein, M., Schiavi, R. C., & Camerino, M. S. Influence of brain and behavior on the immune system. *Science,* 1976, *191,* 435–440.

Strom, T. B., & Carpenter, C. B. Regulation of alloimmunity by cyclic nucleotide. In *Immunopharmacology.* New York: Plenum, 1977.

Tavadia, H. B., Fleming, K. A., Hume, P. D., & Simpson, H. W. Circadian rhythmicity of human plasma cortisol and PHA-induced lymphocyte transformation. *Clinical and Experimental Immunology,* 1975, *22,* 190–193.

Taylor, A. N., Lorenz, R. J., Turner, B. B., Ronnekleiv, O. K., Casady, R. L., & Branch, B. B. Factors influencing pituitary-adrenal rhythmicity: Its ontogeny and circadian variations in stress responsiveness. *Psychoneuroendocrinology,* 1976, *1,* 291.

Taylor, K. M., & Laverty, R. The metabolism of tritiated dopamine in regions of the rat brain in vivo. II. The significance of the neutral metabolites of the catecholamines. *Journal of Neurochemistry,* 1969, *16,* 1367.

Thierry, A. M., Javoy, J., Glowinski, J., & Kety, S. S. Effects of stress on the metabolism of norepinephrine, dopamine, and serotonin in the central nervous system of the rat: I. Modifications of norepinephrine turnover. *Journal of Pharmacology and Experimental Therapeutics,* 1968, *163,* 163.

Trevethan, R. D., & Tatum, J. C. Rarity of occurrence of psychosis and rheumatoid arthritis in individual patients. *Journal of Nervous and Mental Disease,* 1954, *120,* 83.

Unaure, E. R. The regulatory role of macrophages in antigenic stimulation. *Advances in Immunology,* 1972, *15,* 95.

Volpe, R. The pathogenesis of Graves' disease: An overview. *Clinics in Endocrinology and Metabolism,* 1978, *7*(1), 3.

Wayner, E. A., Flannery, G. R., & Singer, G. The effects of taste aversion conditioning on the primary antibody response to sheep red blood cells and *Brucella abortus* in the albino rat. *Physiology and Behavior,* 1978, *21,* 995–1000.

Weiner, H. Some comments on the transduction of experience by the brain: Implications for our understanding of the relationship of mind to body. *Psychosomatic Medicine,* 1972, *34,* 355.

Wolff, P. H. Mother-infant interactions in the first year. *New England Journal of Medicine,* 1976, *295,* 999.

Yalow, R. S. Radioimmunoassay: A probe for the fine structure of biologic systems. *Science,* 1978, *200,* 1236.

Yalow, R. S., Versano-Aharon, N., Echemendia, E., & Berson, S. A. HGH and ACTH secretory responses to stress. *Hormone and Metabolic Research,* 1969, *1,* 3.

Yamada, A., Jensen, M. M., & Rasmussen, A. F., Jr. Stress and susceptibility to viral infections: III. Antibody response and viral retention during avoidance-learning stress. *Proceedings of the Society for Experimental Biology and Medicine,* 1964, *116,* 677.

# 5

# Neuroendocrine Relationships with Stress

*Jane Veith-Flanigan*
*Washington State University, Pullman, United States*

*Curt A. Sandman*
*University of California, Irvine, United States*

Inherent in many psychological and physiological theories of stress is the concept of arousal, which assumes that when an environmental stimulus is of sufficient magnitude and intensity, the organism becomes aroused in order to respond adaptively. Lacy (1967) has argued, however, that the undimensional concept of arousal is both simplistic and false: "Electrocortical arousal, autonomic arousal, and behavioral arousal may be considered to be *different forms* of arousal, each complex in itself. I think the evidence also shows that one cannot easily use one form of arousal as a highly valid index of another" (pp. 16-17). He calls for a broadened interpretation of the role of autonomic activity in governing behavior.

Lacey (1967) bases this need for reinterpretation of the arousal theory on four key concepts derived from his and others' research. First, somatic and behavioral arousal have been shown to be dissociated. Second, autonomic functions considered indicative of arousal have been shown on numerous occasions to be poorly correlated with one another. Third, different stimulus situations reliably produce different patterns of somatic response, a phenomenon termed *stimulus specificity* or *situational stereotypy*. Finally, visceral afferent feedback from the cardiovascular system associated with activation has inhibitory rather than excitatory effects on the CNS.

Another factor, presented by Lacey, that is in opposition to the concept of overall autonomic activation is *response specificity*. This term refers to characteristic, persistent patterns of somatic response displayed by people in response to a variety of environmental events and tasks (Lacey, 1950; Lacey, Bateman, & Van Lehn, 1953). These profiles are characterized by what is termed *organ emphasis*; a person's autonomic responses tend to be arranged in a relatively reproducible, hierarchical pattern with one autonomic index exhibiting the greatest degree of responsivity relative to others (Lacey & Van Lehn, 1952). Lacey has summarized

We would like to express our appreciation to Mark Orling for his work with the graphics and to Don Meyer, Jack George, and J. Dennis Nolan for their helpful comments on an earlier draft of this chapter.

129

what he terms the principle of relative response specificity: "For a given set of autonomic functions (hence, the term relative) subjects tend to respond with an idiosyncratic pattern of autonomic activation in which maximal activation is shown by the same physiological functions, whatever the stress" (Lacey & Lacey, 1958, p. 50). Both the concepts of response specificity and of situational stereotypy, although originally proposed by Lacey in terms of autonomic functioning, may be extended to other areas, for example, neuroendocrine functioning, particularly with regard to hormonal responsivity to stress.

At present, the concept of stress has evolved to encompass all possible extraindividual events capable of evoking a broad spectrum of intraindividual responses mediated by a complex filter labeled "individual differences." In this sense, most present-day theories of stress are essentially hourglass models. Within this general hourglass conception of stress, differing emphases have been placed on critical factors for defining and understanding stress. Three general approaches may be delineated: a focus solely on environmental stimuli, a focus on the bodily response, or a focus on the interaction between the person and the environment. None of these approaches has proved adequate.

Perhaps one means of solving the dilemma of the definition of stress would be to incorporate two models provided by Holmes and Rahe (1967) and Mason (1975a). Holmes and Rahe have proposed that stress may be considered to be any event occurring in the environment, a definition that chooses to ignore the person's response configuration. Therefore, the difficulty of predicting which event will be found to be stressful is short-circuited by assuming that all events possess the potential to evoke a stress response.

The second aspect of the definition is provided by Mason's (1975a) proposal of an analogy between stress and pathogens. Pathogens, such as bacteria or viruses, may be considered to act on the body in a manner parallel to an environmental stressor. Yet pathogens do not act in a similar manner in all people. Whether or not a person will become ill as a function of his or her exposure to pathogens depends on the nature, intensity, and chronicity of the exposure along with the person's bodily defenses. As Mason wrote:

> There is a complex assemblage of intervening "host resistance" machinery which has a major role in determining whether infection will progress into illness or not. In principle, this intervening "host resistance" machinery would seem to be generally analogous to the intervening psychological impact of psychosocial forces upon the organism, although the latter machinery does differ considerably in the greater degree of its complexity. (p. 33)

Combining these two proposals results in a model in which any event may be considered analogous to a pathogen that possesses the potentiality to evoke a stress response. Thereby, one may postulate that any event may be stressful, depending on its nature, intensity, and chronicity and the host resistance of the exposed person.

During the past decade, evidence has accrued supporting the argument that almost all endocrine response systems are responsive to stressful environmental events (Brown & Reichlin, 1972; Mason, 1968b; Noel, Dimond, Earll, & Frantz, 1976; Rose, 1969). However, investigation of human psychoendocrine responses to stress, in spite of this growing body of literature, has been largely limited to the pituitary adrenal (Mason, 1968b), sympathetic–adrenal medullary (Mason, 1968d), and pituitary thyroid (Mason, 1968c) systems.

While the concept of an integrated, overall responsivity of the endocrine system to stress has become generally accepted, investigators continue, as a result of both theoretical assumptions and practical limitations, to limit their research focus to the response of a single system. This trend results in an ever-increasing knowledge of single hormone systems with little understanding of how these systems function in an integrated manner. This conventional research approach is a major impediment to a more complete conceptualization of the endocrine system as a stress-responsive, functioning whole.

Another problem is that investigations examining psychoendocrine response to stress tend to regard the profound frequency of individual differences as a function of psychological aspects such as defense mechanisms and cognitive styles. Although such interpretations have both merit and data to support them, there is an absence of logic in the attempts to view hormonal variations solely in terms of psychological differences. An alternate explanation may be found by examining endocrine bases for individual differences that, as a result, may influence both the psychological mechanisms and variance in psychoendocrine response.

Also there is a noticeable lack of integration in relating psychoendocrine stress responses to known aspects of hormonal influences on behavior (Cohen, 1977). Presumably, changes in hormone levels as a result of perceived environmental events are adaptive, as are hormonally mediated influences on behavior; yet little synthesis has occurred in terms of stress-induced endogenous hormonal fluctuations mediating behavioral coping responses in person-environmental interactions.

## FACTORS INFLUENCING ENDOCRINE
## STRESS RESPONSES

The first thesis we examine assumes that the predispositional status or host resistance of a person interacts with a given environmental event to mediate the occurrence of a stress response, its intensity, and its extent. The term *host resistance* is a broad concept referring to a person's psychological, physiological, endocrinologic, and experiential makeup. The main focus in this discussion is, however, the hormonal facet of functioning. We assume, as we discuss later, that psychoendocrine response to stress is governed, at least in part, by past and present endocrine factors contributing to the overall host resistance.

To prevent a circular argument that endocrine factors determining hormonal responses to stress will, in turn, later influence endocrine responding to environmental events, we assume that this facet of the host resistance is fairly fixed. We also propose that the host resistance consists of two major components; relatively permanent and relatively transitory endocrine factors acting on central processing. Permanent aspects of endocrine responsivity include early organizational influences, sex differences, and resulting dimorphic endocrine functioning and responsivity to stress; whereas, transitory influences consist of, in part, circadian and cyclic variations.

Another assumption is that people exhibit a profile of hormonal response to environmental events that is a relatively fixed hierarchy of different rates of hormonal secretion across a variety of events. This concept of hormonal response specificity is parallel to Lacey's theory of autonomic response specificity.

Furthermore, his concept of organ emphasis may be seen as analogous to the concept of hormone emphasis, so that each person may respond to various environmental events with the release rate of one hormone predominant over all others.

## Organizational Endocrine Influences

The concept of early exposure to endocrine stimulation having a permanent organizational effect, during critical periods of development, on later adult morphology, responsivity to specific hormones, patterns of endocrine secretion, and behavior has been widely accepted by workers examining the relationships between hormones and sexual behavior. Later evidence has suggested that this so-called organizational-activation model is applicable to other endocrine systems controlling a variety of behaviors independent of sexual behavior and reproductive functioning.

Phoenix, Goy, Gerall, and Young (1959) were the first to propose this model, following their investigation of the behavioral and somatic masculinizing effects of prenatal testosterone on adult female guinea pigs. They theorized that the presence of testosterone, independent of the individual's genetic sex, has a masculinizing effect on the soma during certain perinatal periods, whereas the absence of androgens resulted in adult female morphology and sexual behavior. While issues remain to be resolved concerning the parameters and limitations of this concept (Reinisch, 1976; Whalen, 1974), firm support for the concept of the organizational-activational role of the hypothalamic-pituitary-gonadal axis has been obtained across a wide variety of species.

There is growing evidence that the organizational-activational model of hormones is applicable to a number of endocrine axes. One system that apparently plays a crucial role in stress response is the hypothalamic-pituitary-thyroid axis (Mason, 1968c). Early interventions altering this system have a radical impact on later adult capacity to interact with the environment. For example, rats undergoing neonatal thyroidectomy exhibit severe retardation of physiological, reflex, and CNS functioning that persists into adulthood (Eayrs, 1961; Eayrs & Levine, 1963). In contrast, increased activation of the hypothalamic-pituitary-thyroid axis by neonatal administration of thyrotropin-releasing hormone (TRH) during early periods may enhance aspects of rats' later development (Stratton, Gibson, Kolar, & Kastin, 1976).

Also more relevant to the present discussion are the reported effects of early manipulation of the hypothalamic-pituitary-adrenocortical (HPAC) axis. It appears that early handling of rats results in a greater adaptive, or "economical," functioning of the HPAC system in adulthood when presented with stressful events. Rats handled in infancy exhibited a more rapid and intense, yet less prolonged, corticosteroid response to shock in adulthood when compared with nonhandled animals (Bell, Reisner, & Linn, 1961; S. Levine, 1962). Such treatment has also been found to decrease responsivity to novel open-field situations, as indicated by lowered corticosterone secretion (Levine, Haltmeyer, & Denenberg, cited in Levine & Mullins, 1966). It has been suggested by Levine and Mullins (1966) that early HPAC stimulation induced by handling may result in the animals' increased capacity to respond to stressful environmental events in a differential, adaptive manner. Compared with control animals, which tend to exhibit near-maximal adrenocortical responses to any fluctuation in the environment, handled rats respond only moderately to novel situations yet display a near-maximal corticosterone response to physically endangering events.

Overall, the abundant data from handling and prenatal stress investigations are frequently contradictory and difficult to interpret, partially as a function of the inability to isolate the critical endocrine variables responsible for the observed changes in adult functioning. It must be assumed that perinatal stimulation influences all endocrine functioning, thereby resulting in a variety of possible effects present in adulthood.

Another experimental approach that permits delineation between early adeno-hypophyseal and adrenocortical influences on later behavior is the employment of ACTH peptide fragments that do not possess adrenal-stimulating properties yet retain the behaviorally active amino acid sequence contained both in ACTH and α-MSH (ACTH 1-13). It appears that neonatal exposure of rats to α-MSH results in relatively permanent changes in attentional processes. Neonatal administration of α-MSH increased performance efficiency of juvenile rats of both sexes on a number of measures (Beckwith, Sandman, Hotersall, & Kastin, 1977). Both infant and adult treatment with an MSH/ACTH 4-9 analogue exhibited improved visual orientation and reversal learning (Champney, Sahley, & Sandman, 1976), and evidence was obtained indicating that early administration of the peptide increased adult responsivity to the substance. Neonatal injections of α-MSH resulted in increased gregariousness of juvenile female rats but not males (Beckwith, O'Quin, Petro, Kastin, & Sandman, 1977). Although these findings strongly suggest that early exposure to MSH/ACTH 4-10 and other ACTH fragments exerts positive influences on central neural substrates underlying attention and other functions in rats, it is impossible to extrapolate these findings to other species. Moreover, at the present time, no investigations of the effects of early exposure to these peptides on later endocrine responsivity to environmental events have been completed.

Overall, these studies based on the organization-activation model indicate that early endocrine factors may possess the capacity to influence both later hormonal responsivity and central neural substrates underlying a variety of behaviors. Yet because the great majority of these studies have limited their focus to rodents, it is difficult to assess the full impact of early endocrine stimulation on human adult functioning.

## Sex Differences

Outside the realm of endocrine influences on sexual behavior, the factor of sex differences has been largely ignored. Psychoendocrine research all too frequently disregards this variable as a possible contributing factor to individual differences and variations in host resistance. Considering the wide spectrum of evidence implicating sex differences in metabolic and neurochemical functioning (Gram & Gilette, 1969; Redmond, Baulu, Murphy, Loriaux, Zeigler, & Lake, 1976), animal behavior and learning (Beatty & Beatty, 1970; Denti & Epstein, 1972; Wade, 1972), and human cognitive and behavioral functioning (Gates, 1916; Hutt, 1972; Maccoby & Jacklin, 1974; Witkin, Lewis, Hertzman, Machover, Bretnall, Meissner, & Wapner, 1954), it may be argued that greater emphasis should be placed on this variable in future psychoendocrine investigations.

Sex differences have also been implicated in behavioral responses to neuro-peptide administration. Studies employing fragments of ACTH have found that the sex of the subject is an important contributing factor, both in rats (Beckwith, O'Quin, Petro, Kastin, & Sandman, 1977; Beckwith, Sandman, Hothersall, & Kastin, 1977; Champney et al., 1976) and in humans (Sandman & Kastin, 1981; Veith, Sandman, George, & Stevens, 1978).

Gray (1971) has argued that, compared with women, men exhibit lower thresholds to density-induced stress, an overall heightened emotionality, and a tenfold greater predisposition to stress-induced ulcers. Investigations into psycho-endocrine response to stress have failed, however, to report consistent sex-dependent differences in response. For example, several studies have found that men exhibited higher 17-hydroxycorticosterone (17-OHCS) levels than women in response to stressful events such as hospitalization of their child for neoplastic disease (Friedman, Mason, & Hamburg, 1963) or admission into a clinical research unit (Fishman, Hamburg, Handlon, Mason, & Sachar, 1962). Yet the large number of other studies examining the effects of a variety of stressful events on 17-OHCS levels in both men and women failed to report the presence of sex differences, either because there were no significant differences between the sexes on this measure or because it simply was not examined.

One of the major predispositional variables that has received minimal attention is the female menstrual cycle. Although this variable has been found to be a significant influence on endocrine systems other than the pituitary-gonadal axis (Burns, 1975; Genazzani, Lemarchand-Beraud, Aubert, & Felber, 1975) and on visual perception (M. M. Ward, Stone, & Sandman, 1978), cognitive styles (Zingheim, 1973), and affect (Bardwick, 1976; Golub, 1976; Persky, 1974; Wilcoxin, Schrader, & Sherif, 1976), apparently only one study has been executed concerning the relationship between menstrual phase and psycho-endocrine response to stress. Women underwent a mildly stressful interview at one of two points during the menstrual cycle; it was found that cortisol, GH, and reported anxiety levels were unrelated to menstrual phase (Abplanalp, Livingston, Rose, & Sandwisch, 1977). This single negative finding does not provide sufficient evidence to discontinue this line of investigation. Only two points of the menstrual phase were examined. Also, the profound influence of the menstrual cycle suggests that it may be closely linked with stress responding.

There have been no studies directly examining sex steroid fluctuations in men as an influence on host resistance. Most studies examining basal levels of testosterone in humans have attempted to relate this measure to aggression, and with little success (Rada, Kellner, & Winslow, 1976; Rada, Laws, & Kellner, 1976). Probably the best available study relating steroid levels to affect in men correlated plasma testosterone, measured every other day, with affect checklists and daily events obtained at the same time from young men (Doering, Brodie, Kraemer, Becker, & Hamburg, 1974; Doering, Brodie, Kraemer, Moos, Becker, & Hamburg, 1975). Intrasubject plasma testosterone levels fluctuated markedly over this period (contrary to the general notion of tonic androgen secretion); out of over 600 measures, however, only depressive affect was found to be significantly correlated with steroid level.

Although testosterone does not appear, based on the presently available literature, to be a significant determinant of host resistance, it has proved to be markedly susceptible to stressful events in male humans (Rose, 1969; Rose,

Bourne, Poe, Mougey, Collins, & Mason, 1969). Sudden drops in this steroid, which occur in men during times of stress, may be a contributing factor to sex differences in psychoendocrine stress responding.

Perhaps the best-known study is that on the testosterone response to changes in social hierarchy of rhesus monkeys. Plasma testosterone (Rose, Gordon, & Bernstein, 1972) and serum insulin (Hamilton & Chaddock, 1977) were found to be positively correlated with the monkeys' positions in the social hierarchy. Plasma testosterone was also directly affected by experimentally induced changes in social status and exhibited marked depression with increases of socially induced stress (Rose, Bernstein, & Gordon, 1975). Further, the now-classic study of Christian (1955) demonstrated that social crowding of male mice resulted in a marked decrease of endogenous androgen levels.

It has been suggested that drops in circulating testosterone levels following socially induced stresses are adaptive. Rose, Bernstein, and Gordon (1975) have argued that decreases in androgen levels following defeat and loss of social status decrease the probability of aggressive action on the part of the subject, thereby precluding the likelihood of instigation of additional combat and repeated defeats. But although testosterone has been clearly related to aggression in intrahumans (Leshner, 1975), the evidence relating circulating plasma steroid levels with the exhibition of aggression in humans is contradictory.

Overall, on the basis of limited data, a person's sex may be an aspect of host resistance determining the extent of the psychoendocrine response to environmental events. There is little evidence, however, to indicate that determination of this response is directly related to fluctuations in sex steroids. Furthermore, it is difficult to evaluate the degree of importance of sex differences in response to stress as a contributing factor to a person's predispositional status. The presently available literature all too often ignores this variable by limiting subject populations to one sex or by simply failing to examine possible differences between sexes.

## Circadian Factors

While early organizational actions of the endocrine system and sex differences may be considered to be relatively permanent, the daily fluctuation of hormones may be viewed as relatively transitory in comparison. Studies of the relationship between circadian variations and stress responses have employed unidirectional approaches by studying the effects of various stressors on diurnal patterning. To our knowledge, only a single study in human psychoendocrine stress research has employed the alternate approach, studying the influences of circadian fluctuation in determining the host resistance and extent of the evoked stress (Curtis, 1976). Investigations of central regulatory control of diurnal endocrine patterning have been numerous (e.g., Rice & Critchlow, 1976), as have been studies of various circadian-endocrine release patterns (Karacan, Rosenbloom, Londono, Salis, Thornby, & Williams, 1973; Rubin, Gouin, Kales, & Odell, 1973; Smals, Kloppenberg, & Benraad, 1974; Weitzman, Fukushima, Nogeire, Roffwarf, Gallagher, & Hellman, 1971).

Studies of circadian rhythms may be categorized on the basis of whether this factor was employed as the independent or dependent variable. The effects of stress on diurnal patterning of rats indicated that shock disrupted the circadian rhythm of serum LH and reduced the amplitude of corticosterone levels; PRL periodicity was not, however, affected (Dunn, Arimura, & Scheving, 1972). In human subjects, anticipation of major surgery did not disrupt significantly circadian variations in cortisol secretion (Czeisler, Mooreede, Regestein, Kisch, Fang, & Ehrlich, 1976). Frequent sampling, employed to measure the 24-h episodic cortisol secretory pattern of these patients, revealed that most anxiety-evoking events did not induce a cortisol rise and that most observed secretory episodes were part of the endogenous cyclic pattern independent of environmental events.

In contrast, designation of circadian variations as the independent variable has produced evidence that this factor can influence a number of responses in rodents. For example, variations in lighting conditions can influence rats' learning ability (Sandman, Miller, Kastin, & Schally, 1972). Further, naloxone, which antagonizes the effects of opiates, varies in its efficacy in inducing hyperalgesia in rats on a circadian basis (Fredrickson, Burgis, & Edwards, 1977). Studies examining the influence of diurnal factors on endocrine response to stress are limited. It has been reported that rats stressed at either the crest or the trough of the adrenal diurnal rhythm exhibited significantly greater corticosterone and PRL responses when endogenous corticosterone levels were highest (Seggie & Brown, 1975).

Only indirect evidence from human psychoendocrine research supports the thesis that circadian fluctuations are a facet of host resistance. Curtis (1976) exposed people with severe phobias to prolonged live exposure to the feared object during the late-evening phase of minimal cortisol secretion. Frequent sampling of plasma cortisol revealed that there were no significant elevations in response to this experience even though behavioral and subjective criteria indicated that the experience was perceived as unusually substantial and dramatic. These results suggested that the time at which the environmental stress occurs may be a major variable in determining the host resistance and resulting psychoendocrine response to that stress. Furthermore, the data indicated that the occurrence of cortisol night spiking in depressed patients is apparently not a product of high levels of subjective anxiety.

Admittedly, this is limited support for the notion that human diurnal variations may be a contributing factor in determining psychoendocrine response to potential environmental stressors. Yet, the accumulated evidence suggests that circadian influences affect a number of functions. Furthermore, it may be argued that predispositional endocrine factors must necessarily influence the nature of hormonal responsivity to the environment. Organizational, cyclic, and circadian factors, along with sex differences, are variables in psychoendocrine research on the human stress response that require further examination.

## Endocrine Influences on Sensory Processes

Another determinant of host resistance is predispositional afferent receptor sensitivity—the ability to attend to the environment—which in turn influences the appraisal of threat and the resulting stress response. Furthermore, accumulating evidence suggests that the levels of various circulating hormones possess the capacity to influence both receptor sensitivity and central attentional processes. Although we review much of this evidence in the section on hormone stimulus specificity, it is appropriate to discuss some of the literature relevant to this notion briefly here.

Although it has been known for some time that hypothalamic manipulation can result in altered pain perception (Gispen, Van Wimersma Greidanus, & de Wied, 1970), the discovery of peptides capable of altering pain perception has radical implications. The isolation and synthesis of the endorphins, the generic name for the group of naturally occurring peptides possessing opiate-like effects, has provided the strongest support for the thesis that endogenous neuropeptide activity can alter sensory thresholds to incoming environmental stimuli.

Endorphin levels have been shown to be elevated in response to noxious physical stimuli (J. Akil, Madden, Patrick, & Barchas, 1976), and intraventricular administration of these peptides significantly increases pain thresholds in rats (Chang, Fong, Pert, & Pert, 1976; Guillemin, 1977; Walker, Berntson, Sandman, Coy, Schally, & Kastin, 1977; Walker, Sandman, Berntson, McGivern, Coy, & Kastin, 1977). Administration of the specific opiate antagonist naloxone was found to lower pain thresholds in rats (H. Akil, Mayer, & Liebeski, 1976; Walker, Berntson, Sandman, Coy, Schally, & Kastin, 1977) and block acupuncture-induced analgesia in mice (Pomeranz & Chiu, 1976). In humans, administration of naloxone also blocked the reduction of anxiety and tension typically occurring with termination of pain production (Grevert & Goldstein, 1977). Others, however, have found no change in affect following naloxone treatment (Volaka, Mallya, Baig, & Perez-Cruet, 1977).

The preliminary evidence suggests that endorphins possess the capacity to influence the sensory intake of noxious environmental events via their actions on central and peripheral opiate receptors (Sandman & Kastin, 1981). Conceivably, the peptides may alter the perception of and resulting psychoendocrine response to these events. In this sense, the endorphins are important contributors to the organism's host resistance to stressful occurrences because of their ability to reduce the perceptual field. Moreover, it has been suggested that the endorphins may mediate emotional responses related to environmental events (Belluzzi & Stein, 1977) and may interface sensory events with emotional responses (H. Akil, 1977).

Circulating levels of endogenous ACTH have also been implicated in the determination of several sensory thresholds. Henkin (1975), in his review, reported that people with chronic adrenocortical insufficiency (and resulting high levels of ACTH) had significantly enhanced abilities to detect gustatory, olfactory, and auditory stimuli with concomitant impaired recognition and discrimination abilities.

Further evidence, obtained by means of administration of fractions of MSH/ACTH (i.e., MSH/ACTH 4-10) to adult volunteers, suggested that this peptide fragment enhanced a person's ability to attend to the environment, thereby conceivably altering the host resistance to stress. Administration of MSH/ACTH 4-10 to healthy man facilitated selective visual attention, as measured by a concept-formation task (Sandman, George, Nolan, Van Riezen, & Kastin, 1975; Sandman, George, McCanne, Nolan, Kaswan, & Kastin, 1977), and visual memory (Kastin, Miller, Gonzalez-Barcena, Hawley, Dyster-Aas, Schally, Velasco de Parra, & Velasco, 1971; Miller, Harris, Van Riezen, & Kastin, 1976; Miller, Kastin, Sandman, Fink, & Van Veen, 1974; Sandman, George, Nolan, Van Riezen, & Kastin, 1975). MSH/ACTH 4-10 has also been found to counteract fatigue on a self-paced reaction-time task (Gaillard & Sanders, 1975). Further-more, on the Sternberg item-recognition task, the peptide was found to reduce reaction times significantly and in a manner suggestive of facilitated attention rather than memory (M. M. Ward, Sandman, George, & Shulman, 1979). The peptide, however, impaired memory on a bimodal sensory auditory task (Dorn-bush & Nikolovski, 1976). Moment-to-moment anxiety declined significantly following peptide administration to young men (Miller, Kastin, Sandman, Fink, & Van Veen, 1974; Sandman, George, Nolan, Van Riesen, & Kastin, 1975). These data may be among the strongest evidence suggesting that the peptide fragment increases the host resistance to stress.

Women, in contrast to men, exhibited a facilitation in verbal processing without concomitant improvements of visual attention or memory (Veith, Sandman, George, & Stevens, 1978). These sex differences were interpreted as being possibly indicative of the peptide's facilitation of sexually dimorphic dominant modalities.

Even though MSH and ACTH share some behavioral similarities, they have dissociated release patterns both in humans (Kastin, Beach, Hawley, Kendall, Edwards, & Schally, 1973) and in rats (Sandman, Kastin, Schally, Kendall, & Miller, 1973) under conditions of stress. Presumably, appraisal of threatening environmental events can result in the discrete release of these peptides to prepare the individual to meet the demands of the situation. The evidence derived from both the studies employing administration of ACTH fragments as well as from the research examining the effects of high levels of endogenous ACTH on attention and sensory intake, provides strong evidence for the argument that variation in the HPAC axis can influence the perception of the environment, the host resistance, and the resulting psychoendocrine stress response.

Furthermore, the hypothalamic-pituitary-gonadal axis in women appears to possess the capacity to alter sensory thresholds. Women tested at four times during the menstrual cycle exhibited significantly impaired visual detection during the premenstrual session (M. M. Ward, Stone, & Sandman, 1978). Further, the preovulatory phase has been characterized as a period of high arousal, as indicated by habituation patterns to auditory stimuli, followed by a phase of low arousal during the second half of the menstrual cycle (J. Friedman & Meares, 1979).

The evidence obtained from studies examining the endorphins, ACTH and its fragments, and the menstrual cycle support the thesis that endogenous, circulat-ing hormone levels influence receptivity to the environment. This aspect of endocrine functioning influences host resistance by altering the perception and appraisal of the environment. These perceptions, varying as a function of endogenous hormone levels, may in turn influence both the probability and the extent of the psychoendocrine response. Thus, the fluctuating capacity to detect and recognize potential and actual threatening environmental changes will influence the extent and occurrence of the evoked responses to these events.

## Psychoendocrine Response Specificity

As discussed in the introduction, the concept of response specificity, derived from work with autonomic arousal (Lacey & Van Lehn, 1952) may be applied to psychoendocrine functioning based on individual host resistance. Organizational factors such as early exposure to endocrine stimulation, sex differences and cyclic variations, changes in sensory thresholds, and psychological defensive functioning have been suggested as possible contributors to individual overall host resistance. Thus, the response to stressful environmental events may be viewed as idiosyncratic, varying from one person to the next owing to differences in the variables contributing to the overall resistance. All the related factors result in a distinctive individual pattern of psychoendocrine response that may be relatively stable across a wide variety of situations.

Although there is little direct evidence for this concept of psychoendocrine response specificity in the literature, psychosomatic medicine has focused on predisposing risk factors in a variety of stress-based illnesses (Weiner, 1975). For example, hypertensive men were found to excrete significantly higher levels of epinephrine than healthy subjects during laboratory-induced stress (Holmberg, Levi, Mathe, Rosen, & Scott, 1967). Deficits of $\beta$-adrenergic receptor activity have been linked with tendencies toward bronchoconstriction (Weiner, 1975). Asthmatic men in remission were found to secret lower levels of epinephrine during both stress-evoking and control periods when compared with control subjects (Mathe & Knapp, 1971).

These data suggest that some people exhibit a tendency to secrete higher- or lower-than-average amounts of catecholamines across a wide variety of situations. This may result in a greater-than-average likelihood of exhibiting illnesses that result from abnormalities in catecholamine secretion. This trend may be viewed as an example of the psychoendocrine response specificity insofar as these people tend to exhibit these idiosyncratic patterns across a wide number of situations and time periods.

Ranking of individual secretion rates of specific hormones during a number of different events is another feasible approach to examining the concept of endocrine response specificity. For example, levels of 17-OHCS, an index of cortisol, were collected from hemophiliacs during periods when the subjects were at home, in a research center, and undergoing hospitalization (Mattson, Gross, & Hall, 1971). Steroid levels were found to increase across the three settings, presumably as a function of increases in perceived threat. The subjects maintained their rank relative to one another in terms of 17-OHCS levels. Similar findings of stable rank order have been found in women's epinephrine-secretion rates across a variety of pleasant and unpleasant work conditions (Levi, 1967b).

One study indicates that response specificity appears very early in the life-span. Urinary-cortisol levels of 1-year-old infants were measured during a novel play situation and during separation from their mothers (Tennes, Downey, & Vernadakis, 1977). It was found that infants maintained their stable rank order in terms of cortisol secretion across these pleasant and unpleasant situations.

Another important consideration is the relative permanence of endocrine response stereotypy. One study suggests that it may be relatively stable across time. Men exposed to mild sensory and mental annoyances such as noise, flickering lights, and mental-arithmetic tasks responded with significant increases in both cortisol levels and cardiac sympathetic stimulation. Some individuals exhibited particularly exaggerated stress responses that were reproducible 4–5 years later (Raab, 1968).

Differing categories of hormonal-response patterns of neurotic patients have been reported (Miyabo, Asato, & Mizushima, 1979). Subjects rated as defensive and self-controlling exhibited sharp increases in plasma cortisol levels during a mirror-drawing test, whereas subjects prone to exaggeration, hostility, and distorted thinking processes had elevated levels of growth hormone.

Although the cited studies support the notion of psychoendocrine response specificity, no one has directly examined the validity of this thesis. At present, its major support is derived from psychosomatic research concerning predispositional hormonal-release patterns, particularly in terms of the catecholamine system and its relation to stress-induced disease. To achieve scientific support for this notion of endocrine response specificity, three questions must be addressed. The first concerns whether people generally demonstrate fairly stable rank order in levels of specific hormones across a wide variety of stressful and pleasant situations. The second issue concerns the relative stability of these response differences across a significant time period. The third question concerns the hierarchical response patterns of a group of hormones secreted by one person; one may find that each person exhibits a relatively stable endocrine profile but that one hormone exhibits the greatest responsivity in a variety of situations. This concept of hormone emphasis, analogous to Lacey's notion of organ emphasis, may prove important for understanding the origin of stress-related diseases.

## HORMONAL STIMULUS SPECIFICITY

Cannon's (1914) conceptualization of overall autonomic activation governing the emergency response is not dissimilar to Selye's (1936) formulation of the nonspecific stress response. Both concepts postulate that if environmental stimuli constitute a sufficient, significant threat to the homeostatic regulation, a pattern of adaptive physiological responses is initiated. This response pattern is conceived as being relatively invariant; different environmental demands are not viewed by these theories as inducing stimulus-specific autonomic or endocrine patterns of adaptive responses.

The autonomic-activation theory of Cannon has undergone gradual modification in the direction of broadened interpretation and increased complexity (Lacey, 1967). Somatic, physiological, and motor responses are now conceptualized as being imperfectly coupled, complexly interacting systems. Furthermore, autonomic activation is no longer thought of as a relatively fixed pattern independent of varying environmental demands and intended goals. Differing stimulus situations have been found reliably to result in distinct patterns of somatic response (Lacey, 1967), a phenomenon termed *situational stereotypy* or *stimulus specificity*. Moreover, Cannon's theory of the emergency function has been brought into question by evidence that autonomic functioning demonstrates directional fractionalization, characterized by one or more functions moving in directions opposite to those predicted by views of autonomic functioning as energizing and protective. The type of evoked autonomic patterns is presently viewed as determined by the requirements of the situation and the intended goal-directed behavior (Engel, 1960; Graham & Clifton, 1966; Kaiser & Sandman, 1975).

In contrast, the predominant conceptualization of endocrinologic adaptive mechanisms has adhered closely to Selye's original formulation, resulting in the view that hormonal stress responses are relatively nonspecific reactions to all noxious stimuli. This view persists even though research has shown that only the coarsest, or life-threatening, stressors, such as Formalin injection, consistently evoke the nonspecific stress response (Levi, 1967a). This traditional viewpoint is most clearly exemplified in the preponderance of studies examining the patterns of a single hormone's response to an objectively stressful event (Mason, 1972b, 1974). Because many researchers assume that stimuli evoke an overall endocrine arousal, measurement of a single hormone is used to index other unexamined hormonal responses. Furthermore, if the measured hormone fails to exhibit a response to an event, the results are generally interpreted as indicative of an absence of induced stress.

The hypothesis we examine here postulates that arousal-oriented models of endocrine responses to stress are overly simplistic; the increasing number of studies examining multiple endocrine response patterns provide evidence that hormonal profiles are integrated and relatively specific to differing types of noxious stimuli, which poses the question Do endocrine systems exhibit a pattern of response that is specific to the event? We suggest that the endocrine system, as well as the autonomic system (Lacey, 1967), exhibits situational stereotypy, with differing events evoking distinctive patterns of integrated hormonal responses.

Moreover, we present the thesis that differing events result in varying hormonal response patterns that serve an adaptive function not only by preparing a person's metabolism for the anticipated event but by predisposing the person to display adaptive patterns of behavior as a function of selective action on central and peripheral neural processing. The field of behavioral endocrinology has accrued massive evidence indicating that hormones can evoke specific behaviors. Little has been done, however, to relate psychoendocrine stress responses with peptide-induced specific behavior patterns.

## Overall Specific Hormonal-response Patterning

Behavioral endocrinology (Beach, 1948) and psychosomatic medicine (Selye, 1950) have long assumed the integrated and holistic nature of endocrine influences on the organism, but investigative orientations have been predominantly analytic and elementalistic. As mentioned, studies focusing on a single hormone's responsivity to environmental events are predominant in this field of research. Mason and his colleagues, in a series of elegantly designed and executed studies, were the first to examine endocrine responses to a variety of psychological and physical stimuli by measuring a broad spectrum of hormones concurrently.

The first series of studies were designed to examine the scope of interdependent hormonal-response systems in relation to a conditioned avoidance response in the rhesus monkey (Mason, 1968e). Simultaneous measurement revealed that plasma and urinary 17-OHCS (Mason, Brady, & Tolliver, 1968), urinary epinephrine and NE (Mason, Tolson, Brady, Tolliver, & Gilmore, 1968), thyroxine (plasma butanol-extractable iodine, or BEI) (Mason, Mougey, Brady, & Tolliver, 1968), and plasma GH levels (Mason, Wool, Wherry, Pennington, Brady, & Beer, 1968) rose during the initial stress period. In contrast, urinary testosterone (Mason, Kenion, Collins, Mougey, Jones, Driver, Brady, & Beer, 1968); urinary androsterone, etiocholanolone, and dehydroepiandrosterone (Mason, Tolson, Robinson, Brady, Tolliver, & Johnson, 1968); urinary estrone, estradiol, and estriol (Mason, Taylor, Brady, & Tolliver, 1968); plasma insulin (Mason, Wherry, Brady, Beer, Pennington, & Goodman, 1968); and urinary aldosterone levels along with urine volume (Mason, Jones, Ricketts, Brady, & Tolliver, 1968) exhibited a decline during this initial phase. Furthermore, the levels of hormones that rose during the initial avoidance period displayed a monophasic response curve with varying rates of return to base-line levels. In contrast, the levels of hormones that were depressed during the early stress period rose above base line during the recovery period following termination of the conditioned-avoidance sessions, a pattern characterized as a biphasic response curve (Mason, 1968a).

Because the response-provoking situation was mainly psychological in nature, hormonal-response patterning as a means of homeostatic stabilization must be thought of as a result of anticipated rather than an actually occurring physiological disruption. Based on this assumption, Mason (1968a) provided an opposing-action interpretation of the response profile in terms of energy metabolism. Hormones that predominate during the avoidance period, including corticosteroids, catecholamines, GH, and thyroxine, exert catabolic effects on energy metabolism, including hyperglycemia, free fatty-acid release, and increased oxidation rate. Because of their hypoglycemic effects and promotion of protein synthesis, anabolic effects are attributed to the group of hormones, including insulin, estrogen, testosterone, and the androgenic metabolites, that predominate during the recovery period. The anabolic–catabolic conceptualization of hormonal response patterning exhibited during conditioned emotional-response situations suggests that overall endocrine integration is in terms of reciprocal inhibition.

The question concerning the extent to which the anabolic–catabolic profile of hormonal response was consistent across other psychological stressful situations was examined in a series of studies examining endocrine responses of rhesus monkeys in a chair-restraint situation (Mason, 1972a; Mason & Mougey, 1972; Mason, Mougey, & Kenion, 1973). The hormones examined exhibited a surprisingly similar response profile to that seen during the conditioned-avoidance paradigm (Mason, 1974).

Recently, the direction of Mason's investigations has changed toward distinguishing stimulus-specific hormonal profiles by means of separating purely physical stimuli from those that are psychological. As mentioned, endocrine response profiles to psychologically induced factors may exhibit major similarities because of the common quality of anticipation of need or disruption of functioning. Anticipation of a stressful event has been recurrently found to be one of the most effective inducers of psychoendocrine response (Greenwood & Landon, 1966; Kurokawa, Suematso, Tamai, Esaki, Aoki, & Ikema, 1977). Plasma cortisol, NE (Mason, Hartley, Kotchen, Mougey, Ricketts, & Jones, 1973), and TSH (Mason, Hartley, Kotchen, Wherry, Pennington, & Jones, 1973) exhibited significant elevations in young men anticipating an exhausting exercise session. Only cortisol and NE, however, rose during periods of severe or sustained muscular exertion (Hartley, Mason, Hogan, Jones, Kotchen, Mougey, Wherry, Pennington, & Ricketts, 1972a, 1972b), thereby suggesting that psychoendocrine response patterns resulting from anticipation may differ from those resulting from physical stimuli (Sandman, Kastin, Schally, Kendall, & Miller, 1973). Furthermore, initial support for the notion that purely physical stimulus-specific endocrine response profiles exist has been reviewed by Mason (1974) in a series of studies with rhesus monkeys. Hormonal profiles in response to physical stresses such as fasting, heat and cold exposure, and dietary changes were determined; measures were carefully employed to minimize psychological stress. Such techniques included the feeding of nonnutritive fruit-flavored cellulose pellets and the avoidance of sudden or severe temperature change. Distinct response profiles were obtained for each condition that sharply differed from those obtained during the psychologically stressful conditioned-avoidance and chair-restraint studies. For example, heat exposure induced substantial 17-OHCS declines, whereas temperature decreases caused significant cortisol elevations. The obtained endocrine profiles from these two opposing environmental events were apparently diametrically opposed and provided the strongest evidence that integrated endocrine responses are specific to the physical demands imposed by the environment.

In sum, these findings suggested that physical stressors under conditions of minimal psychological arousal provoke stressor-specific endocrine profiles that presumably aid in reestablishing homeostatic regulation according to the specific energy-metabolism demands. This hypothesized specificity of endocrine response was in direct opposition to Selye's nonspecific, adaptive, stress-response concept. Mason (1975a) proposed that the prevailing theory of a nonspecific stress response is a consequent of the contamination of investigations of physical stressors by attendant psychological influences.

Mason postulated that, up to the present time, studies examining psycho-endocrine response to physical stresses have failed to eliminate psychological stress concomitant with the physical trauma. Interpretation of the data has failed, however, to include an examination of the role of psychological stress in inducing the resulting supposed response to physical stress. He propounded the view that the morphological triad determined by Selye (1936) is a product of psychological stress that is prevalent in almost all studies; removing this factor in investigations results, according to Mason, in patterns of endocrine response profiles that not only differ from those following psychological stress but differ from one another on the basis of the demands placed on the organism during the stressful event.

Another important factor in Mason's work is his inclusion of multiple endocrine measurements, which has permitted his delineation of physical, stimulus-specific hormonal profiles. Traditionally, if an investigator employed only a sole hormone measurement, such as cortisol level, and obtained negative results, the common interpretation, as mentioned earlier, would be the absence of stress. Mason's employment of multiple endocrine measurement has revealed that it is possible to delineate a profile wherein cortisol fails to exhibit a response, or even show a decline as in the temperature elevation study, while other hormones exhibit increased secretion rates.

The importance of the concept of relatively stimulus-specific endocrine responses in human beings has yet to be fully determined, but support for the notion comes from studies examining anticipation, as compared with the actual experience, of physical exercise (Hartley et al., 1972a, 1972b; Mason, Hartley, Kotchen, Mougey, Ricketts, & Jones, 1973; Mason, Hartley, Kotchen, Wherry,

Pennington, & Jones, 1973). These studies indicate that cortisol levels exhibited a consistently greater increase during anticipation of such an event than during the actual experience of the exercise.

To test and extend the validity of Mason's notion in terms of human endocrine response to environmental events requires great care in experimental design. The separation of physical from psychological stress demands that the subject be essentially *unaware* of the occurrence of physical stress. This might be accomplished, for instance, by examining human stress response during surgery while a person is anesthetized or by modifying the environment (e.g., temperature) in such small increments that the subject is unaware of the changes.

While such investigations remain to be completed, at present, the work of Mason and his colleagues has provided the strongest and most conclusive evidence of the capacity of psychological stressors to evoke hormonal responses and of the extent to which endocrine responses are integrated and specific to purely physical contingencies. It is the latter body of findings that has the greatest implications not only for Selye's nonspecific stress-response theory but for behavioral endocrinology.

Acceptance of the thesis that the type of response pattern evoked is determined by the nature of the stressor requires the postulation of a virtually infinite array of hormonal profiles. That is, different types of anticipation or psychological stress may also conceivably result in a variety of multiple hormonal profiles. To date, Mason bases his delineation of a single endocrine response profile to psychological stress on the basis of two conditioned emotional response situations in nonhuman species, anticipation of exercise in humans, and the massive literature on human psychoendocrine response to stress that has employed primarily single-hormone indices, and it may be argued that this evidence is only preliminary.

## Psychoendocrine Stimulus Specificity

Identification of psychoendocrine stress responses is based on observed endocrine fluctuations. The absence of significant hormonal changes, particularly adrenocortical elevations, during stressful situations is typically attributed to effective appraisal and coping mechanisms (e.g., S. B. Friedman, Mason, & Hamburg, 1963; Katz, Weiner, Gallagher, & Hellman, 1970). In the absence of employment of multiple hormonal measurements, however, the possibility of differing endocrine stress responses specific to the type of psychological stressor cannot be ruled out. For example, it may be argued that different psychological stressors such as anticipation of physical exertion or injury evoked endocrine response profiles widely different from those evoked by engaging in demanding mental tasks or exposure to chronic environmental stress.

One instance supporting this notion is a study examining men undergoing basic military training. In what might be described as a chronic stress situation, the men were found to have depressed 17-OHCS levels (Rose, Poe, & Mason, 1968). These findings were interpreted as evidence that the men were effectively coping with stress. A second study revealed, however, that concomitant measures of testosterone, epitestosterone, androsterone, and etiocholanolone levels in this group of subjects were significantly depressed (Rose, Bourne, Poe, Mougey, Collins, & Mason, 1969). These data were considered indicative of individual differences and the possible effects of sexual abstinence, which is, in itself, a stress. Testosterone, however, has repeatedly been found to decline in humans under conditions of psychological stress (Kreuz, Rose, & Jennings, 1972; Rada, Kellner, & Winslow, 1976; Rose, 1969). Thus, it is possible to provide an alternate interpretation of Rose et al.'s data by suggesting the androgen depression in the absence of adrenocortical stimulation may be indicative of a specific psychoendocrine profile occurring in men during periods of chronic stress.

It is difficult at this point, to assess the validity of the thesis that psychological stress produces specific and characteristic patterns of endocrine response. Although evidence is available to support the notion that endocrine responses are differentiated on the basis of varying physical stresses (Blake, 1975) or physical versus psychological stress (Sandman, Kastin, Schally, Kendall, & Miller, 1973), most studies examining the concept of stimulus specificity with regard to psychological stress have limited their focus to the responsivity of a single hormone. For example, the length of separation determined infant squirrel monkeys' 17-OHCS response curve following reunion with their mothers (S. Levine, Coe, Smotherman, & Kaplan, 1978). Movies of varying intensity and emotional orientation evoked differing adrenal medullary (Levi, 1972) and corticosteroid responses (Wadeson, Mason, Hamburg, & Handlon, 1963).

The concept of psychoendocrine specificity appears to be also applicable to various states of human psychopathology. Both Cushing's and Addison's disease have been found to induce symptomatic depression (Carpenter & Bunney, 1971; Carroll, 1977), and there have been a large number of studies relating metabolic and hormonal disorders to a variety of types of psychopathology (Altman, Sachar, Gruen, Halpern, & Eto, 1975; Arana, Boyd, Reichlin, & Lipsitt, 1977; Benjafield & Rutter, 1973; Davis, 1970; Howard, 1975; Persky, 1976; Smythies, 1977; Whybrow & Hurwitz, 1976).

The most compelling literature in this field is that relating primary depression to hypercortisolism. The early research in this field was inconsistent and generally related the significantly elevated levels of cortisol in humans suffering from depressive syndromes to elevated levels of psychological stress (Board, Wadeson, & Persky, 1957; Mason, 1975b). Recent work has provided evidence suggesting that increases in adrenocortical secretion in this population are a result of disinhibition of ACTH and CRF secretion rather than a response to stressful affect.

Sachar (1975) suggests that many patients suffering from depression hypersecrete cortisol, but it is difficult to determine the extent to which this phenomenon is a function of psychoendocrine response to psychological stress. He proposes that in reactive neurotic depression, the cortisol fluctuations are closely related to affective arousal, whereas primary endogenous depression may be associated with a central neuroendocrine disturbance. This is supported by his investigations (Sachar, Hellman, Fukushima, & Gallagher, 1970; Sachar, Hellman, Roffwarf, Halpern, Fukushima, & Gallagher, 1973) determining that depressive patients secreted substantially more cortisol, had more secretory episodes, and had more minutes of active secretion than normal subjects. After recovery from depression, these patients were found to exhibit normal cortisol secretion levels. Sachar interprets this data as indicative of abnormal disinhibition of higher neuroendocrine centers in the regulation of ACTH resulting in hypersecretion of cortisol during depression.

In one study examining the cortisol response to dexamethasone administration in a depressed population, Beckwith (1977) found that a subgroup failed to exhibit cortisol suppression, a result that has been repeatedly obtained in a number of studies (Carroll, 1969; Carroll, Martin, & Davies, 1968; Fawcett & Bunney, 1967; Stokes, Stoll, Mattson, & Sollod, 1976). Of importance, the group that failed to exhibit cortisol suppression and therefore had elevated endogenous levels of ACTH demonstrated significantly better performance on a subproblem of a concept-formation task reflecting increased attention, a finding that has also been obtained following MSH/ACTH 4-10 administration in men (Sandman, George, McCanne, Nolan, Kaswan, & Kastin, 1977; Sandman, George, Nolan, Van Riezen, & Kastin, 1975).

This evidence is provocative in terms of the adaptive value of cortisol hypersecretion in depressed populations. One may conjecture that this psycho-endocrine response during depression results in focused attention and expanded capacity to meet the demands unique to a person experiencing stress. Owing to the strong evidence indicating that this response is not merely a breakdown of ego defenses or a function of increases in subjectively experienced anxiety, these HPAC elevations may be a specific response to changes in neurotransmitter regulation that are, in themselves, specific responses to certain environmental events. Furthermore, Beckwith's (1977) findings of increased attentional functioning in this subgroup that exhibited resistance to dexamethasone suppression suggests that changes in behavior may be a function of fluctuation of endogenous peptide levels.

## Endocrine-mediated Behavioral Responses to Stress

The assumption that differing environmental demands induce specific endocrine profiles may be extended from physiological and metabolic responses to include behavior. That is, stimulus-specific psychoendocrine responses may, besides influencing bodily functions, act directly to influence behavioral predispositions that aid in adaptation to environmental events. Moreover, these changes in behavior are specific as a result of the unique peptide-receptor interactions. For example, the isolation, identification, and synthesis of scotophobin, a peptide proposed as inducing specific fear of the dark (Ungar, Desiderio, & Parr, 1972), has been the subject of controversy (Stewart, 1972; de Wied, Sarantakis, & Weinstein, 1973). Its discovery has, however, suggested a conceptualization of peptide-brain interactions in terms of coded information carried in peptides interacting with specific central neural receptors. This concept of "chemo-specificity of innate neural pathways" (Sperry, cited in Ungar, 1976) views peptides as the basis of a recognition system permitting labeling of discrete storage circuits in the brain. Certainly the profound plasticity of specific amino acid sequences adequately serves as a memory-encoding model. The number of possible peptides have been estimated at $3 \times 10^{19}$ permutations, which is far greater than the amount of information (estimated at $10^{15}$ bits) that can be stored in a lifetime (Unger, 1976).

It is assumed that peptides with different structures and conformations have specific interactions with receptor sites that, in turn, determine the specific nature of the observed behavior. Evidence of peptides' specific action on central neural functioning has been provided by studies investigating single-cell activity following applications of various peptides and steroids. For example, application by microiontophoresis of TRH on single neurons at several levels of the neural axis resulted in depressed neural firing in the ventromedial hypothalamus, cuneate nucleus, cerebellar cortex, and particularly the parietal cortex (Renaud & Martin, 1975). Single-cell recordings indicated that TRH, LHRH, and somatostatin also had differential potent depressant effects in widespread extrahypothalamic areas (Renaud, Martin, & Brazeau, 1976). Mechanisms of actions of peptide-mediated changes of neuronal activity have yet to be fully delineated, but the evidence suggests that neuroendocrine action on the brain is specific both in terms of area and neuronal response.

Differential hormonal action on CNS function and peptide-receptor specificity is a key concept in the assumption that specific endocrine response profiles are dependent on the nature of environmental stresses and demands and in turn, exert specific, adaptive influences on behavior. Behavioral neuroendocrinology and endocrine stress research have been delineated as separate fields, and there has been little attempt to integrate the two bodies of knowledge. The concept of endocrine response specificity to differing environmental events may apply to the adaptive and specific nature of these hormonal changes in terms of behavior. We can illustrate this notion by a brief review of the evidence concerning the behavioral effects of corticotropic fragments and the endorphins.

Beta-lipotropin hormone ($\beta$-LPH), a 91–amino acid pituitary peptide, first isolated by Li (Li, 1964, 1972; Chretien & Li, 1967), itself contained in the larger pro-opiomelanocortin (Mains, Eipper, & Ling, 1977), has been proposed as a prohormone for both the endorphins and $\beta$-MSH (Bradbury, Smyth, & Snell, 1976). Structural identification (Hughes, Smith, Kosterlitz, Fothergill, Morgan, & Morris, 1975) has revealed that the amino acid sequences of ACTH 4-10 ($\beta$-LPH 47-53), $\beta$-MSH ($\beta$-LPH 41-58), met-enkephalin ($\beta$-LPH 61-65), and the endorphins ($\alpha$-endorphin = $\beta$-LPH 61-76, $\gamma$-endorphin = $\beta$-LPH 61-77, and $\beta$-endorphin = $\beta$-LPH 61-91) are contained within the larger amino acid sequence.

Because pro-opiomelanocortin has been shown to contain such diverse, behaviorally active peptides, the evidence suggests that it may be an important neurohormonal controlling mechanism. The fact that ACTH, ACTH 4-10, $\beta$-MSH, and the endorphins are contained within this megaprotein is provocative in that these hormones have adaptive but different roles in the stress response. It is possible that the pro-opiomelanocortin may have a major integrative function during periods of physical or psychological stress.

As suggested by Gispen, Van Ree, and de Wied (1977) in their excellent review of $\beta$-LPH, this prohormone may serve as a relatively inactive chemical storage unit of these fragments upon which specific enzymatic action selectively cleaves varying behaviorally active fragments. If this proves to be the case, one can easily see the adaptive value of having behaviorally active peptide fragments almost immediately available in times of need. Although the concept of a prohormone is not new (Steiner & Oyer, 1967), the exact nature of the enzymatic cleavage action of the pro-opiomelanocortin, $\beta$-LPH, and related amino acid structures remains unclear at present (Bloomfield, Scott, & Rees, 1974; Kendall, Tang, & Cook, 1975; Silman, Chard, Rees, Smith, & Young, 1975).

The structure of the endorphin peptides appears to be directly related to their capacity to induce analgesia, with larger fragments of $\beta$-LPH exhibiting greater analgesia-inducing properties (Walker, Sandman, Berntson, McGivern, Coy, &

Kastin, 1977). These differences in ability to raise pain thresholds may also be related to differences in the endorphins' capacity to influence separate classes of behavior. Guillemin (1977) has proposed that $\alpha$-, $\gamma$-, and $\beta$-endorphin may exert differential behavioral actions on the organism. The concept of these peptides having varying effects on behavior as a function of their structure and molecular conformation was supported by a study examining rats systemically administered $\alpha$-, $\gamma$-, or $\beta$-endorphin or a more potent (D-Ala$^2$) analogue of each, which were then tested in an open-field setting (Veith, Sandman, Walker, Coy, & Kastin, 1978). Beta-endorphin was found to induce significantly increased grooming behavior, a finding also obtained following intraventricular administration of the substance (Gispen, Wiegant, Bradbury, Hulme, Smyth, Snell, & de Wied, 1976). Furthermore, the $\alpha$-endorphin analogue appeared to enhance sexual arousal. Both $\gamma$-endorphin and its analogue affected separate measures typically considered indicative of increased emotionality. These results suggested that related structures of the endorphin peptides elicit various patterns of behavior as a function of their biochemical structure and conformation.

The site of receptor action mediating these differences is unclear at present, although it is possible that distinct subgroups of opiate receptors may exist (Lord, Waterfield, Hughes, & Kosterlitz, 1977; Martin, Eades, Thompson, Huppler, & Gilbert, 1976). The possibility of actions unrelated to opiate-receptor interactions must also be considered given that a number of effects of enkephalin (Chang et al., 1976; Hill, Pepper, & Mitchell, 1976; Knoll, 1976) are not reversible by the opiate antagonist naloxone.

Furthermore, the endorphins exert influences on behavior unrelated to analgesia. Met-enkephalin and a more potent analogue facilitated rats' ability to run a complex maze (Kastin, Scollan, King, Schally, & Coy, 1976). A (D-Ala$^2$) analogue of met-enkephalin resulted in spontaneous seminal emissions in male rats (Walker, Berntson, Sandman, Coy, Schally, & Kastin, 1977), whereas $\beta$-endorphin reduced levels of sexual activity of male rats in the presence of estrus females (Meyerson & Terenius, 1977). Centrally administered $\beta$-endorphin was found to exert a dose-dependent suppression of fixed-ratio responding independent of motor-activity inhibition (Lichtblau, Fossom, & Sparber, 1977). Given that naloxone has been shown to suppress central gray self-stimulation, it is possible that endogenous opiate peptides may mediate euphoria or drive-reduction reward (Belluzzi & Stein, 1977).

The evidence reviewed suggests that differing fragments of $\beta$-LPH possess the capacity to elicit different behaviors. There is, however, an additional level of complexity of peptide-behavior relationships. Research suggests that different amino acid sequences also evoke the same behavior to differing extents (Sandman, Beckwith, & Kastin, 1980). This implies that $\beta$-LPH is also coded to contain redundant molecular information, thereby suggesting that the concept of multiplicity of control describes peptide-behavior interactions.

For example, fragments of $\beta$-LPH have been shown to have varying potencies in the elicitation of specific behaviors. In an elegantly designed series of structure-activity analyses, overlapping fragments of $\beta$-LPH were examined for their ability to elicit grooming behavior. ACTH 1-24, ACTH 1-16, $\alpha$-MSH, and $\beta$-MSH had approximately equal capacity to induce grooming behavior, believed to be a function of the common critical sequence of ACTH 5-10 (Gispen, Wiegant, Greven, & de Wied, 1975; Wiegant, Cools, & Gispen, 1977). Furthermore, β-LPH also successfully induced grooming behavior in rats, as did the sequences β-LPH 61-76, 61-91, and 61-65 to decreasing extents (Gispen, Wiegant, Bradbury, Hulme, Smyth, Snell, & deWied, 1976). Thus, two separate amino acid sequences of β-LPH were found capable of inducing the same behavior to differing extents, thereby suggesting that β-LPH has repetitions in molecular coding for predisposing the organism to exhibit specific behaviors.

Moreover, there is evidence that opiate receptors may mediate this grooming behavior evoked by the two separate classes of peptide fragments of β-LPH. Naloxone was found to abolish both ACTH 1-24- and endorphin-induced grooming behavior (Gispen & Wiegant, 1976). Moreover, ACTH antagonized the analgesic effects of morphine in the presence of the adrenal gland. This evidence concerning different peptides' capacity to evoke the same behavior again supports the multiplicity-of-control theory of β-LPH and behavior.

The initial evidence concerning the endorphins suggest that these peptides may possess one of the most apparently adaptive functions in individual-environmental interactions. The modulation of pain response is certainly critical in aiding the individual to function under stressful conditions. Furthermore, one might speculate from the accruing evidence concerning the known behaviorally active fragments contained within β-LPH that differential environmental demands may evoke specific cleavage action in accordance with the metabolic and behavioral needs to meet such contingencies.

The relation of β-LPH to the HPAC axis in altering behavior to meet the demands of the environment is another major aspect of this prohormone. As we have discussed, adrenocortical functioning in response to stressful environmental events is perhaps the most studied aspect of psychoendocrine response to stress. Beyond the influences these steroids have on metabolic and physiological functioning, there is also their role in altering the behavioral predisposition. For example, evidence has been obtained suggesting that the adrenocortical response is not an all-or-nothing reaction to environmental events; it has been demonstrated that this response in monkeys is a function of the degree of control over avoidance of shock (Brady, 1970; Sidman, Mason, Brady, & Thach, 1962). Large bodies of evidence indicate that endogenous pituitary-adrenal fluctuations not only are specific responses to environmental demands in such paradigms but may exert direct adaptive influences on the quality and extent of the ongoing and future behavior.

Intraindividual correlational studies have demonstrated that endogenous levels of circulating corticosteroids (and thus, levels of ACTH) are related to the efficacy of performance. Rats exhibiting the highest plasma corticosteroid response to ether-induced stress also exhibited the greatest proficiency in acquiring the correct response in a Sidman-type avoidance paradigm (Wertheim, Conner, & Levine, 1969). The rate of acquisition of an avoidance response has also been associated with circadian fluctuations of ACTH, facilitated performance being exhibited during the peak of the ACTH cycle (Pagano & Lovely, 1972; Schneider, Weinberg, & Weissberg, 1974). Chronically elevated levels of 17-OHCS in rhesus monkeys have, however, been associated with lower acquisition rate of operant avoidance responding (M.D. Levine, Gordon, Peterson, & Rose, 1970).

Alterations of endogenous ACTH-adrenocorticosteroid levels have also been found to induce changes in performance. Hypophysectomized rats exhibited retarded acquisition and facilitated extinction in both active and passive avoidance situations; ACTH replacement therapy restored performance levels to normal (Applezweig & Baudry, 1955; Weiss, McEwan, Silva, & Kalkut, 1970). Moreover, adrenalectomy induced chronic high elevations of ACTH, which resulted in more pronounced avoidance behavior (P. A. Beatty, W. W. Beatty, Bowman, & Gilchrist, 1970; Weiss et al., 1970).

As might be predicted from these studies, increasing endogenous hormone levels by administering ACTH would also alter the performance of animals in learning paradigms. The earliest explanation of the effects of injecting these peptides was that they influenced the emotional state of the organism and made it more fearful. This explanation relied heavily on the assumption that avoidance situations elicited a fear or anxiety response. The ACTH secretion in response to the stress of shock was considered a manifestation of fear.

A departure from the fear hypothesis was developed by de Wied and Bohus (1966). They interpreted the prolonged extinction after treatment with MSH/ACTH as evidence that these peptides enhanced short-term memory. Refinements of this position suggested the memory effect was secondary to the increased general-motivation state of the organism. Nevertheless, several experiments have implicated MSH/ACTH fragments in the primary retrieval processes. Rigter (Rigter, Janssens-Elbertse, & Van Riezen, 1976; Rigter, Van Riezen, & de Wied, 1974; Rigter & Van Riezen, 1975) trained rats to inhibit a shock-avoidance response and then induced amnesia by applying electroconvulsive shock or partial asphyxiation by $CO_2$. Treatment with MSH/ACTH 4-10 before the test of retention restored the rats' memory of the experience.

Another early depature from classical thinking involved the examination of the effects of peptides in an appetitive rather than an aversive paradigm (Sandman, Kastin, & Schally, 1969). MSH/ACTH was found to prolong extinction even in this appetitive task, casting serious doubt on the fear hypothesis. In a series of studies, it was concluded that the perceptual-attentional functioning of the organism was influenced primarily by MSH/ACTH. The major support for this conclusion was developed with the visual-discrimination and reversal-shift problem in rats. In several studies (Sandman, Alexander, & Kastin, 1973; Sandman, Beckwith, Gittis, & Kastin, 1974; Sandman, Beckwith, & Kastin, 1980; Sandman, Miller, Kastin, & Schally, 1972), rats were tested with a two-choice visual-discrimination and reversal problem of avoiding shock. In the initial studies, treatment of rats with MSH had no significant effect on original learning, but treated rats required approximately 50% *fewer* trials to solve the reversal-learning problem. It was concluded from these data that the MSH/ACTH peptide enhanced attentional processes.

In a recent, refined analysis (Sandman, Beckwith, & Kastin, 1980), the influence of MSH/ACTH 4-10, $\alpha$-MSH (1-13), $\beta_p$-MSH (1-18), $\beta_h$-MSH (1-22), and ACTH 1-24 was determined with tests of learning and attention. This study permitted investigation of the putative effects of the redundant chemical information stored in these related peptide chains. The results of the study indicated that the speed of learning the original problem diminished linearly with administration of the same dose of compounds of increasing molecular weight. The structure-activity relationships were much different for reversal learning and extinction. Maximal enhancement of reversal learning (an index of attention) was achieved with administration of $\alpha$- and $\beta$-MSH but not with administration of MSH/ACTH 4-10 or ACTH 1-24.

If behavioral information was coded redundantly in these related molecules, a linear relationship would be predicted between performance and molecular weight. The results of the reversal learning problem (i.e., attention) indicated, however, that only compounds with MSH-like configurations improved performance. Consistent with the evidence reviewed with endorphin fragments, these findings suggested that behavior may be specific to a particular peptide sequence.

At present, it is difficult to assess pharmacological versus physiological effects of administered corticotropic fragments. Evidence obtained from both studies that examined effects of fluctuations of circadian rhythms on rats' performance along with the findings of elevated ACTH levels following dexamethasone administration in depressed populations (Beckwith, 1977) does, however, lend strong support to the thesis that endogenous ACTH and related peptides facilitate behavioral-environmental interactions through altered cognitive functioning and possible changes in perception of the environment.

## CONCLUSION: A MODEL
## OF PSYCHOENDOCRINE RESPONSE TO STRESS

Through this discussion we have developed the thesis that a change in the environment may result in a stress response as a function of individual host resistance. We have viewed the degree of resistance as a function of permanent and transitory influences of hormones, including permanent organizational endocrine effects along with sex differences and circadian and cyclic factors influencing central neural processes. Furthermore, we have shown that endogenous levels of hormones possess the capacity to alter the perception of the environment, thereby potentially altering the appraisal of potentially stress-producing events.

We have suggested that response stereotypy may evoke consistent endocrine changes resulting in consistent individual-specific patterns of stress response. Also, we developed the hypothesis that differing stimulus configurations may result in consistent patterns of endocrine responses that are differentiated on the basis of the nature of the psychological or physical type of stress. Moreover, we presented the notion that patterns of hormonal profiles may evoke peptide-specific patterns of behavior. This proposal we illustrated by examining the influences of the prohormone β-LPH as one underlying basis of peptide action, with specific enzymatic cleavage action resulting in changes in endogenous levels of hormones. These changes induce specific influences on behavior that aid in the adaptation to environmental demands.

Thus, our proposed model, adapted from Leshner (1978) and represented in Fig. 5.1, is based on this conceptualization of stress. Although we assume, for the purposes of this discussion, that each delineated factor is of equal importance, our primary focus has been aimed at the endocrine influences predominantly determining the individual host resistance.

The ongoing host resistance interacts with central neural processing in such a manner as to influence the perception of potentially stressful events. These interactions may be grouped into two major categories: those enacted on the level of afferent receptors, providing the interface between the individual and the environment and those influencing higher-level host-resistance processes such as attentional functioning. Whether an environmental change will be perceived, how it will be perceived, and the intensity of the perception will be a function of the

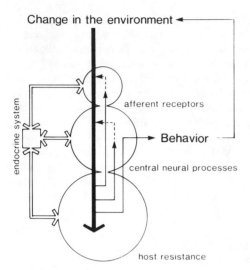

Figure 5.1   A model of stress.

synthetic interaction between the nature of the event and the ongoing host resistance.

The determined perception, in turn, mediates the nature of the endocrine stress response. We assume that the quality of this perception determines the manner and extent of the response. The stress response we assume to be integrated on all levels of endocrine functioning, and furthermore, we conceive it as being relatively specific to both the individual and the nature of the adaptational demands of the perceived event. The response possesses the capacity to alter the event directly, by means of behavior or by altering the perception of the event via its influence on afferent receptor systems of central neural processing.

The first hypothesis, concerning the host resistance as determined by endocrine influences, cannot be directly supported or refuted by the limited available literature. Further research is required in this field to examine both the endogenous and exogenous endocrine fluctuations as independent variables influencing the stress response. Up to now, psychoendocrine response during stress has been viewed as determined mainly by psychological factors; the thesis that endocrine influences play at least an equally important role requires empirical examination. Moreover, the notion of endocrine stress-response stereotypy, which results in stable individual responses across a variety of situations, needs more conclusive research to determine if the concept is applicable to the endocrine as well as the autonomic systems.

The second hypothesis, concerning the specificity of endocrine profiles as a function of the unique demands of the environmental situation resulting in peptide-specific patterns of adaptive behavior, also demands greater investigation. Employment of multiple hormonal profiles across a variety of physical and psychological situations is required. Furthermore, more attention should be focused on the field of behavioral endocrinology to integrate the known influences of peptides on behavior with stress-induced changes in endocrine functioning.

Initial evidence is accumulating to suggest that Selye's concept of the nonspecific stress response is no longer adequate to explain the findings concerning endocrine response to purely physical stressors. Whether this notion of response specificity will be found to be also true of a variety of nonphysical stresses depends on the use of experimental designs employing multiple endocrine measures and delineation of categories of events in terms of the various types of demands made upon the individual. Moreover, the adaptive function of endocrine response is no longer limited in conception to purely physiological or metabolic adaptive effects but must be considered in relation to behavioral changes as well.

Circular definitions of stress such as considering elevated adrenocortical secretion as indicative of responding to stress may prove, as a result of future research, to be misleading. Evidence employing multiple hormonal profiles supports the notion that single hormonal indices are insufficient. Furthermore, present conceptualizations of individual differences in stress responding as solely the product of differences in psychological functioning and appraisal of the environment may be found to be inadequate. Future research may obtain evidence indicating that differential psychoendocrine patterns of stress responding are a product of individual differences in neuroendocrine function. It is possible that these interindividual variations may prove to be a product of stimulus-specific responses to varying demands in the environment, which will, in turn, elicit specific repertoires of behavior.

# REFERENCES

Abplanalp, J. M., Livingston, L., Rose, R. M., & Sandwisch, D. Cortisol and growth hormone responses to psychological stress during the menstrual cycle. *Psychosomatic Medicine,* 1977, *39,* 158–177.

Akil, J., Madden, J., Patrick, R. L., Barchas, J. D. Stress-induced increases in endogenous opiate peptides: Concurrent analgesia and its partial reversal by naloxone. In H. W. Kosterlitz (Ed.), *Opiates and endogenous opioid peptides.* New York: Elsevier, 1976.

Akil, H. Enkephalin: Physiological implications. In F. Usdin, D. A. Hamburg, & J. D. Barchas (Eds.), *Neuroregulators and psychiatric disorders.* New York: Oxford University Press, 1977.

Akil, H., Mayer, D. T., & Liebeski, J. C. Antagonism of stimulation-produced analgesia by naloxone, a narcotic-antagonist. *Science,* 1976, *191,* 961–962.

Altman, N., Sachar, E. J., Gruen, P. H., Halpern, F. S., & Eto, S. Reduced plasma LH concentration in postmenopausal depressed women. *Psychosomatic Medicine,* 1975, *37,* 274–276.

Applezweig, M. H., & Baudry, F. D. The pituitary adrenocortical system in avoidance learning. *Psychological Reports,* 1955, *1,* 417–420.

Arana, G., Boyd, A. E., Reichlin, S., & Lipsitt, D. Prolactin levels in mild depression. *Psychosomatic Medicine,* 1977, *39,* 193–197.

Bardwick, J. M. Psychological correlates of the menstrual cycle and oral contraceptive medications. In E. J. Sacher (Ed.), *Hormones, behavior and psychopathology.* New York: Raven, 1976.

Beach, F. A. *Hormones and behavior.* New York: Cooper Square, 1948.

Beatty, P. A., Beatty, W. W., Bowman, R. E., & Gilchrist, J. C. The effects of ACTH, adrenalectomy and dexamethasone on the acquisition of an avoidance response in rats. *Physiology and Behavior,* 1970, *5,* 939–944.

Beatty, W. W., & Beatty, P. A. Hormonal determinants of sex differences in avoidance behavior and reactivity to electric shock in the rat. *Journal of Comparative and Physiological Psychology,* 1970, *73,* 446–455.

Beckwith, B. E. *Resistance to suppression by dexamethasone: An investigation of some psychological parameters of endocrine dysfunction in depression.* Unpublished doctoral dissertation, Ohio State University, 1977.

Beckwith, B. E., O'Quin, R. K., Petro, M. A., Kastin, A. J., & Sandman, C. A. The effects of neonatal injections of MSH on the open field behavior of juvenile and adult rats. *Physiological Psychology*, 1977, *5*, 295-299.

Beckwith, B. E., Sandman, C. A., Hothersall, D., & Kastin, A. J. Influences of neonatal injections of α-MSH on learning, memory and attention in rats. *Physiology and Behavior*, 1977, *18*, 63-71.

Bell, R. W., Reisner, G., & Linn, T. Recovery from electroconvulsive shock as a function of infantile stimulation. *Science*, 1961, *133*, 1428.

Belluzzi, J. D., & Stein, L. Enkephalin may mediate euphoria and drive reduction reward. *Nature*, 1977, *226*, 556-558.

Benjafield, J. G., & Rutter, L. F. Significance of metabolic disorders in schizophrenia. *Lancet*, 1973, *1*, 783.

Blake, C. A. Effects of stress on pulsatile luteinizing hormone release in ovariectomized rats. *Proceedings of the Society for Experimental Biology and Medicine*, 1975, *148*, 813-815.

Bloomfield, G. A., Scott, A. P., & Rees, L. H. Melanocyte stimulating hormone related peptides in human plasma. *Journal of Endocrinology*, 1974, *63*, 51P.

Board, F., Wadeson, R. W., & Persky, H. Depressive affect and endocrine function. *Archives of Neurology and Psychiatry*, 1957, *78*, 612-620.

Bradbury, A. F., Smyth, D. G., & Snell, C. R. Lipotropin: Precursor to two biologically active peptides. *Biochemical and Biophysical Research Communication*, 1976, *69*, 950-956.

Brady, J. V. Emotion: Some conceptual problems and psychophysiological experiments. In M. B. Arnold (Ed.), *Feelings and emotions*. New York: Academic, 1970.

Brown, G. M., & Reichlin, S. Psychologic and neural regulation of growth hormone secretion. *Psychosomatic Medicine*, 1972, *34*, 45-61.

Burns, J. K. Variation in plasma ACTH during the human menstrual cycle. *Journal of Physiology*, 1975, *249*, 36P.

Cannon, W. B. The emergency function of the adrenal medulla in pain and the major emotions. *American Journal of Physiology*, 1914, *33*, 356.

Carpenter, W. T., & Bunney, W. E. Adrenal cortical activity in depressive illnesses. *American Journal of Psychiatry*, 1971, *128*, 31-40.

Carroll, B. J. Hypothalamic-pituitary function in depressive illness: Insensitivity to hypoglycemia. *British Medical Journal*, 1969, *5*, 27-28.

Carroll, B. J. Psychiatric disorders and steroids. In E. Usdin, D. A. Hamburg, & J. D. Barchas (Eds.), *Neuroregulators and psychiatric disorders*. New York: Oxford University Press, 1977.

Carroll, B. J., Martin, F. I. R., & Davies, B. Resistance to suppression by dexamethasone of plasma 11-OHCS levels in severe depressive illness. *British Medical Journal*, 1968, *3*, 283-287.

Champney, T. F., Sahley, T. L., & Sandman, C. A. Effects of neonatal cerebral ventricular injection of ACTH 4-9 and subsequent adult injections on learning in male and female albino rats. *Physiology, Biochemistry and Behavior*, 1976, *5*(Suppl. 1), 3-9.

Chang, J. K., Fong, B. T. W., Pert, A., & Pert, C. B. Opiate receptor affinities and behavioral effects of enkephalin: Structure-activity relationship of 10 synthetic peptide analogues. *Life Sciences*, 1976, *18*, 1473-1482.

Chretien, M., & Li, C. H. Isolation, purification and characterization of gammalipotropic hormone from sheep pituitary glands. *Canadian Journal of Biochemistry*, 1967, *45*, 1163-1174.

Christian, J. J. Effect of population size on the adrenal glands and reproductive organs of male mice in populations of fixed size. *American Journal of Physiology*, 1955, *182*, 292-300.

Cohen, S. I. Some implications of current neuropeptide studies for clinical psychophysiology of the future. In L. H. Miller, C. A. Sandman, & A. J. Kastin (Eds.), *Neuropeptide influences on the brain and behavior*. New York: Raven, 1977.

Curtis, G. C Are nocturnal cortisol spikes in depressed patients due to stress? In E. J. Sacher (Ed.), *Hormones, behavior and psychopathology*. New York: Raven, 1976.

Czeisler, C. A., Mooreede, M. C., Regestein, Q. R., Kisch, E. S., Fang, V. S., & Ehrlich, E. N. Episodic 24-hour cortisol secretory patterns in patients awaiting elective cardiac surgery. *Journal of Clinical Endocrinology and Metabolism*, 1976, *42*, 273-283.

Davis, J. M. Theories of biological etiology of affective disorders. *International Review of Neurobiology*, 1970, *12*, 145-175.

Denti, A., & Epstein, A. Sex difference in the acquisition of two kinds of avoidance behavior in rats. *Physiology and Behavior*, 1972, *8*, 611–615.

Doering, C. H., Brodie, H. K. H., Kraemer, H. C., Becker, H. B., & Hamburg, D. A. Plasma testosterone levels and psychologic measures in men over a two-month period. In R. C. Friedman, R. M. Richart, and R. L. Vande Wiele (Eds.), *Sex differences in behavior*. New York: Wiley, 1974.

Doering, C. H., Brodie, H. K. H., Kraemer, H. C., Moos, R. H., Becker, H. B., & Hamburg, D. A. Negative affect and plasma testosterone: A longitudinal study. *Psychosomatic Medicine*, 1975, *37*, 484–491.

Dornbush, R. L., & Bikolovski, O. ACTH 4-10 and short-term memory. *Pharmacology, Biochemistry and Behavior*, 1976, *5*(Suppl. 1), 69–72.

Dunn, J. D., Arimura, A., & Scheving, L. E. Effect of stress on circadian periodicity in serum LH and prolactin concentration. *Endocrinology*, 1972, *90*, 29–33.

Eayrs, J. T. Age as a factor determining the severity and reversibility of the effects of thyroid deprivation in the rat. *Journal of Endocrinology*, 1961, *22*, 409–419.

Eayrs, J. T., & Levine, S. Influence of thyroidectomy and subsequent replacement therapy upon conditioned avoidance learning in the rat. *Journal of Endocrinology*, 1963, *25*, 505–515.

Engel, B. T. Stimulus-response and individual-response specificity. *Archives of General Psychiatry*, 1960, *2*, 305–313.

Fawcett, J. A., & Bunney, W. E. Pituitary adrenal function and depression. *Archives of General Psychiatry*, 1967, *16*, 517–535.

Fishman, J. R., Hamburg, D. A., Handlon, J. H., Mason, J. W., & Sachar, E. J. Emotional and adrenal cortical responses to a new experience. *Archives of General Psychiatry*, 1962, *6*, 271–278.

Fredrickson, R. C. A., Burgis, V., & Edwards, J. D. Hyperalgesia induced by naloxone follows diurnal rhythm in responsivity to painful stimuli. *Science*, 1977, *198*, 756–758.

Friedman, J., & Meares, R. A. The menstrual cycle and habituation. *Psychosomatic Medicine*, 1979, *41*, 369–381.

Friedman, S. B., Mason, J. W., & Hamburg, D. A. Urinary 17-hydroxycorticosteroid levels in parents of children with neoplastic disease. *Psychosomatic Medicine*, 1963, *25*, 364–376.

Gaillard, A. W. K., & Sanders, S. Some effects of ACTH 4-10 on performance during a serial reaction task. *Psychopharmacologia*, 1975, *42*, 201–208.

Gates, A. Correlations and sex differences in memory and substitution. *University of California Publications in Psychology*, 1916, *1*, 345–350.

Genazzani, A. R., Lemarchand-Beraud, T. H., Aubert, M. L., & Felber, J. P. Pattern of plasma ACTH, hGH and cortisol during the menstrual cycle. *Journal of Clinical Endocrinology and Metabolism*, 1975, *41*, 431–437.

Gispen, W. H., Van Ree, J. M., & de Wied, D. Lipotropin and the central nervous system. *International Review of Neurobiology*, 1977, *20*, 209–250.

Gispen, W. H., van Wimersma Greidanus, Tj. B., & de Wied, D. Effect of hypophysectomy and ACTH 1-10 on responsiveness to electric shock in rats. *Physiology and Behavior*, 1970, *5*, 143–146.

Gispen, W. H., & Wiegant, V. M. Opiate antagonists suppress ACTH 1-24 induced excessive grooming in the rat. *Neuroscience Letters*, 1976, *2*, 159–164.

Gispen, W. H., Wiegant, V. M., Bradbury, A. F., Hulme, E. C., Smyth, D. G., Snell, C. R., & de Wied, D. Induction of excessive grooming by fragments of lipotropin. *Nature*, 1976, *264*, 794–795.

Gispen, W. H., Wiegant, V. M., Greven, H. M., & de Wied, D. The induction of excessive grooming in the rat by intraventricular application of peptides derived from ACTH: Structure-activity studies. *Life Sciences*, 1975, *17*, 645–652.

Golub, S. The magnitude of premenstrual anxiety and depression. *Psychosomatic Medicine*, 1976, *38*, 4–12.

Graham, F. K., & Clifton, R. K. Heart rate change as a component of the orienting response. *Psychological Bulletin*, 1966, *65*, 305–320.

Gram, T. E., & Gilette, J. R. The role of sex hormones in the metabolism of drugs and other foreign compounds by hepatic microsomal enzymes. In H. A. Salhanick, D. M. Kipnis, and R. L. Vande Wiele (Eds.), *Metabolic effects of gonadal hormones and contraceptive steroids*. New York: Plenum, 1969.

Gray, J. A. *The psychology of fear and stress*. New York: McGraw-Hill, 1971.

Greenwood, F. C., & Landon, J. Growth hormone secretion in response to stress in man. *Nature*, 1966, *210*, 540–541.

Grevert, P., & Goldstein, A. Effect of naloxone on experimentally induced ischemic pain and on mood in human subjects. *Proceedings of the National Academy of Sciences*, 1977, *74*, 1291–1294.

Guillemin, R. Endorphins, brain peptides that act like opiates. *New England Journal of Medicine*, 1977, *296*, 226–228.

Hamilton, D. L., & Chaddock, T. Social interaction and serum insulin values in the monkey (*Macaca mulatta*). *Psychosomatic Medicine*, 1977, *39*, 444–450.

Hartley, L. H., Mason, J. W., Hogan, R. P., Jones, L. G., Kotchen, T. A., Mougey, E. H., Wherry, F. E., Pennington, L. L., & Ricketts, P. T. Multiple hormonal responses to graded exercise in relation to physical training. *Journal of Applied Physiology*, 1972, *33*, 602–606. (a)

Hartley, L. H., Mason, J. W., Hogan, R. P., Jones, L. G., Kotchen, T. A., Mougey, E. H., Wherry, F. E., Pennington, L. L., & Ricketts, P. T. Multiple hormonal responses to prolonged exercise in relation to physical training. *Journal of Applied Physiology*, 1972, *33*, 607–610. (b)

Henkin, R. I. Effects of ACTH, adrenocorticosteroids and thyroid hormone on sensory function. In W. E. Stumpf & L. D. Grant (Eds.), *Anatomical neuroendocrinology*. New York: Karger, 1975.

Hill, R. G., Pepper, C. M., & Mitchell, J. F. Depression of nociceptive and other neurons by iontophoretically applied met-enkephalin. *Nature*, 1976, *262*, 604–606.

Holmberg, C., Levi, L., Mathe, A. A., Rosen, A., & Scott, H. Plasma catecholamines and the effects of adrenergic beta receptor blockade on cardiovascular and mental reactions during emotional stress. In L. Levi (Ed.), *Emotional stress.* New York: Elsevier, 1967.

Holmes, T. H., & Rahe, R. H. The Social Readjustment Rating Scale. *Journal of Psychosomatic Research*, 1967, *11*, 213–218.

Howard, J. S. Psychosis and the thyroid. *Psychosomatics*, 1975, *16*, 61–64.

Hughes, J., Smith, T. W., Kosterlitz, H. W., Fothergill, L. A., Morgan, B. A., & Morris, N. R. Identification of two related pentapeptides from the brain with potent opiate agonist activity. *Nature*, 1975, *258*, 577–579.

Hutt, C. *Male and female.* Baltimore: Penguin, 1972.

Kaiser, D., & Sandman, C. A. Physiological patterns accompanying complex problem solved during warning and nonwarning conditions. *Journal of Comparative and Physiological Psychology*, 1975, *89*, 357–363.

Karacan, I., Rosenbloom, A. L., Londono, J. H., Salis, P. J., Thornby, J. I., & Williams, R. L. The effects of acute fasting on sleep and the sleep-growth hormone response. *Psychosomatics*, 1973, *14*, 33–37.

Kastin, A. J., Beach, G. D., Hawley, W. D., Kendall, J. W., Edwards, M. S., & Schally, A. V. Dissociation of MSH and ACTH release in man. *Journal of Clinical Endocrinology and Metabolism*, 1973, *36*, 770–772.

Kastin, A. J., Miller, L. H., Gonzalez-Barcena, D., Hawley, W. D., Dyster-Aas, K., Schally, A. V., Velasco de Parra, M. L., & Velasco, M. Psychophysiologic correlates of MSH activity in man. *Physiology and Behavior*, 1971, *7*, 893–896.

Kastin, A. J., Scollan, W. L., King, M. G., Schally, A. V., & Coy, D. H. Enkephalin and a potent analog facilitate maze performance after intraperitoneal administration in rats. *Pharmacology, Biochemistry and Behavior*, 1976, *5*, 691–695.

Katz, J. L., Weiner, H., Gallagher, T. F., & Hellman, L. Stress, distress and ego defenses: Psychoendocrine response to impending breast tumor biopsy. *Archives of General Psychiatry*, 1970, *23*, 131–148.

Kendall, J. W., Tang, L., & Cook, D. M. Sites of feedback control in the pituitary-adrenocortical system. In W. E. Stumpf & L. D. Grant (Eds.), *Anatomical neuroendocrinology*, 1975. New York: Karger.

Knoll, J. Neuronl peptide (enkephalin) receptors in the ear artery of the rabbit. *European Journal of Pharmacology*, 1976, *39*, 403–407.

Kreuz, L. E., Rose, R. M., & Jennings, J. R. Suppression of plasma testosterone levels and psychological stress. *Archives of General Psychiatry*, 1972, *26*, 479–482.

Kurokawa, N., Suematso, H., Tamai, A., Esaki, M., Aoki, A., & Ikema, Y. Effect of emotional stress on human growth hormone secretion. *Journal of Psychosomatic Research*, 1977, *21*, 231–235.

Lacey, J. I. Individual difference in somatic response patterns. *Journal of Comparative and Physiological Psychology,* 1950, *43,* 338–350.

Lacey, J. I. Somatic response patterning and stress: Some revisions of activation theory. In M. H. Appley and R. Trumbull (Eds.), *Psychological stress: Issues in research.* New York: Appleton, 1967.

Lacey, J. I., Bateman, D. E., & Van Lehn, R. Autonomic response specificity. *Psychosomatic Medicine,* 1953, *15,* 9–21.

Lacey, J. I., & Lacey, B. C. Verification and extension of the principle of autonomic response stereotypy. *American Journal of Psychology,* 1958, *71,* 50–73.

Lacey, J. I., & Van Lehn, R. Differential emphasis in somatic response to stress. *Psychosomatic Medicine,* 1952, *14,* 71–81.

Leshner, A. I. A model of hormones and agonistic behavior. *Physiology and Behavior,* 1975, *15,* 622–635.

Leshner, A. I. *An introduction to behavioral endocrinology.* New York: Oxford University Press, 1978.

Levi, L. Endocrine reactions during emotional stress. In L. Levi (Ed.), *Emotional stress.* New York: Elsevier, 1967. (a)

Levi, L. Stressors, stress tolerance, emotions and performance in relation to catecholamine excretion. In L. Levi (Ed.), *Emotional stress.* New York: Elsevier, 1967. (b)

Levi, L. Sympathoadreno medullary responses to "pleasant" and "unpleasant" psychosocial stimuli. *Acta Medica Scandinavica,* 1972, *191*(Suppl. 528), 55–73.

Levine, M. D., Gordon, T. P., Peterson, R. H., & Rose, R. M. Urinary 17-OHCS response of high- and low-aggressive rhesus monkeys to shock avoidance. *Physiology and Behavior,* 1970, *5,* 919–924.

Levine, S. Plasma-free corticosteroid response to electric shock in rats stimulated in infancy. *Science,* 1962, *135,* 795–796.

Levine, S., Coe, C. L., Smotherman, W. P., & Kaplan, J. N. Prolonged cortisol elevation in the infant squirrel monkey after reunion with mother. *Physiology and Behavior,* 1978, *20,* 7–10.

Levine, S., & Mullins, R. F., Jr. Hormonal influences on brain organization in infant rats. *Science,* 1966, *152,* 1585–1592.

Li, C. H. Lipotropin, a new active peptide from the pituitary gland. *Nature,* 1964, *258,* 577–579.

Li, C. H. Hormones of the adenohypophysis. *Proceedings of the American Philosophical Society,* 1972, *116,* 365–382.

Lichtblau, L., Fossom, L. H., & Sparber, S. B. β-endorphin: Dose dependent suppression of fixed-ratio operant behavior. *Life Sciences,* 1977, *21,* 927–932.

Lord, J. A., Waterfield, A. A., Hughes, J., & Kosterlitz, H. W. Endogenous opiate peptides: Multiple agonists and receptors. *Nature,* 1977, *267,* 495–499.

Maccoby, E. E., & Jacklin, C. N. *The psychology of sex differences.* Stanford, Calif.: Stanford University Press, 1974.

Mains, R. E., Eipper, B. A., & Ling, N. Common precursor to corticotropins and endorphins. *Proceedings of the National Academy of Sciences,* 1977, *74,* 3014–3018.

Martin, W. R., Eades, C. G., Thompson, J. A., Huppler, R. E., & Gilbert, P. E. The effects of morphine and narlorphine-like drugs in the nondependent and morphine-dependent chronic spinal dog. *Journal of Pharmacology and Experimental Therapy,* 1976, *197,* 517–532.

Mason, J. W. Organization of the multiple endocrine responses to avoidance in the monkey. *Psychosomatic Medicine,* 1968, *30,* 774–790. (a)

Mason, J. W. A review of psychoendocrine research on the pituitary-adrenal cortical system. *Psychosomatic Medicine,* 1968, *30,* 576–607. (b)

Mason, J. W. A review of psychoendocrine research on the pituitary-thyroid system. *Psychosomatic Medicine,* 1968, *30,* 666–681. (c)

Mason, J. W. A review of the psychoendocrine research on the sympathetic–adrenal medullary system. *Psychosomatic Medicine,* 1968, *30,* 631–653. (d)

Mason, J. W. The scope of psychoendocrine research. *Psychosomatic Medicine,* 1968, *30,* 565–575. (e)

Mason, J. W. Corticosteroid response to chair restraint in the monkey. *American Journal of Physiology,* 1972, *222,* 1291–1294. (a)

Mason, J. W. Organization of psychoendocrine mechanism. In N. S. Greenfield and R. A. Sternbach (Eds.), *Handbook of psychophysiology.* New York: Holt, 1972. (b)

Mason, J. W. Specificity in the organization of the neuroendocrine response profiles. In P. Seeman and G. M. Brown (Eds.), *Frontiers in neurology and neuroscience research*. Toronto: University of Toronto, Neuroscience Institute, 1974.

Mason, J. W. A historical view of the stress field. *Journal of Human Stress*, 1975, *1*, 22–36. (a)

Mason, J. W. Psychological stress and endocrine function. In E. J. Sachar (Ed.), *Topics in psychoendocrinology*. New York: Grune & Stratton, 1975. (b)

Mason, J. W., Brady, J. V., & Tolliver, G. A. Plasma and urinary 17-hydroxycorticosteroid responses to 72 hour avoidance sessions in the monkey. *Psychosomatic Medicine*, 1968, *30*, 608–630.

Mason, J. W., Hartley, L. H., Kotchen, T. A., Mougey, E. H., Ricketts, P. T., Jones, L. G. Plasma cortisol and norepinephrine responses in anticipation of muscular exercise. *Psychosomatic Medicine*, 1973, *35*, 406–414.

Mason, J. W., Hartley, L. H., Kotchen, T. A., Wherry, F. E., Pennington, L. L., & Jones, L. G. Plasma thyroid-stimulating hormone response in anticipation of muscular exercise in the human. *Journal of Clinical Endocrinology and Metabolism*, 1973, *37*, 403–406.

Mason, J. W., Jones, J. A., Ricketts, P. T., Brady, J. V., & Tolliver, G. A. Urinary aldosterone and urine volume responses to 72 hour avoidance sessions in the monkey. *Psychosomatic Medicine*, 1968, *30*, 733–745.

Mason, J. W., Kenion, C. K., Collins, D. R., Mougey, E. H., Jones, J. A., Driver, G. C., Brady, J. V., & Beer, B. Urinary testosterone responses to 72-hour avoidance sessions in the monkey. *Psychosomatic Medicine*, 1968, *30*, 721–732.

Mason, J. W., & Mougey, E. H. Thyroid (plasma BEI) response to chair restraint in the monkey. *Psychosomatic Medicine*, 1972, *34*, 441–448.

Mason, J. W., Mougey, E. H., Brady, J. V., & Tolliver, G. A. Thyroid (plasma butanol-extractable iodine) responses to 72-hour avoidance sessions in the monkey. *Psychosomatic Medicine*, 1968, *30*, 682–695.

Mason, J. W., Mougey, E. H., & Kenion, C. K. Urinary epinephrine and norepinephrine responses to chair restraint in the monkey. *Physiology and Behavior*, 1973, *10*, 801–804.

Mason, J. W., Taylor, E. D., Brady, J. V., & Tolliver, G. A. Urinary estrone, estradiol, and estriol responses to 72-hour avoidance sessions in the monkey. *Psychosomatic Medicine*, 1968, *30*, 698–709.

Mason, J. W., Tolson, W. W., Brady, J. V., Tolliver, G. A., & Gilmore, L. R. Urinary epinephrine and norepinephrine responses to 72-hour avoidance session in the monkey. *Psychosomatic Medicine*, 1968, *30*, 654–667.

Mason, J. W., Tolson, W. W., Robinson, J. A., Brady, J. V., Tolliver, G. A., & Johnson, T. A. Urinary androsterone, etiocholanolone and dehydroepiandrosterone responses to 72 hour avoidance sessions in the monkey. *Psychosomatic Medicine*, 1968, *30*, 710–720.

Mason, J. W., Wherry, F. E., Brady, J. V., Beer, B., Pennington, L. L., & Goodman, A. C. Plasma insulin responses to 72-hour avoidance sessions in the monkey. *Psychosomatic Medicine*, 1968, *30*, 746–759.

Mason, J. W., Wool, M. S., Wherry, F. E., Pennington, L. L., Brady, J. V., & Beer, B. Plasma growth hormone response to avoidance sessions in the monkey. *Psychosomatic Medicine*, 1968, *30*, 760–773.

Mathe, A. A., & Knapp, P. H. Emotional and adrenal reactions to stress in bronchial asthma. *Psychosomatic Medicine*, 1971, *33*, 323–430.

Mattson, A., Gross, S., & Hall, T. W. Psychoendocrine study of adaptation in young hemophiliacs. *Psychosomatic Medicine*, 1971, *33*, 215–225.

Meyerson, B. J., & Terenius, L. β-endorphin and male sexual behavior. *European Journal of Pharmacology*, 1977, *42*, 191–192.

Miller, L. H., Harris, L. C., Van Riezen, H., & Kastin, A. J. Neuroheptapeptide influence on attention and memory in man. *Pharmacology, Biochemistry and Behavior*, 1976, *5*(Suppl. 1), 17–21.

Miller, L. H., Kastin, A. J., Sandman, C. A., Fink, M., & Van Veen, W. J., Polypeptide influences on attention, memory and anxiety in man. *Pharmacology, Biochemistry and Behavior*, 1974, *2*, 663–668.

Miyabo, S., Asato, T., & Mizushima, N. Psychological correlates of stress-induced cortisol and growth hormone releases in neurotic patients. *Psychosomatic Medicine*, 1979, *41*, 515–523.

Noel, G. L., Dimond, R. C., Earll, J. M., & Frantz, A. G. Prolactin, thyrotropin, and growth hormone release during stress associated with parachute jumping. *Aviation, Space and Environmental Medicine*, 1976, *47*, 543–547.

Pagano, R. R., & Lovely, R. H. Diurnal cycle and ACTH facilitation of shuttle box avoidance. *Physiology and Behavior*, 1972, *8*, 721–723.

Persky, H. Reproductive hormones, moods, and the menstrual cycle. In R. C. Friedman, R. M. Richart, and R. L. Vande Wiele (Eds.), *Sex differences in behavior.* New York: Wiley, 1974.

Persky, H. Tetrahydrocortisol/tetrahydrocortisone ratio ($H_4 F/H_4 E$) as an indicator of depressive feelings. *Psychosomatic Medicine*, 1976, *38*, 13–18.

Phoenix, C. H., Goy, R. W., Gerall, A. A., & Young, W. D. Organizing action of prenatally administered testosterone propionate on the tissue mediating mating behavior in the female guinea pig. *Endocrinology*, 1959, *65*, 369–382.

Politch, J. A., Herrenkohl, L. R., & Gala, R. R. Effects of ether stress on prolactin and corticosterone levels in prenatally-stressed male rats as adults. *Physiology and Behavior*, 1978, *20*, 91–93.

Pomeranz, B., & Chiu, D. Naloxone blockade of acupuncture analgesia: Endorphins implicated. *Life Sciences*, 1976, *19*, 1757–1762.

Raab, W. Correlated cardiovascular adrenergic and adrenocortical responses to sensory and mental annoyances in man. *Psychosomatic Medicine*, 1968, *30*, 809–818.

Rada, R. T., Kellner, R., & Winslow, W. W. Plasma testosterone and aggressive behavior. *Psychosomatics*, 1976, *17*, 138–142.

Rada, R. T., Laws, D. R., & Kellner, R. Plasma testosterone levels in the rapist. *Psychosomatic Medicine*, 1976, *38*, 257–268.

Redmond, D. E., Baulu, J., Murphy, D. L., Loriaux, D. L., Zeigler, M. G., & Lake, C. R. The effects of testosterone on plasma and platelet monoamine oxidase (MAO) and plasma dopamine-$\beta$-hydroxylase (DBH) activities in the male rhesus monkey. *Psychosomatic Medicine*, 1976, *38*, 315–326.

Reinisch, J. M. Effects of prenatal hormone exposure on physical and psychological development in humans and animals: With a note on the state of the field. In E. J. Sachar (Ed.), *Hormones, behavior and Psychopathology.* New York: Raven, 1976.

Renaud, L. P., & Martin, J. B. Microiontophoresis of thyrotropin-releasing hormone (TRH): Effects on the activity of central neurons. In W. E. Stumpf & L. D. Grant (Eds.), *Anatomical neuroendocrinology.* New York, Karger, 1975.

Renaud, L. P., Martin, J. B., & Brazeau, P. Hypothalamic releasing factors: Physiological evidence for a regulatory action on central neurons and pathways for their distribution in brain. *Pharmacology, Biochemistry and Behavior*, 1976, *5*(Suppl. 1), 171–178.

Rice, R. W., & Critchlow, V. Extrahypothalamic control of stress-induced inhbition of growth hormone secretion in the rat. *Endocrinology*, 1976, *99*, 970–976.

Rigter, H., Janssens-Elbertse, R., & Van Riezen, H. Reversal of anmesia by an orally active ACTH 4-9 analog (Org 2766). *Pharmacology, Biochemistry and Behavior*, 1976, *5*(Suppl. 1), 53–58.

Rigter, H., and Van Riezen, H. Anti-amnesic effects of ACTH 4-10: Its independence of the nature of the amnesic agent and the behavioral test. *Physiology and Behavior*, 1975, *14*, 563–566.

Rigter, H., Van Riezen, H., & de Wied, D. The effects of ACTH and vasopressin analogues on $CO_2$ induced retrograde amnesia in rats. *Physiology and Behavior*, 1974, *13*, 381–388.

Rose, R. M. Androgen response to stress. *Psychosomatic Medicine*, 1969, *31*, 405–412.

Rose, R. M., Bernstein, I. S., & Gordon, T. P. Consequences of social conflict on plasma testosterone levels in rhesus monkeys. *Psychosomatic Medicine*, 1975, *37*, 50–61.

Rose, R. M., Bourne, P. G., Poe, R. O., Mougey, E. H., Collins, D. R., & Mason, J. W. Androgen response to stress. *Psychosomatic Medicine*, 1969, *31*, 418–436.

Rose, R. M., Gordon, T. P., & Bernstein, I. S. Plasma testosterone levels in the male rhesus: Influences of sexual and social stimuli. *Science*, 1972, *178*, 643–645.

Rose, R. M., Poe, R. O., & Mason, J. W. Psychological state and body size as determinants of 17-OHCS excretion. *Archives of Internal Medicine*, 1968, *121*, 406.

Rubin, R. T., Gouin, P. R., Kales, A., & Odell, W. D. Luteinizing hormone, follicle stimulating hormone, and growth hormone secretion in normal adult men during sleep and dreaming. *Psychosomatic Medicine*, 1973, *35*, 309–321.

Sachar, E. J. Hormonal changes in stress and mental illness. *Hospital Practice*, 1975, *10*, 49–55.

Sachar, E. J., Hellman, L., Fukushima, D. K., & Gallagher, T. F. Cortisol production in depressive illness: A clinical and biochemical clarification. *Archives of General Psychiatry*, 1970, *23*, 289–298.

Sachar, E. J., Hellman, L., Roffwarf, H. P., Halpern, F. S., Fukushima, D. K., & Gallagher, T. F.

Disrupted 24-hour patterns of cortisol secretion in psychotic depression. *Archives of General Psychiatry,* 1973, *28,* 19–24.

Sandman, C. A., Alexander, W. D., & Kastin, A. J. Neuroendocrine influences on visual discrimination and reversal learning in the albino and hooded rat. *Physiology and Behavior,* 1973, *11,* 613–617.

Sandman, C. A., Beckwith, B. E., Gittis, M. M., & Kastin, A. J. Melanocyte-stimulating hormone (MSH) and overturning effects on extradimensional shift (EDS) learning. *Physiology and Behavior,* 1974, *13,* 163–166.

Sandman, C. A., Beckwith, B. E., & Kastin, A. J. Are learning and attention related to the molecular weight of MSH/ACTH fragments? *Peptides,* 1980.

Sandman, C. A., George, J. M., McCanne, T. R., Nolan, J. D., Kaswan, J., & Kastin, A. J. MSH/ACTH 4-10 influences behavioral and physiological measures of attention. *Journal of Clinical Endocrinology and Metabolism,* 1977, *44,* 884–891.

Sandman, C. A., George, J. M., Nolan, J. D., Van Riezen, H., & Kastin, A. J. Enhancement of attention in man with MSH/ACTH 4-10. *Physiology and Behavior,* 1975, *15,* 427–431.

Sandman, C. A., & Kastin, A. J. The influence of fragments of the LPH chains on learning, memory and attention in animals and man. *Pharmacology and therapeutics,* 1981, *13,* 39–60.

Sandman, C. A., Kastin, A. J., & Schally, A. V. Melanocyte-stimulating hormone and learned appetitive behavior. *Experienta,* 1969, *25,* 1001–1002.

Sandman, C. A., Kastin, A. J., Schally, A. V., Kendall, J. W., & Miller, L. H. Neuroendocrine response to physical and psychological stress. *Journal of Comparative and Physiological Psychology,* 1973, *84,* 386–390.

Sandman, C. A., Miller, L. H., Kastin, A. J., & Schally, A. V. Neuroendocrine influence on attention and memory. *Journal of Comparative and Physiological Psychology,* 1972, *80,* 54–58.

Schneider, A. M., Weinberg, J., & Weissberg, R. Effects of ACTH on conditioned suppression: A time and strength of conditioning analysis. *Physiology and Behavior,* 1974, *13,* 633–636.

Seggie, J. A., & Brown, G. M. Stress response patterns of plasma corticosterone, prolactin and growth hormone in the rat, following handling or exposure to novel environment. *Canadian Journal of Physiology and Pharmacology,* 1975, *53,* 629–637.

Selye, H. A syndrome produced by diverse noxious agents. *Nature,* 1936, *138,* 32–33.

Selye, H. *The physiology and pathology of exposure to stress.* Montreal: Acta, 1950.

Sidman, M., Mason, J. W., Brady, J. V., & Thach, J. Quantitative reactions between avoidance behavior and pituitary-adrenal cortical activity. *Journal of the Experimental Analysis of Behavior,* 1962, *5,* 353–362.

Silman, R. E., Chard, T., Rees, L. H., Smith, I., & Young, I. M. Observations of melanocyte-stimulating hormone-like peptide in human maternal plasma during late pregnancy. *Journal of Endocrinology,* 1975, *65,* 46P–47P.

Smals, A. G. H., Kloppenberg, P. W. C., & Benraad, T. J. Diurnal plasma testosterone rhythm and the effect of short-term ACTH administration on plasma testosterone in man. *Journal of Clinical Endocrinology and Metabolism,* 1974, *38,* 608–611.

Smythies, J. R. The biochemical organization of the brain and schizophrenia. In C. Shagass, S. Gershon, & A. J. Friedhoff (Eds.), *Psychopathology and brain dysfunction.* New York: Raven, 1977.

Steiner, D. F., & Oyer, P. E. The biosynthesis of insulin and a probable precursor of insulin by a human islet cell adenoma. *Proceedings of the National Academy of Sciences,* 1967, *57,* 473–478.

Stewart, W. W. Comments on the chemistry of scotophobin. *Nature,* 1972, *238,* 202–210.

Stokes, P. E., Stoll, P. M., Mattson, M. R., & Sollod, R. N. Diagnosis and psychopathology in psychiatric patients resistant to dexamethasone. In E. J. Sacher (Ed.), *Hormones, behavior and psychopatholgogy.* New York: Raven, 1976.

Stratton, L. O., Gibson, C. A., Kolar, K. G., & Kastin, A. J. Neonatal treatment with TRH affects development, learning and emotionality in the rat. *Pharmacology, Biochemistry and Behavior,* 1976, *5*(Suppl. 1), 65–67.

Tennes, K., Downey, K., & Vernadakis, A. Urinary cortisol excretion rates and anxiety in normal 1-year-old infants. *Psychosomatic Medicine,* 1977, *39,* 178–187.

Ungar, G. Is there a memory trace? *Israel Journal of Chemistry,* 1976.

Ungar, G., Desiderio, D. M., & Parr, W. Isolation, identification and synthesis of a specific-behavior-inducing brain peptide. *Nature,* 1972, *238,* 198–202.

Veith, J. L., Sandman, C. A., George, J. M., & Stevens, V. C. Effects of MSH/ACTH 4-10 on memory, attention, and endogenous hormone levels in women. *Physiology and Behavior,* 1978, *20,* 43–50.

Veith, J. L., Sandman, C. A., Walker, J. M., Coy, D. H., & Kastin, A. J. Systemic administration of endorphins selectively alters open field behavior of rats. *Physiology and Behavior,* 1978, *20,* 539–542.

Volaka, J., Mallya, A., Baig, S., & Perez-Cruet, J. Naloxone in chronic schizophrenia. *Science,* 1977, *196,* 1227–1228.

Wade, G. N. Gonadal hormones and behavioral regulation of body weight. *Physiology and Behavior,* 1972, *8,* 523–534.

Wadeson, R. W., Mason, J. W., Hamburg, D. A., & Handlon, J. H. Plasma and urinary 17-OHCS responses to motion pictures. *Archives of General Psychiatry,* 1963, *9,* 146–156.

Walker, J. M., Berntson, G. G., Sandman, C. A., Coy, D. H., Schally, A. V., & Kastin, A. J. An analog of enkephalin having prolonged opiate-like effects in vivo. *Science,* 1977, *196,* 85–87.

Walker, J. M., Sandman, C. A., Berntson, G. G., McGivern, R. F., Coy, D. H., & Kastin, A. J. Endorphin analogs with potent and long-lasting analgesic effects. *Pharmacology, Biochemistry and Bheavior,* 1977, *7,* 543–548.

Ward, I. Sexual behavior differentiation: Prenatal hormonal and environmental control. In R. C. Friedman, R. M. Richart, & R. L. Vande Wiele (Eds.), *Sex differences in behavior.* New York: Wiley, 1974.

Ward, M. M., Sandman, C. A., George, J. M., & Shulman, H. MSH/ACTH 4-10 in men and women: Effects upon performance on an attention and memory task. *Physiology and Behavior,* 1979, *22,* 669–673.

Ward, M. M., Stone, S. C., & Sandman, C. A. Visual perception in women during the menstrual cycle. *Physiology and Behavior,* 1978, *20,* 239–243.

Weiner, H. Are "psychosomatic" diseases diseases of regulation? *Psychosomatic Medicine,* 1975, *37,* 289–291.

Weiss, J. M., McEwno, B. S., Silva, M. T. A., & Kalkut, M. S. Pituitary-adrenal alterations and fear responding. *American Journal of Physiology,* 1970, *218,* 864–868.

Weitzman, E. D., Fukushima, D. K., Nogeire, C., Roffwarf, H. P., Gallagher, T. F., & Hellman, L. Twenty-four hour pattern of the episodic secretion of cortisol in normal subjects. *Journal of Clinical Endocrinology,* 1971, *33,* 14–22.

Wertheim, G. A., Conner, R. L., & Levine, S. Avoidance conditioning and adrenocortical function in the rat. *Physiology and Behavior,* 1969, *4,* 41–44.

Whalen, R. E. Sexual differentiation: Models, methods and mechanisms. In R. C. Friedman, R. M. Richart, and R. L. Vande Wiele (Eds.), *Sex differences in behavior.* New York: Wiley, 1974.

Whybrow, P. C. & Hurwitz, T. Psychological disturbances associated with endocrine disease and hormone therapy. In E. J. Sachar (Ed.), *Hormones, behavior and psychopathology,* 1976.

Wied, D. de., & Bohus, B. Long-term and short-term effects on retention of a conditioned avoidance response in rats by treatment with a long acting Pitressin and α-MSH. *Nature,* 1966, *212,* 1484–1488.

Wied, D. de, Saratakis, D., & Weinstein, B. Behavioral evaluation of peptides related to scotophobin. *Neuropharmacology,* 1973, *12,* 1109–1115.

Wiegant, W. M., Cools, A. R., & Gispen, W. H. ACTH-induced excessive grooming involves brain dopamine. *European Journal of Pharmacology,* 1977, *41,* 343–345.

Wilcoxin, L. A., Schrader, S. L., & Sherif, C. W. Daily self-reports on activities, life events, moods and somatic changes during the menstrual cycle. *Psychosomatic Medicine,* 1976, *38,* 399–417.

Witkin, H. A., Lewis, H. B., Hertzman, M., Machover, K., Bretnall, P., Meissner, C., & Wapner, S. *Personality through perception.* New York: Harper, 1954.

Zingneim, P. K. *Physiological responding, cognitive style and affective states in women during the menstrual cycle.* Unpublished masters thesis, Ohio State University, 1973.

# 6

# Hippocampal Inhibition of the Pituitary-Adrenocortical Response to Stress

**Marlene M. Wilson**
*University of Portland, Oregon, United States*

A major component of the physiological response to stress is activation of the pituitary-adrenocortical system. The nervous system detects changes in the environment and stimulates the anterior pituitary to release ACTH. ACTH causes secretion of glucocorticoids from the adrenal cortex, which mobilize the body's resources to deal with the challenge to homeostasis.

Although glucocorticoids are essential for coping with the challenge of the stressor, prolonged exposure to elevated concentrations of these hormones is detrimental to the organism. Increased corticoid concentrations suppress the body's immune system, which may leave the organism vulnerable to pathologies normally controlled by an intact immunologic apparatus. To maintain the body's defense system, the adrenocortical stress response must be limited. This chapter proposes that the hippocampus plays a major role in limiting the degree of activation of the pituitary-adrenocortical system in response to different stressors and that it may be involved in adapting to or coping with various stressors.

The bases of the suggestion that the hippocampus modulates adaptation to stress are the hypothesis of O'Keefe and Nadel (1978) that the hippocampus functions as the core of a neural memory system and the results of numerous studies demonstrating interactions between the hippocampus and the pituitary-adrenal system. The hippocampus receives analyzed, abstracted information from all sensory modalities as well as information about the location of the body in time and space. Current environmental information is continually being fed into an objective spatial framework where the events of an organism's experience are located and interrelated. Constant comparison of incoming information with the body's "cognitive map" of its universe determines the degree of interest in or response to an item. The hippocampus projects out to the hypothalamus, where it can alter the secretion of ACTH, providing a route by which novelty or uncertainty could activate the system or, conversely, where an event that fits into the map could be accepted and a pituitary-adrenal response inhibited. Both ACTH and glucocorticoids alter the neurophysiology of the hippocampal

The author's research reported in this chapter was supported by Grants AM-03385, AM-16794, and AM-01447 from the National Institutes of Health.

neurons, suggesting that items associated with stress states receive special processing.

If the hippocampus is involved in adaptation to stress, one would expect decreased ability to deal with stress following its loss. During senescence the hippocampus is one brain region that shows dramatic anatomic changes that have been correlated with decreased function. A general characteristic of the senescent state is a decreased ability to deal with stressors and impairment of the immunologic apparatus. Needed are data on pituitary-adrenocortical adaptation to stress in elderly subjects and studies linking hippocampal function, physiological stress responses, and immunologic competence. This chapter reviews the way in which the physiological response to stress is assessed and what is known of the interactions between the hippocampus and the pituitary-adrenocortical system.

## CHARACTERISTICS OF THE PITUITARY–ADRENOCORTICAL RESPONSE TO STRESS

Stress is defined as anything that stimulates ACTH secretion. A stressor is the specific stimulus in the transaction, and the stress response is the organism's plasma ACTH and glucocorticoid concentrations following exposure to the stressor.

### Categories of Stress

The stress responsiveness of this system may be discussed under Burchfield's (1979) categories of acute, chronic, and chronic intermittent stress.

*Acute stress* is any event that occurs within a given (usually short) time period and does not recur frequently, if at all. Most studies concerning neural pathways mediating the stress response have used this form of stressor. ACTH is secreted very rapidly into the bloodstream after exposure to stressors and reaches peak concentrations within 2.5 min. The rapidity of the response is independent of the type of stressor, but the amplitude and duration of the response differ with the stressor (Cook, Kendall, Greer, & Kramer, 1973). The adrenocortical response is slower, with peak corticosteroid concentrations being reached 15-30 min after exposure to the stressor (Cook, Kendall, Greer, & Kramer, 1973). Plasma samples taken within the first 3 min of exposure to a noxious stimulus reflect basal, or nonstress, corticosteroid secretion. Although the majority of studies have relied solely on corticosteroid concentrations as an index of ACTH secretion, plasma corticosteroid concentrations are not an accurate indicator of the amount of ACTH secreted. The amplitude of the plasma corticosteroid response to stress is not as great as that of the ACTH response (Cook, Kendall, Greer, & Kramer, 1973; Engeland, Shinsako, Winget, Vernikos-Danellis, & Dallman, 1977), and conversely, the fluctuation of basal plasma corticosteroid levels is greater than the circadian fluctuation in plasma ACTH (Engeland et al., 1977). The limit to the amount of corticosteroid in plasma probably reflects distribution, binding, and metabolism of the hormone as well as maximal adrenal activation.

*Chronic stress* is prolonged, continuous exposure to a stimulus. Plasma corticosterone concentrations decrease with continuous exposure to restraint (Dallman & Jones, 1973; Sakellaris & Vernikos-Danellis, 1975), cold (Sakellaris &

Vernikos-Danellis, 1975), high-intensity sound (Henkin & Knigge, 1963), and immobilization (Bohus, 1969). These findings probably represent adaptation rather than exhaustion of the pituitary-adrenal system because subsequent increases in plasma corticosterone concentrations occurred when the chronic stress was followed by an acute stress (Dallman & Jones, 1973; Sakellaris & Vernikos-Danellis, 1975). The pituitary-adrenal system adapts to chronic stress by decreasing secretion, yet it is still capable of responding to a new stressor and may actually be hypersensitive to new stimuli.

One problem inherent in this type of experiment is that although the administered stimulus is constant, the specific signal that activates receptors leading to a response may vary. For example, during continuous immobilization, body temperature and circulation may gradually be altered, or during continuous exposure to sound some frequency receptors adapt while others do not. Adaptation to chronic stress could reflect altered physiological response to the stressor, adaptation of peripheral receptors, or changes within the central nervous system.

*Chronic intermittent stress* is a discrete stimulus to which the organism is repeatedly exposed, over a given time period, for a specific amount of time (usually less than 1 h). Adaptation to chronic intermittent stress consisting of a decreased adrenocortical response has been demonstrated for trauma in a Noble-Collip drum (Németh & Vigaš, 1973; Németh, Vigaš, & Jurčovičová, 1975), cold exposure (Burchfield, Woods, & Elich, 1980), foot shock (Pollard, Bassett, & Craincross, 1976), and immobilization (Kawakami, Seto, & Kimura, 1972). The pituitary-adrenal response may not adapt to all chronic intermittent stressors. Cook, Allen, Greer, & Allen (1974) found no adaptation in the secretion of ACTH in response to ether, tourniquet, or leg-break stress repeated at 90-min intervals one–three times. Ether stress repeated at 24-h intervals for 3 days did not produce any decrease in either the plasma ACTH or corticosterone response by the third day. The time period of these experiments was so limited, however, that the possibility of eventual adaptation cannot be eliminated.

Burchfield et al. (1980) proposed that an anticipatory response is part of adaptation to chronic intermittent stress. They found that plasma corticosterone concentrations in base-line blood samples taken from rats exposed to 10 min of cold stress per day for 3 months were equal to those secreted during the stress. It would be interesting to see the time course of this anticipatory response.

## Neural Pathways for Stress Responses

The precise neural pathways regulating ACTH secretion in response to acute stressors differ for different stressors. Ascending sensory pathways reach the hypothalamus, which apparently contains the final common-pathway neurons that integrate sensory input with information from higher centers. The secretion of ACTH is regulated by the release of CRF into the hypophyseal portal system. Halász and Pupp (1965) devised a knife that cut all neural connections between the medial basal hypothalamus and the rest of the brain yet preserved the continuity of the medial basal hypothalamus and pituitary and left most of the blood supply to the area intact. The medial basal hypothalamus can be completely isolated by a 360-degree cut, or the input from various areas can be studied separately by smaller cuts placed anteriorly, laterally, or posteriorly.

Using this preparation many investigators demonstrated that certain stressors (e.g., ether) stimulate the pituitary-adrenal axis in the absence of all input to the medial basal hypothalamus (Feldman, Conforti, Chowers, & Davidson, 1970; Greer & Rockie, 1968; Palka, Liebelt, & Critchlow, 1971), whereas other stressors (e.g., auditory) require posterior connections (Siegal, Chowers, Conforti, & Feldman, 1980), and still others (e.g., visual and sciatic-nerve) require anterior connections (Feldman, Conforti, & Chowers, 1975; Siegal et al., 1980). Recently Makara, Stark, and Palkovits (1980) reviewed the literature on hypothalamic isolations and found discrepancies in the ability of the medial basal hypo-thalamus to support pituitary-adrenal and pituitary-gonadal function. Recognizing that there may be previously unrecognized factors complicating these studies, they carefully evaluated cuts histologically. They found that the completeness of the isolation varied and that with complete isolation there was no ACTH response to ether. They suggested that incomplete cuts could be the cause of discrepant findings. Few of the earlier studies have the detailed histology to support the claim of complete isolation of the medial basal hypothalamus. The finding that rats with acute hypothalamic islands, prepared by removing most of the forebrain, show a significant rise in plasma corticosterone after ether inhalation (Dunn & Critchlow, 1969; Matsuda, Duyck, Kendall, & Greer, 1964) supports the proposal that neural connections to the medial basal hypothalamus are not essential for the response to this stressor. Makara et al. (1980) argue, however, that the amputated fibers of CRF-producing neurons may contain significant amounts of releasing factor within 24 h after surgery and may be sensitized by the stressful surgical procedure. The location of the cell bodies of the CRF-producing neurons and the identification of the factor remain to be determined.

Because sciatic-nerve stimulation requires anterior connections to the medial basal hypothalamus (Feldman, Conforti, & Chowers, 1975) and because the projection from the hippocampus enters the medial basal hypothalamus anteriorly, Conforti and Feldman (1976) studied the role of the hippocampal complex in mediating this stress response. They found that the adrenal response to sciatic-nerve stimulation was significantly reduced following hippocampec-tomy.

### Circadian Rhythmicity and Negative-feedback Regulation of Stress Responses

A circadian rhythm in basal plasma corticosterone concentrations is well-established. In the rat, peak concentrations occur in the evening just before the onset of the dark period (Critchlow, Liebelt, Bar-Sela, Mountcastle, & Lipscomb, 1963; Guillemin, Dear, & Liebelt, 1959). Daily fluctuations in basal ACTH concentrations have also been reported (Matsuyama, Ruchmann-Wennhold, & Nelson, 1971; Rees, Cook, Kendall, Allen, Kramer, Ratcliff, & Knight, 1971), although these changes are not of the same magnitude as the variations in plasma glucocorticoids (Engeland et al., 1977).

The influence of this rhythm on the pituitary-adrenal response to stressors has been studied using corticosteroids as an index of the activity of the system, and the results are inconclusive (Ader & Friedman, 1968; Dunn, Sheving, & Millet, 1972; Zimmerman & Critchlow, 1967). It is difficult to compare quantitatively plasma corticosterone responses that start from different initial values. If initial levels are low, infusion of corticosterone at a given rate results in a greater elevation of corticosterone than if initial levels are high. Because of this, neither the incremental response nor the maximum value attained after stress can be used to compare the magnitude of the stress response in the morning and evening (Dallman & Yates, 1969).

More recent studies measuring plasma ACTH directly have tried to determine the role of rhythmicity in stress responses. With high-intensity stimuli such as continuous ether (Yasuda, Takebe, & Greer, 1976) and laparotomy with intestinal traction (Engeland et al., 1977), plasma ACTH concentrations were greater in the morning than in the evening. After low-intensity stimuli, however, the ACTH response appeared to depend on both the lag time before the corticosterone response and the magnitude of the corticosterone response. These results are consistent with the interpretation that corticosterone secretion modifies stress-induced ACTH via a negative-feedback effect. An experiment I did with M. and S. Greer, which found that long-term adrenalectomized rats had similar morning and evening responses to continuous ether (Fig. 1) supports the role of corticosterone in modifying the ACTH response to stress.

The interaction of negative-feedback control and stress responses has been reviewed by Yates, Maran, Cryer, and Gann (1974). The authors state that all the evidence taken together points to the existence of a site for corticosterioid inhibition of release of ACTH at the pituitary and for corticosteroid inhibition of synthesis of CRF through actions at several different points in the brain. There are two separate feedback components, a fast rate-sensitive component and a delayed level-sensitive one. Based on studies using the synthetic corticosteroid dexamethasone as a feedback signal, Yates et al. characterized the relationship among the response of the adrenocortical system to a stressor, the strength of the stressor, and the inhibitory potency of dexamethasone as a signal in the delayed level-sensitive pathway. The primary effect of dexamethasone was to shift the threshold for response of the system to higher stress levels until a dose of dexamethasone was reached beyond which no further increase enhanced inhibition. It appears that both the brain and pituitary play a role in delayed feedback and that the dose of dexamethasone required to saturate the pathway at the pituitary is lower than that required to saturate its effects at the brain. The authors suggested that the brain and pituitary are feedback loci for corticosteroids in the basal circadian-rhythm range of the system and that only the brain elements have sufficient residual sensitivity to changes in corticosteroid levels to modulate stress responses of the system during the circadian peak. One area of the brain that is apparently a target tissue for corticosteroids is the hippocampus. Because of this interaction between circadian rhythmicity and negative-feedback components of the pituitary-adrenal system, the contribution of the hippocampus to control of the system must be assessed at both the trough and crest of the circadian cycle.

## THE HIPPOCAMPUS

Based on physiological, anatomic, and psychological studies, O'Keefe and Nadel (1978) hypothesized that the hippocampus is a cognitive map. They stated that "the hippocampus is the core of a neural memory system providing an

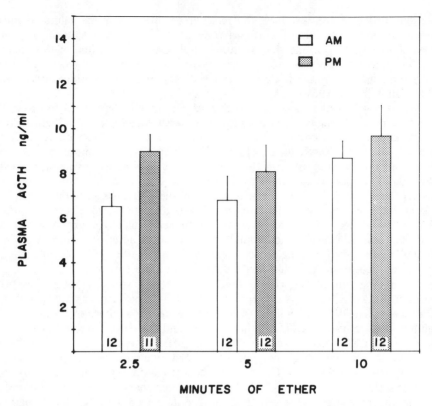

*Figure 6.1*  Ether-stress–induced plasma ACTH concentrations in the morning and evening after 2.5, 5, and 10 min of ether inhalation. There were no significant differences between any of the groups ($p > .05$, Newman-Keuls). In this and subsequent graphs, the bar columns and vertical lines indicate, respectively, group mean and standard error of the mean, and the number of rats per group is shown within each column.

objective spatial framework within which the items and events of an organism's experience are located and interrelated" (p. 232). According to this proposal, the bulk of the hippocampus consists of mapping space that receives continuous input about the environment. In the case of a mismatch between the contents of the map and the current environment, the hippocampus projects to somatic motor areas halting ongoing behavior and to visceral motor areas controlling the internal response to uncertainty. Although this theory suggests that the hippocampus is not involved in fundamental motivational processes such as eating, drinking, and sexual behavior, the hippocampus does indirectly influence these processes as part of coordinating the body's response to novelty or discrepancy and in associating fear with a particular place.

Assuming that mapping space could be provided by a large matrix of identical neurons structured in such a way that each neuron or group of neurons would represent a place in a given environment, the anatomy of the hippocampus is consistent with the functions attributed to it by O'Keefe and Nadel. The hippocampus complex consists of three layers of one basic cell type and associated interneurons that can be divided into four basic components. According to Raisman and Field (1971), these are (1) the dentate gyrus, (2) Field CA3 (of Lorente de No's classification), (3) Field CA1, and (4) the prosubiculum, a field formed by the overlapping of the pyramidal layers of Field CA1 and the subiculum. There are major unidirectional connections among the sectors such that the dentate gyrus projects to CA3, and CA3 projects to CA1. According to the three-stage functional model proposed by O'Keefe and Nadel, the dentate gyrus is the site that organizes environmental input. CA3 is the initial part of the map that represents places in the environment and connections between those places. CA1, the third stage, continues the map and receives information from all preceding levels of the hippocampal complex and contains the misplace system, which signals the presence of something new in a place or the absence of something old. CA1 then projects to the prosubiculum and subicular area, the transitional area between the hippocampus proper and the entorhinal cortex, which projects out via the fimbria of the fornix to the thalamus and hypothalamus to alter somatic and visceral motor activity. The hippocampus proper projects rostrally only to the septum by way of Field CA3 and recieves major input from the septum via the fornix. All areas of the hippocampus and dentate gyrus receive input about environmental items via the entorhinal cortex. There is a cascading of inputs from a number of cortical areas through all adjacent regions leading to the entorhinal cortex, suggesting that the hippocampus receives highly analyzed, abstracted information from all modalities rather than information about any specific modality. The hippocampus also receives information about the location of the body in time and space through afferents from the brainstem.

As summarized in Fig. 6.2, the ultimate output of the hippocampus is from the prosubiculum to the hypothalamus as the medial corticohypothalamic tract. This tract provides a pathway for hippocampal influence over the pituitary-adrenocortical system in addition to the indirect input from the hippocampus to the hypothalamus by way of the septum.

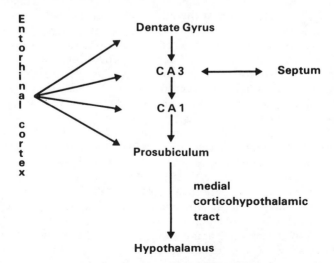

*Figure 6.2* Schematic representation of the medial corticohypothalamic tract as the ultimate emergent pathway from the hippocampal complex.

# HIPPOCAMPAL–HYPOTHALAMIC–PITUITARY–
# ADRENAL INTERACTION

There is strong evidence that the pituitary-adrenocortical system is influenced by, and in turn can influence, the hippocampus. I first present data on hippocampal regulation of pituitary-adrenal function and then on the effect of adrenocorticoids on the hippocampus.

## Hippocampal Regulation
## of the Pituitary-Adrenocortical System

Evaluation of the role of the hippocampus in regulating the pituitary-adrenal system has been difficult because this system appears to be grossly intact in hippocampectomized animals. Following hippocampal or fornix destruction, there is no change in both adrenal weight (Fendler, Karmos, & Telegdy, 1961; Knigge, 1961; Wilson & Critchlow, 1973/1974) and the adrenocortical response to acute stressors (Coover, Goldman, & Levine, 1971; Knigge, 1961; Knigge & Hays, 1963; Lanier, Van Hartesveldt, Weiss, & Isaacson, 1975; Wilson & Critchlow, 1973/1974). Apparently the circadian rhythm in plasma corticosterone is also not dependent on the hippocampus (Lanier et al., 1975; Wilson & Critchlow, 1973/1974). Although Moberg, Scapagnini, De Groot, and Ganong (1971) reported that fornix transection in male rats abolished the diurnal variation in plasma corticosterone 1–2 weeks after surgery, Lengvári and Halász (1973) showed that at 3 weeks after surgery significant diurnal variations had returned. Female rats, which have greater diurnal excursions than males, had significant morning-evening differences 8–11 days after fornix transection or hippocampectomy (Wilson & Critchlow, 1973/1974).

*Response to acute stress.* Ablation of the hippocampus does not result in an increase in stress-induced adrenal corticosteroid hormones. There is, however, a methodological problem with most of the studies that have used adrenocorticoids as an index of neural excitation of the pituitary-adrenal system. As stated earlier, the adrenal response to high ACTH concentrations is nonlinear, and increased secretion of ACTH could go undetected if only plasma glucocorticoids were measured. Increased adrenocorticoid secretion would only be evident if the response of the adrenal cortex were submaximal (Van Hartesveldt, 1975). One way to produce a submaximal adrenocortical response to stress is to suppress the pituitary-adrenal axis by prior treatment with glucocorticoids. In studies done with Critchlow, the hippocampus was removed, and the rats were subjected to a mild stress in the presence of a feedback signal (Wilson, 1975). In rats treated with dexamethasone, hippocampectomy increased the corticosterone response to supination stress in two separate experiments in the evening (Fig. 6.3). Stress levels in hippocampectomized rats were elevated ($p < .01$) compared to those of controls and were higher ($p < .01$) than nonstress levels in dexamethasone-treated groups. There were no significant differences among the saline-injected groups.

When a second series of animals was subjected to similar experiments performed both in the morning and evening, a morning–evening difference in the effect of dexamethasone on the corticosterone response to stress was observed. Dexamethasone-treated hippocampectomized rats had greater ($p < .01$) corticosterone stress responses than did controls in the evening but not in the

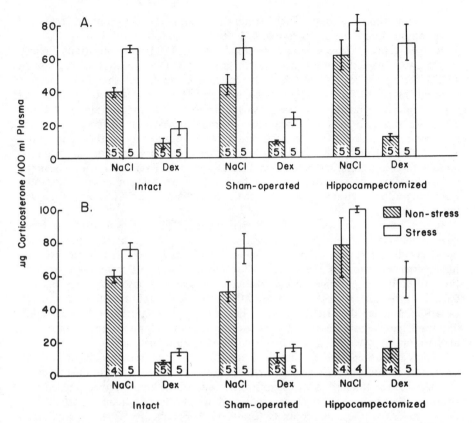

*Figure 6.3* Effect of hippocampectomy on dexamethasone suppression of the response to supination stress in two separate experiments, A and B.

morning. In the morning there were no differences between the groups in nonstress or in stress levels, or in stress responses when rats were injected with either saline or dexamethasone (Fig. 6.4). This experiment was repeated with similar results.

These findings are consistent with the proposal that the hippocampus contributes an inhibitory component to neural mechanisms regulating ACTH release. The greater stress responses in dexamethasone-treated hippocampectomized rats may reflect decreased negative-feedback suppression owing to loss of feedback loci in the brain. The data support the model proposed by Yates et al. (1974), which predicted that, during the circadian peak, only the brain elements have sufficient residual sensitivity to changes in corticosteroid levels to modulate stress responses of the system.

Recently, Feldman and Conforti (1980) demonstrated greater stress responses in hippocampectomized rats in the morning by testing them at 4 h rather than at 2 h after giving dexamethasone. The demonstration of a different response in hippocampectomized rats in the morning probably reflects the interaction among variables involved in these studies, in other words, choice of stressor, feedback signal, and time of day. Their study also supports the concept that the hippocampus limits the stress response.

Recently, my colleagues and I measured plasma ACTH concentrations directly to get away from the problem of nonlinearity of the corticosterone response to ACTH (Wilson, Greer, Greer, & Roberts, 1980). We found that hippocampec-tomized rats had higher ether-stress–induced ACTH concentrations than did cortex-removed controls. Stress plasma corticosterone concentrations did not differ in the two groups. Once again a morning–evening difference was en-countered. Increased ACTH concentrations were found only in the evening and not in the morning. The fact that this increase in hormone concentrations is limited to the evening indicates that there is a circadian variation in hippocampal action that may be related to the feedback effects of endogenous corticosterone. Following adrenalectomy, the effect of the hippocampus on ACTH secretion was lost or masked.

In the same study, we also found that basal ACTH and corticosterone levels were increased in the evening, suggesting that even under basal conditions the pituitary-adrenal system of hippocampectomized rats is overactive in the evening. In previous experiments the tendency for evening basal corticosterone concentra-tions to be higher in saline-treated, lesioned rats was also observed. (Figs. 6.3 and 6.4), but the differences were not statistically significant owing to the overall variation among the eight groups. Feldman and Conforti (1980) observed increased basal plasma corticosterone concentrations in hippocampectomized rats in the morning when all groups had been given dexamethasone.

There are other studies that indicate that the hippocampus participates in activation of the pituitary-adrenal axis. As noted previously, the adrenal response to sciatic-nerve stimulation was significantly reduced in hippocampectomized rats, although the responses to ether stress and to photic and acoustic stimulation were similar to those of controls (Conforti & Feldman, 1976). In studies on fornix-sectioned rats, lesioned rats, like controls, showed significant corticosteroid elevations to food deprivation but unlike controls did not show additional corticosterone elevation in response to handling, transport, and extinction (Osborne, Sivakumaran, & Black, 1979). The authors suggested that some events that influence corticosterone levels are mediated by neural circuits that involve the hippocampus, and others are not. They proposed that simuli that involve the hippocampus are more complex and have indirect modes of action, for example, stimuli that elicit expectancies about motivationally significant events and the violation of such expectancies or elicit mismatches between what is expected and what occurs in a given situation.

*Response to chronic and chronic intermittent stress.* The pituitary-adrenal response to chronic stressors also appears to be greater in hippocampectomized animals. Murphy, Wideman, and Brown (1979) found higher plasma cortico-sterone concentrations in hippocampectomized than in control rats after 5 h of restraint stress and 5 h of restraint plus intermittent shock, suggesting a greater stress response in the lesioned rats. Hippocampectomized rats also developed more gastric ulcers than controls under these conditions. Increased gastric ulceration in hippocampectomized rats has also been reported by Kim, Choi, Kim, Kim, Park, Ahn, and Kang (1976), and although ulcers are a multi-dimensional phenomenon, circulating corticosterone appears to be an important factor (Murphy et al., 1979).

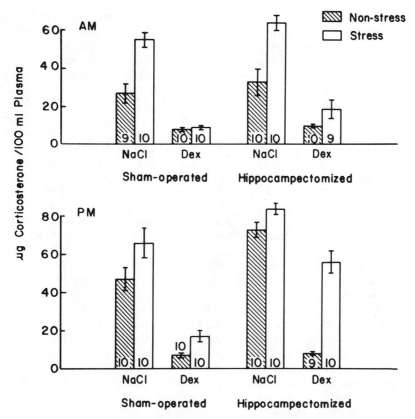

*Figure 6.4* Effect of hippocampectomy on dexamethasone suppression of the response to supination stress in the morning (AM) and evening (PM).

During the process of adaptation to immobilization stress in the rabbit, Kawakami, Kimura, Ishida, and Yanase (1971) monitored the activity of hippocampal-hypothalamic neural pathways with chronically implanted electrodes. During the first immobilization stress (chronic stress), evoked potentials in the medial basal tuberal region decreased in amplitude. Following repeated exposures to the stress (chronic intermittent stress) the amplitude of the initial evoked potentials was also decreased and showed further reduction during the stress. The authors suggest that the hippocampus plays a role in the establishment of an adaptation mechanism by changing responsiveness to the stressful stimuli during repeated exposure to stress.

Kim and Kim (1961) studied the effect of hippocampectomy on the response to chronic intermittent stress using adrenal ascorbic acid content as an index of pituitary-adrenal activity. The rats were chronically stressed by inflicting skin incisions under ether anesthesia daily or on alternate days for up to a total of 11 days. The greatest difference between groups was found when ascorbic acid content was measured in adrenals taken 72 h after the last stress. Their findings suggested that the hippocampus exerts a sustained inhibitory influence over the pituitary-adrenal system. They concluded that the hippocampus acts as a brake to the pituitary-adrenocortical system, protecting it from prolonged excessive activity and facilitating reparative processes in the same system. The above suggestion is supported by the observations of Ely, Greene, and Henry (1977) on hippocampectomized mice. Under conditions of chronic social interaction for 81 days, hippocampectomized mice developed high BP, low HR, and high plasma corticosterone levels during social interaction in a territorial situation. Hippocampectomized mice kept in a nonterritorial situation with minimal social interaction did not show significant cardiovascular or plasma corticosterone changes compared with unoperated-on or cortically lesioned controls.

*Effect of electrical stimulation of the hippocampus on pituitary-adrenal stress responses.* Many experimental parameters and conditions have been identified that determine the outcome of hippocampal stimulation with respect to secretion of adrenocorticosteroid hormones. Studies on the effect of stimulation on pituitary-adrenal stress responses support findings of ablation studies and suggest that the hippocampus has an inhibitory role in regulating stress responses of the pituitary-adrenal axis.

Endröczi, Lissák, Bohus, and Kovács (1959) found that low-frequency hippocampal stimulation attenuated adrenocortical activity in response to electric shock, epinephrine, histamine, and Formalin. In additional studies, Endröczi and Lissák (1962), using progressively higher stimulation frequencies, found that higher-frequency stimulation had little effect or significantly increased the adrenocortical response to stress. Using rabbits and 5-h immobilization stress, Kawakami, Seto, Terasawa, Yoshida, Miyamato, Sekiguichi, and Hattari (1968) found that hippocampal stimulation inhibited corticosteroid biosynthesis under stress conditions while facilitating corticosteroid biosynthesis under normal conditions. Those data indicate that low-frequency stimulation of the hippocampus suppresses or eliminates the adrenocortical response to stress. If low-frequency stimulation enhances the normal function of a structure and hippocampal stimulation causes a decrease in stress-induced adrenocortical activity, then one would conclude that the hippocampus normally inhibits stress-induced secretion of these hormones.

## Effect of Adrenocorticoids on the Hippocampus

For the hippocampus to be an effective regulator of the hypothalamic-pituitary-adrenal system, it must be able to monitor the output of that system. Much of the evidence that the hippocampus is a target tissue for adrenocorticoids comes from the work of McEwen's laboratory on corticosterone receptors in the brain. A review by McEwen and Weiss (1970) is summarized below.

For the brain to act as a sensing device for the regulation of ACTH secretion and as a target organ for corticosterone to influence neural activity and behavior, the hormone must be able to enter the brain in increasing amounts as the blood level increases. Corticosterone concentrations in the cortex, hypothalamus, and septum are proportional to the dose administered. The hippocampus differs from these areas in that its capacity shows a tendency to be saturated by doses within the physiological range. Hippocampal corticosterone receptors must be studied in adrenalectomized rats because in normal rats the hippocampus is saturated by endogenous hormone after the stress of handling and hormone injection. The hippocampus shows the characteristics of a target tissue with a limited-capacity retention mechanism in that it retains the hormone at a higher concentration and for a longer time than other brain structures. In a number of hormone target tissues, the retention of a particular steroid hormone by that tissue is correlated with the presence of high concentrations of that hormone tightly bound within cell nuclei. Hippocampal nuclei had the highest concentration of any cell fraction and showed an interesting time course: Concentration was retained over the first 2 h then lost rapidly in the 3rd and 4th h.

The uptake mechanism in the hippocampus is specific for glucocorticoids in that the tissue concentration can be decreased by prior corticosterone, dexamethasone, and cortisol administration. Pretreatment with cholesterol did not interfere with the uptake mechanism. Binding of a hormone by the cell nucleus appears to involve the action of the hormone on the transcription of genetic information leading to an altered synthesis of protein molecules with the affected cells. Tryptophan hydroxylase, a key step in 5-HT biosynthesis, is reduced by adrenalectomy. Corticosteroid administration to adrenalectomized rats returns the level of tryptophan hydroxylase toward normal in as little as 4 h. The effects of corticosterone can be prevented by intracranial administration of the protein-synthesis inhibitor cycloheximide. This finding not only shows the type of effect corticosterone has in some brain cells but raises intriguing possibilities with respect to the interaction between adrenal steroids and biogenic amines such as 5-HT, NE, and DA.

Studies in which hippocampal activity was recorded support the concept that glucocorticoids alter the activity of the hippocampus. One characteristic of hippocampal activity is the presence of theta waves, which can be elicited by novel stimuli or driven by signals from the reticular formation. Martin, Moberg, and Horowitz (1975) found an increase in theta activity in rabbits 60–90 min after hydrocortisone infusion. The investigators correlated hydrocortisone administration with a change in spontaneous theta activity occurring at times consistent with changing binding and altered enzyme activity. Pfaff, Silva, and Weiss (1971) found a decrease in telemetered unit activity of pyramidal cells following corticosterone injections in rats. Dexamethasone either applied iontophoretically or given intravenously to rats inhibited spontaneous hippocampal activity without apparent interaction with the inhibitory action of NE.

The physiological significance of corticosterone action on the hippocampus leading to altered hippocampal activity has yet to be determined. Putting these studies together with those showing hippocampal regulation of ACTH secretion, the possibility that the hippocampus is involved in negative-feedback control of ACTH secretion is strong. It should be viewed as only one locus of feedback regulation, and its particular role should be clarified.

Rotsztejn, Normand, Lalonde, and Fortier (1975) studied the amount of corticosterone bound to proteins in the anterior pituitary and dorsal hippocampus concurrently with the plasma ACTH concentration in 4-week adrenalectomized rats under steady-state conditions achieved by infusing the steroid at a constant rate for 45 min. Their results suggested that different receptors were involved in the binding of corticosterone by the anterior pituitary and the dorsal hippocampus. A highly suggestive relationship was evident between corticosterone binding by the anterior pituitary and corticosterone-induced inhibition of ACTH release within the physiological range of plasma corticosterone concentrations.

No such relationship could be demonstrated between hippocampal binding of the steroid and the feedback regulation of ACTH secretion. They suggested that specific binding sites in the anterior pituitary may be chiefly involved in the tonic regulation of ACTH secretion and that equally specific hippocampal receptors, though not involved in tonic control, may play a role in transient adjustment of pituitary-adrenocortical activity. This proposal is consistent with the finding that dexamethasone suppresses basal evening corticosterone levels in hippocampectomized, fornix-sectioned, and medial basal hypothalamic-isolated rats (Feldman, Conforti, & Chowers, 1973; Palka et al., 1971; Wilson & Critchlow, 1973/1974) and that suppression of stress responses is impaired in hippocampectomized rats (Feldman & Conforti, 1980; Wilson, 1975).

Two different populations of corticosteroid-binding sites have also been described by Dekloet, Wallach, and McEwen (1975). They found that dexamethasone showed a preference for the anterior pituitary, whereas labeled corticosterone, the predominant endogenous corticosteroid, showed a preference for the hippocampus. Their findings suggested that results of previous studies attempting to define the neural substrate essential for feedback suppression of pituitary-adrenal function might reflect the pharmacology of dexamethasone rather than the physiology of the system. Critchlow and I did an experiment to determine if a physiological level of corticosterone could suppress the pituitary-adrenal system in the absence of the hippocampus. In this study, evening nonstress corticosterone levels were assessed following hippocampectomy and septal ablation in female rats injected with either corticosterone or vehicle. A subcutaneous injection of 1 mg/kg of corticosterone, freshly dissolved in 12% ethanol-normal saline solution, produced a transient elevation of plasma corticosterone levels that was within the range observed in female rats following application of a stress in the afternoon (Zimmerman, Smyrl, & Critchlow, 1972). This dose of corticosterone or ethanol-saline vehicle (0.5 ml) was injected, and nonstress corticosterone levels were assessed in blood and adrenals obtained 1 h later. Hippocampectomy and septal ablation were compatible with suppression of the evening peak in nonstress pituitary-adrenal activity by corticosterone (Fig. 6.5). Adrenal corticosterone levels were lower ($p < .01$) in steroid-injected than in vehicle-injected rats in all groups. Plasma corticosterone levels were lower, but not significantly suppressed, in all groups that received corticosterone compared with those injected with vehicle. Results of these experiments suggest that the hippocampus and septum are not necessary for corticosterone suppression of the evening surge in nonstress corticosterone levels. They are consistent with the view that structures essential for feedback suppression of nonstress pituitary-adrenal function are located within the medal basal hypothalamic-pituitary unit.

The hippocampus may be a locus for the action of pituitary-adrenal hormones on adaptive behavioral responses that in turn regulate the output of these hormones. Bohus (1975) reviewed studies that indicate that an intact pituitary-adrenal system is required for physiological retention or elimination of a learned response but not for learning a response. Implantation of minute quantities of hormones into the hippocampus mimicked the effects of systemic administration of larger quantities of these hormones, suggesting that the hippocampus is involved in mediation of the corticosteroid effect on adaptive behavior.

By examining the role of corticosteroids in fear-motivated behavior, Weiss, McEwen, Silva, and Kalkut (1969) have also explored the possibility that the hippocampus is an important source of internal inhibition affecting behavior.

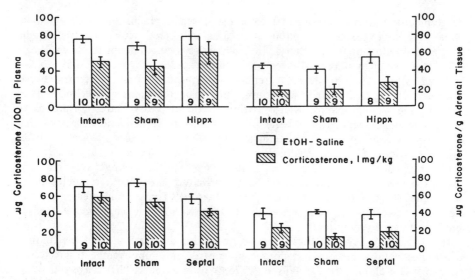

*Figure 6.5* Effect of hippocampectomy and septal ablation on feedback suppression of non-stress adrenal and plasma corticosterone concentrations by corticosterone.

They were concerned with the influence of both ACTH and corticosteroids on behavior and the interaction between the two. Woodbury and Vernadakis (1966) hypothesized that ACTH has general excitatory effects that potentiate fear-motivated responses. ACTH also initiates the "shutoff" of this excitatory influence by stimulating secretion of corticosteroid, which restores excitability to a normal level. Therefore, corticosterone may counteract the excitatory effects of ACTH and not necessarily have a suppressive action of its own in the absence of ACTH. Results of the study by Weiss, McEwen, Silva, and Kalkut (1970) are consistent with this hypothesis. Hypophysectomized rats were deficient in both active and passive avoidance. When they were given ACTH, their performance improved toward normal. Adrenalectomized rats showed more pronounced avoidance behavior. Administration of corticosterone diminished their performance toward normal. The authors also suggest that hormones are maximally effective in influencing behavior when fear is weak and generalized rather than when fear is strong and clearly signaled.

In describing the functions of the hippocampus, O'Keefe and Nadel (1978) stated that the hippocampus projects out to somatic motor areas to alter behavior and to visceral motor areas to control the internal response to uncertainty. This output of the hippocampus is modulated not only by the sensory information it receives from other brain areas but by the concentration of pituitary-adrenal hormones. This feedback effect completes the circuit in the hippocampal-hypothalamic-pituitary-adrenocortical interaction.

## SENESCENCE AND THE HIPPOCAMPAL–HYPOTHALAMIC–PITUITARY–ADRENOCORTICAL SYSTEM

Finch (1976) proposed that age-related changes after maturation result from an extension of the neural and endocrine mechanisms that control earlier development and that produce a regulatory cascade of changing neural, endo-crine, and target-tissue interactions. One area of altered neuroendocrine regula-tion is the ability of the pituitary-adrenocortical system to adapt to stress. Riegle (1973) subjected young and aged male and female rats twice a day to 2-h restraint stress for 20 days. Adrenocortical responsiveness to stressors was decreased during treatment in all groups, but the decrease was smaller in the aged than in the young groups. Riegle attributed the decreased stress responses to negative-feedback regulation of the pituitary-adrenal system and suggested that the sensitivity of this negative-feedback regulation is decreased in aged animals. The suggestion of altered feedback control in aged animals is supported by a study by Riegle and Hess (1972) in which they measured adrenocortical responsiveness to ether-vapor stress in young adult and aged rats subjected to acute and chronic treatments with dexamethasone. They found greater cortico-sterone stress responses in aged animals treated with dexamethasone than in similarly treated young rats.

The similarity between these findings on aged and young rats and the findings of studies comparing stress responses in control and hippocampectomized rats (Conforti & Feldman, 1976; Wilson, 1975; Wilson et al., 1980) suggest that the hippocampus may play a role in the altered stress responses in aged animals. The proposal that the increased stress responses are due to loss of feedback inhibition would be consistent with a proposed role for the hippocampus in negative-feedback control of the pituitary-adrenal axis. Have senescent rats undergone a physiological hippocampectomy?

With increasing age after maturity, substantial anatomic and neuro-physiological changes are seen in the hippocampus. A sizable loss of pyramidal cells and hypertrophic astrocytes were found in the hippocampus of aged animals (Landfield, Rose, Sandles, Wohlstader, & Lynch, 1977; Lindsey, Landfield, & Lynch, 1979). In neurophysiological studies, they found that the aged hippo-campal synaptic responses were clearly deficient when challenged with high-frequency stimulation; that is, synaptic responses were deficient in frequency and long-term potentiation and exhibited a greater tendency to exhaustion or depression. The authors proposed that these deficits in hippocampal synaptic plasticity are relevant to age-related deficits in hippocampal function (see review by Landfield, 1978). Ultrastructural studies provide evidence that this synaptic deficit is related to a quantitative age-related reduction in the population of synaptic vesicles in hippocampal synapses (Landfield, Wurtz, & Lindsey, 1979). Taken as a group, these studies support the concept of decreased function of the hippocampus with increasing age. If the hippocampus serves to limit pituitary-adrenocortical stress responses, then one would expect decreased ability to cope with stress with increasing age, as has been observed.

Landfield (1978) has taken this relationship a step further, by suggesting that the hippocampal changes that lead to altered control mechanisms and, in turn, to endocrine and physiological imbalance are affected, or at least accelerated, by adrenocortical steroids. Normal hormone concentrations could be an early cause of hippocampal deterioration, leading to elevation of adrenocorticoids, additional brain-cell loss, additional deregulation, and so on; in other words, a runaway positive-feedback loop between neuroendocrine regulatory alteration and endocrine-induced neural destruction could be formed. In a study designed to test this proposal, quantitative measures of age-related hippocampal pathology were correlated with plasma corticosterone concentrations and adrenal weight in rats of three different age groups. A quantitative relationship between hippocampal pathology and adrenal activity during aging was observed and provided evidence of a correlative link between brain-endocrine functions in the aging process (Landfield, Waymire, & Lynch, 1978). In an additional study, which has yet to be fully reported, prolonged administration of adrenal hormones was associated with patterns of brain pathology fully consistent with the hypothesis of glucocorticoid acceleration of brain aging (Landfield, Lindsey, & Lynch, 1978).

Because of the profound effects of adrenocorticoid hormones on lipid, protein, and carbohydrate metabolism; calcium balance; and connective tissues, prolonged adrenocorticoid responses to stress could be expected to cause or accelerate many of the changes associated with senescence. An important part of Landfield's proposal is that even normal levels could cause destruction of tissues, and increased concentrations would accelerate those changes. Hyperadrenocorticism in spawning fish is associated with arteriosclerosis, diabetes mellitus, rapid aging, and death. A similar increased secretion of hormones in rats that have been repeatedly bred is associated with diabetes, hypertension, kidney stones, connective-tissue degenerative changes, myocardial infarcts, and arteriosclerosis. Loss of hippocampal inhibition of the pituitary-adrenocortical system may play a significant role in advancing senescence.

## SUMMARY

The studies reviewed in this chapter indicate that there is a two-way interaction between the hippocampus and the pituitary-adrenocortical hormones. It must be emphasized that the role of the hippocampus is one of modulation of hormones and that it is not the major neural site for regulation of ACTH secretion. The hippocampus is not essential for circadian rhythmicity, stress responsiveness, or feedback suppression of the pituitary-adrenal system. A role for the hippocampus in limiting the stress response has been missed in the past owing to technological limitations, and its role in adaptation to stress has not been established. From what is known of the function of the hippocampus, one would expect it to be involved in the response to mild, novel stressors rather than those that inflict physiological trauma, such as ether anesthesia and bleeding stress. It is impressive that even with the rather crude laboratory procedures that have been used, altered pituitary-adrenal function has been demonstrated following hippocampectomy. Although the effects of removing the hippocampus may be subtle, the need to have limits on the pituitary-adrenocortical hormones to prevent destruction of immunologic competence should not be dismissed. A system that fully responded to all changes would be in a constant state of stress that would compromise the well-being of the organism. Following hippocampectomy, one should not expect to find a dramatic increase in the amount of hormone released after a traumatic event; one should instead examine the pattern of hormone output following prolonged or repeated stressors. It is to be hoped future studies will elucidate the mechanism of adaptation to stress.

# REFERENCES

Ader, R., & Friedman, S. B. Plasma corticosterone response to environmental stimulation effects of duration of stimulation and the 24-hour adrenocortical rhythm. *Neuroendocrinology,* 1968, *3,* 378–386.

Bohus, B. Evaluation of the role of the feedback effect of corticosteroids in the control of pituitary ACTH release. *Acta Physiologica Academe of Science Hungary,* 1969, *35,* 141–148.

Bohus, B. The hippocampus and the pituitary-adrenal system hormones. In R. L. Isaacson & K. H. Pribram (Eds.), *The hippocampus.* New York: Plenum, 1975.

Burchfield, S. R. The stress response: A new perspective. *Psychosomatic Medicine,* 1979, *41,* 661–672.

Burchfield, S. R., Woods, S. C., & Elich, M. S. Pituitary-adrenocortical response to chronic intermittent stress. *Physiology and Behavior,* 1980, *24,* 297–302.

Conforti, N., & Feldman, S. Effects of dorsal fornix section and hippocampectomy on adrenocortical responses to sensory stimulation in the rat. *Neuroendocrinology,* 1976, *22,* 1–7.

Cook, D. M., Allen, J. P., Greer, M. A., & Allen, C. F. Lack of adaptation of ACTH secretion to sequential ether, tourniquet or leg-break stress. *Endocrine Research Communications,* 1974, *1,* 347–357.

Cook, D. M., Kendall, J. W., Greer, M. A., & Kramer, R. M. The effect of acute or chronic ether stress on plasma ACTH concentration in the rat. *Endocrinology,* 1973, *93,* 1019–1024.

Coover, G. D., Goldman, L., & Levine, S. Plasma corticosterone levels during extinction of a lever press response in hippocampectomized rats. *Physiology and Behavior,* 1971, *7,* 727–732.

Critchlow, V., Liebelt, R. A., Bar-Sela, M., Mountcastle, W., & Lipscomb, H. S. Sex differences in resting pituitary-adrenal function in the rat. *American Journal of Physiology,* 1963, *205,* 807–815.

Dallman, M. F., & Jones, M. T. Corticosteroid feedback control of ACTH secretion: Effect of stress-induced corticosterone secretion on subsequent stress responses in the rat. *Endocrinology,* 1973, *92,* 1367–1375.

Dallman, M. F., & Yates, F. E. Dynamic asymmetries in the corticosteroid feedback path and distribution-metabolism-binding elements of the adrenocortical system. *Annals of the New York Academy of Sciences,* 1969, *156,* 696–721.

Dekloet, R., Wallach, G., & McEwen, B. S. Differences in corticosterone and dexamethasone binding to the rat brain and pituitary. *Endocrinology,* 1975, *96,* 598–609.

Dunn, J., & Critchlow, V. Pituitary-adrenal response to stress in rats with hypothalamic islands. *Brain Research,* 1969, *16,* 395–403.

Dunn, J. D., Scheving, L. E., & Millet, P. Circadian variation in stress-evoked increases in plasma corticosterone. *American Journal of Physiology,* 1972, *223,* 402–406.

Ely, D. L., Greene, E. G., & Henry, J. P. Effect of hippocampal lesion on cardiovascular, adrenocortical and behavioral response patterns in mice. *Physiology and Behavior,* 1977, *18,* 1075–1083.

Endröczi, E., & Lissák, K. Interrelations between the palaeocortical activity and pituitary adrenocortical function. *Acta Physiologica Academe Science Hungary,* 1962, *21,* 257–263.

Endröczi, E., Lissák, K., Bohus, B., & Kovács, S. The inhibitory influence of archicortical structures on pituitary-adrenal function. *Acta Physiologica Academe Science Hungary,* 1959, *16,* 17–22.

Engeland, W. C., Shinsako, J., Winget, C. M., Vernikos-Danellis, J., & Dallman, M. F. Circadian patterns of stress-induced ACTH secretion are modified by corticosterone responses. *Endocrinology,* 1977, *100,* 138–147.

Feldman, S., & Conforti, N. Participation of the dorsal hippocampus in the glucocorticoid feedback effect on adrenocortical activity. *Neuroendocrinology,* 1980, *30,* 52–55.

Feldman, S., Conforti, N., & Chowers, I. Effect of dexamethasone on adrenocortical responses in intact and hypothalamic deafferented rats. *Acta Endocrinologica* (Copenhagen), 1973, *73,* 660–664.

Feldman, S., Conforti, N., & Chowers, I. Adrenocortical responses following sciatic nerve stimulation in rats with partial hypothalamic deafferentations. *Acta Endocrinologica* (Copenhagen), 1975, *80*, 625-629.

Feldman, S., Conforti, N., Chowers, I., & Davidson, J. M. Pituitary-adrenal activation in rats with medial basal hypothalamic islands. *Acta Endocrinologica* (Copenhagen), 1970, *63*, 405-414.

Fendler, K. G., Karmos, G., & Telegdy, G. Effect of hippocampal lesions on pituitary-adrenal function. *Acta Physiologica* (Budapest), 1961, *20*, 293-297.

Finch, C. E. The regulation of physiological changes during mammalian aging. *Quarterly Review of Biology*, 1976, *51*, 49-83.

Greer, M. A., & Rockie, C. Inhibition by pentobarbital of ether-induced ACTH secretion in the rat. *Endocrinology*, 1968, *83*, 1247-1252.

Guillemin, R., Dear, W. E., & Liebelt, R. A. Nychthemeral variations in plasma free corticosteroid levels of the rat. *Proceedings of the Society for Experimental Biology and Medicine*, 1959, *101*, 394-395.

Halász, B., & Pupp, L. Hormone secretion of the anterior pituitary gland after physical interruption of all nervous pathways to the hypophysiotropic area. *Endocrinology*, 1965, *77*, 553-562.

Henkin, R. I., & Knigge, K. M. Effect of sound on the hypothalamic-pituitary-adrenal axis. *American Journal of Physiology*, 1963, *204*, 710-714.

Kawakami, M., Kimura, F., Ishida, S., & Yanase, M. Changes in the activity of the limbic-hypothalamic neural pathways under repeated immobilization stress. *Endocrinologica Japonica*, 1971, *18*, 469-476.

Kawakami, M., Seto, K., & Kimura, F. Influence of repeated immobilization stress upon the circadian rhythmicity of adrenocorticoid biosynthesis. *Neuroendocrinology*, 1972, *9*, 207-214.

Kawakami, M., Seto, K., Terasawa, E., Yoshida, K., Miyamato, T., Sekiguichi, M., & Hattari, Y. Influence of electrical stimulation and lesion in the limbic structure upon biosynthesis of adrenocorticoid in the rabbit. *Neuroendocrinology*, 1968, *3*, 337-348.

Kim, C., Choi, H., Kim, J. K., Kim, M. S., Park, H. J., Ahn, B. T., & Kang, S. H. Influence of hippocampectomy on gastric ulcers in rats. *Brain Research*, 1976, *109*, 245-254.

Kim, C., & Kim, C. U. Effect of partial hippocampal resection on stress mechanism in rats. *American Journal of Physiology*, 1961, *201*, 337-340.

Knigge, K. M. Adrenocorticoid response to stress in rats with lesions in hippocampus and amygdala. *Proceedings of the Society for Experimental Biology and Medicine*, 1961, *108*, 18-21.

Knigge, K. M., & Hays, M. Evidence of inhibitive role of hippocampus in neural regulation of ACTH release. *Proceedings of the Society for Experimental Biology and Medicine*, 1963, *114*, 67-69.

Landfield, P. W. An endocrine hypothesis of brain aging and studies on brain-endocrine correlations and monosynaptic neurophysiology during aging. In C. E. Finch, D. E. Potter, & A. D. Kenny (Eds.), *Advances in experimental biology and medicine* (Vol. 113): *Parkinson's disease: II. Aging and neuroendocrine relationships.* New York: Plenum, 1978.

Landfield, P. W., Lindsey, J. D., & Lynch, G. Apparent acceleration of brain aging pathology by prolonged administration of glucocorticoids. *Society for Neuroscience Abstracts*, 1978, *4*, 350. (Abstract)

Landfield, P. W., Rose, G., Sandles, L., Wohlstadler, T., & Lynch, G. Patterns of astroglial hypertrophy and neuronal degeneration in the hippocampus of aged, memory-deficient rats. *Journal of Gerontology*, 1977, *32*, 3-12.

Landfield, P. W., Waymire, J. C., & Lynch, G. Hippocampal aging and adrenocorticoids: Quantitative correlations. *Science*, 1978, *202*, 1098-1102.

Landfield, P. W., Wurtz, C., & Lindsey, J. D. Quantification of synaptic vesicles in hippocampus of aging rats and initial studies of possible relations to neurophysiology. *Brain Research Bulletin*, 1979, *4*, 757-763.

Lanier, L. P., Van Hartesveldt, C., Weiss, B. J., & Isaacson, R. L. Effects of differential hippocampal damage upon rhythmic and stress-induced corticosterone secretion in the rat. *Neuroendocrinology*, 1975, *18*, 154-160.

Lengvári, I., & Halász, B. Evidence for a diurnal fluctuation in plasma corticosterone levels after fornix transection in the rat. *Neuroendocrinology*, 1973, *11*, 191-196.

Lindsey, J. D., Landfield, P. W., & Lynch, G. Early onset and topographical distribution of hypertrophied astrocytes in hippocampus of aging rats: A quantitative study. *Journal of Gerontology,* 1979, *34,* 661–671.

Makara, G. B., Stark, E., & Palkovits, M. Reevaluation of the pituitary-adrenal response to ether in rats with various cuts around the medial basal hypothalamus. *Neuroendocrinology,* 1980, *30,* 38–44.

Martin, S. M., Moberg, G. P., & Horowitz, J. M. Glucocorticoids and the hippocampal theta rhythm in loosely restrained unanesthetized rabbits. *Brain Research,* 1975, *93,* 535–542.

Matsuda, K., Duyck, C., Kendall, J. W., & Greer, M. A. Pathways by which traumatic stress and ether induce increased ACTH release in the rat. *Endocrinology,* 1964, *74,* 981–985.

Matsuyama, H., Ruhmann-Wennhold, A., & Nelson, D. H. Radioimmunoassay of plasma ACTH in intact rats. *Endocrinology,* 1971, *88,* 692–695.

McEwen, B. S., & Weiss, J. M. The uptake and action of corticosterone: Regional and subcellular studies on rat brain. In D. deWied & J. A. W. M. Weijner (Eds.), *Progress in brain research* (Vol. 32): *Pituitary, adrenal and the brain.* New York: Elsevier, 1970.

Moberg, G. P., Scapagnini, U., Groot, J. de, & Ganong, W. F. Effect of sectioning the fornix on diurnal fluctuation of plasma corticosterone levels in the rat. *Neuroendocrinology,* 1971, *7,* 11–15.

Murphy, H. M., Wideman, C. H., & Brown, T. S. Plasma corticosterone levels and ulcer formation in rats with hippocampal lesions. *Neuroendocrinology,* 1979, *28,* 123–130.

Németh, S., & Vigaš, M. Rate of disappearance of plasma corticosterone in traumatized rats with special respect to the effect of adaptation. *Endocrinologia Experimentalis,* 1973, *7,* 171–176.

Németh, S., Vigaš, M., & Jurčovičová, J. Shortened ACTH response to trauma in repeatedly injured rats. *Hormones and Metabolism,* 1975, *7,* 101.

O'Keefe, J., & Nadel, L. *The hippocampus as a cognitive map.* Oxford: Oxford University Press, 1978.

Osborne, B., Sivakumaran, T., & Black, A. H. Effects of fornix lesions on adrenocortical responses to charges in environmental stimulation. *Behavioral and Neural Biology,* 1979, *25,* 227–241.

Palka, Y., Liebelt, R. A., & Critchlow, V. Obesity and increased linear growth following partial or complete isolation of ventromedial hypothalamus. *Physiology and Behavior,* 1971, *7,* 187–194.

Pfaff, D. W., Silva, M. T. A., & Weiss, J. M. Telemetered recording of hormonal effects on hippocampal neurons. *Science,* 1971, *172,* 394–395.

Pollard, I., Bassett, J. R., & Craincross, K. D. Plasma glucocorticoid elevation and ultrastructural changes in adenohypophysis of the male rat following prolonged exposure to stress. *Neuroendocrinology,* 1976, *21,* 312–330.

Raisman, G., & Field, P. M. Anatomical considerations relevant to the interpretation of neuroendocrine experiments. In L. Martini & W. F. Ganong (Eds.), *Frontiers in neuroendocrinology.* New York: Oxford University Press, 1971.

Rees, L. H., Cook, D. M., Kendall, J. W., Allen, C. F., Kramer, R. M., Ratcliff, J. G., & Knight, R. A. A radioimmunoassay for rat plasma ACTH. *Endocrinology,* 1971, *89,* 254–261.

Riegle, G. D. Chronic stress effects on adrenocortical responsiveness in young and aged rats. *Neuroendocrinology,* 1973, *11,* 1–10.

Riegle, G. D., & Hess, G. D. Chronic and acute dexamethasone suppression of stress activation of adrenal cortex in young and aged rats. *Neuroendocrinology,* 1972, *9,* 175–187.

Rotsztejn, W. H., Normand, M., Lalonde, J., & Fortier, C. Relationship between ACTH release and corticosterone binding by the receptor sites of the adenohypophysis and dorsal hippocampus following infusion of corticosterone at a constant rate in adrenalectomized rat. *Endocrinology,* 1975, *97,* 223–230.

Sakellaris, P. C., & Vernikos-Danellis, J. Increased rate of response of the pituitary-adrenal system in rats adapted to chronic stress. *Endocrinology,* 1975, *97,* 597–602.

Siegel, R., Chowers, I., Conforti, N., & Feldman, S. Corticotropin and corticosterone secretory patterns following acute neurogenic stress in intact and in variously deafferented male rats. *Brain Research,* 1980, *188,* 399–410.

Van Hartesveldt, C. The hippocampus and regulation of the hypothalamic-hypophyseal-adrenal cortical axis. In R. L. Isaacson & K. H. Pribram (Eds.), *The hippocampus* (Vol. 1). New York: Plenum, 1975.

Weiss, J. M., McEwen, B. S., Silva, M. T. A., & Kalkut, M. S. Pituitary-adrenal influences on fear responding. *Science,* 1969, *163,* 197–199.

Weiss, J. M., McEwen, B. S., Silva, M. T. A., & Kalkut, M. S. Pituitary-adrenal alterations and fear responding. *American Journal of Physiology,* 1970, *218,* 864–868.

Wilson, M. M. Effect of hippocampectomy on dexamethasone suppression of corticosteroid-sensitive stress responses. *Anatomical Record,* 1975, *181,* 511. (Abstract)

Wilson, M., & Critchlow, V. Effect of fornix transection or hippocampectomy on rhythmic pituitary-adrenal function in the rat. *Neuroendocrinology,* 1973/1974, *13,* 24–40.

Wilson, M. m., Greer, S. E., Greer, M. A., & Roberts, L. Hippocampal inhibition of pituitary-adrenocortical function in female rats. *Brain Research,* 1980, *197,* 433–441.

Woodbury, D. M., & Vernadakis, A. Effects of steroids in the central nervous system. In R. L. Dorfman (Ed.), *Methods in hormone research* (Vol. 5). New York: Academic, 1966.

Yasuda, N., Takebe, K., & Greer, M. A. Evidence of nyctohemeral periodicity in stress-induced pituitary-adrenal activation. *Neuroendocrinology,* 1976, *21,* 214–224.

Yates, F. C., Maran, J. W., Cryer, G. L., & Gann, D. S. The pituitary adrenal cortical system and stimulation and inhibition of secretion of corticotrophin. In S. M. McCann (Ed.), *Physiology series one* (Vol. 5); *Endocrine physiology.* Baltimore: University Park, 1974.

Zimmermann, E., & Critchlow, V. Effects of diurnal variation in plasma corticosterone levels on adrenocortical response to stress. *Proceedings of the Society for Experimental Biology and Medicine,* 1967, *125,* 658–663.

Zimmermann, E., Smyrl, R., & Critchlow, V. Suppression of pituitary-adrenal response to stress with physiological plasma levels of corticosterone in the female rat. *Neuroendocrinology,* 1972, *10,* 246–256.

# 7

# The Psychopathology of Stress

## Autonomic Involvement in Myocardial Dysfunction and Pathology

*Karl C. Corley, Jr.*
*Medical College of Virginia, Richmond, United States*

### THE ANS AND STRESS

Cardiovascular disease is the leading cause of death in our society (Cohen & Cabot, 1979). Although the extent to which stress is involved in its etiology in humans is unknown, stress-induced pathophysiology has been demonstrated to be involved with all the cardiovascular disorders (Henry & Stephens, 1977). Because myocardial pathology and dysfunction are evidence of cardiovascular disturbances that can occur after brief exposure to a stressful situation (Corley, Shiel, Mauck, Clark, & Barber, 1977), these disorders necessarily have few antecedent events. Therefore, a relationship with stress should be more easily described than that of atherosclerosis or chronic hypertension, which require longer periods for development of pathological symptoms (Henry, Stephens, & Santisteban, 1975). Although many factors predispose an organism to stress-induced myopathy or arrhythmias, the trigger mechanisms should be identifiable. The rapidity of the occurrence of these phenomena suggests neurogenic, particularly ANS involvement. Although it has been suggested in human reports that psychological factors may be involved in these stress-induced phenomena, their identification and separation in animal studies is difficult.

### Stress and the Nervous System

The reaction of an organism to its environment is manifested by its behavior. This behavior is controlled by the nervous system. Although the divisions are artificial, behavior is controlled by three subdivisions of the nervous system: somatic, autonomic, and neuroendocrine. Each subdivision has important functions that are reflected in the behavioral response to the environment. The somatic motor system controls the skeletal-muscle activity that moves the organism about its environment. The ANS serves not only to support the somatic motor system in its activities but also to regulate visceral organs. A necessary contribution to skeletal-muscle activity is the adjustment of the cardiovascular

Preparation of this chapter was supported in part by Grant HL13454 from the National Heart, Lung and Blood Institute.

system so that nutrients and metabolites necessary for muscular activity are available (Obrist, Webb, Sutterer, & Howard, 1970). Although direct interaction between visceral organs and the environment is seldom thought to be important, the effects of environmental stimuli on these organs are profound. Most internal organs autoregulate and do not require the ANS for normal function, but the ability of the ANS to alter function is extraordinary (Miller, 1969). The neuroendocrine system is also involved. This system does not regulate by direct neural pathways but, rather, depends on the circulation of hormones through the cardiovascular system. Circulation time by necessity limits its involvement in rapid adjustments. Major roles involve initiation of specific behaviors related to survival: thermoregulation, feeding, drinking, and sexual behavior. Through the release of catecholamines and ACTH, autonomic and somatic motor behavior are also sustained.

The activities of these subdivisions in response to stress depend on many factors, but they tend to follow a continuum between the fight-or-flight response (Cannon, 1930) and the playing-dead response (Folkow & Neil, 1971). Psychological variables are very important in determining which response will occur. The fight-or-flight response is a mobilization of all bodily resources to confront and physically oppose or avoid the stress situation. Motor activity at its foremost is exerted, and the cardiovascular response pattern is strikingly similar to that observed during preparation for exercise. Autonomic activity is designed to provide the necessary sustenance for this activity primarily by shunting metabolite-rich blood away from vegetative organs and toward the heart, brain, and skeletal muscles. The endocrine system, by the release of hormones, supports and sustains this behavior by bathing all the important structures with stimulant hormones that reinforce their neurally mediated activity. The playing-dead response, on the other hand, is a conservation-withdrawal response (Engel & Schmale, 1972) in the face of the threat. This response provides animals a means of escape from predators; fainting, being an extreme example in humans. The strategy is not to confront the stress but, rather, to save resources for later use. Motor activity is minimal or nonexistent. Autonomic function and endocrine secretion are reduced to bare necessity.

These two behavior patterns reflect the disposition of the two major components of the ANS: the sympathetic and parasympathetic components. The sympathetic component has functions that are synonymous with the fight-or-flight response. Cardiovascular function is enhanced, with particular emphasis on increased HR, elevated BP, and directing blood flow to vital organs. The parasympathetic component has functions that promote the playing-dead response. Cardiovascular function is reduced, resulting in decreased respiration, HR, BP, and blood flow to most organs.

The autonomic regulatory functions that enable an organism to adjust its behavior in response to stress are also a significant factor in the pathology that may result from stress. The same mechanisms that aid in regulation of the response to stress can also malfunction and lead to organ damage and death. Transmitters released by autonomic nerve endings have been shown in stress situations to produce abnormal effects. The normal process of neural activation is somehow disturbed, and instead of normal activation, dysfunction occurs. Autonomic imbalance can also result because visceral organs, like the heart, are innervated by both sympathetic and parasympathetic inputs. Although these inputs normally act as functional antagonists, the dominance of one input over the other leads to malfunction, which can lead to pathology. Thus, stress-induced pathology and dysfunction can be induced both by the action of autonomic neurotransmitters and by autonomic imbalance.

## ANS and Pathology

Myocardial pathology and dysfunction have been associated with sympathetic innervation of the heart and related to NE. Although many exogenous substances have been shown to induce cardiomyopathy, a nonischemic myofibrillar degeneration has been identified as a distinct myocardiopathy that can be induced by NE released from sympathetic nerve terminals. This NE-induced myopathy is characterized by selective staining with fuchsin. This fuchsinophilia identifies myocardial cells undergoing myofibrillar degeneration, which is early evidence of permanent myocardial damage and fibrosis (Reichenbach & Benditt, 1968). Because these lesions occur in the absence of any evidence of coronary artery obstruction that may lead to anoxia, they are described as a nonischemic cardiomyopathy. The affected muscle fibers are surrounded by apparently normal tissue. Furthermore, these lesions are not localized in any particular region of the myocardium but are scattered throughout the heart (Selye, 1958). Moss and Schenk (1970) have convincingly linked NE to cardiopathy in dogs. Sustained infusions of NE were studied with sympathetic activity blocked by propranolol for β-receptors, by phenoxybenzamine for α-receptors, or by both. Although administration of both blocking agents prevented hemodynamic and pathological changes, each blocker alone revealed the pathophysiological effects of NE. In animals with α-blockade, no significant hemodynamic changes occurred, but extensive subendocardial hemorrhage and fuchsinophilia were observed in the myocardium. In animals with β-blockade, however, these morphological changes were not observed even though a significant decrease in cardiac output and performance occurred. Thus, they concluded that α-receptors mediated primarily hemodynamic abnormalities, that cardiomyopathy was induced by NE acting through β-receptors, and that hemodynamic changes were not necessary for NE-induced lesions.

Although research has also suggested the direct involvement of acetylcholine and parasympathetic input in myocardial pathology, indirect sympathetic activation is a better explanation of these data. Myocardial and coronary-artery damage has been reported to be induced by chronic administration of acetylcholine (Hall, Ettinger, & Banting, 1936) and by stimulation of the intact vagus nerve (Groover & Stout, 1965; Manning, Hall, & Banting, 1937). Horswell (1941) attempted to replicate the acetylcholine experiments, but he found no persistent or abnormal morphological changes. Furthermore, Corley, Shiel, and Mauck (1973) have tested the hypothesis that parasympathetic activation may cause a secondary release of NE. The vagus nerve contains afferent fibers that can initiate a reflex enhancement of sympathetic efferent activity (Randall & Armour, 1974). The release of NE by this reflex could explain the cardiomyopathy that others have produced by vagal stimulation. This contention was supported by the failure to obtain cardiomyopathy from vagal stimulation when β-adrenergic input was eliminated (Corley, Shiel, & Mauck, 1973). Cats had cervical-cord transections, and their cardiac β-receptors were blocked with propranolol. Stimulation of the distal cut end of the vagus nerve for 1- to 4-h intervals produced sustained bradycardia, but no myofibrillar or vascular changes were observed. Thus, parasympathetic innervation per se was not found to induce myocardial damage. Myocardial pathology associated with the ANS results primarily from endogenous release of NE on β-receptors of the myocardium by the sympathetic innervation of the heart.

Whereas the CNS pathways that mediate this sympathetic input to the heart remain to be fully defined, myofibrillar degeneration associated with activation of various levels of the neuraxis has been reported. Acute cervical spinal-cord injury has been shown to produce EKG abnormalities and morphological changes similar to those induced by NE (Greenhoot & Mauck, 1972; Greenhoot, Shiel, & Mauck, 1972). Myofibrillar degeneration has also been induced by electrical stimulation of the brainstems of cats (Greenhoot & Reichenbach, 1969; Melville, Blum, Shister, & Silver, 1963) and rhesus monkeys (Chen, Sun, Chai, Kau, & Kou, 1974; Melville, Garvey, Shister, & Knaack, 1969). A clinical analogy to this stimulation is subdural hemorrhage associated with head trauma. Myofibrillar degeneration has been related to increased intracranial pressure from injection of small volumes of blood in experimental animals (Burch, Sun, Colcolough, DePasquale, & Sohal, 1967; Eichbaum, Gazetta, Bissetti, & Pereira, 1965; Hawkins & Clower, 1971) and brain lesions in humans (Connor, 1969; Greenhoot & Reichenbach, 1969). Inasmuch as the myocardial pathology is similar to that induced by NE and the changes can be prevented by β-adrenergic blockers, these cardiopathies also involve sympathetic release of NE in the myocardium.

Sympathetic activity may also lead to myocardial dysfunction and sudden cardiac death. Ventricular fibrillation, which is a cardiac arrhythmia that can lead to cardiac arrest, has been demonstrated to be related to sympathetic myocardial input. Norepinephrine infusion increases susceptibility to ventricular fibrillation (Rabinowitz, Verrier, & Lown, 1976); manipulations that reduce sympathetic tone decrease this susceptibility (Lown, Verrier, & Rabinowitz, 1977). CNS involvement in the mediation of these phenomena has also been shown. Verrier, Calvert, and Lown (1975) found that posterior hypothalamic stimulation was associated with a marked reduction in ventricular fibrillation threshold, which was dissociated from hemodynamic changes also elicited by the stimulation. Although vagotomy and adrenalectomy did not affect fibrillation threshold, the threshold decrease was abolished by β-adrenergic blockade. Thus, the alteration in fibrillation threshold was due to the direct sympathetic neural action on the myocardium of NE from hypothalamic stimulation.

Depression or cessation of autonomic input to the myocardium may also lead to dysfunction and cardiac arrest. Mauck (1973) reported that stimulation of the cingulate gyrus consistently produced sinus bradycardia and ventricular arrest and frequently elicited atrial flutter and fibrillation. Inasmuch as these arrhythmias were abolished by vagotomy, parasympathetic input to the myocardium was necessary for this dysfunction. Hypotension and bradycardia have also been demonstrated to occur as a result of sympathetic inhibition. Manning, Charbon, & Cotten (1963) studied decreased ventricular contraction, HR, and BP induced by stimulation of the septum. Although these responses were unaffected by vagotomy, decreased ventricular contraction and HR were abolished by surgical denervation or β-adrenergic blockade of sympathetic input to the myocardium. The hypotension, however, remained unaffected by these manipulations. Because this hypotension was inhibited by α-adrenergic agents without affecting the reduction in contraction and HR, these later responses were not secondary to the pressure change. These data suggest that an inhibition in sympathetic tone was responsible for these cardiovascular changes. Therefore, CNS-mediated cardiac dysfunction and arrest may involve autonomic imbalance by sympathetic inhibition, parasympathetic activation, or enhanced sympathetic activity.

## Environmental Stress and Pathology

Myocardial pathology and dysfunction may also be elicited by exposure to environmental stress. Life events have been linked to the occurrence of these psychosomatic disorders. Studies have shown that many people who have suffered a myocardial infarct have had a significant increase of life stress during the 6 months before the attack (Rahe, Romo, Bennett, & Siltanen, 1974; Theorell & Rahe, 1975). Occurrence of death has also been linked to life events. Voodoo deaths in primitive cultures (Cannon, 1957) and contemporary society (Seligman, 1975) appear to be related to the belief of the victim that some person has the power to control her or his life or death. The same results can be seen from overwhelming life events. Deaths among widowers were significantly higher than among other men at a comparable age. Furthermore, a majority of these deaths were related to cardiovascular disease (Parkes, Benjamin, & Fitzgerald, 1969). Retrospective study of a large number of sudden deaths has shown that the victims found themselves overwhelmed by life events over which they had no control, such as loss of job, property, or an important person. The actual threat to life was, in every instance, more imagined than real (Engel, 1971). Thus, many studies indicate a relationship in humans between stress and pathology, but a multiplicity of uncontrollable factors makes it difficult to establish a causal relationship.

Stress experiments have also shown that myocardial pathology and dysfunction can be induced in animals. Cardiomyopathy can be elicited by exposure to noxious stimuli, for example, electrical shock (Hirsch, 1950; Johansson, Jonsson, Lannek, Blomgren, Lindberg, & Poupa, 1974), intense light and sound (Mascitelli-Coriandoli, Boldrini, & Citterio, 1958), and tape presentation to rats of a cat-rat fight (Raab, Chaplin, & Bajusz, 1964). Because the observed pathology was similar to that previously reported for NE-induced lesions, enhanced sympathetic input to the myocardium was suggested as the mechanism for these cardiomyopathies.

Richter (1957) conducted early experiments on stress-induced myocardial dysfunction. He observed that, while most rats in a swimming task survived without difficulty for an average of 60 h, a small number succumbed within 5-10 min. He contended that these deaths were sudden cardiac deaths resulting from a reaction of "hopelessness," which resulted in "giving up" and dying rather than contending or coping with the stress. He arrived at this conclusion from the following observations about the circumstances of these stress-induced deaths. First, face whiskers were important for survival. When rats with whiskers clipped were tested, all died within 1-15 min after water immersion. Richter suggested that trimming the rat's whiskers destroyed an important sensory input. The loss of this input was sufficient to cause the rats to give up contending with the stress and died. Second, EKGs recorded from these rats showed that whereas rats that survived the swimming task showed a persistent tachycardia, a progressive slowing of HR occurred immediately before death in rats that succumbed. This bradycardia, along with slowed respiration and hypothermia, suggested the rats died a "vagal death" as a result of parasympathetic overstimulation. Third, pharmacological data supported parasympathetic involvement in these sudden cardiac deaths. Parasympathetic inhibition by atropine significantly reduced the death rate in rats with whiskers clipped. Moreover, parasympathetic stimulants increased mortality. As adrenalectomy did not prevent these deaths, systemic catecholamines were not necessary for these phenomena. Fourth, the stress-induced death phenomenon was also reduced by adaptation to water immersion. Rats exposed repeatedly to brief immersions survived and showed no signs of giving up. Fifth, while Richter does not discuss directly the possibility that the rats drowned, he observed a rapid reversal of the stress-induced effects. Rats that showed all signs of imminent death in the swimming task were normal again within a few minutes after removal from the swimming tank. If rats were drowning, recovery would not be this rapid.

These basic observations of stress-induced deaths in rats have been replicated by a number of other investigators (Binik, Theriault, & Shustack, 1977; Griffiths, 1960; Hughes, Stein, & Lynch, 1978; Lynch & Katcher, 1974; Rosellini, Binik, & Seligman, 1976). The attribution of these deaths to "hopelessness" and "giving up" has, however, been seriously questioned. Hughes et al. (1978) have suggested that these rats simply drowned, asphyxiated while diving in search of an underwater escape route. Richter's assertions that these deaths were a "giving up" reaction to the "hopelessness" of their attempts to survive the swimming tasks were examined to determine if they could not be more simply explained by drowning. First, rats with whiskers clipped lose an important sensory mechanism necessary to keep the head above the water. Without the whiskers to sense the water level, the nostrils are more often below the surface, and thus, water ingestion reaches lethal proportions more readily. Second, the EKG that was recorded during swimming was studied in more detail. Although bradycardia was observed when the rats sank to the bottom of the tank, the HR increased again in those rats that returned to the surface. The bradycardia is merely a reflection of the "diving response" (Andersen, 1966) that occurred when the rats were exploring the bottom for escape routes. The bradycardia was coincident with drowning during dives rather than a cardiac arrest initiated by a "hopelessness" reaction. Third, the rapidity with which rats recovered from near-fatal exposure to the stress was not unlike human reports of rapid recovery in drowning victims. Thus, these data cannot be taken to eliminate drowning as a factor in these deaths. Fourth, repeated exposure to the swimming task involves more than adaptation. The susceptibility is reduced, because the rats have had the opportunity to improve their swimming ability. The only data not discussed were the pharmacological observations of enhancement and mitigation of susceptibility by manipulation of parasympathetic input to the myocardium. These effects could, however, be synergistic or antagonistic to the effects of anoxia and involve the mechanism per se for the deaths.

An extension of Richter's initial observation of "hopelessness" and "giving up" when confronted with stress is "learned helplessness." Overmier and Seligman (1967) observed that dogs exposed to inescapable shocks performed poorly on a subsequent shuttle-box escape-avoidance task. The source of the interference, they suggested, was "learned helplessness." Learning that was ineffective in coping with an aversive stimulus carried over into the situation where escape or avoidance was possible. Modifications of the initial procedure have demonstrated these phenomena in other animals and humans (Seligman, 1975). Although this cognitive and learning model of "helplessness" has support from many human reports (Engel, 1978), the validity of terms such as *helplessness* for describing a phenomenon in infrahumans has been questioned (Hughes et al., 1978). Because animals cannot verbally communicate their feelings, interpretation of psychological parameters of "helplessness" is impossible. Another problem with the original learned-helplessness experiments is whether learning per se is a necessary concomitant. Weiss, Glazer, and Pohorecky (1976) have proposed a more parsimonious explanation. They suggested that the behavioral deficit reported by Overmier and Seligman (1967) was due to stress-induced physiological changes. The avoidance deficit of Overmier and Seligman was not observed 48 h after the administration of inescapable shocks. This rapid disappearance of the effect is not characteristic of a learned response. Weiss et al. (1976) have also observed in the hypothalamus of rats receiving inescapable shocks, lower levels of NE and a greater reduction in uptake than in rats receiving the same shock in an escape-avoidance situation. Other experiments, which pharmacologically manipulated NE in the brain, have also shown that depletion of NE could mimic the effects of inescapable shock. These data support motor-activation deficit as an alternative explanation for learned helplessness. Inescapable shock causes a deficiency in noradrenergic activity of the brain. This NE deficit limits the amount of motor activity so that motor behavior is reduced below the level necessary to perform and learn the shuttle-box escape-avoidance task. Because brain NE activity is correlated with heart NE activity (Ordy, Samorajski, & Schroeder, 1966), this motor deficit can be extended to autonomic, as well as somatic, activity. Thus, stress-induced behavioral deficits involving motor performance can be explained by physiological rather than psychological factors.

Myocardial dysfunction associated with cardiac arrest can also be explained by enhanced sympathetic activity and ventricular fibrillation. Lown, Verrier, and Corbalan (1973) compared differences of fibrillation threshold in dogs exposed to either a shock or a nonshock environment. They observed an increased susceptibility to fibrillation in the shock situation. This difference, however, was abolished if the dogs were pretreated with a $\beta$-adrenergic blocking agent (Matta, Lawler, & Lown, 1976). This increased susceptibility to fibrillation was also found to be correlated with increased plasma levels of NE and epinephrine (Liang, Verrier, Melman, & Lown, 1979). Thus, a psychological manipulation has been shown to enhance vulnerability to a myocardial dysfunction that can result in sudden cardiac death.

## Conclusions

Myocardial pathology and dysfunction have been shown to be related to autonomic input to the myocardium. Inasmuch as cardiac lesions and arrhythmias induced by environmental stress are similar to those elicited by direct neural activation of autonomic mechanisms, they are considered to be related to the same pathophysiological mechanisms. Sympathetic activity similar to that associated with the flight-or-fight response was shown to induce myofibrillar degeneration and increase susceptibility to ventricular fibrillation. The release of NE on myocardial $\beta$-receptors was demonstrated to be responsible for these phenomena. Although parasympathetic activity may lead to a playing-dead response with cardiac arrhythmias and sudden death, no direct involvement has been found with cardiomyopathy or ventricular fibrillation. Also, sympathetic inhibition and decreased NE may result in parasympathetic-like activity that may lead to motor deficits and cardiac arrhythmias because of the autonomic imbalance created by this reduced neural input. Psychological correlates of some of these pathophysiological phenomena have been suggested, but experimental procedures described so far do not lend themselves to separation of psychological factors from physical aspects of the stress.

## STRESS AND LEARNED BEHAVIOR

### Unsignaled-shock Avoidance

The Sidman avoidance paradigm (Sidman, 1953) was originally developed as a technique of unsignaled-shock avoidance for establishing continuous operant behavior. Unsignaled shock occurs in the absence of a response and is determined by two time intervals. The response–shock interval is the time that shock is postponed following a response. A response at any time postpones or allows immediate escape from shock for the duration of the response–shock interval. The shock–shock interval is the time between shocks if an operant response is not elicited by a shock. Because shocks occur in the absence of responding, the best strategy for avoiding shock is the maintenance of a regular rate of responding with a response interval shorter than the response–shock interval. This behavior is readily obtained from animals exposed to this escape-avoidance paradigm.

Because the responding is motivated by the apparent wish to avoid the consequences of an obnoxious shock, long-term maintenance of this behavior was hypothesized to be a stress that might induce psychosomatic disorders. Numerous experiments have shown pathology concomitant with exposure to unsignaled-shock avoidance. Porter, Brady, Conrad, Mason, Galambos, and Rioch (1958) have observed gastrointestinal lesions in rhesus monkeys subjected to 6 h "on" avoidance alternated with 6 h "off" avoidance. Forsyth (1968, 1969) has also studied the effects of unsignaled-shock avoidance in the rhesus monkey. A change in the hours "on-off" the avoidance schedule, however, produced a sustained hypertension without other evidence of pathology. This cardiovascular dysfunction was elicited by subjecting the monkeys to 12 h "on" unsignaled-shock avoidance alternated with 12 h "off" avoidance. Thus, these data indicate that unsignaled-shock avoidance will induce psychosomatic disorders in primates. The type of disorder would appear to be related to the schedule of stress. Whereas 6 h "on-off" avoidance produced ulcers, 12 h "on-off" resulted in hypertension.

Although these data demonstrated pathological changes not observed in monkeys restrained without shock, a question remained, however, as to whether these changes were caused by response contingencies required by avoidance learning and performance or shock per se. The yoked-pairs procedure controls for the effects of shock. Each avoidance monkey is yoked with a second monkey. This yoked monkey is connected in series with the avoidance monkey so that the yoked monkey receives the same shock delivered to its avoidance partner. Although operant behavior by the yoked monkey will not affect or determine shock occurrence, the yoked monkey has shock experience identical to the avoidance monkey's. Because uncertainty and unpredictability of shock occurrence are a stress, psychological stress is also involved in the yoked situation. Stress-induced ulcers have been shown to occur in both avoidance and yoked situations. Porter et al. (1958) also studied yoked monkey pairs in their 6-h "on-off" avoidance situation. Four pairs of monkeys were studied. The experiment was terminated in each pair at the death of the avoidance monkey. Each avoidance monkey exhibited lesions and perforations of the upper gastrointestinal tract. The yoked monkeys, which were sacrificed when their partners succumbed, revealed no gastrointestinal abnormalities. Experiments in rats, however, have found ulcers more extensive in the yoked than in the avoidance animals. Weiss (1970) observed that rats receiving unpredictable shocks developed more ulcers than rats in a predictable-shock group. These studies provide conflicting data, but still, they suggest that stress specific to each situation can induce ulcers. The reason for the opposite results remains unexplained, but it could be due to variations in species' reactions to stress or to procedural differences as suggested by Weiss (1972).

## Stress-induced Myocardial Pathology and Dysfunction

Squirrel monkeys have also been shown to be susceptible to cardiovascular disorders. Lang (1967) examined the effects of avoidance and restraint on serum cholesterol, urinary 17-ketosteroid levels, and coronary-artery atherosclerosis. Three groups of six squirrel monkeys were studied over 25 months. The first group was daily subjected to 1-h sessions of restraint and unsignaled-shock avoidance. The second group was exposed to the same restraint stress without shock. The third group was a cage control without handling, restraint, or shock. When serum cholesterol and 17-ketosteroid levels were compared among the groups, they were significantly higher in the first two experimental groups than in the caged control group. Coronary-artery atherosclerosis, which was absent in the caged controls, was observed in 9 out of 12 of the experimental monkeys. Furthermore, EKGs recorded from anesthetized monkeys during terminal experiments revealed 3 avoidance-group monkeys and 1 restraint-group monkey that showed EKG abnormalities indicative of cardiovascular disease. Although the cardiovascular effects of avoidance and restraint were not separable, this experiment demonstrated that squirrel monkeys were vulnerable to cardiovascular disorders.

Corley, Shiel, Mauck, and Greenhoot (1973) investigated EKG and myocardial pathology induced by avoidance and restraint in the squirrel monkey. The shock-avoidance-escape parameters used were the same as those used by Lang (1967). Because the experiments with rhesus monkeys suggested that cardiovascular pathology was associated with longer periods "on" avoidance, the sessions were 8 h "on" avoidance alternated with 8 h "off" avoidance. Two groups of squirrel monkeys were studied. Nine avoidance monkeys were trained on shock avoidance in daily 1-h sessions; they were then subjected to 8 h "on-off" avoidance. Eight restraint monkeys were exposed to the same experimental and restraint conditions without shock. All the avoidance and two of the restraint monkeys were implanted with recording electrodes before the experiment, and EKGs were recorded throughout the stress sessions. At the conclusion of the experiments, the monkey were sacrificed, and heart, stomach, and adrenals were examined grossly and microscopically for pathological changes.

Although no pathological changes were observed in the stomach or adrenals and coronary arteries were patent, myocardial fuchsinophilia and fibrosis were observed. No lesions were found in two histological controls, but they were significantly more extensive in the avoidance than in the restraint monkeys (Fig. 7.1). EKG abnormalities were also more evident in avoidance than in restraint monkeys. Whereas restraint monkeys only exhibited HR changes, rhythm disturbances indicative of myocaridal pathology and dysfunction were recorded in the avoidance monkeys. Four avoidance monkeys showed ST-segment elevation and T-wave changes (Fig. 7.2), and two of the monkeys exhibited a profound bradycardia and ventricular arrhythmias with cardiac arrest. Thus, shock avoidance induced not only more myocardial pathology than restraint alone but dysfunction that could result in cardiac arrest.

Corley, Mauck, and Shiel (1975) in their next experiment studied yoked pairs to determine if the myocardial pathology and dysfunction could be related to the response contingencies associated with the avoidance situation. Stress-induced effects on EKG and BP were studied in six yoked pairs. Myocardial pathology was compared among avoidance, yoked, and restraint monkeys. The stress procedures were the same as previously described (Corley, Shiel, Mauck, & Greenhoot, 1973).

The experiment for each pair was terminated because of physical debilitation, EKG abnormalities, or both. Although monkeys that succumbed appeared to be normal and healthy before their final session, they showed minimal movement, did not react to noxious stimuli, and exhibited severe bradycardia when the experiment was stopped. This reaction occurred most often in the yoked

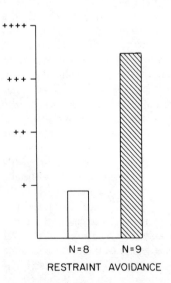

*Figure 7.1* Histograms showing the incidence of myocardial pathology in squirrel monkeys exposed to restraint or 8 h "on" avoidance alternated with 8 h "off" avoidance. The ratings of the avoidance monkeys were significantly higher than those of restraint monkeys (Kolmogorov-Smirnov two-sample test; $p = .01$). 0 = no tissue changes; + = isolated fuchsinophilia (or fibrosis); ++ = widespread fuchsinophilia (or fibrosis); +++ = isolated fuchsinophilia (or fibrosis) combined with widespread fibrosis (or fuchsinophilia); ++++ = widespread fuchsinophilia and fibrosis. (From "Electrocardiographic and Cardiac Morphological Changes Associated with Environmental Stress in Squirrel Monkey" by K. C. Corley, F. O'M. Shiel, H. P. Mauck, and J. Greenhoot, *Psychosomatic Medicine*, 1973, *35*, 361–364. Copyright 1973 by Elsevier North-Holland, Inc. Reprinted by permission.)

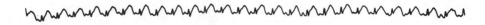

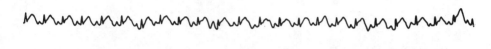

⊢━━━━━━━━━━━━━━━━┤
⊢ I SEC.

*Figure 7.2*  EKG obtained during a 1-h shock-avoidance training session before exposure to
8 h "on-off" avoidance. The top tracing, from the beginning of the session, shows
a normal, steady HR of 270 bpm. The middle tracing, from the middle of the
session, shows an irregular HR between 137 and 198 bpm with a marked ST elevation and T-wave change indicative of myocardial pathology and dysfunction. The
bottom tracing, from the end of the session, shows some return of normal function,
with HR between 224 and 240 bpm and a reduction in the number of ST- and T-
wave abnormalities. A normal EKG was observed in the next training session.

situation. Whereas only one avoidance monkey succumbed to stress before its
yoked partner, five yoked monkeys were affected while their avoidance partners
showed no adverse affects of stress.

Although HR at the beginning of the experiment was not significantly
different between yoked partners, it declined during the course of the experiment, with a significantly greater bradycardia in the yoked than the avoidance
monkeys. Severe bradycardia, which progressed to cardiac arrest, was observed in
the EKGs of the monkeys that succumbed to stress (Fig. 7.3). These HR changes
occurred without noticeable fluctuations in BP. Because BP before cardiac arrest
showed no hypotension until HR declined below 100 bpm, vasopressor syncope
did not appear to be a factor in this ventricular asystole. Stress-induced
pathology was again restricted to the myocardium, with histological evidence of
fuchsinophilia and fibrosis (Fig. 7.4). Although the avoidance situation appeared
to induce more-extensive cardiopathy than the yoked or restraint situations,
these differences were not significant. Because the stress was terminated owing to
the effects on the yoked monkey, longer periods of stress may have been
necessary to demonstrate the differential cardiopathy of the avoidance situation
previously observed (Fig. 7.1). Thus, these experiments suggested that unsignaled-
shock avoidance induced psychosomatic disorders in both the avoidance and
yoked situations. Myocardial dysfunction, which was manifest as severe
bradycardia and cardiac arrest, was most pronounced in the yoked situation, and
myocardial pathology, which did not appear to be a necessary concomitant for
cardiac arrest, was most evident in the avoidance situation.

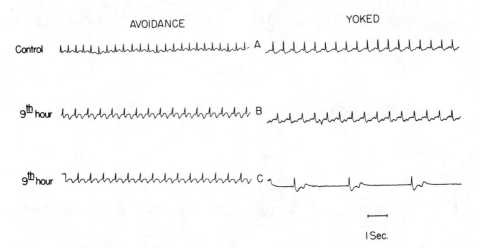

*Figure 7.3*  EKG from a yoked pair of monkeys during their final session of 8 h "on-off" stress.
A is the control record before the 8 h "on" shock stress. The HR is 234 bpm for
the avoidance monkey and 184 bpm for the yoked monkey. B shows that the HRs
at the beginning of the 1st hour "off" shock stress (9th hour) have declined to
153 bpm for the avoidance monkey and 155 bpm for the yoked monkey. C shows
that, whereas the HR of the avoidance monkey remained unchanged throughout
this hour, a severe bradycardia, which decreased to 20 bpm and eventual ventricular
asystole, occurred in the yoked monkey. Physical debilitation, which accompanied
this bradycardia, was only observed in the yoked monkey.

Corley, Shiel, Mauck, Clark, and Barber (1977) in their next experiment
modified the stress procedure so that the occurrence of myocardial pathology
was enhanced in the avoidance situation, and the incidence of cardiac arrest was
reduced in the yoked situation. The stress of the avoidance situation was
intensified by subjecting monkeys to a single 24-h period of continuous,
unsignaled-shock avoidance stress without prior training or adaptation to the
experimental situation. Because dispositional factors of individual monkeys may
contribute to the stress-induced cardiomyopathy and dysfunction, yoked pairs
were randonly assigned to the avoidance or yoked situations, but they were

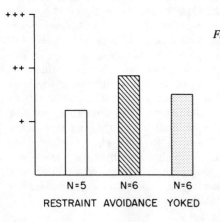

*Figure 7.4*  Histograms showing the incidence of
myocardial pathology in squirrel monkeys exposed to restraint, and yoked
pairs subjected to 8 h "on-off" stress.
No significant differences in myocardial pathology were found among
the situations. See Fig. 7.1 for the
rating scale. (From "Cardiac Responses
Associated with 'Yoked-chair' Shock
Avoidance in Squirrel Monkeys" by
K. C. Corley, H. P. Mauck, and F. O'M.
Shiel, *Psychophysiology*, 1975, *12*,
439–444. Copyright 1975 by Society
for Psychophysiological Research.
Reprinted by permission.)

matched as much as possible on the basis of body weight and aggressive behavior. There were 11 yoked pairs subjected to shock stress. EKGs and BPs were recorded during the experimental sessions. Because the heart tissue was obtained before sufficient time elapsed for damage of the myocardium to elaborate fibrosis, fuchsinophilia and necrosis (clear evidence of tissue damage) were the histological changes assessed.

Myocardial pathology (Fig. 7.5, intact avoidance and yoked monkeys) and cardiac arrest were more readily induced in the avoidance than the yoked monkeys. Although fuchsinophilia was evident in both avoidance and yoked monkeys, a significant number of yoked pairs had higher ratings in the avoidance monkeys than in their yoked partners. Further analysis of these data (Corley, Mauck, Shiel, Barber, Clark, & Blocher, 1979) revealed additional histological differences. Fuchsinophilia of both avoidance and yoked monkeys was significantly greater than that observed in histological control monkeys not exposed to the experimental situation. Necrosis was also observed in eight avoidance and five yoked monkeys. Whereas necrosis was significantly greater in avoidance than in control monkeys, this difference was not evident between control and yoked monkeys. Furthermore, three avoidance monkeys and one yoked monkey succumbed to the shock stress. Again, severe bradycardia with cardiac arrest was observed. These events were very rapid when they occurred in the avoidance monkeys. A sudden cessation of avoidance responding was followed by progressive bradycardia with HR declining from over 200 bpm to ventricular asystole within 5–10 min. The increased incidence in the avoidance situation of cardiac arrest, which had previously been associated with the yoked situation, may be due to the inability of some avoidance monkeys to learn to avoid shock. Thus, unpredictability of shock occurrence became an important factor in the avoidance as well as the yoked situation.

Corley, Mauck, Shiel, Barber, Clark, & Blocher (1979) have most recently studied the incidence of myocardial pathology and dysfunction after the selective removal of sympathetic or parasympathetic input to the myocardium. The effect of 24-h shock stress without prior training was studied in six yoked pairs of monkeys after bilaterial cervical vagotomy removed parasympathetic influences and in six avoidance monkeys with β-adrenergic inputs blocked by propranolol.

Myocardial pathology was increased by vagotomy and reduced by propranolol (Fig. 7.5). The evidence in the vagotomy monkeys of fibrosis, in addition to fuchsinophilia and necrosis, suggested that the removal of parasympathetic input produced cardiomyopathy before the stress session; the over-7 days separating the vagotomy and the stress session was sufficient time for the elaboration of fibrosis. The most logical explanation for this increased cardiomyopathy was that sympathetic activity was enhanced by vagotomy. Such augmented sympathetic activity was also indicated by the vagotomy-induced increase in HR. Thus, vagotomy removed a restraining influence on the sympathetic input, and the resultant increment in NE release and action on β-adrenergic receptors in the myocardium was the mechanism for the cardiomyopathy. Inasmuch as no differences in stress-induced myocardial pathology were observed between avoidance and yoked monkeys, these vagotomy effects may have confounded the more extensive myopathy of the avoidance situation previously observed (Corley, Shiel, Mauck, Clark, & Barber, 1977). The role of β-adrenergic receptors in this pathology was supported by the significant reduction of fuchsinophilia and

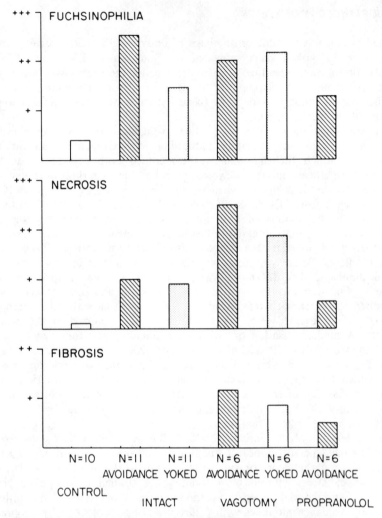

*Figure 7.5* Fuchsinophilia, necrosis, and fibrosis compared among control, intact avoidance and yoked pairs, vagotomy avoidance and yoked pairs, and propranolol avoidance monkeys. Fuchsinophilia was significantly greater than control in all except the propranolol avoidance monkeys. The incidence of necrosis was also greater than control for intact avoidance and vagotomy avoidance and yoked monkeys. Propranolol avoidance monkeys, as well as intact yoked monkeys, failed to show a significant difference from control. Because the experimental procedures excluded the possibility that fibrosis was caused by shock stress, these lesions were attributed to factors preceding the experiment, that is, vagotomy per se and laboratory breeding for the propranolol monkey. 0 = no change; + = small focal areas or diffuse changes involving less than 25% of the myocardium; ++ = a single, large area with 25–50% of the myocardium affected; +++ = 50–75% of the myocardium affected by diffuse changes. (From "Myocardial Dysfunction and Pathology Associated with Environmental Stress in Squirrel Monkey: Effect of Vagotomy and Propranolol" by K. C. Corley, H. P. Mauck, F. O'M. Shiels, J. H. Barber, L. S. Clark, and C. R. Blocher, *Psychophysiology*, 1979, *16*, 554–560. Copyright 1979 by Society for Psychophysiological Research. Reprinted by permission.)

necrosis in the avoidance propranolol monkeys. An isolated incidence of fibrosis in a propranolol monkey was attributed to factors other than the stress experiment.

Stress-induced bradycardia and cardiac arrest have been observed regardless of the autonomic manipulation. Atropine (a parasympathetic inhibitor) sometimes reversed stress-induced HR decreases and prevented cardiac arrest, but not always (Corley & Mauck, 1974). Two examples of HR changes associated with atropine

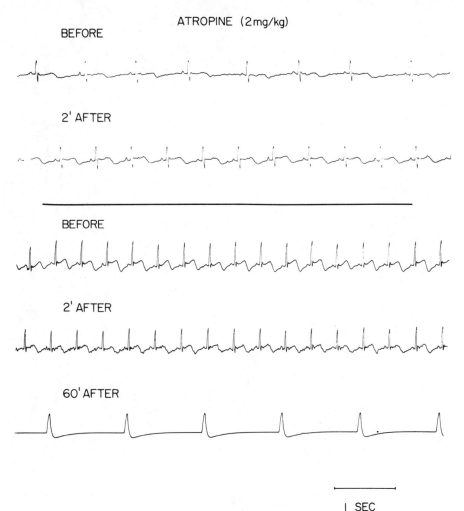

*Figure 7.6*   The effect in two monkeys of 2 mg/kg atropine on bradycardia induced by shock avoidance stress. The upper panel shows reversal of the bradycardia by atropine. An HR of 88 bpm was increased to 120 bpm within 2 min after injection of atropine. No further effects of stress were observed. The bradycardia was not reversed in the lower panel. The HR of 163 bpm in the second monkey was unaffected by atropine. Progressive bradycardia continued, and within 1 h HR declined to 56 bpm, and physical debilitation was followed by cardiac arrest.

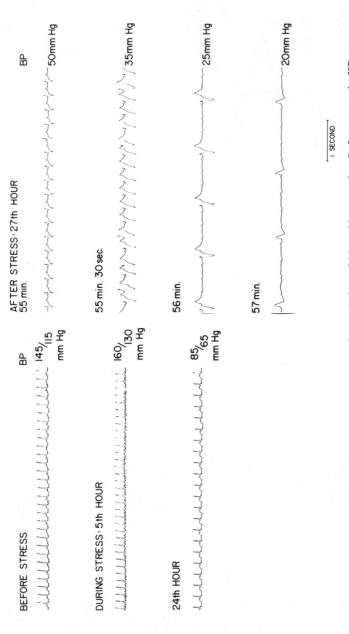

BEFORE STRESS

BP

145/115 mm Hg

DURING STRESS: 5th HOUR

160/130 mm Hg

24th HOUR

85/65 mm Hg

AFTER STRESS: 27th HOUR
55 min.

BP

50mm Hg

55 min. 30 sec.

35mm Hg

56 min.

25mm Hg

57 min.

20mm Hg

1 SECOND

*Figure 7.7* EKG and BP from a vagotomized monkey before and after a 24-h avoidance session. Before stress, the HR was 300 bpm. Tachycardia peaked at 340 bpm during the 5th h, and 217 bpm was the HR at the end of the session. The monkey appeared normal at the end of the session, but physical debilitation suddenly occurred several hours after the session, and the cardiovascular parameters were again monitored. Heart rate was initially a regular 189 bpm, but within seconds the rhythm became irregular and varied between 189 and 264 bpm. During the next 2 min, a severe bradycardia with an incomplete heart block was noted, and rates as low as 37 bpm were recorded immediately before cardiac arrest. Blood pressure increased and decreased with HR. After the session, the pulse width was so small, a single value was indicated for systolic and diastolic measures. The pressure, however, exhibited no sudden drop and declined with the HR.

are presented in Fig. 7.6. While atropine in the first monkey reversed the stress-induced bradycardia, atropine in the second monkey failed to prevent the HR decline and cardiac arrest. Vagotomy also did not prevent cardiac arrest (Fig. 7.7). Stress-induced cardiac arrest occurred in one yoked monkey and two avoidance monkeys, which were survived by their yoked partners. One propranolol avoidance monkey also succumbed. While four other propranolol monkeys appeared to cease operant responding because of behavioral effects of propranolol, only one exhibited severe bradycardia and cardiac arrest. The terminal behavioral and EKG events were comparable to those previously observed for intact monkeys (Corley, Shiel, Mauck, Clark, & Barber, 1977). An autonomic imbalance associated with the removal of either parasympathetic or sympathetic input may be responsible for the cardiac arrest. When atropine or vagotomy removed parasympathetic input, the enhanced sympathetic activity may have led to an electrical instability of the myocardium and cardiac arrest (Lown, Verrier, & Rabinowitz, 1977). The blockade of sympathetic activity by propranolol, on the other hand, left the potential for a parasympathetic-induced asystole (Richter, 1957).

## Conclusions

Experiments with unsignaled-shock avoidance have been shown to induce myocardial pathology and dysfunction manifested as myofibrillar degeneration and cardiac arrest. Although these phenomena were sometimes observed in the same animal, yoked-pair experiments suggested that they may involve different stress factors. Stress-induced myofibrillar degeneration was most prominent in the avoidance situation and was related to an abnormal enhancement of sympathetic activity. Stress factors associated with coping with response contingencies of this situation would appear to be responsible for this cardiomyopathy. Stress-induced cardiac arrest occurred when the animal was not able to cope with stress in the yoked situation or the avoidance situation. The sudden cardiac deaths were related to a marked decrease in sympathetic input, increased parasympathetic activity, or both. The imbalance of autonomic input to the myocardium made the heart susceptible to factors that can induce cariac arrest. Thus, myocardial pathology and dysfunction occurred at both ends of the spectrum of autonomic activity. Abnormal arousal and extreme sympathetic activity led to cardiomyopathy, and marked parasympathetic-like activity resulted in cardiac arrest.

## REFERENCES

Andersen, H. T. Physiological adaptations in diving vertebrates. *Physiological Reviews,* 1966, *46,* 212–243.

Binik, Y. M., Theriault, G., & Shustack, B. Sudden death in the laboratory rat: Cardiac function, sensory, and experiential factors in swimming deaths. *Psychosomatic Medicine,* 1977, *39,* 89–92.

Burch, G. E., Sun, S. C., Colcolough, H. L., DePasquale, N. P., & Sohal, R. S. Acute myocardial lesions following experimentally-induced intracranial hemorrhage in mice. *Archives of Pathology,* 1967, *84,* 517–521.

Cannon, W. B. The Linacre Lecture on the autonomic nervous system: An interpretation. *Lancet,* 1930, *1,* 1109–1115.

Cannon, W. B. "Voodoo" death. *Psychosomatic Medicine,* 1957, *19,* 182–190.

Chen, H. I., Sun, S. C., Chai, C. Y., Kau, S. L., & Kou, C. Encephalogenic cardiomyopathy after stimulation of the brain stem in monkeys. *American Journal of Cardiology*, 1974, *33*, 845–852.

Cohen, D. H., & Cabot, J. B. Toward a cardiovascular neurobiology. *Trends in Neurosciences*, 1979, *2*, 1–3.

Connor, R. C. R. Focal myocytolysis and fuchsinophilic degeneration of the myocardium of patients dying with various brain lesions. *Annals of the New York Academy of Sciences*, 1969, *156*, 261–270.

Corley, K. C., & Mauck, H. P. Autonomic nervous system involvement in cardiac dysfunction. Paper presented at the Society for Neuroscience, St. Louis, 1974.

Corley, K. C., Mauck, H. P., & Shiel, F. O. M. Cardiac responses associated with "yoked-chair" shock avoidance in squirrel monkeys. *Psychophysiology*, 1975, *12*, 439–444.

Corley, K. C., Mauck, H. P., Shiel, F. O'M., Barber, J. H., Clark, L. S., & Blocher, C. R. Myocardial dysfunction and pathology associated with environmental stress in squirrel monkey: Effect of vagotomy and propranolol. *Psychophysiology*, 1979, *16*, 554–560.

Corley, K. C., Shiel, F. O'M., & Mauck, H. P. The effect of vagal stimulation on the myocardium in the cat. *Proceedings of the Society for Experimental Biology and Medicine*, 1973, *144*, 909–911.

Corley, K. C., Shiel, F. O'M., Mauck, H. P., Clark, L. S., & Barber, J. H. Myocardial degeneration and cardiac arrest in squirrel monkey: Autonomic and psychological correlates. *Psychophysiology*, 1977, *14*, 322–328.

Corley, K. C., Shiel, F. O'M., Mauck, H. P., & Greenhoot, J. H. Electrocardiographic and cardiac morphological changes associated with environmental stress in squirrel monkey. *Psychosomatic Medicine*, 1973, *35*, 361–364.

Eichbaum, F. W., Gazetta, B., Bissetti, P. C., & Pereira, C. B. Electrocardiographic disturbances following acute increase of intracranial pressure. *Zietschrift für die gesamte experimentelle Medizin*, 1965, *139*, 721–734.

Engel, G. L. Sudden and rapid death during psychological stress: Folklore or folk wisdom? *Annals of Internal Medicine*, 1971, *74*, 771–782.

Engel, G. L. Psychologic stress, vasodepressor (vagovagal) syncope and sudden death. *Annals of Internal Medicine*, 1978, *89*, 403–412.

Engel, G. L., & Schmale, A. H. Conservation-withdrawal: A primary regulatory process for organismic homeostasis. In R. Porter & J. Knight (Eds.), *Physiology, emotion and psychosomatic illness*. Amsterdam: Elsevier-Excepta Medica, 1972.

Folkow, B., & Neil, E. *Circulation*. New York: Oxford University Press, 1971.

Forsyth, R. P. Blood pressure and avoidance conditioning: A study of 15-day trials in the rhesus monkey. *Psychosomatic Medicine*, 1968, *30*, 125–135.

Forsyth, R. P. Blood pressure responses to long-term avoidance schedules in the restrained rhesus monkey. *Psychosomatic Medicine*, 1969, *31*, 300–309.

Greenhoot, J. H., & Mauck, H. P. The effect of cervical cord injury on cardiac rhythm and conduction. *American Heart Journal*, 1972, *83*, 659–662.

Greenhoot, J. H., & Reichenbach, D. D. Cardiac injury and subarachnoid hemorrhage. *Journal of Neurosurgery*, 1969, *30*, 521–532.

Greenhoot, J. H., Shiel, F. O'M., & Mauck, H. P. Experimental spinal cord injury. *Archives of Neurology*, 1972, *26*, 524–529.

Griffiths, W. J. Responses of wild and domestic rats to forced swimming. *Psychological Reports*, 1960, *6*, 39–49.

Groover, M. E., & Stout, C. Neurogenic myocardial necrosis. *Angiology*, 1965, *16*, 180–186.

Hall, G. E., Ettinger, G. H., & Banting, F. G. An experimental production of coronary thrombosis and myocardial failure. *Canadian Medical Association Journal*, 1936, *34*, 9–15.

Hawkins, W. E., & Clower, B. R. Myocardial damage after head trauma and simulated intracranial hemorrhage in mice: The role of the autonomic nervous system. *Cardiovascular Research*, 1971, *5*, 524–529.

Henry, J. P., & Stephens, P. M. *Stress, health, and the social envornment*. New York: Springer-Verlag, 1977.

Henry, J. P., Stephens, P. M., & Santisteban, G. A. A model of psychosocial hypertension showing reversibility and progression of cardiovascular complications. *Circulation Research*, 1975, *36*, 156–164.

Hirsch, S. Les rôles des petites branches coronaires dans la pathogènese de l'infarctus myocardique. *Acta Medica Scandinavica,* 1950, *138,* 449–456.

Horswell, R. G. Observations on the production of myocardial disease with acetylcholine. *American Heart Journal,* 1941, *22,* 116–121.

Hughes, C. W., Stein, E. A., & Lynch, J. J. Hopelessness-induced sudden death in rats. *Journal of Nervous and Mental Disease,* 1978, *166,* 387–401.

Johansson, G., Jonsson, L., Lannek, N., Blomgren, L., Linberg, P., & Poupa, O. Severe stress-cardiopathy in pigs. *American Heart Journal,* 1974, *87,* 451–457.

Lang, C. M. Effects of psychic stress an atherosclerosis in the squirrel monkey. *Proceedings of the Society for Experimental Biology and Medicine,* 1967, *126,* 30–34.

Liang, B., Verrier, R. L., Melman, J., & Lown, B. Correlation between circulating catecholamine levels and ventricular vulnerability during psychological stress in conscious dogs. *Proceedings of the Society for Experimental Biology and Medicine,* 1979, *161,* 266–269.

Lown, B., Verrier, R. L., & Corbalan, R. Psychological stress and threshold for repetitive ventricular response. *Science,* 1973, *182,* 834–836.

Lown, B., Verrier, R. L., & Rabinowitz, S. H. Neural and psychologic mechanisms and the problem of sudden cardiac death. *American Journal of Cardiology,* 1977, *39,* 890–902.

Lynch, J. J., & Katcher, A. Human handling and sudden death in laboratory rats. *Journal of Nervous and Mental Disease,* 1974, *159,* 362–365.

Manning, J. W., Charbon, G. A., & Cotten, M. deV. Inhibition of tonic cardiac sympathetic activity by stimulation of brain septal region. *American Journal of Physiology,* 1963, *205,* 1221–1226.

Manning, G. W., Hall, G. E., & Banting, F. G. Vagal stimulation and the production of myocardial damage. *Canadian Medical Association Journal,* 1937, *37,* 314–318.

Mascitelli-Coriandoli, E., Boldrini, R., & Citterio, C. Cardiac damage caused by experimental stress. *Nature,* 1958, *181,* 1215–1216.

Matta, R. J., Lawler, J. E., & Lown, B. Ventricular electrical instability in the conscious dog. *American Journal of Cardiology,* 1976, *38,* 594–598.

Mauck, H. P. Neural effects on cardiac rate and rhythm. *MCV Quarterly,* 1973, *9,* 11–12.

Melville, K. I., Blum, B., Shister, H. E., & Silver, M. D. Cardiac ischemic changes and arrhythmias induced by hypothalamic stimulation. *American Journal of Cardiology,* 1963, *12,* 781–791.

Melville, K. I., Garvey, H. L., Shister, H. E., & Knaack, J. Central nervous system stimulation and cardiac ischemic changes in monkeys. *Annals of the New York Academy of Sciences,* 1969, *156,* 241–260.

Miller, N. E. Learning of visceral and glandular responses. *Science,* 1969, *163,* 434–445.

Moss, A. J., & Schenk, E. A. Cardiovascular effects of sustained norepinephrine infusions in dogs. *Circulation Research,* 1970, *27,* 1013–1022.

Obrist, P. A., Webb, R. A., Sutterer, J. R., & Howard, J. L. The cardiac-somatic relationship: Some reformulations. *Psychophysiology,* 1970, *6,* 569–587.

Ordy, J. M., Samorajski, T., & Schroeder, D. Concurrent changes in hypothalamic and cardiac catecholamine levels after anesthetics, tranquilizers and stress in subhuman primate. *Journal of Pharmacology and Experimental Therapeutics,* 1966, *152,* 445–457.

Overmier, J. B., & Seligman, M. E. P. Effects of inescapable shock upon subsequent escape and avoidance learning. *Journal of Comparative and Physiological Psychology,* 1967, *63,* 23–33.

Parkes, C. M., Benjamin, B., & Fitzgerald, R. G. Broken heart: A statistical study of increased mortality among widowers. *British Medical Journal,* 1969, *1,* 740–743.

Porter, R. W., Brady, J. V., Conrad, D., Mason, J. W., Galambos, R., & Rioch, D. McK. Some experimental observations on gastrointestinal lesions in behaviorally conditioned monkeys. *Psychosomatic Medicine,* 1958, *20,* 379–394.

Raab, W., Chaplin, J. P., & Bajusz, E. Myocardial necrosis produced in domesticated rats and wild rats by sensory and emotional stresses. *Proceedings of the Society for Experimental Biology and Medicine,* 1964, *116,* 665–669.

Rabinowitz, S. H., Verrier, R. L., & Lown, B. Muscarinic effects of vagosympathetic trunk stimulation on the repetitive extrasystole (RE) threshold. *Circulation,* 1976, *53,* 622–627.

Rahe, R. H., Romo, M., Bennett, L., & Siltanen, P. Recent life changes, myocardial infarction, and abrupt coronary death. *Archives of Internal Medicine,* 1974, *133,* 221–228.

Randall, W. C., & Armour, J. A. Complex cardiovascular responses to vagosympathetic stimulation. *Proceedings of the Society for Experimental Biology and Medicine,* 1974, *145,* 493–499.

Reichenbach, D. D., & Benditt, E. P. Myofibrillar degeneration: A response of the myocardial cell to injury. *Archives of Pathology,* 1968, *85,* 189–199.

Richter, C. P. On phenomenon of sudden death in animals and man. *Psychosomatic Medicine,* 1957, *19,* 191–198.

Rosellini, R. A., Binik, Y. M. & Seligman, M. E. P. Sudden death in the laboratory rat. *Psychosomatic Medicine,* 1976, *38,* 55–58.

Seligman, M. E. P. *Helplessness: On depression, development, and death.* San Francisco: W. H. Freeman, 1975.

Selye, H. *The chemical prevention of necrosis.* New York: Ronald, 1958.

Sidman, M. Avoidance conditioning with brief shock and no exteroceptive warning signal. *Science,* 1953, *118,* 157–158.

Theorell, T., & Rahe, R. H. Life change events, ballistocardiography and coronary death. *Journal of Human Stress,* 1975, *1,* 18–24.

Verrier, R. L., Calvert, A., & Lown, B. Effect of posterior hypothalamic stimulation on ventricular fibrillation threshold. *American Journal of Physiology,* 1975, *228,* 923–927.

Weiss, J. M. Somatic effects of predictable and unpredictable shock. *Psychosomatic Medicine,* 1970, *32,* 397–408.

Weiss, J. M. Psychological factors in stress and disease. *Scientific American,* 1972, *226,* 104–113.

Weiss, J. M., Glazer, H. I., & Pohorecky, L. A. Coping behavior and neurochemical changes: An alternative explanation for the original "learned helplessness" experiments. In G. Serban & A. Kling (Eds.), *Animal models in human psychobiology.* New York: Plenum, 1976.

# III

# MODERATION
# OF THE STRESS RESPONSE

This part of the book is concerned with what psychological factors influence the physiological reaction to stress. Its four chapters discuss different aspects and kinds of psychological moderator variables, with several overlapping intentionally in order to expose readers to different perspectives and methodologies. The chapters progress from a discussion of the relationship between a specific personality type and its associated physiological responses to chapters delineating traits and coping styles that decrease susceptibility to illness in general. They depict the complexity of stress research in the psychological sphere, whereas those in Part II showed the difficulty of ferreting out specific physiological components of the stress response.

Haney and Blumenthal (Chap. 8) review the research on Type A behavior as a predisposing variable in heart disease. Their discussion raises several questions as to the mechanisms that underlie the relationship between Type A behavior pattern and cardiac disease. One of the most interesting things about Type A construct is that several of the underlying personality traits of these people are similar to those exhibited by extremely healthy people (see Burchfield, Holmes, & Harrington, 1981; Kobasa, 1979; Vaillant, 1978). As Garrity and Marx (Chap. 9) point out, those exhibiting Type A behavior pattern appear to be healthier than those with Type B and to have a higher threshold for stress-induced illness. Do the extremely healthy people identified in several studies have a lower morbidity rate when younger, only to succumb to a heart attack at an early age? This question is important and needs to be answered. Furthermore, it is not known if there are overlapping, as well as independent, traits that characterize Type A individuals and extremely healthy people. Identification of shared and nonshared traits of these groups is important for improving understanding of health and illness.

Garrity's and Marx's chapter provides cohesion between Haney and Blumenthal and Sarason, Sarason, and Johnson (Chap. 10). Garrity and Marx, like Sarason et al., discuss their work on moderators of the relationship between life events and illness, but they also mention Type A behavior as a moderating variable. In their research on life change and moderator variables, Garrity and Marx chose to use Holmes and Rahe's Schedule of Recent Experience (SRE) to measure life change. Sarason et al., on the other hand, thought that the SRE did not explain enough variability, and so they devised their own measurement instrument, the Life Experiences Survey. These two chapters are useful for contrast. They permit investigators to see how two different groups use different methodologies and variables when testing the same hypothesis. It is rare that two chapters such as these are allowed to stand side by side, encouraging comparison of their methods.

J. Wilson (Chap. 11) also works with similar hypotheses, but he focuses on hospitalized patients. He is testing, in an applied setting, the theory that good coping decreases stress-induced pathology. His research investigates differences in postsurgery recovery and physiological arousal among individuals prepared differentially for surgery. Wilson has taken theoretical propositions based on previous work on stress and tested them in an applied setting. By so doing, he has shown that the theories are workable as treatment interventions and that there is a low cost-benefit ratio for these interventions.

# REFERENCES

Burchfield, S. R., Holmes, T. H., & Harrington, R. L. Personality differences between sick and rarely sick individuals. *Social Science and Medicine,* 1981, *15E*, 145–148.
Kobasa, S. C. Stressful life events, personality, and health: An inquiry into hardiness. *Journal of Personality and Social Psychology,* 1979, *37*, 1–11.
Vaillant, G. E. Natural history of male psychological health: VI. Correlates of successful marriage and fatherhood. *American Journal of Psychiatry,* 1978, *135*, 653–659.

# 8

# *Stress and the Type A Behavior Pattern*

*Thomas L. Haney and James A. Blumenthal*
*Duke University Medical Center, Durham, North Carolina, United States*

> Every affliction of the mind that is attended with either pain or pleasure, hope or fear, is the cause of an agitation whose influence extends to the heart.
>
> William Harvey, 1628

The post-World War I era has witnessed a startling rise in the incidence of coronary heart disease (CHD), which cannot be solely explained by improved diagnostic procedures, increased proportions of older people in the population, or simple genetic changes. A series of well-designed and carefully conducted epidemiologic studies have sought to understand the reasons for this development. In the past 25 years, studies of initially healthy individuals have demonstrated that such risk factors as increased levels of blood lipids, cigarette smoking, and elevated BP are significantly associated with higher incidence and prevalence rates of CHD (Epstein, 1965; Keys, 1966; Simborg, 1970). Critical reviews of the epidemiology literature have concluded, however, that these risk factors taken together provide an incomplete explanation for the increased rates of CHD found among those possessing these characteristics (Corday & Corday, 1975; Werko, 1976). Consequently, there has been a call for efforts to identify new risk factors, including psychological and behavioral patterns.

There also has been a more subtle development in the science of medicine as a whole that has had an important impact on increasing understanding of coronary disease. The traditional biomedical approach to the study of disease has come under increased scrutiny in the past 10 years. The reductionistic-mechanistic model, according to which the human organism is regarded as solely a physical object that can be completely understood by the laws of biochemistry and physics, is considered by many to be neither theoretically nor practically tenable. The distinction between the terms *disease* and *illness* emphasizes the necessity to consider patient's condition in a psychosocial context. Illness is a more general concept that includes the cultural, phenomenological, and social forces that directly affect the pathogenesis and clinical expression of both the disease and its treatment. Recognition of the importance of biologic, social, and psychological influences on the disease process has given rise to the biopsychosocial model (Engel, 1977) and the fields of behavioral medicine (Pomerleau, 1979; Schwartz & Weiss, 1977) and behavioral health (Matarazzo, 1980). These new fields are broadly conceived, in their respective interests as the study of psychosocial and physiological interactions in illness and in health. They represent the evolution of a new methodology as well as a new conceptual model for understanding mind–body relationships. The discovery that such hormones as epinephrine and NE also represent neurotransmitter substances found in the brain provides one link between the so-called mind–body dualism. The evidence for a link between different psychobehavioral factors and cardiovascular disease is another major development. While the accumulating research has been the subject of several reviews (see, e.g., Caffrey, 1967; Jenkins, 1971, 1976), this chapter presents an overview of the basic research that has documented an association between the Type A behavior pattern and CHD and provides an interactionist perspective for understanding the relationship.

## HISTORICAL PERSPECTIVE

The behavioral peculiarities of those afflicted with CHD have been noted for as long as the disease has received clinical recognition. Dr. John Hunter, who himself suffered from stress-induced angina pectoris, observed, "My life is at the mercy of any rogue who chooses to provoke me." Dr. Hunter died in 1793 following a heated board meeting at St. George's Hospital in London (cited in Kligfield, 1980, p. 368).

In 1897 Sir William Osler stated, "For this I believe, that the high pressure at which men live and the habit of working the machine to its maximum capacity, are responsible (for arterial degeneration), rather than the excesses of eating and drinking" (p. 154).

The Menningers reported the first clinical study of psychological character-istics in three cardiac subjects evidencing repressed aggression (Menninger & Menninger, 1936). Their observation coincides with that of William Harvey some three centuries earlier:

> *I was acquainted with another strong man, who having received an injury and affront from one more powerful than himself, and upon whom he could not have his revenge, was so overcome with hatred and spite and passion, which he yet communicated to no one, that at last he fell into a strange distemper, suffering from extreme oppression and pain of the heart and breast and in the course of a few years died. His friends thought him poisoned by some maleficent influence, or possessed with an evil spirit. . . . In the dead body I found the heart and aorta so much gorged and distended with blood, that the cavities of the ventricles equalled those of a bullock's heart in size. Such is the force of blood pent up, and such are the effects of its impulse. (Inglis, 1965)*

These and many other clinical observations ranging from anger and aggression to elation and great joy led to the present-day investigations of Type A behavior pattern and CHD. [A more complete historical perspective can be appreciated in a paper by Kowal (1960).] In 1969, following the initiation of the Western Collaborative Group Study (WCGS), Carruthers postulated underlying bio-chemical mechanisms that involved the stresses of modern living giving rise to elevated levels of catecholamines, and he hypothesized that anxiety and aggres-sion along with other predisposing factors lead to atherogenesis. It is this interaction of behavioral processes and underlying physiological mechanisms that serves as the focus for this chapter.

# TYPE A BEHAVIOR AND ITS RELATIONSHIP
# TO THE STRESS RESPONSE

Based on the foregoing literature and their own clinical impressions, Rosenman and Friedman defined the Type A behavior pattern as an "action-emotion complex which is exhibited by those individuals who are engaged in a relatively chronic struggle to obtain an unlimited number of poorly defined things from their environment in the shortest possible period of time, and if necessary, against the opposing efforts of other things or persons in this same environment" (Friedman, 1969). They further stated that those manifesting this behavioral complex exhibit excessive competitiveness, aggressiveness, and impatience and a well-rationalized form of free-floating hostility (Friedman & Rosenman, 1974). Those possessing this behavior pattern are regarded as Type A, or "coronary-prone." Type B behavior pattern is defined as the lack of Type A characteristics; that is, it describes a more leisurely, relaxed, and easy going approach to life. Type B people experience less time pressure and "hurry sickness" and display less of a need to compete in nearly every aspect of living.

Jenkins (1971) offers this supplemental definition:

> *The coronary prone behavior pattern is considered to be an overt behavioral syndrome or style of living characterized by extremes of competitiveness, striving for achievement, aggressiveness (sometimes stringently repressed), haste, impatience, restlessness, hyperalertness, explosiveness of speech, tenseness of facial musculature, and feelings of being under the pressure of time and under the challenge of responsibility. Persons having this pattern are often so deeply committed to their vocation or profession that other aspects of their lives are relatively neglected. Not all aspects of this pattern or syndrome need to be present for a person to be classified as possessing it. The pattern is neither a personality trait nor a standard reaction to a challenging situation, but rather the reaction of a characterologically predisposed person to a situation which challenges him. Different kinds of situations evoke maximal reaction from different people.*

Here, it is important to note that the notion of Type A behavior is neither a psychodynamic concept (although various researchers both past and present have attempted to apply psychological dimensions to the construct) nor a generalized stress response in the usual sense of the word. It is, rather, as Jenkins is careful to point out, a stereotypic response sequence engaged in by a predisposed (Type A) person to a situation which he or she interprets as challenging. In the absence of such a challenging situation, one may not observe Type A behavior (Glass, 1977). As such, it is similar to a stress response as defined by Burchfield (1979) in that it is a response to a perceived challenge from the environment that could be interpreted as "an alteration of psychological homeostatic processes." It should be noted, however, that the emphasis in Type A behavior research remains on the *behavior* and not on any underlying psychodynamic construct. The notion of homeostasis implies an equilibrium of the physiological and psychological states. Typically, the Type A person over compensates for situations she or he perceives as challenging or beyond control. There is also a concomitant physiological and hemodynamic response to the challenge; and in this regard, the behavior pattern is again similar to the stress response. Type A subjects report a reduction in perceived stress when the behavior pattern is activated as a coping response to a perceived challenge; conversely, there is an increase in perceived stress when this behavior is thwarted. The elements of the stress response are thus incorporated in the behavior typology and frequently take an exaggerated form of expression.

## EVOLUTION OF THE TYPE A CONCEPT

The Type A behavior pattern is one of the few risk factors in modern epidemiology to receive careful investigation along a stepwise progression of investigative strategies. The historical basis of the construct, as outlined above, had been observed and recorded by notable physicians since the recognition of CHD as a clinical entity. During the 1950s Rosenman and Friedman, of the Harold Brunn Institute in San Francisco, were struck by the behavioral peculiarities of their patients when comparing them to the general population. They concluded that the observed behavior must enhance the atherogenic potential of more traditional risk factors such as the serum lipids, accounting for the increased risk of CHD (Rosenman & Friedman, 1962). In 1960 they undertook an evaluation of 3,524 middle-aged men in the WCGS for prospective follow-up over the next $8\frac{1}{2}$ years. The purpose of their study was to determine the incidence of CHD in those found to be disease-free at intake and to determine the factors associated with that incidence of disease. Their findings are reported in a series of articles (Rosenman, Brand, Jenkins, Friedman, Straus, & Wurm, 1975; Rosenman, Friedman, Straus, Jenkins, Zyzanski, & Wurm, 1970; Rosenman, Friedman, Straus, Wurm, Kositchek, Hahn, & Werthessen, 1964), and the general conclusion is that Type A behavior confers an overall twofold risk for CHD independent of the other traditional risk factors assessed. Subsequent analyses of the WCGS data using multiple logistic risk models confirmed the earlier findings of an overall twofold risk of CHD for Type A subjects (Brand, Rosenman, Sholtz, & Friedman, 1976; Rosenman, Brand, Sholtz, & Friedman, 1976). The second of these analyses estimated a 31% attributable risk in CHD secondary to the Type A behavior pattern.

These early investigators employed what has become known as the structured interview (SI) to assess Type A behavior. It consists of a series of questions presented by a trained interviewer and designed to elicit the speech characteristics typical of the Type A pattern. The content of the responses, although dealing with Type A characteristics such as impatience, competitiveness, and hostility, was judged to be less important than the voice and speech stylistics of the subject's delivery (Schucker & Jacobs, 1977; Scherwitz, Berton, & Leventhal, 1977; Blumenthal, O'Toole, & Haney, in press).

A second method of assessing Type A behavior was developed and refined by Jenkins, Zyzanski, and co-workers. Theirs is a self-administered, paper-and-pencil evaluation standardized on the WCGS population known as the Jenkins Activity Survey (JAS) for Health Prediction (Jenkins, Rosenman, & Friedman, 1967). Weights were derived for each item to assess overall Type A or B characteristics as well as three factor analytically derived scores that were found to be independent of one another and predictive, either singularly or in combination, of various CHD events (Jenkins et al., 1967; Zyzanski & Jenkins, 1970). For example, in a subgroup of the WCGS study population, high scorers on the JAS Type A scale had twice the incidence of new CHD as did low scorers over a

4-year period (Jenkins, Rosenman, & Zyzanski, 1974). In another study on the same population, high scorers on the Type A-B scale with manifest CHD experienced a higher incidence of recurrent episodes than did low scorers with CHD (Jenkins, Zyzanski, Rosenman, & Cleveland, 1971). Here, however, the JAS assessment was somewhat weaker in predictive power than the SI. Again, using JAS Type A-B assessments in this group, high scorers were found to have a higher risk of new myocardial infarction (MI) than low scorers in that same cohort (Jenkins, Zyzanski, & Rosenman, 1976). High Type A scorers who also had significant records of past achievement were more likely to suffer "silent" (undetected) MIs than were lower scorers with lesser achievement records (Jenkins, 1966).

A third form of assessment was used in the Framingham Heart Study and is reported in a series of articles by Haynes and associates (see Haynes, Levine, Scotch, Feinleib, & Kannel, 1978a, 1978b, 1980). The questionnaire is a 26-item checklist of Type A characteristics on which subjects rate themselves on a 3- or 4-point categorical scale. Both in cross-sectional data and a prospective cohort, Type A behavior as assessed by this instrument was significantly associated with CHD in both men and women, especially in the younger (less than 65) age categories. A number of other psychosocial parameters were also assessed; among them, emotional lability, aging worries, tension, daily stress, and anger were associated with CHD in the cross-sectional data. In the cohort who were initially disease-free and followed over 8 years, suppressed hostility as well as the Type A assessment was significantly and independently related to the incidence of CHD. In a separate paper on the incidence of CHD (Haynes & Feinleib, 1980), Haynes looked at work status in men and women from the Framingham study. She found a twofold risk for women holding menial clerical jobs compared with housewives; suppressed hostility, a nonsupportive boss, and decreased job mobility were significantly associated with their development of CHD. This risk was even greater if the women had children and were married to blue-collar workers.

Waldron (Waldrom, Zyzanski, Shekell, Jankins, & Tannenbaum, 1977) examined the participants of the Chicago Heart Association Detection Project in Industry which included both black and white employed men and women. While differing in geographic region the study population had a wider age distribution than the WCGS and thus she and her collaborators were able to standardize their findings using the JAS to younger and older employed groups. As noted, the JAS was factor analyzed using the WCGS data and three factors were derived using that study population: Speed-and-Impatience, Job-Involvement and Hard-Driving-and-Competitive. Waldron and her associates found similar factors in both older and younger employed white men and women. Black men and women likewise yielded three factor scores but Hard-Driving-and-Competitive was better approximated by Hardworking and Job-Involvement became Striving-to-Advance. The differences between these factors were attributed to cultural differences but caution in interpreting these findings was urged since the long term effects of Type A behavior in blacks has not been assessed.

The Type A concept has also received cross-cultural validation. In Belgium, both the SI and the JAS were translated into Flemish and French for use in a preventive-cardiology study (Kittel, Kornitzer, Zyzanski, Jenkins, Rustin, & Degre, 1978). Using the SI, a similar distribution to that found in U.S. populations was noted, with greater clustering in the central categories. The JAS, using WCGS weightings, yielded scores more in the Type B direction than those found in the U.S. With an interassessment correspondence of 70%, it was concluded that the Type A concept had sufficient cross-cultural validity to determine whether it is a risk factor for CHD in that setting. A similar process was undertaken in the Netherlands, where an independent measurement, the Rating of Statements List (RSL) was compared to assessments made using the SI technique (Dijl, 1978). Three factors similar to those of the JAS were derived: Aggressivity, Activity and Work, and Ambition/Dominance. These factors correlated very highly with the Type A-B ratings of the structured interview, and it was thought that the RSL might well serve a function comparable to the JAS in future epidemiologic studies in that setting. Finally, a retrospective study of MI patients matched with both other medical and healthy controls was undertaken in Inowroclaw, Poland, using a Polish translation of the JAS (Zyzanski, Wrzesniewski, & Jenkins, 1979). As with similar studies in the United States, the coronary cases were found to score significantly higher on the Type A and Hard-driving scales than those free of CHD. This corroboration of the concept of Type A behavior as a risk factor for CHD in a population outside the United States has sparked widespread interest in testing the concept in other cultures of interest.

Clinical studies of anatomic findings show much the same results as were found earlier in autopsy subjects (Friedman, Rosenman, Straus, Wurm, & Kositchek, 1968). In the three different studies of patients undergoing diagnostic coronary angiography, a relationship was found between the Type A assessment and the extent of coronary atherosclerosis (Blumenthal, Williams, Kong, Schanberg, & Thompson, 1978; Frank, Heller, Kornfeld, Sporn, & Weiss, 1978; Zyzanski, Jenkins, Ryan, Flessas, & Everist, 1976). A fourth study failed to confirm these findings (Dimsdale, Hackett, Hutter, Block, & Catanzano, 1978). Zyzanski, Jenkins, and their coinvestigators at the Boston University School of Medicine (Zyzanski, Jenkins, Ryan, Flessas, & Everist, 1976) confirmed the Type A hypothesis in men by using JAS assessments of Type A behavior. In the same study, they also confirmed the hypothesis that "neurotic" traits may be associated with clinical manifestations of angina pectoris or chest pain associated with coronary atherosclerosis (Eastwood & Trevelyan, 1971; Ostfeld, Lebovits, Shekelle, & Paul, 1964). Frank and co-workers (Frank et al., 1978) found in a larger sample of coronary angiography patients including both men and women, the Type A behavior pattern as assessed by the SI to be associated with coronary atherosclerosis to the same extent as other physical risk factors such as age, sex, smoking, and hypertension. Only the association between cholesterol and coronary artery disease (CAD) had a greater magnitude.

Blumenthal, Williams, and coinvestigators (Blumenthal et al., 1978) found similar results regarding the Type A hypothesis when they used the SI in a large sample of both men and women undergoing coronary angiography. Type A in this study when assessed by the SI remained significant even when the effects of age, sex, BP, smoking, and cholesterol levels were statistically adjusted. The association of Type A behavior when assessed by the JAS with coronary disease in this same study population was not significant. Dimsdale and his associates (Dimsdale et al., 1978) at the Massachusetts General Hospital also failed to find the hypothesized association when assessing Type A behavior pattern using the JAS. It has been suggested that the JAS, being a self-report measure, appears to classify people on different aspects of the behavior pattern, whereas the SI constitutes a sample of the behavior itself (Scherwitz, Berton, & Leventhal, 1977). Here, it should also be recalled that the Type A construct is multifaceted and that reanalysis of the WCGS data indicates that certain components of the behavior pattern such as the potential for hostility, competitiveness, and impatience were significantly related to CHD, whereas speed of activity, job involvement, and past accomplishments were not (Matthews, Glass, Rosenman, & Bortner, 1977). Our own recent work has shown that hostility as assessed by a subscale of the MMPI was more strongly associated with the findings at coronary catheterization than was the Type A classification alone (Williams, Haney, Lee, Kong, Blumenthal, & Whalen, 1980).

As noted earlier, Type A behavior as a risk factor for CHD is the only such variable to receive such thorough and well-sequenced documentation of its association with the disease outcome. (The above summary of evidence, although extensive, is far from complete, and readers are referred to other excellent summaries such as Dembroski et al. (Dembroski, McDougall, Herd, Shields, 1977; Dembroski, Weiss, Shields, Haynes, & Feinleib, 1978), Jenkins (Jenkins, 1971, 1976), and Krantz et al. (Krantz, Glass, Schaeffer, & David, 1982)]. That is, the investigative sequence has progressed from historical precedent to clinical observation to cross-sectional studies and from retrospective designs to anatomic findings at autopsy to prospective cohorts and cross-cultural validations to clinical anatomic associations and finally to intervention studies. Given the weight of such evidence, a panel of experts was convened in December 1978 by the National Institutes of Heart, Lung and Blood, and it was established that Type A behavior should be regarded as a "standard risk factor" for CHD. Further, it was considered that Type A behavior is a special form of coronary-prone behavior to be distinguished from other coronary-prone behaviors such as smoking, overeating, noncompliance with pharmacologic regimens, and so on.

There is a well-known truism in epidemiology, however, that association does not prove causality. The final proof of causality relies either on removal of the causative agent and a subsequent improvement or eradication of the disease state or on demonstration of a biologic mechanism between the exposure factor (in this case, "Type A" behavior) and the disease outcome (CHD). Only brief attention to the former is merited because little is known about long-term intervention at this time.

## INTERVENTION STRATEGIES

Suinn initiated intervention strategies for Type A subjects using a behavioral approach known as stress-management training (Suinn & Bloom, 1978). It is aimed at interrupting the vicious cycle of stress so common to Type A people, and it consists of a combination of relaxation techniques and alternative coping strategies for dealing with stress. Such measures have produced significant improvements in Type A behavior, especially the hard-driving factor, and reductions in serum cholesterol and triglyceride levels. Such techniques have also been applied to post-MI patients (Suinn, 1974), and similar results have been achieved through group therapy, suggesting other routes to the same ends. Roskies and her associates in Montreal have employed similar techniques in industrial populations with much the same results and at the same time decreased systolic BP (Roskies, Spevack, Surkis, Cohen, & Gilman, 1978). A 6-month follow-up of the three treatment modalities employed showed that the special behavior therapy group (in those with clinical CHD) maintained the most treatment effects, the healthy subjects receiving regular behavior therapy were intermediate, and the participants receiving psychotherapy the least (Roskies, Kearney, Spewack, Surkis, Cohen, & Gilman, 1979). A recent study of Blumenthal and colleagues (Blumenthal, Williams, Williams, & Wallace, 1980) reveals that a brief (10-week) program of aerobic exercise resulted in significant decreases of participants "cardiovascular risk profiles" including reductions in BP, HR at submaximal workloads, weight, ratio of LDL:HDL cholesterol and Type A behavior as measured by the JAS.

Perhaps the most comprehensive intervention program undertaken is that by Friedman and his associates in attempting to reduce the reinfarction rate of survivors of MIs by reducing their Type A behaviors. His Coronary Recurrence Prevention Program targets the time urgency and excessive competitiveness of the Type A pattern in order to try and reduce the amount of excessive arousal in the daily lives of the subjects. Preliminary results of this project after one year indicate a significant decrement in the incidence of both reinfarction and death in the two intervention groups when compared to the nonintervention control group. A significant decline was also noted in the nonfatal reinfarction rate between those receiving both cardiologic and behavioral counseling compared to those given cardiologic counseling alone (Friedman, Thoresen, Gill, Ulmer, Thompson, Powell, Price, Elek, Rabin, Breall, Piaget, Dixon, Bourg, Levy, & Tasto, 1982).

## BIOBEHAVIORAL MECHANISMS

To date, there have been two lines of evidence linking psychosocial processes to CHD: hemodynamic changes or shifts within the circulatory system itself and a series of neuroendocrine or biochemical changes that have been hypothesized to have some relationship to the atherogenic process. The term *evidence* here is used in the "soft" sense, for many of the following studies and conclusions are based on our current understanding of the atherogenic process, and the factors involved are considered to fit into a general model of atherogenesis without any direct evidence that they actually do so.

It is generally believed that the initiating event in the atherosclerotic process is some type of damage to the inside lining (endothelium) of the artery wall (Duguid, 1946; Gorlin, 1976). This initial insult might be the result of hemodynamic factors in which turbulence and shear forces set the stage for the formation of atherosclerotic buildup, or the initiating event might also occur from biochemical or immunologic processes. Regardless of the initiating event, once the initial insult has occurred, the newly formed lesion can progress along one of two courses; it can follow a self-limiting course in which the arterial wall returns to its normal anatomic state or the injury–healing process can get out of hand and result in a build up of damaged tissue, the residue of the body's attempts at restoring the damaged area (i.e., scar tissue of a sort). The substructures of the arterial wall are lined with smooth muscle cells; once these are exposed to the components of the blood such as platelets that are involved in the normal formation of scar tissue, the atherogenic potential is there (Carruthers, 1969; Ross & Glomset, 1976). Other substances within the circulation are likewise exposed to the injured surface, and some of these, such as certain fractions of cholesterol and blood lipids, are very toxic to the arterial wall (Gorlin, 1976; Williams, 1978). The permeability of the damaged area is thought to be enhanced, and under conditions such as hypertension, the exposure to circulating toxic components and the buildup of plaque (scar tissue) is accelerated. The resultant blockage in the coronary arteries eventually leads to the clinical manifestations of angina pectoris (chest pain), MI (heart attack), or death through decreased or arrested blood flow to that part of the heart muscle being supplied by the blocked coronary arteries.

Many of these atherogenic hemodynamic and neuroendocrine or biochemical factors have been shown to be associated with the Type A behavior pattern. The earliest evidence again comes from the Friedman/Rosenman group and pertains to the excretion of catecholamines and some other metabolites in Type A and Type B men (Friedman, St. George, Byers, & Rosenman, 1960). Resting levels were found to be the same between the two groups, but working-hour levels showed greatly enhanced excretion of NE in the Type A men. This same phenomenon was noted under more experimental conditions of a specific challenge where Type A subjects increased their plasma NE levels by 30%, whereas those of the Type Bs remained the same (Friedman, Byers, Diamant, & Rosenman, 1975). In an experimental paradigm, harassment was added to a uniform competition task for both Type A and B subjects. As responded to harassment with greater elevations in plasma epinephrine than did all the other experimental groups. Plasma NE levels changed in a similar direction but were not reliably different between groups (Glass, Krakoff, Contrada, Hilton, Kehoe, Mannucci, Collins, & Snow, 1980).

Norepinephrine, like epinephrine, is secreted from the adrenal medulla, but it is also secreted from sympathetic nerve endings during periods of arousal. The effects of the catechols relate *initially* to the development of CAD and only secondarily to the clinical manifestations of CHD. They increase HR, BP, and platelet aggregation while releasing lipids and free fatty acids into the blood stream (Carruthers, 1969). Circulating free fatty acids, taken up by the atheromatous plaque, and platelet aggregation contribute both to plaque formation and to certain clinical events such as MI.

Cholesterol metabolism has also been found to be affected in Type A subjects, notable increases occurring during periods of stress. Clotting time and cholesterol levels were monitored in a group of accountants before and during the April 15th deadline for tax returns. Both were found to increase during periods of job stress, and both have been implicated in the pathogenesis of CHD (Friedman, Rosenman, & Carroll, 1958). Similar findings were also confirmed in women (Rosenman & Friedman, 1961) and people under chronic stress (Friedman & Rosenman, 1959) as well as in relationship to physical stress and Type A characteristics (Simpson, Olewine, Jenkins, Ramsey, Zyzanski, Thomas, & Hames, 1974). Likewise, fasting and postprandial serum triglyceride levels were also elevated in Type A subjects (Friedman & Rosenman, 1964) along with postprandial sludging of erythrocytes (Friedman, Byers, & Rosenman, 1965; Friedman & Rosenmen, 1964) which is known to be associated with anginal events (Kuo & Joyner, 1955). Other neuroendocrine and biochemical characteristics associated with the Type A behavior pattern and thought to be associated with the atherogenic process include: (1) elevated levels of ACTH and a depressed response to secreting 17-HOCS following an injection of ACTH (Friedman, Byers, & Rosenmen, 1972); (2) decreased level of GH even following arginine challenge (Friedman, Byers, Rosenman, & Newman, 1971); and (3) hyperinsulinemic response to glucose challenge in the absence of a positive glucose tolerance test (Friedman, Byers, Rosenman, & Elevitch, 1970).

Psychophysiological factors affecting hemodynamic changes are the other group of biobehavioral mechanisms that possibly play a role in atherogenesis. With the development of the relatively new field of behavioral medicine, there has been more integration of the medical-biologic, social, and psychological sciences, with the result that much new research at the interface of these areas is currently underway.

What is known is that the Type A person generally shows a heightened response in sympathetically mediated processes like HR and BP, especially in the face of a challenging situation. In a group of cardiac patients matched with patient controls, Dembroski and his colleages monitored EKG and BP while administering the structured interview for Type A behavior and a brief history quiz, which was considered to be more challenging than the interview in that it called for correct content answers (Dembroski, MacDougall, & Lushene, 1979). As predicated, not only were there more Type As among the patient group, but this group as a whole had significantly elevated systolic and diastolic BP throughout the course of the interview compared with the controls, and this difference became even more pronounced during the challenge of the history quiz. These results are impressive enough; considering the fact that the cardiac patients were all on propranolol (a drug with antihypertensive properties) at the time of the study, they become all the more impressive. The greater sympathetic arousal using the indicators of HR and BP has also been demonstrated in college students undergoing challenging laboratory studies (Dembroski, MacDougall, & Shields, 1977; Manuck, Craft, & Gold, 1978) as well as in working-class adults (Glass et al., 1980). Although groups are essentially comparable at base line and at low levels of challenge, Dembroski has found that highly hostile and competitive Type As show elevated sympathetic arousal even at low levels of challenge (Dembroski, MacDougall, Herd, & Shields, 1979). He likened this group to those found to have the greatest incidence of CHD in the WCGS (Matthews et al., 1977), who were also competitive, impatient, and possessed an increased potential for hostility. Indeed, more recent research involving our data (Dembroski, MacDougall, Williams, Haney, & Blumenthal, in press) found the interaction between the potential for hostility and directing anger inward to be the significant components of the Type A behavior pattern that are associated with disease severity at angiography. Glass (1977) further defined some conditions under which this heightened sympathetic arousal occurs and suggested that the Type A person has a need to "remain in control" of any specific situation.

Two recent studies from our laboratory have focused on Type A/B differences. In our first study, Type As demonstrated increased physiologic arousal (elevated systolic BP, HR, and skeletal muscle vasodilatation) whether a task incentive was present or absent, while Type Bs showed only a heightened cardiovascular response when explicitly challenged by a monetary incentive condition (Blumenthal, Lane, Williams, McKee, Haney, & White, 1983). A second study compared cardiovascular and neuroendocrine response patterns among Type As and Bs during mental arithmetic and reaction time tasks. While performing mental arithmetic, As had greater muscle vasodilatation and elevated levels of norepinephrine, epinephrine, and cortisol compared to Bs and during the sensory intake (reaction time) task showed increased levels of testosterone as well as increased cortisol among those who also had a positive family history of hypertension (Williams, Lane, Kuhn, Melosh, White, & Schanberg, 1982). Williams has identified two sensory modalities, intake and rejection, and the conditions under which these occur (Williams, 1979). He has suggested that the extreme shifts in the hemodynamic and neuroendocrine responses of Type A people, as a result of central and sympathetically mediated processes, may well be associated with the atherogenic process.

## FUTURE DIRECTIONS

Dembroski et al. (1978) offer the model in Fig. 8.1 of various factors involved in CHD. None of the cells nor their interactions in the diagram have been fully explored. Basically, what the foregoing overview reveals is that we know enough about each of the areas involved to formulate and test hypotheses but not enough about any *one* of the areas to account for more than 6-12% of the variance in CHD or more than 45-50% of the variance when considering them altogether.

Regarding Type A behavior and CHD, we know that we have an association that accounts for as much of the variance in CHD as most of the other standard risk factors. We do not know its exact mechanism or mechanisms of action, although several have been suggested. Given future refinements in noninvasive techniques for assessing CHD, expanded study populations will be available to further define the association. In the meantime there are many avenues of exploration left open. Certainly the report by Matthews (Matthews et al., 1977) emphasizes the need to refine the Type A instrument. As Cobb (1977) observed in an editorial, "After 20 years of work in the area, we are back at the starting point, wishing that a sound psychometric approach to the problem had been

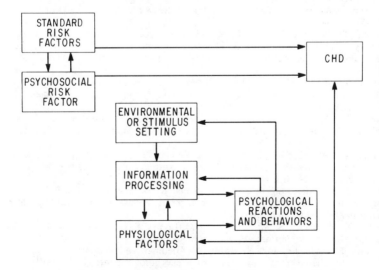

*Figure 8.1* Model of the relationship between psychosocial-physiological variables and CHD. [Adapted from Dembroski et al., 1978, with permission.]

undertaken in the first instance. However, this is often the way of research. One first has to prove that there is a phenomenon to dissect before one can get support to dissect it" (p. 211).

We also need better to understand the interaction between the social environment and behavioral predispositions. Are there intra- or interpersonal effects that modify the Type A–CHD association? Although something is known about cultural and subcultural influences, much remains to be discovered. The questions are endless, and the need for integrative research is evident. The climate in which it can take place is beginning to warm and, we must hope, such research efforts will flourish in the not too distant future.

# REFERENCES

Blumenthal, J. A., Lane, J. D., Williams, R. B., McKee, D. C., Haney, T., & White, A. Effects of task incentives on cardiovascular response in Type A and Type B individuals. *Psychophysiology,* 1983, *20,* 63–70.

Blumenthal, J. A., O'Toole, L., & Haney, T. Behavioral assessment of the Type A behavior pattern. *Psychosomatic Medicine,* in press.

Blumenthal, J. A., Williams, R. B., Kong, Y., Schanberg, S. M., & Thompson, L. W. Type A behavior pattern and coronary atherosclerosis. *Circulation,* 1978, *58,* 634–639.

Blumenthal, J. A., Williams, R. S., Williams, R. B., & Wallace, A. G. Effects of exercise on the Type A (coronary prone) behavior pattern. *Psychosomatic Medicine,* 1980, *42,* 289–296.

Brand, R. J., Rosenman, R. H., Sholtz, R. I., & Friedman, M. Multivariate prediction of coronary heart disease in the Western Collaborative Group Study compared to the findings of the Framingham Study. *Circulation,* 1976, *63,* 348–355.

Burchfield, S. R. The stress response: A new perspective. *Psychosomatic Medicine,* 1979, *41,* 661–672.

Caffrey, B. Factors involving interpersonal and psychological characteristics: A review of empirical findings. *Milbank Memorial Fund Quarterly,* 1967, *45,* 119–139.

Carruthers, M. E. Aggression and atheroma. *Lancet,* 1969, *11,* 1170.

Cobb, S. Coronary disease and Type A behavior. *Psychosomatic Medicine,* 1977, *39,* 211–212.

Corday, E., & Corday, S. R. Prevention of heart disease by control of risk factors: The time has come to face the facts (Editorial). *American Journal of Cardiology,* 1975, *35,* 330–333.

Dembroski, T. M., MacDougall, J. M., Herd, J. A., & Shields, J. L. Perspectives on coronary-prone behavior. In D. S. Krantz, A. Baum, & J. E. Singer (Eds.), *Handbook of psychology and medicine* (Vol. 1): *Cardiovascular disorders.* Hillsdale, N.J.: Erlbaum, 1977.

Dembroski, T. M., MacDougall, J. M., Herd, J. A., & Shields, J. L. Effects of level of challenge on pressor and heart rate responses in Type A and B subjects. *Journal of Applied Social Psychology,* 1979, *9,* 209–228.

Dembroski, T. M., MacDougall, J. M., & Lushene, R. Interpersonal interaction and cardiovascular responses in Type A subjects and coronary patients. *Journal of Human Stress,* 1979, *5,* 28–36.

Dembroski, T. M., MacDougall, J. M., & Shields, J. L. Physiologic reactions to social challenge in persons evidencing the Type A coronary-prone behavior pattern. *Journal of Human Stress,* 1977, *3,* 2–9.

Dembroski, T. M., MacDougall, J. M., Williams, R. B., Haney, T. L., & Blumenthal, J. A. Components of Type A, hostility and anger-in: Relationship to angiographic findings. *Psychosomatic Medicine,* in press.

Dembroski, T. M., Weiss, S. M., Shields, J. L., Haynes, S. G., & Feinleib, M. *Coronary-prone behavior.* New York: Springer-Verlag, 1978.

Dijl, H. van. The A/B typology according to Friedman and Rosenman and an effort to test some of the characteristics by means of a psychological test (RSL or BUL). *Journal of Psychosomatic Research,* 1978, *22,* 101–109.

Dimsdale, J. E., Hackett, T. P., Hutter, A. M., Jr., Block, P. C., & Catanzano, D. Type A personality and extent of coronary atherosclerosis. *American Journal of Cardiology*, 1978, *42*, 583-586.

Duguid, J. B. Thrombosis as a factor in the pathogenesis of coronary atherosclerosis. *Journal of Pathology*, 1946, *58*, 207-212.

Eastwood, M. R., & Trevelyan, H. Stress and coronary disease. *Journal of Psychosomatic Research*, 1971, *15*, 289-292.

Engel, G. L. The need for a new medical model: A challenge for biomedicine. *Science*, 1977, *196*, 129-136.

Epstein, F. H. The epidemiology of coronary heart disease: A review. *Journal of Chronic Diseases*, 1965, *18*, 735-774.

Frank, K. A., Heller, S. S., Kornfeld, D. S., Sporn, A. A., & Weiss, M. B. Type A behavior pattern and coronary angiographic findings. *Journal of the American Medical Association*, 1978, *240*, 761-763.

Friedman, M. *Pathogenesis of coronary artery disease*. New York: McGraw-Hill, 1969.

Friedman, M., Byers, S. O., Diamant, J., & Rosenman, R. H. Plasma catecholamine response of coronary-prone subjects (Type A) to a specific challenge. *Metabolism*, 1975, *24*, 205-210.

Friedman, M., Byers, S. O., & Rosenman, R. H. Effects of unsaturated fats upon lipemia and conjunctival circulation. *Journal of the American Medical Association*, 1965, *193*, 882-886.

Friedman, M., Byers, S. O., & Rosenman, R. H. Plasma ACTH and cortical concentration of coronary-prone subjects. *Proceedings of the Society for Experimental Biology and Medicine*, 1972, *140*, 681-684.

Friedman, M., Byers, S. O., Rosenman, R. H., & Elevitch, F. R. Coronary-prone individuals (Type A behavior pattern): Some biochemical characteristics. *Journal of the American Medical Association*, 1970, *212*, 1030-1037.

Friedman, M., Byers, S. O., Rosenman, R. H., & Neuman, R. Coronary-prone individuals (Type A behavior pattern): Growth hormone responses. *Journal of the American Medical Association*, 1971, *217*, 929-932.

Friedman, M., & Rosenman, R. H. Association of a specific overt behavior pattern with blood and cardiovascular findings: Blood cholesterol level, blood clotting time, incidence of arcus senilis and clinical coronary artery disease. *Journal of the American Medical Association*, 1959, *169*, 1286-1296.

Friedman, M., & Rosenman, R. H. Serum lipids and conjunctival circulation after fat ingestion in men exhibiting Type A behavior pattern. *Circulation*, 1964, *29*, 874-886.

Friedman, M., & Rosenman, R. H. *Type A behavior and your heart*. New York: Knopf, 1974.

Friedman, M., Rosenman, R. H., & Carroll, V. Changes in the serum cholesterol and blood-clotting time in men subjected to cyclic variation of occupational stress. *Circulation*, 1958, *17*, 825-861.

Friedman, M., Rosenman, R. H., Straus, R., Wurm, M., & Kositchek, R. The relationship of Behavior Pattern A to the state of the coronary vasculature: A study of 51 autopsy subjects. *American Journal of Medicine*, 1968, *44*, 525-537.

Friedman, M., St. George, S., Byers, S. O., & Rosenman, R. H. Excretion of catecholamines, 17-ketosteroids, 17-hydroxycorticoids and 5-hydroxindole in men exhibiting a particular behavior pattern (A) associated with high incidence of clinical coronary heart disease. *Journal of Clinical Investiations*, 1960, *39*, 758-764.

Friedman, M., Thoresen, C. E., Gill, J. J., Ulmer, D., Thompson, L., Powell, L., Price, V., Elek, S. R., Rabin, D. C., Breall, W. S., Piaget, G., Dixon, T., Bourg, E., Levy, R. A., & Tasto, D. L. Feasibility of altering Type A behavior pattern after myocardial infarction. Recurrent coronary prevention project study: Methods, baseline results and preliminary findings. *Circulation*, 1982, *66*, 83-92.

Glass, D. C. *Behavior patterns, stress and coronary disease*. Hillsdale, N.J.: Erlbaum, 1977.

Glass, D. C., Krakoff, L. R., Contrada, R., Hilton, W. F., Kehoe, K., Manucci, E. G., Collins, C., & Snow, B. Effects of harassment and competition upon cardiovascular and catecholamine responses in Type A and B individuals. *Psychophysiology*, 1980, *17*, 453-463.

Gorlin, R. *Coronary artery disease*. Philadelphia: Saunders, 1976.

Harvey, W. *De mortu cordis* (1628). Quoted in R. Hunter & D. MacAlpine (Eds.), *Three hundred years of psychiatry, 1535-1860*. London: Oxford University Press, 1963.

Haynes, S. G., & Feinleib, M. Women, work and coronary heart disease: Prospective findings from the Framingham Heart Study. *American Journal of Public Health*, 1980, *70*, 133-141.

Haynes, S. G., Levine, S., Scotch, N., Feinleib, M., & Kannel, W. B. The relationship of psychosocial factors to coronary heart disease in the Framingham Study: I. Methods and risk factors. *American Journal of Epidemiology,* 1978a, *107,* 362–383.

Haynes, S. G., Feinleib, M., Levine, S., Scotch, N., & Kannel, W. B. The relationship of psychosocial factors to coronary heart disease in the Framingham Study: II. Prevalence of coronary heart disease. *American Journal of Epidemilogy,* 1978b, *107,* 384–402.

Haynes, S. G., Feinleib, M., & Kannel, W. B. The relationship of psychosocial factors to coronary heart disease in the Framingham Study: III. Eight-year incidence of coronary heart disease. *American Journal of Epidemiology,* 1980, *111,* 37–58.

Inglis, B. *A history of medicine.* Cleveland: World Publishing, 1965, 179–180.

Jenkins, C. D. Components of the coronary-prone behavior pattern: Their relationship to silent myocardial infarction and blood lipids. *Journal of Chronic Diseases,* 1966, *19,* 599–609.

Jenkins, C. D. Psychologic and social precursors of coronary disease. *New England Journal of Medicine,* 1971, *284,* 244–255; 307–317.

Jenkins, C. D. Recent evidence supporting psychological and social risk factors for coronary disease. *New England Journal of Medicine,* 1976, *294,* 987–994; 1033–1038.

Jenkins, C. D., Rosenman, R. H., & Friedman, M. Development of an objective psychological test for the determination of the coronary-prone behavior pattern in employed men. *Journal of Chronic Diseases,* 1967, *20,* 371–379.

Jenkins, C. D., Rosenman, R. H., & Zyzanski, S. J. Prediction of clinical coronary heart disease by a test for the coronary prone behavior pattern. *New England Journal of Medicine,* 1974, *290,* 1271–1275.

Jenkins, C. D., Zyzanski, S. J., & Rosenman, R. H. Risk of new myocardial infarction in middle-aged men with manifest coronary heart disease. *Circulation,* 1976, *53,* 342–347.

Jenkins, C. D., Zyzanski, S. J., Rosenman, R. H., & Cleveland, G. L. Association of coronary-prone behavior scores with recurrence of coronary heart disease. *Journal of Chronic Diseases,* 1971, *24,* 601–611.

Keys, A. The individual risk of coronary heart disease. *Annals of New York Academy of Sciences,* 1966, *134,* 1046–1063.

Kittel, F., Kornitzer, M., Zyzanski, S. J., Jenkins, C. D., Rustin, R. M., & Degre, C. Two methods of assessing the Type A coronary-prone behavior pattern in Belgium. *Journal of Chronic Dieseases,* 1978, *31,* 147–155.

Kligfield, P. Angina pectoris and medical education. *American Journal of Cardiology,* 1980, *45,* 367–369.

Kowal, S. J. Emotions and angina pectoris: An historical review. *American Journal of Cardiology,* 1960, *5,* 421–427.

Krantz, D. S., Glass, D. C., Schaeffer, M. A., & Davia, J. E. Behavior patterns and coronary disease: A critical review. In J. T. Cacioppo & R. E. Petty (Eds.), *Perspectives on cardiovascular psychophysiology.* New York: Guilford, 1982.

Kuo, P. T., & Joyner, C. R. Angina pectoris induced by fat ingestion in patients with coronary heart disease. *Journal of the American Medical Association,* 1955, *158,* 1008–1013.

Manuck, S. B., Craft, S. A., & Gold, K. J. Coronary-prone behavior pattern and cardiovascular response. *Psychophysiology,* 1978, *15,* 403–411.

Matarazzo, J. I. Behavioral health and behavioral medicine. *American Psychologist,* 1980, *35,* 807–817.

Matthews, K. A., Glass, D. C., Rosenman, R. H., & Bortner, R. W. Competitive drive, Pattern A and coronary heart disease: A further analysis of some data from the Western Collaborative Group Study. *Journal of Chronic Diseases,* 1977, *30,* 489–498.

Menninger, K. A., & Menninger, W. C. Psychoanalytic observations in cardiac disorders. *American Heart Journal,* 1936, *11,* 10.

Osler, W. *Lectures on angina pectoris and allied states.* New York: D. Appleton & Co., Inc., 1897.

Ostfeld, A. M., Lebovits, B. Z., Shekelle, R. B., & Paul, O. A prospective study of the relationship between personality factors and coronary heart disease. *Journal of Chronic Diseases,* 1964, *17,* 265–276.

Pomerleau, O. F. Behavioral medicine: The contribution of the experimental analysis of behavior to medical care. *American Psychologist,* 1979, *34,* 654–663.

Rosenman, R. H., Brand, R. J., Jenkins, C. D., Friedman, M., Straus, R., & Wurm, M. Coronary heart disease in the Western Collaborative Group Study: Final follow-up experience of $8\frac{1}{2}$ years. *Journal of the American Medical Association*, 1975, *233*, 872–877.

Rosenman, R. H., Brand, R. J., Sholtz, R. I., & Friedman, M. Multivariate prediction of coronary heart disease during $8\frac{1}{2}$ year follow-up in the Western Collaborative Group Study. *American Journal of Cardiology*, 1976, *37*, 903–910.

Rosenman, R. H., & Friedman, M. Association of specific behavior pattern in women with blood and cardiovascular findings. *Circulation*, 1961, *24*, 1173–1184.

Rosenman, R. H., & Friedman, M. The role of a specific overt behavior pattern in the occurrence of ischemic heart disease. *Cardiologia Practica*, 1962, *13*, 42–53.

Rosenman, R. H., Friedman, M., Straus, R., Jenkins, C. D., Zymanski, S. J., & Wurm, M. Coronary heart disease in the Western Collaborative Group Study: A follow-up experience of $4\frac{1}{2}$ years. *Journal of Chronic Diseases*, 1970, *23*, 173–190.

Rosenman, R. H., Friedman, M., Straus, R., Wurm, M., Kositcheck, R., Hahn, W., & Werthessen, N. T. A predictive study of coronary heart disease: The Western Collaborative Group Study. *Journal of the American Medical Association*, 1964, *189*, 113–124.

Roskies, E., Kearney, H., Spevack, M., Surkis, A., Cohen, C., & Gilman, S. Generalizability and durability of treatment effects in an intervention program for coronary-prone (Type A) managers. *Journal of Behavioral Medicine*, 1979, *2*, 195–207.

Roskies, E., Spevack, M., Surkis, A., Cohen, C., & Gilman, S. Changing the coronary-prone (Type A) behavior pattern in a non-clinical population. *Journal of Behavioral Medicine*, 1978, *1*, 201–216.

Ross, R., & Glomset, J. A. The pathogenesis of atherosclerosis. *New England Journal of Medicine*, 1976, *295*, 369–377; 420–425.

Scherwitz, L., Berton, K., & Leventhal, H. Type A assessment and interaction in the behavior pattern interview. *Psychosomatic Medicine*, 1977, *39*, 229–240.

Schucker, B., & Jacobs, D. R. Assessment of behavioral risk factors for coronary disease by voice characteristics. *Psychosomatic Medicine*, 1977, *39*, 219–228.

Schwartz, G. E., & Weiss, S. M. What is behavioral medicine? *Psychosomatic Medicine*, 1977, *36*, 377–381.

Simborg, D. The status of risk factors and coronary heart disease. *Journal of Chronic Diseases*, 1970, *22*, 515–552.

Simpson, M. T., Olewine, D. A., Jenkins, C. D., Ramsey, F. H., Zyzanski, S. J., Thomas, G., & Hames, C. G. Exercise induced catecholamines and platelet aggregation in the coronary-prone behavior pattern. *Psychosomatic Medicine*, 1974, *36*, 476–487.

Suinn, R. M. Behavior therapy for cardiac patients. *Behavior Therapy*, 1974, *5*, 369.

Suinn, R. M., & Bloom, L. J. Anxiety management training for Type A persons. *Journal of Behavioral Medicine*, 1978, *1*, 25.

Werko, L. Risk factors and coronary heart disease: Fact or fancy? *American Heart Journal*, 1976, *91*, 87–89.

Waldron, I., Zyzanski, S. J., Shekelle, R. B., Jenkins, C. D., & Tannenbaum, S. The coronary-prone behavior pattern in employed men and women. *Journal of Human Stress*, 1977, *3*, 2–18.

Williams, R. B. Psychophysiological processes, the coronary-prone behavior pattern and coronary heart disease. In T. M. Dembroski, S. M. Weiss, J. L. Shields, S. G. Haynes, & M. Feinleib (Eds.), *Coronary-prone Behavior*. New York: Springer-Verlag, 1978.

Williams, R. B. Physiological mechanisms underlying the association between psychosocial factors and coronary disease. In W. D. Gentry & R. B. Williams (Eds.), *Psychological aspects of myocardial infarction and coronary care*. St. Louis: Mosby, 1979.

Williams, R. B., Haney, T. L., Lee, K. L., Kong, Y., Blumenthal, J. A., & Whalen, R. E. Type A, hostility and coronary atherosclerosis. *Psychosomatic Medicine*, 1980, *42*, 539–549.

Williams, R. B., Lane, J. D., Kuhn, C. M., Melosh, W., White, A. D., & Schanberg, S. M. Type A behavior and elevated physiological and neuroendocrine responses to cognitive tasks. *Science*, 1982, *218*, 483–485.

Zyzanski, S. J., & Jenkins, C. D. Basic dimensions within the coronary-prone behavior pattern. *Journal of Chronic Diseases*, 1970, *22*, 781–795.

Zyzanski, S. J., Jenkins, C. D., Ryan, T. J., Flessas, A., & Everist, M. Psychological correlates of coronary angiographic findings. *Archives of Internal Medicine*, 1976, *136*, 1234–1237.

Zyzanski, S. J., Wrzesniewski, K., & Jenkins, C. D. Cross-cultural validation of the coronary-prone behavior pattern. *Social Science and Medicine*, 1979, *13A*, 405–412.

# 9

# Effects of Moderator Variables on the Response to Stress

*Thomas F. Garrity and Martin B. Marx*
*University of Kentucky College of Medicine,*
*Lexington, United States*

The discussion that follows assumes, and an ever-growing research literature supports the notion, that life changes and events are often experienced as stressful and that the strain provoked leads to health breakdown (Dohrenwend & Dohrenwend, 1974). Yet, common experience, as well as the research literature (Rabkin & Struening, 1976), suggests that not everyone who experiences stress translates this into illness. The usual explanation of this disjuncture is the existence of factors in the person or the environment that buffer or moderate the deleterious effects of stress (Antonovsky, 1979).

In this chapter we examine what is known about the existence and influence of moderating factors of several varieties. Some of these protective factors are more or less stable personal characteristics. Other buffers are more aptly viewed as characteristics of the person's social environment. Still others may be seen as devices injected into the environment with a specific preventive or therapeutic intent. We present examples of moderating factors from each of these categories and, for the sake of coherence, organize them around the theoretical paradigm of Lazarus (1966). But before entering upon the specific discussion of these buffering factors, a brief review of the literature bearing on the stressful life events–illness model is called for because much of the evidence pertinent to moderating factors has been developed in the context of that model.

## THE LIFE-CHANGE–HEALTH-CHANGE PARADIGM

The life-change–health-change hypothesis has its roots in the biologic works of Cannon (1929, 1932) and Selye (1956). Both of these scientists developed perspectives that became useful in explaining the apparent links between a human being's cognitions, especially those relating to threatening stimuli, and physiological responses. It was out of this tradition of psychosomatic medicine that the life-change–health-change theory grew. Holmes and his associates (Holmes, Goodell, Wolf, & Wolff, 1950) began to develop a method for measuring the amount and strength of recent life change experienced and for studying the effects of change on health. It is Holmes's conviction that life changes, both desirable and undesirable, cause a break in the stability and equilibrium of life (Holmes & Masuda, 1974). Thus, the adaptation process may place a person under a psychophysiological strain that, in turn, is thought to increase the likelihood of a negative change in health.

The diagram in Fig. 9.1 is a simple schematic of the model being discussed. The relationship between recent life events and negative health changes is mediated by psychophysiological strain. Simply stated, life changes challenge, causing the organism to struggle emotionally and physically to cope with the change; this struggle results in health breakdown. The diagram suggests two other elements for consideration in this model. It is not unusual for some people with many recent life changes to remain healthy. At least part of the explanation for this resistance may be found in personal and environmental factors that increase coping resources. For example, a person with strong bonds of love and respect with one or a few friends may use them as a source of emotional and informational support for dealing with challenging life disruptions. Such resources, if effectively used, might prevent the person from experiencing psychophysiological strain and, consequently, prevent the onset of illness. In a similar way, certain personality strengths could act to lessen the strain of life change. Hence, a complete representation of the life events–health-change model must include mediating factors capable of reducing the impact of events on health. Conversely, certain environmental and personal factors may potentiate the life-change–health-change relationship.

Figure 9.1 also suggests the existence of factors that influence the occurrence of life-change events themselves. Clearly, some of the changes life brings are largely out of one's control—a home destroyed in an earthquake or flood, the death of a friend, the closing of a place of employment, for example. Nonetheless, many life changes are controllable, such as the taking of a new job, marrying, and moving to a new residence. It is possible that certain personal and environmental factors promote change-seeking behavior. Casual observation of friends and associates reveals that some seem most content in relatively quiet and unchanging lifestyles, whereas others seek excitement, change, and a frenetic pace of life. Hence, no complete picture of the life events–health-change model can exclude mention of factors that predispose to life-change experience.

By 1967 Holmes and his colleague Rahe had developed an instrument useful in measuring recent life-change experience. Their Social Readjustment Rating Scale (Table 9.1) and SRE derived from it included 43 commonly reported life-change events. Using a large panel of judges, the authors were able to assign values or weights to each item in proportion to the amount of readjustment required by each event relative to one other event, namely, marriage, which was given an arbitrary value of 50. The ratings by judges ranged from 100 for the readjustment required after the death of spouse to 11 for minor violations of the law. This approach to the measurement of life change has been criticized for not

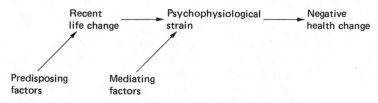

*Figure 9.1* Schematic of the life-change–health-change paradigm.

*Table 9.1*  The Social Readjustment Rating Scale of Holmes and Rahe

| Rank | Life event | Mean value |
|------|------------|------------|
| 1 | Death of spouse | 100 |
| 2 | Divorce | 73 |
| 3 | Marital separation | 65 |
| 4 | Jail term | 63 |
| 5 | Death of close family member | 63 |
| 6 | Personal injury or illness | 53 |
| 7 | Marriage | 50 |
| 8 | Fired at work | 47 |
| 9 | Marital reconciliation | 45 |
| 10 | Retirement | 45 |
| 11 | Change in health of family member | 44 |
| 12 | Pregnancy | 40 |
| 13 | Sex difficulties | 39 |
| 14 | Gain of new family member | 39 |
| 15 | Business readjustment | 39 |
| 16 | Change in financial state | 38 |
| 17 | Death of close friend | 37 |
| 18 | Change to different line of work | 36 |
| 19 | Change in number of arguments with spouse | 35 |
| 20 | Mortgage over $10,000 | 31 |
| 21 | Foreclosure of mortgage or loan | 30 |
| 22 | Change in responsibilities at work | 29 |
| 23 | Son or daughter leaving home | 29 |
| 24 | Trouble with in-laws | 29 |
| 25 | Outstanding personal achievement | 28 |
| 26 | Wife begin or stop work | 26 |
| 27 | Begin or end school | 26 |
| 28 | Change in living conditions | 25 |
| 29 | Revision of personal habits | 24 |
| 30 | Trouble with boss | 23 |
| 31 | Change in work hours or conditions | 20 |
| 32 | Change in residence | 20 |
| 33 | Change in schools | 20 |
| 34 | Change in recreation | 19 |
| 35 | Change in church activities | 19 |
| 36 | Change in social activities | 18 |
| 37 | Mortgage or loan less than $10,000 | 17 |
| 38 | Change in sleeping habits | 16 |
| 39 | Change in number of family get-togethers | 15 |
| 40 | Change in eating habits | 15 |
| 41 | Vacation | 13 |
| 42 | Christmas | 12 |
| 43 | Minor violations of the law | 11 |

*Source.* Table 3, p. 216 in T. H. Holmes and R. H. Rahe, "The Social Readjustment Rating Scale," *Journal of Psychosomatic Research*, 1967, 11. Copyright 1967 by Pergamon Press, Ltd. Reprinted by permission.

covering a sufficient range and variety of life-change events, for assigning readjustment weights that only weakly approximate the responses of most research subjects, for including desirable as well as undesirable life changes, and for other reasons (Rabkin & Struening, 1976). Nevertheless, several studies of the rating scale have demonstrated that in various cultures around the world and with people of differing social and personal characteristics, the rankings of various life changes were quite consistent (Harmon, Masuda, & Holmes, 1970; Masuda & Holmes, 1967; Woon, Masuda, Wagner, & Holmes, 1971). Furthermore, the SRE has proven a reliable predictor of illness outcomes.

An extensive program of studies undertaken by Rahe and his colleagues has shown that the extent of life events experienced by young naval personnel in the 6 months before a 6-month cruise is predictive of their reported illness during sea duty (Rahe, 1974). These findings inspire some confidence because of the use of a rigorous prospective study design that eliminates several biases possible in the less demanding retrospective designs used in most earlier studies. Also, the use of a confined shipboard population minimizes the effects of externally introduced sources of illness. Furthermore, Rahe's findings in this American sample have been largely replicated in studies of Norwegian sailors (Rahe, Floistad, Bergan, Ringdahl, Gerhardt, Gunderson, & Arthur, 1973).

The relationship between recent life events and illness has been documented in a range of study populations and for a range of illness outcomes. In relatively young populations, illness outcomes have generally included minor illness such as upper respiratory infections and accidental injuries (Rahe, 1968; Bramwell, 1971). Rabkin and Struening (1976) concluded from their review, however, that "modest but statistically significant relationships have been found between mounting life change and the occurrence or onset of sudden cardiac death, myocardial infarctions, accidents, athletic injuries, tuberculosis, and the entire gamut of minor medical complaints" (p. 1015). They also pointed out that psychiatric symptoms and disorders have been significantly predicted by life-change scores.

In 1972 we began what has become a series of studies of cohorts of coilege freshmen attempting to adapt to the rigors of college life. We now describe the basic design of our studies because in subsequent sections we draw examples from this work. In late summer of 1972, about two-thirds of the entering freshman class at the University of Kentucky ($n = 1,840$) completed the life events instrument (Anderson, 1972) covering selected changes in the previous 12 months. From this representative sample a random subset of 314 were followed for health changes during their freshman year. As we had hypothesized, those freshmen who brought with them a recent history of many life changes were significantly more at risk for illness during the school year (Marx, Garrity, & Bowers, 1975). We made several additional observations. Students with greater life-change scores not only had more illnesses but illnesses of greater severity, as measured by disability involved (Garrity, Marx, & Somes, 1977). Those students with greater life-change scores also appeared to have greater seriousness-of-illness scores (Wyler, Masuda, & Holmes, 1968; Garrity, Marx, & Somes, 1978). Additionally, in accord with the suggestions of Holmes and Masuda (1974), we found that the life-change scores became more predictive of illness as the school year proceeded (Garrity, Marx, & Somes, 1977), a finding that suggests a latency period between exposure to the stressor and development of illness, especially more severe ones. Findings of significant links between life-change scores and college student illness experience have been confirmed in our own more recent studies (Somes, Garrity, & Marx, 1981) and those of others (Albrecht, 1980). With these basic results regarding the association between life change and illness in hand, it became our goal to study factors that moderated this relationship, such as personality traits (Garrity, Somes, & Marx, 1977a, 1977b), coping resources (Marx, Garrity, & Somes, 1977), and childhood experiences (Marx, Barnes, Somes, & Garrity, 1978). Our results from some of these investigations are discussed in following sections.

Although it is not the purpose of this presentation to review the findings or the criticisms of the life-change–illness model comprehensively, it should be understood that the theory is not without its critics (c.f. Chap. 10). In addition to the criticisms of the Social Readjustment Rating Scale already mentioned, some have argued that the statistically significant correlations found in most of this research are clinically trivial. Some have wondered if these associations are misleading and explainable without reference to the life events–health-change theory. For example, it seems possible that the relationship could be due to the tendency of some people to report many problems, both problems of health and of life in general. Such a propensity would build in a significant life-change–health-change correlation but would not support the psychosomatic links between the two (Garrity, Somes, & Marx, 1977a). It is also possible that the life-change–health-change relationship results from a correlation between the high life events score and the inappropriate overuse of health service. In this case, the apparent life-change–health-change relationship would really be indicative of a relationship between life change and care-seeking behavior rather than actual illness. In spite of this sort of conjecture, the weight of evidence continues to suggest a real link between life change and health; but further research on a number of aspects of the model is needed.

Most of the research to date has used relatively young adult and middle-aged study groups to demonstrate the relationship between life events and illness outcomes. Studies of children, adolescents, and the aged have been rare. Do the correlations found in young and middle-aged adult groups between life events and illness persist for these different age groups? Likewise, few of the studies of this theoretical framework have examined the role of predisposing and mediating factors in the model pictured in Fig. 9.1. We still need to learn if there are more productive approaches to measuring recent life events than the SRE. For example, would it be better to permit each research subject to supply his or her own life-change weights to each item of change he or she has experienced than to impose the weights derived from the 1967 anonymous judgments of the Holmes and Rahe subjects? Are there some dimensions of life change that are more pathogenic than others? For example, are uncontrollable life changes more damaging than controllable ones? Finally, with rare exceptions (McNeil & Pesznecker, 1975), there is almost no research yet on possible interventions for reducing illness likelihood after life change has occurred.

## A MODEL OF STRESS AND COPING

The schematic presented in Fig. 9.1 is a general model of the presumed relationship of life events, mediating or moderating factors, psychophysiological strain, and illness as the outcome. Several authors have presented more detailed conceptualizations of these general elements (Antonovsky, 1979; Lazarus, 1966; Rahe, 1974). We describe Lazarus's model (1966) for its usefulness in suggesting how moderating factors have their beneficial effects.

Lazarus's model, which he traces historically through the contributions of other researchers such as Arnold (1960) and Janis (1962), might be portrayed

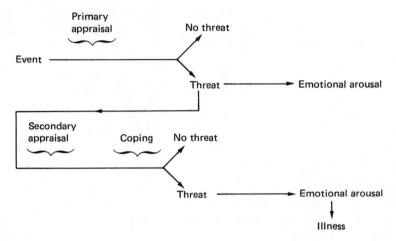

*Figure 9.2*  Schematic of Lazarus's model.

graphically as in Fig. 9.2. This attempt to draw a process model is a vast simplification of both reality and Lazarus's own discussion of a very complex process. The schematic, we hope, is a useful device for communicating some of Lazarus's insights into human responses to threatening stimuli. According to the diagram, an "event" occurs, and a person becomes aware of it. The person then becomes involved in making a primary appraisal of whether the event constitutes a personal threat. It is clear that what is threatening for one person may not be threatening for all and that what threatens at one time under one set of circumstances may not threaten at all times and under all circumstances. This judgment or appraisal of the threat valence of the event, then, is clearly influenced by personal characteristics such as personality and past experience, by characteristics of the event itself, and by characteristics of the environment, all factors that might be viewed as moderators of the events-illness relationship. If the appraisal yields a no-threat judgment, the person is no longer concerned. If, however, the appraisal is one of threat, the person experiences the strain of emotional and physiological arousal. The Cannon (1932) fight-or-flight concept would exemplify this sort of arousal, or psychophysiological strain.

Given a situation of threat, Lazarus identifies a secondary appraisal that is likely to occur. In this appraisal, the person weighs judgments about the kinds of coping strategies that might usefully be employed. Once again personal characteristics and characteristics of the environment and past experience with this or similar threats all come into play as the person considers coping approaches. Coping then occurs and depends on or follows from the decisions made in secondary appraisal. The ideal configuration of coping efforts results in elimination of the threat and, with it, psychophysiological arousal. On the other hand, ineffective coping leaves the threat unalleviated; arousal continues. Chronic arousal may well lead to illness; Selye's (1956) findings would exemplify this eventuality.

## MODERATING FACTORS IN THE PERSON

In the remainder of this chapter we enumerate factors believed to lessen the likelihood that stress-provoked illness will develop. Taking the Lazarus model as a map for our discussion, we begin with an examination of the personal factors thought to influence the occurrence of stressful events. Next, we review personal variables believed to influence the appraisal and coping processes. This division of the discussion is clearly somewhat arbitrary; protective factors may operate simultaneously at several of these and other points in the stress process. Nonetheless, this division should facilitate understanding of the ways in which moderating factors may operate.

## Factors Moderating Exposure to Stressors

Challenging life events are often discussed as though their occurrences are totally outside of personal control. Some clearly are. The sudden appearance of a tornado, the death of a friend, the invasion of one country by another, the arrest and internment of millions as part of the Nazi plan are all examples of events most would consider stressful and beyond the control of their individual victims. There are, however, innumerable potentially stressful events the occurrences of which are clearly manipulable by the people concerned. A reexamination of the list of events in Table 9.1 would indicate that the majority happen because of the choices and decisions made by the people they affect: "change to a different line of work," "marital reconciliation," "divorce" are examples. We propose that certain factors affect the likelihood that challenging events will take place at all.

Hinkle has made major contributions to our understanding of stress-illness links. He and his colleagues (Hinkle, Christenson, Kane, Ostfeld, Thetford, & Wolff, 1958) have suggested a profile of people who tend to remain healthy in the face of life stress. One aspect of these illness-resistant personalities is pertinent in the present context. Hinkle (1974) writes:

> *Many of these people displayed a distinct awareness of their own limitations. . . . They avoided situations that would make demands on them if they felt they could not, or did not want to meet these demands. An employed man or woman might refuse a promotion because he did not want the increased responsibility, refuse a transfer because it was "too much trouble," or refuse to work overtime because it might be too tiring. (p. 41)*

Hinkle noted that this sort of indifference to vocational demands might also manifest itself in family life, as when the person refuses to undertake care for an aged or ill patient or sibling, or an immigrant relative needing a start in the new country. He seems to be describing a tendency to avoid challenges that might test endurance and lead to strain.

In recent research there have been attempts to examine effects of the opposite of this tendency described by Hinkle, namely, the tendency to seek ever more and greater challenges. This pattern sounds similar to the so-called coronary-prone behavior pattern, or what Friedman and Rosenman (1974) call Type A behavior pattern. Jenkins (1979) describes Type As, in part, as "characterized by *extremes* of competitiveness, striving for achievement, aggressiveness (sometimes stringently repressed), haste, impatience, restlessness, hyperalertness" (p. 6). This Type A behavior pattern is now a fairly well-established risk factor for atherosclerotic heart disease. The prospective $8\frac{1}{2}$-year WCGS of Rosenman and Friedman indicates that this behavior pattern is independently predictive of coronary disease (Brand, 1978; Rosenman, Brand, Sholtz, & Friedman, 1976). Reanalysis of behavioral data from the prospective Framingham Heart Study likewise suggests links between behavioral responses similar to the Type A pattern and coronary artery disease (Haynes, Feinleib, Levine, Scotch, & Kannel, 1978; Haynes, Feinleib, & Kannel, 1980). In spite of the growing interest in and research activity focused on the Type A pattern, there is still relatively little known about its relationship to other behavioral traits and tendencies.

Suls, Gastorf, and Witenberg (1979) recently reported an association between Type A pattern and the number of recent life changes experienced by their subjects. Using the JAS adapted for college students by Glass (1977), extreme Type As and Type Bs were identified. The number of life events occurring in the previous 6 months to Type As averaged 8.51 ($n = 63$) and to Type Bs 5.84 ($n = 62$), a difference significant at the .004 probability level. This result is consonant with the view of Type As as change seekers, although it might also suggest a heightening of Type A tendencies in those recently exposed to numerous events. The latter explanation, however, is not consistent with the usual concept of Type A as a stable behavioral trait. Dimsdale, Hackett, Block, and Hutter (1978) also found a significant correlation of .26 ($p < .01$) between Type A score measured by JAS Form B (Jenkins, Rosenman, & Friedman, 1967) and number of recent life changes measured by SRE (Holmes & Rahe, 1967) in a group of 109 patients presenting themselves for cardiac-catheterization studies.

In our own study exploring links between Type A behavior and extent of recent life changes (Somes, Garrity, & Marx, 1981), results were very similar to those of the Suls and Dimsdale groups. Each of the 174 student subjects was interviewed and classified on the A-B dimension using Rosenman's (1978) structured interview method. Each student also completed a life events instrument very similar to the SRE but modified for use in college populations (Anderson, 1972). Subjects closer to the Type A extreme of the continuum ($n = 41$) averaged 1,109 life-change units, whereas more B-like subjects ($n = 104$) averaged only 849 life-change units, a difference significant at the .006 probability level.

These results suggest that people with a certain behavioral pattern, Type A, are more apt to report higher levels of life-change experience. Hence, this personal trait may be a moderating factor operating within the life stress–illness model. In this instance the factor functions to influence likelihood of exposure to stressors themselves. There is evidence now that both Type A pattern (Matteson & Ivancevich, 1980) and recent life changes (Garrity & Marx, 1979) influence onset of manifest coronary disease. We must now wonder if these factors, previously thought to be independent of one another, produce their common outcome because of the relationship we and others have identified between them.

A second example of moderating factors that appear to influence exposure to stress events may be found in the realm of personality characteristics. In an earlier study of life events and illness among 250 college freshmen (Garrity, Somes, & Marx, 1977b), we obtained personality data using the Omnibus Personality Inventory (Heist & Yonge, 1962) scales, factor-analyzed into three composite measures. All three measures correlated significantly with life-change units measured as in the study just described. The first personality trait labeled Liberal Intellectualism, had a Pearson correlation of .33 ($p < .0005$) with life change. This dimension is highly weighted by individual personality scales that involve interest in academic, cognitive, and intellectual issues. It also emphasizes acceptance of attitudes and behaviors generally identified with nonauthoritarianism and liberalism such as flexibility, an acceptance of individual differences, and independence of thinking and action. The second dimension, labeled "Emotional Sensitivity, was significantly correlated with life change at .20 ($p < .0005$). This dimension is highly loaded on individual personality scales that indicate the willingness to express and accept the expression of emotional feelings and concerns. It also loads impressively on scales that indicate the appreciation of the fine arts. The third dimension, labeled Social Conformity, correlated significantly with life change at $-.16$ ($p < .005$). The social-conformity dimension was highly loaded on the scales that indicate the tendency to behave in conventionally approved ways and to espouse attitudes strongly approved in the respondent's social milieu. These results, then, indicate that students scoring high on Liberal Intellectualism and Emotional Sensitivity are likely to have higher life-change scores than their opposites. Conversely, those scoring higher on Social Conformity are less likely to experience a great deal of life change.

This finding leaves open the question of the origin of the significant associations between personality and life change. One explanation is that people with certain personality traits are more likely to place themselves or find themselves in situations of change by virtue of decisions they make or actions they take. It may also be that recent life change has a material effect on response to personality-assessment instruments. The latter explanation runs counter to the notion that personality is a relatively stable characteristic more or less impervious to situational influences. This explanation cannot be rule out, however, inasmuch as more than a few studies have demonstrated personality-test-score responsiveness to life events (Bruhn, Chandler, & Wolf, 1969; Lebovits, Shekelle, Ostfeld, & Paul, 1967). Another explanation is that certain personality types are more apt to report recent life changes. In this view, it is the reporting style rather than the life circumstances that distinguishes those with high and low life-change scores. For now, this issue has to remain open, although later in the chapter we take up the implications again.

There is, unfortunately, not yet much research that would enable us to say that these results have been independently confirmed. Although there is clearly much research still needing to be done, what we have described suggests promise in further work in this area. There do seem to be factors capable of blunting or heightening the exposure to potentially stressful life circumstances.

## Factors Moderating Appraisal or Coping

As we follow the Lazarus paradigm, we now reach the point at which a potentially stressful event has occurred and presented itself to the awareness of the person. In the model, this event only becomes a source of enduring psychophysiological strain that may possibly result in illness when the subject appraises it as threatening and defines an approach to coping that proves less than fully effective in neutralizing the threat. Several individual characteristics have some bearing on appraisal, coping processes, or both. It is not possible to state that these moderating variables act only on one of the appraisals or only on coping; most of these, on the contrary, operate at more than one point in the process. Moreover, the research studies we review have not made the appraisal and coping distinctions we have suggested but have merely studied the impact of variables in modifying the events-illness relationship.

A number of personality traits have been suggested as characteristics that may act as moderators of the stress-illness relationship. Antonovsky (1974) proposed what he called "homeostatic flexibility," which seems to mean the ability to (1) emphasize alternative, unthreatened social roles in one's identity, (2) accept alternative, unthreatened values as legitimate, and (3) recover one's balance and continue daily activities as quickly as possible. Only partial results are presently available from Antonovsky's work testing these propositions. Lazarus (1966) reviewed studies of personality traits that may affect the quality of coping. In these studies, the personality of the adequate coper was sketched. The coper is one who is oriented toward acting directly on the problem rather than avoiding it (Coelho, Silber, & Hamburg, 1962; Goldstein, 1959); the action is not impulsive, however, but tends to be rationally considered (Block & Martin, 1955). The successful coper tends to be optimistic about chances of success (Coelho et al., 1962), tends to have relatively little anxiety about her or his own aggressiveness (Hokanson, 1961), and tends to have strong self-esteem and a willingness to act on the basis of personal conviction (Crowne & Marlowe, 1964; Janis, 1955; Zimbardo & Formica, 1963). There is some evidence that early experience with coping brings about lasting dispositions or tendencies to cope in given ways in adult life (Cohen, Silverman, Zuidema, & Lazar, 1957; Weinstock, 1967). The effect of past coping behavior is shown by Worell (1962) in an experimentally induced conflict situation. Although the findings of these studies are suggestive, none clearly demonstrates the influence of personality traits as factors that promote resistance to health breakdown after exposure to life stress. The studies from which these findings are derived deal with a variety of challenges to the subjects' emotional equilibrium and with varied criteria of good adaptation. Hence, these personality traits may provide some *clues* but not a strong basis for hypothesis building.

Given the relative dearth of specific data on personality dispositions that protect health after the challenge of stressful life events, we think it proper to continue to describe two rather exploratory projects intended to increase our understanding of how personality-mediated resistance operates. We have already explained that initial exposure to more stressful events was found to be influenced by or associated with greater levels of traits of liberal intellectualism and emotional sensitivity and a lower level of social conformity. In the remainder of that study (Garrity, Somes, & Marx, 1977b), we wanted to learn whether these three traits also influenced the process by which illness was produced over the 9 months after assessment of stressful life changes. As we have explained, we conceive of this process as one in which the struggle to meet the adaptive challenges of life events may produce psychophysiological strain. The latter, if unmitigated by the coping response, is likely to bring about breakdowns in health. Hence, we introduced the personality traits not only as moderating variables in relation to the illness status of our subjects but as they may influence production of strain.

We measured psychophysiological strain by the Langner (1962) 22-item scale of psychiatric impairment. The instrument is based on respondent reports of emotional and physical disturbance; it has come to be interpreted as a measure of "psychological stress" and "physical malaise" (Seiler, 1973). As was the case with the earlier-discussed correlations of personality factors with exposure to stressful life events, all three were significantly associated with strain: Social

Conformity ($r = .35$), Liberal Intellectualism ($r = .13$), and Emotional Sensitivity ($r = -.17$). Strain, as expected, was also significantly associated with life change ($r = .32$).

Multiple regression analysis, in which life change and the three personality factors were treated as predictors of strain, revealed that the four, in combination, accounted for 21% of the variance in psychophysiological strain, a significant level of prediction. Social Conformity enters the equation first and accounts for 12.5% of the variance; it is followed by life change and Sensitivity, which explain an additional 7% and 1.5% of the variance respectively. The effect of Intellectualism is negligible after adjustment for the other variables. It appears that the relatively large zero-order relationship between life change and strain is more efficiently explained by the influence of social conformity. In short, knowledge of personality factors adds significantly to the predictive power of life change in the prediction of psychophysiological strain.

The ultimate step in the analysis was to examine the relative contributions of life events, strain, and personality variables in accounting for variance in illness experience. (The latter was a factor-analytically derived composite, weighted score that included number of health problems, number of distinct episodes of illness, number of days with health problems, and number of disability days.) Multiple regression analysis indicated that our strain measure was the strongest predictor of health status, accounting for almost 20% of the total variance in health status. The independent contributions of the several other variables are relatively modest after strain is considered. It appears that the other factors, including personality variables, are most influential in their relationship to strain and that, after they have had their impact on it, their remaining, independent impacts on illness are slight. This result appears to be consistent with the Lazarus model portrayed earlier in that efforts at appraisal and coping, on which we expect behavioral moderating variables to operate, determine level of psychophysiological strain experienced, and this, in turn, directly influences health status. When strain has not been moderated by behavioral factors, illness becomes more likely.

Just as we have examined the role of these three personality dimensions in the production of strain and illness, and earlier, in the extent of stressful life events, so too can the role of the coronary-prone behavior pattern, Type A, be studied. Earlier we showed that Type A subjects were likely to report significantly more recent life changes—a possible indication that Type A people are change seekers. We now present data that indicate that Type A and Type B people are different in the ways they respond to high levels of recent life changes.

The 145 college freshmen from our most recent study (Somes, Garrity, & Marx, 1981), who had been assessed on life change, Type A and B behavior patterns, and prospectively, on illness experience, demonstrated significant life events–illness associations very similar to those of our earlier research subjects (Marx, Garrity, & Bowers, 1975). When the coronary-prone behavior pattern was introduced as a moderating variable, however, a dramatic departure from past results became apparent. We found that in pattern B–like subjects the familiar life-change–illness association held and was even stronger than the same correlation in the total study sample. In A-like subjects, however, the life-events-illness correlation disappeared entirely. In terms of the absolute amount of illness reported by the two types of subjects, there was no significant difference, though on each of the four illness measures, Type A subjects showed somewhat higher averages.

It appears from our data that the coronary-prone behavior pattern acts as a moderating factor in the life events–illness relationship. It is not possible from these data to specify the dynamics of this moderating effect. One possible explanation, consistent with our earlier-described results that Type A subjects accumulate, perhaps seek, more life change, is that Type As are less sensitive to increasing amounts of life change than are Type Bs. The latter, in this explanation, do not relish change and respond to increasing amounts by experiencing more strain and illness. This explanation, however, is not totally consistent with our data. We find that both As and Bs show greater strain reactions [our earlier-described Langner (1962) index] as life events mount. Hence, it cannot be argued that Bs are more sensitive to, and experience greater strain with, increasing numbers of life events compared with Type A subjects.

A second possible explanation, more consistent with our data, would have it that both As and Bs experience mounting strain as life-change challenges increase and hence, a significant life-change–strain correlation. Type Bs respond in the expected way by experiencing greater breakdown of health. Type As may also experience physiological changes describable as illness, but these people refuse to label these changes as "illness," which would require them to take the "sick role" (Parsons, 1951). This view is consistent with Rosenman's (1978) view of Type As as relatively lacking in insight about personal states and characteristics. It is likewise consistent with the notion that As block out stimuli that distract from the job of accomplishing more and more in ever less time (Jenkins, 1979). Illness, for Type A people, may constitute an unwelcome distraction from the press of daily work. Symptoms of illenss are ignored and never fully reach the Type As consciousness. This sort of inattention to the distraction of illness is, of course, most likely when the illness is minor—the predominant situation in our sample of young, generally, robust college freshmen. This line of reasoning, though plausible, will remain conjectural until research specifically designed to test it becomes available.

Reliance on examples from our own research should be taken to indicate the general paucity of data now available on personality as an intervening element of the stress model. In the following section we review a class of moderating factors far more studied in the literature, namely, social supports.

## MODERATING FACTORS IN THE ENVIRONMENT

Of the various categories of factors that moderate the influence of life stress on health, social-support variables have been examined most frequently. *Social support* is a general term that has been applied to several, very different sorts of factors. The general term connotes all resources supplied by other people that might help a person deal with the problems of life (Cassel, 1976). Although these resources can be categorized variously, we suggest that they minimally include emotional, informational, and material supports (Cobb, 1976, 1979). Emotional supports include signals from others that one is loved, appreciated, and considered "one of us." Informational supports connote transmission of messages about how problems may be solved and challenges met; this is tantamount to receiving helpful consultation from others. Material supports include the goods and services provided by others that facilitate the coping process. Money and the materials and efforts it buys are prime examples of this sort of social support.

We discuss social support as a factor that operates to aid coping and appraisal within the stress-illness model. In this sense, social support is a true "moderating" factor; it buffers the impact of stress on health. Some researchers have not treated social support in this way but rather have studied its direct effects on health (Berkman & Syme, 1979; Lin, Simeone, Ensel, & Kuo, 1979). For example, when being married, in other words, having a socially supportive relationship available, is studied as a predictor of health status, social support is being viewed as a variable with a direct impact on health, ignoring any indirect influence it may have on health through its impact on coping and appraisal activities. In the following discussion, however, we present examples from the research literature that appear to demonstrate the effect of social support as an aid in the coping and appraisal processes.

The study of Nuckolls, Cassel, and Kaplan (1972) is probably the single most often cited work that demonstrates the role of social support as a true moderating variable. The subjects of study were 177 white primipara who were cared for at the same medical center obstetric service. Measures of recent life events, social supports, and complications of pregnancy were taken. Although neither life events nor social supports independently predicted the incidence of medical complications, in combination prediction followed the model: 91% of the patients with high life stress before and during pregnancy *and* low social supports experienced complications of their pregnancies. Only 33% of their high-stress–high-social-support counterparts experienced complications, however, indicating, perhaps, that the presence of a variety of assistances from spouses, families, and friends lessens the strain induced by significant life challenges. Patients without such a history of stressful life events, regardless of social-support level, averaged only 46% of patients with pregnancy complications. The latter result may indicate that adequate social supports only become an advantage for health status when the person is engaged in a struggle to adapt to challenging changes in lifestyle.

Similar results emerged from a study by deAraujo, vanArsdel, Holmes, and Dudley (1973). In their study of 36 chronic, intrinsic asthma patients, the influence of life changes and coping ability (one component of which is social support) on need for medication is shown. Once again it was found that patients with high stress and low coping resources demonstrated poorest physical adjustment. This group required about three times the index medication needed by the other three groups. Once again it appears that coping assets, including social support, become crucial for health status when a person is being challenged by stressful life events.

The doctoral research of Gore (1973, 1978) examined the health consequences of being unemployed and the moderating effects of emotional support from the worker's wife. As described elsewhere: "It was found that those men who had the emotional support of their wives while unemployed for several weeks had few illness symptoms, low cholesterol levels. . . . Those who were *both* unemployed and unsupported had the most disturbing health outcomes" (Kaplan, Cassel, & Gore, 1977, p. 53). The unemployed workers with social support returned to work no sooner than those without support, but they appeared to manage this stressful situation with less psychophysiological strain. "Thus, while support did not alter the objective stress, i.e., time unemployed, it evidently buffered the men's perception of its severity, and enabled them to better cope with the experience" (Kaplan, Cassel, & Gore, 1977, p. 53).

The studies of House and Wells (1978) and LaRocco, House, and French (1980) also found evidence that social supports buffer the negative effects of occupational stress on mental and physical health variables. They caution, however, that the moderating influence of social supports may be far more intricate than the relatively simple studies of Nuckolls and colleagues (1972) and deAraujo and colleagues (1973) suggest. The buffering effects may vary by source of support, setting in which support is given, and health outcome in question. For example, in dealing with the health threats of various job stresses and strains, LaRocco and colleagues (1980) found that the support of co-workers had more impact than that of either work supervisors or family members. House and Wells (1978) suggest that even the support of co-workers may fail to moderate occupational stress when the work environment is not conducive to worker communication and group solidarity, as in some noisy, isolating industrial plants. And finally, the complexity of social support's operation as a buffer is evident in its differential influence on various health outcomes. LaRocco and co-workers (1980) showed, for example, that social support played a major role in protecting workers experiencing several types of job stresses from depression, "irritation," and assorted somatic complaints, but not from anxiety. Hence, it seems clear that future research in this area will need to concentrate on understanding the complex interrelationships among types of stressors, types and sources of supports, settings in which stressors are encountered, and kinds of health and performance outcomes potentially affected.

## MODERATING INTERVENTIONS

So far in our review of factors that buffer the effects of stressful life events on health status, we have sampled and discussed characteristics of the person such as personality traits and behavior patterns. We have also examined moderating factors in the person's social environment such as social and emotional supports. In this section we briefly describe interventions developed specifically to buffer the conversion of stressful events into psychophysiological strain, of arousal into illness. In Part IV several intervention strategies are discussed in more detail.

Although stress-moderating interventions are most frequently designed to dampen arousal directly, some operate directly on appraisal and coping and, hence, only indirectly influence arousal. For example, a study of a small number of patients hospitalized for heart attack helps to illustrate the latter. Klein, Kliner, Zipes, Troyer, and Wallace (1968) had come to expect an increase in patients' medical and emotional problems around the time of their transfer from the intensive coronary care unit to the general medical wards for further recuperation. Transfer occurred because the intensive care given in the cardiac unit was no longer needed as cardiac function stabilized during the first several days after the attack. Patients often became anxious about the transfer, however, feeling that the move might place them in danger if further heart trouble was experienced. It was found that catecholamine levels increased as patients became upset around the time of transfer. (These hormones are produced in greater quantity whenever a person experiences emotional distress.) It was also found that a variety of cardiac disturbances occurred in conjunction with these emotional and hormonal responses. In the case of seven transferred patients studied intensively, five experienced a rise in catecholamine excretion, and each also exhibited some cardiac dysfunction ranging from minor rhythm disturbances to recurrent MI and death. Subsequently, a program was implemented to prepare patients for transfer and to provide emotional support before, during, and after the move. Preparation entailed information that might help patients appraise the move as a "promotion" because of improving cardiovascular status. This theme was introduced early in the patient's hospitalization and continued through the time of transfer. After transfer, intensive care unit personnel continued to visit and support the patient in coping with the new environment, emphasizing continuity of care and personal concern. In a series of seven prepared patients, only two developed increased catecholamine levels, and none experienced cardiac complications.

Administration of psychotropic medications may be viewed as another example of a moderating influence. Such drugs can act on the appraisal and arousal components of the model. Some effectively cloud a person's sensorium so that clear appraisal is impossible; this function may be the chemical counterpart of cognitive denial or some other reality-distorting defense. In this instance the person is unable to appraise an actually threatening stimulus as threatening. This results in a lack of psychophysiological arousal. Some psychotropic drugs may act in such a way that the threat appraisal is made and danger is recognized but the physiological arousal response is chemically blocked in one or several of its neural pathways (e.g., Koch-Weser, 1979). The result is a dissociation of cognitive and physiological emotional responses.

Relaxation maneuvers may also be viewed as moderating interventions. They appear to operate in this way by influencing appraisal and arousal. In appraisal it seems that the subject manages to distract himself or herself from thought about the troubling stimulus, achieving the attitude of passivity prescribed by Benson (1977). With awareness of the threat diminished or eliminated, arousal does not occur. There also appears to be a more direct influence on physiological arousal that occurs because of induced progressive muscle relaxation, comfortable posture, easy breathing, and quiet environment.

Biofeedback techniques appear to hold promise as moderating techniques. They seem to operate primarily on aspects of physiological arousal, for example, HR, BP, vascular resistance, and the like. Subjects may learn to exercise direct control over these functions, thereby raising the possibility that pathogenic physical responses may be abolished.

As a final example of a moderating intervention, exercise might be mentioned. Though there is little well-controlled research on exercise as a stress modulator, there is much conjecture, not to mention personal testimonials, that exercise lessens stress-induced arousal. Vigorous exercise, if it does act this way, may operate on appraisal to distract from disturbing thoughts. It may also function temporarily to weaken or modulate some of the body's strain responses as, for example, when muscle tension is lessened because of the overwhelming fatigue of strenuous exercise (Davidson, 1978; Schwartz, Davidson, & Goleman, 1978).

# REFERENCES

Albrecht, M. *The effects of conformity and activity upon illness after recent life change.* Unpublished master's thesis, Montclair State College, 1980.

Anderson, G. *College schedule of recent experience.* Unpublished master's thesis, North Dakota State University, 1972.

Antonovsky, A. Conceptual and methodological problems in the study of resistance resources and stressful life events. In B. S. Dohrenwend & B. P. Dohrenwend (Eds.), *Stressful life events.* New York: Wiley, 1974.

Antonovsky, A. *Health, stress, and coping.* San Francisco: Jossey-Bass, 1979.

Arnold, M. *Emotion and personality.* New York: Columbia University Press, 1960.

Benson, H. Systemic hypertension and the relaxation response. *New England Journal of Medicine,* 1977, *296,* 1152–1156.

Berkman, L. F., & Syme, S. L. Social networks, host resistance, and mortality: A nine-year follow-up study of Alameda County residents. *American Journal of Epidemiology,* 1979, *109,* 186–204.

Block, J., & Martin, B. Predicting the behavior of children under frustration. *Journal of Abormal and Social Psychology,* 1955, *51,* 281–285.

Bramwell, S. *Personality and psychosocial variables in college athletes.* Unpublished medical thesis, University of Washington, 1971.

Brand, R. J. Coronary-prone behavior as an independent risk factor for coronary heart disease. In T. M. Dembroski, S. M. Weiss, J. L. Shields, S. G. Haynes, & M. Feinleib (Eds.), *Coronary-prone behavior.* New York: Springer-Verlag, 1978.

Bruhn, J., Chandler, B., & Wolf, S. A psychological study of survivors and non-survivors of myocardial infarction. *Psychosomatic Medicine,* 1969, *31,* 8–19.

Cannon, W. B. *Bodily changes in pain, hunger, fear, and rage.* New York: Appleton, 1929.

Cannon, W. B. *The wisdom of the body.* New York: Norton, 1932.

Cassel, J. The contribution of the social environment to host resistance. *American Journal of Epidemiology,* 1976, *104,* 107–123.

Cobb, S. Social support as a moderator of life stress. *Psychosomatic Medicine,* 1976, *38,* 300–314.

Cobb, S. Social support and health through the life course. In M. W. Riley (Ed.), *Aging from birth to death: Interdisciplinary perspective.* AAAS Selected Symposium, no. 30, Boulder, Colo.: Westview Press, 1979.

Coelho, G., Silber, E., & Hamburg, D. Use of the student-TAT to assess coping behavior in hospitalized, normal and exceptionally competent college freshmen. *Perceptual and Motor Skills,* 1962, *14,* 355–365.

Cohen, S., Silverman, A., Zuidema, G., & Lazar, C. Psychotherapeutic alteration of a physiologic stress syndrome. *Journal of Nervous and Mental Disease,* 1957, *125,* 112–118.

Crowne, P., & Marlowe, D. *The approval motive.* New York: Wiley, 1964.

Davidson, R. Specificity and patterning in biobehavioral systems: Implications for behavioral change. *American Psychologist,* 1978, *33,* 430–436.

deAraujo, G., van Arsdel, P., Jr., Holmes, T. H., & Dudley, D. Life change, coping ability, and chronic intrinsic asthma. *Journal of Psychosomatic Research,* 1973, *17,* 359–363.

Dimsdale, J. E., Hackett, T. P., Block, P. C., & Hutter, A. M., Jr. Emotional correlates of Type A behavior pattern. *Psychosomatic Medicine,* 1978, *40,* 580–583.

Dohrenwend, B. S., & Dohrenwend, B. P. (Eds.). *Stressful life events: Their nature and effects.* New York: Wiley, 1974.

Friedman, M., & Rosenman, R. H. *Type A behavior and your heart.* New York: Knopf, 1974.

Garrity, T. F., & Marx, M. B. Critical life events and coronary disease. In W. D. Gentry & R. B. Williams (Eds.), *Psychological aspects of myocardial infarction and coronary care.* St. Louis: Mosby, 1979.

Garrity, T. F., Marx, M. B., & Somes, G. W. The influence of illness severity and time since life change on the size of the life change–health change relationship. *Journal of Psychosomatic Research,* 1977, *21,* 377–382.

Garrity, T. F., Marx, M. B., & Somes, G. W. The relationship of recent life change to seriousness of later illness. *Journal of Psychosomatic Research,* 1978, *22,* 7–12.

Garrity, T. F., Somes, G. W., & Marx, M. B. Personality factors in resistance to illness after recent life changes. *Journal of Psychosomatic Research,* 1977, *21,* 23–32. (a)

Garrity, T. F., Somes, G. W., & Marx, M. B. The relationship of personality, life change, psychophysiological strain and health status in a college population. *Social Science and Medicine*, 1977, *11*, 257–263. (b)

Glass, D. C. *Behavior patterns, stress, and coronary disease*. Hillsdale, N.J.: Erlbaum, 1977.

Goldstein, M. The relationship between coping and avoiding behavior and response to fear-arousing propaganda. *Journal of Abnormal and Social Psychology*, 1959, *58*, 247–252.

Gore, S. *The influence of social support in ameliorating the consequences of job loss*. Unpublished doctoral dissertation, University of Michigan, 1973.

Gore, S. The effect of social support in moderating the health consequences of unemployment. *Journal of Health and Social Behavior*, 1978, *19*, 157–165.

Harmon, D., Masuda, M., & Holmes, T. H. The Social Readjustment Rating Scale: A cross-cultural study of Western Europeans and Americans. *Journal of Psychosomatic Research*, 1970, *14*, 391–400.

Haynes, S. G., Feinleib, M., Levine, S., Scotch, N., & Kannel, W. B. The relationship of psychosocial factors to coronary heart disease in the Framingham Study: II. Prevalence of coronary heart disease. *American Journal of Epidemiology*, 1978, *107*, 384–402.

Haynes, S. G., Feinleib, M., & Kannel, W. B. The relationship of psychosocial factors to coronary heart disease in the Framingham Study: III. Eight-year incidence of coronary heart disease. *American Journal of Epidemiology*, 1980, *111*, 37–58.

Heist, P., & Yonge, G. *Omnibus Personality Inventory: Form F*. New York: Psychological Corporation, 1962.

Hinkle, L. E., Jr. The effect of exposure to culture change, social change, and changes in interpersonal relationships on health. In B. S. Dohrenwend & B. P. Dohrenwend (Eds.), *Stressful life events*. New York: Wiley, 1974.

Hinkle, L. E., Jr., Christenson, W. N., Kane, F. D., Ostfeld, A. M., Thetford, W. N., & Wolff, H. G. An investigation of the relation between life experience, personality characteristics, and general susceptibility to illness. *Psychosomatic Medicine*, 1958, *20*, 278–295.

Hokanson, J. Vascular and psychogalvanic effects of experimentally aroused anger. *Journal of Personality*, 1961, *29*, 30–39.

Holmes, T. H., Goodell, H., Wolf, S., & Wolff, H. G. *The nose: An experimental study of reactions within the nose in human subjects during varying life experiences*. Springfield, Ill.: Thomas, 1950.

Holmes, T. H., & Masuda, M. Life change and illness susceptibility. In B. S. Dohrenwend & B. P. Dohrenwend (Eds.), *Stressful life events*. New York: Wiley, 1974.

Holmes, T. H., & Rahe, R. H. The Social Readjustment Rating Scale. *Journal of Psychosomatic Research*, 1967, *11*, 213–218.

House, J. F., & Wells, J. Occupational stress, social support and health. In A. McLean, G. Black, & M. Colligan (Eds.), *Reducing occupational stress: Proceedings of a conference* (HEW, NIOSH, Publication No. 78-140). Washington: U.S. Government Printing Office, 1978.

Janis, I. Anxiety: Indices related to susceptibility in persuasion. *Journal of Abnormal and Social Psychology*, 1955, *51*, 663–667.

Janis, I. Psychological effects of warnings. In G. Baker & D. Chapman (Eds.), *Man and society in disaster*. New York: Basic Books, 1962.

Jenkins, C. D. The coronary-prone personality. In W. D. Gentry & R. B. Williams (Eds.), *Psychological aspects of myocardial infarcation and coronary care*. St. Louis: Mosby, 1979.

Jenkins, C. D., Rosenman, R. H., & Friedman, M. Development of an objective psychological test for the determination of the coronary-prone behavior pattern in employed men. *Journal of Chronic Diseases*, 1967, *20*, 371–379.

Kaplan, B., Cassel, J., & Gore, S. Social support and health. *Medical Care*, 1977, *15*, 47–58.

Klein, R., Kliner, V., Zipes, D., Troyer, W., & Wallace, A. Transfer from a coronary care unit. *Archives of Internal Medicine*, 1968, *122*, 104–108.

Koch-Weser, J. Metoprolol. *New England Journal of Medicine*, 1979, *301*, 698–703.

Langner, T. A twenty-two item screening score of psychiatric symptoms indicating impairment. *Journal of Health and Human Behavior*, 1962, *3*, 269–276.

LaRocco, J., House, J., & French, J. Social support, occupational stress, and health. *Journal of Health and Social Behavior*, 1980, *21*, 202–218.

Lazarus, R. S. *Psychological stress and the coping process*. New York: McGraw-Hill, 1966.

Lebovits, B. Z., Shekelle, R. B., Ostfeld, A. M., & Paul, O. Prospective and retrospective psychological studies of coronary heart disease. *Psychosomatic Medicine,* 1967, *29,* 265–272.

Lin, N., Simeone, R., Ensel, W., & Kuo, W. Social support, stressful life events, and illness: A model and an empirical test. *Journal of Health and Social Behavior,* 1979, *20,* 108–119.

Marx, M. B., Barnes, G., Somes, G. W., & Garrity, T. F. The health script: Its relationship to illness in a college population. *Transactional Analysis Journal,* 1978, *8,* 339–344.

Marx, M. B., Garrity, T. F., & Bowers, F. The influence of recent life experience on the health of college freshmen. *Journal of Psychosomatic Research,* 1975, *19,* 87–98.

Marx, M. B., Garrity, T. F., & Somes, G. W. The effect of imbalance of life satisfactions and frustrations upon illness behavior in college students. *Journal of Psychosomatic Research,* 1977, *21,* 423–427.

Masuda, M., & Holmes, T. H. The Social Readjustment Rating Scale: A cross-cultural study of Japanese and Americans. *Journal of Psychosomatic Research,* 1967, *11,* 227–237.

Matteson, M., & Ivancevich, J. The coronary-prone behavior pattern: A review and reappraisal. *Social Science and Medicine,* 1980, *14A,* 337–351.

McNeil, J., & Pesznecker, B. Altering your response to stress. *Washington State Journal of Nursing,* 1975, *49,* 9–12.

Nuckolls, K. B., Cassel, J., & Kaplan, B. H. Psychosocial assets, life crisis, and the prognosis of pregnancy. *American Journal of Epidemiology,* 1972, *95,* 431–441.

Parsons, T. *The social system.* New York: Free Press, 1951.

Rabkin, J. G., & Struening, E. L. Life events, stress, and illness. *Science,* 1976, *194,* 1013–1020.

Rahe, R. H. Life change measurement as a predictor of illness. *Proceedings of the Royal Society of Medicine,* 1968, *61,* 1124–1126.

Rahe, R. H. The pathway between subjects' recent life changes and their near-future illness reports: Representative results and methodological issues. In B. S. Dohrenwend & B. P. Dohrenwend (Eds.), *Stressful life events.* New York: Wiley, 1974.

Rahe, R. H., Floistad, I., Bergan, T., Ringdahl, R., Gerhardt, R., Gunderson, E., & Arthur, R. J. *Subjects' life changes, symptom recognition and illness reports in the Norwegian Navy* (Unit report). San Diego: U.S. Navy Medical Neuro-psychiatric Research Unit, 1973.

Rosenman, R. H. The interview method of assessment of the coronary-prone behavior pattern. In T. M. Dembroski, S. M. Weiss, J. L. Shields, S. G. Haynes, & M. Feinleib (Eds.), *Coronary-prone behavior.* New York: Springer-Verlag, 1978.

Rosenman, R. H., Brand, R. J., Sholtz, R. I., & Friedman, M. Multivariate prediction of coronary artery disease during $8\frac{1}{2}$ year follow-up in the Western Collaborative Group Study. *American Journal of Cardiology,* 1976, *37,* 903–910.

Schwartz, G. E., Davidson, R. J., & Goleman, D. Patterning of cognitive and somatic processes in the self-regulation of anxiety: Effects of meditation versus exercise. *Psychosomatic Medicine,* 1978, *40,* 321–328.

Seiler, L. The 22-item scale used in field studies of mental illness: A question of method, a question of substance, and a question of theory. *Journal of Health and Social Behavior,* 1973, *14,* 252–264.

Selye, H. *The stress of life.* New York: McGraw-Hill, 1956.

Somes, G. W., Garrity, T. F., & Marx, M. B. The relationship of coronary-prone behavior pattern to the health of college students at varying levels of recent life change. *Journal of Psychosomatic Research,* 1981, *25,* 565–572.

Suls, J., Gastorf, J., & Witenberg, S. Life events psychological distress and the Type A coronary-prone behavior pattern. *Journal of Psychosomatic Research,* 1979, *23,* 315–319.

Weinstock, A. Family environment and the development of defense and coping mechanisms. *Journal of Personality and Social Psychology,* 1967, *5,* 67–75.

Woon, T., Masuda, M., Wagner, N., & Holmes, T. H. The Social Readjustment Rating Scale: A cross-cultural study of Malaysians and Americans. *Journal of Cross-cultural Psychology,* 1971, *2,* 373–386.

Worell, L. Response to conflict as determined by prior exposure to conflict. *Journal of Abnormal and Social Psychology,* 1962, *64,* 438–445.

Wyler, A. R., Masuda, M., & Holmes, T. H. Seriousness of Illness Rating Scale. *Journal of Psychosomatic Research,* 1968, *11,* 363–374.

Zimbardo, P., & Formica, R. Emotional comparison and self-esteem as determinants of affilitation. *Journal of Personality,* 1963, *31,* 142–162.

# 10

## Stressful Life Events

### Measurement, Moderators, and Adaptation

*Irwin G. Sarason and Barbara R. Sarason*
*University of Washington, Seattle, United States*

*James H. Johnson*
*University of Florida, Gainesville, United States*

While the idea that everybody has a breaking point is widely accepted, it is not immediately obvious how individual differences in breaking points can best be assessed. Nor is it clear how breaking points vary as a function of the types of situations that are stress-arousing. Additionally, definitions of the thoughts, behavior, and bodily processes that occur at the breaking point have varied widely. Despite these problems, research on stress and its sequelae has burgeoned during recent years. One of the areas of greatest activity concerns the quantitative assessment of what has come to be called "stressful life events" or "life stress." In this chapter we review the literature on this topic and provide a theoretical perspective for future research.

The evidence that led to efforts at quantifying stressful life events was diverse. Clinical observations have long suggested that personal experiences, such as the loss of a job, often precede illness and psychological maladjustment. Personal experiences that seem especially conducive to later illness or maladjustment are those that involve losses (such as the death of a loved one), sudden environmental changes (natural catastrophes), war, threats to and loss of control over one's life (as experienced, for example, by people in concentration camps), and personal failures or even personal successes.

Although the mechanisms involved are still obscure, researchers interested in stress have long observed that events in a person's life and unwanted outcomes (maladjustment, illness) are linked. These observations led Adolf Meyer to introduce the concept of the "life chart," a recording of significant biographical and medical events in a person's life (Leif, 1948). Later, Wolff (1953) introduced the term *life stress*, by which he meant the responses of people to noxious stimulation and ego threats. Both Cannon (1932) and Selye (1946) gave special emphasis to the body's reaction to environmental events that call for action and the mobilization of bodily resources. Hinkle (1973), recognizing that similar life events do not lead to symptoms in all people, pointed out the need to take

Preparation of this chapter was supported in part by the U.S. Office of Naval Research Contract N00014-80-C-0522, NR 170-908.

account of person variables (personality, general level of health) along with situational variables (life events). It is now clear that a complete understanding of the effects of stressful life events will require investigations at several levels, including the delineation of influential situations, identification of sequelae, and mapping of the psychological and physiological mechanisms that link the two.

We are particularly concerned here with the first level, the events in people's lives that appear to be stressful and to influence future functioning. We begin with a survey of measurement approaches, proceed to an examination of methodological issues surrounding the assessment of stressful life events, and discuss the role of moderator variables that help determine how these events influence behavior. We conclude with a discussion of theoretical considerations and suggestions for future research.

## ASSESSMENT OF STRESSFUL LIFE EVENTS

Measures of stressful life events are becoming so numerous that any comprehensive survey of them would soon be doomed to incompleteness. This review is directed toward illustrating approaches that have been taken in this assessment.

### Schedule of Recent Events

The publication by Holmes and Rahe (1967) of an article describing their attempt to quantify the importance of life changes provided a major impetus to research. Their SRE has been widely used in life stress investigations. The popularity of this instrument is no doubt related to the fact that it provided a convenient measure of the cumulative effects of life changes. (For a detailed description of its development and scoring, please refer to Chap. 9.) Since its initial development, the SRE has been used in numerous studies designed to determine relationships between life stress and indexes of health and adjustment. Retrospective and prospective studies have provided support for a relationship between SRE scores and a variety of health-related variables. Life stress has, for example, been related to sudden cardiac death (Rahe & Lind, 1971), MI (Edwards, 1971; Theorell & Rahe, 1971), pregnancy and birth complications (Gorsuch & Key, 1974), chronic illness (Bedell, Giordani, Amour, Tavormina, & Boll, 1977; Wyler, Masuda, & Holmes, 1971), and other major health problems such as tuberculosis, multiple sclerosis, and diabetes and a host of less serious physical conditions (Rabkin & Struening, 1976). While not providing conclusive evidence, these studies have provided support for the position taken by Holmes and Masuda (1974) that life stress serves to increase overall susceptibility to illness.

### The Life Experiences Survey

Another attempt to quantify the effects of life events is the Life Experiences Survey (LES) developed by I. Sarason, Johnson, and Siegel (1978). Two major features distinguish LES from the SRE. First, it provides both positive and negative life-change scores. Second, it permits individualized ratings of the impact of events and their desirability. These individualized measures have the advantage of providing reflections of person-to-person differences in the perception of events. Evidence in support of this approach was provided by Yamamoto and Kinney (1976), who found life stress scores, based on self-ratings, to be better predictors than scores derived by employing mean adjustment ratings similar to those used with the SRE. Other investigators have also found that individualized self-ratings of the impact of life events aid in the prediction of clinical course (Lundberg, Theorell, & Lind, 1975).

The LES is a 47-item self-report measure that allows subjects to indicate events they have experienced during the past year. Subjects can also indicate the occurrence of significant events they have experienced that are not on the LES list. A special supplementary list of 10 events relevant primarily to student populations is available. Other special adaptations are possible. The LES items were chosen to represent life changes frequently experienced by people in the general population. Others were included because they were judged to be events that occurred frequently and might exert a significant impact on the lives of those experiencing them. Of the events listed in the LES, 34 are similar in content to those found in the SRE, but certain SRE items were made more specific. For example, the SRE contains the item "Pregnancy," which might be endorsed by women but perhaps not by a man whose wife or girl friend has become pregnant. The LES allows both men and women to endorse the occurrence of pregnancy in the following manner: "*Female*: Pregnancy"; "*Male*: Wife's/girl friend's pregnancy. The SRE includes the item "Wife begins or stops work," an item that fails to assess the impact on women whose husbands began or cease working. The LES lists two items: "*Married male*: Change in wife's work outside the home (beginning work, ceasing work, changing to a new job, etc.)," and "*Married female*: Change in husband's work (loss of job, beginning of a new job, etc.)." Examples of events not listed in the SRE but included in the LES are: male and female items dealing with abortion and concerning serious injury or illness of a close friend, engagement, and breaking up with boy friend or girl friend. Of the 10 special school-related items, 9 are unique to the LES.

Subjects respond to the LES by separately rating the desirability and impact of events they have experienced. Ratings are on a 7-point scale ranging from $-3$ to $+3$. A rating of $-3$ indicates a negative event judged to have had an extreme impact on the respondent. A rating of $+3$ indicates a positive event having an extreme impact. Summing the impact ratings of events designated as positive by the subject provides a *positive-change score*. A *negative-change score* is derived by summing the impact ratings of those events experienced as negative by the subject. Scores on the LES do not seem to be influenced by the respondent's mood state at the time of filling out the questionnaire (Siegel, Johnson, & Sarason, 1979b). The LES is presented in the appendix to this chapter.

In an initial study (Sarason, Johnson, & Siegel, 1978), undergraduate psychology students were administered the LES, the State-Trait Anxiety Inventory (Spielberger, Gorsuch, & Lushene, 1970), and a short form of the Marlowe-Crowne Social Desirability Scale (Strahan & Gerbasi, 1972). Grade-point averages were available for the quarter during which the testing occurred. No significant correlations were obtained between LES scores and social desirability, indicating that LES scores are unbiased by a social-desirability response set. Negative change related significantly and in a positive direction with both state and trait anxiety, whereas the positive-change score was unrelated to either measure. (Significant correlations between negative change and anxiety were also found for a sample of naval personnel.) Negative change correlated significantly with grades, with higher levels of negative life change related to poorer academic performance. Knapp & Magee (1979) have replicated this finding.

The relationship between stressful life events and personal maladjustment was estimated by correlating the LES with the Psychological Screening Inventory (PSI) using a student sample. The PSI (Lanyon, 1970, 1973) is a 130-item true-false inventory that yields scores on five subscales; Alienation (Al), Social Nonconformity (Sn), Discomfort (Di), Expression (Ex), and Defensiveness (De). The Al scale was designed for "assessing similarity to psychiatric patients," the Sn scale for "assessing similarity to incarcerated prisoners." The Di scale measures neuroticism; the Ex scale measures introversion–extraversion; and the De scale measures test-taking attitude. Correlations between the LES and the PSI showed a significant relationship between negative life change and two measures of maladjustment, the Sn and Di scales. Only the PSI Ex scale correlated significantly with positive change. Extraverts appear to experience greater degrees of positive change than do introverts.

Scores on the LES, the Beck Depression Scale (Beck, 1967), and the Locus of Control (I-E) Scale (Rotter, 1966) were also obtained for college students. There was a significant relationship between negative change and scores on the Beck Depression Scale, high negative-change scores being associated with depression. Positive change was not significantly correlated with depression. These findings are consistent with evidence presented by Vinokur and Selzer (1975), who found negative change to be related to self-ratings of depression. Subjects who have experienced high levels of negative change appear to be more externally oriented, perceiving themselves as less capable of exerting control over environmental events. No relationship between positive change and locus of control was found.

Although it is a newer instrument and consequently there is a less extensive array of evidence concerning its correlates, the LES has certain advantages over the SRE. Its positive- and negative-change scores have not been found to correlate significantly with the same dependent measures in the same direction. This, together with evidence of the validity of the negative-change score, suggests that the distinction between negative and positive events is a meaningful one. Recent studies have found the LES negative-change score to be related to MI (Pancheri, Bellaterra, Reda, Matteoli, Santarelli, Pugliese, & Mosticoni, 1980), menstrual discomfort (Siegel, Johnson, & Sarason, 1979a), the attitudes of mothers of at-risk infants (Crnic, Greenberg, Ragozin, & Robinson, 1980), and job satisfaction (Sarason & Johnson, 1979).

## THE DIVERSITY OF APPROACHES TO ASSESSMENT

Research on the assessment of stressful life events has explored a wide variety of both populations and assessment devices. Several recent instruments, like the LES, have gone beyond a mere count of life changes in the recent past to provide measures of the undesirability and impact of the events. There seems to be increasing agreement that the perceptions of life events may be as significant as the events themselves (Masuda & Holmes, 1978). Redfield and Stone (1979) have provided striking indications of individual differences in how peopel perceive life events. Tennant and Andrews (1978), using a specially devised list of events, found that the distressing quality of life events, rather than the events themselves, is associated with the onset of neurotic symptoms. Horowitz, Wilner, and Alvarez (1979) were successful in developing a measure of the subjective impact of major life events that reflects psychiatric decompensation.

Several researchers have used interviews to assess stressful life events. Interviews have the advantage of permitting greater individualization and depth than do questionnaires. For example, Paykel (1976) used the interview method in studies of the risk of depression and suicide attempts. On the other hand, the interview method does not lend itself to surveys of large samples because of its cost, primarily a result of the need for qualified and specially trained personnel and of the length of time involved in gathering the data on an individual basis. Furthermore, even standardized interviews by carefully trained interviewers introduce variations that increase the unrealiability of the result. Sometimes it is not possible either to interview subjects or to administer a questionnaire to them. In such cases, Schless and Mendels (1978) have found that "significant others" (family members, friends) can provide useful quantifiable information about subjects' recent life events.

Whereas some researchers have been concerned with the development of measures of these events experienced in the general population, others have been concerned with particular groups within the population. Children have been the most widely studied special population, and there are a number of instruments available that can be used with preschoolers through adolescents (Coddington, 1972; Monaghan, Robinson, & Dodge, 1979; Sandler & Block, 1979). Johnson and McCutcheon (1980) and Yeaworth, York, Hussey, Ingle, and Goodwin (1980) have developed measures specifically directed toward stressful events in the lives of adolescents. These measures include content related to such topics as new school experiences, dating, and work.

The development of methods of recording life events and their impact on people allows researchers to explore personal crises more objectively and conveniently than was the case in the past. Despite a number of methodological problems, life stress scores have been linked to a variety of physical and psychological conditions. Often these linkages have been statistically significant but of limited practical applicability. As solutions to methodological problems are found, the number of practical applications should increase.

## METHODOLOGICAL ISSUES IN ASSESSMENT

Despite the numerous correlates of stressful life events, a certain degree of caution is warranted in interpreting available findings. Studies in this area have been primarily correlational in design, so cause–effect conclusions cannot be drawn with a high level of confidence. Even though it seems reasonable to expect that such events may have a detrimental effect on health and adjustment, significant correlations may be obtained for other reasons. For example, people with problems of health and adjustment may as a result tend to experienced greater degrees of life change, or it may be that both stressful events and problems of health and adjustment covary with some third variable. Some preliminary studies designed to investigate the possibility of causal relationships have been conducted, however, and have yielded data consistent with the hypothesis that stressful life events exert a causal influence (Johnson & Sarason, 1978; Vossel & Froehlich, 1978). Further research concerning the nature of life stress–dependent variable relationships is greatly needed.

In addition to considering the nature of the relationships found in studies of stressful life events and in health and adjustment studies, it is also necessary to examine their magnitude. Although exceptions are to be found, correlations between measures of stressful life events and dependent variables have typically been low, often in the .20–.30 range. These significant relationships are of theoretical interest, but life stress seems to account for a relatively small proportion of the variance in the dependent measures that have been studied. It would seem that, by themselves, life stress measures are not likely to be of much practical value as predictors. A logical question is whether this poor predictive ability is due to the inadequacies of life stress measures (unreliability of measurement, failure to assess separately positive and negative life changes, insensitive methods of quantifying the impact of events) or to other factors. As we have noted, several approaches to the assessment of stressful life events have been employed in the studies published to date. Although instruments that distinguish between positive and negative events typically yield somewhat higher correlations with dependent variables, even these correlations tend to be relatively low. Factors other than inadequacies of measurement may also be related to the low correlations that have typically been found. For example, people may experience stress that is not a product of life change. In addition, researchers have often failed to consider the role of moderator variables.

Life change represents only one type of stressor. Ecological stressors such as crowding and noise pollution are constants for many people, not sudden life changes. There are also a host of other stressors that impinge on people's lives that are not experienced as sudden life events. Examples of these stressors include the knowledge that one has some probability of developing a genetically related disease, or the gradual realization that one will not reach goals set earlier in one's life. Finally, there are undoubtedly a variety of day-to-day situations that do not bring about major life changes but that nevertheless serve as stressors. Examples might be friction with teenaged children over responsibilities and privileges or work deadlines that involve periodic pressures to produce material by a certain date. To the extent that health and adjustment are influenced by stressors other than those assessed by life-change measures, one might expect to find lower correlations between stressful life events and dependent variables.

An example of the critical role methodological issues play in discussions of life stress is provided by research on the relationship between life events and CHD. Over 50 studies have examined this relationship; yet, no unifying explanation has emerged to account for all the reported findings. Although life events and CHD seem to be linked, most studies have been retrospective, life events being assessed *after* occurrence of the heart attack. Brown (1974) has pointed out the confounding role played by *retrospective contamination*, or distortion in life events assessment. Some heart attack victims may want to "blame" their attacks on certain circumstances in their lives. On the other hand, stressful life events can lead to lifestyle changes that aggravate an existing predisposition to coronary heart disease. A sudden change in one's life, such as a heart attack, produces all manner of psychological reactions and behavioral changes (sleep and food-intake disturbances, confusion, and suggestibility) that may produce observable clinical symptoms. A heart attack would seem to be both a consequence of stressful life events and a stressful life event in its own right. The following are some methodological issues concerning which clarifications or improvements in reearch design are needed.

*Types of events.* A wide variety of events may be considered as stressful. Very little is known about the particular types of events that are related to particular types of outcome. The work of Holmes and Rahe (1967) was based on the assumption that symptoms are caused by the total amount of change in a person's life. Later research has suggested that symptoms and maladjustment are related more to negative (unwanted, undesirable) than to positive (wanted, desirable) change (Mueller, Edwards, & Yarvis, 1977; Ross & Mirowsky, 1979). Within the category of negative life events, there may be certain types of events that are more important than others. Research on this possibility is needed. These are some types of events whose properties, correlates, and consequences need to be better understood:

1. Physical illness and injuries
2. Personal failures (loss of job because of inadequate performance)
3. Loss of attachments (bereavement, divorce)
4. Interpersonal changes (a new supervisor, entrance of new member into one's social group)
5. Victimization (being burglarized)
6. Natural disasters (earthquake, volcanic eruption)

In addition to categorizing types of events, it also seems important to determine the degree to which they are or might be predictable or controllable. Unpredictable events and those over which people have little or no control are among the most distressing experiences people go through. Predictability or the lack of it is a major factor in the stress experienced from an event.

*Magnitude of events.* What contributions do particular individual events make to the total level of stressfulness? Research is needed to determine the ways in which events differing in personal significance combine to produce behavioral and physical effects. Is it worse to experience one really major undesirable event or six medium-sized ones? How might events differing in magnitude of stress arousal be optimally weighted and combined?

*Timing of events.* The incubation time for the impact of life events is probably not a constant. It seems reasonable that different types of events exert their influence in different ways and over different periods of time. A tantalizing question concerns the impacts exerted by remote events. At what points do the effects of stressful life events begin to wear off? Brown and Harris (1978) found that one of the major distinguishing features of middle-aged depressed women was the childhood loss of their mothers through death or separation. The interests of psychoanalysts and stress researchers overlap in their attention to stressful life events. They differ in their attention to remote impactful events. Stress researchers are more interested in recent events; psychoanalytically oriented researchers, in events that occurred early in life.

*Meaning of events.* Lazarus and others have pointed out the distinction between events per se and how they are appraised (Folkman, Schaefer, & Lazarus, 1979). It would seem desirable to assess both the things that happen to people and how they appraise them. Some events may be overappraised in that the person attaches more significance to them than they really merit. Other events may be underappraised, with the person failing to appreciate their present or future implications.

*Person variables.* How events are appraised depends on the personality and circumstances of the person experiencing them. This topic, we discuss later in the chapter when we discuss moderator variables.

*Causality versus correlation.* Given that it is desirable ultimately to reach the point where causal inferences can be made and that, for ethical reasons, we will continue to be unable to manipulate life stress experimentally, how then does one proceed? It is likely that no one study, no matter how well-designed, will be capable of providing data sufficient to justify the conclusion that a causal relationship exists. It is, in fact, impossible to "prove" the existence of a causal relationship from correlational data. By conducting a variety of studies, specifically designed to investigate and control for specific variables, it may, however, be possible to accumulate a body of information that, taken together, would allow an inference of causality to be made with some justification.

A large number of studies of life events are retrospective, with all the limitations of that type of research. Prospective or longitudinal studies are valuable both practically and theoretically because assessment of stressful life events takes place before the appearance of symptoms. One potentially fruitful approach to investigating the possibility of a causal relationship would involve the use of a cross-lagged correlational methodology. This quasi-experimental approach, originally suggested by Simon (1954), involves obtaining data on two variables of interest at two points in time and comparing the correlations among these variables from one time period to another.

Johnson and Sarason (1979) measured stressful life events (in the previous 6 months) and obtained several self-report indexes of health and adjustment on a sample of undergraduate psychology studies, contacted subjects again 7 months later, and used these same measures a second time. Negative life-change scores at Time 1 were significantly correlated with the reporting of physical symptoms at Time 2. No significant relationship was found between physical symptoms at Time 1 and subsequent life stress scores. Vossel and Froehlich (1978) examined the relationship between negative life changes, as assessed by the LES, and measures of job tension and task-performance effectiveness. The findings of this study were interpreted as consistent with a causal relationship in the predicted direction (e.g., life stress leads to job tension and decreased performance effectiveness).

*Extraneous variables.* Life stress and indicators of illness and maladjustment may both be influenced by other variables. Socioeconomic status (SES) may function in this way. People low in SES may be more likely to experience negative life changes and to also, for a variety of reasons, be more prone to develop health-related and adjustment problems. Correlations between life stress and illness in this instance might simply result from the fact that both variables covary with SES. Extraneous variables may play important roles in associations among independent and dependent variables. They are extraneous only in the sense that they are neglected.

## MODERATORS

People vary considerably in how they are affected by potential stressors. Some people get divorced; lose their jobs; experience financial hardships, death, and illness in their families; and yet appear to suffer few serious long-term physical or psychological setbacks. Others break down even though they have experienced what would objectively seem to be a relatively low level of stress. An important question concerns the nature of those variables that may determine which people are likely to be most adversely affected by life change.

Although several authors (Jenkins, 1979; Johnson & Sarason, 1979; Rahe & Arthur, 1976) have pointed to the important role of moderator variables, previous studies of life events have usually been designed simply to assess the relationships between life change and other variables without considering that people may vary in how much they are affected by life changes. Lack of attention to moderator variables constitutes a major limitation of much of the research in this area. One might argue that it is unreasonable to expect to find strong correlates of life events unless such variables are examined and taken into account. As the mediators of life stress are identified, measured reliably, and included in research designs, increased effectiveness in prediction is likely to result.

There are three broad categories of moderator variables: (1) relatively stable personal characteristics, such as internal-external locus of control, (2) prior experiences that influence how a person responds to stress, and (3) environmental factors, such as social support. Each type can influence how a person responds to problematic situations. Although the processes by which particular influences act are often not clear, these moderators can generally be thought of as affecting vulnerability to life events. We now describe three variables that illustrate how moderators influence behavior. Two are personality characteristics (sensation seeking and locus of control), and one is social support provided by the environment.

## Sensation Seeking

An example of how a personality characteristic can moderate response to stressful events is sensation seeking. Some people appear to thrive on activities that are exciting and stimulating and that might be expected to increase arousal level. They may enjoy traveling to strange places, prefer the unfamiliar to the familiar, and participate in activities such as skydiving, automobile racing, motorcycle riding, and water skiing. On the other hand, many people shy away from the unfamiliar, would never think of racing cars or going skydiving, and find some everyday situations more arousing than they would like. There are, of course, many people who fall somewhere between these two extremes. They neither consistently seek out nor attempt to avoid stimulation.

Given that people vary in their desire for, or need to seek out, stimulation and also in their tolerance for stimulation, sensation seeking as a personality attribute may well serve as an important moderator of life stress. High sensation seekers might be expected to be relatively unaffected by life changes, particularly if they are not too extreme. These people may be better able to deal with the increased arousal involved in experiencing such changes. On the other hand, life change might have a negative effect on people low in sensation seeking who are less able to cope with arousing stimulus input. To the extent that stimulation seeking mediates the effects of life change, one might expect to find significant correlations between life change and problems of health and adjustment with low, but not high, sensation seekers.

Smith, Johnson, and Sarason (1978) have examined the relationships between the LES, sensation seeking, and psychological distress. Sensation seeking was measured using the Sensation Seeking Scale (Zuckerman, 1979). Distress was assessed by the PSI (Lanyon, 1973), a self-report measure of neuroticism. The LES positive-change score, either alone or in conjunction with sensation seeking, was unrelated to psychological discomfort. The major result was that people with high negative-change scores who were also low in sensation seeking reported high levels of distress. Subjects with high negative-change scores, but also high scores in sensation seeking, did not describe themselves as experiencing discomfort.

Similar results were obtained by Johnson, Sarason, and Siegel (1978), who were specifically interested in anxiety, depression, and hostility. They found that positive change was unrelated to dependent measures regardless of arousal-seeking status. Negative change, on the other hand, was significantly related to measures of both anxiety and hostility. As in the Smith et al. (1978) study, this relationship held only for subjects low in sensation seeking. It is possible that those low on the sensation-seeking dimension are much more likely to be affected by life stress than are those high in sensation seeking.

## Locus of Control

Predictability and controllability are aspects of situations that influence how people respond to them. The more predictable an event and the more confident a person feels about how to handle it, the greater the likelihood of an adaptive response. Are people who perceive themselves as having little control over events more adversely affected by stressful events than are people who feel capable of exerting control over these events?

Johnson and Sarason (1978) have provided some evidence concerning this issue. They administered the LES, the Locus of Control Scale (Rotter, 1966), the State-Trait Anxiety Inventory (Spielberger, Grosuch, & Lushene, 1970), and the Beck Depression Inventory (Beck, 1967) to college students. The Locus of Control Scale is a self-report measure that assesses the degree to which people view environmental events as under their personal control. Subjects scoring low on the measure (internals) tend to perceive events as controllable by their own actions, whereas those scoring high on the scale (externals) tend to view events as influenced by factors other than themselves. The State-Trait Anxiety Inventory assesses anxiety as a relatively stable dispositional variable (trait anxiety) as well as a more transient reaction to specific situations (state anxiety). The Beck scale is a self-report measure of depression.

Based on research findings concerning the controllability or uncontrollability of aversive stimuli, it was predicted that anxiety and depression would correlate with stressful life events only among subjects external in their locus-of-control orientation. This prediction seemed reasonable, as one might expect undesirable life events to be more threatening and hence exert a more negative impact on people perceiving themselves as having little control over such events. Johnson and Sarason found that negative life changes were significantly related to both trait anxiety and depression, but as predicted, this relationship held only for external subjects. Although this study does not permit cause–effect conclusions, its results are consistent with the view that people are more adversely affected by life stress if they perceive themselves as having little control over their environment.

## Social Support

Although methodological rigor has not marked the literature on social supports, there is evidence that close social ties have a protective, stress-buffering effect and that their effect may be more important for some people than for others. This social-support effect may be particularly noticeable among people who bring to certain situations such cognitions as "I'll fail," "I'm all alone," "No one cares about me." To the extent that this is true, social support may play powerful preventive and therapeutic roles in such areas as personality development, mental health, and physical well-being, but these are merely suggestions. At present, neither the situations and circumstances conducive to a social-support effect nor the mechanisms by which such an effect comes about can be specified. Heller (1979) has recently emphasized the need for extensive research into the ingredients and effects of social support. Experimental studies are needed to answer such questions as: Is lack of social support a cause of personal or social unhappiness, or are people low in personal or social competence deficient in the skills needed to elicit supportive social relationships?

Social support is usually defined as the existence or availability of people on whom we can rely, people who let us know that they care about, value, and love us. As Cobb (1976) has pointed out, someone who believes she or he belongs to a social network of communication and mutual obligation experiences social support. Available evidence suggests that social support may facilitate coping with crisis and adaptation to change. Its absence or withdrawal seems to have a negative effect. In this regard, it is interesting that soldiers many of whose buddies have been killed in combat are more likely to develop combat exhaustion than soldiers who belong to intact units.

There is by no means agreement about how to assess a person's level of social support. Both interviews and questionnaires have been used as a basis for identifying social networks and estimating social-support levels. Tolsdorf (1976) content-analyzed interviews to assess subjects' relationships with kin and friends and with religious, political, and fraternal groups. Caplan, Cobb, and French (1975) constructed a 21-item self-report index of the support received from three types of work-related sources: immediate superior, work group or peers, and subordinates. Two factors may be especially important aspects of social support: (1) the amount of social support available and (2) a person's satisfaction with the available support.

*Social support and health.* One study of pregnant women investigated the role of psychosocial assets, an important component of which was defined as social support, in complications of pregnancy (Nuckolls, Cassell, & Kaplan, 1972). Women who had many psychosocial assets had significantly fewer pregnancy complications than women who had relatively few assets. This relationship was particularly dramatic among women who had experienced high levels of life change. For this group, 91% of women who were low in psychosocial assets had birth complications, whereas the comparable figure for those high in psychosocial assets was 33%. It appeared that, though social support was important for all, it was especially important among women high in life stress.

There may be sex differences or other individual differences in response to social support. In a recent study, Whitcher and Fisher (1979) found that, for hospitalized women, being physically and warmly touched by a caring nurse before undergoing surgery resulted not only in lowered anxiety but in a faster return to preoperative BP levels. For male patients, however, Whitcher and Fisher obtained results inconsistent with, and in some cases opposite to, those for women.

Several other studies also indicate that social support functions as a moderator of stressful life events. Lyon and Zucker (1974) found that the post-hospitalization adjustment of discharged schizophrenics was better when social support (friends, neighbors) was present. Burke and Weir (1977) found that the husband–wife helping relationship is an important moderator between ex-perieincing stressful life events and psychological well-being. A helping spouse seems to be particularly valuable in contributing to self-confidence and a sense of security in dealing with the demands of daily living. Brown, Bhrolchain, and Harris (1975) found that the presence of an intimate, but not necessarily sexual, relationship with a male reduced the probability of depression in women following stressful life events. Consistent with these findings, Miller and Ingham (1976) showed that social support (presence of a confidant and friends) reduced the likelihood of psychological and physical symptoms (anxiety, depression, heart palpitations, dizziness) under stress.

In a large-scale epidemiological investigation, Berkman and Syme (1979) found that people who lacked social and community ties were more likely to die during the 9-year period they were studied than those with more extensive contacts. The association between social ties and mortality was independent of self-reported physical health status at the beginning of the 9-year period. It was also independent of physical activity, SES, and use of preventive health services. Gore (1978) studied the relationship between social support and workers' health after being laid off and found that a low sense of social support exacerbated illnesses following the stress of job loss.

*Social support and effective behavior.* Maladaptive ways of thinking and behaving are more common among those with little social support (Silberfeld, 1978). Reliance on others and self-reliance may be not only compatible but complementary. Although the mechanism by which an intimate relationship is protective has yet to be worked out, the following factors are probably involved: intimacy, social integration through shared concerns, reassurance of personal worth, the opportunity to be nurtured by others, a sense of reliable alliance, and guidance.

There are data consistent with the view that adults who are self-reliant, adapt at coping with stress, and able to maintain a task-oriented attitude in the face of challenges frequently had childhoods marked by the personal security that goes along with warm relationships and shared experiences and responsibilities. For example, Ruff and Korchin (1967), in their study of astronauts, found that these self-reliant, adaptable men come from families that provided stable, supportive environments. Reinhardt (1970), in a study of exemplary air force fighter pilots, found that as children they had spent more time in joint activities with their fathers (fishing, making things) than did other pilots.

*Preventive measures based on social support.* Henderson (1980), after review-ing the literature, pointed out three competing hypotheses that have been offered by researchers: (1) A deficiency in social support is a cause of morbidity; (2) a deficiency in social support is a cause of morbidity only when adverse circum-stances and events are present; and (3) a deficiency of socual support is a consequence of a low level of social competence. While acknowledging some discrepant findings and the need to identify the causes of different levels of social support, the available evidence suggests that high levels of social support may play a stress-buffering role and to some degree protect a person from the effects of cumulative life changes. If this is true, there are some important implications for preventive action. As Dean and Lin (1977) have suggested, although it may not be possible for people to avoid experiencing stressful life events, it may be possible to help them mobilize supports within the community and thus, to some extent, protect themselves against the effects of stress. Furthermore, training people in the social skills needed to get help from friends, relatives, and the community when stress reaches high levels might prevent a significant number from experiencing personal difficulties.

An important question concerning which there is little evidence is the matter of the relative contributions of personality, experience, and social support to health and adjustment. Because both experience and social support influence personality, it would seem important wherever possible to incorporate all three types of variables in research designs. One useful starting point is the identification of exemplary people, those who are particularly stress-resistant. Kobasa (1979) took this tack in a study of middle- and upper-level executives who had had comparably high degrees of stressful life events during the previous 3 years. She found that executives who had high levels of life stress but little illness seemed more "hardy" than high-stress–high-illness executives. The defining properties of *hardiness* seemed to include a strong commitment to self, an attitude of vigorousness toward the environment, a sense of the meaningfulness of life, and an internal locus of control. Kobasa's findings seem consistent with Antonovsky's (1979) concept, *resistance resources,* according to which stress-resistant people manage their tensions well and have a feeling of social belongingness. According to Antonovsky, stress-resistant people have a *sense of coherence*, a general orientation that sees life as meaningful and manageable. The sources of the sense of coherence, according to Antonovsky, are to be found in people's upbringing, social relationships, and cultural background. He believes people who have resistance resources are high in flexibility, which includes the capacities to (1) tolerate differences in values and (2) adapt quickly to misfortune.

## COGNITIVE APPRAISAL
## AND THE EXPERIENCE OF STRESS

Any event can be viewed as providing information that must be processed by the one who experiences it. This procedure does not take place in a vacuum; many moderating factors are involved. Personality characteristics, such as personal needs, dispositions, fears, motivations, and also prior experiences influence the particular aspects of an event that are attended to and how they are interpreted. Other moderators include environmental factors such as the presence or absence of social support, and the circumstances surrounding an event also contribute to cognitive appraisal of the situation. Personal characteristics and prior experiences as well as environmental factors also combine in the mobilization of resources to cope with problems posed by the event. In this way, the interaction of person and situation variables can be thought of as important in the way life events are experienced and in reactions to them.

People usually differ in the salience, or pull value, events have for them. Some situations are universally salient because most people have learned the same meaning for a particular cue. For example, when a stop light turns red, most automobile drivers stop. Other situations are universally salient because their overwhelming characteristics evoke similar stress reactions in large numbers of people. Severe earthquakes, catastrophic fires, bridge collapses, mass riots, and nuclear explosions are examples of this type of stress-producing situation. Sometimes, however, when environmental conditions are not stereotyped or extreme, *personal salience* plays a major role in influencing behavior by directing attention to the particular elements of a situation that have personal significance. Hearing a particular song may evoke a grief reaction or feelings of nostalgia or a relaxed state, depending on whether the song was associated with someone who died recently, with someone who is away and whose return is uncertain, or with happy memories of a high school romance. Some situations may not initially be experienced as stressful, but because of learning that subsequently takes place, they become capable of arousing stress responses upon recurrence.

The modeiator variables discussed earlier, personal characteristics (locus of control, sensation seeking), and environmental factors (social support, circumstances surrounding an event) can also be viewed as factors determining vulnerability to a stressful situation. Vulnerable people are those who are especially sensitive and responsive to particular types of life-event stressors. Because vulnerability factors vary among people, the degree to which particular types of events cause problems and require special coping efforts also varies widely. Zubin's and Spring's (1977) vulnerability model, designed to explain the behavior of schizophrenics but which seems to have the potential for wide applicability, is concerned with this problem. Specifically, these writers emphasized the need to develop methods for differentiating those vulnerable to a particular stressor from the rest of the population. Such people might be described as lacking an effective moderator to lessen the effect of the stimulus.

The chain of events involved in the experience of stress begins with a problematic situation. A call for action is issued when either the environment or personal concerns identify the need to do something. The experience of stress follows the call for action when one's capabilities are perceived as falling short of the needed personal resources. For example, in automobile driving, personal ability is usually perceived as commensurate with the situational challenge, and the call for action is handled in a routine, task-oriented manner. Stress may well up, however, on treacherous mountain roads where one is not confident of one's ability in that situation. Experimental and anecdotal evidence from many sources suggests that people use different cognitive strategies in stressful situations and that these cognitions may be important in determining the level of adaptability of ensuring behavior. Some people are able to maintain a task orientation in the face of the call; for others, self-preoccupation often interferes with realistic planning and weighing of alternatives. There are wide individual differences in the frequency and preoccupying character of stress-related cognitions. The most adaptive cognitive response to stressful situations is a task orientation that directs attention to the task at hand rather than to emotional reactions. The ability to set aside unproductive worries and preoccupations seems to be crucial in functioning well under pressure.

Whether danger will be seen in a situation depends on its personal salience. Consequently, an understanding of the effects of stress and prediction of individual behavior must take into account individual perceptions both of the demands of the situation and of one's ability to meet them. The magnitude and manageability of the perceived demand varies among people depending on the particular moderator variables involved.

Research on stressful life events may be on the threshold of progressing from merely assessing whether or not certain events have taken place and correlating the events with outcomes such as illness, to integrating the occurrence of life events into a cognitive theory of stress.

# APPENDIX: THE LES

Listed below are a number of events which sometimes bring about change in the lives of those who experience them and which necessitate social readjustment. *Please check those events which you have experienced in the recent past and indicate the time period during which you have experienced each event.* Be sure that all check marks are directly across from the items they correspond to.

Also, for each item checked below, *please indicate the extent to which you viewed the event as having either a positive or negative impact on your life* at the time the event occurred. That is, *indicate the type and extent of impact that the event had.* A rating of −3 would indicate an extremely negative impact. A rating of 0 suggests no impact either positive or negative. A rating of +3 would indicate an extremely positive impact.

*Section I*

| Event | 0 to 6 mo. | 7 mo to 1 yr | Extremely negative | Moderately negative | Somewhat negative | No impact | Slightly positive | Moderatly positive | Extremely positive |
|---|---|---|---|---|---|---|---|---|---|
| 1. Marriage | | | −3 | −2 | −1 | 0 | +1 | +2 | +3 |
| 2. Detention in jail or comparable institution | | | −3 | −2 | −1 | 0 | +1 | +2 | +3 |
| 3. Death of spouse | | | −3 | −2 | −1 | 0 | +1 | +2 | +3 |
| 4. Major change in sleeping habits (much more or much less sleep) | | | −3 | −2 | −1 | 0 | +1 | +2 | +3 |
| 5. Death of close family member: | | | | | | | | | |
| a. Mother | | | −3 | −2 | −1 | 0 | +1 | +2 | +3 |
| b. Father | | | −3 | −2 | −1 | 0 | +1 | +2 | +3 |
| c. Brother | | | −3 | −2 | −1 | 0 | +1 | +2 | +3 |
| d. Sister | | | −3 | −2 | −1 | 0 | +1 | +2 | +3 |
| e. Grandmother | | | −3 | −2 | −1 | 0 | +1 | +2 | +3 |
| f. Grandfather | | | −3 | −2 | −1 | 0 | +1 | +2 | +3 |
| g. Other (specify) | | | −3 | −2 | −1 | 0 | +1 | +2 | +3 |
| 6. Major change in eating habits (much more or much less food intake) | | | −3 | −2 | −1 | 0 | +1 | +2 | +3 |
| 7. Foreclosure on mortgage or loan | | | −3 | −2 | −1 | 0 | +1 | +2 | +3 |
| 8. Death of close friend | | | −3 | −2 | −1 | 0 | +1 | +2 | +3 |
| 9. Outstanding personal achievement | | | −3 | −2 | −1 | 0 | +1 | +2 | +3 |
| 10. Minor law violations (traffic tickets, disturbing the peace, etc.) | | | −3 | −2 | −1 | 0 | +1 | +2 | +3 |

*Section I (Continued)*

| Event | 0 to 6 mo | 7 mo to 1 yr | Extremely negative | Moderatly negative | Somewhat negative | No impact | Slightly positive | Moderately positive | Extremely positive |
|-------|-----------|--------------|--------------------|--------------------|-------------------|-----------|-------------------|---------------------|--------------------|
| 11. *Male*: Wife/girl friend's pregnancy | | | −3 | −2 | −1 | 0 | +1 | +2 | +3 |
| 12. *Female*: Pregnancy | | | −3 | −2 | −1 | 0 | +1 | +2 | +3 |
| 13. Changed work situation (different work responsibility, major change in working conditions, working hours, etc.) | | | −3 | −2 | −1 | 0 | +1 | +2 | +3 |
| 14. New job | | | −3 | −2 | −1 | 0 | +1 | +2 | +3 |
| 15. Serious illness or injury of close family member: | | | | | | | | | |
| a. Father | | | −3 | −2 | −1 | 0 | +1 | +2 | +3 |
| b. Mother | | | −3 | −2 | −1 | 0 | +1 | +2 | +3 |
| c. Sister | | | −3 | −2 | −1 | 0 | +1 | +2 | +3 |
| d. Brother | | | −3 | −2 | −1 | 0 | +1 | +2 | +3 |
| e. Grandfather | | | −3 | −2 | −1 | 0 | +1 | +2 | +3 |
| f. Grandmother | | | −3 | −2 | −1 | 0 | +1 | +2 | +3 |
| g. Spouse | | | −3 | −2 | −1 | 0 | +1 | +2 | +3 |
| h. Other (specify) | | | −3 | −2 | −1 | 0 | +1 | +2 | +3 |
| 16. Sexual difficulties | | | −3 | −2 | −1 | 0 | +1 | +2 | +3 |
| 17. Trouble with employer (in danger of losing job, being suspended, demoted, etc.) | | | −3 | −2 | −1 | 0 | +1 | +2 | +3 |
| 18. Trouble with in-laws | | | −3 | −2 | −1 | 0 | +1 | +2 | +3 |
| 19. Major change in financial status (a lot better off or a lot worse off) | | | −3 | −2 | −1 | 0 | +1 | +2 | +3 |
| 20. Major change in closeness of family members (increased or decreased closeness) | | | −3 | −2 | −1 | 0 | +1 | +2 | +3 |
| 21. Gaining a new family member (through birth, adoption, family member moving in, etc.) | | | −3 | −2 | −1 | 0 | +1 | +2 | +3 |
| 22. Change of residence | | | −3 | −2 | −1 | 0 | +1 | +2 | +3 |
| 23. Marital separation from mate (due to conflict) | | | −3 | −2 | −1 | 0 | +1 | +2 | +3 |
| 24. Major change in church activities (increased or decreased attendance) | | | −3 | −2 | −1 | 0 | +1 | +2 | +3 |
| 25. Marital reconciliation with mate | | | −3 | −2 | −1 | 0 | +1 | +2 | +3 |
| 26. Major change in number of arguments with spouse (a lot more or a lot less arguments) | | | −3 | −2 | −1 | 0 | +1 | +2 | +3 |
| 27. *Married male*: Change in wife's work outside the home (beginning work, ceasing work, changing to a new job, etc.) | | | −3 | −2 | −1 | 0 | +1 | +2 | +3 |
| 28. *Married female*: Change in husband's work (loss of job, beginning new job, retirement, etc.) | | | −3 | −2 | −1 | 0 | +1 | +2 | +3 |

*Section I (Continued)*

| Event | 0 to 6 mo | 7 mo to 1 yr | Extremely negative | Moderately negative | Somewhat negative | No impact | Slightly positive | Moderately positive | Extremely positive |
|---|---|---|---|---|---|---|---|---|---|
| 29. Major change in usual type and/or amount of recreation | | | −3 | −2 | −1 | 0 | +1 | +2 | +3 |
| 30. Borrowing more than $10,000 (buying home, business, etc.) | | | −3 | −2 | −1 | 0 | +1 | +2 | +3 |
| 31. Borrowing less than $10,000 (buying car, TV, getting school loan, etc.) | | | −3 | −2 | −1 | 0 | +1 | +2 | +3 |
| 32. Being fired from job | | | −3 | −2 | −1 | 0 | +1 | +2 | +3 |
| 33. *Male*: Wife/girl friend having abortion | | | −3 | −2 | −1 | 0 | +1 | +2 | +3 |
| 34. *Female*: Having abortion | | | −3 | −2 | −1 | 0 | +1 | +2 | +3 |
| 35. Major personal illness or injury | | | −3 | −2 | −1 | 0 | +1 | +2 | +3 |
| 36. Major change in social activities, e.g., parties, movies, visiting increased or decreased participation) | | | −3 | −2 | −1 | 0 | +1 | +2 | +3 |
| 37. Major change in living conditions of family (building new home, remodeling, deterioration of home, neighborhood, etc.) | | | −3 | −2 | −1 | 0 | +1 | +2 | +3 |
| 38. Divorce | | | −3 | −2 | −1 | 0 | +1 | +2 | +3 |
| 39. Serious injury or illness of close friend | | | −3 | −2 | −1 | 0 | +1 | +2 | +3 |
| 40. Retirement from work | | | −3 | −2 | −1 | 0 | +1 | +2 | +3 |
| 41. Son or daughter leaving home (due to marriage, college, etc.) | | | −3 | −2 | −1 | 0 | +1 | +2 | +3 |
| 42. Ending of formal schooling | | | −3 | −2 | −1 | 0 | +1 | +2 | +3 |
| 43. Separation from spouse (due to work, travel, etc.) | | | −3 | −2 | −1 | 0 | +1 | +2 | +3 |
| 44. Engagement | | | −3 | −2 | −1 | 0 | +1 | +2 | +3 |
| 45. Breaking up with boy friend/ girl friend | | | −3 | −2 | −1 | 0 | +1 | +2 | +3 |
| 46. Leaving home for the first time | | | −3 | −2 | −1 | 0 | +1 | +2 | +3 |
| 47. Reconciliation with boy friend/girl friend | | | −3 | −2 | −1 | 0 | +1 | +2 | +3 |

*Other recent experiences which have had an impact on your life. List and rate.*

| Event | 0 to 6 mo | 7 mo to 1 yr | Extremely negative | Moderately negative | Somewhat negative | No impact | Slightly positive | Moderately positive | Extremely positive |
|---|---|---|---|---|---|---|---|---|---|
| 48. _____ | | | −3 | −2 | −1 | 0 | +1 | +2 | +3 |
| 49. _____ | | | −3 | −2 | −1 | 0 | +1 | +2 | +3 |
| 50. _____ | | | −3 | −2 | −1 | 0 | +1 | +2 | +3 |

*Section II* Student only

| Event | 0 to 6 mo | 7 mo to 1 yr | Extremely negative | Moderately negative | Somewhat negative | No impact | Slightly positive | Moderately positive | Extremely positive |
|---|---|---|---|---|---|---|---|---|---|
| 51. Beginning a new school experience at a higher academic level (college, graduate school, professional school, etc.) | | | −3 | −2 | −1 | 0 | +1 | +2 | +3 |
| 52. Changing to a new school at same academic level (undergraduate, graduate, etc.) | | | −3 | −2 | −1 | 0 | +1 | +2 | +3 |

Section II   Student only (Continued)

| Event | 0 to 6 mo | 7 mo to 1 yr | Extremely negative | Moderatl negative | Somewhat negative | No impact | Slightly positive | Moderately positive | Extremely positive |
|---|---|---|---|---|---|---|---|---|---|
| 53. Academic probation | | | −3 | −2 | −1 | 0 | +1 | +2 | +3 |
| 54. Being dismissed from dormitory or other residence | | | −3 | −2 | −1 | 0 | +1 | +2 | +3 |
| 55. Failing an important exam | | | −3 | −2 | −1 | 0 | +1 | +2 | +3 |
| 56. Changing a major | | | −3 | −2 | −1 | 0 | +1 | +2 | +3 |
| 57. Failing a course | | | −3 | −2 | −1 | 0 | +1 | +2 | +3 |
| 58. Dropping a course | | | −3 | −2 | −1 | 0 | +1 | +2 | +3 |
| 59. Joining a fraternity/sorority | | | −3 | −2 | −1 | 0 | +1 | +2 | +3 |
| 60. Financial problems concerning school (in danger of not having sufficient money to continue) | | | −3 | −2 | −1 | 0 | +1 | +2 | +3 |

# REFERENCES

Antonovsky, A. *Health, stress, and coping.* San Francisco: Jossey-Bass, 1979.

Beck, A. T. *Depression: Clinical, experimental, and theoretical aspects.* New York: Harper, 1967.

Bedell, J. R., Giordani, B., Amour, J. L., Tavormina, J., & Boll, T. Life stress and the psychological and medical adjustment of chronically ill children. *Journal of Psychosomatic Research,* 1977, *21,* 237–242.

Berkman, L. F., & Syme, S. L. Social networks, host resistance, and mortality: A nine-year follow-up study of Alameda County residents. *American Journal of Epidemiology,* 1979, *109,* 186–204.

Brown, G. W. Meaning, measurement, and stress of life events. In B. S. Dohrenwend & D. P. Dohrenwend (Eds.), *Stressful life events: Their nature and effects.* New York: Wiley, 1974.

Brown, G. W., Bhrolchain, M., & Harris, T. Social class and psychiatric disturbances among women in an urban population. *Sociology,* 1975, *9,* 225–254.

Brown, G. W., & Harris, T. *Social origins of depression: A study of psychiatric disorder in women.* New York: Free Press, 1978.

Burke, R., & Weir, T. Marital helping relationships: Moderators between stress and well-being. *Journal of Psychology,* 1977, *95,* 121–130.

Cannon, W. B. *The wisdom of the body.* New York: Norton, 1932.

Caplan, R. D., Cobb, S., & French, J. Relationship of cessation of smoking with job stress, personality, and social support. *Journal of Applied Psychology,* 1975, *60,* 211–219.

Cobb, S. Social support as a moderator of life stress. *Psychosomatic Medicine,* 1976, *38,* 300–312.

Coddington, R. D. The significance of life events as etiological factors in the diseases of children: I. A survey of professional workers. *Journal of Psychosomatic Research,* 1972, *17,* 7.

Crnic, K. A., Greenberg, M. T., Ragozin, A. S., & Robinson, N. M. *The effects of life stress and social support on the life satisfaction and attitudes of mothers of newborn normal and at-risk infants.* Paper presented at the Western Psychological Association annual conference, Honolulu, May 1980.

Dean, A., & Lin, N. The stress-buffering role of social support. *Journal of Nervous and Mental Disease,* 1977, *165,* 403–417.

Edwards, M. K. *Life crisis and myocardial infarction.* Master of Nursing thesis, University of Washington, Seattle, 1971.

Folkman, S., Schaefer, C., & Lazarus, R. S. Cognitive processes as mediators of stress and coping. In V. Hamilton and D. M. Warburton (Eds.), *Human stress and cognition: An informtion processing approach.* Chichester: Wiley, 1979.

Gore, S. The effect of social support in moderating the health consequences of unemployment. *Journal of Health and Social Behavior,* 1978, *19,* 157–165.

Gorsuch, R. L., & Key, M. K. Abnormalities of pregnancy as a function of anxiety and life stress. *Psychosomatic Medicine,* 1974, *36,* 352.

Heller, K. The effects of social support: Prevention and treatment implications. In A. P. Goldstein & F. H. Kanfer (Eds.), *Maximizing treatment gains: Transfer enhancement in psychotherapy.* New York: Academic, 1979.

Henderson, S. A development in social psychiatry: The systematic study of social bonds. *Journal of Nervous and Mental Disease,* 1980, *168,* 63–69.

Hinkle, Jr., L. E. The concept of "stress" in the biological and social sciences. *Science, Medicine, and Man,* 1973, *1,* 31–48.

Holmes, T. H., & Masuda, M. Life change and illness susceptibility. In B. S. Dohrenwend & B. P. Dohrenwend (Eds.), *Stressful life events: Their nature and effects.* New York: Wiley, 1974.

Holmes, T. H., & Rahe, R. H. The Social Readjustment Rating Scale. *Journal of Psychosomatic Research,* 1967, *11,* 213–218.

Horowitz, M. J., Wilner, N., & Alvarez, W. Impact of Event Scale: A measure of subjective stress. *Psychosomatic Medicine,* 1979, *41,* 209–218.

Jenkins, C. D. Psychosocial modifiers of response to stress. In J. E. Barrett, R. Rose, & G. Klerman (Eds.), *Stress and mental disorder.* New York: Raven, 1979.

Johnson, J. H., & McCutcheon, S. Assessing life stress in older children and adolescents: Preliminary findings with the Life Events Checklist. In I. G. Sarason & C. D. Spielberger (Eds.), *Stress and anxiety* (Vol. 7). Washington: Hemisphere, 1980.

Johnson, J. H., & Sarason, I. G. Life stress, depression, and anxiety: Internal–external control as a moderator variable. *Journal of Psychosomatic Research,* 1978, *22,* 205–208.

Johnson, J. H., & Sarason, I. G. Recent developments in research on life stress. In V. Hamilton & D. M. Warburton (Eds.), *Human stress and cognition: An information processing approach.* Chichester: Wiley, 1979.

Johnson, J. H., Sarason, I. G., & Siegel, J. M. *Arousal seeking as a moderator of life stress.* Unpublished manuscript, University of Washington, 1978.

Knapp, S. J., & Magee, R. D. The relationship of life events to grade point average of college students. *Journal of College Student Personnel,* November 1979, 497–502.

Kobasa, S. C. Stressful life events, personality, and health: An inquiry into hardiness. *Journal of Personality and Social Psychology,* 1979, *37,* 1–11.

Lanyon, R. I. Development and validation of a psychological screening inventory. *Journal of Consulting and Clinical Psychology,* 1970, *35,* 1–24.

Lanyon, R. I. *Psychological Screening Inventory manual.* Goshen, N.Y.: Research Psychologists Press, 1973.

Leif, A. (Ed.). *The commonsense psychiatry of Dr. Adolf Meyer.* New York: McGraw-Hill, 1948.

Lundberg, V., Theorell, T., & Lind, E. Life changes and myocardial infarction: Individual differences in life change scaling. *Journal of Psychosomatic Research,* 1975, *19,* 27–32.

Lyon, K., & Zucker, R. Environmental supports and post-hospital adjustment. *Journal of Clinical Psychology,* 1974, *30,* 460–465.

Masuda, M., & Holmes, T. H. Life events: Perceptions and frequencies. *Psychosomatic Medicine,* 1978, *40,* 236–261.

Miller, P., & Ingham, J. G. Friends, confidants, and symptoms. *Social Psychiatry,* 1976, *11,* 51–58.

Monaghan, J. H., Robinson, J. O., & Dodge, J. A. The children's Life Events Inventory. *Journal of Psychosomatic Research,* 1979, *23,* 63–68.

Mueller, D. P., Edwards, D. W., & Yarvis, R. M. Stressful life events and psychiatric symptomatology: Change or undesirability? *Journal of Health and Social Behavior,* 1977, *18,* 307–317.

Nuckolls, K. B., Cassell, J., & Kaplan, B. H. Psychosocial assets, life crisis, and the prognosis of pregnancy. *American Journal of Epidemiology,* 1972, *95,* 431–441.

Pancheri, P., Bellaterra, M., Reda, G., Matteoli, S., Santarelli, E., Pugliese, M., & Mosticoni, S. *Psycho-neural-endocrinological correlates of myocardial infarction.* Paper presented at the NIAS International Conference on Stress and Anxiety, Wassenaar, Netherlands, June 1980.

Paykel, E. S. Life stress, depression, and suicide. *Journal of Human Stress,* 1976, *2,* 3–14.

Rabkin, J. G., & Struening, E. L. Life events, stress, and illness. *Science*, 1976, *194*, 1013-1020.

Rahe, R. H., & Arthur, R. J. *Life change and illness studies: Past history and future directions* (Tech. Rep. No. 76-14). San Diego: Naval Health Research Center, 1976.

Rahe, R. H., & Lind, E. Psychosocial factors and sudden cardiac death: A pilot study. *Journal of Psychosomatic Research*, 1971, *15*, 19.

Redfield, J., & Stone, A. Individual viewpoints of stressful life events. *Journal of Consulting and Clinical Psychology*, 1979, *47*, 147-154.

Reinhardt, R. F. The outstanding jet pilot. *American Journal of Psychiatry*, 1970, *127*, 732-736.

Ross, C. E., & Mirowsky, J., II. A comparison of life-event-weighting schemes: Change, undesirability, and effect-proportional indices. *Journal of Health and Social Behavior*, 1979, *20*, 166-177.

Rotter, J. B. Generalized expectancies for internal versus external control of reinforcement. *Psychological Monographs*, 1966, *80*(1, Whole No. 609).

Ruff, G. E., & Korchin, S. J. Adaptive stress behavior. In M. H. Appley & R. Trumbull (Eds.), *Psychological stress: Issues in research*. New York: Appleton, 1967.

Sandler, I. N., & Block, M. Life stress and maladaptation of children. *American Journal of Community Psychology*, 1979, *7*, 425-440.

Sarason, I. G., & Johnson, J. H. Life stress, organizational stress, and job satisfaction. *Psychological Reports*, 1979, *44*, 75-79.

Sarason, I. G., Johnson, J. H., & Siegel, J. M. Assessing the impact of life changes: Development of the Life Experiences Survey. *Journal of Consulting and Clinical Psychology*, 1978, *46*, 932-946.

Schless, A. P., & Mendels, J. The value of interviewing family and friends in assessing life stressors. *Archives of General Psychiatry*, 1978, *35*, 565-567.

Selye, H. The general adaptation syndrome and the diseases of adaptation. *Journal of Clinical Endocrinology*, 1946, *6*, 117.

Siegel, J. M., Johnson, J. H., & Sarason, I. G. Life changes and menstrual discomfort. *Journal of Human Stress*, 1979, *5*, 41-46. (a)

Siegel, J. M., Johnson, J. H., & Sarason, I. G. Mood states and the reporting of life changes. *Journal of Psychosomatic Research*, 1979, *23*, 103-108. (b)

Silberfeld, M. Psychological symptoms and social supports. *Social Psychiatry*, 1978, *13*, 11-17.

Simon, H. A. Spurious correlation: A causal interpretation. *Journal of the American Statistical Association*, 1954, *49*, 467-479.

Smith, R. E., Johnson, J. H., & Sarason, I. G. Life change, the sensation seeking motive, and psychological distress. *Journal of Consulting and Clinical Psychology*, 1978, *46*, 348-349.

Spielberger, C. D., Gorsuch, R. L., & Lushene, R. E. *Manual for the State-Trait Anxiety Inventory*. Palo Alto, Calif.: Consulting Psychologists Press, 1970.

Strahan, R., & Gerbasi, K. C. Short homogeneous versions of the Marlowe-Crowne Social Desirability Scale. *Journal of Clinical Psychology*, 1972, *28*, 191-193.

Tennant, C., & Andrews, G. The pathogenic quality of life event stress in neurotic impairment. *Archives of General Psychiatry*, 1978, *35*, 859-863.

Theorell, T., & Rahe, R. H. Psychosocial factors and myocardial infarction: I. An inpatient study in Sweden. *Journal of Psychosomatic Research*, 1971, *15*, 25-31.

Tolsdorf, C. Social networks, support, and coping: An exploratory study. *Family Process*, 1976, *15*, 407-417.

Vinokur, A., & Selzer, M. L. Desirable versus undesirable life events: Their relationship to stress and mental distress. *Journal of Personality and Social Psychology*, 1975, *32*, 329-337.

Vossel, G., & Froehlich, W. D. *Life stress, job tension, and subjective reports of task performance effectiveness: A causal-correlational analysis.* Paper presented at the NATO Conference "Environmental Stress, Life Crisis, and Social Adaptation," Cambridge, England, August 1978.

Whitcher, S. J., & Fisher, J. D. Multidimensional reaction to therapeutic touch in a hospital setting. *Journal of Personality and Social Psychology*, 1979, *36*, 87-96.

Wolff, H. G. *Stress and disease*. Springfield, Ill.: Thomas, 1953.

Wyler, A. R., Masuda, M., & Holmes, T. H. Magnitude of life events and seriousness of illness. *Psychosomatic Medicine,* 1971, *33,* 115–122.

Yamamoto, K. J., & Kinney, O. K. Pregnant women's ratings of different factors influencing psychological stress during pregnancy. *Psychological Reports,* 1976, *39,* 203–214.

Yeaworth, R. C., York, J., Hussey, M. A., Ingle, M. E., & Goodwin, T. The development of an adolescent life change event scale. *Adolescence,* 1980, *25*(57), 91–98.

Zubin, J., & Spring, B. Vulnerability: A new view of schizophrenia. *Journal of Abnormal Psychology,* 1977, *86,* 103–126.

Zuckerman, M. *Sensation seeking: Beyond the optimal level of arousal.* Hillsdale, N.J.: Erlbaum, 1979.

# 11

# Stress, Coping Styles, and Physiological Arousal

*John F. Wilson*
*University of Kentucky College of Medicine,*
*Lexington, United States*

In a popular comic strip, Charlie Brown is unable to speak as the little red-haired girl he had dreamed about walks by. He is promptly afflicted with a stomachache. On a popular television show, a newspaper editor complains of his hectic schedule. He is advised to slow down in order to avoid a heart attack. Shoppers waiting in lines at grocery stores can browse through books, magazines, and newspapers that tell them how to cope with marriage, divorce, work, and unemployment. Radar Willie, an air traffic controller for 25 years at Chicago's O'Hare International, is the subject of an Associated Press news release because he is *not* ill.

All of the above scenes reflect the extent to which the topics of stress, coping, and illness have penetrated popular American culture. The themes in these scenarios are deceptively simple. Stress causes emotional upheaval. This state of physiological arousal results in illness. Some people, who are more effective copers, do not get sick. The world for researchers in the social sciences, however, has not been so easily simplified. The patterns of physiological arousal that lead to illness and the coping patterns that might protect one from illness have not yet been clearly identified. More subtle interactions between individual temperament, specific coping styles, and physiological links to stress have been even less clearly revealed. But common sense and an increasing number of studies suggest that coping styles are indeed crucial variables linking stress, physiological arousal, and illness. In this chapter I attempt to discuss critical issues facing researchers studying interactions between coping styles and physiological response to stress. I make no attempt to review comprehensively the massive literature that has addressed this question. Instead, I highlight research with three different stressful situations and with the personality trait of repression–sensitization. I then discuss recurrent problems and current trends in this subarea of stress research.

Comprehensive reviews of the literature on psychosomatic illness (Weiner, 1977), on the effects of stress on social behavior (S. Cohen, 1980), and on psychological factors involved in treatment of diseases such as hypertension (Harrell, 1980) all point to the importance of understanding interaction between coping styles and physiological arousal.

## COPING STYLE, AROUSAL, AND MILITARY STRESS

Stresses placed on military personnel during wartime provide an opportunity to view the short- and long-term effects of stress. Such research, however, has most often focused on combat neurosis (Pace, Schaeffer, & Elmadjan, 1956) or on the adjustment of prisoners of war (Ford & Spaulding, 1973; Lifton, 1954). Such research reports are often eloquent descriptions of coping but seldom provide physiological measures of arousal. Peacetime settings that allow for physiological data seldom provide the realism of combat or have a limited number of subjects (Radloff & Helmreich, 1968).

A classic study in a controlled situation was, however, devised by military researchers in the post-Korean War era (Berkun, Bialek, Kern, & Yagi, 1962). Military trainees were subjected to carefully staged experimental stressors. Some recruits were led to believe that the plane on which they were riding was about to ditch into the ocean. Others were isolated in remote areas and led to believe that they were endangered by a forest fire, a radiation leak, or misdirected artillery fire. The realism of the situation was enhanced by elaborate staging that included smoke bombs and realistic radio transmissions. The performance of the recruits in the simulated emergencies was carefully monitored. Physiological measures included urinary 17-HOCs. Measures of coping style were behavioral rating scales that judged degree of denial and effective sublimation or minimization of fear. Three findings from this study have relevance for questions of coping style and arousal.

First, the quantification of "coping" failed to capture the complexity of real-life adaptive processes. Rapid changes in cognitive appraisal processes and in behavioral attempts to manage the stress frustrated the researchers' efforts to match particular coping styles with measures of arousal. Second, individual differences in the physiological indexes of stress were enormous, minimizing the power of the statistical methods. Third, no attempt was made to examine the complex three-way relationship among degree of arousal, type of coping mechanism, and success of adaptive efforts. This elaborate set of studies, which for obvious ethical and monetary reasons could not be duplicated today, reflects basic problems of the field setting: difficulty in adequately measuring coping style and arousal. It also illustrates a tendency to underestimate the complexity of this topic, which demands that interactions among coping, arousal, and performance be the focus of the study rather than an afterthought addressed only when main effects are not significant.

Although studies of coping and response to stress in military settings are numerous, they have seldom included the components necessary to study complex interactions.

## COPING STYLE, AROUSAL, AND THE STRESS FILM

Methodological and ethical problems connected with using experimental stressors in field settings made the development of effective laboratory methods imperative. A series of studies devised by Lazarus and his colleagues (Lazarus, Speisman, Mordkoff, & Davison, 1962) focused on the response to films that depicted emotionally disturbing events. Typical of this genre of stressors is the 17-min film entitled *Subincision*. Filmed by an anthropologist studying an

Australian aborigine tribe, it depicts a series of rituals in which stone knives are used to lacerate the genitals of adolescent boys. Other stressful films included *It Shouldn't Have Happened*, a safety film depicting woodshop accidents. Control films, which were presumably less stressful for the viewers, included travelogues such as *Corn Farming in Iowa*. Physiological arousal during the film was measured with HR and skin conductance.

The original study demonstrated the validity of the film as a stressor. Peaks of arousal coincided with the bloodiest portions of the film. Additional studies (Speisman, Lazarus, Mordkoff, & Davison, 1964) attempted to channel the arousal of the subjects by altering the sound track. One version emphasized the traumatic aspects of the film. A second minimized the harm, emphasizing how happy the adolescents were. A third suggested adopting the detached attitude of a clinical observer. These attempts to channel the arousal levels of the subject were effective and also tended to be most effective when the coping style of the subject was matched with the appropriate sound track. The hypothesis that threat and arousal could be cognitively short-circuited with appropriate coping instructions was extended to other films (Lazarus, Opton, Momikos, & Opton, 1965), to preparatory instructions (Lazarus & Alfert, 1964), to the timing of waiting periods before the film (Nomikos, Opton, Averill, & Lazarus, 1968), and to the use of rehearsal and relaxation procedures (Folkins, Lawson, Opton, & Lazarus, 1968).

This approach to the study of stress, personality, and arousal provides a dramatic demonstration of the effects cognitive appraisal processes can have on psychophysiological indexes of arousal. The meaning of the interactions between arousal and coping style, however, remains unclear. First, these film studies investigated a narrow range of coping styles, weighted heavily toward scales derived from the MMPI. Second, measures of arousal never included any endocrine indicators of response to stress. Third, the personality correlates of arousal and arousal reduction are unclear.

In the original study, Lazarus (Lazarus, Speisman, Mordkoff, & Davison, 1962) reported that subjects who were self-centered, shrewd, and ambitious reacted *less* strongly to the film than did more mature, moderate, and self-controlled subjects. Roessler and Collins (1970) used a similar methodology and reported that high scorers on the Barron ego-strength scale of the MMPI reacted *more* strongly to the film than did subjects low in ego-strength. Finally, in the study by Lazarus and Alfert (1964), high scorers on the denial scale showed greater reactivity to the film than did low scorers. Thus, in some studies, the most well-adjusted subjects reacted most strongly to the film, and in others the reverse was found. Is arousal good or bad?

The question is further clouded by a study (Opton & Lazarus, 1967) in which subjects' stress responses to the woodshop film and to the threat of electrical shock were recorded. A 795-item personality battery composed mainly of the MMPI and the Berkeley Psychological Inventory found only chance numbers of items that discriminated high-arousal subjects from low-arousal subjects. When an ipsative analysis was done, however, significant findings emerged. Subjects were divided into those who reacted more strongly to shock then to the film and vice versa. The group who responded with higher levels of arousal to the film than to the threat of shock saw themselves as insecure, anxious, socially inhibited, submissive, and not caring.

From all these results it is not clear whether high arousal levels to threatening films are characteristic of good or poor psychological adjustment or whether the "short-circuiting" of threat through appraisal techniques should be a goal of stress reduction. It is also unclear whether results of personality and arousal studies generalize at all from one type of stressful stimulus to another. It is clear that use of laboratory stressors in studying correlation between coping styles and measures of arousal requires more careful assessment of coping styles and arousal and perhaps a closer analysis of the process by which different personality types cope with the stressor. Horowitz and his associates (Horowitz & Becker, 1971a, 1971b; Horowitz & Wilner, 1976) have used similar stress-film methods in studying the compulsive repetition of intrusive thoughts after viewing different types of stress films. Their more microscopic analysis of cognitive processes that are occurring not only during the stressor but at later times may provide a way to categorize coping styles more adequately and extend Lazarus's concepts of appraisal.

## LEARNING TO COPE, AROUSAL, AND PARACHUTE JUMPING

A compromise between the laboratory settings of the stress films and the experimentally created military stressor is sport parachute jumping. As a naturally occurring stressor that attracts volunteers, it provides a possibly biased sample but a most definitely stressful setting for research.

A series of studies by Fenz and his associates focused on the manner in which jumpers learned to control fear as they moved from novice to experienced jumping. Fenz and Jones (1972b) monitored HR and respiration of jumpers at eight points in the jump sequence, starting when the jumper first arrived at the airport and concluding after the jumper had landed. Performance ratings in terms of jump accuracy were also obtained for each jumper. The arousal level of the typical novice jumper increased from the moment of arrival at the airport throughout the jump sequence. The arousal level of experienced jumpers, on the other hand, showed a curvilinear trend, characteristically increasing until the plane was ready to take off and then decreasing throughout the jump sequence. This typical inverted-V arousal curve of the experienced jumper was also related to accuracy of the jump.

But even for experienced jumpers, psychological factors could affect the shape of their arousal curve. Fenz and Jones (1972a) reported a case study using an experienced jumper who had jumped more than 1,000 times. This man was told that, in a series of 10 jumps, he would be given a faulty main parachute once. This would force the experienced jumper to cut away his main parachute and rely on reserve chutes. During this sequence of jumps that contained the possibility of chute failure, three control, or normal, jumps were also tested. Although the experiment was a sham and no faulty parachutes were used, the uncertainty in the mind of the jumper affected his control over level of arousal. Although the curve generally approximated the traditional inverted V, there were wide fluctuations up and down. Control jumps showed the stable inverted-V curve of arousal. Fenz and Jones concluded that control over arousal level, or coping ability, was a learned function.

Two additional points should be made about Fenz and Jones's sport-parachuting research. First, unlike many other applied researchers, they have been able to move comfortably back and forth between the laboratory and applied settings. The inverted-V–shaped curve of arousal has been duplicated in laboratory settings (Fenz, 1964, 1975). Second, although coping was defined as a learnable skill rather than in more traditional trait terminology, some traditional trait approaches were used. Fenz (1975) used a version of the TAT and demonstrated that experienced jumpers exhibit a higher $n$ cognizance, or need to think about a problem, to plan, or to strive for knowledge. Poor jumpers and novices tended to either use denial or report very high levels of fear. In terms of this chapter's question concerning the relationship between coping styles and arousal, the contribution of Fenz and his colleagues lies in defining coping as a learned control over an arousal state, a learned control that is manifested in the timing of arousal and in arousal reduction that is subject to disruption by environmental or psychological factors.

Once again, however, the definition of arousal was limited to psychophysiological measures such as HR and respiration. Hansen and his co-workers (Hansen, Stoa, Blix, & Ursin, 1978), however, did measure catecholamine output before and after parachute jumps during training for Swedish sky divers. Even in experienced jumpers they observed a short-lasting sympathetic activation before the jump. But as "coping" developed, the prejump values of epinephrine were reduced, although this decrease was not shown for NE. This data is also consistent with that of Bloom, von Euler, and Frankenhäuser (1963), who reported that habituation of maximum epinephrine level does not occur after practice, although there may be a decline in total amount secreted during an entire sequence of jumps. The crucial question regarding the exact timing of that short-lasting sympathetic activation, however, is not easily resolved using urinary measures of catecholamines. The endocrine evidence, however, is generally supportive of Fenz's contentions for the inverted-V–shaped curve.

## STRESS, AROUSAL, AND REPRESSION–SENSITIZATION

The research reviewed here up to this point has focused on the problem of interactions between coping and arousal by first defining a stressful situation: a simulated emergency in the army, an emotionally disturbing film, or a life-threatening sporting event. The special characteristics of each stressful setting determined how coping was measured and what was the meaning of adaptation or "good performance." It can be argued that in each case the situation or the population used in those studies was so special that results relating coping styles to levels of arousal are not generalizable to even slightly different groups or situations.

A different and much more commonly used approach to the study of coping styles and response to stress is one that defines a dimension of coping style or personality that is said to be a relatively enduring "trait," then varies the type of stressful situation, and finally, correlates the personality trait or disposition with a measure of arousal or adaptation. This approach emphasizes stable individual differences that are relevant to many different stressors.

Critiques of the traditional trait approach to personality have emphasized the typically small amount of variability explained by personality-stress correlations and the importance of examining situational and interactional components of

variance (Endler & Magnusson, 1976; Mischel, 1969, 1973). Others have persua-
sively argued that behavior is far more stable than supposed and that relatively
enduring personality dispositions explain much larger components of the variability in human behavior when experiments are designed to include aggregation
over many different stimuli in many different occasions or when experimental
settings include implicitly ego-involving events, such as the parachute studies
previously reviewed (Epstein, 1980).

Epstein's position suggests that if the trait approach is useful, it should be
most evident in research that involves realistically stressful situations. My purpose
here is to trace the development of a commonly used dimension of personality,
repression–sensitization (R–S), as it has evolved in the stress literature. This
dimension provides an example with which to discuss the shortcomings and
potentials the trait approach to coping may have for explaining interactions
between coping styles and physiological arousal.

R–S is a global dimension of personality functioning that purports to measure
the extent to which a person tries to escape anxiety through the use of
avoidance or repressive strategies or tends to focus upon anxiety through the use
of ruminative or sensitizing strategies. It was developed 20 years ago (Byrne,
1961) during a period in which personality researchers were concerned with the
topic of perceptual defense and the relationship between Freudian conceptions of
repression and learning theory concepts of approach and avoidance (for a
discussion, see Byrne, 1964).

An attempt was made to psychometrically define a scale of R–S using items
from subscales of the MMPI that presumably measured topics relevant to
approach and avoidance tendencies (e.g., depression, defensiveness). These efforts
resulted in an inventory consisting of 127 items plus some filler items (item
numbers are listed in Bell & Byrne, 1978, pp. 454–455; Byrne, Barry, & Nelson,
1963).

Some general questions can be asked about the use of this inventory and its
related revisions. First, how does the scale overlap with other measures of
personality? The most telling problem concerns the scale's relationship to
measures of anxiety. Correlations between the Repression–Sensitization Scale and
the Taylor Manifest Anxiety Scale are on the order of .90 (Abbot, 1972).
Because there is considerable item overlap between the two scales, this relationship is to some degree a spurious one. Even when common items are excluded,
however, the correlation remains at .76 (Sullivan & Roberts, 1969). Similar
problems can be found in the relationship between R–S and measures of social
desirability. The R–S Scale correlates $-.90$ with the social-desirability scale of the
MMPI (Abbot, 1972) and on the order of $-.40$ with the Marlowe-Crowne Social
Desirability Scale (Feder, 1967).

Even when efforts are made to minimize the correlation between anxiety and
the R–S dimension, the correlation between trait anxiety and R–S remains in the
order of magnitude of .50 (Epstein & Fenz, 1967). Although one can argue that
the magnitude of the correlation leaves room for at least some noncommon
variance, and one can maintain that R–S is a better construct than trait anxiety
for some purposes, the magnitude of correlations between traits is a serious
source of conceptual confusion and a serious limitation to much of the research
in personality and stress.

A second question about the R–S Scale concerns how one should view middle scorers on the R–S Scale. Byrne (1961) was originally attempting to measure two maladaptive personality types who fell at extremes of repression and sensitization. This poses considerable difficulties for researchers who have basically tested linear hypotheses about adaptability or arousal with a scale that may be curvilinear in nature. Bell and Byrne (1978) review literature relevant to this question and find some support for the contention that middle scorers on the R–S Scale are the best adjusted, but they caution that the evidence is difficult to interpret because of problems in defining "adjustment." Other researchers have sidestepped the problem (Shipley, Butt, & Horowitz, 1979; Shipley, Butt, Horowitz, & Fabry, 1978) by simply deleting from the sample those who fall at the median. Such an approach is unsatisfying on both statistical and conceptual grounds. If middle scorers truly show a different style of responding in stressful situations, the problem should be more directly addressed.

A third question that is directly related to the topic of this chapter concerns the physiological-arousal levels of repressors and sensitizers who are placed in stressful situations. In a recent review, Bell and Byrne (1978) noted that the results are mixed. On measures such as skin conductance, repressors show evidence of being more aroused during stressful experimental settings. Bell and Byrne noted, however, that other researchers have found no difference and that there are some reports that sensitizers show higher arousal. Given the complexity of psychophysiological measurements, of adequately controlling a stressful stimulus, and of taking into account the possible curvilinearity of the R–S dimension, such confusion should not be surprising. Under stress, however, the effectiveness of a repressor's attempts to avoid anxiety may depend on type and level of stress involved in the experiment. Level of physiological arousal, therefore, may be determined by the degree to which the repressor is able cognitively or behaviorally to remove himself or herself from the stressor. If this is true, determining the effects of R–S on the level of physiological arousal would require a detailed analysis of cognitive, behavioral, and physiological recordings. An indication that complex behavioral avoidance processes may be occurring is reported by Haley (1974), who used the industrial accident film discussed previously and measured the eye movements of repressors and sensitizers. Haley found that repressors tended to look away from stressful scenes during the film, whereas sensitizers did not.

If Epstein (1980) is correct in asserting that ego-involving, realistic stressful situations will be the most profitable area in which to look for trait-outcome relationships, then medically stressful settings may provide an appropriate test of the validity of R–S. The results are disappointing in studies using the R–S Scale with surgical patients. F. Cohen and Lazarus (1973) reported no significant relationships between measure of recovery from surgery and the R–S Scale. In this same study, however, the authors interviewed and categorized the patients as avoidant, vigilant, or middle-level in coping style. Vigilant patients recovered more poorly. A doctoral dissertation by Walseth (1968) reported no significant findings with the R–S Scale, and although repression was marginally related to a measure of relinquishing the sick role in a sample of open-heart surgery patients (Brown & Rawlinson, 1975), the overall pattern of results is disappointing. The surgical setting has been a source of several studies investigating the concept of denial and avoidance (Andrew, 1970; Janis, 1958; Wilson, 1981). The lack of results with the R–S Scale raises serious questions about its construct validity.

One could argue, however, that the surgical settings and the largely correlational designs are not sufficiently controlled stressors. Shipley and his co-workers (Shipley, Butt, & Horowitz, 1979; Shipley, Butt, Horowitz, & Fabry, 1978) randomly assigned patients to viewing videotapes of a stressful medical procedure that patients would undergo the next morning. The pattern of results suggests that repressors who viewed the videotape only once had increased HR during the medical procedure, whereas sensitizers showed decreased levels of arousal. Particularly interesting was the finding that repressors who viewed the tape only once had the highest arousal levels, whereas repressors who viewed the tape three times had lower arousal levels. This result is similar to the conclusions of Fenz from the parachute studies, in which coping as measured by control of arousal was considered to be a process. This raises the possibility that the R-S Scale might more profitably be seen as a measure of a state within a larger coping process rather than a fixed "trait."

As can be seen from the results discussed previously, it is impossible to describe clearly what is being measured by the R-S Scale. This scale has generated a complex pattern of sometimes significant results that lead in no clear direction. For example, repression was found to be a premorbid personality characteristic that distinguished cancer patients from noncancer patients (Dattore, Shontz, & Coyne, 1980). Although the results are significant statistically, they do not lead anywhere because the effect is so small that one cannot use the R-S Scale to isolate a high-risk group, and the meaning of the scale is so diffuse that the finding has little heuristic value. As it stands, the scale is simply too complex to be of practical use.

Coupled with such problems is the possible contaminating effect of defensive or socially desirable reporting. Kahn and Schill (1971) and Lefcourt (1969) have demonstrated that people categorized as repressors on the R-S Scale who are also high scorers on measures of social desirability have patterns of anxiety and response to stress that differ from repressors who are low on measures of social desirability or defensiveness. The problem is similar to that faced by researchers who try to measure denial by asking subjects if they are frightened. If subjects say no, are they really unafraid or are they "deniers"? Repressor–social desirability differences extend into the realm of physiological arousal. Weinberger, Schwartz, and Davidson (1979) reported significant differences in measures of muscle tension and HR among subjects who were categorized into four groups by their scores (high or low) on trait anxiety and the Marlowe-Crowne scale of social desirability. It is clear that the R-S Scale is not one dimension. Therefore, use of the R-S Scale in stressful settings requires at least the simultaneous administration of another measure of defensiveness.

To summarize, the original purpose and validity of the scale has gradually been forgotten as the scale has become reified. If one wants to measure denial, avoidance, or repression, the R-S Scale is used in spite of the fact that its construct validity is far from established. The problem may become clearer by examining a sample of items from the R-S Scale and a sample of three different stressful situations.

Items from the R-S Scale

1. I sweat very easily even on cool days.
2. I am not easily awakened by noises.

3. Sex education should not be part of the high school curriculum.

4. When things go wrong, I cannot rest until I've corrected the situation.

5. Everything is turning out just like the prophets of the Bible said it would.

Stressful situations

1. Threat of electric shock based on performance in paired associate learning task.

2. Training in skydiving

3. Tachistoscopic presentation of emotionally neutral and emotionally laden words (e.g., whore)

It is difficult to imagine that the same items would be predictive of physiological arousal or performance in those different situations. As a whole, the items that comprise the R–S Scale certainly measure something, but as a global dimension of practical usefulness the R–S Scale still has not demonstrated an adequate level of validity.

At least for the field of stress research, the use of global personality traits as predictors of performance or arousal is not likely to lead to increased understanding of the complex processes that link coping, arousal, and performance under stress.

## LEVEL OF AROUSAL AND LEVEL OF ADAPTATION

Having presented different approaches to studying coping style and physiological arousal, consider implications for current and future work in this area of stress research. Much of the research on stress has made four implicit or explicit assumptions about relationships among the concepts of stress, arousal, and adaptation. First, the level of stress is directly proportional to the level of physiological arousal. Second, adaptation or performance under stress improves as arousal and stress decrease. Third, these relationships are true regardless of which psychophysiological or endocrinologic indicator of arousal is used. Fourth, the relationship between arousal and performance is essentially linear. If the Yerkes-Dodson law suggesting an inverted-U-shaped relationship between stress and performance is considered at all, the assumption seems to be that the levels of stress being studied are beyond the inflection point of the U-shaped curve.

These assumptions also filter into the society at large. Conventional wisdom in the form of television and films that focus on stress maintain that the fight-or-flight response used to be adaptive but is now outmoded in our more cerebral and less action-oriented society (*Managing Stress,* CRM Publications and Films). But considerable evidence supports the contention that the "wisdom of the body's" response to stress goes well beyond traditional fight-or-flight situations.

In regard to arousal as measured by endocrine responses of the sympathetic-adrenal medullary system, Levi (1972) demonstrated that a significant increase in level of epinephrine occurs in response to amusing films such as *Charley's Aunt* as well as to more threatening movies. One need only ride a roller coaster at amusement parks for a graphic illustration of our willingness to pay for increases in arousal. Frankenhäuser and her colleagues have also demonstrated in applied settings that levels of epinephrine are related to performance. Output of epinephrine in school children was positively correlated with adjustment and performance during an arithmetic test (Johansson, Frankenhäuser, & Magnusson, 1973). Decrease in epinephrine levels in response to stress was found to indicate a failure in adaptation (Frankenhäuser, 1980). Similar results were reported in a medical setting by a team of Russian researchers (Genzdilov, Alexandrin, & Simonov, 1972). Catecholamine levels of patients who underwent surgery for rectal cancer were negatively correlated with development of postoperative complications. Patients at extremely low levels of catecholamine output were particularly likely to exhibit difficult recoveries.

A similar relationship is evident in regard to the pituitary-adrenocortical system. Hennessy and Levine (1979) reviewed literature suggesting that performance in stressful situations is optimal at moderately increased levels of ACTH and corticosteroids. Injections that depress normal activity of the pituitary-adrenal axis can actually impair animals' performance in learning tasks. When pituitary-adrenocortical activity was at moderately increased levels, performance was superior to that at higher and lower levels of activity (Gold & Van Buskirk, 1976).

Although levels of endocrine arousal are associated with performance in stressful situations, understanding the interaction between the process of coping and arousal requires exploring patterns of arousal. The Gemini space program provided a unique opportunity to obtain detailed measurements of endocrine arousal during a stressful space flight. Levels of 17-OHCSs were so low during the orbital flight that researchers suspected a malfunction in their recording devices. After careful checking they reported their readings accurate. Levels of epinephrine and NE did not show such a precipitous decline (Lutwak, Whedon, Tachance, Reid, & Lipscomb, 1969).

Lack of simple relationships among measures of arousal should not be surprising. Lacey (1967) was the first to show systematically that psychophysiological indicators of arousal were not highly correlated. Similar variations among endocrine indicators of arousal (Ellertsen, Johnse, & Ursin, 1978) should lead us to look for patterns of arousal that may help unravel the puzzling relationships between coping processes and arousal (Knight, Atkins, Eagle, Evans, Finkelstein, Fukushima, Katz, & Weiner, 1979; Mason, 1975; Ursin, 1978).

In a study of parachutists, Ellertsen and colleagues (1978) used factor analysis to discover two distinct factors that were defined by epinephrine-NE and cortisol. In the case of the astronauts, Ellertsen's and Frankenhäuser's research suggests a possible solution. A psychosocial environment that does not provide a person with a sense of control will increase cortisol levels; but when the sense of control is present, cortisol levels may be drastically decreased (see discussion in Frankenhäuser, 1980). The situation of the astronauts may be one of confident task involvement and the sense of control. Their moderately high levels of epinephrine and drastically decreased levels of cortisol are consistent with such an interpretation. Perhaps for them the orbital space flight was simply a grand roller coaster ride.

The importance of coping styles in such a situation should not be underestimated. It is not just the situation that provides a sense of control but the interaction between characteristics of the situation and characteristics of the person (Magnusson & Endler, 1977). A person with a lesser estimate of her or his own abilities or with a more avoidant coping style would most likely not have shown the same endocrine pattern as the astronauts.

It is interesting to note that the astronauts' cortisol levels were elevated during periods of the mission in which they were not in command, both before and after landing. Johansson and Frankenhäuser (1973) found that people who rapidly returned to base-line levels following a stressor showed better performance under stress than did those who showed a slow and gradual decrease. Temporal factors and phases of activation may be particularly important in determining the larger configuration of arousal, coping style, and performance.

Identified relationships between coping and arousal have been largely confined either to psychophysiological measures such as skin conductance, HR, and respiration rate or to the levels of circulating hormones. Brain chemistry, however, may provide additional insight into the coping process. The word *endorphin* is an acronym for endogenous morphine-like substances. These brain peptides have been found to increase dramatically following stress (Rossier, Bloom, & Guillemin, 1980) and have been implicated in the process of relief from pain. N. E. Miller (1980) summarized additional research suggesting that performing an effective coping response will increase levels of NE in the brain. On the other hand, when levels of NE in the brain are decreased with the use of drugs, performance during subsequent stressful episodes is impaired. Increasing sophistication of measurement may also allow easier investigation of the effects of coping styles on brain neurotransmitters such as NE.

## MORE CONCRETE APPROACHES
## TO MEASURING COPING STYLE

Although increased understanding of the sequencing of physiological arousal under stress and the pattern formed by different measures of physiological arousal will help clarify questions about coping-arousal interactions, it is important that the level of specificity and concreteness in measuring coping styles be increased. If coping styles can be more specifically tied to how people think and act when placed in a stressful situation, the problems of interpretation of the R–S Scale can be minimized.

An example of a measure of coping style that meets this requirement is the Miller Behavioral Style Scale (S. M. Miller, 1979, 1980). This scale purports to measure a person's reactions to signals of danger from the environment. Miller emphasizes two approaches to coping after an appraisal of danger has been made. One approach, called "monitoring," consists of thoughts and actions that seek out information, that look for predictability, and that generally indicate vigilance in the face of threat. A second approach is called "blunting" and consists of thoughts and actions that tend to remove the person psychologically from the situation.

Scores on these dimensions are obtained by presenting the person with a hypothetical situation that involves a signal of danger from the environment. For example, a person may be asked to

*Vividly imagine that you are on an airplane, 30 minutes from your destination, when the plane unexpectedly goes into a deep dive and then suddenly levels off. After a short time, the pilot announces that nothing is wrong, although the rest of the ride may be rough.*

The subject is then asked to select from a list of responses all the thoughts and actions that would apply to him or her in that situation. For example, in the situation described above, a subject would be rated high on monitoring tendencies if she or he checked responses such as

I would carefully read the information provided about the safety features of the
plane and make sure I knew where the emergency exits were.
I would call the stewardess and ask her exactly what the problem was.
I would listen carefully to the engines for unusual noises and would watch the
crew to see if their behavior was out of the ordinary.

A person would be rated high on blunting tendencies for selecting responses such as:

I would watch the end of the movie, even if I had seen it before.
I would settle down and read a book or magazine or write a letter.

The monitoring and blunting coping styles are similar in many respects to the concepts of R–S, coping–avoidance, and vigilance–denial that are often used to describe coping behavior. The methodology used in obtaining the scores, however, offers definite advantages. First, the subject is provided with a concrete stimulus situation and concrete alternative responses. Second, the scale does not assume that a person's response to stress is unidimensional. The scale allows separate scores to be generated for monitoring, blunting, and also for total coping attempts.

The initial studies using this scale show promising results. In a laboratory experiment that involved the threat of impending electrical shock, monitors preferred listening to a warning signal and exhibited increased arousal in the form of EDRs. Blunters, on the other hand, chose to distract themselves and not to listen to warning signals, and they exhibited less physiological arousal (S. M. Miller, 1979).

The scale has also been used in the stressful setting of a gynecologic examination. Monitors and blunters were randomly assigned to groups in which they were given either augmented information or minimal information about the impending examination. As a group, monitors had higher self-ratings and observer ratings of distress than did blunters. A second major finding was that, although monitors showed reduced HR when they had been placed in the high-information condition, blunters increased their level of arousal when given more extensive information. Effects on self-ratings of mood also persisted beyond the period of the examination.

Although research using the monitoring and blunting coping styles is still in its initial stages, several aspects of this program are especially encouraging. First, the scale is much more easily administered in field settings and medical settings than the long paper-and-pencil derivatives of the MMPI. Second, the typical approaches using paper-and-pencil or interview assessments of coping effectiveness (Wolff, Friedman, Hofer, & Mason, 1964; Wolff, Hofer, & Mason, 1964) do not measure the actual process of coping. Miller's (1979) methodology could be altered so that subjects would also check their responses to the situation in the order in which they would probably occur. In this manner, a time line of coping could be generated that would provide a tool allowing systematic examination of the process of coping.

Third, by simply varying the characteristics of the situations used as stimuli for the scale, it would be possible to investigate the influence different situations have on a person's hierarchy of responsiveness to stressful situations. For example, the situations described by S. M. Miller (1979, 1980) are ones in which there was little opportunity or probability that direct action would remove the danger signal. Inclusion of situations in which direct action might be more appropriate or useful, such as hearing a strange noise or smelling gas fumes, would allow the researcher to chart configurations of defenses based on estimates of behavior in stressful settings. Miller suggested that the results she observed in the study of gynecologic patients might well be different if the stressful situation allowed one to make more direct use of information or if the situation had been longer in duration than that of a diagnostic examination. In addition, the tendency of a person to shift from monitoring to blunting or vice versa as well as the conditions that would permit such a switch could be easily obtained using this methodology.

The approach used by Miller in measuring monitoring and blunting provides a method to measure easily the situation-person interactions that have complicated so much of the work in the stress field. Methods such as Miller's that provide for more specific and concrete definition and measurement of coping styles may help researchers more adequately conceptualize and map phenomenological aspects of the coping process that have remained so elusive.

## ILLUSTRATIONS OF INTERACTIONS BETWEEN COPING STYLES AND AROUSAL

A recurring theme here has been that global dimensions of coping and global conceptions of arousal do not adequately capture the complexity of the coping process. I have suggested that many of the problems encountered in interpreting relationships between coping style and stress could be remedied if patterns of arousal were considered and if coping styles were operationalized in a less global, more specific manner. I now illustrate types of interactions between coping styles and physiological arousal that are more likely to be discovered when coping styles are tied to the specific behavior of people in stressful situations.

The data that illustrate these interactions between arousal and coping style are taken from a larger project that examined determinants of recovery from gallbladder surgery, hysterectomy, and the effects of behavioral interventions in reducing the stress of hospitalization. More detailed descriptions of that project can be found in Wilson (1977, 1981, 1982).

The first type of interaction illustrates the need to examine configurations of coping styles rather than relying on global dimensions of coping ability. Several authors have suggested that two parallel processes of coping are activated after a person has appraised a situation as stressful (Anderson, 1976; Lazarus, Averill, & Opton, 1974; Leventhal, 1970). One process can be labeled the "emotional response system." This system is concerned with the organism's response to physiological sensations of emotion produced by the appraisal that a stressor is present. A second process is called the "instrumental response system." This system is concerned with influencing or removing the stress through active or instrumental behavior. Thus the emotional response system is responsible for maintaining a relatively steady state of the internal milieu, and the instrumental response system is responsible for reaching out to solve the problem by influencing or eliminating the stressor.

Measures of individual differences in style of functioning for these two systems form the basis for the first example of coping-arousal interactions. A person's ability to modulate the emotional response system effectively was labeled "fear control." Scores on fear control were obtained from responses to Likert-type statements such as:

I am able to be calm and controlled when faced with disturbing things.
I have trouble sleeping when I am worried or nervous about something that is going to happen the next day.

A person's ability to act instrumentally to minimize the impact of a stressor through anticipatory action was labeled "danger control." Scores on danger control were obtained through responses to statements such as:

If I've got a lot of things that have to be done, I line them up in my mind and then go and do them one at a time.
If I am going on a trip, I make sure that everything is packed ahead of time so I don't have to rush around at the last minute.

Abilities on these coping dimensions should be particularly important immediately before surgery. One measure of level of physiological arousal before surgery is the amount of sodium Pentothal necessary to bring a patient below the level of full consciousness in preparation for the general anesthetic. The more "aroused" the patient, the more Pentothal is required. Patients high in fear control required significantly less Pentothal than patients low in fear control ability (all results in this section from Wilson, 1977, pp. 140–141). Patients high in danger control required more Pentothal than did patients low in danger control.

The results appear to indicate that fear control ability results in lower arousal and that danger control ability results in higher levels of arousal. But when patients are categorized into four groups according to median splits on the fear control and danger control dimensions, the importance of configurations of coping styles can be demonstrated.

As is shown in Table 11.1, the only group that showed elevated requirements for Pentothal, and thus elevated arousal levels, consisted of patients high in danger control and low in fear control. Patients low in danger control but high in fear control showed no elevations in Pantothal requirements, and neither did patients high in both dimensions or low in both dimensions. Thus, it is a combination of defensive styles that is most predictive of level of arousal.

It is important to note that fear control and danger control are positively correlated ($r = .44$). Coping abilities may often intercorrelate, but it would be a mistake to combine the scales automatically into one measure of coping ability. Interactions will not be discovered nor individual differences fully explained unless coping abilities are defined in configurations that allow for interactive effects.

A second type of interaction illustrates the manner in which coping style may be a factor that mediates the relationship between level of arousal and level of

Table 11.1   Mean number of milligrams of sodium Pentothal required for induction into anesthesia for surgical patients at high and low levels of danger control and fear control

| Group | | | |
|-------|------|---|---|
| Danger control | Fear control | n | Pentothal (mg) |
| Low  | Low  | 18 | 274.5 |
| Low  | High | 13 | 238.6 |
| High | Low  | 12 | 375.9 |
| High | High | 22 | 277.6 |

adjustment to a stressful situation. Level of arousal during the period of recovery was assessed by measuring total urinary output of epinephrine during the first 3 postoperative days. A median split was used to classify patients as high or low epinephrine responders. Level of recovery was assessed by a recovery index composed of indicators of mood, physical symptoms, ambulation, and pain; by numbers of injections for pain; and by length of hospital stay. Coping style for this analysis was level of fear control, divided by a median split.

When arousal-recovery relationships were analyzed, no significant linear or curvilinear effects were found between level of epinephrine and any of the measures of recovery from surgery. Statistically significant ($p < .05$) effects were discovered, however, for the recovery index and for number of injections for pain, when fear control was used as a mediating variable. The shape of the interaction between epinephrine level and fear control for the recovery index and for use of injections for pain is shown in Table 11.2.

Increased level of arousal was related to improved recovery only for patients who were high in fear control ability. High levels of epinephrine coupled with low levels of fear control was indicative of poor scores on the recovery index and increased need for medications for pain.

This finding suggests that coping styles may be important mediators in determining whether arousal reflects the active, involved coping described by Frankenhäuser (1980) or whether it reflects too high a level of arousal for the patients with limited fear control ability.

These findings also illustrate a major difficulty of research with interactions. It

Table 11.2   Mean standardized recovery score and number of injections for pain of surgical patients at high and low levels of epinephrine and fear control

| Group | | | | |
|-------|------|---|---|---|
| Epinephrine | Fear control | n | Recovery index | Injections |
| Low  | Low  | 13 | −0.18 | 8.8 |
| Low  | High | 25 | 0.24 | 9.7 |
| High | Low  | 16 | −1.42 | 14.1 |
| High | High | 10 | 1.70 | 9.6 |

would have been desirable to analyze the results in greater detail, including level of danger control as well as level of fear control. The sample size, however, limited the analysis of higher-order interactions. Investigation of higher-order interactions will require a greater investment in sample size than has often occurred in stress research.

It should also be noted that measures of cortisol would have allowed a more satisfactory test of Frankenhäuser's (1980) contention that active, involved coping would be related to increased epinephrine level and decreased cortisol level. Lack of sufficient measures of arousal in this study limits ability to unravel the relationships among arousal, coping style, and adaptation. In spite of such limitations, even this limited use of interaction-oriented analysis increases the ability to discover patterns between coping style and arousal.

## CONCLUSIONS

In a textbook on methodology for behavioral scientists, Kaplan (1964) tells a story about endocrinologists who were searching for the secret of the incredible fertility of the rabbit. No matter what single blocking approach was used, the rabbits still ovulated. I believe this story contains a message for those interested in studying relationships between coping style and physiological arousal. If progress is to be made, our concepts and research designs must be able to match the complexity of human adaptation.

The research reviewed in the initial section of this chapter illustrated this point. Problems in interpreting the results produced using global coping styles such as R-S should underscore the need to articulate our concepts. The section on the meaning of endocrine arousal provides evidence that the use of multiple endocrine measures has increased our understanding of endocrine–coping style relationships. S. M. Miller's (1979, 1980) methodology suggests a promising direction for future research in coping style. Finally, the examples of interactions between measures of coping style and arousal during recovery from surgery suggest that researchers interested in understanding relationships between coping styles and arousal must also consider the three-way relationships among coping, arousal, and adaptation.

Averill (1973) has talked about the frustrating, will-o'-the-wisp nature of relationships between personality and stress. Replication of findings has proved a difficult task, and advances will remain ephemeral until the fertility of our concepts of arousal, coping, and stress do justice to the complexity of human adaptive processes.

## REFERENCES

Abbot, R. D. On confounding of the Repression–Sensitization and Manifest Anxiety scales. *Psychological Reports*, 1972, *30*, 392–394.

Anderson, C. R. Coping behaviors as intervening mechanisms in the inverted-V stress-performance relationship. *Journal of Applied Psychology*, 1976, *61*, 30–34.

Andrew, J. M. Recovery from surgery, with and without preparatory instruction, for three coping styles. *Journal of Personality and Social Psychology*, 1970, *15*, 223–226.

Averill, J. R. Personal control over aversive stimuli and its relationship to stress. *Psychological Bulletin*, 1973, *80*, 286–303.

Bell, P. A., & Byrne, D. Repression-sensitization. In H. London & J. E. Exner (Eds.), *Dimensions of Personality*. New York: Wiley, 1978.

Berkun, M. M., Bialek, H. M., Kern, R. P., & Yagi, K. Experimental studies of psychological stress in man. *Psychological Monographs*, 1962, *76*, Whole No. 534).

Bloom, G., von Euler, U. S., & Frankenhäuser, M. Catecholamine excretion and personality traits in paratroop trainees. *Acta Physiologica Scandinavica*, 1963, *58*, 77–89.

Brown, J. S., & Rawlinson, M. Relinquishing the sick role following open-heart surgery. *Journal of Health and Social Behavior*, 1975, *16*, 12–26.

Byrne, D. The Repression–Sensitization Scale: Rationale, reliability, and validity. *Journal of Personality*, 1961, *29*, 334–349.

Byrne, D. Repression-sensitization as a dimension of personality. In B. A. Maher (Ed.), *Progress in experimental personality research* (Vol. 1). New York: Academic, 1964.

Byrne, D., Barry, J., & Nelson, D. Relation of the revised Repression–Sensitization Scale to measures of self-description. *Psychological Reports*, 1963, *13*, 323–334.

Cohen, F., & Lazarus, R. S. Active coping processes, coping dispositions, and recovery from surgery. *Psychosomatic Medicine*, 1973, *35*, 375–389.

Cohen, S. After effects of stress on human performance and social behavior: A review of research and theory. *Psychological Bulletin*, 1980, *88*, 82–108.

Dattore, P. T., Shontz, F. C., & Coyne, L. Premorbid personality differentiation of cancer and noncancer groups: A test of the hypothesis of cancer proneness. *Journal of Consulting and Clinical Psychology*, 1980, *48*, 388–394.

Ellertsen, B., Johnsen, T. B., & Ursin, H. Relationship between the hormonal responses to activation and coping. In S. Levine, J. Weinberg, & H. Ursin (Eds.), *Psychobiology of stress: A study of coping men*. New York: Academic, 1978.

Endler, N. S., & Magnusson, D. Toward an interactional psychology of personality. *Psychological Bulletin*, 1976, *83*, 956–974.

Epstein, S. The stability of behavior: II. Implications for psychological research. *American Psychologist*, 1980, *35*, 790–806.

Epstein, S., & Fenz, W. D. The detection of areas of emotional stress through variations in perceptual threshold and physiological arousal. *Journal of Experimental Research in Personality*, 1967, *2*, 191–199.

Feder, C. F. Relationship of repression-sensitization to adjustment status, social desirability, and acquiescence response set. *Journal of Consulting Psychology*, 1967, *31*, 401–406.

Fenz, W. D. Conflict and stress as related to physiological activation and sensory, perceptual, and cognitive functioning. *Psychological Monographs*, 1964, *78* (Whole No. 585).

Fenz, W. D. Strategies for coping with stress. In I. G. Sarason & C. D. Spielberger (Eds.), *Stress and anxiety* (Vol. 1). Washington: Hemisphere, 1975.

Fenz, W. D., & Jones, G. B. The effect of uncertainty on mastery of stress: A case study. *Psychophysiology*, 1972, *9*, 615–619. (a)

Fenz, W. D., & Jones, G. B. Individual differences in physiologic arousal and performance in sport parachutists. *Psychosomatic Medicine*, 1972, *34*, 1–8. (b)

Folkins, C. H., Lawson, K. D., Opton, E. M., & Lazarus, R. S. Desensitization and the experimental reduction of threat. *Journal of Abnormal Psychology*, 1968, *73*, 100–113.

Ford, C. V., & Spaulding, R. C. The Pueblo incident: A comparison of factors related to coping with extreme stress. *Archives of General Psychiatry*, 1973, *29*, 340–343.

Frankenhäuser, M. Psychoneuroendocrine approaches to the study of stressful person-environment transactions. In H. Selye (Ed.), *Selye's guide to stress research* (Vol. 1). New York: Van Nostrand Reinhold, 1980.

Genzdilov, A. V., Alexandrin, G. P., & Simonov, N. N. The role of stress, factors in the postoperative course of patients with rectal cancer. *Journal of Surgical Oncology*, 1977, *9*, 517–523.

Gold, P. E., & Van Buskirk, R. Enhancement and impairment of memory processes with post-trial injections of adrenocorticotrophic hormone. *Behavioral Biology*, 1976, *16*, 387–400.

Haley, G. Eye movement responses of repressors and sensitizers to a stressful film. *Journal of Research in Personality*, 1974, *8*, 88–94.

Hansen, J. R., Stoa, K. F., Blix, A. S., & Ursin, H. Urinary levels of epinephrine and norepinephrine in parachutist trainees. In S. Levine, J. Weinberg, & H. Ursin (Eds.), *Psychobiology of stress: A study of coping men*. New York: Academic, 1978.

Harrell, J. P. Psychological factors and hypertension: A status report. *Psychological Bulletin*, 1980, *87*, 482–501.

Hennessy, J. W., & Levine, S. Stress, arousal, and the pituitary-adrenal system: A psychoendocrine hypothesis. *Progress in Psychobiology and Physiological Psychology,* 1979, *8*, 133–178.

Horowitz, M. J., & Becker, S. S. Cognitive responses to stressful stimuli. *Archives of General Psychiatry,* 1971, *25*, 419–428. (a)

Horowitz, M. J., & Becker, S. S. The compulsion to repeat trauma: Experimental study of intrusive thinking after stress. *Journal of Nervous and Mental Disease,* 1971, *152*, 32–40. (b)

Horowitz, M., & Wilner, N. Stress films, emotion, and cognitive response. *Archives of General Psychiatry,* 1976, *33*, 1339–1344.

Janis, I. L. *Psychological stress: Psychoanalytic and behavioral studies of surgical patients.* New York: Wiley, 1958.

Johansson, G., & Frankenhäuser, M. Temporal factors in sympathoadrenomedullary activity following acute behavioral activation. *Biological Psychology,* 1973, *1*, 63–73.

Johansson, G., Frankenhäuser, M., & Magnusson, D. Catecholamine output in school children as related to performance and adjustment. *Scandinavian Journal of Psychology,* 1973, *14*, 20–28.

Kahn, M., & Schill, T. Anxiety report in defensive and nondefensive repressors. *Journal of Consulting and Clinical Psychology,* 1971, *36*, 300.

Kaplan, A. *The conduct of inquiry: Methodology for behavioral science.* Scranton, Pa.: Chandler, 1964.

Knight, R. B., Atkins, A., Eagle, C. J., Evans, N., Finkelstein, J. W., Fukushima, D. K., Katz, J. L., & Weiner, H. Psychological stress, ego defenses, and cortisol production in children hospitalized for elective surgery. *Psychosomatic Medicine,* 1979, *41*, 40–49.

Lacey, J. I. Somatic response patterning and stress: Some revisions of activation theory. In M. H. Appley & R. Trumbull (Eds.), *Psychological stress: Issues in research.* New York: Appleton, 1967.

Lazarus, R. S., & Alfert, E. The short-circuiting of threat. *Journal of Abnormal and Social Psychology,* 1964, *69*, 195–205.

Lazarus, R. S., Averill, J. R., & Opton, E. M. Psychology of coping: Issues of research and assessment. In C. V. Coelho, Hamburg, D. A., & J. E. Adams (Eds.), *Coping and adaptation.* New York: Basic Books, 1974.

Lazarus, R. S., Opton, E. M., Nomikos, M. S., & Rankin, N. O. The principle of short-circuiting of threat: Further evidence. *Journal of Personality,* 1965, *33*, 622–635.

Lazarus, R. S., Speisman, J. E., Mordkoff, A. M., & Davison, L. A. A laboratory study of psychological stress produced by a motion picture film. *Psychological Monographs,* 1962, *76*(2, Whole No. 553).

Lefcourt, H. Need for approval and threatened negative evaluation as determinants of expressiveness in a projective test. *Journal of Consulting and Clinical Psychology,* 1969, *33*, 96–102.

Leventhal, H. Findings and theory in the study of fear-arousing communications. In L. Berkowitz (Ed.), *Advances in experimental social psychology* (Vol. 5). New York: Academic, 1970.

Levi, L. (Ed.). *Stress and distress in response to psychosocial stimuli.* Oxford: Pergamon, 1972.

Lifton, R. J. Home by ship: Reaction patterns of American prisoners of war repatriated from North Korea. *American Journal of Psychiatry,* 1954, *110*, 732–739.

Lutwak, L., Whedon, G. D., Lachance, P. A., Reid, J. M., & Lipscomb, H. S. Mineral, electrolyte, and nitrogen balance studies of the Gemini VII (14-day orbital space flight). *Journal of Clinical and Endocrinological Metabolism,* 1969, *29*, 1140–1156.

Magnusson, D., & Endler, N. S. (Eds.). *Personality at the crossroads: Current issues in interactional psychology.* Hillsdale, N.J.: Erlbaum, 1977.

Mason, J. W. Emotion as reflected in patterns of endocrine intergration. In L. Levi (Ed.), *Emotions: Their parameters and measurement.* New York: Raven, 1975, 153–181.

Miller, N. E. Effects of learning on physical symptoms produced by stress. In H. Selye (Ed.), *Selye's guide to stress research* (Vol. 1). New York: Van Nostrand Reinhold, 1980.

Miller, S. M. Coping with impending stress: Psychophysiological and cognitive correlates of choice. *Psychophysiology,* 1979, *16*, 572–581.

Miller, S. M. When is a little information a dangerous thing? Coping with stressful events by monitoring vs. blunting. In S. Levine & H. Ursin (Eds.), *Coping and health: Proceedings of a NATO conference.* New York: Plenum, 1980.

Miller, S. M., & Grant, R. P. The blunting hypothesis: A view of predictability and human stress. In P. O. Sjoden, S. Bates, & W. S. Dockens III, (Eds.), *Trends in behavior therapy.* New York: Academic, 1979, 135–161.

Mischel, W. Continuity and change in personality. *American Psychologist,* 1969, *24,* 1012–1018.

Mischel, W. Toward a cognitive social learning reconceptualization of personality. *Psychological Review,* 1973, *80,* 252–283.

Nomikos, M. S., Opton, E. M., Averill, J. R., & Lazarus, R. S. Surprise versus suspense in the production of a stress reaction. *Journal of Personality and Social Psychology,* 1968, *8,* 204–208.

Opton, E. M., & Lazarus, R. S. Personality determinants of psychophysiological response to stress. *Journal of Personality and Social Psychology,* 1967, *6,* 291–303.

Pace, N., Schaeffer, F. L., & Elmadjian, F. Physiological studies on infantrymen in combat. *University of California Publication in Physiology,* 1956, *10,* 1–48.

Radloff, R., & Helmreich, R. *Groups under stress: Psychological research in Sea Lab II.* New York: Appleton, 1968.

Roessler, R., & Collins, F. Personality correlates of physiological responses to motion pictures. *Psychophysiology,* 1970, *6,* 732–748.

Rossier, J., Bloom, F. E., & Guillemin, R. Endorphins and stress. In H. Selye (Ed.), *Selye's guide to stress research* (Vol. 1). New York: Van Nostrand Reinhold, 1980.

Shipley, R. H., Butt, J. H., Horowitz, E. A. Preparation to reexperience a stressful medical examination: Effect of repetitious videotape exposure and coping style. *Journal of Consulting and Clinical Psychology,* 1979, *47,* 485–492.

Shipley, R. H., Butt, J. H., Horowitz, B., & Farbry, J. E. Preparation for a stressful medical procedure: Effect of amount of stimulus preexposure and coping style. *Journal of Consulting and Clinical Psychology,* 1978, *46,* 499–507.

Speisman, J. C., Lazarus, R. S., Mordkoff, A., & Davison, L. Experimental reduction of stress based on ego-defense theory. *Journal of Abnormal and Social Psychology,* 1964, *68,* 367–380.

Sullivan, P. F., & Roberts, L. K. Relationship of manifest anxiety to repression–sensitization on the MMPI. *Journal of Consulting and Clinical Psychology,* 1969, *33,* 763–764.

Ursin, H. Activation, coping, and psychosomatics. In S. Levine, J. Weinberg, H. Ursin (Eds.), *Psychobiology of stress: A study of coping men.* New York: Academic, 1978.

Walseth, H. K. *Repression-sensitization and reaction to surgery.* Unpublished doctoral dissertation, University of Missouri, 1968.

Weinberger, D. A., Schwartz, G. E., & Davidson, R. J. Low-anxious, high-anxious, and repressive coping styles: Psychometric patterns and behavioral and physiological responses to stress. *Journal of Abnormal Psychology,* 1979, *88,* 369–380.

Weiner, H. *Psychobiology and human disease.* New York: Elsevier, 1977.

Wilson, J. F. *Determinants of recovery from surgery: Preoperative instruction, relaxation training, and defensive structure.* Unpublished doctoral dissertation, University of Michigan, 1977.

Wilson, J. F. Recovery from surgery and scores on the Defense Mechanisms Inventory. *Journal of Personality Assessment,* 1982, *46,* 312–319.

Wilson, J. F. Behavioral preparation for surgery: Benefit or harm? *Journal of Behavioral Medicine,* 1981, *4,* 79–102.

Wolff, C. T., Friedman, S. B., Hofer, M. A., & Mason, J. W. Relationship between psychological defenses and mean urinary 17-hydroxycorticosteroid excretion rates: I. A predictive study of parents of fatally ill children. *Psychosomatic Medicine,* 1964, *26,* 576–591.

Wolff, C. T., Hofer, M. A., & Mason, J. W. Relationship between psychological defenses and mean urinary 17-hydroxycorticosteroid excretion rates: II. Methodologic and theoretical considerations. *Psychosomatic Medicine,* 1964, *26,* 592–608.

# IV

# TREATMENT
# OF THE STRESS RESPONSE

The previous chapters in this book have been concerned with theoretical discussions of different variables that affect the stress response. By incorporating these data, treatments to decrease the negative consequences of stress have been developed. Treatments for stress-related disorders have been developed based on the assumption that if the negative consequences of stress are due to physiological arousal, then effective treatment should result in relaxation. Physiological relaxation can be produced with treatments that have either a somatic or a cognitive orientation. Cognitively oriented therapies use techniques from thought restructuring (e.g., "I can handle this. I'm not upset.") to clearing the mind of all thoughts. Somatically oriented treatments primarily disregard what thoughts a person has and focus instead on relaxing muscles either directly (as in progressive muscle relaxation) or indirectly (as in biofeedback). These treatments are also used to decrease autonomic arousal.

The major theme in this book, that cognitive and physiological systems interact, is reflected in the treatment effects discussed in Part IV. Chapter 12, by Andrasik, Blanchard, and Edlund, discusses a purely physiological treatment, biofeedback. Shapiro (Chap. 13) describes the effects of a purely cognitive relaxation technique, meditation. The remaining two chapters describe treatments with both psychological and physiological components. Lavey and Taylor (Chap. 14) describe their work with progressive muscle relaxation. They stress that muscle relaxation in the absence of internal focusing and clearing the mind of other thoughts is not effective. Thus, their treatment combines both mental and muscular relaxation. Finally, Smith and Ascough (Chap. 15) close the book by describing a stress-management program that uses cognitive restructuring, teaching of coping skills, muscle relaxation, and induced-affect training. Induced affect refers to the process of increasing the emotional-physiological arousal to an imagined stressor and then actively coping, thereby decreasing, the arousal.

In addition to describing different types of cognitive and physiological treatments and their effects on similar disorders, these chapters show how applied research is done and how treatment protocols are modified in response to research results. Furthermore, they provide the interested practitioner with up-to-date information on four different treatments, and they encourage cross-treatment comparisons. Thus, the clinician can use these chapters as a reference when trying to find a treatment that best fits a client's needs. Smith and Ascough include a step-by-step description of their stress-management training program for the practitioner who is unfamiliar with stress management but interested in beginning work in it.

Each of the first three chapters in this part presents data comparing its featured treatment to other relaxation techniques. The conclusions in each chapter are similar: All relaxation-type treatments are more effective than control treatments and are roughly equivalent in efficacy. Depending on the target problem, one treatment may be preferable to another. Shapiro discusses in great detail the issue of how to choose a treatment strategy. He notes that somatic treatments are often more effective for somatic complaints, whereas cognitive treatments are preferred for complaints of anxiety and obsessiveness. Each chapter also discusses methodological problems in assessing treatment efficacy and proposes areas for further study. In general, each chapter supplements the others and provides an increased understanding of the parameters of each treatment's effectiveness.

Although Smith and Ascough's treatment is not a relaxation type like the previous three, it does have the same goals: to reduce stress-induced pathology and to improve coping skills. Because Smith and Ascough's treatment is less well known than the others, they describe it in great detail. By so doing, they encourage replication of their program and comparison of it to the other treatments. Because their treatment affects both psychological and physiological systems, it is an appropriate final chapter for the part. It integrates research results in both spheres, as discussed throughout the book, and it shows how theory can be tested in an applied setting. Formulating a treatment package based on research results is a major goal of stress research. Research on stress also has as its goal understanding the mechanisms and reactions to stress so as to improve the quality of life.

Thus, the book ends where it began: discussing cognitive–physiological inter-actions. But now, these principles are applied to treatment, and their utility is assessed. If integration of mind and body is the desired result—a biopsychosocial model as suggested at the beginning of the book—then a treatment that integrates these two systems should be preferred, and more effective, than one that focuses on only one system. To date, outcome literature is sparse and noncommittal on this issue. It may be hoped that this part will inspire people to consider implementation of these treatments and evaluation of their effectiveness. Then, in several years, we may know whether a diverse treatment package that includes treatment of many different systems is more effective than a single-system strategy.

# 12

# Physiological Responding during Biofeedback

*Frank Andrasik, Edward B. Blanchard, and S. Rebecca Edlund*
*State University of New York, Albany, United States*

Biofeedback is one of the major treatment technologies for stress-related disorders. Its use has been steadily increasing since the mid-1960s. This interest in biofeedback is reflected in the recent surge of scientific and lay articles and books devoted to the topic. Although there are many claims of clinical efficacy of biofeedback, researchers have frequently neglected certain critical aspects of methodology when investigating the treatment process and its physiological underpinnings. Consequently, the evidence firmly supporting biofeedback is weak in many areas of application. We discuss some of these problems in terms of treatment outcome and treatment process.

As is all too often the case, in the rush to provide treatment, many researchers have failed to incorporate appropriate control procedures to support their claims of successful treatment outcome. After nearly a decade of research, Shapiro and Surwit (1976) concluded in their review of the available literature that "there is not one well-controlled scientific study of the effectiveness of biofeedback and operant conditioning in treating a physiological disorder" (p. 113). Similar statements have been made by other critical reviewers (e.g., Alexander & Smith, 1979; Andrasik, Coleman, & Epstein, 1982; Blanchard & Epstein, 1977, 1978; Rice & Blanchard, 1982; Blanchard & Young, 1974; Miller & Dworkin, 1977). A common criticism voiced by these and other reviewers is that researchers have neglected to include controls for placebo responsivity, expectancy effects, and credibility differences. Early researchers were cognizant of these issues but chose to address them by using false or yoked feedback procedures as controls. Recently, however, researchers have begun to question the adequacy of this type of procedure (Alexander & Smith, 1979; Andrasik et al., 1982; Andrasik & Holroyd, 1980; Beaty & Haynes, 1979; Miller & Dworkin, 1977; Shapiro & Surwit, 1976). Research addressing this issue is slowly accruing, but at present, the data base is too limited to permit firm conclusions.

Although many of the therapies (e.g., cognitive therapy) used for stress-related and other disorders are quite difficult to analyze from a process perspective, biofeedback affords unique opportunities for performing such

Preparation of this chapter was supported in part by Grant NS-15235 from the National Institute of Neurological and Communicative Disorders and Stroke and by the Research Foundation of the State University of New York.

analyses. Unfortunately, just as researchers have ignored important controls for evaluating treatment outcome, so have they failed in most instances to examine the process of biofeedback. Although in this chapter we choose to make a distinction between treatment outcome and process, this distinction does not always hold in biofeedback. For example, one typical biofeedback treatment for essential hypertension involves direct feedback of systolic BP. Within this paradigm, questions of outcome and process would both be addressed by examining the same data set. For many other biofeedback treatments, such as the use of hand-temperature biofeedback for migraine headache, the assessment of outcome and process are distinct and would be approached from different perspectives. To assess outcome, the researcher could have subjects make regular recordings of their headache activity and compare the results of a group treated with biofeedback to those obtained from a group of subjects provided an equally credible but "nonactive" procedure. Investigations of treatment process would focus on the amount of control subjects were able to exert over their hand temperature and possibly on the collateral changes in other response systems as a function of the biofeedback training. As can be seen, there are two distinct focuses for research, each attempting to answer very different but equally important questions. In the ideal state, researchers would focus on both domains.

Unfortunately, in the existing treatment studies, such process analyses have been extremely rare, except in those instances where process and treatment are essentially one and the same. There is, however, an extensive body of research on the process of biofeedback, although nonclinical populations were used primarily. It is this body of research that we examine in our chapter. Before reviewing this literature it is necessary to delineate the factors we believe one needs to consider in evaluating the process of biofeedback.

## EVALUATING THE PROCESS

In all biofeedback treatment paradigms, ability to regulate physiological responding is assumed to be the chief mediator of treatment. Thus, the changes in physiological responding that occur during biofeedback must be examined in order to evaluate the process. Before we discuss *feedback control* of a response (i.e., the ability to alter a response in the presence of feedback), however, it seems appropriate to determine to what extent subjects have *instructional control* of the response, that is, the ability to alter the response before any biofeedback training. This potential phenomenon has been assessed in two ways, both of which are comparisons of instructional and feedback control. In the first method, within-subject comparisons are made of subjects' ability to show instructional control followed by tests of ability to show feedback control. In the second method, separate groups of subjects are asked to demonstrate either feedback control or instructional control.

The next important consideration in any area of biofeedback research is whether there is a true effect or a phenomenon to study. This is answered by determining whether there is a significant effect of feedback control over that obtainable through instructional control. In addition, because of cost-benefit considerations, it is important to determine if the effect produced by biofeedback is greater than the effect produced by alternative procedures, such as relaxation training. If not, one would have to begin to question the clinical utility of biofeedback for altering physiological responding.

The logical goal or end point of most biofeedback training in the clinical area, as noted by Epstein and Blanchard (1977), is for the subject to control the response in the absence of feedback. They termed this *self-control* and differentiated it from instructional control in that it is the degree of control available *after* biofeedback training. In one sense, the best evaluation of the utility of a biofeedback training regimen would be to compare self-control to instructional control.

Our review, in examining physiological responding during biofeedback, seeks to provide answers to the following questions: (1) Can subjects display significant effects from biofeedback over and above those obtained from mere instructions alone or from alternative, nonbiofeedback procedures? (2) Following training, can subjects demonstrate self-control of the relevant response? (3) And, finally, is the magnitude of these effects sufficient to be of clinical benefit? Our review is limited to three types of biofeedback that have been sufficiently well-investigated and that appear to have some clinical utility as techniques for coping with stress: HR, skin temperature (ST), and electromyographic (EMG) biofeedback. While our review draws most heavily on research studies with nonclinical populations, we have included research on clinical populations when possible.

## HR BIOFEEDBACK

Heart rate, or the number of times the heart contracts per unit of time, is not a fundamental property of the cardiovascular system. Rather, the fundamental temporal characteristic is the interbeat interval (IBI), or the length of time between two contractions. This is usually measured as time between R waves of the EKG. This parameter, IBI, is then converted into HR by taking its reciprocal. There are electronic devices that make this conversion automatically. Despite the fact that HR is not a fundamental property of the cardiovascular system, most biofeedback studies and psychophysiological studies describe HR and changes in it in response to varying conditions. We thus follow this convention.

Many factors affect HR in an unconditioned or reflexive manner. By and large, increases in HR are associated with "arousal," or the defense-alarm reaction, whereas decreases in HR are associated with quiescence. A fair number of the "control loops" for the heart are closed loops, for example, mild-to-vigorous exercise will result in varying increases in heart rate.

To some degree, however, HR is controlled, or at least influenced, by both branches of the ANS. Increased sympathetic firing leads to an increase in rate of beating as well as an increase in the strength of contractions. Increased parasympathetic firing tends to inhibit basal sympathetic activity and thus leads to a decrease in rate of beating. Inasmuch as the phasic, and perhaps tonic, levels of activity of these two branches of the ANS are thought to be partially under central control, a potential mechanism exists for "voluntary" control of HR.

As noted in several reviews of the biofeedback literature (Blanchard & Epstein, 1978; Williamson & Blanchard, 1979b), there has been a large volume of research devoted to elucidating the parameters of feedback control of HR. This is somewhat in contrast to the smaller volume of research devoted to the clinical applications of HR biofeedback. By and large the latter falls in two areas: use of HR biofeedback training to treat cardiac arrhythmias and use of HR biofeedback as an antianxiety treatment (Blanchard & Epstein, 1978).

## Instructional Control

Compared with an uninstructed, resting group of subjects, subjects instructed to increase HR showed a statistically reliable increase of about 5 bpm over eight 20-min sessions conducted on separate days (Blanchard, Young, Haynes, & Scott, 1975). In another study (Blanchard, Young, Scott, & Haynes, 1974), we showed that instructional control led to reliable increases in HR maintained over several sessions when compared with HR measured during relaxation in an uninstructed state. Bergman and Johnson (1971, 1972) and White, Holmes, and Bennett (1977) have also shown that for brief trials there is a reliable instructional-control effect for raising HR.

There have been no clear demonstrations of instructional control for HR lowering. White et al. (1977) found no differences in HR between subjects who received instructions to lower HR and those who sat quietly. This same failure was noted by Cuthbert and Lang (1976). Thus there is fairly good evidence that there is an instructional-control effect for HR increasing but not for HR slowing.

## Instructional Control Versus Biofeedback Control

Of some 26 studies that have assessed this issue, 20 (Bell & Schwartz, 1975; Bergman & Johnson, 1972; Blanchard, Scott, Young, & Edmundson, 1974; Blanchard, Scott, Young, & Haynes, 1974; Blanchard & Young, 1972; Blanchard, Young, Scott, & Haynes, 1974; Blankstein, Zimmerman, & Egner, 1976; Brener, 1974; Brener, Kleinman, & Goesling, 1969; Colgan, 1977; Dale, Anderson, & Spencer, 1980; Davidson & Schwartz, 1976; Johns, 1970; Lang & Twentyman, 1974, 1976; Ray, 1974; Stephens, Harris, Brady, & Shaffer, 1975; Wells, 1973; Whitehead, Drescher, Heiman, & Blackwell, 1977; Young & Blanchard, 1974) found significantly greater feedback control than instructional control of HR raising. Only 6 studies did not find this effect (Bergman & Johnson, 1971; Johnston, 1976; Lang, Troyer, Twentyman, & Gatchel, 1975; Levenson, 1976; Manuck, Levenson, Hendricksen, & Gryll, 1975; White et al., 1977). All but 1 of the latter studies (Lang et al., 1975) used only one or two training sessions, which may help account for the discrepancy. On the balance, the evidence seems to support the conclusion that a significant feedback-control effect for HR raising can be shown.

For HR lowering, the results are less clear-cut. Of 17 studies that investigated this phenomenon, 10 reported a failure to find a feedback-control effect greater than the instructional-control effect (Blanchard & Young, 1972; Cuthbert & Lang, 1976; Davidson & Schwartz, 1976; Holmes, Soloman, & Buchsbaum, 1979; Levenson, 1976; Manuck et al., 1975; Twentyman, Malloy, & Green, 1979; Wells, 1973; White et al., 1977; Young & Blanchard, 1974). Holmes, Frost, and Bennett (1977), in a very cleverly designed study, showed that length of adaptation period plays a major role in demonstration of a feedback-control effect for HR lowering. With a brief (3-min) adaptation period, HR lowering is relatively easy to show, whereas with a longer (20-min) adaptation period, it is very difficult to show the effect. Two studies compared instructional control and feedback control to simple instructions to relax (Cuthbert & Lang, 1976; Twentyman et al., 1979) and found no advantage in HR lowering for instructional control or feedback control over simple relaxation. In conclusion, it would seem there is a reliable feedback-control effect for HR increasing but not for HR decreasing.

## Magnitude of Effect

A conclusion drawn by Blanchard and Young's (1973) early review of this literature was that only small-magnitude changes in HR had been demonstrated. In a more recent review, Williamson and Blanchard (1979b) noted that at least 10 studies had reported average HR increases across all subjects of at least 10 bpm, with 5 studies reporting average increases of at least 15 bpm (Blanchard, Haynes, Young, & Scott, 1977; Blanchard, Young, Scott, & Haynes, 1974; Colgan, 1977; Gatchel, 1974, Experiment I; Obrist, Galosy, Lawler, Gaebelein, Howard, & Shanks, 1975). When individual subject data are reported, a wide range of abilities to increase HR is found. Stephens et al. (1975) reported that 22.5% of their sample showed increases of 20 bpm; Wells (1973) reported that 67% of his sample showed increases in HR of at least 15 bpm; seven of eight subjects in Blanchard, Young, Scott, and Haynes (1977) showed at least a 15-bpm increase.

Only five studies have reported group-average decreases in HR of more than 5 bpm (Bouchard & Granger, 1977; Colgan, 1977; Gatchel, 1976; Sirota, Schwartz, & Shapiro, 1974, 1976). In most of these, very short adaptation periods (see Holmes, Frost, & Bennett, 1977) were used. In examining studies of HR slowing for which individual subject data are available (Bell & Schwartz, 1975; Colgan, 1977; Stephens et al., 1975; Wells, 1973), only 1 subject of 81 total could lower HR by 10 bpm over the entire session. Moreover, Twentyman et al. (1979), using people with high resting HR, failed to show a significant feedback-control effect.

The present state of knowledge seems to be that some substantial proportion of subjects can produce sizable HR increases, but marked HR decreases are rare and probably only found in patients with tachycardia who are given extended training.

## Effects of Extended Training

Most of the early research on biofeedback and HR used relatively brief training regimens of one or two sessions. In the past few years, however, there have been at least 15 studies that used more than two training sessions. All but one of these (Manuck et al., 1975) found sizable HR increases and a trend for later sessions to show more of a feedback-control effect than earlier sessions. Lang (1974) has reported that the largest proportion of the total HR increase occurs in the first session; but in three studies for which individual subject data are available (Blanchard, Scott, & Young, 1974; Colgan, 1977; Wells, 1973), there is fairly clear evidence of continuing improvement throughout training regimens of up to 24 separate sessions.

For HR decreases, the picture is less clear. Colgan (1977) and Lang and Twentyman (1974) have reported continued improvement in HR lowering over repeated sessions, yet, Blanchard, Scott, Young, and Haynes (1974), McCanne and Sandman (1975), and Wells (1973) have not confirmed this effect. Most of the inconsistency may well be due to the generally poor results in feedback-assisted HR lowerings.

## Self-control

Evidence of ability to exert self-control over HR in excess of that displayed during instructional control would provide the most compelling support for the clinical utility of HR biofeedback. Unfortunately, data for such comparisons are relatively scarce. Four group studies (Bell & Schwartz, 1975; Colgan, 1977; Lang & Twentyman, 1974; Whitehead et al., 1977) and two multiple single-subject reports (Blanchard, Young, Scott, & Haynes, 1974; Wells, 1973) have included the conditions necessary for this evaluation. In three of the group studies (Colgan, 1977; Lang & Twentyman, 1974; Whitehead et al., 1977), there were clear indications of greater-magnitude changes in HR acceleration during self-control than during instructional control. In the studies reporting individual subject data, Wells (1973) found six of eight subjects had better self-control than instructional control of HR acceleration, whereas Blanchard, Young, Scott, and Haynes (1974) reported this finding in only two of six subjects. The one failure (Bell & Schwartz, 1975) used heart sounds as the feedback stimulus, which, as noted earlier, is not as effective as other forms of feedback.

For HR lowering, three studies (Bell & Schwartz, 1975; Colgan, 1977; Lang & Twentyman, 1974) found better self-control than instructional control, whereas two other studies (Wells, 1973; Whitehead et al., 1977) did not. Given the overall unreliability of demonstrations of feedback control of HR lowering, the finding of inconsistency in self-control of HR lowering is not surprising.

A final feature of self-control that has received little attention is the durability of self-control (i.e., how long the effect remains). Three studies that evaluated self-control over multiple sessions (Blanchard, Young, Scott, & Haynes, 1974; Colgan, 1977; Whitehead et al., 1977) found decreasing ability to achieve self-control over HR over repeated assessments. Obviously, one area in need of research is the development of strategies for maintaining self-control after cessation of biofeedback training.

## Maintenance of Self-control

Three strategies for achieving maintenance of self-control have been empirically tested. Blanchard, Haynes, Young, and Scott (1977) used a stimulus-control procedure to assist subjects who had shown good (at least 15-bpm change) feedback control of HR increasing in the laboratory, to maintain this ability in the absence of feedback. For six of eight subjects, this was successful, and self-control was maintained for up to 12 sessions. In four cases, self-control was demonstrated outside of the laboratory. In two cases, a second strategy was added to the basic stimulus-control package. This strategy consisted of "booster" feedback-control training sessions that were included as needed. The idea of regular, periodic booster training sessions has not been studied systematically. Finally, a different strategy has been successfully demonstrated in a patient population by Weiss and Engel (1971). In their study, feedback was faded out of the feedback training trails for gradually longer intervals. This procedure has also not been studied systematically. In fact, a major area in need of research is the effect of most of the parameters described above for feedback control on self-control over time.

## Conclusions

At this point a fair amount is known about various parameters that affect the feedback control of HR acceleration; moreover, relatively large-scale increases, of the order of 20% to 30% of resting HR, are routinely obtainable. There is also a model that accounts for many of these results, the so-called motor-skills model of Engel (1974) and Lang (1974).

The picture is unclear for HR deceleration. In fact, it is not clear that one can achieve HR deceleration in excess of that obtained by merely having subjects rest quietly. The magnitude of change is usually less than 10% of resting HR.

Future research should certainly focus on three areas: (1) the effects of various feedback training parameters on self-control, (2) the continued exploration of methods to acquire and maintain self-control, and (3) the development of reliable strategies for obtaining HR deceleration under feedback control.

## ST BIOFEEDBACK

Feedback from peripheral skin sites chiefly owes its clinial application to work stemming from the Menninger Clinic, where it was observed in one subject that recovery from a migraine attack was accompanied by a rapid, large-scale increase in hand temperature (Sargent, Green, & Walters, 1973). This serendipitous finding quickly led to the study and application of temperature biofeedback as a migraine treatment, the efficacy of which has since been replicated by a number of different research teams (e.g., Blanchard, Theobald, Williamson, Silver, & Brown, 1978; Mitch, McGrady, & Iannone, 1976; Turin & Johnson, 1976). Temperature biofeedback has been attempted with a number of different problems, including Raynaud's disease (Blanchard & Haynes, 1975; Surwit, 1973) and chronic pain from causalgia (Blanchard, 1979) or burns (Bird & Colborne, 1980).

The procedure developed by the Menninger group and subsequently adopted by others involves the simultaneous application of temperature biofeedback and autogenic training, resulting in autogenic feedback therapy. Autogenic training, developed by Schultz and Luthe (1969), uses passive concentration on phrases whose semantic content embodies heaviness and warmth in order to facilitate relaxation. Thermal imagery is frequently incorporated into the training as well. In the initial applications, temperature monitoring was accomplished from two different sites (e.g., right hand and left hand or hand and forehead), with subjects being instructed to raise or lower the temperature differentially from one site relative to the other. Subsequent applications have increasingly focused on temperature regulation from a single site, typically the hand or finger. To the basic paradigm of temperature feedback and autogenic training, others have added additional components (e.g., incentives, positive expectancies, graphed performance data, etc.) in an attempt to maximize training effects. In our review here, we attempt to partial out these various factors so that we can carefully examine the independent contributions of the various components.

In their writings, the Menninger group speculated that hand warming was effective with patients because it enabled them to "turn off" excessive sympathetic outflow and thus interrupt the vasomotor cycle of migraine. This account assumes a high degree of correspondence between peripheral blood flow, autonomic activity, and surface temperature. Although factors such as fluctuations in the temperature gradient between the recording site and the body core underlying the recording site and experimental or recording error resulting from laboratory environmental factors, sensor placement, and the buildup of heat in the thermistor and conductive leads (King & Montgomery, 1980) affect this relationship, preliminary findings have validated the notion that hand temperature warming leads to reduced sympathetic outflow (Sovack, Kunzel, Sternbach, & Dalessio, 1978).

## Magnitude of Effect during Varied Experimental Conditions

In the subsections that follow, we review the literature that has addressed the extent to which subjects can exert control over finger or hand temperature in varied experimental conditions. Even though data have been reported in both centigrade and Fahrenheit temperature units in the research articles, we have converted all temperature values given in centigrade to Fahrenheit to facilitate comparisons. Also, in instances where specific figures have not been provided, we have attempted to estimate amount of change by extrapolation from tables or figures. Finally, because basal temperatures do change from session to session, we have calculated amount of change for within, rather than between, sessions in cases where researchers have not done so.

*Instructional control.* Several groups of researchers have examined subjects' abilities to raise temperature under instructions to do so. All have reported subjects being unable to exhibit any marked, consistent increases in response to these instructions (Keefe, 1978; King & Montgomery, 1981—Experiment I, in press; Experiments I and II; Stoffer, Jensen, & Nesset, 1979). Four additional studies have examined changes in temperature as a function of sitting quietly or relaxing for extended periods of time in the absence of instructions to change temperature. Again, all four showed no significant effects (Keefe, 1978; Largen, Mathew, Dobbins, Meyer, & Claghorn, 1978; Mathew, Largen, Dobbins, Meyer, Sakai, & Claghorn, 1980; Ohno, Tanaka, Takeya, & Ikemi, 1977). Changes as a function of noncontingent temperature feedback have been examined in four studies. Three of the four investigations found that the provision of nonveridical feedback, either in the presence or in the absence of instructions to increase, also resulted in minimal changes in temperature (King & Montgomery, in press, Experiments I and II; Ohno et al., 1977). The fourth study, however, found that subjects given false feedback and instructed to raise temperature produced a small degree of change, $0.9°$ F (Stoffer et al., 1979). We could find no studies examining subjects' abilities to lower hand or finger temperature in response to instructions to do so. Thus, with one exception, the literature reveals that mere instructions, alone or in combination with other "control" procedures, are insufficient to produce meaningful increases in hand temperature.

*Feedback control.* Many investigators have sought to determine the degree to which subjects can exert feedback control over hand or finger temperature. Single-case reports and investigations performed with highly selected subjects have shown remarkable abilities to regulate hand or finger temperature during biofeedback alone or in combination with hypnosis, relaxation, or autogenic training. For example, one burn patient was able to increase his hand temperature an astounding $21°$ F during biofeedback, with minimal loss of regulation ability once the feedback was removed (Bird & Colborne, 1980). Increases of approximately $10°$ F have been reported for Raynaud patients (Surwit, 1973). Highly selected nonpatients have also displayed similarly robust abilities to regulate hand temperature by 10°-14° F in both upward and downward directions during feedback (Taub & Emurian, 1976; Willerman, Skeen, & Simpson, 1976).

*Group studies.* In this section we review the evidence for magnitude of feedback control displayed in group studies, which are presumably more representative of the changes that can be expected under typical training conditions.

There have been 13 investigations that have studied subjects' abilities to increase hand temperature during *feedback alone* (with or without the use of mental imagery). Of these, 4 found mean increases to be quite small, ranging from 0.5° to 1.0° F (King & Montgomery, in press, Experiments I and II; Ohno et al., 1977; Stoffer et al., 1979). Of the remaining 9 studies, 4 found increases ranging from 1.0° to 2.0° F (Keefe, 1975, 1978; O'Connell, Frerker, & Ross, 1979; Turin & Johnson, 1976), and 5 found larger changes ranging from 2.0° to 3.1° F (Keefe & Gardner, 1979, Experiments I and II; Largen et al., 1978; Mathew et al., 1980; Taub & Emurian, 1976).

Results from the limited investigations of abilities to lower temperature during feedback alone are slightly more consistent. Four studies found mean temperature reductions ranging from 0.7° to 2.0° F (Keefe, 1975; Largen et al., 1978; Mathew et al., 1980; Ohno et al., 1977). Two additional studies investigating feedback control of temperature decreases revealed decreases of 2.6° F (Taub & Emurian, 1976) and 2.9° F (Keefe & Gardner, 1979, Experiment II).

These studies indicate that, during feedback, subjects can increase or decrease peripheral temperature in modest amounts. A central concern in applications of biofeedback is safeguarding against somatic mediation of change. Most of these studies have acknowledged this concern and have attempted to minimize the chances of somatic mediational factors producing temperature changes artifactually. Taub (1977; Taub & Emurian, 1976) has investigated this issue systematically (as well as possible effects of cheating and other sources of confounding) and has, in all instances, found minimal-to-no effects of somatic activities (e.g., altered respiration, tensing and contracting of muscles, etc.).

One set of investigators (King & Montgomery; 1981, in press) has more directly tested for effects of somatic mediation in a series of four studies. Basically, King and Montgomery's findings indicate that when firm controls are used to minimize or neutralize somatic maneuvering, subjects are unable to produce meaningful increases during temperature feedback; results were 0.5° F and −0.3°F (King & Montgomery, in press, Experiment I) and 0.8° F (King & Montgomery, in press, Experiment II). In another series of studies, three groups of subjects were instructed to employ various somatic maneuvers during biofeedback. One group showed minimal increases (1.0° F) (King & Montgomery, 1981, Experiment I) but the other two displayed relatively large-scale increases—3.1° F (King & Montgomery, 1981, Experiment I) and 5.2° F (King & Montgomery, in press, Experiment II)—surpassing those found in the studies previously reviewed. King and Montgomery (1981) also examined the effects obtained when temperature feedback and somatic maneuvers are used to decrease temperature and found this procedure produced changes consistent with those of the previously reviewed studies—2.6° F (Experiment II).

Taken together, these results indicate that subjects can regulate hand or finger temperature when provided feedback alone, but only in a modest fashion. The largest temperature increase has been reported by King and Montgomery (in press), who attributed the increase primarily to somatic mediation. Only future research can determine whether this indeed accounts for the effects or whether the effects are attributable to some other sources (e.g., subject selection, method variance, etc.).

Given the history and development of temperature biofeedback it is also instructive to review findings from studies that have examined changes in hand temperature as a function of temperature feedback alone, *autogenic training*, or the two combined (i.e., autogenic feedback). Only one study has directly compared all three procedures and found them to produce modest increases of similar magnitude, ranging from 1.7° to 2.0° F (Keefe, 1978). These three procedures were in turn found to be superior to the varying-control conditions previously presented. Because the autogenic training component in this study was modified somewhat, it may be argued, however, that this test was inadequate. A second investigation compared autogenic training and autogenic feedback with Raynaud's patients and, contrary to expectations, found mean temperatures for both groups actually decreased over trials (Surwit & Fenton, 1980). Subjects provided with autogenic feedback displayed less of a decrement (−0.9° F), however, than subjects provided with autogenic training alone (−2.9° F). The remaining investigator to use autogenic feedback found a temperature increase of 8.0° F (Leeb, Fahrion, & French, 1976). The Leeb et al. results were based on change scores calculated from base line during all sessions to the end of training, and thus, this data is not directly comparable to the previous studies where we have been able to report changes in terms of mean within-session changes.

Results from these very limited studies are equivocal and indicate that additional comparative investigations are warranted. There is a hint that the combination of temperature feedback and autogenic training may produce larger and more consistent effects, but this remains unconfirmed.

Three investigative teams have examined changes that occur as a function of *differential feedback.* Roberts, Kewman, and MacDonald (1973) found that subjects provided with right-hand–left-hand temperature feedback combined with autogenic phrases and hypnotic induction were able to achieve a temperature difference of 2.5° F. A subsequent investigation (Roberts, Schuler, Bacon, Zimmerman, & Patterson, 1975) found that omission of hypnotic induction did not appreciably affect subjects' abilities to maintain a temperature difference between the two sites. In fact, a larger temperature differential was achieved in this study, on the order of approximately 5.0° F. In another study, Keefe (1975) found an increase of 1.9° F and a decrease of 1.5° F during differential (hand-forehead) temperature feedback alone (in the absence of autogenic training or other relaxation strategies). Thus, results from the differential-feedback studies are consistent with results from studies using single feedback sites.

*Effects of extended training.* In the studies reviewed, the number of training sessions varied from a low of 1 to a high of 20. Results from early clinical interventions led some investigators to recommend the use of extensive trials to achieve maximum clinical effectiveness (e.g., Sargent et al., 1973). Taub and Emurian (1976), after carefully examining the individual performance of each of 21 subjects during four to six sessions, reported 33% of the subjects showed continued improvement across sessions, 43% displayed abrupt initial changes that tended to remain stable throughout the remainder of training, and the remaining

24% evidenced either ambiguous or nonapparent learning. Two subjects selected on the basis of pronounced initial abilities to regulate hand temperature exhibited continued improvement through several additional training sessions. Taken together, these findings suggest there may be some value in increased frequencies of training sessions.

We could find only one study that has specifically addressed this issue in a controlled fashion. Keefe and Gardner (1979, Experiment II) administered 20 sessions of temperature biofeedback for raising hand temperature (in the absence of autogenic or thermal instructions) to six subjects. Significant increases in hand temperature first occurred in Session 3. Subjects continued to raise their hand temperatures during the remaining 17 sessions, but the size of the increases was no greater than that achieved in Session 3. Unfortunately, ability to regulate hand temperature in the absence of feedback was not assessed. It may be that increased training sessions are needed to affect regulation abilities markedly in the absence of feedback.

*Self-control.* Only two research teams have investigated abilities to increase or decrease temperature during self-control periods. King and Montgomery found that subjects provided temperature feedback alone, but instructed to refrain from somatic maneuvers, produced only small increases in temperature (1.1° F and 0.8° F, in press, Experiments I and II, respectively), whereas subjects given feedback coupled with instructions to employ somatic manipulations displayed increased self-control abilities (3.5° F and 1.6° F, 1981, Experiments I and II, respectively, and 4.4° F, in press, Experiment I). Stoffer et al. (1979) found subjects could produce a mean temperature increase of only 0.7° F following feedback alone. The only investigation to examine abilities to self-control temperature decreases found that subjects provided with feedback combined with somatic maneuvers were able to produce only small-scale decreases (−1.1° F) (King & Montgomery, 1981, Experiment II). The limited available data indicate that performance during self-control periods is modest and quite variable. More important, no studies have shown that subjects can self-control temperature in the absence of specific instructions to engage in somatic manipulations.

## Conclusions

Results from a wide range of studies reveal that subjects are able to exert modest control over skin temperature as a function of biofeedback alone and that the magnitude of change is superior to that produced by instructions alone. Thus, biofeedback does produce some effect. How the effects obtained from biofeedback compare to those obtained from autogenic feedback or autogenic training is unknown at present. The limited data suggest that the initially promising regulation abilities displayed by Raynaud's disease patients in case studies do not hold up to group scrutiny. The findings of King and Montgomery (1981, in press) raise anew the "mediation controversy." The mediation issue remains central because of its very important implications for clinical practice. If a significant portion of the temperature effect is indeed found to be due to somatic maneuvers, then the presumed mechanism of therapeutic change, alterations in sympathetic activity, will be unsupported. Last, additional research is needed to assess self-control abilities and the parameters affecting their acquisition and maintenance.

# EMG BIOFEEDBACK

Electromyographic biofeedback is rapidly becoming accepted as a therapeutic tool for the treatment of problems caused by or associated with excessive muscular tension, such as muscle-contraction headache (e.g., Budzynski, Stoyva, & Adler, 1970), chronic anxiety (e.g., Townsend, House, & Addario, 1975), and spastic movement or torticolis (e.g., Amato, Hermsmeyer, & Kleinman, 1973), as well as problems of decreased muscle activity from muscle damage or disuse (e.g., Andrews, 1964). Our review in this section is limited to those studies that have used EMG feedback to produce a state of relaxation, which is the most typical use of EMG biofeedback. When used in this manner, feedback is generally provided from forehead or frontal electrode placements with subjects being instructed to lower the tension levels in the monitored muscles. The typical application combines home practice in relaxation with EMG biofeedback to augment training effects.

Electromyographic biofeedback training of this type has been claimed to produce a generalized deep-muscle relaxation response (Budzynski & Stoyva, 1972; Stoyva & Budzynski, 1974). To test this assumption, researchers have collected, from subjects receiving frontal EMG biofeedback, other measures indicative or relaxation, such as changes in muscle-tension levels in other muscle groups, changes in other physiological response systems, and self-reports of overall relaxation. DeGood and Chisholm (1977) found EMG biofeedback did produce a consistent pattern of lowered arousal as measured by heart and respiratory rate and by EEG and EMG activity levels. They caution against oversimplification of their results, however, because fingertip vasoconstriction, indicative of increased arousal, occurred during training.

The majority of research investigations, however, have found minimal-to-no support for the notion of EMG biofeedback producing a state of "cultivated low arousal" (Surwit & Keefe, 1978). For example, Alexander, White, and Wallace (1977) found no evidence for a general relaxation response accompanying EMG training as assessed by changes in heart and respiration rates, ST, and skin conductance, and subjective ratings of relaxation. Furthermore, three researchers testing for generalization of effects to other muscles as a function of EMG biofeedback have found no consistent significant effects (Alexander, 1975; Freedman, 1976; Shedivy & Kleinman, 1977). There is one study that has provided subjects with frontal feedback in order to *increase* frontal muscle tension as a control procedure in a treatment-outcome investigation (Andrasik & Holroyd, 1980). Surprisingly, subjects exposed to this condition displayed significant clinical improvement and reported attendant feelings of decreased tension. Thus, firm support is lacking for the notion that frontal EMG feedback produces a cultivated low-arousal response.

## Instructional Control Versus Biofeedback Control

The issue of the relative efficacy of instructional and biofeedback control has been addressed in 18 studies conducted with nonclinical populations. Instructional control of the EMG response has been assessed through varying types of conditions, which fall into five basic approaches: (1) no instructions to relax (resting control-group procedure), (2) general instructions to relax, (3) specific instructions to relax, (4) Jacobsen or Wolpe relaxation training, and (5) noncontingent feedback. Nielson and Holmes (1980), who included an uninstructed, resting control group, found no treatment effect for this group, nor for the remaining groups under investigation (biofeedback, general relaxation instructions, or attention-placebo).

Of the 18 studies, 4 employed some type of generalized instructions to relax. Of these, 3 (Carlson, 1980; Carlson & Feld, 1978; Freedman & Glares, 1979) found biofeedback significantly more effective in reducing EMG. Schandler and Grings (1976) found biofeedback and progressive relaxation more effective than generalized instructions to relax.

Of 6 studies (Alexander, 1975; Alexander, French, & Goodman, 1975; Alexander, White, & Wallace, 1977; Edwards & Murphy, 1980; Gersten & Pope, 1976; Kinsman, O'Banion, Robinson, & Staudenmayer, 1975) that provided more specific instructions to subjects by informing them to relax their entire bodies, devoting specific attention to facial and forehead muscles, only Alexander, White, and Wallace (1977) failed to find a significant effect for biofeedback.

Reinking and Kohl (1975) found that biofeedback produced lower EMG levels than Jacobson or Wolpe relaxation training focused on facial relaxation (specific instructions), and both were in turn more effective than general instructional control.

Of the 6 studies employing noncontingent feedback as a control for the instructional effect of feedback, 4 found biofeedback more effective (Gatchel, Korman, Weis, Smith, & Clarke, 1978; Le Boeuf, 1980; Wickramasekera, 1973; Zeisig & Simkims, 1976). Haynes, Moseley, and McGowan (1975) found both biofeedback and Wolpe-type relaxation training more effective than Jacobsontype relaxation training, noncontingent feedback, and an instructed general relaxation group. Yock (1978) found no differences among feedback, noncontingent feedback, and instructional self-relaxation.

Thus, 15 of the 18 studies reviewed support the efficacy of biofeedback control compared with an instructional-control procedure. There is some evidence, however, supporting a claim for equally significant effects of relaxation procedures such as progressive relaxation.

A number of the studies that employed frontal EMG as a treatment for muscle-contraction headache also reported data on changes in EMG level during treatment. Four of these studies compared EMG feedback to false- or pseudofeedback procedures and found contingent feedback procedures superior in all instances (Andrasik & Holroyd, 1980; Budzynski, Stoyva, Adler, & Mullaney, 1973; Kondo & Canter, 1977; Philips, 1977). Biofeedback has also been found superior to a pseudo-meditation procedure in reducing muscle activity (Holroyd, Andrasik, & Noble, 1980). Another study compared EMG feedback to a stress-coping procedure as a treatment for headache. The EMG procedure used in this study produced significant reductions in muscle-tension level, but the stress-coping procedure did not (Holroyd, Andrasik, & Westbrook, 1977). Finally, three studies compared EMG feedback to varying forms of relaxation training and, in all instances, found that both procedures produced significant reductions of similar magnitude in EMG level (Cox, Freundlich, & Meyer, 1975; Gray, Lyle, McGuire, & Peck, 1980; Hutchings & Reinking, 1976).

In all but two of these treatment studies, EMG biofeedback was used in conjunction with home relaxation training, making it impossible to identify the independent contributions of biofeedback and relaxation. The two studies that omitted home relaxation practice did find equivalent effects, however (Andrasik & Holroyd, 1980; Kondo & Canter, 1977).

Thus, subjects provided with EMG biofeedback are capable of producing reductions in muscle activity superior to those obtained by subjects instructed to relax, provided with noncontingent feedback, or trained in pseudo meditation or stress coping. But various forms of relaxation training have been shown, in a number of studies, to produce effects equivalent to those obtainable by biofeedback.

## Magnitude of Effect

Most clinical applications of EMG feedback have concentrated on the psycho-physiological disorders associated with high muscle-tension levels. Hence, magnitude of decrease has most often been the dependent variable of interest. The majority of the studies have concentrated on the comparison of EMG bio-feedback training to control groups. In these studies, results are most often tested on the basis of significant differences between groups, ignoring the issue of what amount of change is clinically significant. In this section, percentage of change in EMG, from base line to posttreatment, has been calculated for all studies that have presented absolute values of EMG levels.

Kondo, Canter, and Bean (1977), in studying the effects of intersession intervals of EMG control, found that short intervals resulted in the largest drops in EMG (on the order of 70%), whereas long intersession intervals produced reductions of about 25%. Three studies showed reductions of about 45%: Haynes et al. (1975) with normal subjects, Le Boeuf (1977) with anxious introverts and extroverts, and Le Boeuf (1980) with subjects with elevated muscle-tension levels. DeGood and Chisholm (1977) had normal subjects both increase and decrease muscle-tension levels. The EMG-down group decreased about 80%, and the EMG-up group increased about 150%.

There have been 12 studies conducted with headache patients and reporting a significant magnitude of change in EMG levels during feedback. In every instance, mean decreases were sizable, ranging from a low of approximately 40% of base line to a high of approximately 75% of base line (Andrasik & Holroyd, 1980; Borgeat, Hade, Larouche, & Bedwani, 1980; Bruhn, Olesen, & Melgaard, 1979; Budzynski, Stoyva, Adler, & Mullaney, 1973; Cox, Freundlich, & Meyer, 1975; Epstein & Abel, 1977; Gray et al., 1980; Holroyd, Andrasik, & Noble, 1980; Holroyd, Andrasik, & Westbrook, 1977; Hutchings & Reinking, 1976; Kondo & Canter, 1977; Philips, 1977).

Results, thus, are quite uniform and clearly indicate various subject populations can produce large-scale reductions in frontal EMG during biofeedback training.

## Effects of Extended Training

EMG biofeedback training has varied in number of sessions from 1 (e.g., Gersten & Pope, 1978) to 32 (Masi, Moore, & Weston, 1976). Although Caronite (1972) postulates that overlearning may be the crucial factor in retention, little research has systematically investigated the effects of length of training.

Two studies examined the effects of length of training in order to aid clinicians in planning a course of treatment and to minimize extinction of the acquired response. Le Boeuf and Hurrell (1975), who employed five feedback sessions, reported rapid extinction assessed at 2 and 7 days posttreatment. Pairing verbal stimuli with low EMG levels did not significantly increase resistance to extinction, whereas fading out feedback over trials, either by the experimenter or the subject, increased resistance to extinction at the 2-day assessment only.

DeGood, Klaus, Tennenbaum, and Greenwald (1978) investigated the effects of 4, 8, or 12 weekly EMG feedback sessions with 1- and 3-month follow-up sessions for adults with mild, but chronic, stress-related physiological symptoms. Although only modest changes in EMG level occurred beyond the fourth session, at both the 1-month and 3-month follow-ups, the 8- and 12-session groups appeared to be more effective in maintaining EMG self-regulation abilities. DeGood et al. concluded that 8 sessions appeared to be the optimal number in terms of response control, time, and money for the patient population employed in their study.

Cox, Klee, and Meyer (1976) reported that approximately 75% of the total amount of EMG reduction in their study was obtained by the end of the second session. It is of interest to note that similar findings were reported for relaxation training.

On the basis of these limited investigations, it appears that, whereas only limited training is necessary for response acquisition (from 2 to 4 sessions), additional sessions are necessary to produce durable effects. Although the exact number of sessions needed is undetermined, the preliminary data suggest 8 to 12 sessions may be adequate with most people.

## Self-control

Despite the large number of experimental investigations of EMG biofeedback, there are only a limited number of studies that have assessed subjects' self-control abilities. Of the seven studies directly assessing this, all but one found that reductions displayed during self-control periods were similar in magnitude to those obtained during feedback periods (Andrasik & Holroyd, 1980; Budzynski, Stoyva, Adler, & Mullaney, 1973; Carlson, 1980; Carlson & Feld, 1978; Holroyd, Andrasik, & Noble, 1980; Holroyd, Andrasik, & Westbrook, 1977). The remaining study (Epstein & Abel, 1977) found that none of six headache subjects could produce decreases in the absence of feedback, even though five subjects had been able to produce significant decreases during feedback.

Two of the above seven studies selected subjects on the basis of displaying high initial frontal-EMG levels. Of these two studies, Budzynski, Stoyva, Adler, and Mullaney's (1973) subjects could display abilities to self-control EMG, whereas Epstein and Abel's (1977) could not. Thus, elevated basal muscle-tension levels appeared to serve as a limiting factor in one of the two studies. To determine the generality of this finding, future research is needed.

## Conclusions

On the basis of the reviewed studies, we conclude that most subjects can indeed display pronounced abilities to decrease frontal EMG both with and without feedback after a modest number of training sessions. There is some suggestion, however, that subjects with elevated initial EMG levels may have difficulty acquiring the ability to decrease frontal-EMG levels.

The evidence from the EMG biofeedback research as a whole suggests that biofeedback is indeed effective as a training technique in learned EMG control. These demonstrations of training effectiveness do not, however, delve into the issue of the mechanism of treatment. Future research is needed to determine how EMG control mediates the relief and control of muscle-tension disorders such as tension headaches.

## OVERALL CONCLUSIONS

For two of the three biofeedback approaches under review, results are somewhat disappointing: Whereas subjects can increase HR to a sizable degree during biofeedback, it is questionable whether they can reliably decrease it in excess of the level obtainable from mere instructions alone. Subjects can regulate temperature during biofeedback, but the magnitude is quite modest (from $1.0°$ to $3.0°$ F) and no different from that obtained by alternative relaxation procedures. Although evidence is more clear that subjects can produce sizable reductions in frontal-EMG levels during biofeedback, it is unclear how this mediates clinical outcome and, as with temperature biofeedback, alternative procedures have been shown to produce similar size reductions in frontal EMG. These findings echo those of Silver and Blanchard (1978) and raise questions about the utility of biofeedback for affecting change in physiological functioning.

Evidence for self-control of HR and temperature is similarly disappointing, owing in part to a lack of research attention. Studies have shown subjects able to self-regulate EMG to a meaningful degree in the laboratory; but in virtually all instances, assessments of self-control abilities have been conducted in the relaxed laboratory environment. While demonstration of self-control of physiology in the laboratory seems to use to be a minimum condition for providing support for the utility of biofeedback, it is by no means sufficient. Although it is a difficult criterion to meet, research must demonstrate that subjects can retain self-control abilities in the presence of demanding life situations or circumstances or in the presence of meaningful simulations of these circumstances. Researchers are beginning to address this issue in the realms of EMG biofeedback (Gatchel et al., 1978; Nielson & Holmes, 1980) and temperature training (Stoffer et al., 1979; Taub & Emurian, 1976). Such investigations are sorely needed.

Research needs to advance on several additional fronts as well, the first being to determine ways to optimize biofeedback training effects. Considerable research has already been conducted on this topic in the area of HR feedback (see Williamson & Blanchard, 1979b), with research indicating, for example, increased effects of analogue-visual versus binary-feedback displays (e.g., Blanchard, Scott, Young, & Haynes, 1974; Colgan, 1977; Lang & Twentyman, 1974), immediate versus delayed feedback (e.g., Gatchel, 1974; Williamson & Blanchard, 1979a), and incentives versus no incentives (e.g., Lang & Twentyman, 1976). In EMG biofeedback, one of the more consistent findings is an increased magnitude of effect for short rather than long intersession intervals (Gersten & Pope, 1978; Kondo et al., 1977). Less is known about critical parameters of temperature training. Researchers have suggested, however, that positive experimenter expectancies affect results (Leeb et al., 1976; Taub, 1977; Taub & Emurian, 1976).

A second neglected research area concerns factors affecting acquisition and maintenance of self-control. In HR biofeedback, we described some initial approaches for accomplishing this, which include stimulus-control procedures, with and without booster sessions (Blanchard, Haynes, Young, & Scott, 1977) and fading of biofeedback (Weiss & Engel, 1971). Lynn and Freedman (1979) suggested some additional procedures that may be useful in this respect. These include training under stressful or stimulating conditions, varying the stimuli associated with training (e.g., therapists, settings, distractions, etc.), and using other behavioral procedures to augment effects (e.g., stress-inoculation training). The utility of these procedures awaits further research.

Epstein and Blanchard (1977) stated that for subjects to self-regulate their physiological responding, they need to be able to discriminate when to do so. The importance of this is aptly demonstrated by a case report by Gainer (1978) in which a migraine client learned to warm her hands reliably in the presence of feedback but saw no change in headache activity until discrimination training was instituted. We found in our review minimal assessment of abilities to discriminate level of physiological responding. Such assessments need to be attempted in the future to provide increased support for the utility of biofeedback as a means for coping with stress.

# REFERENCES

Alexander, A. B. An experimental test of assumptions relating to the use of electromyographic biofeedback as a general relaxation technique. *Psychophysiology*, 1975, *12*, 656–662.

Alexander, A. B., French, C. A., & Goodman, N. J. A comparison of auditory and visual feedback in biofeedback assisted muscular relaxation training. *Psychophysiology*, 1975, *12*, 119–123.

Alexander, A. B., & Smith, D. D. Clinical applications of electromyographic biofeedback. In R. J. Gatchel & K. Price (Eds.), *Clinical applications of biofeedback: Appraisal and status.* Elmsford, N.Y.: Pergamon, 1979.

Alexander, A. B., White, P. D., & Wallace, H. M. Training and transfer of training effects in EMG biofeedback assisted muscular relaxation. *Psychophysiology*, 1977, *14*, 551–559.

Amato, A., Hermsmeyer, C. A., & Kleinman, K. M. Use of electromyographic feedback to increase inhibitory control of spastic muscles. *Physical Therapy*, 1973, *53*, 1063–1066.

Andrasik, F., Coleman, D., & Epstein, L. H. Biofeedback: Clinical and research considerations. In D. M. Doleys, R. L. Meredith, & A. R. Ciminero (Eds.), *Behavioral psychology in medicine: Assessment and treatment strategies.* New York: Plenum, 1982.

Andrasik, F., & Holroyd, K. A. A test of specific and nonspecific effects in the biofeedback treatment of tension headache. *Journal of Consulting and Clinical Psychology*, 1980, *48*, 575–586.

Andrews, J. M. Neuromuscular re-education of the hemiplegic with the aid of the electromyograph. *Archives of Physical Medicine and Rehabilitation*, 1964, *45*, 530–532.

Beaty, E. T., & Haynes, S. N. Behavioral intervention with muscle contraction headache: A review. *Psychosomatic Medicine*, 1979, *41*, 165–180.

Bell, I. R., & Schwartz, G. E. Voluntary control and reactivity of human heart rate. *Psychophysiology*, 1975, *12*, 339–348.

Bergman, J. S., & Johnson, H. J. The effects of instructional set and autonomic perception on cardiac control. *Psychophysiology*, 1971, *8*, 180–190.

Bergman, J. S., & Johnson, H. J. Sources of information which affect training and raising of heart rate. *Psychophysiology*, 1972, *9*, 30–39.

Bird, E. I., & Colborne, G. R. Rehabilitation of an electrical burn patient through thermal biofeedback. *Biofeedback and Self-regulation*, 1980, *5*, 283–288.

Blanchard, E. B. The use of temperature biofeedback in the treatment of chronic pain due to causalgia. *Biofeedback and Self-regulation*, 1979, *4*, 183–188.

Blanchard, E. G., & Epstein, L. H. Clinical applications of biofeedback. In M. Hersen, R. M. Eisler, & P. M. Miller (Eds.), *Progress in behavior modification* (Vol. 4). New York: Academic, 1977.

Blanchard, E. B., & Epstein, L. H. *A biofeedback primer.* Reading, Mass.: Addison-Wesley, 1978.

Blanchard, E. B., & Haynes, M. R. Biofeedback treatment of a case of Raynaud's disease. *Journal of Behavior Therapy and Experimental Psychiatry,* 1975, *6,* 230–234.

Blanchard, E. B., Haynes, M. R., Young, L. D., & Scott, R. W. The use of feedback training and a stimulus control procedure to obtain large magnitude increases in heart rate outside of the laboratory. *Biofeedback and Self-regulation,* 1977, *2,* 81–91.

Blanchard, E. B., Scott, R. W., Young, L. D., & Edmundson, E. D. Effect of knowledge of response on the self-control of heart rate. *Psychophysiology,* 1974, *11,* 251–264.

Blanchard, E. B., Scott, R. W., Young, L. D., & Haynes, M. R. The effects of feedback signal information content on the long-term self-control of heart rate. *Journal of General Psychology,* 1974, *91,* 175–187.

Blanchard, E. B., Theobald, D. E., Williamson, D. A., Silver, B. V., & Brown, D. A. Temperature biofeedback in the treatment of migraine headaches. *Archives of General Psychiatry,* 1978, *35,* 581–588.

Blanchard, E. G., & Young, L. D. The relative efficacy of visual and auditory feedback for self-control of heart rate. *Journal of General Psychology,* 1972, *87,* 195–202.

Blanchard, E. B., & Young, L. D. Self-control of cardiac functioning: A promise as yet unfulfilled. *Psychological Bulletin,* 1973, *79,* 145–163.

Blanchard, E. B., & Young, L. D. Clinical applications of biofeedback training: A review of evidence. *Archives of General Psychiatry,* 1974, *30,* 573–589.

Blanchard, E. B., Young, L. D., Haynes, M. R., & Scott, R. W. Long term instructional control of heart rate without exteroceptive feedback. *Journal of General Psychology,* 1975, *92,* 291–292.

Blanchard, E. B., Young, L. D., Scott, R. W., & Haynes, M. R. Differential effects of feedback and reinforcement in voluntary acceleration of human heart rate. *Perceptual and Motor Skills,* 1974, *38,* 683–691.

Blankstein, K. R., Zimmerman, J., & Egner, K. Within-subject control designs and voluntary bidirectional control of cardiac rate: Methodological comparison between preexperimental and pretrial baseline. *Journal of Experimental Psychology,* 1976, *95,* 161–175.

Borgeat, F., Hade, B., Larouche, L. M., & Bedwani, C. N. Effect of therapist's active presence on EMG biofeedback training of headache patients. *Biofeedback and Self-regulation,* 1980, *5,* 275–282.

Bouchard, M., & Granger, L. The role of instructions versus instructions plus feedback in voluntary heart rate slowing. *Psychophysiology,* 1977, *14,* 475–482.

Brener, J. Factors influencing the specificity of voluntary control. In L. V. DiCara (Ed.), *Limbic and autonomic nervous system research.* New York: Plenum, 1974.

Brener, J., Kleinman, R. A., & Goesling, W. J. The effects of different exposures to augmented sensory feedback on the control of heart rate. *Psychophysiology,* 1969, *5,* 510–516.

Bruhn, P., Olesen, J., & Melgaard, B. Controlled trial of EMG feedback in muscle contraction headache. *Annals of Neurology,* 1979, *6,* 34–36.

Budzynski, T. H., & Stoyva, J. M. Biofeedback techniques in behavior therapy. In D. Shapiro, T. X. Barber, L. V. DiCara, J. Kamiya, N. E. Miller, & J. Stoyva (Eds.), *Biofeedback and self-control, 1972.* Chicago: Aldine, 1972.

Budzynski, T. H., Stoyva, J. M., & Adler, C. S. Feedback-induced muscle relaxation: Application to tension headache. *Journal of Behavior Therapy and Experimental Psychiatry,* 1970, *1,* 205–211.

Budzynski, T. H., Stoyva, J. M., Alder, C. S., & Mullaney, D. J. EMG biofeedback and tension headache: A controlled outcome study. *Psychosomatic Medicine,* 1973, *35,* 484–496.

Carlson, J. G. Proportional and discrete feedback EMG training. *Proceedings of the 11th Annual Meeting of the Biofeedback Society of America,* 1980, 22–25.

Carlson, J. G., & Feld, J. L. Role of incentives in the training of the frontal EMG relaxation response. *Journal of Behavioral Medicine,* 1978, *1,* 427–436.

Caronite, S. C. The effects of biofeedback variables on the acquisition and retention of a differentiated electromyographic response. *Dissertation Abstracts International,* 1972, *33,* 1812.

Colgan, M. Effects of binary and proportional feedback on bi-directional control of heart rate. *Psychophysiology,* 1977, *14,* 187–191.

Cox, D. J., Freundlich, A., & Meyer, R. G. Differential effectiveness of electromyographic feedback, verbal relaxation instructions, and medication placebo with tension headaches. *Journal of Consulting and Clinical Psychology,* 1975, *43,* 892–989.

Cox, D. J., Klee, S., & Meyer, R. G. Predictive variables in EMG responsiveness to varied relaxation training techniques. *Proceedings of the American Association of Tension Control,* 1976, 151–158.

Cuthbert, B. N., & Lang, P. J. *Biofeedback and cardiovascular self-control.* Unpublished manuscript, 1976.

Dale, A., Anderson, D., & Spencer, K. Voluntary heart-rate changes med. d by muscular tension and respiration. *Perceptual and Motor Skills,* 1980, *50,* 875–881.

Davidson, R. J., & Schwartz, G. E. Patterns of cerebral lateralization during cardiac biofeedback versus the self-regulation of emotion: Sex differences. *Psychophysiology,* 1976, *13,* 62–68.

DeGood, D. E., & Chisholm, R. C. Multiple response comparison of parietal EEG and frontalis EMG biofeedback. *Psychophysiology,* 1977, *14,* 258–265.

DeGood, D., Klaus, D., Tennenbaum, D., & Greenwald, D. "Length of training" as a factor in the biofeedback treatment of psychosomatic symptoms. *Proceedings of the Ninth Annual Meeting of the Biofeedback Society of America,* 1978, 88–91.

Edwards, C., & Murphy, P. Performance motivation in EMG biofeedback. *Proceedings of the 11th Annual Meeting of the Biofeedback Society of America,* 1980, 33–34.

Engel, B. T. Comment on self-control of cardiac functioning: A promise as yet unfulfilled. *Psychological Bulletin,* 1974, *84,* 43.

Epstein, L. H., & Abel, G. G. An analysis of biofeedback training effects for tension headache patients. *Behavior Therapy,* 1977, *8,* 37–47.

Epstein, L. H., & Blanchard, E. B. Biofeedback, self-control and self-management. *Biofeedback and Self-regulation,* 1977, *2,* 201–211.

Freedman, R. Generalization of frontalis EMG biofeedback training to other muscles. *Proceedings of the Seventh Annual Meeting of the Biofeedback Research Society,* 1976. (Summary)

Freedman, R. R., & Glares, A. A generalization gradient in frontal EMG training. *Proceedings of the 10th Annual Meeting of the Biofeedback Society of America,* 1979, 167–169.

Gainer, J. C. Temperature discrimination training in the biofeedback treatment of migraine headache. *Journal of Behavior Therapy and Experimental Psychiatry,* 1978, *9,* 185–188.

Gatchel, R. J. Frequency of feedback and learned heart rate control. *Journal of Experimental Psychology,* 1974, *103,* 274–283.

Gatchel, R. J. The effect of voluntary control of heart rate deceleration on skin conductance level: An example of response fractionation. *Biological Psychology,* 1976, *4,* 241–248.

Gatchel, R. J., Korman, M., Weis, C. B., Smith, D., & Clarke, L. A multiple-response evaluation of EMG biofeedback performance during training and stress-induction conditions. *Psychophysiology,* 1978, *15,* 253–258.

Gersten, C. D., & Pope, A. T. EMG feedback gain as a determinant of muscle tension reduction. *Proceedings of the Seventh Annual Meeting of the Biofeedback Research Society,* 1976, 26. (Summary)

Gersten, C. D., & Pope, A. T. Continuous vs. intermittent EMG feedback effects on muscle tension reduction during Jacobsonian relaxation training. *Proceedings of the Ninth Annual Meeting of the Biofeedback Society of America,* 1978, 230–231.

Gray, C. L., Lyle, R. C., McGuire, R. J., & Peck, D. F. Electrode placement, EMG feedback, and relaxation for tension headaches. *Behaviour Research and Therapy,* 1980, *18,* 19–23.

Haynes, S. N., Moseley, D., & McGowan, W. T. Relaxation training and biofeedback in the reduction of frontalis muscle tension. *Psychophysiology,* 1975, *12,* 547–552.

Holmes, D. S., Frost, R. O., & Bennett, D. H. Influence of adaptation period length on the ability of humans to increase and decrease heart rate with instructions and biofeedback. *Behavioral Biology,* 1977, *20,* 261–269.

Holmes, D. S., Solomon, S., & Buchsbaum, H. K. Utility of control of respiration and biofeedback for increasing and decreasing heart rate. *Psychophysiology,* 1979, *16,* 432–437.

Holroyd, K. A., Andrasik, F., & Noble, J. A comparison of EMG biofeedback and a credible pseudotherapy in treating tension headache. *Journal of Behavioral Medicine,* 1980, *3,* 29–39.

Holroyd, K. A., Andrasik, F., & Westbrook, T. Cognitive control of tension headache. *Cognitive Therapy and Research*, 1977, *1*, 121–133.

Hutchings, D. F., & Reinking, R. H. Tension headaches: What form of therapy is most effective? *Biofeedback and Self-regulation*, 1976, *1*, 183–190.

Johns, T. R. *Heart rate control in humans under paced respiration and restricted movement: The effect of instructions and exteroceptive feedback.* Unpublished doctoral dissertation, University of Miami (Florida), 1970.

Johnston, D. Criterion level and instrumental effects in the voluntary control of heart rate. *Biological Psychology*, 1976, *4*, 1–17.

Keefe, F. J. Conditioned changes in differential skin temperature. *Perceptual and Motor Skills*, 1975, *40*, 283–288.

Keefe, F. J. Biofeedback versus instructional control of skin temperature. *Journal of Behavioral Medicine*, 1978, *1*, 383–390.

Keefe, F. J., & Gardner, E. T. Learned control of skin-temperature: Effects of short- and long-term biofeedback training. *Behavior Therapy*, 1979, *10*, 202–210.

King, N. J., & Montgomery, R. M. Biofeedback induced control of human peripheral temperature: A critical review of the literature. *Psychological Bulletin*, 1980, *88*, 738–752.

King, N. J., & Montgomery, R. M. The self-control of human peripheral (finger) temperature: An exploration of somatic maneuvers as aids to biofeedback training. *Behavior Therapy*, 1981, *12*, 263–273.

King, N. J., & Montgomery, R. M. A component analysis of biofeedback induced self-control of peripheral (finger) temperature. *Biological Psychology*, in press.

Kinsman, R. A., O'Banion, K., Robinson, S., & Staudenmayer, H. Continuous biofeedback and discrete posttrial verbal feedback in frontalis muscle relaxation training. *Psychophysiology*, 1975, *12*, 30–35.

Kondo, C., & Canter, A. True and false electromyographic feedback: Effect on tension headache. *Journal of Abnormal Psychology*, 1977, *86*, 93–95.

Kondo, C. Y., Canter, A., & Bean, J. A. Intercession interval and reductions in frontalis EMG during biofeedback training. *Psychophysiology*, 1977, *14*, 15–17.

Lang, P. J. Learned control of human heart rate in a computer directed environment. In P. A. Obrist, A. H. Black, J. Brener, & L. V. DiCara (Eds.), *Cardiovascular psychophysiology.* Chicago: Aldine, 1974.

Lang, P. J., Troyer, W. G., Twentyman, C. T., & Gatchel, R. J. Differential effects of heart rate modification training on college students, older males, and patients with ischemic heart disease. *Psychosomatic Medicine*, 1975, *37*, 429–446.

Lang, P. J., & Twentyman, C. T. Learning to control heart rate: Binary vs. analog feedback. *Psychophysiology*, 1974, *11*, 619–629.

Lang, P. J., & Twentyman, C. T. Learning to control heart rate: Effects of varying incentive and criterion of success on past performance. *Psychophysiology*, 1976, *13*, 378–385.

Largen, J. W., Mathew, R. J., Dobbins, K., Meyer, J. S., & Claghorn, J. L. Skin temperature self-regulation and non-invasive regional cerebral blood flow. *Headache*, 1978, *18*, 203–210.

Le Boeuf, A. The effects of EMG feedback training on state anxiety in introverts and extroverts. *Journal of Clinical Psychology*, 1977, *33*, 251–253.

Le Boeuf, A. Effects of frontalis biofeedback on subjective ratings of relaxation. *Perceptual and Motor Skills*, 1980, *50*, 99–103.

Le Boeuf, A., & Hurrell, M. E.M.G. feedback training: Increasing resistance to extinction. *Proceedings of the Sixth Annual Meeting of the Biofeedback Research Society*, 1975, 7. (Summary)

Leeb, C., Fahrion, S., & French, D. Instructional set, deep relaxation, and growth enhancement: A pilot study. *Journal of Humanistic Psychology*, 1976, *16*, 71–78.

Levenson, R. W. Feedback effects and respiratory involvement in voluntary heart control of heart rate. *Psychophysiology*, 1976, *13*, 108–114.

Lynn, S. J., & Freedman, R. R. Transfer and evaluation of biofeedback treatment. In A. P. Goldstein & F. Kanfer (Eds.), *Maximizing treatment gains: Transfer enhancement in psychotherapy.* New York: Academic, 1979.

Manuck, S. B., Levenson, R. W., Hendricksen, J. J., & Gryll, S. L. Role of feedback in voluntary control of heart rate. *Perceptual and Motor Skills*, 1975, *40*, 747–752.

Masi, N., Moore, R. H., & Weston, A. A. A skeptical look at EMG training in the reduction of blood pressure in essential hypertensives. *Proceedings of the Seventh Annual Meeting of the Biofeedback Research Society,* 1976, 48. (Summary)

Mathew, R. J., Largen, J. W., Dobbins, K., Meyer, J. S., Sakai, F., & Claghorn, J. L. Biofeedback control of skin temperature and cerebral blood flow in migraine. *Headache,* 1980, *20,* 19–28.

McCanne, T. R., & Sandman, C. A. Determinants of human operant heart rate conditioning: A systematic investigation of several methodological issues. *Journal of Comparative and Physiological Psychology,* 1975, *88,* 609–618.

Miller, N. E., & Dworkin, B. R. Critical issues in therapeutic applications of biofeedback. In G. E. Schwartz & J. Beatty (Eds.), *Biofeedback: Theory and research.* New York: Academic, 1977.

Mitch, P. S., McGrady, A., & Iannone, A. Autogenic feedback training in migraine: A treatment report. *Headache,* 1976, *15,* 267–270.

Nielson, D. H., & Holmes, D. S. Effectiveness of EMG biofeedback training for controlling in subsequent stressful situations. *Biofeedback and Self-regulation,* 1980, *5,* 235–248.

Obrist, P. A., Galosy, R. A., Lawler, J. E., Gaebelein, C. J., Howard, J. L., & Shanks, E. M. Operant conditioning of heart rate: Somatic correlates. *Psychophysiology,* 1975, *12,* 445–455.

O'Connell, M. F., Frerker, D. L., & Ross, K. L. The effects of feedback sensory modality, feedback information content, and sex on short-term biofeedback training of three responses. *Psychophysiology,* 1979, *16,* 438–444.

Ohno, Y., Tanaka, Y., Takeya, T., & Ikemi, Y. Modification of skin temperature by biofeedback procedures. *Journal of Behavior Therapy and Experimental Psychiatry,* 1977, *8,* 31–34.

Philips, C. The modification of tension headache pain using EMG biofeedback. *Behaviour Research and Therapy,* 1977, *15,* 119–129.

Ray, R. J. The relationship of locus of control, self-report measures, and feedback to the voluntary control of heart rate. *Psychophysiology,* 1974, *11,* 527–534.

Reinking, R. H., & Kohl, M. L. Effects of various forms of relaxation training on physiological and self-report measures of relaxation. *Journal of Consulting and Clinical Psychology,* 1975, *43,* 595–600.

Rice, R. M., & Blanchard, E. B. *Biofeedback in the treatment of anxiety disorders. Clinical Psychology Review,* 1982, *2,* 557–577.

Roberts, A. H., Kewman, D. G., & MacDonald, H. Voluntary control of skin temperature: Unilateral changes using hypnosis and feedback. *Journal of Abnormal Psychology,* 1973, *82,* 163–168.

Roberts, A. H., Schuler, J., Bacon, J. G., Zimmerman, R. L., & Patterson, R. Individual differences and autonomic control: Absorption, hypnotic susceptibility, and the unilateral control of skin temperature. *Journal of Abnormal Psychology,* 1975, *84,* 272–279.

Sargent, J. D., Green, E. E., & Walters, E. D. Preliminary report on the use of autogenic feedback training in the treatment of migraine and tension headaches. *Psychosomatic Medicine,* 1973, *35,* 129–135.

Schandler, S. L., & Grings, W. W. An examination of methods for producing relaxation during short-term laboratory sessions. *Behaviour Research and Therapy,* 1976, *14,* 419–426.

Schultz, J. H., & Luthe, W. *Autogenic therapy* (Vol. 1). New York: Grune & Stratton, 1969.

Shapiro, D., & Surwit, R. S. Learned control of physiological function and disease. In H. Leitenberg (Ed.), *Handbook of behavior modification and behavior therapy.* Englewood Cliffs, N.J.: Prentice-Hall, 1976.

Shedivy, D. I., & Kleinman, K. M. Lack of correlation between fontalis EMG and either neck EMG or verbal ratings of tension. *Psychophysiology,* 1977, *14,* 182–186.

Silver, B. V., & Blanchard, E. B. Biofeedback and relaxation training in the treatment of psychophysiological disorders: Or are the machines really necessary? *Journal of Behavioral Medicine,* 1978, *2,* 217–239.

Sirota, A. D., Schwartz, G. E., & Shapiro, D. Voluntary control of human heart rate: Effect on reaction to aversive stimuli. *Journal of Abnormal Psychology,* 1974, *83,* 261–267.

Sirota, A. D., Schwartz, G. E., & Shapiro, D. Voluntary control of human heart rate: Effect on reaction to aversive stimulation: A replication and extension. *Journal of Abnromal Psychology,* 1976, *85,* 473–477.

Sovak, M., Kunzel, M., Sternbach, R. A., & Dalessio, P. J. Is volitional manipulation of hemodynamics a valid rationale for biofeedback therapy of migraine? *Headache,* 1978, *18,* 197-202.

Stephens, J. H., Harris, A. H., Brady, J. V., & Shaffer, J. W. Psychological and physiological variables associated with large magnitude voluntary heart rate changes. *Psychophysiology,* 1975, *12,* 381-387.

Stoffer, G. R., Jensen, J. A. S., & Nesset, B. L. Effects of contingent versus yoked temperature feedback on voluntary temperature control and cold stress tolerance. *Biofeedback and Self-regulation,* 1979, *4,* 51-61.

Stoyva, J. M., & Budzynski, T. H. Cultivated low arousal: An antistress response? In L. V. DiCara (Ed.), *Limbic and autonomic nervous systems research.* New York: Plenum, 1974.

Surwit, R. S. Biofeedback: A possible treatment for Raynaud's disease. *Seminars in Psychiatry,* 1973, *5,* 483-489.

Surwit, R. S., & Fenton, C. H. Feedback and instructions in the control of digital skin temperature. *Psychophysiology,* 1980, *17,* 129-132.

Surwit, R. S., & Keefe, F. J. Frontalis EMG feedback training: An electronic panacea? *Behavior Therapy,* 1978, *9,* 779-792.

Taub, E. Self-regulation of human tissue temperature. In G. E. Schwartz & J. Beatty (Eds.), *Biofeedback: Theory and research.* New York: Academic, 1977.

Taub, E., & Emurian, C. S. Feedback-aided self-regulation of skin temperature with a single feedback locus: I. Acquisition and reversal training. *Biofeedback and Self-regulation,* 1976, *1,* 147-168.

Townsend, R. E., House, J. F., & Addario, D. A comparison of biofeedback-mediated relaxation and group therapy in the treatment of chronic anxiety. *American Journal of Psychiatry,* 1975, *132,* 598-601.

Turin, A., & Johnson, W. G. Biofeedback therapy for migraine headaches. *Archives of General Psychiatry,* 1976, *33,* 517-519.

Twentyman, C. T., Malloy, P. F., & Green, A. S. Instructed heart rate control in a high heart rate population. *Journal of Behavioral Medicine,* 1979, *2,* 251-261.

Weiss, T., & Engel, B. T. Operant conditioning of heart rate in patients with premature ventricular contractions. *Psychosomatic Medicine,* 1971, *33,* 301-321.

Wells, D. T. Large magnitude voluntary heart rate changes. *Psychophysiology,* 1973, *10,* 260-269.

White, T. H., Holmes, D. S., & Bennett, D. H. Effects of instructions, biofeedback, and cognitive activities on heart rate control. *Journal of Experimental Psychology: Human Learning and Memory,* 1977, *3,* 477-484.

Whitehead, W. E., Drescher, V. M., Heiman, P., & Blackwell, B. Relation of heart rate control to heart beat perception. *Biofeedback and Self-regulation,* 1977, *2,* 371-392.

Wickramasekera, I. Effects of electromyographic feedback on hypnotic susceptibility: More preliminary data. *Journal of Abnormal Psychology,* 1973, *82,* 74-77.

Willerman, L., Skeen, J. T., & Simpson, J. S. Retention of learned temperature changes during problem solving. *Perceptual and Motor Skills,* 1976, *43,* 995-1002.

Williamson, D. A., & Blanchard, E. B. Effect of feedback delay upon learned heart rate control. *Psychophysiology,* 1979, *16,* 108-115. (a)

Williamson, D. A., & Blanchard, E. B. Heart rate and blood pressure feedback: I. A review of the recent experimental literature. *Biofeedback and Self-regulation,* 1979, *4,* 1-34. (b)

Yock, T. J. Electromyographic feedback as a relaxation procedure: A psychophysiological evaluation. *Proceedings of the Ninth Annual Meeting of the Biofeedback Society of America,* 1978, 245-246.

Young, L. D., & Blanchard, E. B. Effects of auditory feedback of varying information and content on the self-control of heart rate. *Journal of General Psychology,* 1974, *91,* 61-68.

Zeisig, J., & Simkims, L. Sensory mode of feedback and incentive effects on muscle relaxation. *Proceedings of the Seventh Annual Meeting of the Biofeedback Research Society,* 1976, 94. (Summary)

# 13

## Meditation and Behavioral Medicine

## Application of a Self-regulation Strategy to the Clinical Management of Stress

*Deane H. Shapiro, Jr.*
*University of California, Irvine, United States*

It has been suggested, based on clinical observation, that between 50% and 70% of patients seen in general medical practice have an illness that is either stress induced or exacerbated by stress (Pelletier, 1977). There is also evidence that stress is associated with increased utilization of health care services (Roghmann & Haggerty, 1973) and with increased morbidity (Holmes & Rahe, 1967; Levi, 1971; Rabkin & Struening, 1976).

Concommitant with these findings is a growing dissatisfaction among health care professionals in our culture who find themselves treating stress-related disorders with pharmacological solutions (Benson, 1975; Coates & Thoresen, 1978; Glueck & Stroebel, 1975). This has resulted in attempts to find non-drug-related self-regulation strategies by which people may learn to manage their own internal and external behaviors better (D. H. Shapiro & J. Shapiro, 1980). Meditation is viewed as one such potential self-regulation strategy.

The interest of the Western scientific community in meditation was catalyzed in the mid-1960s by reports from India and the Orient detailing extraordinary feats of bodily control and altered states of consciousness by meditation masters (Anand, Chinna, & Singh, 1961; Kasamatsu, Okima, Takenaka, Koga, & Ikada, 1957; Wenger & Bagchi, 1961). These reports were not summarily dismissed because they paralleled a rather major shift in Western scientific zeitgeist and models. For example, Miller and DiCara, among others, were showing that voluntary control of the autonomic system was possible (DiCara, 1970; Miller, 1969; D. H. Shapiro, Tursky, Schwartz, & Schwartz, 1971); and Tart (1971) was pointing out how a variety of arcane, seemingly incomprehensible phenomena of non-Western psychologies could be rendered understandable within the framework of state-dependent technologies. Further, increased sophistication in scientific instrumentation gave rise to the possibility of replicating and substantiating these anecdotal reports.

The past decade has seen an exponential rise in the number of studies looking at the physiological and psychological effects of meditation as well as at the phenomenological experiences occurring during it. Meditation is a technique developed in an Eastern philosophical and religious framework, and it is important that Western scientists recognize that fact when using meditation for ends other than those for which it was intended. As a way of making that distinction, meditation has been referred to both as a self-regulation strategy for dealing with stress and tension, the addictions, and hypertension and as an altered state of consciousness, a means for developing a new and harmonious relationship with oneself, with others, and with the surrounding world (D. H. Shapiro, 1980; D. H. Shapiro & Giber, 1978).

In this chapter I look primarily at meditation as a self-regulation strategy for the clinical management of stress; hence I couch it in the framework of behavior therapy or behavioral medicine. The chapter is in four sections. In the first, I briefly review behavioral approaches and behavioral medicine and comment on how other orientations have used meditation. In the second section, I provide a working definition of meditation and discuss the different types. In the third, I review the literature on psychological and physiological changes relating to meditation as an independent variable and stress as a dependent variable, and in the fourth section, I review additional clinical considerations that need to be taken into account when using mediation as a self-regulation strategy for stress management.

## BEHAVIORAL APPROACHES
## AND BEHAVIORAL MEDICINE

Behavior modification uses principles derived from the experimental analysis of behavior (Skinner, 1953) and social learning theory (Bandura, 1969, 1977) to modify maladaptive behaviors or inculcate more adaptive habits. Behavior therapy consists of activities implying a contractual agreement between therapist and patient (or client) to modify a designated problem behavior, with particular application to neurosis and affective disorders (Wolpe, 1969; Lazarus, 1971).

Behavioral medicine is the application of these principles to physical disease. As Schwartz and Weiss (1977) have noted, "Behavioral medicine is the field concerned with the development of behavioral science knowledge and techniques relevant to the understanding of physical health and illness and applications of this knowledge and these techniques to diagnosis, prevention, treatment and rehabilitation" (p. 379). Pomerleau (1979) defines behavioral medicine as "(a) the clinical use of techniques derived from the experimental analysis of behavior—behavior therapy and behavior modification—for the evaluation, prevention, management or treatment of physical disease or physiological dysfunction; and (b) the conduct of research contributing to the functional analysis and understanding of behavior associated with medical disorders and problems in health care (p. 655). Thus, behavioral medicine becomes an "interdisciplinary field concerned with the development and integration of behavioral and bio-medical science, knowledge, and techniques relevant to the understanding of health and illness, and the application of this knowledge and these techniques to prevention, diagnosis, treatment, and rehabilitation" (*Behavioral Medicine Abstracts*, 1980).

The behaviorally oriented people who use meditation in their research or practice view it primarily as a self-regulation strategy for dealing with clinical, health-oriented, and stress-related concerns. Thus it may be conceptualized as a self-regulation strategy with potential applications in health psychology (Stone, Cohen, & Adler, 1979) and behavioral medicine (P. O. Davidson & Davidson, 1980; McNamara, 1979; Pomerleau & Brady, 1979; Stroebel & Glueck, 1977) or as a clinical tool for the management of anxiety and the addictions within a behavioral framework (Berwick & Oziel, 1973; D. H. Shapiro, 1978b; Shapiro & Zifferblatt, 1976a; Woolfolk & Franks, in press). From this perspective, meditation is considered to be a successful treatment if it proves effective in significantly reducing the target behavior problem (Bandura, 1969, 1977; Lazarus, 1971; Skinner, 1953; Wolpe, 1969).

Conceptualizing meditation within a behavioral framework is not meant to imply that there is no overlap between the ways different orientations conceptualize meditation or the end results that may occur. For example, those from the humanistic and holistic medicine persuasion would argue that whenever individual responsibility is being taught, one is operating within the framework of holistic medicine (Hastings, Fadiman, & Gordon, 1980; Pelletier, 1979). Those within the framework of behavioral medicine would argue similarly that they are advocates of individual responsibility (e.g., Benson, 1978). Thus, there is both overlap and difference between orientations in their use of meditation in clinical problems and human concerns.

## MEDITATION: TOWARD A WORKING DEFINITION

One of the problems in determining the clinical applications of meditation to stress is the lack of a clear definition of meditation. Because of its effects, some have tried to define it as a relaxation technique (Benson, 1975). This raises problems similar to those encountered in the relaxation literature (R. J. Davidson & Schwartz, 1976) where a relaxation technique is defined as one producing certain effects, for example, decreased skeletal-muscle tension or decreased sympathetic arousal. Defining the independent variable by its dependent-variable effects is, however, tautological and unsatisfactory as a complete definition.

Another problem with defining meditation is that there are so many different techniques. Some involve sitting quietly and produce a state of quiescence and restfulness (Wallace, Benson, & Wilson, 1971). Some involve sitting quietly and produce a state of excitement and arousal (Corby, Roth, Zarcone, & Kepell, 1978; Das & Gastaut, 1955). Some such as the Sufi dervish whirling, tai chi, hatha yoga, isiguro Zen, involve physical movement to a greater or lesser degree (Hirai, 1974; Naranjo, & Ornstein, 1971). Sometimes these "movement meditations" result in a state of excitement, sometimes a state of relaxation (J. Davidson, 1976; Fischer, 1971).

Accordingly, depending on the type of meditation, the body may be active and moving or relatively motionless and passive. Attention may be actively focused on one object of concentration to the exclusion of the other objects (Anand et al., 1961) (concentrative meditation). Attention may be focused on one object, but as other objects, thoughts, or feelings occur, they too are noticed, and then attention is returned to the original focal object (e.g., vipassana, TM). Attention may not be focused exclusively on any particular object (e.g., Zen's Shikan-taza) (Kasamatsu & Hirai, 1966; Krishnamurti, 1979) (mindfulness meditation). There do, however, seem to be three broad, general groupings of attentional strategies in meditation; either a focus on the field (mindfulness meditation), a focus on a specific object within the field (concentrative meditation) (Goleman, 1972; Narajo & Ornstein, 1971), or a shifting back and forth between the two (Washburn, 1978). These groupings fit nicely with brain attentional mechanisms, which Pribram (1971) has described as similar to a camera and of two types. In the first, paralleling mindfulness meditation, the focus is similar to that achieved with a wide-angle lens—a broad sweeping awareness taking in the entire field. In the second type, paralleling concentrative meditation, the focus is similar to that achieved with a zoom lens—a specific focusing on a particular restricted segment of the field.

Therefore, using attentional mechanisms as the basis for a definition, *meditation* refers to a family of techniques that have in common a conscious attempt to focus attention in a nonanalytical way and also an attempt not to dwell on discursive, ruminating thought. This definition has several important features. First, the word *conscious* is used. Meditation involves intention: the intention to focus attention either on a particular object in the field, or on whatever arises. Second, the definition is noncultic. Understanding it does not depend on knowledge of any religious framework or orientation. This does not imply that meditation does not or cannot occur within a religious framework. It does suggest, however, that what meditation is, and the framework within which it is practiced, through interactive, are two separate issues and must be viewed as such. Therefore, although there may be overlap in terms of the concentration on a particular object, or repetition of a sound or phrase, meditation cannot be equated a priori with prayer. This is particularly true when the intent of the prayer has a goal-directed focus outside oneself (e.g., asking a higher power to absolve one of one's sins).

Third, the word *attempt* is used throughout. This points to the process of meditation. Because meditation is an effort to focus attention, it also involves how one responds when one's attention wanders or how one responds when a thought arises. There is a continuum of instructions, from quite strong to quite mild, for dealing with thoughts (Carrington, 1978). For example, Benson (1975) instructs students to "ignore" the thoughts; Deikman (1966) to exclude them; a fifth-century Buddhist treatise to "with teeth clenched and tongue pressed against the gums ... by means of sheer mental effort hold back, crush and burn out the thought" (Conze, 1969, p. 83); the vipassana tradition merely to notice and label the thought (e.g., thinking thinking); or in Zen, merely to notice, observe with equanimity, and when weary of watching, let go (Herrigel, 1953).

Fourth, there is an important metamessage implicit in the definition: namely, the *content* of thoughts is not so important; they should be allowed to come and go. Consciousness, or awareness of the *process* of thoughts coming and going is more important. The context—conscious attention—is stated to be the most important variable. Although cognitions and images may arise, they are not the final goal of meditation. Thus, although there may be overlapping content, meditation may not be equated a priori with techniques of guided imagery (Kretschmer, 1969); daydreaming (Singer, 1975); covert self-instructional training (Meichenbaum & Cameron, 1974); heterohypnosis (Paul, 1969); self-hypnosis (Fromm, 1975); or other cognitive strategies (cf. Tart, 1969).

Meditation can be practiced either formally or informally. Formal meditation refers to the practice of meditation at certain times during the day, usually in a consistent, specified place and generally in a specific posture (classically the lotus or half-lotus position). Informal meditation is practiced throyghout the day, in no specific posture or specified place. It involves an attempt to be conscious of everything that one does, to attend very closely to one's everyday actions, without judging or evaluating. As Rahula (1959) noted,

*Be aware and mindful of whatever you do, physically or verbally, during the daily routine of your work and your life. Whether you walk, stand, sit, lie down, or sleep, whether you stretch or bend your legs, whether you look around, whether you put your clothes on, whether you talk or keep silent, whether you eat or drink, whether you answer the calls of nature—in these and other activities you should be fully aware and mindful of the act performed at the moment, that is to say, that you should live in the present moment, the present action. (p. 71)*

In informal meditation, conscious attention becomes a way of life. I mention informal meditation here because most Western researchers focus primarily on formal practice. The final goal of meditation is not simply to be able to make an effort consciously to focus attention twice a day during formal sittings, however, but to maintain and generalize that conscious attention to all parts of the day.

## MEDITATION AND STRESS: ROUND-ONE STUDIES

Almost without exception the studies viewing meditation as self-regulation strategy have focused on its relaxation (stress-reduction) component. This is true in the stress studies, the therapy studies, the majority of the addiction studies, and the hypertension research. The first round of studies viewing meditation as a self-regulation strategy helped establish interest in the field. These early studies suggested that meditation may be quite promising for a variety of clinical problems. Generally these first-round studies consisted of anecdotal case reports; intensive design studies containing nonspecific variables; combining techniques for treatment; comparing meditation to control groups but not to other, similar techniques, and combinations of these methods. Because this first-round literature has been reviewed at length elsewhere, including both clinical and therapeutic effects (Shapiro & Giber, 1978; Smith, 1975) and physiological effects (J. Davidson, 1976; Woolfolk, 1975), I provide only a brief summary here. As this first-round literature is generally quite flawed methodologically, I confine myself to general comments on methodological issues.

### Stress and Stress Disorders: Fears, Phobias, and Stress and Tension Management

There have been 20 round-one studies concerned with the reduction of fears and phobias and with stress and tension management (Berwick & Oziel, 1973; Bondreau, 1972; Daniels, 1975; R. J. Davidson, Goleman, & Schwartz, 1976; Dillbeck, 1977; Ferguson & Gowan, 1976; French & Tupin, 1974; Girodo, 1974; Goleman & Schwartz, 1976; Hjelle, 1974; Honsberger & Wilson, 1973; Lazar, Farwell, & Farrow, 1977; Linden, 1973; Otis, 1974; D. H. Shapiro, 1976; Smith, 1976; Tulpule, 1971; Vahia, Doongaji, & Jeste, 1972, 1973; Woolfolk, Carr-Kaffashan, McNulty, & Lehrer, 1976). These studies suggest that meditation may be a promising clinical-intervention technique for several stress-related dependent variables. All studies reported successful outcomes on dependent variables ranging from fear of enclosed places, examinations, elevators, being alone (Bondreau, 1972) to "generalized anxiety" (D. H. Shapiro, 1976), anxiety neurosis (Girodo, 1974), pain from bullet wounds, back pain (French & Tupin, 1974), fear of heart attack (French & Tupin, 1974), rehabilitation after MI (Tulpule, 1971), and bronchial asthma (Honsberger & Wilson, 1973). Many of these studies involved within-subject design (Bondreau, 1972; French & Tupin, 1974; Girodo, 1974; D. H. Shapiro, 1976) and a combination of meditation and other techniques, with meditation sometimes first (Girodo, 1974), sometimes second (Bondreau, 1972), sometimes concurrent (Daniels, 1975; D. H. Shapiro, 1976) with other modes; the data were gathered by subjective measures (patient verbal self-report). Girodo (1974) also used an anxiety-symptom questionnaire, and D. H. Shapiro (1976) had the patient monitor daily feelings of anxiety using a wrist counter.

The study by Vahia et al. (1972), the first to use control groups, reported a consistent and greater reduction in anxiety for the treatment group. The control group consisted of a "pseudo-yogic treatment" with only superficial use of postures and breathing exercises. Data were gathered from patient notebooks, from the Taylor Manifest Anxiety Scale, and from relatives, friends, and colleagues. Its conclusions are discussed in greater detail in the following section on meditation and psychotherapy.

Other studies, using control-group designs, have also reported a consistent reduction in anxiety for the meditating treatment group. The data have been gathered primarily by pretest and posttest questionnaires, including Spielberger's State-Trait Anxiety Inventory (R. J. Davidson, Goleman, & Schwartz, 1976; Dillbeck, 1977; Ferguson & Gowan, 1976; Goleman & Schwartz, 1976; Smith, 1976); the IPAT anxiety questionnaire (Cattell anxiety scale) (Ferguson & Gowan, 1976; Lazar, Farwell, & Farrow, 1977), the Bendig anxiety scale (Hjelle, 1974), and the Text Anxiety Scale for Children (Linden, 1973). Other data measuring anxiety-related behaviors include HR and phasic skin conductance [meditators recovered more quickly after viewing a stressful film (Goleman & Schwartz, 1976)] and insomnia [meditators showed substantial improvement on variables of sleep onset and rated difficulty of falling asleep (Woolfolk, Carr-Kaffashan, McNulty, & Lehrer, 1976)].

The drug studies have been discussed elsewhere (D. H. Shapiro, 1980) and do not seem of primary interest to this chapter, so I now turn to the literature on hypertension.

## Hypertension

Seven first-round studies have involved the use of meditation in reducing BP (Benson, Marzetla, Rosner, & Klemchuk, 1974; Benson, Rosner, Marzetla, et al., 1974; Benson & Wallace, 1972; Datey, Deshmukh, S. H. Dalviica et al., 1969; Patel, 1973, 1975, 1975b; R. A. Stone & DeLeo, 1976). Certainly, from a research standpoint, BP is one of the "cleanest" dependent variables to measure. All these studies indicate a reduction in BP in the treatment group. Several reported a reduction in the use of hypertensive medication (Datey et al., 1969; Patel, 1973) and one a reduction in reports of somatic symptoms (Datey et al., 1969). Follow-up data have shown that treatment gains were maintained during a 12-month period (Patel, 1975b).

Although the treatment effect seems relatively clear, there are still several unanswered questions as to what is causing that effect. The treatment interventions have ranged from a combination of yoga breathing, concentration, and muscle relaxation (Datey, K., Deshmuk, S. H. Dalviica et al., 1969); the relaxation-response technique (Benson, Marzetla, Rosner, & Klemchuk, 1974; Benson, Rosner, Marzetla, & Wallace, 1972; Benson, 1974); and a combination of yoga, breath meditation, muscle relaxation, concentration, and biofeedback (Patel, 1973) to a Buddhist meditation procedure (R. A. Stone & DeLeo, 1976). Future research should attempt to isolate the variance of treatment success owing to different aspects of the intervention. Further research should also determine whether the results are maintained. For example, Pollack, Weber, Case, and Laragh (1977) found that changes in BP had disappeared after 6 months. For a more detailed discussion of possible variables influencing treatment outcome, readers are referred to an excellent review of the literature by Jacob, Kraemer, and Agras (1977).

## Physiological Changes

The studies discussed previously suggest that meditation may be a promising therapeutic intervention strategy for several different clinical applications. One hypothesis that attempts to explain its effectiveness is that meditation helps a person relax. There seems general agreement that meditation does, in fact, produce a state of relaxation (Benson, Beary, & Carol, 1974; Smith, 1975) variously described as an activity [effortless breathing (D. H. Shapiro & Zifferblatt, 1976b)], a "state" [the hypometabolic state (Wallace, Benson, & Wilson, 1971)]; and a response [the relaxation response (Benson, Beary, & Carol, 1974)].

Briefly, the physiological changes evidenced in round-one studies during the act of meditation itself were: reduced HR (Anad et al., 1961; Bagchi & Wenger, 1957; Das & Gastaut, 1955; Goyeche, Chihara, & Shimizu, 1972; Karambelkar, Vinekar, & Bhole, 1968; Wallace, 1970; Wenger & Bagchi, 1961), decreased oxygen consumption (Allison, 1970; Goyeche, Chilhara, & Shimizu, 1972; Hirai, 1974; Karambelkar et al., 1968; Sugi & Akutsu, 1968; Treichel, Clinch, & Cran, 1973; Wallace, 1970; Wallace et al., 1971; Watanabe, Shapiro, & Schwartz, 1972; Wenger & Bagchi, 1961), decreased BP (Bagchi & Wenger, 1957; Krambelkar et al., 1968; Wallace et al., 1971; Wenger & Bagchi, 1961), increased skin resistance (Akishige, 1970; Bagchi & Wenger, 1957; Karambelkar et al., 1968; Orme-Johnson, 1973; Wallace, 1970; Wallace et al., 1971; Wenger & Bagchi, 1961), and increased percentages of time, regularity, and amplitude of alpha activity (Akishige, 1970; Anand et al., 1961; Bagchi & Wenger, 1957; Banquet, 1972, 1973; Das & Gastaut, 1955; Hirai, 1974; Kasamatsu & Hirai, 1966; Wallace, 1970; Wallace et al., 1971; Watanabe et al., 1972; Williams & West, 1975).

## Physiological Comparison with Self-regulation Strategies

There was initial enthusiasm that meditation might be a unique strategy (Mulchman, 1977) different from all other self-regulation strategies. This position was based on certain first-round clinical studies and physiological findings. Benson (1975, 1977) argued, however, that the physiological response pattern was not unique to meditation per se but common to any passive relaxation strategy. This view has been supported and replicated by a number of studies that suggest no physiological differences between meditation and other self-regulation strategies and often no differences between meditation and a "just sit" control group.

For example, early first-round studies suggested that skin resistance significantly increased within subjects (Wallace, 1970; Wallace et al., 1971) and in a TM group versus a control group (Orme-Johnson, 1973). Later studies, however (Boswell & Murray, 1979; Cauthen & Prymak, 1977; Curtis & Wessberg, 1975/1976; Morse, Martin, Furst, & Dubin, 1977; Travis, Condo, & Knott, 1976; Walrath & Hamilton, 1975) show no significant differences on galvanic skin response between meditation and other self-regulation strategies including self-hypnosis, progressive relaxation, and other instructional-relaxation control groups. Further, these studies also showed no difference between meditation and other self-regulation strategies in HR or respiration decrease.

Morse et al. (1977), in a rather complex study, noted that neither respiration rate, pulse rate, nor systolic and diastolic BP differentiated experimental conditions. The authors noted that the physiological responses of TM and simple word meditation were similar and that relaxation, meditation, and relaxation hypnosis yielded similar physiological responses suggestive of deep relaxation. Other studies found no difference of respiratory rate between meditation and progressive relaxation (Pagano, Warrenburg, & Woods, 1978) or between meditation and listening to music (Fenwick, Donaldson, & Gillis, 1977). Fenwick et al. noted that subjects that were tense to begin with showed a greater relaxation effect than subjects who were not and suggested that the findings of Wallace et al. (1971) may have been due to high initial levels of metabolism and tension.

Early literature also suggested that meditation may be characterized by a unique EEG pattern, the synchronization of slow alpha (Glueck & Stroebel, 1975). Travis et al. (1976) noted, however, that a striking effect was the *lack* of alpha EEG occurring during TM compared with previous reports, and Morse et al. (1977) noted that there was interhemispheric EEG synchronicity in all experimental conditions; that is, when synchronization of slow alpha occurred, it was not unique to TM but found in all the relaxation conditions.

A similar lack of metabolic uniqueness has been found by other investigators. Michaels, Huber, and McCann (1976) attempted to differentiate meditators from resting controls biochemically. Because stress increases blood catecholamines, experimenters looked at plasma epinephrine and NE as well as at lactate. Subjects were 12 experienced meditators (with more than 12 months experience); they were compared with controls matched for sex and age who rested instead of meditating. There were no significant fluctuations of plasma epinephrine during meditation. Neither were significant differences observed between controls and meditators. The same held true for plasma lactic acid concentration. Earlier TM findings (Wallace, 1970) thus were not replicated.

More recent studies further call into question the uniqueness of meditation's effects. In an earlier study, Goleman and Schwartz (1976) showed increased responsiveness of meditators to an upcoming stressful event on a film and their quicker recovery time compared with a relaxing control group. From a cognitive standpoint, however, in terms of number of poststress intrusive thoughts, significant differences between meditators and controls have not been detected (Kanas & Horowitz, 1977). Further, earlier theories that suggested that TM was unrelated to sleep have recently been called into question by Pagano and Frumkin (1977) and by Younger, Adrianne, and Berger (1975), who note that at least beginning meditators may spend an appreciable part of their time in Sleep Stages 2, 3, and 4.

Thus it appears that the original belief that meditation could be discriminated as a unique physiological state has not been confirmed—either on an autonomic or a metabolic level, or in terms of EEG pattern. Although it does seem clear that meditation can bring about a generalized reduction in multiple physiological systems, thereby creating a state of relaxation (J. Davidson, 1976; Shapiro & Giber, 1978), it is not yet clear from the available data that this state is differentiated from relaxation effects of other techniques, whether they be hypnosis (Walrath & Hamilton, 1975) or deep-muscle relaxation (Cauthen & Prymak, 1977; Curtis & Wessberg, 1975/1976; Morse et al., 1977; Travis et al., 1976). The constellation of changes is, in most studies, significantly different between meditation and placebo control groups but not between self-regulation treatment groups.

In fairness, it should be noted that although the results thus far seem to indicate quite convincingly that there is no physiological difference between meditation and other self-regulation strategies, they are not unequivocal. For example, Elseon, Hauri, and Cunis (1977) compared meditation with a "wakefully relaxed" group and a group of ĀnandaMarga meditators. They noted that meditation was characterized by a marked increase in basal skin resistance and by a decrease in respiratory rate; changes which were not observed in the controls. Further, they stated that 6 of the 11 controls fell asleep, while none of the meditators fell asleep—rather meditators remained in a relatively stable state at alpha and theta EEG activity. Also, Jevning and O'Halloran (1980, in press) suggest blood flow as a metabolic measure unique to meditation.

In addition to there being findings which are not in accord with the above review of the physiological literature, there are also others who would disagree with the way in which I have interpreted the literature. For example, Jevning and O'Halloran (in press) believe that additional unique physiological response patterns will be found in meditators and that current findings do not reflect this simply because we do not have sensitive enough physiological measures to ferret out the unique aspects of meditation patterns as compared with other self-regulation strategies. They also note that one must be careful in generalizing from beginning meditators who may in fact fall asleep and whose physiological changes may not be different from those of people practicing other self-regulation strategies. There is no assurance, they correctly note, that beginning practitioners will have anywhere near the dramatic physiological changes of advanced meditators who have spent decades perfecting their practice. As the authors themselves point out, however, to determine whether meditation is truly unique, advanced TM practitioners would have to be compared to advanced practitioners of other self-regulation strategies.

## Clinical Comparison with Other Self-regulation Strategies

Similar findings of meditation's nonuniqueness are also now being reported on a clinical level. Meditation appears to be equally, but no more, effective than other self-regulation strategies for dependent variables ranging from anxiety (Beiman, Johnson, Puente, Majestic, & Graham, in press; Boswell & Murray, 1979; Goldman, Domitor, & Murray, 1979; Kirsch & Henry, 1979; Smith, 1976; Thomas & Abbas, 1978; Zuroff & Schwartz, 1978) and anxiety in alcoholics (Parker, Gilbert, & Thoreson, 1978) to alcohol consumption (Marlatt, Pagano, Rose, & Margues, in press), insomnia (Woolfolk et al., 1976), and borderline hypertension (Sururt, Shapiro, & Good, 1978). Self-regulation strategies compared included progressive relaxation (Boswell & Murray, 1979; Elson et al., 1977; Marlatt et al., in press; Thomas & Abbas, 1978; Woolfolk & Franks, 1976), Benson's relaxation response (Bieman et al., in press), a pseudo-meditation treatment (Smith, 1976), antimeditation treatments (Boswell & Murray, 1979; Goldman, Domitor, & Murray, 1979; Smith, 1976), self-administered systematic desensitization (Kirsch & Henry, 1979), and cardiovascular and neuromuscular biofeedback (Hager & Sururt, 1978; Sururt et al., 1978).

Thus it seems that the data from these clinical studies indicate that meditation does not appear to be any more effective than other self-regulation strategies on a wide variety of clinically relevant dependent variables. It should be noted, however, that my interpretation of the data is not without its critics. The critics point to studies in which meditation was more effective than a pseudo-yoga procedure (Vahia et al., 1972, 1973) and than biofeedback (Glueck & Stroebel, 1975). I believe it could be argued, however, that therapist's belief in treatment credibility may have been a critical confounding factor in Vahia's studies (Smith, 1975). Further, the fact that Glueck and Stroebel's study was conducted at the Institute for Living, where a great deal of TM research was being conducted, could have caused strong confounding demand characteristics, possibly accounting for subjects' continuing to adhere to the TM program while dropping out of the biofeedback treatment group.

## Adverse Effects and Contraindications

Carrington and Ephron (1975) as well as Stroebel and Glueck (1977) point out the importance, with psychiatric patients, of having the therapist available to aid with any material that comes into the patient's awareness. Therefore Carrington (1978) noted that borderline psychotics or psychotic patients should not be prescribed meditation unless their practice of it can be supervised by a psychotherapist familiar with meditation. In this regard, almost all meditation researchers and those who use it in their clinical practice are cautious in stating that there should be careful instruction, training, and follow-up observation by the therapist. This is especially true as we become more sensitive to unpleasant and adverse experiences patients sometimes have during meditation (French, Schmid, & Ingalls, 1975; Kohr, 1977; Lazarus, 1976; Osis, K. Bokert, & Carlson, 1973; Otis, in press; D. H. Shapiro, 1980; Van Nuys, 1973). These feelings may include occasional dizziness, feelings of disassociation, and other adverse feelings produced by the release of images, thoughts, and other material that patients had not been sensitive to. In addition to anecdotal reports, there have been three case reports in the literature suggesting the negative effects of meditation (French et al., 1975; Lazarus, 1976; D. H. Shapiro, 1980). There is also one study (Otis, in press) with a large number of subjects that discusses potential adverse effects of meditation.

Otis (in press) reanalyzed data he had collected previously and examined particular subjects who had reported a considerable increase (51% or over) of feelings in a negative or adverse direction. He found that the longer a person meditated, the more likely it was that adverse effects would occur. These adverse effects included increased anxiety, boredom, confusion, depression, restlessness, and withdrawal. He also noted that teacher-trainees who were long-term meditators reported more adverse effects than long-term meditators who had not made a commitment to become teachers. Although there are many ways to analyze the data, it seems that there is a percentage of people for whom meditation will have negative effects.

For example, certain people seem to be attracted to meditation for inappropriate reasons, seeing it as a powerful cognitive-avoidance strategy or to be attracted to the technique of concentrative meditation as a way of blocking out unpleasant areas of their lives. Similarly, many people lacking basic social skills (i.e., those shy or withdrawn) may be attracted to meditation. For these people meditation may not be a useful therapeutic intervention (certainly not as a sole intervention strategy). Rather, it may be more appropriate for them to have some kind of social-skill or assertiveness training either in place of or in addition to the meditation treatment (D. H. Shapiro, 1980). Further meditation may not be a useful therapeutic intervention for chronically depressed people, who may need to have their arousal level activated (cf. also hypotensives, hyperactive children). Also, many therapists consider arousal one of the prime conditions facilitating therapetic change (Yalom, Bend, Bloch, Zimmerman, & Friedman, 1977) and therefore would not consider meditation a treatment of choice to calm or relax a person. In addition, it may not be a useful strategy for people with high somatic, but low cognitive, activity (R. J. Davidson & Schwartz, 1976). Meditation may not be the treatment of choice for people with a high external locus of control (Beiman et al., in press) or with clinical problems such as migraine headaches or Raynaud's disease, which as Stroebel and Glueck (1977) note are not as amenable to amelioration by meditation as to temperature and EMG biofeedback for eliciting vasodilation and muscle relaxation.

Additional issues to be considered regarding negative effects are the following: Is the person meditating for too long a time, thereby impairing reality testing (French et al., 1975; Lazarus, 1976)? Is the person spending too much time letting go of thoughts (not analyzing them) and therefore not gaining pinpointed cause-and-effect awareness. If so, then, even though affect may be lessened, has the person learned the antecedent conditions that cause reflex inappropriate, maladaptive behaviors? Has the person learned, in addition to skills of letting go of thoughts and goals, the skills of setting goals, existentially choosing who he or she wants to be and how he or she wants to act?

There is also the important issue of preparation. Negative effects may occur if the person has not been given sufficient preparation for meditation. For example, a self-critical, perfectionistic, Western, goal-oriented person who learns meditation will probably bring that same cognitive orientation to the task of meditation. She or he may, therefore, be highly critical (e.g., I am not doing it right); each thought may be seen as defeat; and an internal fight may ensue to stop "thoughts." As one patient noted to me, "I became distracted by thoughts, then worried about being distracted; but I couldn't stop the flood of thoughts; I started crying; it was almost impossible for me to then return to breathing."

My hope in presenting this discussion of adverse effects is twofold. On the one hand I would like to insert a note of caution into the hosannahs many bestow on meditation. The transpersonal, or spiritual, perspective gives an answer elegant in its simplicity for dealing with adverse effects, namely: Watch the process; do not get caught up in it; let it be a learning experience for yourself, a new awareness of your resistance and defenses; keep the context. The answer to every dilemma becomes: adverse effects are only part of the path. Stay centered. It takes years of practice. Eastern philosophy, with the world view espousing acceptance, says all things, good and bad, should be accepted with equanimity. Philosophically and theoretically, once a person can do that, life becomes free from suffering, as Buddah noted in his Four Noble Truths. On the one hand, I subscribe to this advice. On the other hand, I find it too absolute; it strikes me as similar to the classical psychoanalytic dictum: Insight causes cure. If you are not cured, by definition more insight is needed. Similarly, if you are not keeping the context, practice keeping it more.

Therefore, as clinicians, I believe we need extreme caution in using a technique such as meditation, and we need to be sensitive to some of the adverse effects that may occur with patients to whom we prescribe it. On the other hand, my second purpose in presenting the adverse effects, is that I believe meditation is an extremely powerful technique that can bring a great deal of good to many patients. I do not want it to be too readily dismissed by the scientific community just because the initial global claims of its effectiveness do not appear to be warranted. My hope is that we can develop a cautious approach to the use of meditation, neither overstating its worth nor arbitrarily dismissing it.

## Directions Clinically Oriented Research Might Profitably Pursue

Let me suggest five different directions I think need to be pursued. First I believe we need to look more carefully at the context of meditation. In particular this would involve an understanding of what peoples' expectations are in learning meditation as well as some assessment of the demand characteristics of the teacher-training organization (Malec & Sipprelle, 1977; Orne, 1962). Most religious traditions have a series of preparations that must be performed before a person is thought to be ready to begin the spiritual practice of meditation (Brown, 1977; Deikman, in press). These preparations range from the highly structured and complex—changing dietary habits, cultivating feelings of love and compassion, decreasing thoughts of selfishness and greed—to the much less complex—preparatory lectures and instructional training. Additional contextual variables would include the issue of motivation and the role of individual responsibility (Globus, 1980; J. Shapiro & D. H. Shapiro, 1979).

Second, a component analysis of meditation must be undertaken in order to be able to separate the active from the inert aspects. In other words, how much of meditation's effects are due to antecedent variables of preparation and environmental planning, how much to components of the behavior itself— physical posture, attentional focus and style, and breathing? By breaking meditation into its various components, it might be possible to determine which aspects might be profitably combined with other self-regulation strategies (D. H. Shapiro, 1978; D. H. Shapiro & Zifferblatt, 1976b; Woolfolk, in press).

A third direction that might profitably be pursued is refinement of the dependent variable. For example, as noted, Davidson and Schwartz (1976) have suggested that anxiety actually has both a cognitive and a somatic component and that meditation may be effective for reducing cognitive anxiety while doing relatively little for somatic anxiety. A fourth direction is examining subject variables (Beiman et al., in press; Smith, 1978). This approach would attempt, based on certain pretest indicators, to develop a subject profile of those for whom meditation is likely to provide a successful clinical intervention and a profile of those for whom there may be adverse effects (Walsh & Rauche, 1979). These refinements would enable us to become more precise in choosing the correct clinical intervention (or combination of interventions) for a specific person with a specific clinical problem.

A fifth direction is looking at the phenomenology of meditation. This approach, valued by the Eastern tradition for centuries, is just beginning to gain favor within the Western scientific community. Despite methodological and conceptual problems (Walsh, 1980), researchers are beginning to note its importance. For example, although Morse et al. (1977) found that physiological responses failed to show significant differences among the three relaxation states, they point out that subject evaluation *did* show significance (cf. also Gilbert, Parker, & Claiborn, 1978). Therefore, they cite and concur with Tart's remark that "in a subject's own estimate of his behavior, an internal state is a rich and promising source of data which some experimenters tend to ignore in their passionate search for objectivity" (Morse et al., 1977). Similarly, Curtis and Wessberg (1975/1976) noted that there were more positive subjective changes in the meditation group than in the control "relaxation group" even though there was no difference in physiological measures. They suggest that if meditation has a unique effect, it is apparently different from a visceral or neuromuscular one.

If meditation is a unique technique, its uniqueness may not be as a self-regulation strategy, and therefore it will not be seen as different from other self-regulation strategies on either a clinical or a physiological basis. It may be seen instead in the way the person experiences it. This literature on the phenomenological or subjective experiences during meditation—on meditation as an altered state of consciousness—(J. Davidson, 1976; D. H. Shapiro, 1980; D. H. Shapiro & Giber, 1978) may be an important and critical source for future scientific examination.

Setting aside the question of meditation's uniqueness, however, the issue that now confronts us is to develop more precision as to when to use meditation versus other self-regulation strategies. Although it appears that meditation is no more effective as a clinical intervention than other self-regulation strategies, this is neither a reason to use or not to use it. It appears that we now have several self-regulation strategies that are more effective than controls in the alleviation of certain clinical problems. We are now faced with the task of designing more sophisticated and precise research strategies in order to clarify which self-regulation strategy is the treatment of choice for which patient with what clinical problem.

## GENERAL CLINICAL CONSIDERATIONS

Meditation, though an effective self-control strategy for the clinical management of stress when regularly practiced by the client, is not a magical cure. It is a treatment strategy that requires the patient's cooperation and thus raises important issues including those of preparation, adherence and compliance, and evaluation.

## Preparation

*Motivation.* Before introducing a self-control strategy such as meditation, it is necessary, at least informally, to assess patient motivation. Does the patient really want to decrease or manage stress? For example, some people may feel that stress is the "glue" that holds them together. Even though at times they may wish to reduce stress or are aware of the dangers of a stressful life-style, they also fear what would happen if they did not have stress as a motivation. Often the classic Type A personality who feels that a hard-driving and competitive life-style is necessary for success may risk potential myocardial infarction in exchange for avoiding failure (Friedman & Roseman, 1974). The stress reactions some people experience, or their illnesses exacerbated by stress, may also include a component of secondary gain. Despite apparent misery and distress, a patient may be resistant to change because of the attention received from an otherwise aloof and preoccupied family.

In addition to assessing barriers to change, the physician or clinician must also evaluate positive motivation. Is the patient aware of positive reasons to adopt a self-control strategy or is he or she merely giving pro forma acquiescence? Focusing the patient on positive consequences, such as feelings of competence, inner relaxation and calm, and more positive energy to enjoy and experience, can often be a powerful motivator.

*Individual responsibility.* The concept of self-control implies a person performing these strategies under her or his own volition. Old models of the dependent, passive patient without any involvement in or responsibility for his or her own health care will not work in the context of self-control skills (J. Shapiro & D. H. Shapiro, 1979). The physician or clinician needs to use her or his traditional high status and aura of omnipotence to communicate firmly and supportively the importance of responsibility for self in the health care process.

*Relationship.* A related factor is the patient's relationship with the physician (Antonovsky, 1979) or therapist (Truax & Carkuff, 1967). Successful implementation of a self-control strategy, indeed of any prescribed medical regimen, depends in part on the patient's rapport with and trust in the physician. By adopting a warm, sincere, and empathetic attitude toward the patient, the physician can facilitate the teaching of these skills and encourage and support their practice. Attention to the whole person (Baker & Cassata, 1978) will stimulate both the development of individual responsibility and the successful adoption of the self-control practice.

*Assessing types of stress.* People respond differently to stress. Generally client's self-observation of a potential stressor is necessary to determine what role this stimulus in fact plays in his or her life. The clinician should work with the patient to ensure sensitivity to cognitive, physiological, and symbolic (i.e., imaginal) manifestations of stress.

*Assessing client characteristics.* Generally, if a patient or client appears highly dependent, with a high external locus of control, the therapist or physician will need to take a stronger initial posture in teaching self-control strategies (Houston, 1972; Rotter, 1966). The health care professional may also need to work on the patient's belief in her or his own ability to exercise some mastery over self and environment (Glass, 1977).

The therapist should also assess the patient's beliefs about and attitudes toward the different self-control strategies available. Each of the several stress-

toward the different self-control strategies available. Each of the several stress-management techniques has gone through popular phases where it has been embraced by the lay community and thus already has some face recognition. Some patients may not like the scientific precision of biofeedback; some may be attracted to it for precisely this reason. Similarly, the terms *hypnosis* and *meditation* may evoke either positive or negative responses. At this point in the state of our knowledge (with the few exceptions mentioned below), all self-control techniques appear to work equally well in stress management; all work better than a placebo but none better than another (D. H. Shapiro, 1980). Therefore the choice of a strategy should take into consideration the patient's attitude toward it.

## Choosing a Strategy

One of the reasons why the self-control strategies may be equally effective, names and labels aside, is that almost all the techniques involve attentional focusing, cognitive statements, imagery, or combination of these components. Further, a general antistress response in the person has been posited (Stoyva & Budzynski, 1975); it is supposed to be a common pathway shared by all the self-control techniques and to promote a pattern of psychobiologic responding antithetical to the stresses of daily living. Thus, as a general rule, selection of a particular technique depends largely on the individual practitioner's own familiarity and comfort with the technique, pragmatic considerations in training (e.g., access to biofeedback equipment), and patient attitude.

Preliminary research indicates the following differentiations among strategies that also need to be taken into consideration:

1. For detecting a precise functional relationship between the patient's environment and stress, behavioral self-observation is the treatment of choice (Thoresen & Mahoney, 1974).

2. For tension headache, EMG biofeedback is the treatment of choice; for migraine headache, the choice is temperature training (Budzynski, Stoyva, Adler, & Mullaney, 1973).

3. Between meditation and biofeedback, for "general relaxation," meditation is the treatment of choice; for a specific stress area, the choice is biofeedback (Schwartz, 1973).

4. For cognitive stress, a cognitive strategy such as hypnosis or meditation appears more effective than a somatic strategy (Schwartz, Davidson, & Goleman, 1978).

5. For somatic stress, exercise or progressive relaxation appears to be more effective (Schwartz, Davidson, & Goleman, 1978).

6. For a person with a primarily auditory response system,

    a. when using biofeedback, a visual feedback stimulus is preferable (Branstrom, 1978).

    b. when using meditation or hypnosis, an auditory stimulus is preferred (Davidson & Schwartz, 1976).

## Adherence and Compliance

In considering any treatment strategy, issues of adherence and compliance must always be in the physician's mind. In addition to assessing initial motivation, the clinician should also be sensitive to decreasing motivation over time and possible negative experiences the patient might undergo. Once initial enthusiasm for the technique has dissipated, patients may not structure practice periods unless they receive continued encouragement and attention from the physician (Glueck & Stroebel, 1975). Also, because negative experiences (e.g., feelings of sadness, depression, withdrawal, unpleasant images) occasionally occur during the practice of a technique, the clinician must be vigilant in continuing to monitor the patient's experience of the self-control practice and must deal in a therapeutic manner with any such occurrence.

Maintaining the self-control behaviors may often be facilitated by the pleasurable nature of the experience itself or by the reduction in symptoms. In addition, it may be useful to enlist the family or other social contacts as a support system. It is often possible to make the practice of meditation or progressive relaxation a family exercise, which may have unintended benefits as well in improving family togetherness and harmony. Setting up a contract with the client (Kanfer, 1977) and specifying special instructions and reminders (Weiss, 1975) will also ensure improved compliance.

## Evaluation and Follow-up

Despite research and clinical findings currently reported in the literature, because people are unique, no one strategy will necessarily be "right" for an individual patient. At this state of our knowlege, practicing physicians and health care professionals, functioning as scientist-observers, need to evaluate carefully the efficacy of the self-control strategies they employ. Is this client following instructions? Adhering? Making progress? If not, why not? Might another strategy be more beneficial? How will a decrease in stress in one family member affect the entire family system? These and similar questions deserve careful attention, and answers to them will help contribute to a more complete science of the clinical management of stress.

## REFERENCES

Akishige, Y. (Ed.). *Psychological studies on Zen.* Tokyo: Zen Institute of the Komazawa University, 1970.

Allison, J. Respiratory change during transcendental meditation. *Lancet,* 1970, *1*, 833–834.

Anand, B., Chinna, G., & Singh, B. Some aspects of electroencephalographic studies in yogis. *Electroencephalography and Clinical Neurophysiology,* 1961, *13*, 452–456.

Antonovsky, A. *Health, stress and coping.* San Francisco: Jossey-Bass, 1979, 198–220.

Bagchi, B. K., & Wenger, M. A. Simultaneous EEG and other recordings during some yogi exercises. *Electroencephalography and Clinical Neurophysiology,* 1957, 7(Suppl.), 132–149.

Baker, E. M., & Cassatta, D. M. The physician–patient relationship. In R. B. Taylor (Ed.), *Family medicine: Principles and practice.* New York: Springer-Verlag, 1978, 143–148.

Bandura, A. *Principles of behavior modification.* New York: Holt, 1969.

Bandura, A. *Social learning theory.* Englewood Cliffs, N.J.: Prentice-Hall, 1977.

Banquet, J. P. EEG and meditation. *Electroencephalography and Clinical Neurophysiology,* 1972, *33*, 454.

Banquet, J. P. Spectral analysis of the EEG in meditation. *Electroencephalography and Clinical Neurophysiology,* 1973, *35*, 143–151.

*Behavioral Medicine Abstracts,* 1980, *1*(1), p. iii.

Beiman, I. H., Johnson, S. A., Puente, A. E., Majestic, H. W., & Graham, L. E. Client characteristics and success in TM. In D. H. Shapiro & R. N. Walsh (Eds.), *The science of meditation.* New York: Aldine, in press.

Benson, H. *The relaxation response.* New York: Morrow, 1975.

Benson, H. Reply to Muchlman. *New England Journal of Medicine,* 1977, *297*(9), 513.

Benson, H. *The mind body effect.* New York: Simon & Schuster, 1978.

Benson, H., Beary, J. F., & Carol, M. P. The relaxation response. *Psychiatry,* 1974, *37,* 37–46.

Benson, H., Marzetla, B. R., Rosner, B. A., & Klemchuk, H. M. Decreased blood pressure in pharmacologically treated hypertensive patients who regularly elicited the relaxation response. *Lancet,* 1974, *785,* 289–291.

Benson, H., Rosner, B. A., Marzetla, B. R., et al. Decreased blood pressure in borderline hypertensive subjects who practiced meditation. *Journal of Chronic Diseases,* 1974, *27,* 163–169.

Benson, H., & Wallace, R. Decreased blood pressure in hypertensive subjects who practice meditation. *Circulation,* 1972, *2*(Suppl.), 516.

Berwick, P., & Oziel, L. J. The use of meditation as a behavioral technique. *Behavior Therapy,* 1973, *4,* 743–745.

Boswell, P. C., & Murray, G. J. Effects of meditation on psychological and physiological measures of anxiety. *Journal of Consulting and Clinical Psychology,* 1979, *47,* 606–607.

Boudreau, L. Transcendental meditation and yoga as reciprocal inhibitors. *Journal of Behavior Therapy and Experimental Psychiatry,* 1972, *3,* 97–98.

Branstrom, M. *The efficacy of preferred and nonpreferred feedback mode for auditory and visual persons.* Unpublished doctoral dissertation, Pacific Graduate School of Psychology, Palo Alto, Calif.

Brown, D. A model for the levels of concentrative meditation. *International Journal of Clinical & Experimental Hypnosis,* 1977, *25,* 236–273.

Budzynski, T. H., Stoyva, J. M., Adler, C. S., & Mullaney, D. J. EMG biofeedback and tension headache: A controlled outcome study. *Psychosomatic Medicine,* 1973, *35,* 484–496.

Carrington, P. *Freedom in meditation.* New York: Doubleday, Anchor, 1978.

Carrington, P., & Ephron, H. Meditation as an adjunct to psychotherapy. In S. Arieti & G. Chrzanowski (Eds.), *The world biennial of psychotherapy and psychiatry* (Vol. 3). New York: Wiley, 1975.

Cauthen, N., & Prymak, C. Meditation versus relaxation. *Journal of Consulting and Clinical Psychology,* 1977, *45,* 496–497.

Coates, T. J., & Thoresen, C. E. What to use instead of sleeping pills. *Journal of the American Medical Association,* 1978, *240,* 2311–2314.

Conze, E. *Buddhist meditation.* New York: Harper, 1969.

Corby, J. C., Roth, W. T., Zarzone, V. P., & Koppell, B. S. Psychophysiological correlates of the practice of tantric yoga meditation. *Archives of General Psychiatry,* 1978, *35,* 571–580.

Curtis, W. D., & Wessberg, H. W. A comparison of heart rate, respiration, and galvanic skin response among meditators, relaxers, and control. *Journal of Altered States of Consciousness,* 1975/1976, *2,* 319–324.

Daniels, L. Treatment of psychophysiological disorders and severe anxiety by behavior therapy, hypnosis and transcendental meditation. *American Journal of Clinical Hypnosis,* 1975, *17,* 267–270.

Das, H., & Gastaut, H. Variations de l'activité électrique du cerveau, du coeur et des muscles squellettiques an cours de la méditation et de l'extase yogique. *Electroencephalography and Clinical Neurophysiology,* 1955, *6*(Suppl.), 211–219.

Datey, K., Deshmukh, S. H., Dalviica, et al. "Shavasana": A yogic exercise in the management of hypertension. *Angiology,* 1969, *20,* 325–333.

Davidson, J. Physiology of meditation and mystical states of consciousness. *Perspectives in Biology and Medicine,* 1976, *19,* 345–380.

Davidson, P. O., & Davidson, S. M. (Eds.). *Behavioral medicine: Changing health lifestyles.* New York: Brunner/Mazel, 1980.

Davidson, R. J., & Goleman, D., & Schwartz, G. E. Attentional and affective concomitants of meditation: A cross-sectional study. *Journal of Abnormal Psychology,* 1976, *85,* 235–238.

Davidson, R. J., & Schwartz, G. E. The psychobiology of relaxation and related states: A multi-process theory. In D. I. Mostofsky (Ed.), *Behavior control and the modification of physiological activity*. Englewood Cliffs, N.J.: Prentice-Hall, 1976.

Deikman, A. J. Deautomatization and the mystic experience. *Psychiatry*, 1966, *29*, 324–338.

Deikman, A. J. The state of the art of meditation. In D. H. Shapiro & R. N. Walsh (Eds.), *The science of meditation*. New York: Aldine, in press.

DiCara, L. V. Learning in the autonomic nervous system. *Scientific American*, 1970, *222*, 30–39.

Dillbeck, M. The effect of the transcendental meditation technique on anxiety level. *Journal of Clinical Psychology*, 1977, *33*, 1076–1978.

Elson, B., Hauri, P., Cunis, D. Physiological changes in yoga meditation. *Psychophysiology*, 1977, *14*, 52–57.

Fenwick, P. B., Donaldson, S., & Gillis, L. Metabolic and EEG changes during transcendental meditation: An explanation. *Biological Psychology*, 1977, *5*, 101–118.

Ferguson, P. C., & Gowan, J. C. Transcendental meditation: Some preliminary findings. *Journal of Humanistic Psychology*, 1976, *16*(3), 51–60.

Fischer, R. A cartography of the ecstatic and meditative states. *Science*, 1971, *174*, 897–904.

French, A. P., Schmid, A. C., & Ingalls, E. Transcendental meditation, altered reality testing, and behavioral change: A case report. *Journal of Nervous and Mental Disease*, 1975, *161*, 55–58.

French, A. P., & Tupin, J. Therapeutic application of a simple relaxation method. *American Journal of Psychotherapy*, 1974, *28*, 282–287.

Friedman, M., & Rosenman, R. H. *Type A behavior and your heart*. New York: Knopf, 1974.

Fromm, E. Self-hypnosis. *Psychotherapy: Theory, Research and Practice*, 1975, *12*, 295–301.

Gilbert, G. S., Parker, J. C., & Claiborn, C. D. Differential mood changes in alcoholics as a function of anxiety management strategies. *Journal of Clinical Psychology*, 1978, *34*, 229–232.

Girodo, M. Yoga meditation and flooding in the treatment of anxiety neurosis. *Journal of Behavior Therapy and Experimental Psychiatry*, 1974, *5*, 157–160.

Glass, D. C. Stress, behavior patterns, and coronary disease. *American Scientist*, 1977, *65*, 178–187.

Globus, G. On "I": The conceptual foundations of responsibility. *American Journal of Psychiatry*, 1980, *137*, 417–422.

Glueck, B. C., & Stroebel, C. F. Biofeedback and meditation in the treatment of psychiatric illness. *Comprehensive Psychiatry*, 1975, *16*, 303–321.

Goldman, B. L., Domitor, P. J., & Murray, E. J. Effects of Zen meditation on anxiety reduction and perceptual functioning. *Journal of Consulting and Clinical Psychology*, 1979, *47*, 551–556.

Goleman, D. The Buddha on meditation and states of consciousness: II: A typology of meditation techniques. *Journal of Transpersonal Psychology*, 1972, *4*, 151–210.

Goleman, D., & Schwartz, G. E. Meditation as an intervention in stress reactivity. *Journal of Consulting and Clinical Psychology*, 1976, *44*, 456–466.

Goyeche, J., Chihara, T., & Shimizu, H. Two concentration methods: A preliminary comparison. *Psychologia*, 1972, *15*, 110–111.

Hager, J. L., & Suruit, R. S. Hypertension self-control with a portable feedback unit or meditation-relaxation. *Biofeedback and Self-regulation*, 1978, *3*, 269–275.

Hastings, A., Fadiman, J., & Gordon, J. S. *Health for the whole person*. Boulder, Colo.: Westview, 1980.

Herrigel, E. *Zen in the art of archery*. New York: McGraw-Hill, 1953. (Now entitled *Method of Zen*.)

Hirai, T. *Psychophysiology of Zen*. Tokyo: Igaku Shin, 1974.

Hjelle, L. A. Transcendental meditation and psychological health. *Perceptual and Motor Skills*, 1974, *39*, 623–628.

Holmes, T. H., & Rahe, R. H. The Social Readjustment Rating Scale. *Journal of Psychosomatic Research*, 1967, *11*, 213–218.

Honsberger, R., & Wilson, A. P. Transcendental meditation in treating asthma. *Respiratory Therapy: Journal of Inhalation Technology*, 1973, *3*, 79–81.

Houston, B. D. Control over stress, locus of control, and response to stress. *Journal of Personality and Social Psychology*, 1972, *21*, 249–255.

Jacob, R. G., Kraemer, H. C., & Agras, W. S. Relaxation therapy in the treatment of hypertension: A review. *Archives of General Psychiatry,* 1977, *34,* 1417-1421.

Jevning, R., & O'Halloran, J. P. Metabolic effects of transcendental meditation. In D. H. Shapiro & R. N. Walsh (Eds.), *The science of meditation.* New York: Aldine, in press.

Kanas, N., & Horowitz, M. Reactions of TMers and non-meditators to stress films. *Archives of General Psychiatry,* 1977, *34,* 1431-1436.

Kanfer, F. H. The many faces of self-control. In R. B. Stuart (Ed.), *Behavioral self-management: Strategies, techniques and outcomes.* New York: Brunner/Mazel, 1977.

Karambelkar, P., Vinekar, S., & Bhole, M. Studies on human subjects staying in an air-tight pit. *Indian Journal of Medical Research,* 1968, *56,* 1282-1288.

Kasamatsu, A., & Hirai, T. An electroencephalographic study of the Zen meditation (zazen). *Folia Psychiatria et Neurologica Japonica,* 1966, *20,* 315-336.

Kasamatsu, A., Okima, T., Takenaka, S., Koga, E., & Ikada, K. The EEG of "Zen" and "yoga" practitioners. *Electroencephalography and Clinical Neurophysiology,* 1957, *9*(Suppl.), 51-52.

Kirsch, I., & Henry, I. Self-desensitization and meditation in the reduction of public speaking anxiety. *Journal of Consulting and Clinical Psychology,* 1979, *47,* 536-541.

Kohr, E. Dimensionality in the meditative experience: A replication. *Journal of Transpersonal Psychology,* 1977, *9,* 193-203.

Kretschmer, W. Meditative techniques in psychotherapy. In C. Tart (Ed.), *Altered states of consciousness.* New York: Wiley, 1969.

Krishnamurti, J. *Meditation.* Ojai, Calif.: Krishnamurti Foundation, 1979.

Lazar, Z., Farwell, L., & Farrow, J. Effects of transcendental meditation program on anxiety, drug abuse, cigarette smoking, and alcohol consumption. In D. W. Orme-Johnson & J. Farrow (Ed.), *Scientific research on the transcendental meditation program* (Vol. 1, 2nd ed.). Maharishi European Research University Press, 1977.

Lazarus, A. A. *Behavior therapy and beyond.* New York: McGraw-Hill, 1971.

Lazarus, A. A. Psychiatric problems precipitated by transcendental meditation. *Psychological Reports,* 1976, *10,* 39-74.

Levi, L. (Ed.). *Society, stress and disease: The psychosocial environment and psychosomatic disease.* London: Oxford University Press, 1971.

Linden, W. The relationship between the practice of meditation by school children and their levels of field dependence-independence, test anxiety, and reading achievement. *Journal of Consulting and Clinical Psychology,* 1973, *41,* 139-143.

Malec, J., & Sipprelle, C. N. Physiological and subjective effects of Zen meditation and demand characteristics. *Journal of Consulting and Clinical Psychology,* 1977, *44,* 339-340.

Marlatt, G., Pagano, R., Rose, R., & Margues, J. K. Effect of meditation and relaxation training upon alcohol use in male social drinkers. In D. H. Shapiro & R. N. Walsh (Eds.), *The science of meditation.* New York: Aldine, in press.

McNamara, J. R. (Ed.). *Behavioral approaches to medicine: Application and analysis.* New York: Plenum, 1979.

Meichenbaum, D., & Cameron, R. The clinical potential of modifying what clients say to themselves. In M. J. Mahoney & C. E. Thoresen, *Self-control: Power to the person.* Monterey, Calif.: Brooks/Cole, 1974.

Michaels, R., Huber, M., & McCann, D. Evaluation of transcendental meditation as a method of reducing stress. *Science,* 1976, *192,* 1242-1244.

Miller, N. E. Learning of visceral and glandular responses. *Science,* 1969, *163,* 434-445.

Morse, D. R., Martin, S., Furst, M. L., & Dubin, L. L. A physiological and subjective evaluation of meditation, hypnosis, and relaxation. *Psychosomatic Medicine,* 1977, *39,* 304-324.

Muchlman, M. Transcendental meditation. *New England Journal of Medicine,* 1977, *297,* 513.

Naranjo, C., & Ornstein, R. *On the psychology of meditation.* New York: Viking, 1971.

Orme-Johnson, D. W. Autonomic stability and transcendental meditation. *Psychosomatic Medicine,* 1973, *35,* 341-349.

Orne, M. T. On the social psychology of the psychological experiment: With particular reference to demand characteristics and their implications. *American Psychologist,* 1962, *17,* 776-783.

Osis, K., Bokert, E., & Carlson, M. L. Dimensions of the meditative experience. *Journal of Transpersonal Psychology,* 1973, *5,* 109-135.

Otis, L. S. If well-integrated but anxious, try TM. *Psychology Today,* 1974, *7,* 45–46.

Otis, L. S. Adverse effects of meditation. In D. H. Shapiro & R. N. Walsh (Eds.), *The science of meditation.* New York: Aldine, in press.

Pagano, R., & Frumkin, L. Effect of TM in right hemispheric functioning. *Biofeedback and Self-regulation,* 1977, *2,* 407–415.

Pagano, R., Warrenburg, S., & Woods, M. *Oxygen consumption during transcendental meditation and progressive muscle relaxation.* Unpublished manuscript, University of Washington, Seattle, 1978.

Parker, J. C., Gilbert, A. S., & Thoreson, R. W. Reduction of autonomic arousal in alcoholics. *Journal of Consulting and Clinical Psychology,* 1978, *46,* 879–886.

Patel, C. H. Yoga and biofeedback in the management of hypertension. *Lancet,* 1973, *2,* 1053–1055.

Patel, C. H. Randomized control trial of yoga and biofeedback in management of hypertension. *Lancet,* 1975, *11,* 93–94. (a)

Patel, C. H. Twelve-month follow-up of yoga and biofeedback in the management of hypertension. *Lancet,* 1975, *1,* 62–65. (b)

Paul, G. L. Physiological effects of relaxation training and hypnotic suggestion. *Journal of Abnormal Psychology,* 1969, *74,* 425–437.

Pelletier, K. R. *Mind as a healer, mind as slayer: A holistic approach to stress disorders.* New York: Dell, Delacorte, 1977.

Pelletier, K. R. *Holistic medicine.* New York: Dell, Delacorte, 1979.

Pollack, A. A., Weber, M. A., Case, D. B., & Laragh, J. H. Limitations of transcendental meditation in the treatment of essential hypertension. *Lancet,* 1977, *8,* 71–73.

Pomerleau, O. F. Behavioral medicine: The contribution of the experimental analysis of behavior to medical care. *American Psychologist,* 1979, *34,* 654–663.

Pomerleau, O. F., & Brady, J. P. (Eds.). *Behavioral medicine: Theory and practice.* Baltimore: Williams & Wilkins, 1979.

Pribram, K. *Languages of the brain: Experimental paradoxes and principles in neuropsychology.* Englewood Cliffs, N.J.: Prentice-Hall, 1971.

Rahula, W. *What the Buddha taught.* New York: Grove, 1959.

Rabkin, J. G., & Struening, E. L. Life events, stress, and illness. *Science,* 1976, *194,* 1013–1020.

Roghmann, K. J., & Haggerty, R. J. Daily stress, illness, and use of health services in young families. *Pediatric Research,* 1973, *7,* 520–526.

Rotter, J. B. Generalized expectancies for internal versus external control of reinforcement. *Psychological Monographs,* 1966, *80,*(1, Whole No. 609).

Schwartz, G. E. Biofeedback as therapy: Some theoretical and practical issues. *American Psychologist,* 1973, *28,* 666–673.

Schwartz, G. E., Davidson, R. J., & Goleman, D. Patterning of cognitive and somatic processes in the self-regulation of anxiety: Effects of meditation versus exercise. *Psychosomatic Medicine,* 1978, *40,* 321–328.

Schwartz, G. E., & Weiss, S. M. What is behavioral medicine? *Psychosomatic Medicine,* 1977, *36,* 377–381.

Shapiro, D., Tursky, B., Schwartz, G. E., & Schnidman, S. R. Smoking on cue: A behavioral approach to smoking reduction. *Journal of Health and Social Behavior,* 1971, *12,* 108–113.

Shapiro, D. H. Zen meditation and behavioral self-management applied to a case of generalized anxiety. *Psychologia,* 1976, *19,* 134–138.

Shapiro, D. H. Instructions for a training package combining Zen meditation and behavioral self-management strategies. *Psychlogia,* 1978, *21,* 70–76. (a)

Shapiro, D. H. *Precision nirvana.* Englewood Cliffs, N.J.: Prentice-Hall, 1978. (b)

Shapiro, D. H. *Meditation: Self-regulation strategy and altered state of consciousness.* New York: Aldine, 1980.

Shapiro, D. H., & Giber, D. Meditation and psychotherapeutic effects. *Archives of General Psychiatry,* 1978, *35,* 294–302.

Shapiro, D. H., & Shapiro, J. The clinical management of stress: Nonpharmacological approaches. *Family Practice Recertification,* 1980, *2*(10), 55–63.

Shapiro, D. H., & Zifferblatt, S. M. An applied clinical combination of Zen meditation and behavioral self-management techniques: Reducing methadone dosage in drug addiction. *Behavior Therapy,* 1976, *7,* 694–695. (a)

Shapiro, D. H., & Zifferblatt, S. M. Zen meditation and behavioral self-control: Similarities, differences and clinical applications. *American Psychologist,* 1976, *31*, 519-532. (b)

Shapiro, J., & Shapiro, D. H. The psychology of responsibility. *New England Journal of Medicine,* 1979, *301*, 211-212.

Singer, J. L. Navigating the stream of consciousness: Research in daydreaming and related inner experience. *American Psychologist,* 1975, *30*, 727-738.

Skinner, B. F. *Science and human behavior.* New York: Macmillan, 1953.

Smith, J. Meditation and psychotherapy: A review of the literature. *Psychological Bulletin,* 1975, *32*, 553-564.

Smith, J. Psychotherapeutic effects of TM with controls for expectations of relief and daily sitting. *Journal of Consulting & Clinical Psychology,* 1976, *44*, 630-637.

Smith, J. Personality correlates of continuation and outcome in meditation and erect sitting control treatments. *Journal of Consulting and Clinical Psychology,* 1978, *46*, 272-279.

Stone, G. C., Cohen, F., & Adler, N. E. *Health psychology.* San Francisco, Calif.: Jossey-Bass, 1979.

Stone, R. A., & DeLeo, J. Psychotherapeutic control of hypertension. *New England Journal of Medicine,* 1976, *294*, 80-84.

Stoyva, J. M., & Budzynski, T. H. Cultivated low arousal: An anti-stress response. In L. V. DiCara, T. X. Baber, J. Kamiya, N. E. Miller, D. H. Shapiro, & J. M. Stoyva (Eds.), *Biofeedback and self-control.* Chicago: Aldine, 1975.

Stroebel, C. F., & Glueck, B. C. Passive meditation: Subjective and clinical comparison with biofeedback. In G. E. Schwartz & D. Shapiro (Eds.), *Consciousness and self-regulation.* New York: Plenum, 1977.

Sugi, Y., & Akutsu, K. Studies on respiration and energy metabolism during sitting in zazen. *Research Journal Physical Education,* 1968, *12*, 190-206.

Sururt, R. S., Shapiro, D. H., & Good, M. I. Comparison of cardiovascular biofeedback, neuromuscular feedback, and meditation in the treatment of borderline hypertension. *Journal of Consulting and Clinical Psychology,* 1978, *46*, 252-263.

Tart, C. (Ed.). *Altered states of consciousness.* New York: Wiley, 1969.

Tart, C. A psychologist's experience with T.M. *Journal of Transpersonal Psychology,* 1971, *3*, 135-140.

Thomas, D., & Abbas, K. A. Comparison of transcendental meditation and progressive relaxation in reducing anxiety. *British Medical Journal,* 1978, *2*, 17.

Thoresen, C. E., & Mahoney, M. J. *Behavioral self-management.* New York: Holt, 1974.

Travis, T., Kondo, C., & Knott, J. Heart rate, muscle tension, and alpha production of transcendental meditation and relaxation controls. *Biofeedback and self-regulation.* 1976, *1*(4), 387-394.

Treichel, M., Clinch, N., & Cran, M. The metabolic effects of transcendental meditation. *Physiologist,* 1973, *16*, 472. (Abstract)

Truax, C. B., & Carkuff, R. R. *Toward effective counseling and psychotherapy.* New York: Aldine, 1967.

Tulpule, T. Yogic exercises in the management of ischaemic heart disease. *Indian Heart Journal,* 1971, *23*, 259-264.

Vahia, H. S., Doengaji, D. R., Jeste, D. V., et al. A deconditioning therapy based upon concepts of patanjali. *International Journal of Social Psychiatry,* 1972, *18*, 61-66.

Vahia, H. S., Doengaji, D. R., Jeste, D. V., et al. Psychophysiologic therapy based on the concepts of patanjali. *American Journal of Psychotherapy,* 1973, *27*, 557-565.

Van Nuys, D. Meditation, attention, and hypnotic susceptibility: A correlational study. *International Journal of Clinical and Experimental Hypnosis,* 1973, *21*, 59-69.

Wallace, R. K. The physiological effects of transcendental meditation. *Science,* 1970, *167*, 1751-1754.

Wallace, R. K., Benson, H., & Wilson, A. F. A wakeful hypometabolic physiologic state. *American Journal of Physiology,* 1971, *221*, 795-799.

Walrath, L., & Hamilton, D. Autonomic correlates of meditation and hypnosis. *American Journal of Clinical Hypnosis,* 1975, *17*, 190-197.

Walsh, R. Behavioral sciences and the consciousness disciplines. *American Journal of Psychiatry,* 1980, *137*(6), 663-673.

Walsh, R., & Rauche, L. The precipitation of acute psychoses by intensive meditation in individuals with a history of schizophrenia. *American Journal of Psychiatry,* 1979, *138*, 1985-1986.

Washburn, M. Observations relevant to a unified theory of meditation. *Journal of Transpersonal Psychology,* 1978, *10,* 45–66.

Watanabe, T., Shapiro, D. H., & Schwartz, G. E. Meditation as an anoxic state: A critical review and theory. *Psychophysiologia,* 1972, *9,* 279.

Weiss, S. M. (Ed.). *Proceedings of the National Heart and Lung Institute: Working Conference on Health Behavior* (DHEW Publication No. (NIH) 79. Washington: U.S. Government Printing Office, 1975.

Wenger, M. A., & Bagchi, B. K. Studies of autonomic functions in practitioners of yoga in India. *Behavioral Science,* 1961, *6,* 312–323.

Williams, P., & West, M. EEG responses to photic stimulation in persons experienced at meditation. *Electroencephalography and Clinical Neurophysiology,* 1975, *39,* 519–522.

Wolpe, J. *The practice of behavior therapy.* Elmsford, N.Y.: Pergamon, 1969.

Woolfolk, R. L. Psychophysiological correlates of meditation. *Archives of General Psychiatry,* 1975, *32,* 1326–1333.

Woolfolk, R. L. Self-control, meditation and the treatment of chronic anger. In D. H. Shapiro & R. N. Walsh (Eds.), *The science of meditation.* New York: Aldine, in press.

Woolfolk, R. L., Carr-Kaffashan, L., McNulty, T. F., & Lehrer, P. Meditation training as a treatment for insomnia. *Behavior Therapy,* 1976, *7,* 359–365.

Woolfolk, R., & Franks, C. Meditation and behavior therapy. In D. H. Shapiro and R. N. Walsh (Eds.), *The science of meditation.* New York: Aldine, in press.

Yalom, I., Bend, D., Bloch, S., Zimmerman, E., & Friedman, L. The impact of a weekend group experience on individual therapy. *Archives of General Psychiatry,* 1977, *34,* 399–415.

Younger, J., Adrianne, W., & Berger, R. Sleep during transcendental meditation. *Perceptual and Motor Skills,* 1975, *40,* 953–954.

Zuroff, D., & Schwartz, J. Effects of TM and muscle relaxation on trait anxiety, maladjustment, locus of control, and drug use. *Journal of Consulting and Clinical Psychology,* 1978, *46,* 264–271.

# 14

## The Nature of Relaxation Therapy

**Robert S. Lavey**
*Duke University Medical Center, Durham, United States*

**C. Barr Taylor**
*Stanford University School of Medicine, Stanford,
California, United States*

The popularity and spectrum of application of relaxation therapy have expanded rapidly in the past decade. "Relaxation," however, remains a poorly defined entity variously considered as a procedure, a mental state, and a physiological response. Clues to its fundamental nature are nonetheless emerging from the recent flurry of investigations. In this chapter we draw on the accumulating body of information on the techniques, physiological effects, and clinical efficacy of relaxation training to examine more critically the nature of relaxation therapy.

## RELAXATION AND RELATED TECHNIQUES

### Relaxation Methods

Practices analogous to the relaxation methods currently in clinical use have been mainstays of medical treatment in some cultures for millennia. The Egyptian physician-priests 7,000 years ago commonly cured disease through forms of hypnosis and imagery relaxation, a modern technique we discuss later (Sigerist, 1951). Zen, Buddhist, Tibetan, and yogic healing all relied on having the patient in a "relaxed" state, making use of all the elements often cited as being the basis of our current methods: a quiet environment, comfortable position, reduced muscle activity, and an attention-focusing device (MacHovec, 1975). The kavanah state of relaxation and concentration, achieved by controlled breathing exercises and repetitive chanting, was therapeutic for disease-stricken ancient Hebrews (Bokser, 1954; Bowers and Glasner, 1958). Additional examples are provided by the early-Christian meditative practices described by Benson (1974).

Relaxation was introduced into modern Western medicine by Jacobson as a treatment for "fatigue, debility, and lowered resistance" as well as "nervous disorders." He believed that "the nervous system cannot be quieted except in conjunction with the muscular system . . . the whole organism rests as neuromuscular activity diminishes" (Jacobson, 1929, p. xii). The progressive-relaxation (PR) program he developed therefore consists solely of relaxation of the skeletal mus-

Sincerest thanks to Jacqueline Dunbar, Barbara Newman, and Todd Rogers for their critical reading of and contributions to the manuscript and to Ellen Nachtrieb for her secretarial assistance. This work was supported in part by Grant HL07034-06 from the National Heart Lung and Blood Institute.

culature. Patients are required to practice 1 to 2 h per day for "weeks or months, perhaps years" to learn to achieve complete relaxation within a few minutes. Each session involves tensing a particular muscle group (i.e., left forearm or tongue) while lying (or sitting) still with eyes closed in a quiet environment, gaining awareness of the sensation of tension within that part of the body, and then concentrating on eliminating this sensation by relaxing the muscles completely. The program "progresses" around the body. The client spends about 6 days learning to relax the right arm, then the left, followed by each leg, the trunk, neck, and head. Relaxation of mental activities is considered to follow naturally from relaxation of the muscles of speech and the eyes (Jacobson, 1957).

Jacobson (1934, 1967) reported consistent success in treating hypertension, insomnia, asthma, indigestion, and anxiety with PR. The extensive training time has, however, been a major impediment to its more widespread use. Jacobson (1938) admitted that "for purely clinical purposes in acute conditions, treatments may be made very brief and few in number" (p. 40), but he discouraged this practice. It was not until Wolpe and Lazarus reported that an abbreviated form of PR was effective as an anxiety-inhibiting procedure in systematic desensitization that the technique gained widespread use (Wolpe, 1958). This version of PR, with minor individual modifications, is still the most extensively studied and applied type of relaxation therapy.

Another popular modern relaxation technique was derived from traditional Judeo-Christian and Eastern religious meditative practices. Benson, Beary, and Carol (1974) noted that although stemming from widely disparate cultures (including Islam, Buddhism, Shinto, Taoism, Shamanism, Judaism, and Christianity), these meditation procedures shared certain basic elements: a quiet environment, comfortable position, repetitive mental stimulus, and passive attitude. Benson combined these elements with muscle relaxation to produce the technique of Bensonian relaxation (BR). As with PR, the subjects assume a comfortable position in a quiet room with eyes closed. Sitting is advocated in place of reclining to discourage sleep. After relaxing their muscles, subjects focus attention on their breathing and repeat the word *one* silently with each breath for 20 min. There is no instruction given in how to eliminate muscle tension, but it is emphasized that all muscles are to be deeply relaxed. Repetition of "one" or an alternate phrase (often "relax" or a phrase having religious significance) is used to prevent distracting thoughts from interfering with relaxation.

The third basic, commonly practiced relaxation method uses mental imagery alone or in conjunction with related techniques (i.e., PR, hypnosis, or systematic desensitization). Imagery was originally used by Jacobson to *increase* tension in his patients' muscles of vision and speech by having them imagine seeing objects or talking. They were trained to recognize the sensation of tension thus produced in these muscles and to practice eliminating it. During imagery relaxation (IR) the subject creates vivid relaxing images involving all five senses with the purpose of decreasing tension (Kroger & Fezler, 1976; Singer & Pope, 1978; Wolpe, 1958). The preliminary steps of IR are the same as in BR or PR, with the subject comfortably placed in a quiet environment, eyes closed and muscles relaxed. Attention to breathing may be included, but it is not a part of many IR sequences. IR practitioners then relax by reliving in their minds a particularly restful experience (e.g., an afternoon at the seashore or sunning in the backyard).

Using the same procedure for opposite ends reveals a fundamental difference in philosophy of relaxation between Jacobson and adherers to IR. Classical PR looks strictly to inactivity of the skeletal musculature as the source of relaxation, and Jacobson (1967) points out that local EMG activity is increased during visualization or imagined phonation. Proponents of IR believe, however, that the mental calmness that results from experiencing a tranquil image is of greater significance. Kroger and Fezler (1976) argue that "the depth of relaxation produced is largely a function of the subject's concentration and sensory recall. The more vivid the patient's relaxing image the greater will be the relaxation" (p. 38). We discuss the various concepts of the mechanism of relaxation more extensively later in this chapter.

## Related Techniques

Biofeedback, meditation, hypnosis, and autogenic training are distinct from the three relaxation techniques described above, but they often produce subjective feelings analogous to those reported during the relaxation exercises. Biofeedback-aided relaxation usually consists of one of the relaxation techniques with the addition of auditory or visual feedback indicating to the subject the level of some physiological parameter, perhaps EMG or skin conductance (SC), that supposedly reflects the degree of relaxation (Budzynski & Stoyva, 1969; Patel & Carruthers, 1977; Patel & North, 1975). The feedback may guide and reassure the person that he or she is indeed producing the desired changes.

As we already noted, several forms of meditation are very similar to, and in fact serve as the models for, BR. People in a hypnotic trance frequently report generalized sensations of warmth and heaviness. These have been proposed as psychological perceptions of peripheral vasodilation and muscular inactivity, which are changes associated with relaxation (Pelletier, 1977). Autogenic training was developed as a program teaching patients to induce these sensations in themselves, thereby allowing them to achieve all the phenomena otherwise obtainable through hypnosis (Schultz, 1953). This is accomplished by daily practice in a quiet room while lying or sitting in a comfortable position with eyes closed such that "muscular tension should be totally absent" (Pelletier, 1977, p. 234). The practitioner focuses his or her attention on a single body part each session, gradually progressing around the body over the course of weeks, just as in PR. Instead of attending to the sensation of muscle tension, however, he or she concentrates on heaviness, warmth, slow respirations, or heartbeat while continuously repeating a simple phrase (e.g., "My right arm is heavy," or "It breathes me").

While these related techniques can *involve* relaxation and use similar procedures for achieving it, their goals generally go beyond simple relaxation. Biofeedback is more often used to achieve control over a particular physiological variable, such as heart rate (HR) (Pickering & Miller, 1977; Weiss & Engel, 1974) or anal sphincter tone (Engel, Nikoomanesh, & Schuster, 1974), than to induce a relaxed state. Relaxation and visualization are the preliminary steps in the autogenic training program, necessary preconditions allowing the patient to create realistic scenes of conflict or turmoil for analysis and resolution. Investigation of the physiological effects of hypnosis led to the conclusion that "neutral hypnosis is synonymous with relaxation" (Edmonston, 1979, p. 455). As with autogenic training, hypnosis then uses the relaxed state as the basis for engaging in technique-specific procedures such as age regression or posthypnotic suggestion. Practice of the other relaxation-related technique, meditation, is likewise associated with physiological changes suggestive of decreased sympathetic autonomic nervous system (SANS) activity among novices (Kanellakos & Lukas, 1974; Wallace, 1970; Wallace, Benson, & Wilson, 1971; Woolfolk, 1975), but experienced meditators show the opposite effect of *increased* arousal (Corby, Roth, Zarcone, & Kopell, 1978; Das & Gastaut, 1957; Wenger & Bagchi, 1961).

In clinical practice, training in these techniques often includes instruction in the use of the relaxation method in stressful situations as well as under the ideal conditions of a quiet, comfortable environment and an unhurried pace. Little study has been made, however, of the generalizability of relaxation or the effectiveness of these practices while the subject is involved in other activities such as driving a car or giving a speech. While we note that it is important clinically to teach generalization techniques, we focus here on those aspects of relaxation that have been experimentally investigated.

## CRITICAL ELEMENTS IN THE INDUCTION OF RELAXATION

Although the procedures we have discussed differ in approach and purpose, they share an emphasis on a few basic features: a tranquil setting, reduced muscle activity, internal focus of attention, and passive frame of mind. How critical are these elements to the induction of relaxation? Exploration of this issue is particularly handicapped by our lack of a definition or measure of the relaxed state. Most work in the field has assessed relaxation by its effects on physiological variables, focusing especially on EMG, SC, HR, respiratory rate (RR), and BP. These are measures of biologic activities whose complex regulation is at best incompletely understood and which are affected only *indirectly* by relaxation, which presumably exerts its primary action on the CNS. Table 14.1 summarizes the controlled trials that compared the changes occurring during relaxation with those during an alternate activity. These studies fail to demonstrate a characteristic pattern of physiological changes that could be used as an index of relaxation. The relaxation condition did, however, consistently prove superior to control conditions in producing a subjective increase in relaxation or decrease in anxiety. Before discussing the implications of these studies for a unified concept of relaxation, we return to the consideration of the essential components of relaxation.

### Tranquil Setting

In all the relaxation techniques, the subject is seated or lying motionless in a comfortable position with eyes closed in a quiet environment. There is a general feeling that relaxation is easiest under these conditions, but it is unclear whether any of them are required for relaxation. Jacobson, whose concern was solely with muscular contraction, insisted that relaxation not only could, but should, be practiced in all circumstances by reducing motor activity to the minimum required for carrying out the desired action (Jacobson, 1957). It appears that physical exertion *is* compatible with relaxation, as "tense" subjects have reported subjective relaxation and a decrease in anxiety while exercising (Driscoll, 1976).

*Table 14.1* Summary of Controlled Studies Assessing the Changes Occurring during Relaxation as Compared with an Alternate (Control) Activity

| | Relaxation method | Control | Number of subjects in relaxation | Experienced subjects | Effects of relaxation | | | | | Subjective measure |
|---|---|---|---|---|---|---|---|---|---|---|
| | | | | | HR | RR | EMG | SC | BP | |
| Grossberg, 1966 | Taped PR | Self-relaxation | 30 | No | NS[a] | | NS | NS | | |
| Matthews & Gelder, 1969 | Taped PR | Listen to tape-recorded lesson | 14 | Yes | NS | NS | -[b] | - | | + |
| Paul, 1969 | Live PR | Self-relaxation | 20 | No | - | - | | | | + |
| Beary & Benson, 1974 | BR | Sit with eyes closed | 17 | No | - | - | - | NS | | |
| Redmond, Gaylor, McDonald, & Shapiro, 1974 | Live PR | Rest | 6 | Yes | | | | | NS | |
| M. H. Pollack & Zeiner, 1976 | BR | Sit with eyes closed | 10 | No | + | NS | NS | NS | | |
| Benson, Dryer, & Hartley, 1978 | BR during exercise | Exercise | 8 | Yes | NS | NS | NS | NS | | |
| Borkovec, Grayson, & Cooper, 1978 | Taped PR | Self-relaxation | 36 | Yes | NS | NS | | | | + |
| Christoph, Luborsky, Kron, & Fishman, 1978 | BR | Read | 18 | No | - | - | | | NS | |
| D. N. Davidson, Winchester, Taylor, Alderman, & Ingels, 1979 | Taped PR | Rest | 6 | Yes | NS | | | | NS | + |

[a] NS = intrasession change not significantly different between the two groups ($p > .05$).
[b] + (or -) = relaxation group significantly increased (or decreased) during session as compared with control group ($p \leq .05$).

To obtain objective support for this finding, Benson et al. (1978) had eight adults experienced in BR practice this technique while riding a stationary bicycle. Pooled results showed that, at fixed work intensity, there was a 3% decrease in mean oxygen consumption ($VO_2$) during the relaxation period as compared with pre- and postrelaxation. This was not accompanied by a change in mean HR, however, and on an individual basis only three of the eight showed significant decrease during BR in either measure. Unfortunately, no other measures of relaxation, including subjective reports of ability to relax while active, were taken.

Although sitting (or lying) quietly with eyes closed may facilitate relaxation, it appears clear that this is not sufficient to induce it. Paul (1969) instructed 20 college coeds to "get completely comfortable and rest quietly with your eyes closed" for 45 min while he measured their HR, RR, EMG, and SC. These measures were compared both with values taken with eyes open before the rest period and with values from a comparable group practicing PR for the first time. Although most of the group exhibited a significant decrease in at least one of the variables during the resting period, the PR group had a significantly greater decline in all measures except mean SC both during the initial session and on repetition 1 week later. Of greater significance, anxiety-differential tests administered immediately before and after both sessions showed no treatment effect in the resting subjects, whereas the PR trainees reported a significant decrease in anxiety during each period. Another study compared reading with having one's eyes closed while sitting quietly in a comfortable position. There was no significant difference between conditions in any of the parameters studied: $VO_2$, $CO_2$ production, or RR. This same group of 16 young adults showed a significant mean decrease in all measures while practicing BR (Beary & Benson, 1974).

## Reduced Muscle Activity

Inasmuch as the deliberate tensing of muscles is an element of PR only, one is led to believe that it is not essential to relaxation induction. This notion is supported by the work of Brokovec and Sides (1979), who compared the effects of traditional PR with similar training focused on identifying and eliminating muscular tension but not actually tensing the muscles. Subjects were 36 undergraduates who reported high levels of subjective daily tension; they were randomized to one of the two treatment conditions or to no treatment. There was no significant difference between the two treatment groups in self-reported daily tension, either after the 5-week training period or on follow-up 5 months later. Both full PR and training without muscle tensing resulted in a significant reduction in self-reported daily frequency and severity of tension as compared with the no-treatment group. The treated groups did not differ in their decrease in anxiety-differential scores after individual relaxation sessions but, combined, they showed a significantly greater change than the control group, which just sat quietly through the sessions. These results confirm the findings of Edelman (1971), who noted no significant difference between the mean decreases in subjective anxiety, EMG, and SC occurring during sessions of either traditional PR or a version of PR with muscle tensing eliminated.

The importance of muscle relaxation itself is also questionable. Muscle relaxation alone does not produce mental calmness, as totally curarized subjects having no detectable peripheral muscle activity still report experiencing anxiety (Davison,

1966). Other studies have found that EMG activity does not correlate with reported mental calmness or decreased anxiety (Edelman, 1971; Matthews & Gelder, 1969). The apparent compatibility of exercise with relaxation was discussed previously.

## Deep, Regular Breathing

Although the role of breathing is not emphasized in traditional PR or IR, relaxation procedures derived from them commonly include instructions to breathe deeply and slowly, to attend to the feeling of "relaxation" that accompanies exhalation, or both (Taylor, 1978). Breathing techniques similar to that used in BR also have a major role in several meditation and natural childbirth practices, possibly serving to induce relaxation. Such changes in respiratory pattern modify plasma oxygen, carbon dioxide, and hydrogen ion concentrations, which have an effect on all organ systems. The common hyperventilation syndrome, for example, consists of apprehension, lightheadedness, peripheral numbness, and decreased BP sometimes leading to panic, all resulting from the lowered carbon dioxide and hydrogen ion concentrations of overbreathing. Aside from its physiological effects, the practice of deep, regular breathing may itself bring about relaxation. This subject has not been investigated experimentally.

## Internal Focusing of Attention

Internal focusing of attention and passive frame of mind, two elements that may form the basis of relaxation, are particularly difficult to evaluate because they are abstract concepts not readily measured or understood. Complex classification systems of attention and awareness operations have been developed (Fromm, 1979), but researchers have tended to favor dichotomous schemes, categorizing attentional states, for example, as either restrictive or expansive (Ornstein, 1972), active or passive (R. J. Davidson & Schwartz, 1976), or focused on internal sensations as opposed to external stimuli (Fromm, 1979). This last approach to dividing the continuum of attention is particularly relevant to the consideration of relaxation. The Borkovec et al. study of the role of muscle tensing already summarized concluded that "frequent attempts to relax while focusing on internal sensations are sufficient to promote tension reduction" (Borkovec, Grayson, & Cooper, 1978, p. 527). Results of an investigation of behavioral treatments for insomnia (discussed later) had earlier led Borkovec and Fowles (1973) to suggest that the active ingredient in relaxation therapy is "to focus on the pleasant *internal feelings*" of relaxation (p. 157). Several other prominent researchers have proposed that a restriction of attention to internal events is a critical element of relaxation (Jacob, Kraemer, & Agras, 1977; Matthews & Gelder, 1969; Paul, 1969). It is present in all the relaxation techniques discussed here; in fact, the major difference between the methods is the sensation on which they choose to direct attention. Whereas PR focuses on muscle tension, BR concentrates on breathing, and IR uses a vivid image.

Other elements common to these techniques—a quiet environment, closed eyes, and lack of movement—may have their importance in limiting external input, thereby allowing attention to remain inwardly focused. They are not themselves sufficient to produce relaxation, but together they serve to minimize external sources of stress. Stress is defined here as "anything which causes an alteration of psychological homeostatic processes" (Burchfield, 1979, p. 662), in other words, an alteration in the maintenance of the mood state of a relaxed person. As the practitioner becomes more skilled at restricting his or her attention, external stimuli can be present without becoming stressors. Thus, a practitioner could report subjective relaxation while physically active or in a noisy office.

## Passive Frame of Mind

A person's own thoughts and attitude are also potential threats to her or his establishing or maintaining a state of relaxation. To reduce the effects of these internal stressors and help keep attention focused on sensations, each of the relaxation techniques we have discussed uses the power of "passive concentration" discussed by Schultz (1953). All include specific directions in their instruction sets to maintain a passive attitude while undertaking the prescribed concentration device. Benson (1974) warns "one should not scrutinize his performance or try to force the [relaxation] response, because this may well prevent the response from occurring. When distracting thoughts enter the mind, they should simply be disregarded" (p. 54). In PR, the trainee is told, "At no time should you make an *effort* to stop thinking or 'make your mind a blank.' Throughout the course your sole purpose is to relax muscles progressively, letting other effects come as they may" (Jacobson, 1957, p. 117). The phenomenon of the "relaxation paradox" is well known in biofeedback. The harder one tries to change a physiological variable in the direction associated with relaxation, the further it goes in the opposite direction. This "active concentration" acts in opposition to relaxation. The same theme is discussed in autogenic training. The trainee is to have "functional passivity toward the intended outcome of his concentrated activity" (Luthe, 1969) and is advised that "too strong an effort of purpose volition immediately interrupts movement toward deep relaxation" (Pelletier, 1977, p. 231).

The significance of passive concentration goes beyond its role in supporting attention focusing. It establishes a functional mind state void of goal setting, desire, or concern—in other terms, the abandonment of conscious will. Such a condition of passivity to psychological or physiological events, the equivalent of mental calmness, may be required to allow relaxation to occur. The interaction between the passive mental state and somatic sensation-restricted attention has not been investigated. They appear complementary, but either may induce relaxation on its own, or there may be other elements key to relaxation.

Having reviewed the elements common to the relaxation techniques, it seems that muscle relaxation, a quiet environment, and a comfortable position are not necessary; and those that may be critical in the induction of relaxation—internal focusing of attention and a passive frame of mind—are abstract concepts describing difficult-to-measure phenomena. What we know as scientists and do as clinicians are different, however, and a few observations are relevant here. First, elements useful or necessary to acquire a relaxation skill may not be necessary to maintain it. Thus, muscle-tension release, which creates a sense of phsyical relaxation, and a tranquil setting may facilitate the development of relaxation skills. One could probably begin to teach a traffic officer to relax in the middle of rush hour, but it seems easier to be in a quiet office and a comfortable chair.

Also, certain techniques may be more helpful or appealing to some people than others. For example, there are clients who require feedback from instruments to be convinced that they can affect changes in their physiology. For them, an indication of reduced neuromuscular activity can be an important factor in promoting relaxation.

## THE MECHANISM OF RELAXATION

Although the elements critical to the induction of relaxation have yet to be unambiguously defined, the practice of relaxation techniques does seem consistently to produce a feeling of relaxation and improvement in some clinical disorders. How might relaxation work? In this section we examine the most prominent explanations of its underlying mechanisms.

### Decreased Proprioceptive Impulses

Jacobson (1938) first brought attention to the psychophysiology of relaxation with his hypothesis that tension exists in the brain as a result of afferent proprioceptive impulses from the skeletal musculature. This input decreases, and mental tension dissolves, as the muscles are relaxed. "We know that there is only one way to be sure that a patient is really relaxed," he stated, "and this requires electrical (EMG) measurement" (Jacobson, 1967, p. 19). As noted earlier, however, repeated tests have provided evidence against this point of view (Davison, 1966; Edelman, 1971; Matthews & Gelder, 1969), which now has few supporters.

### Decreased CNS Arousability

The level of CNS "arousal" or "activation" is a measure of the organism's physiological and emotional excitation. It ranges from the hyperaroused states of terror and rage to unresponsiveness to external stimuli at the opposite end of the continuum. Middle-to-high levels of activation correspond to vigilance, a watchful state of preparedness to react appropriately to an effective stimulus, and are indicated by peripheral vasoconstriction, tachycardia, and high EMG and SC levels (Lader & Wing, 1966; Sokolov, 1957). Changes in the environment transiently increase an animal's arousal, producing the behavioral and physiological adaptations termed the *orientation reaction* or the *startle reflex*. This integrated set of responses includes changes in sense organ function, skeletal musculature activity, brain-wave frequencies, and hemodynamics (Berlyne, 1960) as outlined in Table 14.2.

This broad spectrum of responses suggests that they are centrally rather than peripherally mediated. How it is that CNS arousal is regulated and how changes in arousal produce these physiological effects has been the subject of much research and speculation. Animal experiments have shown that lesion of the midbrain reticular formation (MRF) produces a comatose state (Bremer, 1935; Lindsley, Schreiner, Knowles, & Magoun, 1950), whereas stimulation of this area is an alerting device (French, Verzeano, & Magoun, 1953; Moruzzi & Magoun,

Table 14.2  The Sets of Physiological Changes Characterizing an Acute Increase in CNS Arousal (Startle Reflex), Ergotropic Stimulation, and Trophotropic Stimulation

| | Muscles affecting sense organs | General musculature | Hemodynamics | EEG | Sweat gland activity | Serum hormones |
|---|---|---|---|---|---|---|
| Acute increase in CNS arousal (startle reflex) | Pupils dilate; nictitating membrane retracts; palpebral fissure widens; head and eyes turn toward stimulus. | Skeletal muscle tone increases; ongoing actions cease. | HR increases, then slows; vessels supplying skeletal musculature dilate; vessels supplying skin and splanchnic areas constrict. | Alpha and slower waves disappear; desynchronization | Increases. | |
| Ergotropic stimulation | Pupils dilate; nictitating membrane retracts. | Skeletal muscle tone increases; intestinal motility decreases; piloerector muscles contract. | HR increases; BP increases. | Desynchronization occurs. | Increases | Epinephrine, adrenocortical steroids increase. |
| Trophotropic stimulation | Pupils constrict; nictitating membrane relaxes. | Skeletal muscle tone decreases; intestinal motility increases. | HR decreases; BP decreases. | Synchronization occurs. | Decreases. | Insulin increases. |

Adapted from Lader and Wing (1966) and Gellhorn and Kiely (1972).

1949). This work gives strong credence to the hypothesis that the mesencephalic and diencephalic reticular formations regulate arousal through activation of the cerebral cortex. In turn, it appears that there exist both positive- and negative-feedback systems whereby the cortex can adjust the degree of stimulation it receives from the MRF (Hugelin & Bonvallet, 1957; Segundo, Arana, & French, 1955). Inhibitory control over the MRF also comes from below in the bulbar reticular formation (Bonvallet & Bloch, 1961). MRF activity thus seems to be closely regulated, as would be expected for an essential biologic function.

Acute activation of the cerebral cortex by the MRF produces an orienting, or startle, response that translates into an increased level of CNS arousal if prolonged. The general physiological effects of increased arousal are essentially the same changes produced by stimulation of the ergotropic system (Table 14.2). The response to facilitation of this system, as described in the next section, is mediated by the SANS, and the strong similarities suggest that the arousal response may involve the same mechanism, as suggested by Sternbach (1960) and Gellhorn and Kiely (1972).

It has been suggested that relaxation involves a decrease in CNS arousability (Taylor, 1978). Lowered arousability is defined by an increase in the degree of input change (stimulus) required to produce a measurable phasic change in a physiological indicator (e.g., BP) or behavioral indicator (e.g., head turning) over base line or a decrease in the response produced by that stimulus. Miller (1926) noted during her experimentation with the PR technique that subjects showed a lessened or absent startle response while relaxing. Based on this observation is the practice of systematic desensitization, which uses the presentation of anxiety-evoking stimuli during relaxation to weaken the connection between the stimuli and the anxiety reaction (Wolpe, 1958). Interest in this clinical technique has prompted a number of controlled studies that have demonstrated a muted physiological response to arousing stimuli in relaxed subjects (Brenner, 1974; Connor, 1974; Grings & Uno, 1968; Hyman & Gale, 1973; Paul, 1969; Van Egeren, Feather, & Hein, 1971). Frequency of spontaneous fluctuation in SC, a variable affected by arousal, was also found to be significantly decreased during relaxation as compared with control conditions. Furthermore, this measure corresponded better than any other taken (frontalis EMG, SC level, HR, and RR) to subjective report of relaxation (Matthews & Gelder, 1969).

## Trophotropic Stimulation

The sympathetic arousal system is also the focus of Gellhorn's concept of relaxation (Gellhorn, 1967). Relaxation, he believes, is a result of a "loss in ergotropic tone of the hypothalamus, a diminution of hypothalamic-cortical discharges, and, consequently . . . dominance of the trophotropic system through reciprocal innervation" (Gellhorn & Kiely, 1972, p. 404). This concept stems from Hess's (1957) observations of the effects of electrical stimulation of the cat brain. The ergotropic zone is located in the posterior hypothalamus, encompassing the mammillary, ventrolateral, lateral, and posterior nuclei. Stimulation of this area produces an increase in BP, RR, motor excitability, and pupil size, as well as the other characteristics listed in Table 14.2. This integrated response is mediated by the SANS and is equivalent to the emergency reaction, or fight-or-flight response, to threatening environmental situations noted by Cannon (1914). Electrical stimulation of the trophotropic zone—which covers the preoptic, supraoptic, suprachiasmatic, and anterior nuclei of the anterior hypothalamus—results in a markedly contrasting set of responses, including decreased BP, RR, and pupil size, as well as hypo- or adynamia of the skeletal musculature. Hess (1957) viewed this parasympathetic autonomic nervous system (PANS)-mediated set of changes as "protective mechanisms against over-stress . . . promoting restorative processes" (p. 40). Benson agreed that relaxation involves a distinct mechanism opposing the fight-or-flight response, with a separate locus of control and means of regulation, and he labeled it the "relaxation response" (Wallace et al., 1971).

As mentioned earlier, the results of controlled trials comparing the changes occurring during relaxation to those during a period fo alternate activity (e.g., sitting quietly, resting, or reading) are presented in Table 14.1. The "integrated set of physiologic changes associated with decreased sympathetic nervous system activity" (the relaxation response) that Benson argues characterizes relaxation (Greenwood & Benson, 1977, p. 342) is not evident in these studies, even those using Benson's technique for eliciting these changes. The relaxation response is said to consist of significant simultaneous decreases in HR, BP, RR, SC, and $VO_2$ (Benson, Kotch, & Crassweller, 1977; Greenwood & Benson, 1977). In each of their tests of this hypothesis, however, Benson's group measured only two of these parameters. Mean RR and $VO_2$ did decrease in their group of 17 young adults when practicing BR as compared with conditions of sitting with eyes closed or reading (Beary & Benson, 1974). It should be noted that the BR technique has the subjects focus on their breathing, so changes in these respiratory measures might be expected ad hoc and could be independent of a relaxation-mediated effect. In addition, data are given only for the group, and attempts to ascribe these effects to individuals are unjustified (the fallacy of particularization). This is demonstrated in their other study of eight exercising adults experienced in BR. While their overall decrease in $VO_2$ during exercise was significant, such a change occurred in only three of the subjects, and an equal number actually had a *higher* $VO_2$ when relaxing. Among the six subjects in whom HR was monitored, there was no significant change in mean rate, but on an individual basis HR increased slightly during relaxation in four, was unchanged in one, and decreased in only one. A replication of the Beary and Benson experiment found no change in mean RR, frontalis EMG, or SC during BR and a significant *increase* in HR as compared with sitting quietly with eyes closed in the 10 people studied (M. H. Pollack & Zeiner, 1976). The only other investigation of physiological changes occurring with BR made the unfortunate choice of comparing it to the active process of reading, whose potential stimulatory effects were not checked (Christoph et al., 1978).

Only in studies of PR was confirmation sought, by either subjective report or psychometric testing, that the subjects were more relaxed during the relaxation period. This is especially important in those experiments using tape-recorded, as opposed to live PR, instruction, as the efficacy of this method has been questioned (Borkovec & Sides, 1979). Yet even in the three taped PR studies in which the subjects achieved relaxation by these criteria, only one showed a change in *any* parameter measured (Borkovec, Grayson, & Cooper, 1978; D. N. Davidson et al., 1979; Matthews & Gelder, 1969). Notably, each of these studies used people who had extensive training and practice in PR before the test period. The Matthews and Gelder (1969) investigation, showing a decrease in mean frontalis EMG (predictably, as the PR technique is directed toward muscle relaxation) and SC among 14 relaxing subjects, found no effect on HR or respiratory rate. The control condition to which PR was compared in this study involved listening to a tape describing alternative relaxation techniques to be tried at home; the effect this learning situation may have on SC and the other parameters measured is uncertain.

The only studies demonstrating a decrease in HR with relaxation as compared with sitting quietly were the two using live experimenter-guided PR (Paul, 1969; Redmond et al., 1974). Paul also noted a significant relaxation-associated drop in mean respiratory rate and EMG in his 20 subjects, but no change in SC. In addition to their decrease in HR, the six experienced subjects in Redmond et al.'s investigation were the only group to change their BP significantly during relaxation; there was no recording of the other physiological parameters responsive to changes in SANS activity. This study introduced an important confounding element in the assessment of any relaxation-associated physiological or therapeutic effects. After being instructed to "make your heart beat slower and less forcefully, and your vessels lessen resistance to the flow of blood" without relaxing, subjects were able to decrease their BP and HR from base-line values to levels even *lower* than during PR through mental imagery. Using imagery, they could also significantly raise their BP and HR. This ability to change physiological functions that are under autonomic control at will by mental processes was evident even without training or feedback. The changes we have been discussing in this section may therefore have occurred, not as a direct effect of relaxation, but rather in response to the subjects' desires or expectations. The role of these factors was investigated by Christoph et al. (1978), who subjectively rated their subjects' attitudes toward the relaxation procedure being learned on a 5-point scale. They found that positive attitude was highly correlated ($p < .005$) with subsequent decrease in HR during BR, and this crude rating system alone accounted for 51% of the variance in HR response. Another study manipulated subject expectations by informing half of the recruits that PR would acutely lower their BP during the first session, while the other half were told that there would be no immediate effect. Questionnaires following the three relaxation sessions, all carried out in a single day, showed no significant difference between the two groups' confidence in, credibility rating of, or subjective relaxation achieved during the PR training. Neither could the groups be distinguished by an investigator's rating of residual forearm-muscle tension during the relaxation procedures. Despite their apparent identity in all other respects (including initial BP), the group that expected its BP to decrease had a significantly greater average drop in systolic pressure during the relaxation sessions. The expectancy effect leading to a therapeutic response to placebo treatments is well-documented for numerous disorders, including hypertension (Goldring, Chasis, Schreiner, & Smith, 1956; Grenfell, Briggs, & Holland, 1962).

The pattern of relaxation-induced physiological changes (or absence of change) varies considerably between studies, as we have noted. Part of this variability may be accounted for by differences in subject expectation and credibility of the procedures as well as by actual relaxation elicited by the treatment. The concept of a relaxation, or trophotropic, response is based on an integrated *set* of changes occurring simultaneously in the relaxing person owing to a decrease in SANS activity. Thus one would expect not only a drop in HR, BP, RR, and $VO_2$, but all the effects of trophotropic stimulation listed in Table 14.2 plus decreases in plasma catecholamine levels, gastric acid secretion, and cardiac contractility, and an increase in airway resistance and peripheral blood flow, all triggered by the single factor of decreased SANS output. The few studies that have disclosed data on individuals have failed to support such a central mechanism. Christoph et al. (1978), who noted a mean decrease in HR and RR without significant change in BP during BR, found that individual subjects' changes in RR did *not* correlate with change in HR. Neither was there a correlation between RR and BP change. Only 2 of their 18 subjects showed an increase in RR as compared with the control condition, suggesting a failure of these people to relax; but at the same time, one of the two exhibited a decreased HR and the other had a significant drop in BP. The only group to measure catecholamine levels during relaxation found a decrease in plasma NE in five of six subjects and a significant correlation between relaxation-associated change in NE and HR. In these subjects, NE change did not correlate with decrease in BP, however. Mean epinephrine and dopamine levels were not affected by relaxation, nor did they correlate with HR or BP changes on an individual basis (D. N. Davidson et al., 1979). The only other study giving data for individual subjects showed no correlation between $VO_2$ and HR change during relaxation (Benson, Dryer, & Hartley, 1978). These results support the notion that the physiological response to relaxation is not uniform but, insted, varies between persons (Christoph et al., 1978; Schwartz, 1975). Individual patterns of change in physiological parameters have been observed in response to other standardized challenges (Engel & Bickford, 1961; Lacey, 1967).

## Servocontrol Mechanisms

Both an increase in trophotropic dominance and a decrease in CNS arousability involve alterations in general CNS activity. Instead of a unified change in CNS activity, it is possible that relaxation responses are produced by independent servocontrol mechanisms. *Servocontrol* refers to the set of feedback mechanisms that regulate the activity of components in the systems they mediate (Yates, 1980), and it has been demonstrated that alterations can occur in servocontrol mechanisms affecting a specific function without impinging on other systems. For example, baseline testosterone levels are noted to decrease in animals moved from a dominant to subordinate social status (Henry & Stephens, 1977). The mechanism of this chemical resetting may include any point at which control of testosterone secretion is exerted but does not appear to involve more general changes in the animal's physiology. Similarly, primary (i.e., essential) hypertension may involve an upward resetting of arterial baroreceptors (Bali, 1979; Kezdi, 1962).

Yates (1980) sees biofeedback as a procedure training patients to alter specified servocontrol mechanisms. Thus, a person who achieves HR reduction with relaxation does so by adjusting one of the servocontrol mechanisms controlling HR. This alteration could occur at any level of the nervous system without involving any aspect of sympathetic activity. The data presented in Table 14.1 is, of course, consistent with the servocontrol mechanism hypothesis, but a direct demonstration of changes in servocontrol mechanisms with relaxation or related techniques has not been done.

## Mental Calmness

Each of the preceding four approaches assumes that relaxation has as its basis a characteristic physiological change. It may be more appropriate to consider relaxation a mental or emotional state instead. As mentioned earlier, anxiety is the only parameter that has consistently been found to be affected by relaxation (see Table 14.1). This change was measured by both self-report (D. N. Davidson et al., 1979; Matthews & Gelder, 1969) and psychometric testing (Brokovec, Grayson, & Cooper, 1978; Paul, 1969). Rachman (1968) has argued that mental calmness, rather than any physiological change, is responsible for the efficacy of relaxation in treating stress-related disorders.

## Relaxation and Systems

Perhaps it is premature to define a mechanism of relaxation categorically. With other conditions for which there is no empirical measure, such as phobia, it is important to consider the relationships among the measures that serve to define them. Phobia involves self-report, behavior, and physiology; and changes in one of these parameters are often not reflected by the others. People claiming to have overcome a phobia, for example, may still be unable to approach the phobic situation or may show no modification in their physiological response to it (Taylor & Agras, in press). In asking how relaxation works, we imply a single phenomenon of relaxation when, in fact, it may consist of an individually determined interaction among systems, each of which contributes to the phenomenon without any one *being* it.

# EFFECTS OF RELAXATION ON STRESS–RELATED DISORDERS

There is a growing literature suggesting relaxation is effective in reducing symptoms of several disorders thought to be induced or exacerbated by stress. Of course the fact that relaxation may lead to improvement in a disorder does not prove that relaxation reduces stress or that the condition is caused by stress. The clinical effects of relaxation have been extensively discussed elsewhere (Blanchard & Ahles, 1979; Seer, 1979; Taylor, 1980a), and we review this area only briefly here. The focus of this section is on learning more about the fundamental nature of relaxation through an examination of its efficacy in treating primary hypertension, chronic headache, asthma, and insomnia—the illnesses for which it has been most extensively studied.

## Hypertension

The hemodynamic basis of established primary (essential) hypertension considered to be a steady-state increase in peripheral vascular resistance. This resistance to blood flow occurs mainly in the arterioles, whose degree of constriction is regulated by $\alpha$-adrenergic receptors sensitive to circulating NE. The therapeutic effect of two classes of antihypertensive agents appears to be based on their decreasing peripheral resistance by diminishing sympathetic stimulation of the arterioles. The commonly used drugs clonidine, α-methyldopa, and reserpine all act centrally within the brain to decrease sympathetic tone. Prazosin exercises its BP-lowering effect at the local level by blocking the normal constriction response to NE binding. With this knowledge, one would expect that relaxation, if it decreases sympathetic tone, might have the same therapeutic action.

Substantial BP decreases in hypertensives during relaxation were first reported in 1937 by Buck, whose therapy was based on the premise that "sedation and relaxation are the two objectives to be sought in the therapy of hypertensive patients" (p. 515). Shortly thereafter, Jacobson (1938, 1957) reported the successful treatment of several hypertensives with PR. There were no controlled studies on the long-term value of relaxation training for lowering BP, however, until the mid-1970s. Brady, Luborsky, and Kron's (1974) pioneering investigation and those that have followed are summarized in Table 14.3. Seven of the eight studies found a significant treatment effect on systolic BP, diastolic BP, or both soon after relaxation training was completed. In only four of the studies was a follow-up BP check performed to assess long-term effect. All three of those noting an initial decrease saw the difference between treatment and control groups maintained at their single follow-up point of 3, 6, or 12 months (Bali, 1979; Patel & North, 1975; Taylor et al., 1977). In the other study, the small relaxation-associated decrease in systolic BP became more pronounced and reached statistical significance at the 6-month follow-up (Brauer et al., 1977). The powerful factor of patient expectation was considered in only half the studies, which attempted to counteract it by providing "supportive psychotherapy" to their control groups; but the credibility of this procedure is questionable. Other significant influences on BP—antihypertensive medications, smoking, weight, sodium intake, and environmental stress—either were not measured or were noted to change during the course of the investigations.

Although it has not been possible to measure the effects of relaxation on SANS activity in hypertensives, two studies have used as indirect measures the plasma levels of hormones whose activity supposedly reflects sympathetic function. Both demonstrated no change in plasma renin activity among hypertensives who had practiced a BR-like procedure as compared with the no treatment control group (A. A. Pollack, Case, Weber, & Laragh, 1977; Stone & DeLeo, 1976). Stone and DeLeo also took single measures of dopamine β-hydroxylase (DBH) activity before and after 6 months of treatment, finding it significantly reduced in the relaxation group when measured in the standing, but not the supine, position. Based on the work of Weinshilboum and Axelrod (1971), they interpreted this decrease in upright DBH activity as indicating a relaxation-associated drop in SANS activity. Weinshilboum (1976) responded, however, that "the situation is not as simple as was originally assumed . . . there are many potential pratfalls associated with [DBH's] use as a measure of sympathetic nervous system function, and a great deal more must be learned before we will be in a position to interpret the results of such measurements adequately" (p. 786).

Relaxation training appears to reliably produce significant decreases in BP among hypertensives, a result consistent with the hypothesis that relaxation diminishes SANS activity. One cannot confidently attribute the BP effect to the practice of relaxation per se, however, as the work up to this point has not adequately controlled for several other potentially active factors. The amount of BP drop for individuals in these studies correlated with their initial BP levels (i.e.,

*Table 14.3*  Effects of Relaxation on Hypertension

| | | | | Treatment effects | | |
| Investigators | Relaxation procedure | Alternate activity | Number of subjects in relaxation | Systolic BP decrease | Diastolic BP decrease | Follow-up |
|---|---|---|---|---|---|---|
| Brady et al. (1974) | PR and metronome | Reversal | 4 | | $+^a$ | |
| Patel & North (1975) | BR and biofeedback | NT | 17 | + | + | Maintained at 3 months |
| Shoemaker & Tasto (1975) | PR | NT | 5 | + | + | |
| Stone & DeLeo (1976) | BR | NT | 14 | + | + | |
| Patel & Carruthers (1977) | BR and biofeedback | Nonspecific psychotherapy | 22 | + | + | |
| Taylor, Farquhar, Nelson, & Agras (1977) | PR | Nonspecific psychotherapy | 10 | + | − | Maintained at 6 months |
| Bali (1979) | PR | Nonspecific psychotherapy | 9 | + | + | Maintained at 12 months |
| Brauer, Horlick, Nelson, Farquhar, & Agras (1979) | PR | Nonspecific psychotherapy | 20 | − | + | Systolic BP decreased, no effect on diastolic BP at 6 months |

[a] + (or −) diastolic BP decrease = significant ($p \leqslant .05$) decrease (or no significant decrease) in diastolic BP.

the higher the BP, the more it can be expected to decrease). Treatment effect was usually not strong enough, unfortunately, to bring patients' pressures down to the normal range (<140/90). This topic has been reviewed more extensively elsewhere (Agras & Jacob, 1979; Blanchard & Miller, 1977; Frumkin, Nathan, Prout, & Cohen, 1978; Taylor, 1980b).

## Tension Headache

Recurrent muscle-contraction (tension) headache is a particularly common and disturbing ailment in our society for which relaxation therapy is becoming an increasingly popular treatment. Tension headaches are characterized by steady, dull, bilateral pain, usually originating in the frontal or suboccipital area. Their cause is generally considered to be sustained, excessive contraction of the head, neck, or shoulder musculature in the resting state or by an increased stress re-activity of these muscles (Ostfeld, 1962; Phillips, 1977; Wolff, 1963).

PR alone or in combination with EMG biofeedback would thus appear ideally suited for this condition, as suggested by Jacobson (1938). A summary of the controlled studies investigating the effect of PR on subjective headache activity is presented in Table 14.4. These headache studies are subject to many short-comings; therapist attention, patient expectancy, medication intake, and social and environmental factors have not been controlled. Cox et al. (1975) compared PR with a placebo "muscle-relaxant" pill for improvement on an hourly weighted average in subjective headache activity in 18 chronic tension-headache sufferers. After 4 weeks of training there was a trend toward decreased activity in the PR group ($p < .10$) that reached significance at a single follow-up measure 4 months later. It was not indicated whether patients had continued practicing relaxation during the follow-up period or if practice correlated with decreased headache activity. Another study measured self-reported frequency, duration, and severity of tension headaches during 1-week periods before and after participation in a PR, frontalis-muscle EMG feedback, or no-treatment program. Compared with the no-treatment group, the six relaxation subjects experienced a decreased mean frequency of headaches but no change in the duration or severity of those that did occur. Duration of headaches actually increased slightly for the biofeed-back group, and this is the only measure that differentiated it from the relaxation group. There were not data collected on headache activity, except for the weeks immediately before and after treatment (Chesney & Shelton, 1976). Haynes, Griffin, Mooney, and Parise (1975) found the same pattern as Chesney and Shelton, with mean headache frequency, but not duration or severity, decreased in their PR group in relation to no treatment controls. None of these measures distinguished between the relaxation and biofeedback groups.

In each of these studies, frontalis-muscle tension was a poor indicator of head-ache activity. Haynes, Griffin, Mooney, and Parise (1975) found no correlation between headache onset and elevated frontalis EMG. Neither has EMG activity been noted to correlate with headache pain level (Epstein & Abel, 1977; Epstein & Cinciripini, in press; Hart & Cichanski, 1975). Chesney and Shelton (1976) did not record electromotor activity, but their frontalis EMG feedback group showed no treatment effect. In addition, reduction in EMG accounted for only 18% of the variance in treatment effect achieved by Cox et al.'s (1975) relaxa-tion group. Possible explanations for these findings are that (1) the frontalis is

*Table 14.4* Effects of Relaxation Therapy on Tension Headache

| Study | Treatment | Number of subjects in relaxation | Controls | Headache characteristics | | | | Follow-up |
|---|---|---|---|---|---|---|---|---|
| | | | | Frequency | Duration | Severity | Activity[a] | |
| Cox, Freundlich, & Meyer (1975) | PR | 9 | Placebo medication | | | | NS[b] | Activity decreased at 4 months |
| Haynes, Griffin, Moody, & Parisa (1975) | Taped relaxation instructions | 7 | Frontalis EMG feedback | NS | NS | NS | NS | |
| | | | NT | _[c] | NS | NS | — | |
| Chesney & Shelton (1976) | PR | 6 | Frontalis EMG feedback | NS | — | NS | | |
| | | | NT | — | NS | NS | | |

[a] Activity = rating of overall headache activity, combining measures of frequency, duration, and severity.
[b] NS = difference between groups not significant ($p > .05$).
[c] _ = decrease in subjective report of this headache characteristic from pre- to posttreatment monitoring periods is significantly ($p < .05$) greater in the relaxation, as compared with the other, group.

not an important muscle in tension headaches *and* that reduction in frontalis activity does not generalize to the nearby muscle groups that do play a role or (2) factors other than muscle contraction, such as *mental* tension (anxiety), are of primary importance in tension headache (Chesney & Shelton, 1976). The therapeutic success of PR could be explained by its effect on mental state as well as by muscle relaxation per se. If anxiety is the key factor in tension headache, one would predict that other forms of relaxation therapy that do not involve decreased head- and neck-muscle activity would be equally effective.

Although we have few studies upon which to base our evaluation, there is some indication that relaxation training as well as biofeedback therapy decreases the frequency of tension headaches without affecting the duration or severity of headaches that do occur. The onset of tension headaches has long been associated with stress, and relaxation may exert its effect by producing mental calmness, by decreasing SANS activity, or both. The determinants of the subjective characteristics of an ongoing headache (e.g., duration and severity) are unknown, but investigation of this differential effect of relaxation may yield valuable information on its mechanism of action.

## Asthma

Bronhcial asthma is a chronic disease characterized by recurrent attacks of paroxysmal dyspnea owing to spasmotic contraction of the bronchial smooth muscle, which increases resistance to outflow of air from the lungs. Various factors, including irritation of the bronchial mucosa by allergens, physical exertion, and anxiety may precipitate these attacks, but their underlying cause remains uncertain. It is PANS activity that is associated with normal bronchoconstriction, while the SANS mediates dilation of the bronchi through its stimulation of local $\beta_2$-adrenergic receptors. Medical management of asthmatics relies heavily on the use of drugs that act as SANS transmitters (e.g., isoproterenol, a synthetic epinephrine-like beta agonist) or that enhance the effect of these transmitters (e.g., theophylline). Abnormally low epinephrine levels owing to decreased central stimulation of the adrenal medulla have been postulated as the cause of bronchial asthma based on findings of significantly lower urinary epinephrine secretion and adrenal response to hormonal stimulation among asthmatics (Mathé & Knapp, 1969, 1971; Robson & Kilborn, 1965). With this in mind, treatments that decrease SANS activity should be contraindicated for asthma. There is some evidence, however, that asthmatics react to psychological stress with pulmonary function changes opposite to those found in normals. Several independent investigators noted that although 1-sec forced expiratory volume ($FEV_1$) increases during emotional arousal in healthy subjects, corresponding to SANS-mediated bronchodilation, it actually decreases in asthmatics (Mathé & Knapp, 1971; Miklich, Chai, Purcell, Weiss, & Brady, 1974; Smith, Colebatch, & Clarke, 1970; Tal & Miklich, 1976). Clinical observation has led many physicians to recommend physical inactivity or "relaxation" to their asthmatic patients for relief during acute attacks.

It is, therefore, difficult to predict what effect relaxation would have on bronchial asthma, even if it did decrease SANS activity, owing to its concurrent effect on mental state. Several investigators have measured improvement in pulmonary function with relaxation training among their asthmatic subjects

(Alexander, 1972; Alexander, Miklich, & Hershkoff, 1972; British Tuberculosis Association, 1968; Davis, Saunders, Creer, & Chai, 1973), but several shortcomings limit the applicability of their work. First, the measures of pulmonary function used in these studies—$FEV_1$ or peak expiratory flow rate (PEFR)—are highly dependent on subject effort and may reflect patient expectation. They also reflect predominantly large-airway resistance, ignoring the important small-airway component of asthma. Furthermore, the change in pulmonary function test performance may have reached statistical significance, but in no study did relaxation training produce *clinically* significant improvement. While the most impressive mean PEFR increase was 11% (Alexander, Miklich, & Hershkoff, 1972), this small change is not subjectively detectable, nor does it approach the degree of improvement routinely obtained with the medications described above (Alexander, Cropp, & Chai, 1979; Taylor, 1980a). In each case, the physiological measures were taken immediately before and after treatment; there were no follow-up tests, measures of subjective improvement, or examination of treatment effect on medication taking, attack rate or severity, or wheezing. Alexander, Cropp, and Chai (1979) repeated their earlier work with the goal of filling some of these gaps. Fourteen severely asthmatic children participated in a longitudinal study design in which they simply sat quietly the first three sessions, next underwent combined PR and autogenic training, and then relaxed themselves during the final three sessions. A treatment effect could be found only for $FEV_1$ and PEFR, not in the more objective effort-*independent* measures of large-airway resistance (specific airway conductance), or small-airway resistance (maximum mid-expiratory flow rate), or expiratory wheezing. In contrast, isoproterenol inhalation produced dramatic improvement in each of these parameters. Relaxation training also failed to bring about a long-term change in PEFR, medication requirements, or serious asthma attacks. There is thus little experimental support for the use of relaxation therapy in treating bronchial asthmatics. Here too our findings match what was expected based on the hypothesis that relaxation decreases sympathetic tone.

## Insomnia

*Insomnia* is a broad descriptive term referring to a chronic inability to obtain "adequate" sleep, and it encompasses a variety of complaints and deviations from the norm. Insomniacs have been categorized according to the point at which sleep is disturbed: (1) sleep onset (difficulty in falling asleep), (2) sleep maintenance (frequent awakening during sleep), or (3) terminal (difficulty getting back to sleep after awakening) (Bootzin & Nicassio, 1978; Thoreson, Coates, Zarcone, Kirmil-Gray, & Rosekind, in press). Relaxation therapy for insomnia is based on the premise that primary, or idiopathic, insomnia (as opposed to that secondary to physical or psychological disturbances) results from CNS hyperarousal. Several studies have indicated that poor sleepers rate significantly higher than normal ones in both physiological and psychological measures of anxiety (Coursey, Buchsbaum, & Frankel, 1973; Haynes, Woodward, Moran, & Alexander, 1974; Johns, Gay, Masterson, & Bruce, 1971; Monroe, 1967; Nicassio & Bootzin, 1974). If this is an important factor in sleep disturbance, then PR, which is quite effective in reducing at least subjective anxiety, would be expected to be a useful treatment.

The controlled studies assessing the effects of relaxation have all used PR and

Table 14.5  Effects of Relaxation Therapy on Insomnia

| Study | Relaxation procedure | Number of subjects in relaxation | Controls | Sleep-onset time | | Subjective number of awakenings | Subjective sleep quality | Objective total waking time | Follow-up subjective sleep-onset time |
|---|---|---|---|---|---|---|---|---|---|
| | | | | Objective | Subjective | | | | |
| Borkovec & Fowles (1973) | PR | 9 | Hypnotic relaxation<br>Self-relaxation<br>NT | | NS[a]<br>NS[b]<br>– | NS<br>NS<br>– | NS<br>NS<br>+ | | |
| Woodward, Moran, & Alexander (1974) | PR | 7 | Nonspecific psycho-therapy | | NS | NS | | | |
| Nicassio & Bootzin (1974) | PR | 8 | Autogenic training<br>Self-relaxation<br>NT | | NS<br>–<br>– | NS<br>NS<br>NS | NS<br>NS<br>NS | | NS at 6 months<br>– at 6 months |
| Steinmark & Borkovec (1974) | PR | 12 | Desensitization<br>Placebo desensitization<br>NT | | NS<br>NS<br>– | NS<br>NS<br>NS | NS<br>NS<br>+ | | NS at 5 months<br>– at 5 months |
| Borkovec, Kaloupek, & Slama (1975) | PR | 14 | Physiological attention focusing<br>Placebo desensitization<br>NT | | NS<br>– | NS<br>NS | NS<br>NS | | NS at 5 months<br>NS at 5 months |

| Study | | N | Treatment | | | | | |
|---|---|---|---|---|---|---|---|---|
| Borkovec & Weerts (1976) | PR | 11 | Placebo desensitization<br>NT | NS<br>– | | NS<br>NS | | – at 12 months |
| Freedman & Papsdorf (1976) | PR | 6 | Frontalis feedback<br>Physical exercise | NS<br>– | | NS<br>NS | | NS at 2 months<br>NS at 2 months |
| Woolfolk, Carr-Kaffashan, McNulty, & Lehrer (1976) | PR | 8 | Meditation<br>NT | NS<br>– | NS<br>– | | | |
| Lick & Heffler (1977) | PR | 14 | Placebo feedback<br>NT | NS<br>– | NS<br>– | NS<br>+ | NS<br>NS | |
| Borkovec, Grayson, O'Brien & Weerts (1979) | PR | 9 | NT of physiological attention focusing | –[c] | – | NS | NS | |

[a]NS = no significant difference ($p > .05$) between change in characteristic from pre- to posttreatment monitoring periods in the relaxation, as compared with the other, group.

[b]– (or +) = decrease (or increase) in characteristic from pre- to posttreatment monitoring periods is significantly greater ($p < .05$) in the relaxation, as compared with the other, group.

[c]Sleep-onset time was affected only in the idiopathic insomniac group, whose subjective/objective latency ratio was less than 1.5.

generally recruited people with the complaint of prolonged time to sleep onset. Their results are summarized in Table 14.5. Most have found a significant *subjective* decrease in onset time compared with no treatment conditions, but no difference between the relaxation group and other subjects receiving some degree of therapist attention. The findings of the three studies that obtained objective measures of sleep activity (using EEG criteria) conformed to this pattern. Relaxation training consistently decreased reported time to sleep onset to about 50% of mean pretreatment values (approximately 20 to 30 min), a noticeable change for the subjects, but still leaving their latency time higher than the normal range (0 to 20 min).

Much less attention has been paid to the other parameters of sleep quality. Freedman and Papsdorf (1976) found that total time spent moving or awake during the night as measured by EEG did not differ among groups practicing PR, biofeedback, or stretching exercises. Neither did PR affect self-reported number of awakenings during the night in five of six studies (see Table 14.5). It is important to remember that insomnia is a subjective problem, usually referring to complaints of poor sleep or daytime drowsiness. Decreases in sleep latency or an increased total sleep time may not impinge on the primary complaint. It is, therefore, noteworthy that in none of the five studies in which subjects were asked to rate their quality of sleep did the PR group report significantly greater improvement during training than the control treatment group, and in only three were they improved in comparison with untreated subjects (see Table 14.5). The results of relaxation on sleep are nonetheless again consistent with reduced SANS activity.

## SUMMARY

Although the popularity and clinical testing of relaxation therapy have greatly increased in the past decade, relaxation remains a poorly defined entity, variously considered as a procedure, a mental state, and a physiologic response. Relaxation techniques share an emphasis on four basic components: a tranquil setting, reduced muscle activity, internal focusing of attention, and a passive attitude. The last two, attention focusing and passive attitude, may be the key elements in the induction of relaxation. A quiet environment, comfortable position, and skeletal muscle relaxation do not appear to be necessary or sufficient for relaxation, but serve to eliminate externally and internally generated stressors that might disturb the process.

The practice of relaxation techniques is associated with a reproducible improvement in certain stress-related disorders, most notably primary hypertension, tension headache, and insomnia. It does not appear to be effective in the treatment of bronchial asthma. The mechanism by which relaxation exerts its effects is uncertain, but these clinical results are consistent with the hypothesis that it reduces SANS activity. Current evidence does not support the proposal that relaxation is produced by a reduction in proprioceptive impulses to the CNS or that it involves trophotropic stimulation (the "relaxation response"). Instead, it may act centrally by reducing CNS arousability, with a resultant dampening of sympathetic tone. The lack of a characteristic pattern of physiologic change with relaxation also raises the possibility that local servocontrol mechanisms mediate the individual's response.

*ses* to relaxation, we may be diverting our attention
n underlying it. While it cannot be defined by any
ion is consistently accompanied by unexplained changes
gs of mental calmness and decreased anxiety charac-
exact nature of relaxation, the mental state and how
ng to be explored.

## REFERENCES

ypertension. In O. F. Pomerleau & J. P. Brady (Eds.), *Behavioral*
ice. Baltimore: Williams & Wilkins, 1979.

elaxation and flow rates in asthmatic children: Relationship to
anxiety. *Journal of Psychosomatic Research*, 1972, *16*, 405–

J. A., & Chai, H. Effects of relaxation training on pulmonary
asthma. *Journal of Applied Behavior Analysis*, 1979, *12*, 27–

R., & Hershkoff, H. The immediate effects of systematic relaxa-
atory flow rates in asthmatic children. *Psychosomatic Medicine*,

f relaxation on blood pressure and anxiety levels of hypertensive
*Psychosomatic Medicine*, 1979, *41*, 637–646.

Beary, J. F., & Benson, A simple psychophysiologic technique which elicits the hypometabolic changes of th. relaxation response. *Psychosomatic Medicine*, 1974, *36*, 115–
120.

Benson, H. Your innate asset for combating stress. *Harvard Business Review*, 1974, *52*, 49–
60.

Benson, H., Beary, J. F., & Carol, M. P. The relaxation response. *Psychiatry*, 1974, *37*, 37–46.

Benson, H., Dryer, T., & Hartley, L. H. Decreased VO$_2$ consumption during exercise with
elicitation of the relaxation response. *Journal of Human Stress*, June 1978, 38–42.

Benson, H., Kotch, J. B., & Crassweller, K. D. The relaxation response: A bridge between
psychiatry and medicine. *Medical Clinics of North America*, 1977, *61*, 929–938.

Berlyne, D. E. *Conflict, arousal, and curiosity*. New York: McGraw-Hill, 1960.

Blanchard, E. B., & Ahles, T. A. Behavioral treatment of psychophysical disorders. *Behavior
Modification*, 1979, *3*, 518–549.

Blanchard, E. B., & Miller, S. T. Psychological teratment of cardiovascular disease. *Archives
of General Psychiatry*, 1977, *34*, 1402–1413.

Bokser, B. Z. *From the world of the cabbalah*. New York: Philosophical Library, 1954.

Bonvallet, M., & Bloch, V. Bulbar control of cortical arousal. *Science*, 1961, *133*, 1133–1134.

Bootzin, R. R., & Nicassio, P. M. Behavioral treatments for insomnia. In M. Hersen, R. M.
Eisler, & P. M. Miller (Eds.), *Progress in behavior modification* (Vol. 6). New York:
Academic, 1978.

Borkovec, T. D., & Fowles, D. Controlled investigation of the effects of progressive relaxation and hypnotic relaxation on insomnia. *Journal of Abnormal Psychology*, 1973, *82*,
153–158.

Borkovec, T. D., Grayson, J. B., & Cooper, K. M. Treatment of general tension: Subjective
and physiologic effects of progressive relaxation. *Journal of Consulting and Clinical Psychology*, 1978, *46*, 518–528.

Borkovec, T. D., Grayson, J. B., O'Brien, G. T., & Weerts, T. C. Relaxation treatment of
pseudoinsomnia and idiopathic insomnia: An electroencephalographic evaluation. *Journal
of Applied Behavior Analysis*, 1979, *12*, 37–54.

Borkovec, T. D., Kaloupek, D. G., & Slama, K. M. The facilitative effect of muscle tension
release in the relaxation treatment of sleep disturbance. *Behavior Therapy*, 1975, *6*, 301–
309.

Borkovec, T. D., & Sides, J. K. Critical procedural variables related to the physiological effects
of progressive relaxation: A review. *Behaviour Research and Therapy*, 1979 *17*, 119–125.

Borkovec, T. D., & Weerts, T. C. Effects of progressive relaxation on sleep disturbance: An
electroencephalographic evaluation. *Psychosomatic Medicine*, 1976, *38*, 173–180.

Bowers, M., & Glasner, S. Auto-hypnotic aspects of the Jewish cabbalistic concept of kavanah. *Journal of Clinical and Experimental Hypnosis,* 1958, *6,* 50–70.

Brady, J. P., Luborsky, L., & Kron, R. E. Blood pressure reduction in patients with essential hypertension through metronome-conditioned relaxation: A preliminary report. *Behavior Therapy,* 1974, *5,* 203–209.

Brauer, A. P., Horlick, L., Nelson, E., Farquhar, J. W., & Agras, W. S. Relaxation therapy for essential hypertension: A Veterans Administration outpatient study. *Journal of Behavioral Medicine,* 1979, *2,* 21–29.

Bremer, F. Cerveau "isole" et physiologie du sommeil. *Comptes Rendus Société de Biologie,* 1935, *118,* 1235–1241.

Brenner, J. Factors influencing the specificity of voluntary cardiovascular control. In L. V. Di Cara (Ed.), *Limbic and autonomic nervous system research.* New York: Plenum, 1974.

British Tuberculosis Association. Hypnosis for asthma. A controlled trial. *British Medical Journal,* 1968, *4,* 71–76.

Buck, R. W. Class method in therapy of essential hypertension. *Annals of Internal Medicine,* 1937, *11,* 514–518.

Budzynski, T. H., & Stoyva, J. M. An instrument for producing deep muscle relaxation by means of analogy information feedback. *Journal of Applied Behavior Analysis,* 1969, *2,* 231–237.

Burchfield, S. R. The stress response: A new perspective. *Psychosomatic Medicine,* 1979, *41,* 661–672.

Cannon, W. B. The emergency function of the adrenal medulla in pain and the major emotions. *American Journal of Physiology,* 1914, *33,* 356–372.

Chesney, M. A., & Shelton, J. L. A comparison of muscle relaxation and electromyogram biofeedback treatments for muscle contraction headache. *Journal of Behavior Therapy and Experimental Psychiatry,* 1976, *7,* 221–225.

Christoph, P., Luborsky, L., Kron, R. E., & Fishman, H. Blood pressure, heart rate and respiratory responses to a single session of relaxation: A partial replication. *Journal of Psychosomatic Research,* 1978, *22,* 493–501.

Connor, W. H. Effects of brief relaxation training on autonomic response to anxiety-evoking stimuli. *Psychophysiology,* 1974, *11,* 591–599.

Corby, J. C., Roth, W. T., Zarcone, V. P., & Kopell, B. S. Psychophysiological correlates of the practice of tantric yoga meditation. *Archives of General Psychiatry,* 1978, *35,* 571–577.

Coursey, R. D., Buchsbaum, M., & Frankel, B. L. Personality measures and evoked responses in chronic insomniacs. *Journal of Abnormal Psychology,* 1973, *82,* 124–133.

Cox, D. J., Freundlich, A., & Meyer, R. G. Differential effectiveness of electromyograph feedback, verbal relaxation instructions, and medication placebo with tension headaches. *Journal of Consulting and Clinical Psychology,* 1975, *43,* 892–898.

Das, N. N., & Gastaut, H. Variations de l'activité électrique du cerveau, du coeur et des muscles squelettiques au cours de la méditation et de l'extase yogique. *Electroencephalography and Clinical Neurophysiology,* 1957, *6*(Suppl.), 211–219.

Davidson, D. N., Winchster, M. A., Taylor, C. B., Alderman, E. A., & Ingels, N. B. Effects of relaxation therapy on cardiac performance and sympathetic activity in patients with organic heart disease. *Psychosomatic Medicine,* 1979, *41,* 303–309.

Davidson, R. J., & Schwartz, G. E. The psychobiology of relaxation and related states: A multi-process theory. In D. I. Mostofsky (Ed.), *Behavioral control and the modification of physiological activity.* Englewood Cliffs, N.J.: Prentice-Hall, 1976.

Davis, M. H., Saunders, D. R., Creer, T. L., & Chair, H. Relaxation training facilitated by biofeedback apparatus as a supplemental treatment in bronchial asthma. *Journal of Psychosomatic Research,* 1973, *17,* 212–128.

Davison, G. C. Anxiety under total curarization: Implications for the role of muscular relaxation in the desensitization of neurotic fears. *Journal of Nervous and Mental Disease,* 1966, *143,* 443–448.

Driscoll, R., Anxiety reduction using physical exertion and positive images. *Psychological Record,* 1976, *26,* 87–94.

Edelman, R. I. Desensitization and physiological arousal. *Journal of Personality and Social Psychology,* 1971, *17,* 259–266.

Edmonston, W. E. The effects of neutral hypnosis on conditioned responses: Implications for hypnosis as relaxation. In E. Fromm & R. E. Shor (Eds.), *Hypnosis: Developments in research and new perspectives* (2nd ed.). New York: Aldine, 1979.

Engel, B. T., & Bickford, A. F. Response specificity: Stimulus response and individual response specificity in essential hypertension. *Archives of General Psychiatry*, 1961, *5*, 82–93.

Engel, B. T., Nickoomanesh, P., & Schuster, M. M. Operant conditioning of rectosphincteric responses in the treatment of fecal incontinence. *New England Journal of Medicine*, 1974, *290*, 646–649.

Epstein, L. H., & Abel, G. G. An analysis of biofeedback training effects for tension headache patients. *Behavior Therapy*, 1977, *8*, 34–47.

Epstein, L. H., & Cinciripini, C. M. Behavioral control of tension headaches. In J. M. Ferguson & C. B. Taylor (Eds.), *The comprehensive handbook of behavioral medicine* (Vol. 2). Jamaica, N.Y.: SP Medical & Scientific, in press.

Freedman, R., & Papsdorf, J. D. Biofeedback and progressive relaxation treatment of sleep-onset insomnia: A controlled, all-night investigation. *Biofeedback and Self-regulation*, 1976, *1*, 253–271.

French, J. D., Verzeano, M., & Magoun, H. W. An extralemniscal sensory system in the brain. *Archives of Neurology and Psychiatry*, 1953, *69*, 505–518.

Fromm, E. The nature of hypnosis and other altered states of consciousness: An ego-psychological theory. In E. Fromm & R. E. Shor (Eds.), *Hypnosis: Developments in research and new perspectives* (2nd ed.). New York: Aldine, 1979.

Frumkin, K., Nathan, R. J., Prout, M. F., & Cohen, M. C. Nonpharmacologic control of hypertension in man: A critical review of the experimental literature. *Psychosomatic Medicine*, 1978, *40*, 294–320.

Gellhorn, E. *Principles of autonomic-somatic integrations: Physiological basis and psychological and clinical implications*. Minneapolis: University of Minnesota Press, 1967.

Gellhorn, E., & Kiely, W. F. Mystical states of consciousness: Neurophysiological and clinical aspects. *Journal of Nervous and Mental Disease*, 1972, *154*, 399–405.

Goldring, W., Chasis, H., Schreiner, G. E., & Smith, H. W. Reassurance in the management of benign hypertensive disease. *Circulation*, 1956, *14*, 260–264.

Greenwood, M. M., & Benson, H. The efficacy of progressive relaxation in systematic desensitization and a proposal for an alternate competitive response–the relaxation response. *Behaviour Research and Therapy*, 1977, *15*, 337–343.

Grenfell, R. F., Briggs, A. J., & Holland, W. C. Antihypertensive drugs: A controlled evaluation. *Journal of the Mississippi State Medical Association*, 1962, *3*, 93–98.

Grings, W. W., & Uno, T. Counterconditioning: Fear and relaxation. *Psychophysiology*, 1968, *4*, 479–485.

Groosberg, J. M. *The physiological effectiveness of brief training in differential muscle relaxation* (Tech. Rep. No. 9). La Jolla, Calif.: Western Behavioral Science, 1966.

Hart, J. D., & Cichanski, K. A. *Biofeedback as a treatment for headache: Conceptual and methodological issues*. Paper presented at the Ninth Annual Convention of the Association for the Advancement of Behavior Therapy, San Francisco, 1975.

Haynes, S. N., Griffin, R., Mooney, D., & Parise, M. Electromyographic feedback and relaxation instructions in the treatment of muscle contraction headaches. *Behavior Therapy*, 1975, *6*, 672–678.

Haynes, S. N., Woodward, S., Moran, R., & Alexander, D. Relaxation treatment of insomnia. *Behavior Therapy*, 1974, *5*, 555–558.

Henry, J. P., & Stephens, P. M. *Stress, health and the social environment*. New York: Springer-Verlag, 1977.

Hess, W. R. *Functional organization of the diencephalon*. New York: Grune & Stratton, 1957.

Horne, M., Taylor, C. B., & Agras, W. S. *The expectation effects of the blood pressure response to relaxation*. Manuscript submitted for publication, 1980.

Hugelin, A., & Bonvallet, M. Tonus cortical et contrôle de la facilitation matrice d'origine réticulaire. *Journal de Physiologie*, 1957, *49*, 1171–1200.

Hyman, E. T., & Gale, E. N. Galvanic skin response and reported anxiety during systematic desensitization. *Journal of Consulting and Clinical Psychology*, 1973, *40*, 108–114.

Jacob, R. G., Kraemer, H. C., & Agras, W. S. Relaxation therapy in the treatment of hypertension: A review. *Archives of General Psychiatry*, 1977, *34*, 1417–1427.

Jacobsen, E. *Progressive relaxation*. Chicago: University of Chicago Press, 1928.

Jacobson, E. *You must relax*. New York: McGraw-Hill, 1934.

Jacobson, E. *Progressive relaxation*. Chicago: University of Chicago Press, 1938.

Jacobson, E. *You must relax.* New York: McGraw-Hill, 1957.

Jacobson, E. *Tension in medicine.* Springfield, Ill.: Thomas, 1967.

Johns, M., Gay, T., Masterson, J., & Bruce, D. Relationship between sleep habits and adreno-cortical activity and personality. *Psychosomatic Medicine,* 1971, *33,* 499–508.

Kanellakos, D. P., & Lukas, J. S. (Eds.). *The psychobiology of transcendental meditation: A literature review.* Menlo Park, Calif.: W. A. Benjamin, 1974.

Kezdi, P. Mechanism of the carotid sinus in experimental hypertension. *Circulation Research,* 1962, *11,* 145–151.

Kroger, W. S., & Fezler, W. D. *Hypnosis and behavior modification: Imagery conditioning.* Philadelphia: Lippincott, 1976.

Lacey, J. I. Somatic response patterning and stress: Some revisions of activation theory. In M. H. Appley & R. Trumbull (Eds.), *Psychological stress: Issues in research.* New York: Appleton, 1967.

Lader, M. H., & Wing, L. *Physiological measures, sedative drugs, and morbid anxiety.* New York: Oxford University Press, 1966.

Lick, J., & Heffler, D. Relaxation training and attention placebo in the treatment of severe insomnia. *Journal of Consulting and Clinical Psychology,* 1977, *45,* 153–161.

Lindsley, D. B., Schreiner, L. H., Knowles, W. B., & Magoun, H. W. Behavioural and E.E.G. changes following chronic brain stem lesions in the cat. *Electroencephalography and Clinical Neurophysiology,* 1950, *2,* 483–498.

Luthe, W. (Ed.). *Autogenic therapy* (Vols. 1, 3). New York: Grune & Stratton, 1969.

MacHovec, F. J. Hypnosis before Mesmer. *American Journal of Clinical Hypnosis,* 1975, *17,* 215–220.

Mathé, A. A., & Knapp, P. H. Decreased plasma free fatty acids and urinary epinephrine in bronchial asthma. *New England Journal of Medicine,* 1969, *281,* 234–238.

Mathé, A. A., & Knapp, P. H. Emotional and adrenal reactions to stress in bronchial asthma. *Psychosomatic Medicine,* 1971, *33,* 323–340.

Matthews, A. M., & Gelder, M. G. Psychophysiological investigations of brief relaxation training. *Journal of Psychosomatic Research,* 1969, *13,* 1–12.

Miklich, D. R., Chair, H., Purcell, K., Weiss, J. H., & Brady, K. Naturalistic observation of emotions preceding low pulmonary flow rates. *Journal of Allergy and Clinical Immunology,* 1974, *53,* 102. (Abstract)

Miller, M. Changes in response to electric shock produced by varying muscular conditions. *Journal of Experimental Psychology,* 1926, *9,* 26–44.

Monroe, L. J. Psychological and physiological differences between good and poor sleepers. *Journal of Abnormal Psychology,* 1967, *72,* 255–264.

Moruzzi, G., & Magoun, H. W. Brain stem reticular formation and activation of the E.E.G. *Electroencephalography and Clinical Neurophysiology,* 1949, *1,* 455–473.

Nicassio, P. M., & Bootzin, R. R. A comparison of progressive relaxation and autogenic training as treatments for insomnia. *Journal of Abnormal Psychology,* 1974, *83,* 253–260.

Ornstein, R. *The psycholgy of consciousness.* San Francisco: W. H. Freeman, 1972.

Ostfeld, A. M. *The common headache syndromes: Biochemistry, pathophysiology, and therapy.* Springfield, Ill.: Thomas, 1962.

Patel, C. H., & Carruthers, M. Coronary risk factor reduction through biofeedback-aided relaxation and meditation. *Journal of the Royal College of General Practice,* 1977, *27,* 401–405.

Patel, C. H., & North, W. R. Randomized controlled trial of yoga and biofeedback in management of hypertension. *Lancet,* 1975, *2,* 93–95.

Paul, G. L. Physiological effects of relaxation training and hypnotic suggestion. *Journal of Abnormal Psychology,* 1969, *74,* 425–437.

Pelletier, K. R. *Mind as healer, mind as slayer: A holistic approach to stress disorders.* New York: Dell, Delacorte, 1977.

Pendleton, L. R., & Tasto, D. L. Effects of metronome-conditioned relaxation, metronome-induced relaxation, and progressive muscle relaxation in insomnia. *Behaviour Research and Therapy,* 1976, *14,* 165–166.

Phillips, C. The modification of tension headache pain using EMG biofeedback. *Behaviour Research and Therapy,* 1977, *15,* 119–129.

Pickering, T. G., & Miller, N. E. Learned voluntary control of heart rate and rhythm in two subjects with premature ventricular contractions. *British Heart Journal,* 1977, *39,* 152–159.

Pollack, A. A., Case, D. B., Weber, M. A., & Laragh, J. H. Limitations of transcendental meditation in the treatment of essential hypertension. *Lancet,* 1977, *1,* 71–73.

Pollack, M. H., & Zeiner, A. R. Physiological correlates of Bensonian relaxation training with controls for relaxation and sitting. *Psychophysiology,* 1976, *13,* 185. (Abstract)

Rachman, S. The role of muscular relaxation in desensitization therapy. *Behaviour Research and Therapy,* 1968, *6,* 159–166.

Redmond, D. P., Gaylor, M. S., McDonald, R. H., & Shapiro, A. P. Blood pressure and heart rate response to verbal instruction and relaxation in hypertension. *Psychosomatic Medicine,* 1974, *36,* 285–297.

Robson, A. D., & Kilborn, J. R. Studies of adrenocortical function in continuous asthma. *Thorax,* 1965, *20,* 93–98.

Schultz, J. H. *Das autogene training.* Stuttgart: Georg-Thieme, 1953.

Schwartz, G. E. Biofeedback, self-regulation, and the patterning of physiological processes. *American Scientist,* 1975, *63,* 314–325.

Seer, P. Psychological control of essential hypertension: Review of the literature and methodological critique. *Psychological Bulletin,* 1979, *86,* 1015–1043.

Segundo, J. P., Arana, R., & French, J. D. Behavioral arousal by stimulation of the brain in the monkey. *Journal of Neurosurgery,* 1955, *12,* 601–613.

Sigerist, H. E. *A history of medicine* (Vol. 1). New York: Oxford University Press, 1951.

Singer, J. L., & Pope, K. S. *The power of human imagination.* New York: Plenum, 1978.

Smith, M. M., Colebatch, H. J. H., & Clarke, P. S. Increase and decrease in pulmonary resistance with hypnotic suggestion in asthma. *American Review of Respiratory Disease,* 1970, *102,* 236–242.

Sokolov, E. N. Higher nervous activity and the problem of perception. In B. Simon (Ed.), *Psychology in the Soviet Union.* Stanford, Calif.: Stanford University Press, 1957.

Steinmark, S., & Borkovec, T. D. Active and placebo treatment effects on moderate insomnia under counterdemand and positive demand instructions. *Journal of Abnormal Psychology,* 1974, *83,* 157–163.

Sternbach, R. A. A comparative analysis of autonomic responses in startle. *Psychosomatic medicine,* 1960, *22,* 204–210.

Stone, R. A., & DeLeo, J. Psychotherapeutic control of hypertension. *New England Journal of Medicine,* 1976, *294,* 80–84.

Tal, A., & Miklich, D. R. Emotionally induced decreases in pulmonary flow rates in asthmatic children. *Psychosomatic Medicine,* 1976, *38,* 190–200.

Taylor, C. B. Relaxation training and related techniques. In W. S. Agras (Ed.), *Behavior modification: Principles and clinical applications.* Boston: Little, Brown, 1978.

Taylor, C. B. Adult medical disorders. In A. S. Bellack, M. Hersen, & A. E. Kazdin (Eds.), *International handbook of behavior modification and therapy.* New York: Plenum, 1980. (a)

Taylor, C. B. Behavioral approaches to hypertension. In J. M. Ferguson & C. B. Taylor (Eds.), *The comprehensive handbook of behavioral medicine* (Vol. 1). Jamaica, N.Y.: SP Medical and Scientific, 1980. (b)

Taylor, C. B., & Agras, W. S. Assessment of phobia. In D. H. Barlow (Ed.), *Behavioral assessment of adult disorders.* New York: Guilford, in press.

Taylor, C. B., Farquhar, J. W., Nelson, E., & Agras, W. S. Relaxation therapy and high blood pressure. *Archives of General Psychiatry,* 1977, *34,* 339–342.

Thoreson, C. E., Coates, T. J., Zarcone, V. P., Kirmil-Gray, K., & Rosekind, M. R. Treating the complaint of insomnia: Self-management perspectives. In J. M. Ferguson & C. B. Taylor (Eds.), *The comprehensive handbook of behavioral medicine* (Vol. 2). Jamaica, N.Y.: SP Medical and Scientific, in press.

Van Egeren, L. F., Feather, B. W., & Hein, P. L. Desensitization of phobias: Some psychophysiological propositions. *Psychophysiology,* 1971, *8,* 213–228.

Wallace, R. K. Physiological effects of transcendental meditation. *Science,* 1970, *167,* 1751–1754.

Wallace, R. K., Benson, H., & Wilson, A. F. A wakeful hypometabolic physiologic state. *American Journal of Physiology,* 1971, *221,* 795–799.

Weinshilboum, R. Letter to the editor. *New England Journal of Medicine,* 1976, *294,* 786–787.

Weinshilboum, R., & Axelrod, J. Serum dopamine-beta-hydroxylase activity. *Circulation Research,* 1971, *28,* 307–315.

Weiss, T., & Engel, B. T. Operant conditioning of heart rate in patients with premature ventricular contractions. *Psychosomatic Medicine*, 1974, *36*, 411–419.

Wenger, M. A., & Bagchi, B. K. Studies of autonomic functions in practitioners of yoga in
India. *Behavioral Science*, 1961, *6*, 312–323.

Wolff, J. G. *Headache and other head pain*. New York: Oxford University Press, 1963.

Wolpe, J. *Psychotherapy by reciprocal inhibition*. Stanford, Calif.: Stanford University Press,
1958.

Woolfolk, R. L. Psychophysiological correlates of meditation. *Archives of General Psychiatry*,
1975, *32*, 1326–1333.

Woolfolk, R., Carr-Kaffashan, L., McNulty, T., & Lehrer, P. Meditation training as a treatment
for insomnia. *Behavior Therapy*, 1976, *7*, 359–365.

Yates, A. J. *Biofeedback and the modification of behavior*. New York: Plenum, 1980.

# 15

# Induced Affect in Stress-management Training

**Ronald E. Smith**
*University of Washington, Seattle, United States*

**James C. Ascough**
*Purdue University, West Lafayette, Indiana, United States*

The 1970s witnessed a growing interest in the antecedents and consequences of psychological stress and in methods of coping with it. The development of learning-based anxiety-reduction techniques and cognitive therapies has served to stimulate the development of educational programs designed to help people acquire specific coping responses they can use to prevent or reduce stress responses (e.g., Goldfried, 1971; Goldfried, Decenteceo, & Weinberg, 1974; Meichenbaum, 1972, 1977; Smith, 1980a, b; Suinn & Richardson, 1971; Turk, 1976). Such methods usually provide for the acquisition and rehearsal of cognitive and/or somatic relaxation skills which presumably have transsituational generalizability.

The development and evaluation of programs designed to enhance emotional self-control is a desirable approach to reducing the widespread incidence of stress and its negative effects on physical health and personal functioning. We describe here a conceptual model of stress that emphasizes reciprocal relationships among stressors, cognitive appraisal processes, affective arousal, and instrumental behaviors, as well as the cognitive-affective stress management training program designed to modify certain critical components of the model. Intervention strategies in our approach are directed toward the development of cognitive and somatic coping skills that become part of an *integrated coping response*. A technique known as *induced affect* is used to permit rehearsal of the integrated coping response in reducing high levels of induced emotional arousal. We describe this technique in some detail and also present preliminary evidence relating to the effectiveness of the program.

## A CONCEPTUAL MODEL OF STRESS

The term *stress* generally is used in two major ways: to label situations ("stressors") that tax a person's physical or psychological resources and to refer to the emotional response of the person to such situations. These two uses of the term are not synonymous, for people vary widely in how "stressful" they find the same objective situations to be as well as in their idiosyncratic responses to stressful situations. In our discussion here, we use the term in the second sense to refer to the cognitive-affective response. Moreover, we use the term in a broad

359

sense to include not only anxiety but other negative or aversive emotional states such as anger.

The conceptual model that underlies the cognitive-affective stress-management training program is derived from the contributions of several theorists, including R. S. Lazarus (1966), Schachter (1966), Arnold (1967), and Ellis (1962). The model, presented in Fig. 15.1, emphasizes relationships involving cognition, physiological responses, and behavior; and it has four major elements: (1) the situation, (2) the person's cognitive appraisal of the situation, his or her ability to cope with it, and its possible consequences, (3) physiological arousal responses, and (4) instrumental behaviors. Personality and motivational variables are assumed to influence each of the elements. The stimuli that constitute the situation may be either external or internal in origin. Although one ordinarily thinks of emotion as being evoked by external situations, internal cues in the form of thoughts, images or memories may also be stimuli to which one may respond with a stress response. Whatever the exact nature of the situation, it is one which taxes the resources of the person.

Nonmeditational models of behavior (e.g., Wolpe, 1958) often conceptualize the situation as directly stimulating the physiological component of the emotional response. One major contribution of the theorists cited above was to emphasize the crucial role of cognitive mediators of emotionality. Appraisal processes create the psychological reality to which people respond, and the nature and intensity of emotional responses are a function of their perceptions and expectancies about the situation, their ability to deal with it, and its potential consequences for them. R. S. Lazarus (1975) used the terms *primary* and *secondary* appraisal to refer, respectively, to subjective judgments about the nature and meaning of the situation and to judgments about one's ability to cope successfully with it. Bandura (1977) emphasized the role of expectancies of self-efficacy in effective behavior.

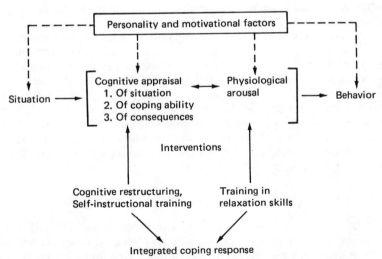

*Figure 15.1*  Mediational model of stress underlying the cognitive-affective stress-management program together with the major intervention techniques used in development of the integrated coping response.

Expectancies that one can cope successfully with situational demands form a close conceptual link with the concept of secondary appraisal. Ellis's (1962) major contribution was to specify the manner in which maladaptive emotional reactions are a function of irrational beliefs that are manifested in internal self-statements. Most other cognitive mediational concepts such as perceptions, attributions, and self-instructions can be readily conceptualized within the appraisal component of the model.

A third component, physiological responses, is related in a bidirectional or reciprocal fashion to appraisal processes. Whether and to what extent people respond with emotional arousal depends largely on cognitive mediational responses. Even in the case of classically conditioned emotional responses, cognitive mediators can markedly affect the course of acquisition and extinction (Notterman, Schoenfeld, & Bersh, 1952). On the other hand, physiological responses provide feedback concerning the intensity of the emotion being experienced (Schachter, 1966). Such feedback contributes to the ongoing process of appraisal and reappraisal. Thus, a person who becomes aware of somatic cues of increasing arousal may appraise the situation as one that is very stressful or upsetting. It is not difficult to understand how a spiraling acceleration of emotional arousal can result from the intimate relationship between cognitions and physiological response systems. Conversely, a person who experiences evidence of low physiological arousal in a potentially stressful situation is likely to appraise the situation as less threatening or as one with which he or she can cope successfully (Valins & Ray, 1967).

The fourth component consists of the instrumental responses that are made within the situation. These include task-oriented, social, and coping behaviors. Their nature, appropriateness, and efficacy are assumed to be affected by the cognitive and physiological processes within the bracket as well as the learned response capabilities of the person.

Each of the four primary components of the model—situation, appraisal processes, physiological arousal, and instrumental behaviors—can be influenced by motivational and personality vairables. Individual differences in personality and motivation influence the kinds of situations to which people expose themselves; the manner in which internal and external stimuli, as well as response capabilities and the "meaning" of potential consequences, are appraised; the quality, intensity, and duration of emotional arousal; and the ways in which people attempt to cope with the situation as perceived.

The practical as well as conceptual advantage of the mediational model of stress is that it has clear implications for the development of intervention strategies. Intervention at any of the four primary component levels may serve to reduce stress, as may motivational and personality changes. At the situational level, changes in certain features of the environment may alter its capacity to generate distress. In industrial settings, for example, intervention programs may be directed at changing the physical environment (e.g., through noise reduction or greater privacy), the work requirements (e.g., by decreasing workloads), or the interpersonal environment (e.g, through changes in leadership or human relations training of supervisors and co-workers). Lack of real or anticipated success in achieving change may result in perhaps the most elementary means of managing a situation: leaving or avoiding it. For example, in a study of 8- and 9-year-old sport nonparticipants and children who had dropped out of sport programs, Orlick

(1972) found that 75% of the children indicated as their main reason for non-participation fear of performing poorly or failing to make the team.

Environmental change can also be produced by changes in the behavioral component. While behavior is influenced by the environment, the opposite is also true. People tend to underestimate the extent to which their environment is created by their behavior, and acquisition of various skills may alter the environment significantly. For example, interpersonal-skills training can help people create a more benign interpersonal environment for themselves. Besides affecting the situational component, behavioral changes affect future situational appraisals and self-efficacy expectancies.

The third point at which distress can be reduced is at the level of physiological arousal. Many measures, including use of alcohol and certain drugs, eating, and various meditative techniques, can be used to dampen emotional arousal. Behaviors incompatible with arousal, such as muscular relaxation and vigorous muscular activity, can also be applied voluntarily to reduce arousal. Muscular relaxation has been found to be a highly effective means of preventing or reducing physiological arousal (Delman & Johnson, 1976), and people who acquire the ability to induce in themselves a state of deep muscular relaxation have a highly generalizable means of counteracting emotional arousal.

Finally, intervention strategies can be directed at modifying cognitive mediational responses. This is in many respects the key component in the model because many interventions that might be directed at other components ultimately are mediated by, or exert their effects through, the appraisal processes. Distress is not triggered directly by the situation but by what people tell themselves about the stressful situation and their ability to cope with it. Thus, a situation may be regarded by one person as positive and enjoyable and by another as dangerous and aversive. Even if a situation cannot be changed, as is often the case, people can be trained to discover, challenge, and change the internal self-statements that are generating their stress responses (Ellis, 1962). The person who is described as "mentally tough" may be one who is able to emit cognitive responses that keep arousal within manageable limits and that facilitate attentional processes and task performance under adverse conditions.

Several intervention strategies may be used to modify cognitive processes, including cognitive restructuring (A. A. Lazarus, 1971) and self-instructional training (Meichenbaum, 1977). Cognitive restructuring is derived from rational-emotive therapy (Ellis, 1962) and is directed at identifying and modifying the specific irrational self-statements that cause the person to appraise the situation as stressful. It has been applied successfully to reduce responses to stress in several experimental investigations (e.g., Maes & Heimann, 1970; Moleski & Tosi, 1976; Trexler & Karst, 1972). In self-instructional training, people are taught to emit specific covert instructions designed to enhance attentional and problem-solving processes. Performance increments following self-instructional training have been demonstrated with a variety of tasks and subject populations (Labouvie-Vief & Gonda, 1976; Meichenbaum, 1975; Meichenbaum & Cameron, 1973).

Although various intervention strategies may appear to be directed at modification of a particular component of the conceptual model, it is important to emphasize again the reciprocal influences that the components exercise in relation to one another. Environment, internal processes, and overt behavior are intertwined in a system of reciprocal influences. Therefore, modification of any component, be it situation, appraisal processes, physiological arousal, or behavior, almost certainly will influence other components as well.

## INDUCED AFFECT

A critical aspect of the cognitive-affective stress management training program is the use of a procedure known as induced affect (IA) to facilitate the rehearsal of cognitive and somatic coping skills under conditions of moderate-to-high affective arousal. Although IA as a clinical technique has existed for more than 15 years, it is perhaps less well known than some other affect-elicitation techniques. We therefore describe the historical development of IA, the method itself, and research related to its efficacy and to procedural and subject variables that influence its effects.

IA was developed by C. N. Sipprelle (1967) as a learning-based psychotherapy technique designed to elicit affective arousal and to facilitate awareness of cues and situations related to the arousal. Like many other clinicians who have used psychodynamic therapy procedures, Sipprelle noted that a flood of affect during treatment is sometimes accompanied by memories and thoughts that are functionally related to the client's problems. Sipprelle also felt that in many instances, behavior change seemed directly related to the amount of affective arousal that occurred during therapy. In the mid 1960s Sipprelle began to experiment with techniques, including hypnosis, that might allow a therapist to bypass psychological defenses and elicit the arousal that was typically controlled by these learned avoidance responses. Hypnosis was soon abandoned in favor of an operant conditioning framework. Several studies showed that increases and decreases in cardiac rate could be brought about through operant reinforcement (Ascough & Sipprelle, 1968; Cox & Sipprelle, 1971). The prospect of using an operant approach to elicit affective responses seemed promising. As therapists using such techniques would most likely reinforce overt behavioral manifestations of emotionality, a study was conducted in which specified musculoskeletal affective responses were verbally reinforced. Conditioned changes in these behaviors occurred, and they were accompanied by positively correlated changes in respiration, cardiac rate, and skin conductance (Jordan & Sipprelle, 1972).

The therapeutic technique that evolved from Sipprelle's clinical and laboratory research involved first training clients in voluntary muscle relaxation techniques as in systematic desensitization (Wolpe, 1958). After relaxation had been mastered, the next phase of treatment involved the elicitation of affective arousal through suggestion, encouragement, and reinforcement by the therapist. The client was asked to report memories, images, or other cognitions that occurred during arousal and then to "relax away" the arousal while continuing to imagine these affect-related cues. The procedure was first viewed as a counterconditioning technique for reducing arousal to specific cues (C. N. Sipprelle, 1967), but Sipprelle later reconceptualized the procedure in terms of a coping response hypothesis (C. N. Sipprelle, 1971). He believed that while processes such as insight, extinction, habituation, and abreaction might account for some part of the total change variance, the emotional arousal associated with typically avoided cues could be controlled by a complex coping response that would *begin* with relaxation training and include a variety of physiological, behavioral, and cognitive aspects. Clients would leave therapy with coping skills that would allow continued improvement.

An elaboration of this coping skills model was advanced by Ascough (1972) and is still being refined. For purposes of this review, three important aspects will be noted. First, the development of IA has been guided largely by the assumption that it is highly desirable to elicit the affective responses that are the focus of treatment within the therapy room. Here, "behavior" implies a response complex that includes cognitive, physiological, and musculoskeletal components. A second assumption is that people must face typically avoided cues, as occurs in implosive therapy or in flooding, but that use of nonspecific suggestions and instructions (as opposed to specific anxiety-arousing scenes) allows for emotional arousal that is more isomorphic with the problem-eliciting cues than are the therapist-generated cues or hierarchies of other therapies. A third assumption is that adequate behavior change must be based on more than just extinction or habituation of affective responses to typically avoided cues. The person will show greatest improvement and generalization of treatment effects if specific coping skills are acquired that can be used in a range of stressful situations.

## IA Therapy

Having summarized briefly the historical background and theoretical framework underlying IA, let us now describe how it is traditionally used as a therapeutic technique. The specific procedures for IA therapy vary somewhat among therapists but generally conform to the sequence we describe (see Ascough, 1980b).

*Evaluation and case conceptualization.* The first two sessions are used for evaluation and case conceptualization. Interview and objective data are entered into Pascal's (1959) conceptual method (also see Swensen, 1968). Therapists should have a working knowledge of this scheme if they intend to use IA as it was originally formulated. Briefly, the client's problem, or psychological deficit, is viewed as a function of: (1) internal or environmental stressors; (2) learned maladaptive feelings, attitudes, or expectancies; (3) maladaptive coping responses; (4) strengths or assets; (5) adaptive habits; and (6) environmental supports. Assessment and case conceptualization is carried out in terms of this framework. As part of the assessment process, personality measures may be administered. Some therapists use the MMPI as a screening device. Anxiety measures allow some prediction of responsiveness to IA procedures (Korn, Ascough, & Kleemeier, 1972).

*Relaxation training.* Relaxation training is introduced in the first session, and we provide a cassette tape (Ascough, 1979) with progressive relaxation on one side and general relaxation on the other, with instructions to use both sides each day for 2 weeks. In the second session, final interview and objective data are obtained, and further relaxation training is administered.

*Rationale.* A rationale is presented in the second session or at the beginning of the third. It includes a general explanation of the purpose, the assumptions, the procedures, the process, and the goals of treatment. This information about IA is helpful in that therapy is stressful no matter what type is selected. Clients have expectancies for what occurs in therapy, and IA may differ considerably. The rationale suggests that the client may experience tension reduction from the release of arousal and derive benefits from learning about thoughts and stimuli that result in distress. It is emphasized, however, that the most important aspect of IA is learning a coping response. Clients are told that they will have a series of trials in which arousal is induced and they are trained to "turn off" the arousal. Relaxation training is conceptualized as the *initial* step in learning a complex coping response that includes behavior, ANS activity, and cognitive responses that clients can use to withstand stressful cues in future situations outside therapy.

*Baseline.* Baseline measures for clinical or research assessment may include scores from measures administered in the first two sessions, scores from state and trait paper-and-pencil measures, and physiological measures obtained in an initial phase of each therapy session.

The following phases occur within each treatment session once assessment and relaxation training have been completed and the client understands the treatment rationale:

*Relaxation phase.* There are several reasons for including an initial relaxation phase. First, the therapist can pair reinforcement with client compliance, and cooperation can be assessed. Second, it provides a low behavioral baseline above which any affective behaviors can be reinforced. Finally, it engenders an expectancy that relaxation can be achieved. Some therapists use progressive or tension-release instructions for the initial relaxation phase, but general relaxation instructions are more common. The initial relaxation phase usually lasts somewhere between 6 and 10 min.

It is not essential that this phase be included. When people are highly anxious, it may be more efficient to reinforce and increase existing affect rather than to attempt to induce relaxation.

*Arousal phase.* In the arousal phase, the client is told to focus attention inward and it is suggested that she or he will experience feelings that will begin to grow stronger. In its traditional form, IA differs from most other affect-elicitation therapies in that no specific content cues are used in most cases to generate arousal. The feeling is left unspecified until the client labels it. The following approaches can be used to generate and reinforce arousal: (1) The therapist can continue the instructions to "feel"; (2) the therapist can make suggestions that the feelings are getting stronger and stronger; (3) the therapist can give specific verbal reinforcements such as "good" when signs of arousal occur; and (4) the instructions may take the form of an elicitation-reinforcement model. That is, the instructions specify behaviors, and then the client is reinforced or shaped toward the behaviors, for example, "Your hands are trembling and the feelings are becoming stronger." In general, the therapist reinforces any overt signs of arousal, whether monitored by polygraph or directly observed.

*Verbalization, or stimulus-elicitation, phase.* This portion of the arousal phase usually does not occur in nonclinical research. In therapy, the client is asked during high levels of arousal to verbalize the feelings, thoughts or images being experienced if he or she has not already done so spontaneously. This allows the therapist to monitor the ongoing affect state and to use it to increase arousal by reflecting the client's thoughts and feelings or by elaborating cues as is done in implosive therapy. The arousal phase usually lasts from 6 to 10 min, but some clinicians continue as long as 15-to-20 min.

*Arousal-reducing relaxation phase.* The final relaxation phase may involve progressive or general relaxation instructions, but we prefer the latter. Two aspects are quite important. First, the therapist reiterates the material obtained during the verbalization procedure of the arousal phase at the onset of relaxation, once or twice as relaxation deepens, and again shortly before termination of relaxation. Second, the client is soon asked to "do it yourself." By the second or third session the client is encouraged to emit relaxation responses as an initial attempt at developing a coping response. The simultaneous presentation of relaxation instructions with suggestions to focus on affect and content, continued over sessions, allows the client to learn to inhibit the emotional response.

*Discussion phase.* After arousal has been reduced through relaxation, the therapist asks the client to describe his or her experiences during arousal and offers reflection, reassurance, clarification, support and interpretation. The intent is to facilitate the client's integration of the material, to explore with the client the significance and meaning of the experience, and to engage in cognitive restructuring that will allow the client to perceive future situations with similar cues in a more adaptive manner. Here the case conceptualization is of importance, and some therapists may use a chalk board to diagram the material.

The process of IA has several interesting characteristics. Figure 15.2 shows mean HR for each minute in three groups of six sessions each for an obsessive-compulsive client. Note that relaxation phases reflect a continuing ability to achieve lowered rate. Arousal appears to increase over sessions and then to decrease as the client learns to relax more effectively, as he or she appraises more accurately, and as the appraisal process results in finer discriminations about affect. In early sessions it is not unusual to obtain physiological arousal with vague, undifferentiated reports about the type of arousal, or the feeling state. Over several sessions the client begins to make discriminations about feelings and perhaps to elaborate on an identifiable theme such as anger. After general feelings of anger occur in several sessions, the client may begin to make discriminations about the anger such as anger *and* resentment toward parents, anger *and* bitterness in a school situation, anger *and* loneliness for interpersonal relationships

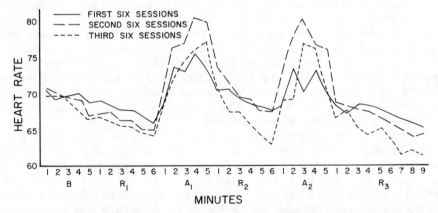

*Figure 15.2*   The course of physiological responding by an obsessive-compulsive client over 18 IA sessions. Mean HR is shown for each minute in three groups of six sessions during base line (B), relaxation ($R_1$), arousal ($A_1$), a second relaxation phase ($R_2$), a second arousal ($A_2$), and a final relaxation phase ($R_3$).

with peers, and rage. Such data can be regarded as typically avoided cues and as "insights" into the contingencies that affect ongoing behavior.

During the arousal phase, it is necessary to reinforce whatever feelings occur. If anger is presented, the therapist reinforces anger rather than trying to deflect the affect. The current procedure in traditional IA therapy is to obtain relatively strong arousal without overwhelming the client. This is a moderate approach in relation to speculation in the affective elicitation literature about a possible positive relationship between intensity of arousal and outcome.

It is not always clear when to terminate a client, but several criteria have been suggested for IA. One is to terminate the procedure when physiological arousal begins to level out and it is difficult to obtain an affective response during the arousal phase. Another sign of change is the occurrence of positive affect during the arousal phase. Of course the most important criterion is behavioral evidence of coping in weekly reports or observations.

## IA Research

The IA technique has stimulated a broad range of empirical research on subject and procedural variables. Although space does not permit a detailed description of research findings, it is worth noting that personality variables such as trait anxiety (Korn et al., 1972), neuroticism (R. C. Sipprelle, Ascough, Detrio, & Horst, 1977), and need for social approval (Detrio, 1975) have been shown to influence the intensity and quality of emotional responses exhibited by IA in experimental settings. Instructional sets and subject expectancies have also been shown to affect physiological and self-report responses to the technique (Burns & Ascough, 1971; R. C. Sipprelle, 1974, 1977). Finally, there is evidence that spaced IA sessions (weekly for 8 weeks) result in larger decreases in test anxiety than an equal amount of massed training given daily or twice weekly (Childers, 1971).

Use of unselected introductory psychology students in early IA research revealed that the typical undergraduate often shows positive affect during arousal phases rather than the negative affect encountered in clients. This is especially likely if the subject has low scores on anxiety, neuroticism, and need for approval measures. The IA procedure has also proven to be a means of evoking positive affect and of systematically manipulating the state (R. C. Sipprelle, 1974, 1977). Repeated training sessions may help people evoke positive affect in themselves for simple pleasure or for inhibiting negative affect such as anxiety, anger, and depression (Ascough, 1978; Burns, 1977; Lange-Schmelter & Ascough, 1976).

Much of the outcome research on IA has been performed on subclinical student populations in analogue studies (see Ascough, 1980a, for a summary), but a number of investigations have also been done with clinical problems. Although no large body of outcome studies exists for any single problem, IA has been applied with moderate-to-high success to such psychological and medical problems as schizophrenia (Cockshott & Ascough, 1973; Friedberg, 1969), drug abuse (Bereika, 1976; Boer & Sipprelle, 1969; Jordan, 1973), alcoholism (Paquette & Costelloe, 1973), and obesity (Bornstein & Sipprelle, 1973a, 1973b). In comparative studies, IA compares well with other therapies, but the strength of the method seems to be in the treatment of highly anxious clinic patients rather than the subclinical difficulties used in analogue research. Unfortunately, although dramatic case studies have been reported (e.g., Moore, 1973; Noonan, 1971), this conclusion must be regarded as speculative rather than empirically established in the absence of large-scale controlled outcome studies of such patients.

Two studies precede the development of the current cognitive-affective stress management program. Boer (1970) conceptualized IA as a potential stress inoculation strategy. After three sessions in either verbal psychotherapy, systematic desensitization, IA, or no-treatment control conditions, undergraduate psychology majors were exposed to a stress film. Five physiological and nine behavioral measures were obtained as dependent measures of stress. The results indicated that both systematic desensitization and IA reduced the stress response, with IA being the most effective.

Korn & Ascough (1972) assessed IA as an inoculation or preventive intervention for freshmen who reported anxiety about entering college. Treatment groups received either group discussion with IA, group IA alone, group discussion alone, or simple relaxation training. Subjects in each condition met for six sessions. Various dependent measures of outcome for anxiety and school performance showed no differences between the groups. Subsequent analyses indicated that all of the treatment groups had changed significantly, whether or not they received IA treatment. Follow-up interviews with subjects suggested that there were so many adjustment aids instituted by the university in question that most freshmen were likely to change for the better with or without a formal program.

## COGNITIVE-AFFECTIVE STRESS-MANAGEMENT TRAINING

As the conceptual model of stress presented earlier suggests, coping with stress is a complex process, and many separate coping skills may prove effective in preventing or reducing responses to stressful cues. There are both individual and situational determinants of how effective a coping skill will be. One person may find it easier to acquire and effectively employ a particular skill (e.g., cognitive restructuring) than another, who may, in turn, be remarkably talented at voluntary muscle relaxation. Certain coping skills may be especially useful in specific situations while being less useful in others. It therefore follows that a training program should teach a variety of coping skills and should provide the opportunity not only for acquisition of skills but also for practice in rehearsing and applying them. Our program is labeled a cognitive-affective approach because the coping skills are explicitly directed at modifying the appraisal and physiological arousal components of the conceptual model (see Fig. 15.1), and an affective arousal technique, modified from the clinical IA procedure, is used for rehearsal purposes.

Like other coping skills programs (e.g., Goldfried, 1971; Goldfried, Decenteceo, & Weinberg, 1974; Meichenbaum, 1972; Novaco, 1975; Suinn & Richardson, 1971), the cognitive-affective approach represents an attempt to combine a number of clinical treatment techniques into an educational program for self-control of emotion. Originally developed for use in individual and group psychotherapy with clinical populations, the program components have been adapted and combined to form a training package that can be administered in either an individual or a group format. Over the past 7 years, the program has been applied to a variety of clinical and nonclinical populations, including social welfare caseworkers, university administrators, bankers, business executives, test-anxious college students, medical students, heavy social drinkers, and athletes. The latter group has included preadolescents, college athletes, and professionals in a variety of individual and team sports. Athletes have proven to be an especially interesting target population because they are able to acquire a number of the coping skills (e.g., muscular relaxation) somewhat more quickly than other groups; they are typically exposed to the stressful athletic situations frequently enough to permit careful monitoring of their progress; and behavioral performance measures are readily obtained for assessment and research purposes (Smith, 1980a; Smith & Smoll, 1978).

## Treatment Phases

For descriptive purposes, we may divide the program as administered on an individual basis into five partially overlapping phases: (1) pretreatment assessment, (2) treatment rationale, (3) skill acquisition, (4) skill rehearsal, and (5) posttreatment evaluation. When administered on a group basis, the preliminary-assessment phase typically involves primarily paper-and-pencil measures.

*Pretreatment assessment.* When the program is administered to individuals, several sessions may be devoted to assessing the nature of their stress responses, the circumstances under which stress occurs, and its effects on performance and other behaviors. Assessment is also directed toward evaluating their behavioral and cognitive skills and deficits so that the program can be tailored to the person's special needs. We want to know, for example, how well the person can voluntarily relax and how aware she or he is of the cognitive processes that elicit emotionality and impair performance or, conversely, reduce stress and improve behavioral efficiency. In short, we try to specify the component variables in the conceptual model and the relationships among them so that we can build on the person's strengths and help him or her acquire new coping skills in deficit areas. For example, the focus of training for a person who already has fairly good relaxation skills but who has little control over self-defeating thought processes will tend to be concentrated on developing stress-reducing and performance-enhancing cognitive skills. On the other hand, a primary focus on the development of relaxation and self-instructional skills may be the preferred approach for an intellectually dull and chronically tense person.

A variety of assessment techniques can be employed during this phase. Much information can be obtained through careful interviewing. Interview data can be supplemented by a number of self-report questionnaires and inventories. The MMPI can provide valuable information on potential sources of stress. In our work with athletes and test anxious students, we have developed questionnaires that assess both the frequency or *extensity* with which stress is experienced in particular situations (e.g., "the night before the game" or "after you've made a playing mistake") and the *intensity* of the upset experienced when it does occur. We find that in some populations, the frequency and intensity dimensions correlate only around +.30, so that assessment of both dimensions is advisable. Another questionnaire we have found useful is the Irrational Beliefs Scale (Jones, 1968). This instrument is based on Ellis's (1962) description of commonly held irrational beliefs that tend to elicit emotional disturbance. This measure can be useful in suggesting target beliefs for cognitive restructuring.

Self-monitoring by subjects can be an extremely useful assessment procedure. We frequently employ a 100-point "tension thermomenter" and ask subjects to give "readings" of their degree of tension in various situations. They are also asked to monitor the situations under which particular kinds of thoughts occur.

*Treatment rationale.* The training program begins with a conceptualization phase to help subjects understand the nature of their stress response in terms of the conceptual model presented earlier. As Meichenbaum (1977) has emphasized, the initial conceptualization of the problem is of crucial importance in obtaining commitment to a training program. The conceptualization should therefore be understandable and plausible, and it should have clear intervention implications.

We have found it fairly easy to ensure that subjects arrive at the conceptual model on their own simply by asking them to describe their stress responses. Questions like When did it happen? What was it like? and What were your thoughts like? are usually sufficient to elicit descriptions of situational, physiological, and cognitive elements. Labeling these elements and the relationships among them provides an introduction to a description of the conceptual model and of its implications for the acquisition of specific cognitive and behavioral coping skills. An overview of the following elements of the training program is then presented.

### Course of Training in the Cognitive-Affective Stress-Management Program

1. Orientation and relaxation training. The nature of emotion and stress is discussed, as in the nature of coping with stress. Training is begun in muscular relaxation, which serves as a physical coping response.

2. Continuation of relaxation training and discussion of the role of cognitive appraisal processes in coping with stress.

3. Practice in the use of relaxation to control emotional responses elicited during the session by means of IA. Development of cognitive coping responses.

4. Practice in using relaxation and stress-reducing self-statements to control emotional reactions to IA.

5. Continued practice in use of coping skills with emphasis on development of the end product of the program: the integrated coping response.

6. Training in the use of Benson's meditation technique as a generalized stress-management technique.

Two important points are emphasized during the conceptualization phase and throughout training. One is that the program is not psychotherapy, but an educational program. It is stressed that the basic difference between people who are negatively affected by stress and those who cope successfully is that the latter group has been fortunate in having previous life experiences that enabled them to learn the kinds of coping skills to be taught in the program. The second point emphasized is that it is a program in *self*-control and the coping abilities that result from the program are a function of how much effort the person devotes to their acquisition. Our goal is to ensure that positive changes are attributed by the subject to herself rather than to the actions of the trainer, because self-attributed behavioral changes are more likely to endure (Davison & Valins, 1968, 1969). It is interesting to note in this regard that test-anxious college students who took part in the program showed significant gains on a measure of general self-efficacy (Nye, 1979).

*Skill acquisition.* The training program is directed toward the development of an *integrated coping response* having somatic and cognitive elements. The skill-acquisition phase thus consists of the learning of muscular relaxation and a concomitant analysis of thought processes and replacement of stress-eliciting self-statements with specific cognitions designed to reduce stress and improve performance.

Training in voluntary muscle relaxation begins immediately, using a variant of Jacobson's (1938) progressive muscle relaxation technique. Individual muscle groups are tensed, slowly relaxed half way, and then slowly relaxed completely. This procedure is designed to enhance discrimination of slight changes in muscle tension. The written exercises are presented elsewhere (Smith, Sarason, & Sarason, 1978, pp. 258–260). As training proceeds, increasingly larger groups of muscles are combined until the entire body is being relaxed as a unit. Although some of the relaxation training is done by the trainer, most of it is accomplished on a daily basis as homework assignments.

During the course of relaxation training, special emphasis is placed on the use of deep breathing to facilitate relaxation. Deane (1964) has shown experimentally that respiration amplitude and frequency can affect HR as well as subjective feelings of anxiety. Subjects are asked to breathe slowly and deeply and to emit repeatedly the mental command, "Relax" during exhalation. The command is thus repeatedly paired with the relaxation that occurs with exhalation so that in time the command becomes an eliciting cue for inducing relaxation (see A. A. Lazarus, 1971) as well as an important component of the integrated coping response.

Training in cognitive coping skills begins with a didactic description and the reading of written materials on the manner in which emotional responses are elicited by internal sentences or self-statements. Subjects are told that because such thought patterns are well-practiced and automatized, people generally have limited awareness of precisely what they are telling themselves. It is emphasized, however, that with practice and effort, people can learn to tune in to their internal dialogue, to evaluate logically the beliefs that underlie their self-statements, and to develop new self-statements to replace dysfunctional ones. A book by Ellis and Harper (1975) and a chapter in Rudestam (1980) based on rational-emotive therapy are recommended as outside reading, as a basis for later discussions, and as a source of potentially adaptive self-statements. To facilitate identification of stress-inducing cognitions and development of adaptive self-statements, subjects are given daily homework forms on which they list a situation that upset them, the emotion they experienced, what they must have told themselves about the situation in order to have been upset, and what they might have told themselves instead in order to have prevented their upset. These exercises, discussions with the trainer, and written materials form the basis for an "antistress" log on which subjects list their habitual stress-producing self-statements (usually five or fewer) and an "antistress" substitute for each. The latter form the basis for later practice and rehearsal.

In analyzing their stress-eliciting thoughts, subjects are shown how the beliefs that underlie their self-statements, though widely embraced in our culture, are often quite irrational (e.g., "It is terrible, awful, and catastrophic when things (me, others, events) are not the way I *demand* they be"; "I must always be successful in order to be worthwhile"; "I cannot be worth anything unless I earn the constant approval and love of everyone who matters to me."). Replacing such statements with substitutions like "Don't catastrophize—I may not like this, but I can certainly live with it"; "I can do no more than give 100% and I'm still the same person whether I succeed or not" provides a person with a potential tool for preventing or reducing self-induced stress responses.

The approach described thus far is a form of cognitive restructuring, inasmuch as its objective is to rationally evaluate and replace irrational beliefs that cause disturbance (see A. A. Lazarus, 1971, and Goldfried & Davison, 1976, for a more detailed description of this approach). The important contributions of Meichenbaum (1977) and his colleagues have resulted in the addition of self-instructional training elements to the cognitive coping skills training. As its name implies, the focus of this approach is on development of specific task-relevant self-commands that can be emitted in relevant situations. Examples of such commands are: "Don't think about fear; just think about what you have to do"; "One step at a time. Develop a plan to deal with it"; "Take a deep breath and relax." A number of studies have shown that self-instructional training can be valuable in enhancing performance and in reducing emotional arousal under stressful conditions (see Meichenbaum, 1977, for a review). Not only is self-instructional training a useful supplement to cognitive restructuring in generating adaptive cognitions, but it is the approach of choice with certain people. Some subjects are simply not psychologically minded or introspective enough to be ideal subjects for cognitive restructuring. Additionally, as we have begun to apply the program to preadolescent children, we have found that in most cases self-instructional training is more helpful and more readily applied than is restructuring.

*Skill rehearsal.* Stress coping skills are no different than any other kind of skill. To be most effective, they must be rehearsed and practiced under conditions that approximate the real-life situations in which they will eventually be employed. A skill-rehearsal phase should thus be an integral component of any coping-skills program. Meichenbaum and Cameron (1972) found that phobic clients who received only self-instructional training without the opportunity to rehearse their coping responses in the face of a stressor reported low anxiety when initially confronting the phobic object but a precipitous rise in anxiety as the task demands increased.

Stress management programs can employ a variety of stressors so as to give subjects the opportunity to practice and experiment with various coping skills. These can include stress-inducing films (R. S. Lazarus & Opton, 1966), unpredictable electrical shock (Klepac, 1975), imagining stressful situations (Goldfried, 1971; Meichenbaum, 1972; Suinn & Richardson, 1971), the cold pressor test (Turk, 1976), and other physical and psychological stressors. In our program, a modification of IA is the procedure used to generate high levels of emotional arousal, which the subject then reduces by using the coping responses acquired in the preceding phase of training.

As employed in the present program, IA is designed to allow rehearsal of coping responses in the presence of two kinds of cues: (1) imaginal representations of external cues that tend to elicit stress and (2) internal cues resulting from the emotional arousal. Although the external cues are fairly specific to certain situations, the internal cues are probably common to differing emotional responses that may occur in a wide variety of situations. Practice in dealing with the latter class of cues should therefore maximize the generalizability of the coping skills across a variety of affect-eliciting situations (Goldfried, 1971; Suinn & Richardson, 1971). In contrast, conventional systematic desensitization (Wolpe, 1958) deals primarily with relaxation in response to imagined external cues, and an attempt is made to prevent the experiencing of anxiety. It is therefore not surprising that fear reduction accomplished through this technique typically does not generalize to other anxiety arousing situations (Meichenbaum & Cameron, 1972; Meyer & Gelder, 1963; Wolpe, 1958, 1961).

In our use of IA, clients are asked to imagine as vividly as possible a stressful situation. They are then asked to focus on the feeling that the situation has elicited, and we suggest that as they concentrate on it, it will begin to grow and to become stronger and stronger. The suggestions continue as the client begins to respond to them with increasing emotional arousal, and physical indications of arousal are verbally reinforced and encouraged ("That's good, that's fine. . . . Now just let that feeling grow. . . . It's getting bigger and bigger. . . . Just let it come. . . . It will grow all by itself. . . . It's OK to let it come, because in a minute you'll see how easily you can turn it off . . ."). At intervals during the arousal phase, the trainer asks the client what kinds of thoughts are occurring, and this information is used to elaborate upon the arousal. It also provides information on the nature of the cognitions that accompany (and, it is hypothesized, mediate) the arousal.

When a high level of arousal is obtained, the client is instructed to "turn it off" with the coping responses. Initially, relaxation alone is used as the active coping skill. In the second stage of rehearsal, self-statements alone are used. Finally, the two types of coping responses are combined into an integrated coping response that ties both the self-statements and the relaxation response into the breathing cycle. As clients inhale, they emit one of their stress-reducing self-statements (e.g., "I may not like this, but I can definitely stand it" or "I need to concentrate, not to make myself tense," etc.). At the peak of inhalation, they say the word *so,* and as they slowly exhale, they instruct themselves to "Relax" and induce muscular relaxation. Recall that, during relaxation training, exhalation, the mental command to relax, and voluntarily relaxing were repeatedly combined with one another. The introduction of the self-statement during inhalation results in the integration of cognitive and physiological coping responses within the breathing cycle.

Subjects trained individually typically report that the level of arousal experienced during IA is *more* intense than that experienced in the real-life situations. Their ability to control this high level of arousal very quickly with their coping skills increases their confidence that they can deal successfully with actual stressors. It is worth noting that the present program differs sharply in this regard from Meichenbaum's (1977) stress-inoculation procedure. As the name implies, Meichenbaum's emphasis is on immunizing the person to large stresses by "learning to cope with small, manageable units of stress" (p. 149). In our program, the emphasis is quite the opposite in that the person practices successfully managing emotional responses that are frequently more intense than those elicited by *in vivo* stressors. Which of the two approaches will ultimately prove more effective in developing stress-management skills is an important empirical question, because it has theoretical as well as practical implications. Because the IA procedure elicits higher levels of arousal in individual than in group settings (in which we make no effort to elicit high arousal), the most appropriate test of the two models will be in individual training. Nye (1979) found the two procedures to be roughly comparable in the group treatment of test-anxious college students.

After the skill-rehearsal phase is completed, the program ends with training in Benson's (1975) meditation procedure, which is presented as a general relaxation and stress-reduction technique that can be used in nonstressful situations.

*Evaluation.* An integral part of a training program of any kind should be an evaluation of its effects. In nonexperimental or single-subject studies, the most elementary type of design is the pre-post design whereby dependent variable measures are obtained before and after training. In the absence of credible attention-placebo and nontreated control groups, pre-post results—particularly those based on self-report measures—must be interpreted with great caution. In one recently completed nonexperimental study, a total of 142 child welfare caseworkers were administered, in groups of 10-15, a six-session cognitive-affective program. Highly significant decreases in self-reported stress on the job were reported on anonymous (number-coded) questionnaires. The fact that the program extended over a 9-month period and that the time of year during which caseworkers participated in the program was unrelated to magnitude of change would appear to rule out the influence of systematic temporal factors.

As noted earlier, athletes have been an important target population in recent applications of the program. A major assessment advantage in working with athletes is that behavioral measures of athletic performance are often available. For example, football players are frequently graded on each play in which they participate by coaches who observe game films. Using these measures, it was possible to demonstrate improved performance on the part of high-anxiety college players who participated in the program (Smith & Smoll, 1978). As in the caseworker project, however, the absence of control groups renders the results suggestive at best.

When performance measures are available for a series of performances before and after training, a time series analysis of performance data may provide evidence of outcome in instances where high anxiety appears to be adversely affecting performance. As an example, a highly skilled and talented adolescent figure skater continually performed poorly in competitive events and always placed in the lower half of the standings. In the previous six competitions, extending over about a year, she had not placed above eighth. The cognitive-affective program was administered to her over a three-week period. Subsequent to completion of the cognitive-affective training program, a dramatic performance reversal occurred, as she placed first in three of her next four competitions and second in the remaining one. She also exhibited a large decrease in her score in the Sport Competition Anxiety Test (Martens, 1977) and reported that her coping skills were very successful in allowing her to control her anxiety during her routines under competitive conditions. Onlookers who were unaware that she had been in the program frequently remarked that she appeared more relaxed and confident than was previously the case.

While positive results obtained in single-subject case studies and uncontrolled group studies are somewhat encouraging, more confident assertions concerning the efficacy of the program require controlled outcome studies. Nye (1979) compared a group administration of the cognitive-affective program with Meichenbaum's (1972) covert rehearsal stress inoculation procedure; a nonrehearsal condition in which subjects were given information and self-instructional materials on a variety of coping skills; and a nontreated control group. The subjects were college students who suffered from high test anxiety. All three treatment groups exhibited significant decreases in scores on Sarason's (1978) Test Anxiety Scale, with the greatest decrease being exhibited by the cognitive-affective training group. The cognitive-affective and covert modeling groups both exhibited large decreases in state anxiety during actual classroom tests. All three treatment groups showed significant increases on a measure of general self-efficacy. In academic performance, only the cognitive-affective group showed an increase in test grades following training, but the magnitude of change was not statistically significant. It is interesting to note that the nonrehearsal group showed a level of improvement on self-report measures that approximated that of the two rehearsal conditions. The former group did not differ from the rehearsal conditions on either pre- or post-treatment credibility reatings made by subjects. Unlike the Meichenbaum and Cameron (1972) results (in which the nonrehearsal condition was not demonstrated to be equally credible), Nye's results did not support the need for skill rehearsal. It is also the case, however, that performance limits were not assessed in Nye's study. It may be that incremental effects of rehearsal are likely to appear only under high task demands.

As noted earlier, the IA technique is particularly effective in eliciting intense emotional responses in individual sessions, and our experience indicates that the cognitive-affective program is likely to be most effective in training individuals. When training is administered to groups, the level of affective arousal is attenuated both by the trainer's instructions and by group processes, and the level of affect exhibited is similar to that which occurs in Goldfriend's (1971) self-control variant of systematic desensitization. Assuming that rehearsal of the integrated coping response to reduce high levels of affect facilitates treatment gains, an experimental-outcome study involving individual rather than group rehearsal under IA would be desirable. Such a study is currently being carried out in our laboratory with heavy social drinkers whose drinking behaviors tend to occur under stress. It is hypothesized that the acquisition of adaptive coping skills will reduce dependence on alcohol as a means of reducing stress. Posttreatment and 6-month follow-up changes in drinking rates as well as indexes of subjectively experienced stress and general adjustment are being assessed in the experimental group and in a control condition that receives only meditation training.

The cognitive-affective stress management program incorporates a number of techniques that have proven to be successful components of other programs. The feature that most clearly differentiates the program from other stress-management programs is the use of IA during the rehearsal phase after development of cognitive and somatic coping skills. Induced affect has proven to be an effective clinical tool in its own right (Ascough, 1980a; Bornstein & Sipprelle, 1973a, 1973b; Hamilton & Bornstein, 1977; C. N. Sipprelle, 1967), and it appears well-suited for a training program that emphasizes the rehearsal of coping skills under conditions of high affective arousal.

# REFERENCES

Arnold, M. B. Stress and emotion. In M. H. Appley & R. Trumbull (Eds.), *Psychological stress: Issues in research.* New York: Appleton, 1967.
Ascough, J. C. *Induced anxiety: Toward a theory.* Paper presented at the meeting of the Southeastern Psychological Association, Atlanta, April 1972.

Ascough, J. C. *Research on positive affect and positive affect training.* Paper presented at the meeting of the Southeastern Psychological Association, Atlanta, March 1978.

Ascough, J. C. *The standard relaxation training tape.* West Lafayette, Ind.: Center for Induced Affect, 1979.

Ascough, J. C. *Case studies and research in induced affect.* West Lafayette, Ind.: Center for Induced Affect, 1980. (a)

Ascough, J. C. *A manual for induced affect.* West Lafayette, Ind.: Center for Induced Affect, 1980. (b)

Ascough, J. C., & Sipprelle, C. N. Operant verbal conditioning of autonomic responses. *Behaviour Research and Therapy, 1968, 6,* 363–370.

Bandura, A. Self-efficacy: Toward a unifying theroy of behavior change. *Psychological Review, 1977, 84,* 191–215.

Benson, H. *The relaxation response.* New York: Morrow, 1975.

Bereika, G. M. *The effects of induced affect on selected characteristics of drug dependent patients.* Unpublished doctoral dissertation, Purdue University, 1976.

Boer, A. P. *Toward preventative psychotherapy: Experimental reduction of psychophysiological stress through prior behavior therapy training.* Unpublished doctoral dissertation, University of South Dakota, 1970.

Boer, A. P., & Sipprelle, C. N. Induced anxiety in the treatment of LSD effects. *Psychotherapy and Psychosomatics, 1969, 17,* 108–113.

Bornstein, P. H., & Sipprelle, C. N. Group treatment of obesity by induced anxiety. *Behaviour Research and Therapy, 1973, 11,* 339–341. (a)

Bornstein, P. H., & Sipprelle, C. N. Induced anxiety in the treatment of obesity: A preliminary case report. *Behavior Therapy, 1973, 4,* 141–143. (b)

Burns, J. M. *An initial investigation into positive affect training.* Unpublished doctoral dissertation, Purdue University, 1977.

Burns, J. M., & Ascough, J. C. A psychophysiological comparison of two approaches to relaxation and anxiety induction. *Behavior Therapy, 1971, 2,* 170–176.

Childers, J. *Induced anxiety as a function of massed versus spaced practice.* Paper presented at the meeting of the Southeastern Psychological Association, Miami, April 1971.

Cockshott, J. B., & Ascough, J. C. *An evaluation of the efficacy of induced anxiety for treatment of schizophrenia.* Paper presented at the meeting of the Southeastern Psychological Association, New Orleans, April 1973.

Cox, D. E., & Sipprelle, C. N. Coercion in participation as a research subject. *American Psychologist, 1971, 26,* 726–728.

Davison, G. C., & Valins, S. On self-produced and drug-produced relaxation. *Behaviour Research and Therapy, 1968, 6,* 401–402.

Davison, G. C., & Valins, S. Maintenance of self-attributed and drug-attributed behavior change. *Journal of Personality and Social Psychology, 1969, 11,* 25–33.

Deane, G. Human heart rate responses during experimentally induced anxiety: A follow-up with controlled respiration. *Journal of Experimental Psychology, 1964, 67,* 193–195.

Delman, R., & Johnson, H. Biofeedback and progressive muscle relaxation: A comparison of psychophysiological effects. *Psychophysiology, 1976, 13,* 181.

Detrio, D. M. *Effects of need for approval and pre-experimental rationale on response to induced affect.* Unpublished master's thesis, Purdue University, 1975.

Ellis, A. *Reason and emotion in psychotherapy.* New York: Lyle Stuart, 1962.

Ellis, A., & Harper, R. A. *A new guide to rational living.* Englewood Cliffs, N.J.: Prentice-Hall, 1975.

Friedberg, F. T. *The effects of induced anxiety under verbal and nonverbal conditions on withdrawal in chronic hospitalized schizophrenics.* Paper presented at the meeting of the Southeastern Psychological Association, New Orleans, March 1969.

Goldfried, M. R. Systematic desensitization as training in self-control. *Journal of Consulting and Clinical Psychology, 1971, 37,* 228–234.

Goldfried, M. R., & Davison, G. *Clinical behavior therapy.* New York: Holt, 1976.

Goldfried, M. R., Decenteceo, E., & Weinberg, L. Systematic rational restructuring as a self-control technique. *Behavior Therapy, 1974, 5,* 247–254.

Hamilton, S. B., & Bornstein, P. H. Modified induced anxiety: A generalized anxiety reduction procedure. *Journal of Consulting and Clinical Psychology, 1977, 45,* 1200–1201.

Jacobson, E. *Progressive relaxation.* Chicago: University of Chicago Press, 1938.

Jones, R. G. *A factored measure of Ellis' irrational belief system, with personality and maladjustment correlates.* Unpublished doctoral dissertation, Texas Technological College, 1968.

Jordan, C. S. *Some initial findings on the treatment of addiction with induced anxiety.* Paper presented at the meeting of the Southeastern Psychological Association, New Orleans, April 1973.

Jordan, C. S., & Sipprelle, C. N. Physiological correlates of induced anxiety in normal subjects. *Psychotherapy: Theory, Research and Practice,* 1972, *9,* 18–21.

Klepac, R. Successful treatment of avoidance of dentistry by desensitization or by increasing pain tolerance. *Journal of Behavior Therapy and Experimental Psychiatry,* 1975, *6,* 307–310.

Korn, E. J., & Ascough, J. C. *The effectiveness of induced anxiety in group counseling as a preventative intervention procedure for freshmen.* Paper presented at the meeting of the Southeastern Psychological Association, Atlanta, April 1972.

Korn, E. J., Ascough, J. C., & Kleemeier, R. B. The effect of induced anxiety on state-trait measures of anxiety in high, middle, and low trait-anxious individuals. *Behavior Therapy,* 1972, *3,* 547–554.

Labouvie-Vief, G., & Gonda, J. Cognitive strategy training and intellectual performance in the elderly. *Journal of Gerontology,* 1976, *31,* 327–332.

Lange-Schmelter, B. S., & Ascough, J. C. *Recent developments in positive affect training.* Paper presented at the meeting of the Indiana Psychological Association, Indianapolis, November 1976.

Lazarus, A. A. *Behavior therapy and beyond.* New York: McGraw-Hill, 1971.

Lazarus, R. S. *Psychological stress and the coping process.* New York: McGraw-Hill, 1966.

Lazarus, R. S. The self-regulation of emotions. In L. Levi (Ed.), *Emotions: Their parameters and measurement.* New York: Raven, 1975.

Lazarus, R. S., & Opton, E. The use of motion picture films in the study of psychological stress. In C. D. Spielberger (Ed.), *Anxiety and behavior* (Vol. 1). New York: Academic, 1966.

Maes, W. R., & Heimann, R. A. *A comparison of three approaches to the reduction of test anxiety in high school students* (Final Rep., Project 9-1049). Washington: DHEW, Office of Education, Bureau of Research, 1970.

Martens, R. *Sport Competition Anxiety Test.* Champaign, Ill.: Human Kinetics, 1977.

Meichenbaum, D. Cognitive modification of test anxious college students. *Journal of Consulting and Clinical Psychology,* 1972, *39,* 370–380.

Meichenbaum, D. Enhancing creativity by modifying what subjects say to themselves. *American Educational Research Journal,* 1975, *12,* 129–145.

Meichenbaum, D. *Cognitive-behavior modification.* New York: Plenum, 1977.

Meichenbaum, D., & Cameron, R. *Stress inoculation: A skills training approach to anxiety management.* Unpublished manuscript, University of Waterloo, 1972.

Meichenbaum, D., & Cameron, R. Training schizophrenics to talk to themselves: A means of developing attentional controls. *Behavior Therapy,* 1973, *4,* 515–534.

Meyer, V., & Gelder, M. Behavior therapy and phobic disorders. *British Journal of Psychology,* 1963, *109,* 19–28.

Moleski, R., & Tosi, D. J. Comparative psychotherapy: Rational-emotive therapy versus systematic desensitization in the treatment of stuttering. *Journal of Consulting and Clinical Psychology,* 1976, *44,* 309–311.

Moore, C. H. *New directions for induced affect: Lessons from unusual cases.* Paper presented at the meeting of the Southeastern Psychological Association, New Orleans, April 1973.

Noonan, J. R. An obsessive-compulsive reaction treated by induced anxiety. *American Journal of Psychotherapy,* 1971, *25,* 293–299.

Notterman, J. M., Schoenfeld, W. N., & Bersh, P. J. A comparison of three extinction procedures following heart rate conditioning. *Journal of Abnormal and Social Psychology,* 1952, *47,* 674–677.

Novaco, R. *Anger control: The development and evaluation of an experimental treatment.* Lexington, Mass.: Heath, 1975.

Nye, S. L. *Self-instructional stress management training: A comparison of the effects of induced affect and covert modeling in a cognitive restructuring treatment program for test anxiety.* Unpublished doctoral dissertation, University of Washington, 1979.

Orlick, T. D. *A socio-psychological analysis of early sports participation*. Unpublished doctoral dissertation, University of Alberta, 1972.

Paquette, E. D., & Costelloe, C. A. *Induced anxiety in the treatment of alcoholism*. Paper presented at the meeting of the Southeastern Psychological Association, New Orleans, April 1973.

Pascal, G. R. *Behavioral change in the clinic*. New York: Grune and Stratton, 1959.

Rudestam, K. E. *Methods of self-change: An ABC primer*. Monterey, Calif.: Brooks-Cole, 1980.

Sarason, I. G. The Test Anxiety Scale: Concept and research. In C. D. Spielberger & I. G. Sarason (Eds.), *Stress and anxiety* (Vol. 5). Washington: Hemisphere, 1978.

Schachter, S. The interaction of cognitive and physiological determinants of emotional state. In C. D. Spielberger (Ed.), *Anxiety and behavior* (Vol. 1). New York: Academic, 1966.

Sipprelle, C. N. Induced anxiety. *Psychotherapy: Theory, Research, and Practice, 1967, 4*, 36–40.

Sipprelle, C. N. *Development and theory of induced anxiety*. Paper presented at the meeting of the Southeastern Psychological Association, Miami, April 1971.

Sipprelle, R. C. *Demand characteristics and affective tone in induced affect*. Unpublished master's thesis, Purdue University, 1974.

Sipprelle, R. C. *Person and situation determinants of response to stress*. Unpublished doctoral dissertation, Purdue University, 1977.

Sipprelle, R. C., Ascough, J. C., Detrio, D. M., & Horst, P. A. Neuroticism, extroversion, and response to stress. *Behaviour Research and Therapy, 1977, 15*, 411–418.

Smith, R. E. A cognitive-affective approach to stress management training for athletes. In C. H. Nadeau, W. Halliwell, K. M. Newell, & G. C. Roberts (Eds.), *Skillfulness in movement: Psychology of motor behavior and sport*. Champaign, Ill.: Human Kinetics, 1980. (a)

Smith, R. E. Development of an integrated coping response through cognitive-affective stress management training. In I. G. Sarason & C. D. Spielberger (Eds.), *Stress and anxiety* (Vol. 7). Washington: Hemisphere, 1980. (b)

Smith, R. E., Sarason, I. G., & Sarason, B. R. *Psychology: The frontiers of behavior*. New York: Harper & Row, 1978.

Smith, R. E., & Smoll, F. L. Psychological intervention and sports medicine: Stress management training and coach effectiveness training. *University of Washington Medicine, 1978, 5*, 20–24.

Suinn, R. M., & Richardson, F. Anxiety management training: A nonspecific behavior therapy program for anxiety control. *Behavior Therapy, 1971, 2*, 498–510.

Swensen, C. H. *An approach to case conceptualization*. Boston: Houghton Mifflin, 1968.

Trexler, L. D., & Karst, T. D. Rational emotive therapy, placebo, and no treatment effects on public speaking anxiety. *Journal of Abnormal Psychology, 1972, 79*, 60–67.

Turk, D. *An expanded skills training approach for the treatment of experimentally-induced pain*. Unpublished doctoral dissertation, University of Waterloo, 1976.

Valins, S., & Ray, A. A. Effects of cognitive desensitization on avoidance behavior. *Journal of Personality and Social Psychology, 1967, 7*, 345–350.

Wolpe, J. *Psychotherapy by reciprocal inhibition*. Stanford, Calif.: Stanford University Press, 1958.

Wolpe, J. The systematic desensitization treatment of neurosis. *Journal of Nervous and Mental Disease, 1961, 132*, 189–203.

# CONCLUSIONS

# 16

---

# *Stress*

---

## An Integrative Framework

### *Susan R. Burchfield*
### *University of Washington, Seattle, United States*

Stress is a concept that has generated a lot of research interest yet still remains elusive. Various definitions (Lazarus & Launier, 1978; Selye, 1956) and theories (Mason, 1975; Selye, 1975) of stress abound in the literature. In this chapter, stress is defined as any transactional process (cf. Lazarus & Launier, 1978) in which the organism experiences an alteration of psychological homeostasis. Psychological homeostasis and mechanisms to maintain it have been hypothesized to represent and maintain the "normal" psychological state of the person (Flaek & Britton, 1974; Klinger, 1975). The relevance of this concept to stress and its implications has been discussed in detail elsewhere (Burchfield, 1979). Here, then, *stress* is a process and *stressor* is the specific stimulus eliciting a "stress response" in an organism. The "nonspecific" stress response as described by Selye (1956) is probably elicited by a psychological stressor. If the stressor is not subjectively perceived as such (e.g., is a pure physiological stressor), then the response pattern is composed of compensatory changes initiated to return the organism to physiological homeostasis (cf. Mason, 1974).

## THE PATTERN OF THE STRESS RESPONSE

Burchfield (1979) proposed a model of the stress response based on learning predictive and consequential cues. The model contends that organisms learn which environmental stimuli precede stressor onset, thereby better enabling them to initiate their physiological stress response before the stressor actually occurs. After repeated exposure to a stressor, organisms learn the consequences, or threat potential, of that stressor. They then modulate their physiological reactivity to achieve adequate defense against the stressor without overtaxing the system or creating too much imbalance. It is presumed that one goal of all organisms is the maintenance of homeostasis and that physiological conditioning helps promote this goal. Hence, an organism exposed to a chronic intermittent stressor may cope most efficiently and achieve a more rapid return to homeostasis if it responds in a compensatory manner immediately before stressor onset and increases arousal to a minimal amount necessary to cope with the stressor.

This model was derived from research performed by Burchfield, Woods, and Elich (1980). Male Wistar rats were exposed to 10 min of daily cold stress or no stress for either 3 weeks or 3 months. On the 1st day of the experiment, blood samples were obtained either immediately after stressor exposure or instead of it. The results, depicted in Fig. 16.1, indicated that the plasma corticosterone response to stress decreased over time in rats chronically stressed throughout ($p <$ .01), whereas there was no difference in basal levels of rats that were not stressed. The most interesting result was found for rats that were daily stressed but received no stress on the test day. Blood samples were obtained at the same time of day as stress would normally have occurred. Results indicated that, after three months, the plasma corticosterone levels of this group equaled those of the 3-month stressed-throughout group and were significantly higher than their 3-week, daily stress–no stress on test day counterparts ($p < .01$). It was hypothesized that a conditioned corticosterone response to cues predictive of stress accounted for these results. Additionally, the decreased stress response seen in the 3-month stressed-throughout group was hypothesized to be due to adaptation achieved through learning of consequential cues (How much arousal is necessary to adequately cope with this stressor?). Although the hypothesis concerning ability to learn consequential cues has not been tested, we have begun to examine the conditionability of the hormonal response to stress.

Male Wistar rats were exposed to an unconditioned stimulus (loud noise) paired with a click (CS). After 1 week of daily click-noise pairings (Burchfield, 1980,

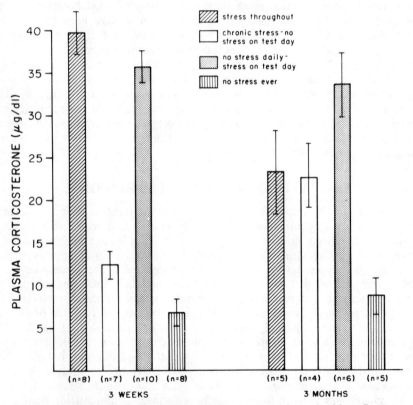

*Figure 16.1*  Mean ± SE levels of plasma corticosterone, as determined by a fluorometric assay, for all groups in Experiment 1 of Burchfield, Woods, and Elich (1980).

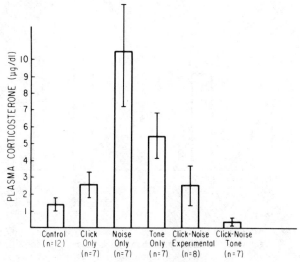

*Figure 16.2* Mean ± SE levels of plasma corticosterone, as determined by a specific radioimmunoassay, for rats exposed to a conditioning paradigm (click-noise, experimental) for 7 days. There was no conditioned corticosterone response to a click paired with loud noise.

1981), blood was collected 3 min after exposure to the click alone, and the serum was assayed for corticosterone and testosterone levels. The results, depicted in Figs. 16.2 and 16.3, suggested that conditioning of corticosterone did not occur, but that conditioning of testosterone did. There were no differences in serum corticosterone levels between the experimental and control groups, but there were significant ($p < .05$) differences of serum testosterone levels between these groups. Testosterone levels of the experimental group, which received daily click-noise pairings except on Day 8, when they were exposed to the click alone, equaled those of the noise-only group (one-time exposure to noise) and were significantly higher than those of the controls, which were either never exposed to noise or daily exposed to the click-noise sequence except on Day 8. These data indicated that testosterone was conditioned to the cue (click), which predicted stress (loud noise). We are currently running several experiments to rule out alternative hypotheses, such as sensitization, and to determine why there was no conditioned corticosterone response.

Overall, these data indicate that the hormonal system is conditionable to cues predictive of stress. Although several other studies have examined the condition-ability of hormones (Coover, Goldman, & Levine, 1971; Coover, Sutton, & Hey-bach, 1977; Corson & Corson, 1976), few have used appropriate controls, and none has directly attempted to condition a stimulus paired with a stressor. It is possible to conclude from these data that the anticipatory increase in physio-logical arousal that occurs before stressor onset is probably due to conditioning. Furthermore, the physiological stress response per se may, in some cases, repre-sent classical conditioning of a situation paired with a stimulus that caused a

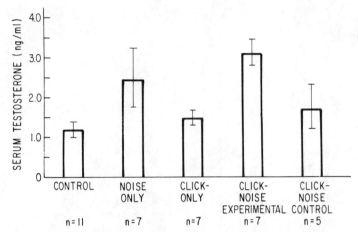

*Figure 16.3*   Mean ± SE levels of serum testosterone for rats exposed
to a conditioning paradigm (click-noise, experimental)
for 7 days. There was a conditioned testosterone response
to a click paired with loud noise.

reflexive startle reaction. Further investigation is needed to determine whether
the physiological stress response in humans is, itself, a reflexive response or
whether it is due to learning. Because the pattern of arousal is fairly consistent
across individuals and species (see Burchfield, 1979), it is likely that organisms
are genetically predisposed to exhibit this response pattern.

Within this response pattern of anticipatory arousal followed by decreased
arousal during stressor exposure, more specific response patterns occur. Veith-
Flanigan and Sandman (Chap. 5) hypothesized that the Laceys' hypothesis (Lacey
& Lacey, 1958) about organ specificity could be extended to the psychoendocrine
system. Individuals may tend to respond to all stimuli by increasing arousal more
in one system than in another (response specificity); yet, they may also exhibit
a hormonal response pattern during the stressor that is specific to the stressor
(stimulus specificity). For example, an organism may always respond with an
increase in catecholamines to any threatening stimulus (response specificity),
but it may also respond with an increase in thyroid hormone, glucagon, and cortisol
to cold stress and with a different pattern of release of these hormones to a different, specific, threatening stimulus (stimulus specificity). Veith-Flanigan and
Sandman cited a study investigating glucocorticoid response to several stressors
in 1-year-old infants. It showed that certain infants were already displaying preferential use of the glucocorticoid system when responding to different stressors.
Hence, psychoendocrine response specificity begins before 1 year of age. Follow-
up research is needed in this area to discover whether response specificity occurs
in newborns and what role learning plays in this process.

In addition, longitudinal research is necessary to determine if environment
and aging modify this response. It is important to know whether predispositions
to diseases, such as idiopathic hypertension, which apparently result from increased sensitivity of the involved system to stress, are present from birth or
whether they develop secondary to learning and environmental stimulation.

Effective treatment and prevention of these illnesses is predicated on acquisition of relevant longitudinal data. Furthermore, if the psychoendocrine response pattern to stress occurs early in life, then the relationship among thoughts, feelings, and physiological arousal may be very different from the currently accepted theories of emotion. As Veith-Flanigan and Sandman suggest, hormonal change may be not only the response to stressful stimuli but the stimuli that predispose a person to different thoughts, feelings, and behaviors.

Riley and Furedy (Chap. 1) suggested that psychological and physiological systems learn information using different modalities. The cognitive system learns CS-unconditioned stimulus (UCS) contingencies (i.e., relational learning), whereas the ANS learns S-R connections. Conditioning of the ANS occurs not because the ANS has learned the CS-UCS contingency but because it has learned a reaction. Predictions and contingencies are learned at a higher level. This formulation explains why a person may rationally understand his or her phobia yet not be able to rid himself or herself of it. Treatment of phobias (e.g., flooding, systematic desensitization) in which the CS-CR connection is extinguished and replaced by learning a new, nonfear response are often very effective despite the fact that propositional learning (CS-UCS contingencies) is absent. Riley and Furedy concluded that because the stress response is multidimensional, researchers investigating behavior or treatment must examine both systems and their interactions. Treatment of only the cognitive or only the physiological response to stress will not be as effective as a treatment method including both learning a new response to the CS and learning the CS-UCS contingencies.

Burchfield, Stein, and Hamilton's chapter (Chap. 2), in which test anxiety was used as a model to study cognitive–physiological interrelationships, supported the interactive theory of psychological and physiological processing. Psychological treatments (cognitive restructuring, etc.) and physiological treatments (relaxation, etc.) were equally effective in decreasing test anxiety. Test anxiety apparently results from maladaptive cognitions, as hypothesized by Wine (1971), which transact with the physiological system. Although little physiological research of test anxiety has been performed, it appears that there is no general difference of physiological arousal during testing in high- versus low-test-anxious people but there are specific differences in cardiac wave forms. Both groups are highly aroused, although the pattern of the arousal and their interpretations of it are different. Interpreting Riley and Furedy's conceptualization of learning, high-test-anxious people may learn different CS-UCS contingencies associated with arousal during a test than do low-anxious people.

Although this hypothesis is supported by current research, many more investigations are needed before test anxiety can be succinctly understood. Research that includes simultaneous measurement of physiological and psychological arousal before, during, and after testing must be performed. The pattern of the physiological response to chronic intermittent stress (i.e., anticipatory increase–consequential decrease) apparently differs between high- and low-test-anxious people. Thus, test anxiety may be useful as a model of maladaptive (high–test anxiety) and adaptive (low–test anxiety) responses to chronic intermittent stress. Examining cognitive and physiological reactions concomitantly may provide insight into the interdependency of these two systems and their role in the stress response.

Test anxiety, like most stressors experienced by humans, is psychological in nature; the physiological response originates through S-R learning, whereas the psychological interpretation of the situation is relational learning. Riley and Furedy's hypothesis explains why insight does not change physiological behavior and how the stress response (especially organ or hormonal specificity) may, given a genetic predisposition for the physiological system to react in a specific way, generalize to situations that are not physically taxing. The hypothesis that cognitions interact with the ANS is helpful in explaining how the stress-response pattern may become maladaptive so that anticipatory and consequential cues are disregarded.

## MECHANISMS OF THE STRESS RESPONSE

The precise physiological mechanisms of the stress response are described in this volume by Anisman, Kokkinidis, and Sklar; M. Wilson; Corley; Veith-Flanigan and Sandman; and Solomon, Amkraut, and Rubin. Anisman et al. (Chap. 3) focused on neurotransmitter changes during stress and the role of coping in modifying these changes. M. Wilson (Chap. 6) described a specific negative-feedback system within the brain in which glucocorticoid stimulation of the hippocampus inhibits ACTH release, thereby decreasing levels of plasma glucocorticoids. Norepinephrine is the likely transmitter substance involved in hippocampal inhibition of the hypothalamus, although further investigation of the neural circuits is needed. As Anisman et al. reported, NE and DA increase transiently after stress and then drop to below-normal levels. These neural changes are responsible for many behavioral and other physiological effects noted by other researchers. The relationship between neurotransmitter release and hormonal secretion has been investigated by Sachar and his colleagues (Asnis, Sachar, Halbreich, Nathan, Novacenko, and Ostrow, 1981; Sachar, 1979). For example, Sachar reported that DA inhibits PRL secretion and that antipsychotic medications, such as chlorpromazine, which decrease DA, cause increased PRL secretion. In the noradrenergic system, NE inhibits ACTH. People who are depressed have high circulating levels of cortisol that are not suppressed by dexamethasone (a drug that usually prevents cortisol release). The low NE in endogenous depression presumably disinhibits cortisol release. By integrating these data, one control mechanism of the pituitary-adrenocortical response to stress can be delineated: Given that hippocampal release of NE to the hypothalamus inhibits ACTH release from the anterior pituitary, then whenever this system is depleted of NE, as after exposure to an acute stressor, ACTH will rise and cause cortisol to be secreted from the adrenal cortex. Anisman et al. caution, however, that stress-induced changes in catecholamine concentration vary depending on the length and type of stressor and availability of coping resources. As more neurotransmitters are identified, it is likely that other mechanisms underlying the physiological stress response will be discovered.

Veith-Flanigan and Sandman also discussed the role of neurotransmitters in the stress response and discussed the exciting theory of prohormones. Identification of enzymes that split off substances like $\beta$-endorphin and MSH from $\beta$-LPH as well as determination of changes in the concentration of these peptides following enzyme activation is needed before the prohormone theory can be accepted. The implications of this theory are important, however; especially as it relates to the functioning of the neuroendocrine system under stress. Furthermore, with the recent identification of Valium receptors, the probability is high that an antianxiety system exists within the brain and is larger than the encephalon system. These findings, as well as those of peptides as transmitter substances ("Neuroactive Peptides," 1980), add to the excitement in the field of neurobiology. If two pain systems exist, as Anisman et al. suggest, and if they are activated by stress, as is indicated by the literature, then they probably serve in part as the basis for stress-induced alterations of pain perception, attention, and memory. It seems likely that this system must have evolved as a response to physical stress. If millions of years ago animals and humans were primarily faced with physical stressors of survival, then, when subjected to an acute stressor, the most adaptive coping mechanism would have been mobilization of all defenses to escape from or subdue the threatening stimulus as opposed to reaction to the bodily insult with pain or swelling. Hence, the mechanisms of increased release of endorphins, glucocorticoids, and catecholamines and decreased immunocompetence may have promoted survival. Because present-day humans primarily face psychological stressors of a chronic, intermittent nature, the physiological alterations, when occurring for a prolonged period of time, are no longer adaptive. According to Burchfield's model, organisms are genetically predisposed to react to chronic intermittent stress with an anticipatory arousal decreasing toward basal levels during and after stressor exposure. Alterations from this pattern in humans presumably are the result of cognitive mediation.

Perception, either conscious or unconscious, of an event will determine whether or not a response occurs. If the event is perceived as stressful, processes such as rumination that tend to perpetuate the mental representation of the stimulus should result in maintenance of the physiological stress response following this line of thinking. Hypothetically, hysteroid people who overstate and overreact to stressful stimuli should, in general, exhibit maladaptive physiological stress-response patterns and experience more stress-induced illness than normal people. Research has found that these people do report more illness, undergo more operations, and report greater amounts of anxiety than normal people (Hinkle, Christenson, Kane, Ostfeld, Thetford, & Wolff, 1958; Horowitz, 1977). On the other hand, people who ignore or suppress their psychological reactions to stress should display less physiological arousal and report fewer illnesses and less anxiety than normal people. Research on healthy people (Burchfield, Holmes, & Harrington, 1981; Kobasa, 1979; Vaillant, 1978) and on nonresponders to stress (Wolff, Friedman, Hofer, & Mason, 1964) supports this hypothesis. Any variables that increase or prolong the physiological stress response increase the probability of illness, whereas variables that decrease the intensity or length of the arousal decrease the likelihood of stress-induced illness. These hypotheses are addressed in the chapters on immunity, cardiac function, and moderator variables.

## STRESS AND ILLNESS

Solomon, Amkraut, and Rubin (Chap. 4) described the research on stress-induced immunosuppression. Apparently, altered immunocompetence occurs secondarily to cortisol release but is also a direct result of stress-induced changes in the thymus and T-cell production. Hence, because of immune alterations, the probability of getting a viral or bacterial disease increases after a person is chronically stressed. Other stress-induced illnesses, such as hypertension and heart disease, are due to other, nonimmunological changes that occur under stress. Ader and

Cohen (1975) have shown that immunosuppression is conditionable. Given that the normal response to a pathogen is an increased immune response, the finding that immunosuppression occurs because a CS is present, is remarkable. The implications of conditioning are vast: The cognitive representation of an event may serve as a CS initiating a stress response with concurrent immunosuppression. Patients who undergo organ transplants are treated with immunosuppressive drugs. It is likely that their immune response becomes conditioned to stimuli associated with the drugs (time of day, a certain nurse, sight of the medicine). A more common occurrence of conditioned immunosuppression may be found in people who ruminate, thereby increasing their anxiety. Does immunosuppression occur whenever they worry, or does this response adapt to chronic stress exposure, as Anisman et al. showed that NE levels do? Because immunosuppression is a major mechanism linking stress and illness, more research is needed in this area.

The other type of stress-induced illness occurs from response specificity, or increased sensitivity of one system, making it hyperresponsive to stimuli such as stress. Corley (Chap. 7) discussed mechanisms of sudden cardiac death and their psychological correlates. Overactivity of the sympathetic input to the heart contributes to cardiac fibrillation, whereas parasympathetic influences can cause slowing and eventual stopping of the heart. Helplessness and giving up are apparently correlated with sudden cardiac death owing to parasympathetic input, whereas chronic severe tension (as in the executive monkey syndrome) more often results in ventricular fibrillation. Corley's research showed, however, that these cardiac changes are not simply the result of overactivity of one system. A complex interaction between systems is responsible for both normal and abnormal cardiac activity. Lown, DeSilva, Reich, and Murawski (1980), reviewing different studies of sudden cardiac death, concurred that psychophysiological mechanisms may produce death from ventricular fibrillation. Lown et al. cited human research showing that certain healthy men frequently experienced ventricular premature beats when exposed to psychological stress. Patients treated for ventricular arrhythmias also displayed this pattern. This stress-induced arrhythmia rarely occurred, however, in these people during the traditional cardiac-stress test, in which the stressor is physical. Lown et al. suggested that certain people are predisposed to experience sudden cardiac death secondary to stress and that these people are those who tend to respond with arrhythmias when exposed to psychological stress.

Haney and Blumenthal (Chap. 8) examined the cardiovascular system in terms of personality characteristics that predispose people to cardiac arrest. The Type A personality, a well-researched concept, seems to exemplify a person with an overactive SNS. Corley's search for the mechanisms of sudden cardiac death are important in understanding MI in Type As. Garrity and Marx (Chap. 9) also discussed Type A personality as a moderator between stress and illness. An important area for future research in this topic is to determine whether or not the correlation between Type A behavior and MI is due to some third variable that causes both cardiovascular overreactivity and Type A personality traits.

## MODERATION OF THE STRESS RESPONSE

The way that moderator variables affect stress-induced physiological arousal was discussed by J. Wilson (Chap. 11). He pointed out the ambiguity and difficulty of using global trait measures, such as R-S, in the study of stress. Although the concept of R-S is relevant to stress research, it is not clear what R-S is and whether or not the R-S Scale actually measures it. Weinberger, Schwartz, and Davidson (1979) showed that people who report that they have low anxiety levels actually consist of two groups: true low-anxious people and repressors. The true low-anxious people are physically unaroused during stress, whereas the repressors, although verbally reporting low anxiety, are highly aroused. Therefore, it is impossible to determine whether or not a person is actually a "repressor" from paper-and-pencil measures.

The process of repression may be conceptualized using Riley and Furedy's framework as an example of the distinctiveness of the processing modes of psychological and physiological systems. This process may be more adequately assessed by using Miller's (1980) exciting technique of identifying monitors and blunters. Monitors are similar to sensitizers in that they seek information and search the environment for cues to help them cope with a stressor. Blunters, on the other hand, try to suppress and ignore information about a stressor over which they have no control. This method seems to have more predictive validity than that of the identification of R-S. Wilson emphasized that consideration of these individual differences is important—especially when planning interventions with patients seeking medical treatment. Identification of those patients who will be helped instead of harmed by the psychological intervention is mandatory. This identification can only be accomplished by studying moderator variables to determine how they interact with each other and with a person's coping style. Moderation and modification of the stress response were discussed in the remaining chapters of this book.

The chapters by Sarason, Sarason, and Johnson (Chap. 10) and Garrity and Marx (Chap. 9) were included in this book so readers could see how scientists whose research is spawned from the same theoretical framework can take different perspectives and use different techniques to test their hypotheses about moderation of the stress-illness relationship. Garrity and Marx used Holmes and Rahe's (1967) SRE in their research and, although they noted methodological weaknesses in this instrument, sought to decrease variability by examining specific moderator variables and populations. Sarason et al., on the other hand, reacted to the methodological problems of the SRE by developing a questionnaire, the LES, that measures not only life change but also one's perception of the valence and intensity of the change. Sarason et al. cited several studies that reported correlations of .4-.6 between scores on the negative LES scale and dependent variables (anxiety, depression, grade-point average) as well as a study (Pancheri, De Martino, Spiombi, Biondi, and Mosticoni, 1979) that correlated both the LES and the SRE with illness. The LES surpassed the SRE in predictive validity. Sarason et al. have been able to increase further the predictability of a health alteration following high levels of life stress by including measurement of moderator variables such as locus of control, sensation seeking, personality, and social supports. Garrity and Marx examined the moderator variables of psychophysiological strain, personality, Type A or B behavior, and social supports.

Despite these different perspectives, both groups of investigators have reported similar variables as important modifiers of the stress-illness relationship. Garrity and Marx discussed social support as an intervening variable and cited support for its role as a moderator of stress-induced illness. Sarason et al. discussed the methodological difficulties of measuring social supports, factors that influence response to social supports, the relative lack of research in this area, and the role of social supports in stress research.

Social support can moderate the physiological stress response either directly or indirectly. Most investigators conceptualize the impact of social supports as indirectly being due to the psychosocial components, including listening and caring, of a support system that promotes a person's growth, insight, and coping. Recent evidence has accumulated to suggest that one component of social supports (the touch of another person) directly alters biologic rhythms. Given that human beings are social animals, then one would expect that people would live in groups and would be, physiologically, more relaxed when with a group than when isolated. Drescher, Gantt, and Whitehead (1980) found that subjects responded to the experimenter's touching their wrists by significantly reducing their HR compared with their basal levels when sitting alone. This effect of touching on HR is very complex, however, Witcher and Fisher (1979) found that, when female nurses touched female patients, the patients' HR decreased, but when they touched male patients, HR increased. Drescher et al. found no sex differences in their experiment, although the meaning of the act of touching was directly stated to the subjects and was unambiguous, whereas the purpose of touching was not told to the Witcher and Fisher subjects, who may have interpreted it as sexual instead of as caring. Drescher et al. hypothesized that touching results in a reflexive decrease in HR in humans. If this hypothesis is proven, it may be a mechanism whereby social-support systems (in which members touch each other) directly affect the physiological stress response. It would be worthwhile to examine whether social-support systems that employ a lot of touching have a stronger moderating effect on the stress response than do those in which touching is absent. Distinction of touching as expressing caring and love versus sexual interest may also be important for understanding the impact of social supports on stress.

Another interesting finding reported by Garrity and Marx was that Type A people experienced greater amounts of life change than Type Bs yet similar amounts of illness. Garrity and Marx hypothesized that Type A personalities seek change as part of their aggressive, competitive lifestyle. Sensation seekers, identified in Sarason et al.'s chapter by using Zuckerman's Sensation Seeking Scale, are also people who, as a group, have a low correlation between life stress and illness despite the high levels of life stress experienced. It would be worthwhile to determine the correlation between sensation seeking and Type A personality because these two traits may share a lot of variance. Furthermore, although the data indicate that Type As are very likely to have a cardiac-related illness (CHD, MI, atherosclerosis), the data are lacking concerning the incidence of other illnesses in this group. Garrity has suggested that these people may, in fact, be relatively healthy until the heart disease is diagnosed. This issue needs to be further explored because it has implications for treatment of Type A behavior patterns and for understanding response specificity and its relationship to general health. Longitudinal research must be undertaken to examine the relationship between Type A behavior and general health both in youth and in aging adults.

Further research is also needed in measurement of moderator variables such as personality needs and traits, coping mechanisms, and environmental resources. Examination of the types of life change relevant to a person's needs and the person's ability to fulfill those needs or be supported when they are unfilled is another way to improve our understanding of stress-induced illness. In a study just completed in our laboratory, Burchfield, Hamilton, and Banks (1982) found that highly interpersonally stressed people with high unfulfilled affiliative needs reported higher illness rates than highly stressed people with fulfilled affiliative needs ($p < .01$). McClelland, Floor, Davidson, and Saron (1980) reported that people with a high need for power who experienced many life changes in the area of achievement and power reported significantly more illness than people with a high need for power who experienced many affiliative life changes. McClelland et al. (1980) also measured physiological and immunological variables and found that subjects who had a high need for power, high activity inhibition, and high stress levels exhibited more sympathetic arousal and immunosuppression during stress than did controls. These data exemplify the type of multivariate approach needed in stress research. Understanding the interactions between subject (psychological and physiological) and environmental variables would improve the treatment of stress-response syndromes. Currently, there are no reported studies of the effects of group treatment to reduce stress and anxiety in which individual differences were included as independent variables.

## TREATMENT OF THE STRESS RESPONSE

The chapters on treatment of the stress response explore three methods of decreasing physiological arousal and one method that includes both cognitive and physiological elements. The primary conclusion drawn from these chapters is that meditation, biofeedback, and relaxation training (PMR) are all effective in decreasing anxiety, although their effectiveness varies with the symptom being treated. Andrasik, Blanchard, & Edlund (Chap. 12) reviewed the literature on biofeedback and reported disappointing findings. Biofeedback seems to be effective in increasing HR, increasing finger ST and decreasing muscle tension in the frontalis muscle. The magnitude of these effects is not great, however, and they frequently disappear after training is stopped. Biofeedback is effective in the treatment of tension headache and results in a decreased incidence of headaches, although, when they occur, they are equal in intensity and duration to pretreatment levels. The mechanism for biofeedback's effects is unclear, and Andrasik et al. suggest that more research should be done to clarify whether the effects are due to physiological changes induced by biofeedback or to somatic changes secondary to movement or to psychological responses of the client. Cohen, McArthur, and Rickles (1980) hypothesized, for example, that biofeedback's effects on headache reduction were due to the client's perception of increased control.

Shapiro (Chap. 13) also noted that biofeedback has only been proven effective in the treatment of headaches. He reviewed the history and research on meditation. Meditation has been found effective in producing a relaxation response and in decreasing certain tension-associated symptoms such as insomnia and hypertension. In general, it is equally as effective as other relaxation methods.

Lavey and Taylor (Chap. 14) discussed Jacobson's PMR and Benson's relaxation-response method and concluded that muscle relaxation is more effective in reducing somatic anxiety, whereas Benson's treatment is more effective in reducing cognitions and feelings of anxiety. Relaxation therapy was found to be equally as effective as meditation and biofeedback in the treatment of stress-induced anxiety and symptomatology including headache, insomnia, and hypertension.

Differences between somatic anxiety-reduction methods (PMR and biofeedback) and cognitive methods (meditation and Benson's relaxation) may be due to the different modalities under which these systems operate. According to Riley and Furedy, in a method that teaches somatic relaxation (such as PMR), the ANS learns that the response is relaxation. In a cognitive-based treatment, psychological contingencies are learned.

Warrenburg, Pagano, Woods, and Hlastala (1980) examined the physiological effects of TM and PMR and reported an extremely interesting result. Significant between-group differences were found on the first day of the experiment (usually a stressful time for subjects). Meditators reported low anxiety but physiologically appeared aroused, whereas subjects trained in PMR reported high anxiety but appeared physiologically relaxed. On Day 2 both groups were similar in the degree of their cognitive and physiological relaxation. These data indicate the independent processing of the two systems and the possibility that the primary site of action of a relaxation strategy depends on the type of strategy. Relaxation of the non-targeted system occurs after the targeted system has learned the strategy. Hence, it would be beneficial to use a treatment that acts at both the cognitive and the physiological levels in order to increase the probability that the treatment would have a greater effect.

Smith and Ascough (Chap. 15) reported their work on treatment of the stress response using IA. This treatment program includes both psychological (self-monitoring and coping-skills training) and physiological (PMR and IA) components. Smith and Ascough reported data that showed that this treatment was slightly more effective in reducing test anxiety than Meichenbaum's covert-rehearsal training and significantly more effective than placebo controls. It is important to determine the comparative effectiveness of treatments that affect either psychological or physiological systems or both. No research has been done to compare IA training with other stress-management programs. Well-controlled treatment-outcome studies are desperately needed. The data in these chapters appear consistent with the predictions of Riley and Furedy based on differences in processing modes of physiological and psychological systems. And so, we have come full circle: Results in the penultimate chapter are explained by predictions made by the authors of the first chapter.

## CONCLUSIONS

Although this book contains different perspectives on stress, there are many commonalities, and each approach complements another. Yet there is still a lot to learn. Determination of the effects of moderator variables on the physiological response to stress and examination of the mechanisms that promote their protective influence must be performed. Investigations of the effects of stress-management training on health-related variables must also be undertaken. Although it is known that relaxation-type treatments decrease anxiety and associated symptoms, their effect on illness is unclear. (If high anxiety predisposes one to illness owing to alterations of the immune system, then decreasing anxiety should return immunocompetence to normal.) Identification of objective treatment-outcome variables must be made if the effects of stress-reduction techniques on illness are to be learned. Measurement of the physiological stress response before and after treatment may provide one such objective outcome variable. This presupposes that an adaptive hormonal-response pattern to psychological stress can be identified. If specific adaptive-response patterns can be identified, then a new treatment approach based on the possibility that maladaptive neuroendocrine responses can be modified through conditioning will be explored.

These hypotheses and more are waiting to be examined by investigators in the field. Yet the answers will never be complete unless researchers determine interactions between psychological and physiological variables and analyze the data for individual differences. Even variability within subjects is high because of stimulus-specific response patterns. It is practically impossible to decrease variability totally, but much can be understood if scientists examine as many variables as possible and remember that the organism is an open system. It interacts with larger social systems, and these affect the working of the many different physiological systems contained within.

The purpose of this book was to provide a framework from which to understand the complexities of the stress response. Our aim has been to provide an integrated approach, fill in gaps, extend the knowledge base, and engender questions for readers to explore in future studies.

# REFERENCES

Ader, R., & Cohen, N. Behaviorally conditioned immunosuppression. *Psychosomatic Medicine, 1975, 37*, 333–340.

Asnis, G. M., Sachar, E. J., Halbreich, U., Nathan, R. S., Novacenko, H., & Ostrow, L. C. Cortisol secretion in relation to age in major depression. *Psychosomatic Medicine, 1981, 43*, 235–242.

Burchfield, S. R. The stress response: A new perspective. *Psychosomatic Medicine, 1979, 41*, 661–672.

Burchfield, S. R. *Conditioned corticosterone secretion to stimuli associated with stress.* Paper presented at the Society for Neuroscience Annual Meeting, Cincinnati, November 14, 1980.

Burchfield, S. R. *Anticipatory hormonal conditioning to stress.* Unpublished manuscript, 1981.

Burchfield, S. R., Hamilton, K. L., & Banks, K. L. Affiliative needs, interpersonal stress and symptomatology. *Journal of Human Stress, 1982, 8*, 5–10.

Burchfield, S. R., Holmes, T. H., & Harrington, R. L. Personality differences between sick and rarely sick individuals. *Social Science and Medicine, 1981, 15E*, 145–148.

Burchfield, S. R., Woods, S. C., & Elich, M. S. Pituitary adrenocortical response to chronic intermittent stress. *Physiology and Behavior, 1980, 24*, 297–302.

Cohen, M. J., McArthur, D., & Rickles, W. H. Comparison of four biofeedback treatments for migraine headache: Physiological and headache variables. *Psychosomatic Medicine, 1980, 42*, 463–480.

Coover, G. D., Goldman, L., & Levine, S. Plasma corticosterone increases produced by extinction of operant behavior in rats. *Physiology and Behavior, 1971, 6*, 261–263.

Coover, G. D., Sutton, B. R., & Heybach, J. P. Conditioning decreases in plasma corticosterone level in rats by pairing stimuli with daily feedings. *Journal of Comparative and Physiological Psychology, 1977, 91*, 716–726.

Corson, S. A., & Corson, E. O'L. Constitutional differences in physiological adaptation to stress and distress. In G. Serban (Ed.), *Psychopathology of Human Adaptation.* New York: Plenum, 1976.

Drescher, V. M., Gantt, W. H., & Whitehead, W. E. Heart rate response to touch. *Psychosomatic Medicine, 1980, 42*, 559–566.

Falek, A., & Britton, S. Phases in coping: The hypothesis and its implications. *Social Biology, 1974, 21*, 1–7.

Hinkle, L. E., Jr., Christenson, W. N., Kane, F. D., Ostfeld, A. M., Thetford, W. N., & Wolff, H. G. An investigation of the relation between life experience, personality characteristics, and general susceptibility to illness. *Psychosomatic Medicine, 1958, 20*, 278–295.

Holmes, T. H., & Rahe, R. The Social Readjustment Rating Scale. *Journal of Psychosomatic Research,* 1967, *11,* 213–218.

Horowitz, M. J. (Ed.). *Hysterical personality.* New York: Aronson, 1977.

Klinger, E. Consequences of commitment to and disengagement from incentives. *Psychological Review,* 1975, *82,* 1–25.

Kobasa, S. C. Stressful life events, personality, and health: An inquiry into hardiness. *Journal of Personality and Social Psychology,* 1979, *37,* 1–11.

Lacey, J. I., & Lacey, B. C. Verification and extension of the principle of autonomic response stereotypy. *American Journal of Psychology,* 1958, *71,* 50–73.

Lazarus, R. S., & Launier, R. Stress-related transactions between person and environment. In L. A. Pervin and M. Lewis (Eds.), *Perspectives in international psychology.* New York: Plenum, 1978.

Lown, B. DeSilva, R. A., Reich, P., & Murawski, B. J. Psychophysiological factors in sudden cardiac death. *American Journal of Psychiatry,* 1980, *137,* 1325–1335.

Mason, J. W. Specificity in the organization of neuroendocrine response profiles. In P. Seeman & G. M. Brown (Eds.), *Frontiers in neurology and neuroscience research.* Toronto: University of Toronto, Neuroscience Institute, 1974.

Mason, J. W. A historical view of the stress field. *Journal of Human Stress,* 1975, *1*(1), 6–12, *1*(2), 22–36.

McClelland, D. C., Floor, E., Davidson, R. J., & Saron, C. Stressed power motivation, sympathetic activation, immune function and illness. *Journal of Human Stress,* 1980, *6,* 11–19.

Miller, S. M. When is a little information a dangerous thing? Coping with stressful events by monitoring vs. blunting. In S. Levine & H. Ursin (Eds.), *Coping and health: Proceedings of a NATO conference.* New York: Plenum, 1980.

Neuroactive peptides. *Proceedings of the Royal Society,* Series B, 1980, *210.*

Pancheri, P. De Martino, V., Spiombi, G., Biondi, M., & Mosticoni, S. Life stress events and state-trait anxiety in psychiatric and psychosomatic patients. In I. G. Sarason & C. D. Spielberger (Eds.), *Stress and Anxiety* (Vol. 6). Washington: Hemisphere, 1979.

Sachar, E. J. Neuroendocrine strategies in psychiatric research. In E. Meyer, III, & J. V. Brady (Eds.). *Research in the psychobiology of human behaior.* Baltimore: Johns Hopkins Press, 1979.

Selye, H. *The stress of life.* New York: McGraw-Hill, 1956.

Selye, H. Confusion and controversy in the stress field. *Journal of Human Stress,* 1975, *1,* 37–44.

Vaillant, G. E. Natural history of the male psychological health: VI. Correlates of successful marriage and fatherhood. *American Journal of Psychiatry,* 1978, *135,* 653–659.

Warrenburg, W. S., Pagano, R. R., Woods, M., & Hlastala, M. A comparison of somatic relaxation and EEG activity in classical progressive relaxation and transcendental meditation. *Journal of Behavioral Medicine,* 1980, *3,* 73–93.

Weinberger, D. A., Schwartz, G. E., & Davidson, R. J. Low-anxious, high-anxious, and repressive coping styles: Psychometric patterns and behavioral and physiological responses to stress. *Journal of Abnormal Psychology,* 1979, *88,* 369–380.

Wine, J. Test anxiety and direction of attention. *Psychological Bulletin,* 1971, *76,* 92–104.

Witcher, S. J., & Fisher, J. D. Multidimensional reaction to therapeutic touch in a hospital setting. *Journal of Personality and Social Psychology,* 1979, *36,* 87–96.

Wolff, C. T., Friedman, S. B., Hofer, M. A., & Mason, J. W. Relationship between psychological defenses and mean urinary 17-hydroxycorticosteroid excretion rates: I, II. *Psychosomatic Medicine,* 1964, *26,* 576–609.

# Index

Acetylcholine:
  and CHD, 187
  conditioning of, 83
  and coping, 78
  stress response of, 88
ACTH, 42, 108, 147–151, 163, 166–167, 175,
    178
  changes under stress, 85–86, 108,
      386
  circadian rhythm of, 167
  in depression, 145
  effect on hippocampus, 174–175
  and hypothalamus, 69, 165, 175
  role of hippocampus as regulator, 170
Affective responding, 6, 7, 11, 14, 18, 385
Anger, 105, 208, 366–367
Anxiety, 58, 236–237, 268, 270, 309, 312,
    315–318, 330, 335, 364, 367, 374
  relationship to: cardiac
      disturbances, 236–237
    depression, 250
    social supports, 252
  treatment of, 296, 311
  types of, 38–39, 58
  (*See also* Test anxiety)
Arthritis, 99
Autogenic training, 291, 336

Autonomic nervous system (ANS), 11, 21,
    185, 264–267
  response modalities, 6–7, 11, 14,
    18, 385
  response specificity, 129, 138–140,
    142, 147, 384
  stimulus specificity, 129, 140–141,
    143–146, 384
Avoidance behavior, 27, 176, 192, 273

Behavioral medicine, 207, 263, 308
Benson, H., 330, 334, 340, 374
Biofeedback, 24–25, 237, 285, 316,
    321, 331, 342, 391
  EMG changes, 296, 391
  heart rate changes, 287
  Reynaud's disease, 293
Blood pressure, 186, 195, 216, 314,
    332, 339–341, 344
  (*See also* Hypertension)

Cancer, 100, 102, 272
Cannon, W. B., 140, 223, 241, 339
  (*See also* Fight or flight response)
Cardiac changes and hopelessness, 191